# Reconsidering Formulary Apportionment in the Post-BEPS Era

**Series on International Taxation**

---

VOLUME 92

---

*Series Editors*

Prof. Ruth Mason, University of Virginia School of Law
Prof. Dr Ekkehart Reimer, University of Heidelberg

*Introduction & Contents*

The Series on International Taxation deals with a wide variety of topics in the global tax arena. The authors include many of the field's leading experts as well as talented newcomers. Their expert views and incisive commentary have proven highly useful to practitioners and academics alike.

*Objective*

The volumes published in this series are aimed at offering high-quality analytical information and practical solutions to international tax practitioners.

*Readership*

Practitioners, academics and policy makers in international tax law.

*Frequency of Publication*

2-3 new volumes published each year.

*The titles published in this series are listed at the end of this volume.*

# Reconsidering Formulary Apportionment in the Post-BEPS Era

Jie Wang

Wolters Kluwer

*Published by:*
Kluwer Law International B.V.
PO Box 316
2400 AH Alphen aan den Rijn
The Netherlands
E-mail: lrs-sales@wolterskluwer.com
Website: www.wolterskluwer.com/en/solutions/kluwerlawinternational

*Sold and distributed by:*
Wolters Kluwer Legal & Regulatory U.S.
920 Links Avenue
Landisville, PA 17538
United States of America
E-mail: customer.service@wolterskluwer.com

ISBN 978-94-035-2729-1

e-Book: ISBN 978-94-035-2739-0
web-PDF: ISBN 978-94-035-2749-9

# About the Author

**Jie Wang** is an assistant professor at Wuxi University, China. He obtained his PhD in International Taxation from Erasmus University Rotterdam in 2024. He specializes in general tax law theory, Chinese tax law, and international taxation. His recent research focuses on the digital transformation of the economy and the historical evolution of the international tax regime in the modern era. This book is based on the author's doctoral thesis and was funded by the China Scholarship Council and the Wuxi University Start-Up Research Grant.

# Table of Contents

# List of Abbreviations

| | |
|---|---|
| ALP | Arm's Length Principle |
| ALS | Arm's Length Standard |
| AOA | Authorized OECD Approach |
| APA | Advance Pricing Arrangement |
| AtP | Ability to Pay |
| BEPS | Base Erosion and Profit Shifting |
| BP | Benefit Principle |
| BRI | Belt and Road Initiative |
| CbC | Country-by-Country |
| CCCTB | Common Consolidated Corporate Tax Base |
| CCTB | Common Corporate Tax Base |
| CEN | Capital Export Neutrality |
| CFC | Controlled Foreign Corporation |
| CIN | Capital Import Neutrality |
| CON | Capital Ownership Neutrality |
| CPM | Comparable Price Method |
| CSFM | Community with a Shared Future for Mankind |
| CUP | Comparable Uncontrolled Price |
| DEMPE | Development, Enhancement, Maintenance, Protection, and Exploitation |
| DEMPE-P | Development, Enhancement, Maintenance, Protection, Exploitation, and Promotion |
| DST | Digital Service Tax |
| DTA | Double Tax Agreements |
| EITL | Enterprise Income Tax Law |
| FA | Formulary Apportionment |

| | |
|---|---|
| FDI | Foreign Direct Investment |
| FTC | Foreign Tax Credit |
| GILTI | Global Intangible Low-Taxed Income |
| GLOBE | Global Anti-Base Erosion Rules |
| ICC | International Chamber of Commerce |
| IIR | Income Inclusion Rule |
| IITL | Individual Income Tax Law |
| ITRC | International Tax Regime of China |
| LON | League of Nations |
| LSA | Location Specific Advantages |
| MFN | Most-Favoured-Nation |
| MLC | Multilateral Convention |
| MLI | Multilateral Instrument |
| MN | Market Neutrality |
| MNE | Multinational Enterprise |
| MTC | Model Tax Convention |
| OECD | Organization for Economic Co-operation and Development |
| PE | Permanent Establishment |
| PSM | Profit Split Method |
| RBT | Residence-Based Taxation |
| RCEP | Regional Comprehensive Economic Partnership |
| ROT | Residence-Oriented Tax |
| RPM | Residual Profit Method |
| S-H-S | Schanz-Haig-Simons |
| SBT | Source-Based Taxation |
| SOR | Switch-Over Rule |
| SOT | Source-Oriented Tax |
| SRF | Silk Road Fund of China |
| STA | State Taxation Administration of China |
| STTR | Subject-to-Tax Rule |
| TNMM | Transactional Net Margin Method |
| TPG | OECD Transfer Pricing Guidelines for Multinational Enterprises and Tax Administrations |
| TPS | OECD/G20 Two-Pillar Solution |
| TPSM | Transactional Profit Split Method |
| TRA | Tax Rental Agreements |
| UDITPA | Uniform Division of Income for Tax Purposes Act |
| UN | United Nations |
| US | United States of America |
| UTPR | Undertaxed Payment Rule |

| | |
|---|---|
| VCAM | Value Contribution Apportionment Method |
| WTO | World Trade Organization |

# List of Equations

# List of Figures

# List of Tables

CHAPTER 1

# Introduction

## 1.1 THE BACKGROUND AND MOTIVATION OF THE RESEARCH

### 1.1.1 The International Tax System in Turbulence: BEPS 1.0, 2.0 and the Beyond

Leaving aside the difficult question of what the 'system' of international taxation is or even whether the 'system' truly exists, the field of international taxation has experienced significant turbulence in the past decade – and this turbulence shows no signs of abating.

This reminds the author of the 'Big Bang' era of international taxation in the 1920s, when the League of Nations (LON) championed the inception of the system by laying down the fundamentals and core framework of international taxation. However, before that and in the long days following the LON reform, international taxation had been caught in a long trajectory of autonomous harmonization or systemization, where conflicts and uncertainties were mainstream.

The Base Erosion and Profit Shifting (BEPS) Project hosted by the Organization for Economic Co-operation and Development (OECD) and the ensuing Two-Pillar reform taken over by the Inclusive Framework, respectively, marks the era of BEPS 1.0 and 2.0, both of which have made a substantial number of tweaks to the international tax system. As a result, multinational enterprises (MNE) and governments around the world are now having to deal with tax rules with greater complexities and weigh the implications of those which are yet to be (or may never be) finalized.

To what extent the BEPS 1.0 and 2.0 reforms deliver the historical and normative significance for international taxation of the LON-led work is still to be revealed. However, the turbulence and uncertainties that are widespread nowadays have presented a *déjà vu* of the old days of a century ago.

### 1.1.2 The International Tax System after the BEPS Project

The BEPS Project originated from a consensus within international communities - comprising society, business, and governments - that the existing international tax system required significant reform, particularly in addressing the taxation of MNEs in the post-financial crisis era. The project sought to address systemic gaps and inefficiencies that had become unbearable over time.

With the political mandate of the G20, the OECD was ambitious in implying destructive innovation to the system as conveyed in the earlier framework documents. Subsequently, it announced that the reform will be organized around three pillars, namely, coherence, economic substance and transparency, and each of them encompasses several action items.

The outcome of the BEPS Project is multi-layered. The action items target different aspects of international taxation, of which the internal connections are somewhat remote; the enforcing approach is contrasting as there are minimum standards, a common approach, and pure guidance drawing on best practices. Even within the minimum standards, the abiding countries are offered a variety of options as to how they may specifically implement those standards. The latter two categories are basically imposing pressure on states to act in a certain way.

The specifics of how the BEPS Project has unfolded, and the degree to which it has achieved its objectives, will be thoroughly analysed in later chapters. At this stage, it is important to recognize the ongoing nature of these reforms and the continuing efforts to adapt international tax systems to the realities of the modern global economy.

The story can be shorter if one takes into account the heated wave of the Two-Pillar campaign, which, in essence, is making up for the inadequacies of the BEPS Project. Should the project achieve its great ambitions that are asserted in the BEPS Action Plan, the two pillars would have no ground to stand on in the first place.

### 1.1.3 The International Tax System Emerging from the Two-Pillar Solution

The BEPS Action 1[1] gives birth to the Two-Pillar program by laying down the path of tackling digitalization. Since 2019, the OECD has carried out a series of studies around the tax challenges brought about by the digitalization of the economy. Eventually, it formed the 'Two-Pillar' tax reform plan for the digital economy. In October 2020, the OECD/G20 BEPS Inclusive Framework released a comprehensive Blueprint for Pillar One and Pillar Two, refining key aspects and adjusting and perfecting the ideas,

1. OECD, 'Addressing the Tax Challenges of the Digital Economy, Action 1: 2015 Final Report' (OECD 2015) https://www.oecd.org/content/dam/oecd/en/publications/reports/2015/10/addressing-the-tax-challenges-of-the-digital-economy-action-1-2015-final-report_g1g58cdd/9789264241046-en.pdf accessed 27 March 2025.

structure, and methods.[2] From then on, the Two-Pillar Solution (TPS) has gradually matured.

On 8 October 2021, the OECD/G20 BEPS Inclusive Framework issued a statement on the TPS for addressing the tax challenges of the digitalization of the economy.[3] This statement not only introduced significant innovations to the existing rules for the international allocation of taxing rights and the dispute prevention and resolution mechanisms, but it will also deeply touch the domestic tax systems of all countries, requiring a series of modifications and adjustments in domestic legislation and existing tax treaties. On 31 October 2021, the declaration was approved by the G20 Leaders' Summit in Rome, marking a historic step in the restructuring of the international tax rules system.[4]

From the perspective of Pillar One, with the rapid development of the digital economy, the division of the international tax pie based on supply factors has become inappropriate. The Pillar One innovatively proposed the concept of 'market country' formally in international tax taxonomy, recognizing the significant contribution of market ends to value creation, granting new taxing rights to market countries, allocating part of the residual profits to the market countries for taxation, and breaking the profit manipulation of multinational companies through a formula-based allocation method. It is a revolutionary reform plan reflecting fairness. From the perspective of Pillar Two, the plan aims to curb harmful tax competition through multilateral governance, marking a key step in the transition from bilateral mechanism to multilateral mechanism in the international tax field. Overall, the TPS is beneficial for reducing the risk of double taxation brought about by unilateral measures, further curbing tax base erosion and profit shifting, and ensuring the tax revenues of governments.

The TPS also brings new challenges to international taxation. Pillar One allocates only a small portion of the residual profits of qualifying multinational enterprise groups to market countries, which is also pending to be implemented. Reaching a consensus in the international community on the determination of the calculation formula is somewhat difficult, and it is not easy to establish a completely new tax collection and management mechanism. The Pillar Two plan, originating from the US' GILTI (Global Intangible Low-Taxed Income) tax system, predominantly reflects the tax interests of developed countries but overlooks the goal of developing countries at different stages of economic development. This is particularly true for countries with lower domestic

2. OECD, 'Tax Challenges Arising from Digitalisation: Report on Pillar One Blueprint – Inclusive Framework on BEPS' (OECD 2020) https://www.oecd.org/en/publications/tax-challenges-arising-from-digitalisation-report-on-pillar-one-blueprint_beba0634-en.html accessed 29 April 2025; OECD, 'Tax Challenges Arising from Digitalisation: Report on Pillar Two Blueprint' (2020) https://www.oecd.org/en/publications/2020/10/tax-challenges-arising-from-digitalisation-report-on-pillar-two-blueprint_4c7eaa3d.html accessed 26 August 2025.
3. OECD, 'Statement on a Two-Pillar Solution to Address the Tax Challenges Arising from the Digitalisation of the Economy' (2021) https://www.oecd.org/tax/beps/statement-on-a-two-pillar-solution-to-address-the-tax-challenges-arising-from-the-digitalisation-of-the-economy-october-2021.pdf accessed 26 August 2025.
4. 'G20 Rome Leader's Declaration' https://www.governo.it/sites/governo.it/files/G20ROMELEADERSDECLARATION_0.pdf accessed 1 June 2024.

tax rates in Africa and Latin America, as well as countries like Vietnam that attract foreign direct investment (FDI) through tax benefits.[5] Therefore, the extent to which the Pillar Two is reasonable and inclusive has been questioned by these countries.

The general content and structure of the two pillars and their relationship with the BEPS Project are presented in the following Figure 1.1.

*Figure 1.1 General Content and Structure of the Two Pillars*

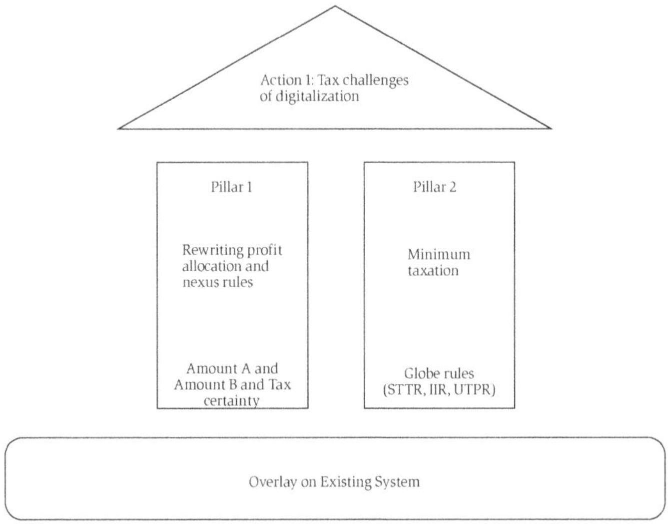


### 1.1.4 Formulary Apportionment Brought to the Stage as an Expedient Fix

Either the BEPS Project or the Two-Pillar program is effectively carried out by the OECD, which is notoriously known as a repudiator of formulary apportionment (FA) and an advocate of the Arm's Length Principle (ALP). As such, the OECD assiduously maintains the Transfer Pricing Guidelines, where it documents its unwavering adherence to the ALP. In contrast, formulary apportionment is repudiated as not in alignment with economic reality, may result in double taxation or unintended non-taxation, hard to achieve international consistency, and has significant potential for manipulation and (in-)compatibility with existing treaties. These also mirror what the OECD endorses in the ALP.

This contrast of preference continues with the development of the BEPS Project. The OECD vowed to bring in some fundamental changes to the underlying ideas of international taxation and revamp the transfer pricing practice with the new thought of value creation. The BEPS Actions 8-10 are centred on further calibrating the ALP.

5. Heydon Wardell-Burrus, 'Pillar Two and Developing Countries: The STTR and GloBE Implementation' (16 September 2022) https://papers.ssrn.com/abstract=4221115 accessed 21 September 2024.

Action 1, however, did not render any meaningful outcomes but accommodated the subsequent Two-Pillar reform.

The Policy Note of the Inclusive Framework published in January 2019 seems to be the first piece of work that explicitly announced the Two-Pillar conception.[6] The first pillar was assigned to reallocate taxing right, for which the proposals under consideration all go beyond the ALP. The ensuing developments from then on till mid-2023 basically laid down both the framework and content of the two pillars.

With the benefits of hindsight, the deployment of FA as a result of the asserted deviation from the ALP seems to be a patch put on the existing international tax architecture. The use of FA may, therefore, be an expedient measure under the mandate of taxing digitalization.

First, on the surface of it, formulary apportionment has actually not been seriously reflected upon by the OECD or the Inclusive Framework, apart from the limited discussions in academia. This is the case before and after either the BEPS Project or the Two-Pillar reform. In the relevant technical output, even the specific term of formulary apportionment has been discreetly evaded, as 'fractional', rather than 'formulary' apportionment is used. Throughout the outcomes, the overall tone is restrained and strictly technical, which makes the collision with ALP seem unreal. Questions around the origin, rationale and repercussions of formulary apportionment have barely been dealt with.

Second, and most profoundly, the Pillar One that utilizes formulary apportionment is an overlay above the existing architecture. This not only means that the scope of formulary apportionment is limited but also that the majority of how international taxation works remains unchanged. After all, only Amount A in the two pillars ever employs formulary apportionment (apart from the mechanism of 'UTPR' (Undertaxed Payment Rule) in Pillar Two to a limited degree), which just reallocates a small portion of the defined residual profits of the in-scope MNEs.

All in all, the (re-)emergence of formulary apportionment is not intended to revolutionize the international tax system. Instead, it serves the narrow purpose of directing an additional piece, which may also be tiny, of the tax pie to market countries. By concealing formulary apportionment within the Amount A, the practical instrumentality in doing so is fortified. Therefore, all these reforms are not initiated on the basis of the ALP-FA antithesis, and perception of the ALP's well-grounded dominance.

## 1.2 RESEARCH QUESTIONS

Against the background as introduced above, the main research question guiding this research is:

6. OECD/G20 Base Erosion and Profit Shifting Project, 'Addressing the Tax Challenges of the Digitalisation of the Economy: Policy Note' (2019) https://www.oecd.org/tax/beps/policy-note-beps-inclusive-framework-addressing-tax-challenges-digitalisation.pdf accessed 26 August 2025.

**Main Question**: *Should formulary apportionment be reconsidered a fundamental reform option in the evolving context of international taxation?*

There are four subsidiary questions as follows.

**Research Question 1:** Is formulary apportionment, as opposed to the dominant ALP, something 'real', or in other words, a practical reality or merely a theoretical construct?

This question stirs a historical analysis of the FA, that is, to contextualize FA in the evolution of the international tax system. The analysis will dig into the following secondary questions:

- What are the key phases in the evolution of the international tax system, and how have economic and political concerns shaped these phases? How does understanding these phases help explain the reconsideration of formulary apportionment as a potentially viable option today?
- How did the ALP gain dominance in the international tax system, and to what extent is this dominance based on historical contingency rather than theoretical superiority?
- Has formulary apportionment played some role in the evolution of the international tax system?
- How have formulary apportionment and the ALP evolved historically, and in the most recent times, in relation to each other? What does it mean for the potential role of FA in the coming years of international taxation?

After understanding the role FA has historically played and the factors that once hindered its further application, the Main Question naturally leads to a subsidiary inquiry:

**Research Question 2:** To what extent does FA exist in the current tax landscape, and if it does, what insights can the various forms of FA provide for designing an international FA system, envisioning a positive future for FA?

This question reflects the goal of examining real-world applications of formulary apportionment to provide practical insights for reform on a global level, with respect to highlighting how they function, what lessons can be drawn, and how they can contribute to future international tax reform. At a more specific level, this question will guide the thesis to inspect FA from implementation perspectives, which will, for example, structurize the FA into its components, horizontally compare the FA systems (if any), the internal and external conditions required for the successful implementation of a FA system and so forth.

As a new potential method for taxing MNEs, aside from the lack of direct practical experience, it is clearly equally important to determine what normative foundation can serve as the justification for formulary apportionment, guide its design, and provide the basis for its evaluation. Therefore, constructing an analytical framework is essential for answering the main research question.

The principles in the analytical framework can provide a normative justification of formulary apportionment beyond the practical or political concerns. They guide the assessment of whether this reform aligns with the core values of fairness, efficiency, and justice, offering a structured way to measure its suitability within the evolving global tax landscape.

Furthermore, the analytical framework is vital for understanding the broader impact of formulary apportionment on the global tax system. They help determine whether the reform could better balance taxing rights between countries compared to the current system. By grounding the analysis in these principles, formulary apportionment can be assessed not only as a technical solution but also as a reform that fits within the broader socio-legal context of international taxation.

Additionally, the analytical framework allows for the identification and resolution of potential conflicts between competing values and ensures that formulary apportionment's compromises are also identified. This framework also offers a comparative lens for evaluating formulary apportionment against the ALP, revealing where the ALP may fall short and whether formulary apportionment provides better alignment with modern international tax values.

Therefore, the next subsidiary research question is:

**Research Question 3:** What is the analytical framework for the normative analysis of formulary apportionment, and what does it inform for formulary apportionment?

Under this question, there is a set of secondary questions that need to be addressed, including:

- How can international tax principles be derived and reinterpreted for the application of formulary apportionment at the international level, considering the dual structure of international tax law? This question focuses on understanding the need for reinterpreting and reformulating domestic tax principles to fit within the international context, particularly for implementing formulary apportionment.
- What are the key principles to be put in the analytical framework that should guide the analysis and design of an international formulary apportionment system? This question explores the foundational values and principles that need to be considered when developing an analytical framework for formulary apportionment, especially emphasizing justice/fairness and efficiency.
- Why is the principle of neutrality contested in its application to formulary apportionment, and how can its role be redefined in the analytical framework? This addresses the critical examination of neutrality as a principle, probing into why its usefulness may be limited in the design of formulary apportionment and how it can be better applied in evaluating tax systems.
- With each of the principles in the analytical principle determined and (re-)formulated, what do they inform or instruct regarding the design and implementation of FA at the international level?

If all the above questions are sufficiently addressed, many key aspects of the Main Question should already be answered. However, there remains a significant gap due to the lack of a specific perspective. The current analysis, no matter how thoroughly it concludes that FA should be introduced or how well it proposes a design, remains relatively distant from the practical realities of the tax world. Equally important is the question of how FA should be implemented in practice. This is not merely a legal or tax issue but also a political one. A straightforward answer would be to implement FA through international political consensus, via a comprehensive multilateral tax treaty. However, as seen with the challenges faced by Amount A, this path remains untested and filled with significant hurdles.

Additionally, the answers provided in addressing preceding questions will largely be from a multilateral perspective, lacking sufficient exploration of unilateral, bilateral, or regional perspectives.

In this context, it seems valuable to explore an alternative approach, starting from a more focused, micro-level perspective. When FA is presented to a specific country, it becomes crucial to study how that country assesses the feasibility of FA – both from its own standpoint and from the perspective of FA itself – and to investigate what concrete steps it might take to lead FA's international implementation.

This research, therefore, selects China as a quasi-case study. By doing so, it bridges the global theoretical discussions in the previous chapters with the real-world dynamics of one of the largest economies, making the analysis more comprehensive. The China study also contextualizes FA within a real, evolving economic environment, demonstrating both its feasibility and its broader implications for the global tax system.

Accordingly, the final research question of this study is:

**Research Question 4**: Is China in a position to adopt formulary apportionment, and if so, what could be the potential pathway for its implementation, and what formula would be recommended?

## 1.3 RESEARCH STRUCTURE AND CHAPTER SUMMARIES

### 1.3.1 Part I: Formulary Apportionment at the Historical Turning Point

Part I includes Chapter 2, which assembles and distils crucial historical documents to outline the development path of formulary apportionment. The prevailing system of global taxation, which has a history spanning over a century, can be segmented into four distinct phases, each characterized by particular guiding themes. Comprehending the underlying issues specific to each phase is essential for grasping the evolutionary trajectory of the international tax system.

To be specific, it aims to elucidate the historical role that formulary apportionment played in the evolution of the global tax system, emphasizing the reasons behind its decline and the rise of the ALS as the dominant paradigm in international taxation. Contrary to common misperceptions that formulary apportionment is way too simplistic or illusory, this method has persistently played a role throughout various phases in the historical development of international taxation. Initially, formulary apportionment was a widely used legal tool and was even considered a viable alternative for alleviating double taxation on a global scale. Subsequently, it fell out of favour due to pragmatic concerns, failing to separate accounting or the independent entity approach for allocating taxation rights over MNEs. While its prominence declined in the later stage, its foundational elements persist within the existing treaty frameworks. With the digital transformation exacerbating existing system flaws to an intolerable level for most stakeholders, the re-emergence of formulary apportionment is becoming an increasingly concrete reality.

Retrospectively, the ALS has acquired its preeminent and normative position due more to historical contingencies than to its theoretical merits. It originated and matured during specific phases tailored for economic and political conditions that are markedly different from today's context. The standard has primarily served the interests of MNEs and the developed nations that host them, at the expense of source states that have been systematically exploited. The proliferation of aggressive tax avoidance strategies employed by MNEs has exposed the unsustainable nature of the anti-avoidance measures in place.

Additionally, this chapter places the exploration of formulary apportionment within the broader context of the origins of the modern international tax structure, specifically focusing on how this system fails to adequately address the issue of stateless income, a gap that the BEPS Project has not successfully tackled. Formulary apportionment is not a standalone entity but represents a synthesis of various principles and theories. One of its major conceptual affinities is with the economic allegiance theory, which allocates taxing rights based on the geographical distribution of value-creating factors. The international taxation system was originally designed to mirror the process by which value is generated. However, core elements like the residence-source division and the ALS have become rigid to the point where they perpetuate issues of base erosion and profit shifting.

The BEPS Project represents the pinnacle of pushing the boundaries of established norms concerning source and allocation, which has ever sidelined formulary apportionment. The principles of fairness and inter-nation equity in taxation have taken on unprecedented salience, as dissatisfaction with the current allocation framework has grown among both developing and developed nations.

### 1.3.2 Part II: Experience from the Real World

Part II consists of Chapter 3, which introduces how formulary apportionment regimes exist in the real world, though mostly within national borders. The existential being of formulary apportionment itself is significant. By lining up the national regimes, additionally, including the TPS for comparative analysis, the 'skeleton' of a formulary apportionment system is established.

Chapter 3 sorts out five structural components of the formulary apportionment regime under two broad categories for a more organized analysis: internal and external components. This chapter conducts a comparative study of the current formulary apportionment systems in the United States, Canada, the European Union's Common Consolidated Corporate Tax Base (CCCTB) Proposal, and the newly introduced Pillar One Amount A. Instead of employing a country-by-country analysis, the chapter initially deconstructs the formulary apportionment systems into their constituent elements. Subsequent to this deconstruction, the chapter then offers a component-by-component analysis and extracts lessons for the future architecture of international formulary apportionment.

The primary objective of this comparative evaluation is not to reveal any concealed realities but to lay down a foundational framework for the investigation of formulary apportionment within the modern global setting. In certain summary sections, explicit recommendations are made; for instance, a group approach is advocated over Canada's separate reporting method when addressing the issue of the taxable unit, and a harmonized tax base is also favoured.

Beyond these specific recommendations, one consistent observation across the discussions is the absence of any incontrovertible choices concerning the design of formulary apportionment. There is pervasive disagreement not only over what constitutes 'good' or 'bad' design elements but also over what is 'feasible' or 'unfeasible'. Moreover, different choices among the various alternatives for each component could lead to markedly different outcomes in formulary apportionment.

By scrutinizing these aspects, the chapter aims to offer valuable insights and provoke thought on the multifaceted and contested design options within formulary apportionment in international taxation.

### 1.3.3 Part III: Constructing the Analytical Framework for Formulary Apportionment

Part III, comprising Chapters 4-6, turns the view to abstract thinking. Technical discussions would be frivolous without the guiding light of principles. The ultimate motivation for weighing formulary apportionment is its potential to build an international tax system that is more consistent with these principles. Or the other way round, these principles can also shed light on where the technical inspection is inadequate or ambiguous.

Chapters 4-6 constitute an attempt to determine the analytical principles for formulary apportionment. Two primary discourses are noteworthy within the extant body of international taxation literature. First, the shortcomings and adverse implications of an ALP-based international taxation system have been examined, particularly in how they deviate from common benchmarks. Second, there is an exploration of specific merits that FA holds over ALP, such as its recognition of MNEs as unitary entities. Given the objectives of this research and recognizing the gaps in existing literature, it appears both timely and necessary to construct a set of principles and theories that not only support FA at a normative level but also provide guidelines for its prospective design and development.

To this end, Chapter 4 revisits the principle of equity in international taxation. It goes beyond existing discussions by formulating more specific approaches that can substantiate formulary apportionment at a foundational level. As the outcome of the discussion, the equity principle can provide the critical driving force to adopt formulary apportionment in the very first place. Second, it can also provide some instructions on the concrete design of formulary apportionment, where the latter embodies ambiguities.

The chapter begins by acknowledging the complexity of defining equity in taxation. It establishes that equity, as a norm of fairness, is concerned with the allocation of a country's total tax burden and is inherently derived from the principle of equality. The discussion sets the stage for a 'three-step' approach to examining the equity principle in international taxation, starting with its application to individuals in a unitary fiscal setting. In this setting, it highlights two key principles: the Ability to Pay Principle (AtP) and the Benefit Principle (BP), which influence the foundational design of tax systems. The section explores how these principles materialize the claims of inter-individual equity and how they shape national tax systems. The chapter then moves on to examining equity in the international context. It questions whether principles like AtP and BP, which are grounded in domestic contexts, can be directly applied to international taxation. The analysis suggests that the direct internationalization of these domestic equity norms is problematic due to differences in underlying relationships and circumstances in the international setting.

This chapter then turns to focus on redefining criteria for international tax equity. It introduces concepts such as 'inter-nation equity' developed by Peggy B. Musgrave[7] and explores its relationship with inter-individual equity. Various approaches, such as the Equal Earned Income and the Equal Allegiance approaches, are proposed for apportioning international income among different taxing jurisdictions.

As the last step of the discourse, Chapter 4 extends the equity standards developed for individuals to corporations in the international setting. This involves analysing the potential influences and adaptations required when shifting the focus from individuals to corporate entities.

In essence, this chapter emphasizes that equity in international taxation requires a departure from merely extending domestic equity norms to the global context. It provides an in-depth theoretical analysis of equity in taxation, highlighting the complexity and nuances involved in applying equity principles from domestic to international tax contexts. The construction of equity principle in international taxation requires critical insights into the challenges of developing equitable international tax systems, particularly in the context of globalization and the growing interdependence of national economies.

Utilizing a similar methodology, Chapter 5 undertakes a redevelopment of the legitimacy principle. Similar to equity, this chapter proves that legitimacy also undergirds formulary apportionment and provides instructions on the design specifics, even to a greater extent.

The chapter begins by establishing the significance of legitimacy in the international tax order, emphasizing its dual impact on both the taxpayer-tax authority relationship and the interactions between taxing states. The chapter is methodically divided into several sections, each tackling a different aspect of legitimacy.

7. Richard A Musgrave and Peggy B Musgrave, 'Inter-Nation Equity' in Richard M Bird and John G Head (eds), *Modern Fiscal Issues: Essays in Honour of Carl S. Shoup* (University of Toronto Press 1972).

As a key contribution, this chapter distinguishes between 'normative legitimacy' and 'descriptive legitimacy' in the context of international tax law. Normative legitimacy focuses on the substantive aspects of law and its alignment with the common interest of constituents, while descriptive legitimacy centres on the formal and procedural aspects, especially regarding the democratic creation of laws and their acceptance by stakeholders.

A significant portion of the chapter revisits the concept of normative legitimacy, highlighting its historical evolution and its implications in the modern international tax setting. The discussion includes an in-depth analysis of the theories and models proposed by notable scholars like Lorenz von Stein and Klaus Vogel, who contribute significantly to understanding tax legitimacy. Their models, which evolve from a 'state-individual' interaction to a more complex 'state-society-economy' framework, provide a foundational basis for re-examining legitimacy in the constantly changing tax order.

Furthermore, the chapter looks into the modernization of normative legitimacy in the context of the evolving international tax order. It scrutinizes the historical underpinnings of international tax law and contrasts them with contemporary realities, thus highlighting the need for a re-evaluation of legitimacy principles. This section also explores the operationalization of legitimacy in taxation and the challenges it presents in an international context.

In the end, the chapter addresses the issue of descriptive legitimacy, particularly in relation to the taxation of multinational enterprises. It critically examines the current international tax system and its alignment with descriptive legitimacy principles, focusing on aspects such as cooperation among states, the norm-making process, and the role of the ALP in shaping the descriptive legitimacy of international tax law.

Chapter 5 concludes by reinforcing the importance of legitimacy in international taxation and advocating for a re-evaluation of both normative and descriptive legitimacy in light of the evolving global tax landscape. This re-evaluation is crucial for ensuring that the international tax regime remains just, equitable, and reflective of contemporary economic and social realities.

Chapter 6 engages in a comprehensive discourse on neutrality. It argues, from the standpoint of normative thinking, that neutrality cannot serve as a guiding principle. Consequently, considerations of neutrality and efficiency are relegated to secondary roles within the framework being established.

The chapter commences with an exploration of what neutrality in taxation fundamentally dictates. It is established that neutrality, though not originally one of Adam Smith's canons of good tax design, has become a significant concept in taxation discourse, especially in its application to minimize the distortive effects of taxation on economic activities.

The discourse then divides into an examination of neutrality in domestic and international tax contexts. Its application in domestic policymaking remains limited due to prevalent tax expenditure schemes. In contrast, neutrality in international tax literature is often elevated to a principle status akin to traditional concepts like equity or equality. The chapter critically assesses the current status of neutrality in international tax discussions, arguing that its significance might be overemphasized due to a lack of alternative benchmarks for economic efficiency.

Subsequent sections of the chapter look into the basic propositions of Capital Export Neutrality (CEN) and Capital Import Neutrality (CIN), providing economic rationales, illustrative examples, and discussions on the tax systems satisfying each form of neutrality. It also scrutinizes the questionable grounds for choosing either CEN or CIN in real-world scenarios, emphasizing their mutual exclusivity without tax harmonization.

The chapter further explores the problems associated with favouring CEN over CIN in academic literature, highlighting the criticisms and limitations of CEN, including its disconnection from real-world tax policy and the opt-out problem, where only a few countries adopt CEN-endorsed tax policies. Similarly, the interpretations of CIN are dissected for their inconsistencies and varying efficiency contexts.

Chapter 6 also introduces newer generations of neutralities like capital ownership neutrality (CON) and Market Neutrality (MN), evaluating their potential as better alternatives.

This chapter concludes with a call for a new philosophy of international tax neutrality, advocating a shift from viewing neutrality as a guiding principle to treating it as an evaluative benchmark in tax policy design. The chapter emphasizes that global cooperation, rather than competition, should be the main theme in international taxation in the foreseeable future and the need to balance efficiency with other principles like equity and simplicity.

### 1.3.4 Part IV: The China Test and Experiment of Formulary Apportionment

Part IV is the concluding segment of the main research process. This section encompasses an analysis divided into three primary stages. Initially, it informs readers about the current state of China's international tax regime and, more importantly, its ongoing changes. Subsequently, the discussion reverts to the theme of formulary apportionment; it reveals the fundamental enigma of whether China is an appropriate sovereign candidate for experimenting with formulary apportionment. Predicated on these considerations, a route is proposed that China might deliberate upon for the trial implementation of formulary apportionment in the context of international taxation.

Chapter 7 serves as an introductory section concerning China's international tax regime. Distinct from conventional literature that introduces China's taxation system, this chapter centres its focus on the impact and shaping influence of the Belt and Road Initiative (BRI) on China's tax policies. It delineates a series of changes in the tax system, covering both treaty and domestic law dimensions, to expose a hidden transition in China's international tax paradigm. Specifically, China is gradually shifting its stance from a typical source country to a residence-based taxation country.

Chapter 8 adopts a narrower focus, questioning the suitability of China for further exploration into formulary apportionment. The chapter enhances its argument by revealing China's international tax strategy beyond the implicit trends described in Chapter 7 and the underlying principles that potentially govern it. The chapter highlights both the formal declarations by China's state tax authority and the inherent tension in China's dual role as an origin state and a market state. Such a contradiction, however, may augment China's strategic momentum to explore multi-factor formulary apportionment models. The chapter also briefly discusses the viability of applying the classical three-factor formula in the Chinese context.

Assuming that China becomes the subject country tested for pioneering the advancement of formulary apportionment, Chapter 9 concludes the research by outlining potential paths on two fronts. The first pertains to the substantive design of the prospective regime, drawing upon the philosophical discussions laid out in previous chapters, notably in Part III, which focuses on normative principles, and Part III, which looks into comparative analysis.

As for the potential pathways to implement this tentative regime, Chapter 9 considers two contrasting approaches: the first is through multilateral tax treaties, and the second leverages existing trade and investment relations. As both approaches have yet to be manifested in real-world applications, they remain speculative and are essentially thought experiments. While their practical relevance remains uncertain, it is hoped that these theoretical frameworks will provide valuable insights when the day of actual implementation arrives.

The conclusion in Chapter 10 encapsulates the research process of all the above chapters.

# PART I Formulary Apportionment at the Historical Turning Point

CHAPTER 2

# Historical Analysis: Formulary Apportionment as a Key Indicator

*This chapter is a diachronic study of formulary apportionment against the evolution of the international tax system. Such a topic is massive since there are numerous facets of the story to be told, even though the history of international taxation is rather short compared to other areas of law or the law itself. In this light, this chapter mainly serves three purposes. First, the history matters itself. This chapter collects and extracts the most relevant historical materials and delineates a historical trajectory of formulary apportionment. Based on this, the second purpose is to unveil the historical status of formulary apportionment in the emergence of the international tax system, focusing on understanding how and why formulary apportionment finally faded and the arm's length standard ascended as the international tax norm. Last but not least, the quest for formulary apportionment will put into perspective the genesis of the modern international tax system, particularly in relation to the key foundations of the system that underlie the homeless income problems to which the BEPS Project fails to address its core. Within the general framework of the thesis, this chapter also contributes to unfolding a matter of fact that formulary apportionment is not a chimera but an alternative design of the system for taxing international business that had been seriously contemplated as well as deployed by tax treaties and domestic tax laws. It is to be established that the effacement of formulary apportionment is attributed to preserving the economic/political order of the world long before we are currently living rather than based on some genuine theoretical superiority of the existing foundations, particularly the arm's length standard and that an international tax system employing formulary apportionment is an alternative facing to the future.*

## 2.1 INTRODUCTION

Chapter 2 examines the intricate historical development of formulary apportionment as a pivotal concept in the evolution of the international tax system, offering a diachronic study that unearths its historical significance. The history of international taxation may be relatively short compared to other legal areas, but it is rich with important milestones and shifts, particularly when it comes to the role of formulary apportionment. This chapter serves three key purposes: first, it extracts the most relevant historical materials and delineates the historical trajectory of formulary apportionment; second, it examines how and why formulary apportionment faded as the ALS ascended to dominance; and third, it contextualizes the modern international tax system's failure to address 'homeless income' problems, which the BEPS Project does not fully resolve.

Setting the stage, this chapter reviews the work of scholars like Avi-Yonah and Benshalom, using their insights to periodize the evolution of the international tax system. It highlights how formulary apportionment was once seriously considered and deployed by tax treaties and domestic laws, positioning it as a credible alternative design for taxing international businesses. By tracing the early existence of formulary apportionment and its formalization through institutions like the International Chamber of Commerce (ICC) and the LON, this chapter reveals its importance in shaping the foundations of the current system.

As we progress through the different phases – Revenue, Trade, and Anti-avoidance – the chapter highlights key turning points, such as the divergence between the Mexico and London Models and the adoption of the arm's length standard (ALS) as the prevailing method of taxation. This analysis culminates in a reflection on how formulary apportionment was sidelined during the rise of anti-avoidance measures, despite its continued relevance in addressing the complexities of MNE taxation.

Finally, the chapter turns to the emerging Allocation Phase, where the digital economy and the TPS have reignited discussions about formulary apportionment. This section explores how the evolving global economy demands a re-evaluation of international tax norms, positioning formulary apportionment as a key indicator for the future of a post-BEPS international tax system.

Ultimately, this chapter contributes to the broader thesis by establishing that formulary apportionment is not a historical chimera but a serious alternative that was once considered a key part of the international tax landscape. Through its detailed historical analysis, the chapter positions formulary apportionment as an enduring concept, ready to face the challenges of a post-BEPS international tax system, where unresolved issues like 'homeless income' still demand innovative solutions.

## 2.2 SETTING THE STAGE: PERIODIZING THE EVOLUTION OF THE INTERNATIONAL TAX SYSTEM

'Without periodization ... history risks becoming just one damn fact after another ...'

– Avi-Yonah[8]

Since the discussions of the history of formulary apportionment in this chapter are revisited in the changing environment of international taxation rather than insulated as in a vacuum, it is advisable to shed some light on how the international tax system has evolved to the status quo. Compared to the approach of a comprehensive yet lengthy investigation, this part relies on a shortcut method of periodizing the history of international taxation so as to provide a panorama with legible dividing lines while avoiding piling the international tax events one after another. Instead of starting from scratch, this part draws insights from two studies that explore the periodization of international taxation. A caveat should also be made that such a shortcut way is at the peril of being crude and probably inaccurate in details, yet it does not diminish the overall value of periodization.

### 2.2.1 Avi-Yonah

There are several possible ways of dividing the historical evolution in question into different stages. The most basic way is a chronological list of high-profile events of international taxation, such as the launch of the BEPS Project or the earliest entry of LON in the 1920s, which was employed by Woodward in his discussion of the evolution of the international corporate tax regime between 1920 and 2008.[9] Other approaches may rely on different anchors, yet they all present the narrative in forward chronology. Numerous studies in this respect have revolved around certain components of the international tax system,[10] yet many fewer take the system as a whole for a macro view. Avi-Yonah's work on the periodization of the international tax policy of the United States is roughly the first of those efforts with a global outlook, even though the perspective is within the US national policy domain.[11] The author has provided his

8. Reuven S Avi-Yonah, 'All of a Piece Throughout: The Four Ages of U.S. International Taxation' (2005) 25 Virginia Tax Review 313, 315.
9. Richard Woodward, 'Chapter 1: The Evolution of the International Corporate Tax Regime, 1920 - 2008' in Richard Eccleston and Ainsley Elbra (eds), *Business, Civil Society and the 'New' Politics of Corporate Tax Justice* (Edward Elgar Publishing 2018). Similar view was also expressed by Sunita Jogarajan, 'Prelude to the International Tax Treaty Network: 1815-1914 Early Tax Treaties and the Conditions for Action' (2011) 31 Oxford Journal of Legal Studies 679 https://doi.org/10.1093/ojls/gqr021 accessed 26 August 2025.
10. The probably most typical sample is the studies on the history of the arm's length standard, *see*, for example, the Chapter 1: The Emergence of the ALP, in Collier Richard and Joseph L Andrus, *Transfer Pricing and the Arm's Length Principle After BEPS* (Oxford University Press 2017) 6-50. For miscellaneous components of tax law as the subjects of historical studies, *see* Studies in the History of Tax Law series, Vols 1-9, Hart Publishing, 2004-2019.
11. Avi-Yonah, 'All of a Piece Throughout' (n. 8).

unique basis for dividing the US international tax policy history into different stages, that is, the main international tax principles underlying major legislative moves. Accordingly, history is cut into four pieces. The first is the Age of Benefits (1918-1960), when the benefit principle was widely invoked as the justification for taxation in the international context. The US history in this stage largely converged with the developments in the international tax forum as the main contributors on the US side were also active on the international side. The second stage is Neutrality (1961-1980), when the CEN dominated the US policymakers' arguments for enacting the controlled foreign corporations (CFC) regime in the 1960s to put an end to deferral or as their expression of the general preference for residence-based taxation. When the CEN increasingly lost its appeal among the US international tax community, the third Age of Competition (1981-1997) emerged in competitiveness terms, which led to the shrunk residence-based taxation and US source tax base. With respect to the last stage, the author was not as steadfast as the earlier ones in that it approaches the present times. Marked by the US cooperation with the OECD's 1998 harmful tax competition campaign, this period onwards was designated as an Age of Cooperation (1998 onwards) in deviation from the previous unilateral pro-competition position. As a general comment, among the insights drawn from Avi-Yonah's diachronic analysis for application to the international context, first and foremost, periodization is a powerful tool to systematize the evolution of the international tax system. It has exhibited a dynamic process of international tax policy that keeps adjusting itself to the changing international political, economic, and societal order. Thus, it dismisses the evolution of international taxation as an erratic or discontinuous process independent of the general environment of the global political economy. In addition, the author's specific methodology of periodization also reveals that constructing a principle-based evolution of the international tax system is tenable, which is not only of significance to comprehending the past but also to evaluating the present and predicting or guiding the future.

It is a pity that, to my best knowledge, Avi-Yonah's successful periodization of the US international tax history seems to have not stirred enough academic interest in the evolution of the international tax system as a whole. One of the rare exceptions is Benshalom's two consecutive studies on the international taxation of interest/financial income.[12] The issue in question was not approached as a static or insulated matter; rather, the whole international tax regime was periodized into four stages, of which the evolving conventions on sourcing interest income are emblematic. Specifically, the periodization of the international tax regime in these studies served multiple purposes that reflect the above insights drawing on the analysis of Avi-Yonah: it aimed to provide an explanation of the historical backdrop in which a certain international tax policy arose; the stages in the evolution of the international tax system were important yet expedient signposts for judging the system itself; usually, the most recent stage of

12. Ilan Benshalom, 'The Quest to Tax Interest Income in a Global Economy: Stages in the Development of International Income Taxation' (2007) 27 Virginia Tax Review 631; Ilan Benshalom, 'The Quest to Tax Financial Income in a Global Economy: Emerging to an Allocation Phase' (2008) 28 Virginia Tax Review 165.

the evolution embodies the clues for future direction based on a value judgment of the historical developments.

### 2.2.2 Benshalom

Continuing Avi-Yonah's spirit of acknowledging the evolution of international taxation as a contrived process, Benshalom's methodology of periodizing the international tax system is to identify the distinguishing themes of the phases of development. In each of the phases, with particular reference to the source rules of interest, a roughly unique set of considerations dominated the policy-making of international taxation in the minds of the players over the considerations in the earlier stages.[13] The four phases in chronological order are: the Revenue Phase, the Trade Phase, the Anti-Avoidance Phase, and the last the author sees emerging, the Allocation Phase. The Revenue Phase spreads between the end of WWI and the end of WWII (1918-circa 1948), which is a period when revenue allocation between capital exporting and importing countries was the states' dominant concern over the making of international tax rules. It is revealing that the author emphasized that although the substantial developments in this phase were alleged primarily to alleviate double taxation, the allocation of revenues among sovereign states was the true linchpin that actuated the progress in this period. As is also commonly known, this phase is the formative period of the modern international tax system, whose general framework, terminology and principles were forged during these two decades. As to the period between post-WWII and the 1990s, the author observed a transition of the theme from revenue allocation to the liberalization of international commerce, which is coined as the Trade Phase. More specifically, the Trade Phase was identified because the concerns of international trade gradually overflowed into the area of international taxation and finally marginalized the traditional normative considerations with regard to revenue allocation. The tangible implications for the international tax system are the worldwide trend of reducing withholding tax at source, the expansion of the tax treaty network, and, more profoundly, an opened Pandora's Box of tax avoidance.[14] Anti-avoidance, as the theme of the third phase between the late 1980s and 2000s, marks a shift of focus from the period of the Trade Phase. The scale of tax avoidance exponentially increases against the backdrop of the changing picture of the global economy, including the higher integration, the booming international market, and the prosperous MNEs. As a response, the major developments of the international tax system in this phase were the proliferation of anti-tax avoidance rules, based on the premise that abusive transactions can be singled out from regular transactions, and which was disproved by the author as fictitious. The last Allocation Phase was still in embryo form, which was predicted from the author's case studies, corroborating that the ALS was increasingly

13. Benshalom, 'The Quest to Tax Interest Income in a Global Economy: Stages in the Development of International Income Taxation' (n. 12) 633-634.
14. *Ibid.*, 671.

questioned and avoided.[15] The leitmotiv of this phase seems to be a revitalization of the trajectory searching for appropriate sourcing norms of incomes that have failed in the previous phases. As a thought experiment, the author in the second and third volumes of research explored a proposal of employing unitary and formulary apportionment to tax the financial incomes of MNEs.[16]

### 2.2.3 Interconnection of Avi-Yonah and Benshalom

Based on the above introductions, Avi-Yonah and Benshalom have set good examples of why periodization, how to periodize, and what periodization yields in terms of the evolution of international taxation. In fact, the two discourses are complementary to each other, for one is on the international tax policy of a sovereign state while the other is on the tax system of international wide, and one's approach is principle-based while the other is a synthesis of the principal concerns of policymakers and global political economy circumstances. On the surface, the two pieces of periodization seem to have rendered distinct results based on varying philosophies. Nevertheless, they are closely interlinked. Avi-Yonah's Age of Benefits largely corresponds with Benshalom's Revenue Phase both in the time range and the underlying rationale since the benefit principle is to justify the revenue concerns of taxing states; so is the case for the Age of Neutrality and the Trade Phase where both served to promote cross-border investment flows; the Age of Competition and the Anti-Avoidance Phase are connected by the inner link between tax competition and international tax arbitrage; and the link between the Age of Cooperation and the Allocation Phase is even more solid taking into consideration of the latest developments under the G20/OECD BEPS Project. What Benshalom's analysis adds to Avi-Yonah is that it has presented how a certain component of international taxation miniatures the evolution of the system as an organic whole, and at the mirror side, and of more significance, how the changing era tunes its various components – sourcing convention for interest income is the example, the changing role of formulary apportionment should not be an exception.

Back to the theme of this chapter, in what follows, Avi-Yonah and especially Benshalom's discourses on periodizing the international tax system evolution will be the analytical context for conducting the diachronic analysis of formulary apportionment. The embedded value of introducing this section on the periodization of an international tax system evolution, to repeat, lies in putting the development of formulary apportionment into the dynamics of international taxation. The history of formulary apportionment should resonate with the historical picture of the international tax system rather than be a melody played in a vacuum. This is a cautious but probably fair deduction; the formulary apportionment must have experienced a similar

15. Benshalom, 'The Quest to Tax Financial Income in a Global Economy: Emerging to an Allocation Phase' (n. 12) 181-193; Benshalom, 'The Quest to Tax Interest Income in a Global Economy: Stages in the Development of International Income Taxation' (n. 12) 703-707.
16. Benshalom, 'The Quest to Tax Financial Income in a Global Economy: Emerging to an Allocation Phase' (n. 12). Ilan Benshalom, 'Taxing the Financial Income of Multinational Enterprises by Employing a Hybrid Formulary and Arm's Length Allocation Method' (2008) 28 Virginia Tax Review 619.

tortuous life track, and more intriguing is its prospect from a diachronic perspective of the organic whole of the international system. The following sections will contribute to filling the gap between this deduction and the details.

### 2.2.4 The Periodization Adopted by This Research

Largely based on the periodization contributed by Benshalom and its inner connection with Avi-Yonah's, and considering the latest developments of international tax events, this chapter thus adopted the following division of the developments of international taxation. The first Revenue Phase extends roughly between the two World Wars; the second Trade Phase covers the period from the post-WWII to the late 1990s; the third Anti-avoidance Phase extends from the late 1990s to the publication of the Final Reports of the BEPS Project in 2015; the last Allocation Phase, however, refers to the post-BEPS era.

## 2.3 THE PROLOGUE: FORMULARY APPORTIONMENT BEFORE THE 'BIG BANG'

History cannot begin at the beginning.[17] In international tax literature, the history of international taxation has commonly been traced back to the 1920s. However, as historians agree, the remote past can continuously bear on the later part of the historical track. International taxation is not an exception, considering the periodization of the evolution of international tax. Contrary to the intuition of many that tax treaty is the end product following the developments in the early twentieth century, for instance, the first recorded international tax agreement was dated back to 1843 between France and Belgium,[18] and the first international double taxation agreement on income taxation was concluded in 1869 between Prussia and Saxony, earlier than many incorrectly referred to,[19] both of which laid important foundations for the modern international tax system such as the principle of reciprocity, the double taxation elimination methods and the concept of PE.[20] In the same vein, formulary

17. Theodore Frank Thomas Plucknett, *A Concise History of the Common Law* (The Lawbook Exchange, Ltd 2001) 3.
18. Jogarajan, 'Prelude to the International Tax Treaty Network' (n. 9) 687; League of Nations, 'Double Taxation and Tax Evasion Report and Resolutions Submitted by the Technical Experts to the Financial Committee of the League of Nations' (1925) F.212 (hereinafter '1925 Technical Report'), as reprinted in Joint Committee On Internal Revenue Taxation, *Legislative History of United States Tax Conventions* (US GPO 1962) 4083 (hereinafter 'Legislative History').
19. The first international double taxation treaty was often wrongly deemed as the tax treaty between Prussia and Austria-Hungary in 1899, *see* Jogarajan, 'Prelude to the International Tax Treaty Network' (n. 9) 690. Michael Kobetsky, *International Taxation of Permanent Establishments: Principles and Policy* (Cambridge University Press 2011) 109. Such mistake was pointed out by Maikel Evers, 'Tracing the Origins of the Netherlands' Tax Treaty Network' (2013) 41 Intertax 379 https://doi.org/10.54648/taxi2013033 accessed 26 August 2025.
20. For the implications of this treaty for the later international tax law, *see* the detailed introduction and analysis in Johann Hattingh, 'On the Origins of Model Tax Conventions: 19th Century German Tax Treaties and Laws Concerned with the Avoidance of Double Taxation' (2013) 6

apportionment has similar origins that have long been forgotten. This section is the archaeological effort to dig it out.

### 2.3.1 Global Economy Prior to WWI

The decades before the First World War in 1914 were the era of Europe, where most of the colonial empires were 'found'. Possibly, to many legal scholars' surprise, in economics, the familiar phenomenon of globalization as it is accustomed to today is frequently deemed as having its roots in this period of time.[21] The nineteenth century witnessed the First and Second Industrial Revolutions, which provided the material basis for globalization as an unprecedented event in mankind's history. The widespread usage of steam engines in ships and railroads had shrunk the geographical dispersion of markets, the invention of the telegraph and telephone had facilitated communication dramatically, and the construction of canals like the Suez and Panama had greatly shortened the shipping route. To sum up, all these developments are major drivers of the first epoch of globalization in trade, capital and population migration.[22] Statistics show that the percentage of trade in world production has increased from one-thirtieth to one-third from the 1800s till the outbreak of WWI, and the absolute trade volumes have expanded more than twenty times.[23]

With the economic activities going global, so arose the rudiments of (multinational) companies, income tax and international taxation. The emblems of the earliest multinational companies, the Dutch East India Company and English East India Company, carried the characteristics of that age. They are truly multinational in the sense of doing business across borders; they are not multinational enough in that the business was established still within the colonial empire of the Great Britain and The Netherlands.[24] When it comes to determining the liabilities of income tax or other analogues across jurisdictions, the preliminary issue of income allocation thus emerged. In relative terms, the double taxation was still mild in that income tax was yet to become global, and the tax rates were low. As a result, the tax agreements in the early stages either revolved around administration issues or were concluded between contiguous states.[25] One should not be surprised at finding few clues of formulary

---

Studies in the History of Tax Law 31, 34-42. *See also* Evers (n .19) 378-379; Jogarajan, 'Prelude to the International Tax Treaty Network' (n. 9) 681-684.

21. George Ritzer and Dean Paul, *Globalization: The Essentials* (John Wiley & Sons 2019) 59-60; C Fred Bergsten, 'The Backlash Against Globalization' (2000) https://www.piie.com/commentary/speeches-papers/backlash-against-globalization accessed 24 November 2023.
22. Alan Taylor, 'Globalization, Trade, and Development: Some Lessons From History' (National Bureau of Economic Research 2002) w9326 http://www.nber.org/papers/w9326.pdf accessed 18 November 2023.
23. Estevadeordal, Antoni, Brian Frantz, and Alan M. Taylor. 'The rise and fall of world trade, 1870–1939.' The Quarterly Journal of Economics 118.2 (2003): 359-407.
24. Mira Wilkins, 'Chapter 1 The History of Multinational Enterprise' in Alan M Rugman and Thomas L Brewer (eds), *Oxford Handbook of International Business* (Oxford University Press 2001) 18.
25. For example, the Austro-Hungarian Empire and certain constituent states of the German Empire had concluded double taxation agreements before the war, *see* League of Nations, 'Double

apportionment in the earliest tax treaties that were still in preliminary forms;[26] the following is thus principally to sketch its existence in national practices.

### 2.3.2 The Earliest Existences of Formulary Apportionment

Before the international tax system entered its formative period, it drew most of the attention of observers to the forging of the earliest model double taxation conventions, and as sketched above, the emerging issue of cross-jurisdiction allocation of profits for tax purposes began to demand solutions. Since then, the formulary apportionment has already been widely employed in national practices within the border, which the following aims to briefly outline.[27]

*The United States.* The United States is a true pioneer in the application of formulary apportionment, both in terms of the early adoption and the intellectual debates that have contributed ever since. In the last decades of the nineteenth century, the taxing authorities of US states began to use the formulary methodology for property tax or capital tax purposes[28] in relation to the transportation and communication businesses, including railways, toll bridges, express services and telegraphs, which were also sanctioned by adjudications.[29] These sectors are common in their nature of crossing several tax jurisdictions and have identifiable factors as the basis of apportionment. The rationale is straightforward. Instead of assessing the value of property separately in each state where the business is conducted, the formulary apportionment views the business operators as a single unit and attributes as the basis of state taxation a proportion of the total property value calculated by the proportion of the mileage or length of lines or track within the state relative to the total mileage or length of lines or

Taxation and Tax Evasion: Report and Resolutions Submitted by the Technical Experts to the Financial Committee of the League of Nations (Document F.212)' (n. 18) 4071.

26. To the author's best knowledge, within this period, only Germany and Holland entered a tax treaty employing formulary apportionment in 1899. The following will introduce more about it. *See* John G Herndon, *Relief from International Taxation, the Development of International Reciprocity for the Prevention of Double Taxation* (Callaghan & Co 1932) 15.
27. The 'national practice' used here does not mean the nation-wide application of formulary apportionment, but is to differentiate the utilization of it through tax treaties.
28. The corporate income tax was first introduced in the United States by the State of Wisconsin in 1911. Harley L Lutz, 'The Progress of State Income Taxation Since 1911' (1920) 10 American Economic Review 66; Joann Martens Weiner, *Formulary Apportionment and Group Taxation in the European Union: Insights from the United States and Canada* (Directorate General Taxation and Customs Union, European Commission 2005) 11.
29. *See*, for example, the case of *Western Union Tel. Co. v. Taggart*, 163 US 1, 16 S. Ct. 1054 (1896), adjudicating a Statute of Indiana enacted in 1983 that directed the tax authority to tax a telegraph company on its property within the state at the proportion of the whole capital stock, a proportion calculated by the length of the lines within the state divided by the total line length everywhere. Similar cases include *Pittsburgh C. & St. L. Ry. v. Backus*, 154 US 421, 14 S. Ct. 1114 (1894); State Railroad Tax Cases, 92 US 575, 608 (1875); Delaware Railroad Tax, 85 US (18 Wall.) 206 (1873). *See* Jerome R Hellerstein and Walter Hellerstein (eds), *Hellerstein & Hellerstein: State Taxation (WGL)* (Thomson Reuters 2010) s. 8.05 https://www.westlaw.com/Browse/Home/SecondarySources/TaxSecondarySources/TaxTextsTreatises/HellersteinHellersteinStateTaxationWGL?rs=tran3.0&vr=3.0&originationContext=vendcc accessed 6 December 2023.

track.[30] The bedrock philosophy of this formulary apportionment method had been sanctioned as the 'unit rule' by the US Supreme Court in the State Railroad Tax Cases in 1875.[31] The unit rule, refined subsequently in a series of court decisions and applied to a certain range of business sectors, is justified by the internal interconnectivity, unity of use, and the unique character of the businesses.[32] It becomes the predecessor of the modern 'unitary business principle' of devising more sophisticated formulary solutions in the area of state corporate income taxation.[33]

*Germany*. In 1884, the state of Baden in Germany enacted the law of income tax. It was provided that the tax base of the corporate income was determined in proportion to the capital employed in the state relative to the total capital of the corporation.[34] The Prussian law of 1867, just as the contemporaneous US laws but for income tax purposes, stipulated that the taxable income in the state from cross-jurisdictional railroads was assessed by the proportion of gross receipts calculated by the ratio of the length of the railroad in the state relative to the total length of the railroad.[35] In 1885, the Prussian local tax law extended this formulary apportionment approach to banking/insurance companies and transportation companies. For the former, the taxable corporate income was allocated to each district for taxation in proportion to the share of gross profits; and for the latter, the allocation key is the share of salaries and wages expenses.[36]

Besides these experiences, Germany may have also concluded the first bilateral tax treaty that employed formulary apportionment. In 1899, Germany and Holland entered a convention with respect to taxing the profits from a cross-border railroad, which provided that the operating profits were assessed and taxed according to the length of the section within the territory relative to the total length of the line.[37] In summary, Germany and the United States almost developed the approach of formulary apportionment in the same period and applied it to similar fields of business as well. It is to be noted that in both countries, the formulary apportionment had been confined

30. For the details of the formulary apportionment applications in the several states, *see* Joann Martens Weiner, 'Company Taxation for the European Community: How Sub-National Tax Variation Affects Business Investment in the United States and Canada' (PhD dissertation, Harvard University 1994).
31. State Railroad Tax Cases, 92 US 575, 608 (1875).
32. The following cases gradually extended the spirit of unit rule from 1875 to similar businesses for the application of the formulary apportionment: *Wallace v. Hines*, 253 US 66, 40 S. Ct. 435 (1920); *Norfolk & W. Ry. v. Missouri State Tax Comm'n*, 390 US 317, 88 S. Ct. 995 (1968); *Adams Express Co. v. Ohio*, 165 US 194, 17 S. Ct. 305 (1897); *see also* the developments of the unit rule in Elcanon Isaacs, 'The Unit Rule', 35 Yale Law Journal 838 (1926) https://doi.org/10.2307/789461 accessed 26 August 2025.
33. Hellerstein and Hellerstein (n. 29) s. 8.05.
34. Badisches Einkommensteuergesetz Vom. 20 Juni, 1884, Art. 5, lit. B. In FinanzArckiv, III, 368, referred to in Edwin RA Seligman, 'The Taxation of Corporations. III' (1890) 5 Political Science Quarterly 636, 660 https://doi.org/10.2307/2139532 accessed 26 August 2025.
35. 4 Law of 16 March 1867, §9, referred to in *Ibid*.
36. Kommunalsteuer-Notgesetz Vom 27. Juli 1885, referred to in *Ibid*.
37. League of Nations, 'Double Taxation and Fiscal Evasion Collection of International Agreements and Internal Legal Provisions for the Prevention of Double Taxation and Fiscal Evasion' (League of Nations 1928) C.345 M.102 111.

to sub-national rather than nationwide implementation, and in the US, the early adoption experiences were not for income tax purposes.

*France.* In the late nineteenth century, with the increased fiscal needs of the French government and movable capital like stocks and bonds becoming a substantial source of revenue, France introduced in 1872 a tax on the dividend, interest, and other incomes from French transferable securities.[38] What draws attention here is that, in the context of foreign companies having a French branch or subsidiary, the company is liable to pay the French income tax on a fraction of, rather than a sum total of, the actual, dividend, interest or other incomes distributed by the branch or subsidiary corporation. The taxable fraction is determined by multiplying the total and actual distributed income by a ratio, the so-called taxable quota ('quotité imposable').[39] The taxable quota in turn is the proportion of the value of the French assets relative to the total value of the company's assets, or the French turnover relative to the total turnover, or any other factors deemed appropriate by the tax commission.[40] Compared to the applications of formulary apportionment in the United States and Germany, the French system is closer to the modern scenario where formulary apportionment has been frequently proposed as a solution to international taxation of multinational enterprises.

*United Kingdom, The Dominion Income Tax Relief System.*[41] In 1920, the United Kingdom introduced the system for the purpose of relieving double taxations between the UK and its dominions or colonies.[42] The Dominion Income Tax Relief System had been used until the modern double tax treaties that superseded it. The general objective of the system was to provide a total credit equal to the lower half of the UK rate or the dominion rate. The net effect is the same, sharing of relief between the taxing jurisdictions. Besides that, the concepts of residence and source, and characterization of incomes were basically irrelevant.[43] These features share many properties of a formulary apportionment system, as recognized by the experts of the LON in 1923.[44]

38. Mitchell B Carroll, *Taxation of Business in France* (US Government Printing Office 1931) 43.
39. League of Nations, 'Taxation of Foreign and National Enterprises Vol. 1. A Study of the Tax Systems and the Methods of Allocation of the Profits of Enterprises Operating in More than One Country in France, Germany, Spain, the United Kingdom, and the United States of America' (League of Nations 1932) C.73.M.38.1932.II.A 80-81.
40. Mitchell B Carroll, 'Observations on Report of The Committee of the National Tax Association on Uniformity and Reciprocity on State Tax Legislation, Especially with Regard to the Allocation of Income of International Enterprises' (1931) 24 Proceedings of The Annual Conference on Taxation Under the Auspices of The National Tax Association 337.
41. For a detailed introduction of the system, *see* Staples Ronald, *Income Tax Relief: Dominion (Including the Irish Free State) Income Tax Relief, Law and Practice, Over Seventy Examples; Appropriate Rate Tables* (Gee & Co 1925).
42. At s. 27 of the Finance Act 1920 (UK) 10 & 11 Geo 5, c 18.
43. C John Taylor, 'Twilight of the Neanderthals, or Are Bilateral Double Taxation Treaty Networks Sustainable' (2010) 34 Melbourne University Law Review 290.
44. Gijsbert Weijer Jan Bruins et al., 'Report on Double Taxation Submitted to the Financial Committee by Professors Bruins, Einaudi, Seligman, and Sir Josiah Stamp' in Joint Committee on Internal Revenue Taxation (ed.), *Legislative History of United States Tax Conventions* (US GPO 1962) 4051.

### 2.3.3 Summary of the Primeval Formulary Systems

Formulary tax systems had been widely in use before the 'big bang' in the 1920s, which led to the essentials of the modern international tax system. However, their applications were restricted to a limited scope and certain kinds of taxes, most of which were subnational rather than international. It is also noteworthy that these formulary systems were all statutory, not just being pure practices.

## 2.4 THE REVENUE PHASE, EPISODE ONE: FORMULARY APPORTIONMENT AND INTERNATIONAL CHAMBER OF COMMERCE

### 2.4.1 Post-war Economic and Fiscal Implications

As indicated above, although the world had undergone the first wave of globalization before WWI, international taxation was still a nascent phenomenon. Thus, the complaints for double taxation and solutions developed thereto were relatively rare.[45] The picture changed dramatically in the aftermath of the war, probably less for the subjective lessons learned from the war, but more for the objective implications for taxation by the economic and fiscal circumstances in the immediate post-war times.[46] One of the most direct outcomes of war on taxation is the increased level of taxation, especially among combatant states that yearned for revenue,[47] and that had made double taxation more salient and costly for cross-border capital flow.[48] In addition, the trend of liberalizing cross-border trade and investment continued, albeit interrupted by the war, and the justification of double taxation as a shield to protect national interests had been further undermined after the war.[49] These two points are in congruence with Benshalom's Revenue Phase, when international taxation at this period revolved around the competing revenue claims of capital exporting and importing countries debating over the proper method of double tax relief. Furthermore, consistent with the

45. Stanley I Langbein, 'The Unitary Method and the Myth of Arm's Length' (1986) 30 Tax Notes 630.
46. *See* for the slightly different explanations for the increasing importance of double taxation after the war, in Richard and Andrus (n. 10) para. 1.08., and Philipp Genschel and Thomas Rixen, 'The International Tax Regime: Historical Evolution and Political Change' [2012] SSRN Electronic Journal s. 3 http://www.ssrn.com/abstract=2139665 accessed 18 November 2023. Brian D Lepard, 'Is the United States Obligated to Drive on the Right: A Multidisciplinary Inquiry into the Normative Authority of Contemporary International Law Using the Arm's Length Standard as a Case Study' (1999) 10 Duke Journal of Comparative & International Law 43, 60.
47. For example, the UK income tax rate had risen to a combined rate of 52.5% in 1918-1919 compared to 5.8% in the period of 1911-1912, and similar increases of rates can also be observed in Australia (the highest at 40.625%), Japan (the highest at 30%), Canada (the highest at 72.9 %), and the United States (the highest at 77 %), see John F Avery Jones, 'Sir Josiah Stamp and Double Income Tax' in John Tiley (ed.), *Studies in the History of Tax Law*, vol. 6 (Hart Publishing 2013), pp.2-3.
48. *Ibid.*, 635. Mitchell B Carroll, *Prevention of International Double Taxation and Fiscal Evasion: Two Decades of Progress Under the League of Nations* (League of Nations 1939) 7-8.
49. Genschel and Rixen (n. 46) 8-9.

French experience, taxation in many countries has seen increasing reliance on mobile capitals and activities that can cross the border more easily, and new direct taxes like those on individual and corporation incomes have gradually risen,[50] both of which have led to more frequent international double taxation.[51]

Against such a background, the modern problem of international double taxation emerged to the top of the global agenda of post-war reconstruction. As a result, the advances of international tax norm-setting in the aftermath of the WWI were unprecedented in terms of total volume, density or the spirit of enterprise. Rather than a comprehensive narrative of international taxation as a whole within this period, this part, as the main body of the historical analysis, centres on the advances in broad relation to formulary apportionment, either in terms of its historical status, the emergence and effacement, theoretical advantage and practical constraints, and so forth.

### 2.4.2 The Legacies of the International Chamber of Commerce

*What is ICC*? The ICC is a private international organization founded in 1920 following a call in 1919, immediately after the end of WWI.[52] With the aim of filling the gap where no governmental world system of trade, investment, or finance existed, a group of 'merchants of peace' was convicted of promoting trade, investment, and an open market by setting global standards for businesses.[53] The ICC has now become a permanent business organization focusing on promoting international commerce and was granted Observer Status at the UN General Assembly in 2016.[54]

*The Forerunner of Addressing Double Taxation*. With a few exceptions, the establishment of modern international tax institutions has been solely attributed in recent times to the work of the LON, whereas the ICC was neglected as another international organization in parallel that had engaged even earlier than the LON or other institutions[55] in addressing the international double taxation problem.[56] As early as in the organization meeting of 1920 that officially created the ICC, 'duplicate

50. For example, the Unites States introduced the progressive income tax in 1913, and the France introduced in 1914.
51. Edwin RA Seligman, *Double Taxation and International Fiscal Cooperation* (Macmillan 1928) 5-11.
52. *See* the detailed introduction of the early history of the ICC in Shane R Tomashot, 'Selling Peace: The History of the International Chamber of Commerce, 1919-1925' (PhD Dissertation, Georgia State University 2015) 1919-1925.
53. International Chamber of Commerce, 'About ICC' https://iccwbo.org/about-icc-2/ accessed 26 November 2023.
54. United Nations, 'List of Non-Member States, Entities and Organizations Having Received a Standing Invitation to Participate as Observers in the Sessions and the Work of the General Assembly' (2019) A/INF/74/3 3 https://undocs.org/en/A/INF/74/3.
55. For example, the International Intermediary Institute and the Committee for the Advancement of International Law, as referred to in Sunita Jogarajan, *Double Taxation and the League of Nations* (1st edn, Cambridge University Press 2018) 85.
56. Ke Chin Wang, 'International Double Taxation of Income: Relief Through International Agreement 1921-1945' (1945) 59 Harvard Law Review 73, 63 https://doi.org/10.2307/1335505 accessed 26 August 2025; Michael J Graetz and Michael M O'Hear, 'The Original Intent of US International Taxation' (1996) 46 Duke Law Journal 1021, 1066-1074 https://doi.org/10.2307/

taxation' was already adopted as Resolution 2 among the other three. Knowing its status of consultancy, the ICC was resolved to 'urge prompt agreement between the Governments of the allied countries in order to avoid that individuals or companies of any one country may be liable to more than one tax on the same income ...'.[57] It is thus safe to conclude that the elimination of double taxation has been the foundational tenet of the ICC. In addition, taking into consideration that when the LON had just begun to act on double taxation in 1921, the ICC had already presented a report of double taxation for its First Congress in London (hereinafter 'ICC Proceedings 1921'),[58] thus the ICC was deemed as the first, the forerunner to advocating a consensus solution to the double taxation phenomenon.[59]

*Momentary yet Momentous*. The ICC had not worked long on international taxation when the LON gradually took over the agenda, arguably from 1924,[60] whereas the contributions of the ICC were truly momentous as regards providing groundbreaking intellectual debates to the international tax system formation. Subsequent to the First Congress, the Committee on Double Taxation of the ICC met in Paris in 1922, and the Second Congress of the ICC was convened in Rome in 1923. In 1924, the Council of the ICC adopted some revisions to the previous Resolutions. These are almost all the ICC actions on double taxation by 1925, and after this, the ICC decided to endorse the LON's leadership. Many of the discussions of the ICC were rudimentary as viewed today. However, as the institution leading the agenda of double taxation in this period, the ICC had contributed, among others, the following legacies:

(i) the ICC had successfully rung the alarm through clearly formulating the seriousness of the problem of double taxation;
(ii) the classification and assignment approach to taxing the different categories of income was brought to the international tax forum for the first time;[61]

---

1372916 accessed 26 August 2025; Bret Wells and Cym H Lowell, 'Income Tax Treaty Policy in the 21st Century: Residence vs. Source' (2014) 5 Columbia Journal of Tax Law 1, 13-17.

57. International Chamber of Commerce, *Proceedings Organization Meeting, Paris, France, June 23-30, 1920* (International Headquarters 1920) 40 and Annex B.
58. International Chamber of Commerce, *First Congress, London (June 27-July 1, 1921) Double Taxation, Brochure No. 11. Double Taxation, Part I, Report of the Select Committee of the Chamber* (International Headquarters 1921); International Chamber of Commerce, *First Congress, London (June 27-July 1, 1921) Double Taxation, Brochure No. 12. Double Taxation, Part II, Special Report by the British National Committee* (2nd edn, International Headquarters 1921).
59. Herndon (n. 26) 8.
60. Richard and Andrus (n. 10) para. 1.28; or, it was the year of 1925, in Graetz and O'Hear (n. 56) 1073.
61. As sanctioned in Resolutions Adopted by the Committee on Double Taxation on 20 December 1922: ... 7. Considered settled:
    (a) Income from real estate [acquired in the country] in which it is situated.
    (b) Interest from loans and dividends from shares [acquired] in the country where the debtor or company issuing the shares is domiciled, or in the country in which the creditor or shareholder is domiciled.
    (c) Income from movable property [acquired] in the country in which it happens to be.
    (d) Income derived from a business of any kind (trade, industry, etc.) or of a profession (office, etc.) [acquired] in the country in which the business is carried on, or the profession exercised.

(iii) the residence-source paradigm was established to accommodate the competing tax claims of capital exporting and capital importing countries, even though it failed to reconcile the two sides following this paradigm that brought itself to the impasse;[62]

(iv) the ICC envisioned a multilateral tax treaty as the proper instrument to eliminate double taxation, while a bilateral tax treaty seemed to be a tax ad hoc solution pending the consensus on basic international tax principles;[63]

(v) the implicit starting point of the ICC's approach to double taxation relief is its perception of the 'single tax principle', namely, an income should be taxed only once;[64]

(vi) the relief of double taxation was indicated as inseparable from the international allocation of income. The general principle conceived was 'to tax income where it is earned'. In particular, for taxation of cross-border businesses that spread in multiple countries, when the profits accrued in each country cannot be ascertained, the ICC had suggested, albeit not insisted on, a formulary apportionment approach.[65] The following section will elaborate on this point.

### 2.4.3 The ICC Model of International Business Taxation

The oblivion of the contributions made by the ICC in terms of international business taxation constitutes a loss in retrieving the 'ancient' wisdom of international taxation. The income allocation with regard to cross-border businesses contemplated by the ICC represents an alternative intellectual design of international business taxation (hereinafter, the 'ICC Model'). Although the ICC Model was ultimately taken over by the approach of the LON, it is a road not taken that deserves to be revisited, in which the hidden value rests in the normative differences between the ICC Model and the LON approach. As pointed out above, the ICC Model adopted the formulary apportionment methodology rather than the ALS as the bedrock.

This is extracted by Jogarajan, *Double Taxation and the League of Nations* (n. 55) apps 4-1922 ICC Resolutions.

62. This is typically manifested in the confrontation between the UK as capital exporters and the European countries as capital importers, *see* Graetz and O'Hear (n. 56) 1070-1073.
63. Such preference to the multilateral convention was maintained till 1928 in the ICC's submission to the LON, *see* League of Nations, 'Double Taxation and Fiscal Evasion. General Meeting of Government Experts October 1928' (League of Nations 1928) C.495.M.147.1928.II; *see also* Richard and Andrus (n. 10) para. 1.27.
64. International Chamber of Commerce, *Proceedings Organization Meeting, Paris, France, June 23-30, 1920* (n. 57) Annex B.
65. Richard and Andrus (n. 10) para. 1.23; International Chamber of Commerce, *Second Congress, Rome (March 18-25, 1923) Brochure No. 23 Programme of the Congress and Drafts of Resolutions* (International Headquarters 1923) 34-35. And International Chamber of Commerce, *Second Congress, Rome (March 18-25, 1923) Brochure No. 25 Double Taxation* (International Headquarters 1923) 26-27.

What exactly is the ICC Model? The ICC Model is not a sophisticated design of international taxation by the ICC within a short period of time, but what the foundations of the international tax system would be like had the ICC's proposal of international business taxation been adopted as the model in the formative period of international taxation. The proposal, contained in the 1922 Resolutions for the ICC Second Congress, as reproduced below, provided that for business operated in more than one country (in modern discourse, the MNE), the countries can employ the sales-based formulary apportionment method to allocate the income from the multinational business if they cannot agree on the specific allocation:

> 8. If a business is being carried on, or a profession exercised in more than one country, the profits derived from such work, or profession should be taxed in each country, in proportion to the profit realised therein.
>
> 9. Should it be impossible to prove the exact amount of profits accruing in each country, the portions pertaining to each country should be determined in a *lump sum* according to rules to be established by the countries concerned. For example, that portion of the profits realised in each of the countries concerned other than that in which the business is being worked, would be presumed to be *proportional to the whole or a portion of the turn-over* realised in these countries by the enterprise to be taxed.
>
> 10. In no case should the portions of incomes taxed in the different countries concerned exceed the total fixed by the competent authority in the country of domicile.

**– ICC 1922 Resolutions**[66]

There are at least five characteristics of the ICC Model of international taxation following the ICC proposal:

(i) income is sourced to the countries where the business is carried on, not dependent on the artificial classification of the income; however, under the default rule of sales-based formulary apportionment, income is sourced on the destination basis;[67]

(ii) it acknowledges the communal interest of both the residence country and source country in the combined income of the cross-border business;

(iii) in light of the first point, the residual income is thus to be allocated to all the countries proportionally to the specified factor;

(iv) the legal structure, i.e., PE, subsidiary, or interim holding company, in which the cross-border business is conducted, is not relevant to the taxation on the income from it;

(v) the most basic one, following a different perception of double taxation that a country cannot get a portion more than the formula apportioned, the

66. This is extracted by Jogarajan, *Double Taxation and the League of Nations* (n. 55) apps 4-1922 ICC Resolutions.

67. Richard Krever and François Vaillancourt (eds), *The Allocation of Multinational Business Income: Reassessing the Formulary Apportionment Option* (Alphen aan den Rijn: Kluwer Law International 2020) 21.

formulary allocation will automatically prevent double taxation on the income from cross-border business.

At a glance, the LON approach that eventually prevails, having constituted the basis of modern tax treaties, contrasts with the above sketches of the ICC Model. The implications for the problem of base erosion and profit shifting of this historical move will be elaborated on later. The normative differences between the ICC Model and the LON approach are summarized as follows.[68]

First, compared to point (i), the LON approach relies heavily on the categorization of the income, which is generally carried out by domestic rules, and then the treaty assigns the taxing right to either the residence or source country;

Second, as to the point (ii) above of the ICC Model, the LON approach instead adopted an all-or-nothing methodology to assign the taxing right of income to either the residence or source country, and this has been discussed in the evaluation chapter of the BEPS Project in terms of its adverse impact on international tax competition. On the surface, such methodology, as enshrined in the classification and assignment approach, is manifested in the single tax principle; at the root, it is the product of the traditional perception of preserving tax sovereignty. The original proposal of the ICC also aims to accommodate this perception of sovereignty, in that a specific allocation arrangement of combined income can be agreed by the countries before a factor-based formulaic allocation applies by default.

Third, in relation to point (iii), the residual income following the LON approach is solely allocated to the residence country, while the source country is entitled to tax the routine profits. Put in another way, the source country is allowed to tax the local operations but not the functions actually performed or according to the overall position in the business;

Fourth, for point (iv), legal structure matters to the LON approach, which has a different set of rules for PE or subsidiary, and a subsidiary by no means constitutes a PE, and the country hosting an interim holding company is treated as the residence country. The transfer pricing rule is thus at the core of intra-group profit allocation. As a cumulative effect of the above points, one-sided transfer pricing methods that inspect the separate accounts at source are the mainstream.

Fifth, the point (v). The perception of double taxation under the LON approach is that the number of levies on the income matters, which should be exactly one.[69] In contrast, each dollar of the combined income is taxed multiple times, each time for a given portion as determined by the formula.[70]

68. For general reference, *see* Wells and Lowell (n. 56) 15-17, 27, 33.
69. Daniel N Shaviro, *Fixing U.S. International Taxation* (Oxford University Press 2014) 6-7; Luís Eduardo Schoueri and Guiherme Galdino, 'Single Taxation as a Policy Goal: Controversial Meaning, Lack of Justification and Unfeasibility' in Jonna Wheeler (ed.), *Single Taxation?* (IBFD Publications 2018) para. 3.2.1.
70. Michael J McIntyre, 'Contrasting Methodologies: A Systematic Presentation of the Differences between an Arm's-Length/Source-Rule System and a Combined-Reporting/Formulary-Apportionment System', *Proceedings of the Annual Conference on Taxation Held under the Auspices of the National Tax Association-Tax Institute of America* (National Tax Association 1994) 231.

## 2.5 THE REVENUE PHASE, EPISODE TWO: THE INVOLVEMENT OF THE LON

The LON was founded in 1920 following the end of World War I, which was the first worldwide intergovernmental organization in the history of mankind. Partly due to the lobbying of the ICC, as noted above, immediately in the next year of its establishment, the LON decided to engage in exploring solutions to the increasing double taxation arising from international trade and business under restoration.

### 2.5.1 Formulary Apportionment in the 1923 Academic Report

The Report entrusted to the four scholars in 1921 and issued in 1923, hereinafter, the Academic Report,[71] represents the first of the outputs on international taxation under the auspices of the LON. Compared to those that came after, this Report is unique in that it was drawn up quite independently by experts from academia instead of representatives from governments, which makes the report more theoretical and principled. Rather than starting from the investigation of the prevalent systems, the Academic Report approached the subject of double taxation with discussions on the principles of taxation and closed the Report with the application of the principles. Although it is a matter of fact that the Report did not truly precede many existing developments or contributions,[72] for example, the work of ICC as indicated above, the Academic Report has been commonly referred to as the intellectual basis or the fountainhead of the modern international tax system.[73] This is a fair recognition of the Academic Report's historic status, which is attributed partly to the fact that it predated the rest of the LON reports, but more to its abundance of intellectual discourse. Especially entering into the new stage of the development of international taxation opened by the BEPS Project, the academia and policymakers' interest in this piece of work is growing,[74] and this section is also among them. One of the explanations is that, as discussed in the periodization section, the allocation phase of international taxation resembles many aspects of the revenue phase, both of which involve the apportionment of the tax base in a nascent economic reality. The following discussions of this

71. Bruins et al. (n. 44) 4003.
72. Graetz and O'Hear (n. 56) 1079-1091.
73. Hugh J Ault, 'Corporate Integration, Tax Treaties and the Division of the International Tax Base: Principles and Practices' (1991) 47 Tax Law Review 565, 567; Richard Krever and François Vaillancourt (eds), *The Allocation of Multinational Business Income: Reassessing the Formulary Apportionment Option* (Wolters Kluwer 2020) 21-22; Avi-Yonah, 'All of a Piece Throughout' (n. 8) 322; Jogarajan, *Double Taxation and the League of Nations* (n. 55) 34, 81-82.
74. For example, the OECD has rereferred to the economic allegiance theory from the 1923 Academic Report, in the OECD, 'Addressing Base Erosion and Profit Shifting' (OECD Publishing 2013) 35 https://doi.org/10.1787/9789264192744-en accessed 26 August 2025; Such theory has also been triggered by scholars as justification for future reforms of international tax system, *see* Stanley I Langbein and Max R Fuss, 'The OECD/G20-BEPS-Project and the Value Creation Paradigm: Economic Reality Disemboguing into the Interpretation of the "Arm's Length" Standard' (2018) 51 International Lawyer 259., and Jinyan Li, Jinjian Bao and Huaning Li, 'Value Creation: A Constant Principle in a Changing World of International Taxation' (2019) 67 Political Economy: Taxation 1107 https://doi.org/10.32721/ctj.2019.67.4.sym.li accessed 26 August 2025.

report intend to rediscover its value against the new phase of international taxation in which the formulary apportionment is going to play a role.

#### *2.5.1.1 Economic Allegiance and Its Natural Affinity with Formulary Apportionment*

Double taxation arises intrinsically from the competing or overlapping tax jurisdictions on cross-border income. The experts of the Academic Report, after discussing briefly the economic consequences of double taxation, advocated the 'economic allegiance' theory as the theoretical basis of the solutions to the double taxation problem.[75] The economic allegiance, vis-à-vis the political allegiance whose force was regarded as considerably weakened, has drawn the values from the ability to pay principle, which is in turn superior to the benefit principle. The economic allegiance is a theory for relieving double taxation from addressing both the basis of jurisdiction to tax and the allocation of the tax base, namely, the whole ability to pay of the taxpayer. Without denying that several constraints certainly exist when 'engrafting' the rationale of economic allegiance to the modern international business taxation scenario,[76] the Academic Report's formulation of the economic allegiance theory has unravelled an astonishing, yet apparent once reflected on, connection to the conception of formulary apportionment:

> The ideal solution is that the individual's whole faculty should be taxed, but that it should be taxed only once, and that *the liability should be divided among the tax districts according to his relative interests in each*. The individual has certain *economic interests* in the place of his permanent residence or domicile, as well as in the place or places where his property is situated or *from which his income is derived.*[77]

This natural affinity, as noted above, between the division of tax liability on the whole faculty of taxpayer in line with his relative economic allegiance (as the proxies of tax liabilities) with the tax districts and allocating the taxing rights on a combined tax base relative to the presence of value creation factors (also as the proxies of tax liabilities) among tax jurisdictions, has revealed that the rationale of formulary apportionment to taxing MNEs is deeply rooted in the intellectual foundation of the modern international tax system.

---

75. One of the experts, Seligman, who is the steadfast supporter of the economic allegiance theory, already in 1900 foreshadowed the prevalence of this theory, 'We see then that each of the last three principles – temporary residence, domicile and location of property – has a certain, but none a complete justification. There is, however, one final principle, toward which all modern governments are tending, which reconciles the three preceding tests. This is the principle of *economic interest or economic allegiance*, as against the antiquated doctrine of political allegiance.', Edwin RA Seligman, *Essays in Taxation* (The Macmillan Company 1905) 110.
76. For example, the economic allegiance theory was discussed in the context of individual's ability to pay, while the ability to pay of an organization is still disputed, which involves the understanding of the role of corporation income tax in relation to individual income tax. *See* George F. Break and Joseph A. Pechman, 'Relationship Between the Corporation and Individual Income Taxes' (1975) 28 National Tax Journal 341; Conor Clarke and Wojciech Kopczuk, 'Business Income and Business Taxation in the United States since the 1950s' (2016) 31 Tax Policy and The Economy 121.
77. Bruins et al. (n. 44) 4024.

Tracing back to the very genesis of the economic allegiance theory in the arena of international taxation, such affinity is even more conspicuous. The German legal scholar Georg von Schanz, in an article dated 1892,[78] put forward the idea of economic allegiance as the best-suited alternative to determining who is liable to pay tax and to whom the tax is owed. The other three alternatives, including the geographical presence, residence and citizenship, were rejected as appropriate bases for international income allocation. Also, as the contributor to the modern Schanz-Haig-Simons concept of income, Schanz defended his economic allegiance theory from the double-sided nature of income taxation: it is linked to the reimbursement for the benefits enjoyed from the public services; and it is the taxpayer's economic wellbeing at stake to determine who and how much to pay his shares to the community.[79] To Schanz, the taxpayer's economic allegiance with the community connects the two sides of income taxation. Applied to international taxation, the countries to which the taxpayer has economic allegiance are determined by either where the income is finally consumed (the residence country) or where the income is derived (the source country). In the cross-border scenario, decisions must be made as to translating the taxpayer's economic allegiance with residence or source into an arrangement of taxing right allocation so as to avoid international double taxation and entail fairness and equity in the distribution of the tax burden.[80] Schanz's position is that the economic allegiance to the source country substantially outweighs the residence country, and interestingly, he suggested a proportional allocation of one-fourth of income taxed at residence, while three-fourths of income is taxed at source.[81]

Schanz did not provide additional explanations on the specific portions assigned to the residence or source, so the exact numbers should not arouse controversies. What the economic allegiance theory tells in its original discourse is threefold. The first is that economic allegiance theory directs a straightforward allocation of income between residence and source, for purposes of avoiding double taxation as well as fair and equitable international taxation. The second is that the weight of economic allegiance as proxies of taxing the right allocation can be crystallized and compared. This point is not explicitly announced in the article, yet it is embedded in the general economic formulation. It represents the author's conception of using objective indicators as the basis for international income allocation between residence and source. In the original proposal, the indicator is a fixed proportion. Last but not least, the economic allegiance theory discards the pure residence or mere physical presence as a priori bases of international taxation; they are nevertheless evaluated collectively and equally within the framework of economic allegiance as regards their economic contribution to the production and consumption of income. Schanz clearly prefers source taxation and also makes it plain that the economic allegiance theory applies

78. George von Schanz, 'Zur Frage Der Steuerpflicht' (1892) 9 FinanzArchiv/Public Finance Analysis 1-74.
79. *Ibid.*, 10.
80. Klaus Vogel, 'Worldwide vs. Source Taxation of Income: A Review and Re-Evaluation of Arguments (Part I)' (1988) 16 Intertax 219 https://doi.org/10.54648/taxi1988068 accessed 26 August 2025.
81. von Schanz (n. 78) 11.

equally to corporations.[82] Developed in a world far simpler than the current one, the theory of economic allegiance may look primitive, but its three connotations have jointly laid the foundation for using formulary apportionment to tax MNEs in the modern context.

#### 2.5.1.2 *The Residence- Source (Origin) Paradigm*

The Report next identified four constituent elements of economic allegiance and concluded that: (i) the production/origin of wealth; and (iv) the consumption of wealth at residence/domicile[83] are the most important considerations over the; (ii) *situs* of wealth; and (iii) the enforceability of rights to wealth, and that the latter two elements are merely auxiliary to the origin and consumption of wealth.[84] Therefore, the focus is on the concepts of origin and residence. For one thing, there are few disputes over the determination of the residence or domicile of a taxpayer; the origin draws much more attention in the Report. For another, the experts especially reasoned with an assumption to illustrate that the residence does not have priority per se. If the relative importance of origin outweighs the residence in the considerations of economic allegiance, the origin is thus the predominant element.[85] The origin, or the production of wealth, has been hotly debated ever since.[86] The experts' understanding of origin is explicit: it is not merely the output of wealth. Instead, it refers to all the stages involved up to the fruition of wealth, including the original physical appearance, the intermediate adaptations, and the final sales.[87] All in all, the economic allegiance theory has underscored the residence and origin as the dominant elements to assign taxing rights between competing jurisdictions.

#### 2.5.1.3 *The Classification and Assignment Approach*

The experts surveyed different categories of wealth and determined which of the four elements of economic allegiance is preponderant for each category of wealth. The result was summarized succinctly in a table;[88] it is easily observed as a sharp line was drawn for the economic allegiance assignment: local and physical operations were considered having predominant allegiance at origin, while the rest of the wealth had

82. *Ibid.*, 53; Luzius U Cavelti, *International Tax Cooperation: The Sovereignty Conflict between the Residence and the Source Country* (Stämpfli Verlag 2016) 22.
83. The following will only use residence rather than domicile for simplification reasons. For difference between domicile and residence, *see* Bruins et al. (n. 44) 4029.
84. *Ibid.*, 4024, 4026-4027.
85. 'If the first three principles are of overwhelming importance as compared with the fourth, i.e., if situs and the place of enforcement re-enforce the place of origin to such an extent as to make it far more important than domicile, the presumption is clearly in favor of the composite principle of origin being predominant.' *Ibid.*, 4030. Residence is not indispensable.
86. *See* Eric C.C.M. Kemmeren, 'Principle of Origin in Tax Conventions: A Rethinking of Models' (Tilburg University, School of Economics and Management 2001).
87. Bruins et al. (n. 44) 4028.
88. The tale is as follows, *Ibid.*, 4043.

predominant allegiance at domicile. Prior to considering the Report's actual recommendations of income allocation,[89] it is safe, based on this assignment, to conclude that almost all intangible wealth, at present the core of the profitability of MNEs, was allocated principally to the residence country for taxation purposes, whereas the origin country was allowed to tax only the corporeal wealth. Notwithstanding that such a conclusion was based on the experts' inspection of the role of the four elements of economic allegiance, respectively, several serious concerns undermine the authority of their analysis.

First, the experts themselves, on the one hand, had made the caveat in discussing the concept of origin that the production of wealth is not the physical appearance of wealth but the result of a whole apparatus, on the other hand, their analysis that follows to crystallize the economic allegiance was strictly based on the classification of wealth being the final product or the physical emblem of economic activities, rather than on the contributions of business activities to the production of economic value per se.[90] The differences may not be that salient when international business was still embryonic, but they will be dramatic when economic reality becomes more sophisticated. The Report's analysis of business enterprise is a good demonstration.[91]

---

| *Category of Wealth* | | *Preponderant Element* | |
|---|---|---|---|
| | | *Origin* | *Domicile* |
| I. | Land | ✓ | |
| II.a | Mines, oils, etc. | ✓ | |
| II.b | Commercial establishments | ✓ | |
| III.a | Agricultural implements, machinery, flocks, and herds | ✓ | |
| III.b | Money, jewellery, furniture, etc. | | ✓ |
| IV. | Vessels | ✓ (registration) | |
| V.a | Mortgages | ✓ (property) | ✓ (income) |
| V.b | Corporate shares | | ✓ |
| V.c | Corporate bonds | | ✓ |
| V.d | Public securities | | ✓ |
| V.e | General credits | | ✓ |
| VI. | Professional earnings | | ✓ |

89. The reader should cautiously differentiate the outcome in the above table from the experts' recommendation of double taxation elimination and income allocation, because the former serves only as the theoretical basis of the latter, and it is yet to be revealed how and to what extent the authors apply this economic allegiance theory.
90. For similar criticism, *see* Wells and Lowell (n. 56) 21.
91. The business enterprise was categorized by the experts into three groups: 'those directly dependent upon the land, like mines and oil wells; those where land plays a somewhat less important role like industrial establishments; and those where other elements become of increasing importance, as in commercial establishments.', which is far from catching the economic reality of current international business, *see* Seligman, *Double Taxation and International Fiscal Cooperation* (n. 51) 126. and Bruins et al. (n. 44) 4033-4035.

Second, another bitter truth is that the Report's categorization of economic allegiance may be ascribed to the experts', principally, Seligman's subjective preference for pure residence-based taxation and the underlying disparagement of income taxation at source.[92] As is well known, the Report explicitly repudiated the origin as a principle of international taxation,[93] and optimistically predicted that the source-based taxation would diminish in the long run,[94] which, as it currently turns out, contradicts the subsequent developments.[95]

Third, as one can read from the experts' classification of wealth, it is emblematic of the economic realities and the international division of labour at that time. As discussed earlier, in the post-WWI era, when mercantilism dominated, the typical model of international commerce was between the imperial countries (creditors) and the colonies countries (debtors), in which the former as residence countries, provided capital and know-how[96] to the latter source countries principally as suppliers of minerals and agricultural commodities.[97] By restraining the economic and tax connotations of the concept origin to local and physical operations, the origin countries (colonies) will be precluded from all residual profits, including interest, royalties, service fees, and lease transfer payments, which will be solely with the residence countries (the imperial powers). The lack of consideration of the actual business activities that produce the profits unavoidably leads to the scenario in which: (i) such misallocation by base eroding the colonies is not fair, and 'outrageous and contradicted principles held by all countries';[98] (ii) the imperials powers, for example, Great Britain, are utilizing tax rules to recover and maintain its dominance in the world; and (iii) the most relevant as well as unexpected, with residence countries in the latter periods becoming reluctant to tax the extra-territorial income out of tax competition concerns, double non-taxation and homeless income arise unavoidably.[99]

*From Classification and Assignment to All-or-Nothing Paradigm of Residence and Source.* Frankly noting that the analysis based on the economic allegiance theory only mirrored the existent discussions on origin and residence,[100] it seems that through the classification and assignment approach, the Report had established the residence-origin (source) paradigm. However, it is only part of the paradigm, and the rest of the Report complements the picture.[101] First of all, it is noteworthy that the blank cells

92. *See* a detailed introduction of Seligman's devotion to residence taxation, in comparison to Graetz and O'Hear (n. 56) 1075-1076., the text and the accompanying footnotes, and Michael J Graetz, 'The David R. Tillinghast Lecture Taxing International Income: Inadequate Principles, Outdated Concepts, and Unsatisfactory Policies' (2000) 54 Tax Law Review 261, 297.
93. 'Can origin, then, be so sacred a principle?', Bruins et al. (n. 44) 4044.
94. 'as semi-developed countries become more industrialised, with the resulting attenuation of the distinctions between debtor and creditor countries ...', *Ibid.*, 4055.
95. Richard and Andrus (n. 10) para. 1.35.
96. As illustrated in the category V in the table at Bruins et al. (n. 44) 4043.
97. As illustrated in the categories I, II, III and IV in the table above.
98. Georg von Schanz, Die Doppelbesteuerung und der Volkerbund, 40 FinanzArchiv 353, 363 (1923), referred to in Bret Wells and Cym Lowell, 'Tax Base Erosion and Homeless Income: Collection at Source Is the Linchpin' (2011) 65 Tax Law Review 550.
99. Wells and Lowell (n. 56) 13.
100. Bruins et al. (n. 44) 4029.
101. The author found there has been a common mistake to referred to the results in the table of classification and assignment as the Report's basis of recommending their approach of relieving double taxation, for example, in Wells and Lowell (n. 56) 19-20. Such mistake is not

without a mark in the table that presents the experts' classification of wealth and assignment of economic allegiance do not mean that they are not assigned any value of economic allegiance. Instead, those marked cells, either origin or domicile, are 'preponderant' rather than exclusive elements of economic allegiance. Accordingly, with respect to the task of converting the classification and assignment of economic allegiance into an operable solution of taxing right allocation and double taxation, it is a natural response to ask how much economic allegiance is there respectively in residence and the origin. Such a response also finds an echo with the natural affinity between formulary apportionment and economic allegiance. Rather than heading directly to answer that question, the experts abruptly rejected the underlying philosophy of their own and turned to hold that economic allegiance was not possible to be apportioned scientifically in and by itself,[102] and in the meantime, taxation at origin was inevitable for the present.[103]

With the above ideas as the guideline, the Report considered four methods to relieve double taxation:[104] (i) reduction of origin tax in the residence country; (ii) elimination of origin tax by exempting non-residents at the origin country; (iii) proportional allocation of taxation between the origin and residence; and (iv) classification of income into various categories and assignment of the taxing right on each category to residence or origin, to be specific, an all-or-nothing approach where exclusive taxation of origin on income from local and physical wealth and exclusive taxation of residence on other categories of income. The method (i) was flatly ruled out because it violated the ability to pay principle,[105] which instead directed that the method (ii) was the desirable option as highly recommended by the experts.[106] Such preference, as noted above, is also attributed to the experts' disparagement of taxation at origin on the grounds that it is based on an antiquated benefit principle and discourages foreign investment. In spite of being a theoretical and intellectual piece of study, the experts did not fully disregard realistic constraints. Acknowledging that the elimination of origin-based taxation may be unacceptable to debtor countries, the Report still cautiously disagreed with the method (iv) and presented some caveats for its adoption.[107] Intriguingly, it was the method (iii) that took up the majority of the experts' explanations.[108]

Ostensibly, method (iii) and method (iv) were in general congruence with the 'apportionment' spirit of the economic allegiance theory, the spirit where the formulary apportionment is also rooted. The method (iii) was viewed in the Report as a

---

consistent with the Report's flow of thoughts and logic, and causes the risk of missing much of experts' discourse of refusing apportionment methodology.

102. 'To allocate the exact proportion of economic allegiance to origin or domicile in each particular category is well-nigh impossible. Such an attempt would savor too much of the arbitrary. However, where any two countries desire to make such an allocation, they would do well to be guided, ideally at least, by the above analysis.', Bruins et al. (n. 44) 4043.
103. *Ibid.*, 4044.
104. *Ibid.*, 4045-4046.
105. *Ibid.*, 4052.
106. *Ibid.*, 4052, 4055.
107. *Ibid.*, 4055.
108. *Ibid.*, 4049-4052.

modification or a concretization of the method (iv).[109] However, they have important differences not explicitly indicated by the experts. The method (iii), in essence, does not rely on the classification of incomes but only allocates the income on a combined basis; the relative economic allegiance between residence and origin serves as a guideline for determining the proportion. The allocation following method (iv) is strictly based on the categorization of incomes. In addition, method (iii) acknowledges the contribution of both residence and origin, whereas method (iv) is overly generous to one side by wholly disregarding the other side under certain categories of income. However, with the benefit of hindsight, the experts' formulation of both methods is problematic.

First of all, the two methods share a common presumption, as established in the closing remarks of Part II: the economic allegiance theory in and by itself dictates scientific accuracy for income allocation between residence and origin. Accordingly, if exact apportionment cannot be achieved in practice, the acceptable alternatives are a fixed proportional allocation guided by the economic allegiance or nullifying wholly the portion of the side where the economic allegiance was not preponderant. Without actually looking into the Report's later arguments against the adoption of the two methods, the experts' presumption above is not a faithful interpretation of the economic allegiance theory. The economic allegiance theory, drawing on the strengths of the benefits principle and the ability to pay principle, is a composite rationale for the justification of taxation and international taxing right allocation. It is not an exact science to find out where income arises, nor does it presume income has a geographic location. Such perception was obviously harboured by the experts before addressing the content of the economic allegiance,[110] while the authors somehow seemingly had dropped it when turning to the application of the economic allegiance theory, which explains their presumption as noted above and thus had profoundly shaped, in fact, distorted the Report's stance on the two double taxation relief methods that should have been in accord with the economic allegiance theory.

The method (iii), with a prototype of the British Dominion Tax Relief System and once labelled as a 'formulary apportionment' method, was, in fact, deconstructed by the experts in the latter part of the Report as a mechanical approach to double taxation relief devoid of any economic rationale. It is perplexing that for the original introduction of this method, the experts had envisioned a formalist apportionment methodology therein, that is, the [*x% : 1–x%*] model of allocation of income, yet in the subsequent formulation, method (iii) was stirred away from this and became a model of a preset [x% : y%] reduction of tax claims at residence and source.[111] Regardless of

109. *Ibid.*, 4049.
110. As seen in the 'Java' example given by the authors, *Ibid.*, 4027.
111. 'We are driven to ask, therefore, whether we should not endeavor to commute or compound the rights and difficulties of the fourth method by adopting the third, that is, not to attempt to get at exact elements of economic allegiance but to adopt a broad line and to say that where double taxation of income is involved each country shall give up *a flat or fixed proportion of the sum due to it.*', *Ibid.*, 4049. From this formulation, the value of x and y are not necessarily the same, neither is their sum total necessarily 1. As a result, such approach most of times only reduces double taxation rather than eliminates it.

this change in the trajectory, the formulary approach was in general rejected for practical reasons, such as lack of exchange of information, heavy compliance and administration burden, intrinsic complexity, and low level of cooperation on tax matters and so forth. In noting the successful application of similar methods by the British Empire, the authors attributed it to the common language, income tax systems, conceptions of income, and more effective political connections among the dominions of the Empire. All these may constitute real obstacles to the application of apportionment methods, yet as to whether they are decisive and irresistible factors especially under modern circumstances, the answer, as far as the author can see, is negative.

In a similar vein, method (iv) was also disparaged by the experts for two reasons - less for theoretical and more for practical reasons. As explained above, the theoretical reason is that since economic allegiance cannot be quantified, it cannot be used to assign the resultant income. Following this, all income allocation attempts to simulate the distribution of economic allegiance are arbitrary.[112] Bewilderingly, as instructed by method (iv), to allocate income based on the economic allegiance theory between the residence and origin in an all-or-nothing fashion was acceptable preliminarily as rough justice.[113] Therefore, the experts' overall disagreement with this method falls on practical reasons as well. Particularly, the Report referred to the major difficulty of systematic valuation of annual yields on business lines, a precondition for the application of method (iv). This is not an issue under the current sophisticated accounting practice, nor should it be a material impediment back to the Report's times either. The actual problem with the experts' discourse of the method (iv) is its inconsistency. If the economic allegiance theory fails to scientifically guide the exact apportionment of income between residence and origin, why should it be acceptable if one side's pie is wholly surrendered to the other side?

#### *2.5.1.4 Summary*

Based on the above discussions of the 1923 Academic Report, several conclusions can be drawn:

(1) The history of economic allegiance theory is as long as the intellectual history of international taxation itself. Formulated originally in 1892, the concept was adopted by Seligman and formally introduced into the norm-making forum of international taxation by the 1923 Academic Report.

(2) The economic allegiance theory has a natural affinity with the formulary apportionment discussed in the modern context, which is evidenced by both the original conception of international taxation backed by the economic allegiance and the formulation of economic allegiance in the Academic Report. With international taxation entering a new age of allocation, the economic allegiance has been increasingly contemplated as a theoretical

112. *Ibid.*, 4049.
113. *Ibid.*, 4043.

foundation for a fundamental reform of the international tax system that the BEPS Project failed to render.[114] Therefore, further study may be required to orient this theory in the modern context.

(3) However, the Academic Report endorsed the economic allegiance theory in the beginning but did not apply it faithfully in the latter parts. The experts had essentially deviated from and practically headed toward the opposite of the economic allegiance theory and turned to pure residence-based taxation in their final discussions.[115] The inconsistencies in the Report have been ascribed to the manner in which the different parts were compiled and (un-) coordinated.[116] As a result, the Report is self-contradictory and thus weak in its arguments for the final recommendations.

(4) The historical importance of the Report for international taxation is not unanimously recognized,[117] yet it seems more widely acknowledged that the Report has contributed to the nomenclature of the modern international tax system. In particular, it has presented systematically for the first time the interminable conflict between residence and source. It is not the specific double taxation relief measures as recommended by the Report that have the greatest influence, but the Report's ultimate preference for the all-or-nothing paradigm of residence and source, thus having a deterrent effect on the prospect of international tax sharing through formulary apportionment. Some attributed the paradigm to the dilemma of sovereignty conflict between residence and source,[118] whereas the experts neglected the applications of formulary apportionment that already existed at international and sub-national level, and more importantly, the potential of formulary apportionment as an alternative intellectual design of international taxation (as contemplated by the ICC) was stifled by the Report through a twisted application of the economic allegiance theory.

(5) Following the all-or-nothing paradigm of residence and source, the model of classifying incomes and assigning active income to the source while assigning passive income to the residence has become the emblem of modern bilateral tax treaties.[119] Many of the international tax problems, especially the modern ones in the ongoing allocation phase haunting policymakers and commentators, are rooted in or with great relevance to this model, including but not

114. Langbein and Fuss (n. 74). and Li, Bao and Li (n. 74); Jinyan Li, 'Global Profit Split: An Evolutionary Approach to International Income Allocation' (2002) 50 Canadian Tax Journal 823.

115. Vogel, 'Worldwide vs. Source Taxation of Income: A Review and Re-Evaluation of Arguments (Part I)' (n. 80) 220.

116. Sunita Jogarajan, 'Stamp, Seligman and the Drafting of the 1923 Experts' Report on Double Taxation' (2013) 5 World Tax Journal 368 https://doi.org/10.59403/szqg31 accessed 26 August 2025; Richard and Andrus (n. 10) para. 1.32.

117. Graetz and O'Hear (n. 56) 1021.

118. Cavelti (n. 82) 68-69; *see* the 'great compromise', in Avi-Yonah, 'All of a Piece Throughout' (n. 8) 322.

119. Reuven S Avi-Yonah, 'The Structure of International Taxation: A Proposal for Simplification' (1996) 6 Texas Law Review 1301, 1305-1310 https://doi.org/10.2139/ssrn.3920264 accessed 26 August 2025; Avi-Yonah, 'All of a Piece Throughout' (n. 8) 322-323.

limited to the homeless income conundrum, the lack of adaptation to the digitalization of the economy, the increasingly conflicting tax claims between the developed and developing countries, the emerging disputes over the inter-nation equity of the international tax system, and the race to the bottom problem of international tax competition.

(6) The formulary system considered in the Report in relation to Method 3 should be understood as a general design for double taxation relief, rather than specifically for the allocation of income of MNEs where, in comparison, what the Addendum contemplated seemed more applicable.

### 2.5.2 Formulary Apportionment in the 1925 Technical Report

Prior to the completion of the 1923 Academic Report, a Committee of Technical Experts was appointed by the LON to further study the questions of international double taxation and tax evasion. The end product of the work of the Committee is a four-part report published in 1925.[120] The Technical Report is another milestone of the evolution of the international tax system since it drew on the intellectual contributions of the Academic Report[121] and served as the foundation of the first LON model tax treaties.[122] Therefore, the Technical Report is a decisive event in the historical track of formulary apportionment, yet just as the Academic Report, it means another defeat for formulary apportionment as an alternative design of the international tax system.

A stark difference between the Technical Report from the Academic Report is its practical nature. The Report made it clear in the beginning that its mission was to search for the 'best possible', in other words, the most practical solutions acceptable to the states, while relying on few, if at all, overarching principles or economic theories.[123] One of the direct consequences is the Report's firm acknowledgement of taxes at source. On this basis, the Report's general approach is the division of personal (global)income tax/impersonal (schedular) taxes.[124] However, since the division itself is devoid of any economic doctrine or theory,[125] but is based on the existence of source taxes,[126] the experts were confused about the difference as well.[127]

120. League of Nations, 'Double Taxation and Tax Evasion: Report and Resolutions Submitted by the Technical Experts to the Financial Committee of the League of Nations (Document F.212)' (n. 18).
121. The Technical Report had specifically restated the analysis of the Academic Report and specified its benefits from it, *see ibid.*, 4069-4070.
122. Jogarajan, *Double Taxation and the League of Nations* (n. 55) 22.
123. League of Nations, 'Double Taxation and Tax Evasion: Report and Resolutions Submitted by the Technical Experts to the Financial Committee of the League of Nations (Document F.212)' (n. 18) 4065.
124. *Ibid.*, 4075.
125. 'The division which we have established between the impôts réels or schedular taxes, and the general or personal income tax has been made for purely practical purposes and no inference in regard to economic theory or doctrine should be drawn from this fact.', *Ibid.*, 4065.
126. *Ibid.*, 4074.
127. As corroborated by the minutes of the meetings, *see* Jogarajan, *Double Taxation and the League of Nations* (n. 55) 23, 35.

The recommendations thereby developed, for practical ease and compromise, were seriously questioned in terms of their validity.[128]

Following the approach, the Technical Report altered the Academic Report's strong pro-residence position by suggesting that personal taxes should be imposed by the residence state while impersonal taxes should exclusively be imposed by the source state.[129] The source country was thus allowed to tax the incomes from local business activities, typically the real properties, agricultural undertakings, and industrial businesses or commercial enterprises, but not the global income of non-resident taxpayers, which is imposed by the residence country. While the Academic Report originally set up the residence-source nomenclature, it is the Technical Report which decidedly recognizes that source taxation is, although only in the form of impersonal taxes, as valid as residence taxation.[130] There are several explanations for this shift,[131] but none of them are principle-driven, and such a spirit of pragmaticism also dominated the Report's overall rejection of formulary options for double taxation relief.

Having established the above framework of taxing right allocation, the Report suggested two methods for double taxation relief:[132] the first is relief by the residence state providing exemption or credit for taxes imposed at source, and the second is proportional allocation of income between residence and source. It is noteworthy that both methods were to operate under the general approach of personal/impersonal tax division, which is to say, the proportional allocation under the second method has decisive differences from the formulary division as contemplated by the Academic Report.[133] The experts did not suggest an exact ratio of allocation, nor were any lists of the specific taxes to be allocated defined. This method was finally dropped in the later Draft Models.

In considering the method (iii) in the Academic Report, the formulary approach to relieving double taxation was summarily rejected as being too complicated in the international field. More generally, the very idea of apportioning the combined income to residence and source was dismissed, as the Report claimed that personal taxes based on residence and the taxes based on the conception of origin were incompatible. Assigning income to residence and source was thus deemed as improperly mixing the two different taxes or transforming the income tax into pure origin-based taxation.[134]

128. WH Coates, 'Double Taxation and Tax Evasion' (1925) 88 Journal of the Royal Statistical Society 403 https://doi.org/10.2307/2341417 accessed 26 August 2025; Seligman, *Double Taxation and International Fiscal Cooperation* (n. 51) 145-146.
129. League of Nations, 'Double Taxation and Tax Evasion: Report and Resolutions Submitted by the Technical Experts to the Financial Committee of the League of Nations (Document F.212)' (n. 18) 4075, 4091.
130. 'In the case of the impôts réels, we have recognised the primary importance of the idea of origin, that is to say, the system of the assignment of income', *Ibid.*, 4074-4091; Graetz and O'Hear (n. 56) 1081; Richard and Andrus (n. 10) para. 1.39.
131. For example, the spirit of compromise, the need for revenue, and the experts as technicians, and that the majority of the experts are from debtor nations. Jogarajan, *Double Taxation and the League of Nations* (n. 55) 27-31.
132. League of Nations, 'Double Taxation and Tax Evasion: Report and Resolutions Submitted by the Technical Experts to the Financial Committee of the League of Nations (Document F.212)' (n. 18) 4078, 4079, 4093.
133. Taylor (n. 43) 275.
134. 'However, the evolution of fiscal practice, by adding personal taxes to taxes founded on the idea of origin or by substituting the former for the latter, and our desire to attain universality in

Once again, if there must be a guiding principle of the Report, it is the division of personal/impersonal taxes, which in turn is merely founded on practice. There were minority voices by the experts from The Netherlands and Belgium claiming that the division method between residence and source was more just and moral, but it did not become mainstream.[135]

Though the formulary approach was not accepted as a general method to eliminate double taxation, the Report was nevertheless open-minded about its application for the cross-border taxation of business profits. Following its personal/impersonal tax methodology, the profits from industrial and commercial business activities were the income that the source state could impose on its impersonal tax.[136] Where business activities are carried on in more than one state, the problem of potential overlapped taxation arises. In this case, referring to the Addendum of the Academic Report as discussed above, the Report upheld the principle of division of income between the states hosting these business activities. In this spirit, the Report mentioned the methods of profit allocation in the tax treaties and regulations of several Central European states as accurate and feasible examples, including the treaty between Austria and Czechoslovakia in 1922, Danzig and Poland in 1924,[137] and the Royal Decree of Belgium.[138] These examples share one common thing: they employed various factors such as kilometric length, receipts, sales, and purchase of economic production in different businesses to divide the profits thereby accrued. The Report clearly approved the application of the formulary division,[139] for it confirmed that such practices of above contracting states were not restrained by the internal division of personal/impersonal tax.

To summarize, the 1925 Technical Report made a major contribution to incarnating the residence versus source paradigm of international taxation, particularly for the recognition of source taxing rights, by drawing a hard line of assigning personal tax to the residence state while assigning impersonal tax to the source state. The Report is almost a product wholly to accommodate practical concerns and then existent practices, and feasibility rather than any other economic or ethical principles dominates. The overwhelming pragmatism in the formative period of the international tax system has the advantage of breaking the impasse in the short term, yet in every sense,

our decisions, made it necessary for us to take into account the difficulties caused by differences in the various fiscal systems.', League of Nations, 'Double Taxation and Tax Evasion: Report and Resolutions Submitted by the Technical Experts to the Financial Committee of the League of Nations (Document F.212)' (n. 18) 4074.

135. Jogarajan, *Double Taxation and the League of Nations* (n. 55) 33.
136. League of Nations, 'Double Taxation and Tax Evasion: Report and Resolutions Submitted by the Technical Experts to the Financial Committee of the League of Nations (Document F.212)' (n. 18) 4091.
137. League of Nations, 'Double Taxation and Fiscal Evasion Collection of International Agreements and Internal Legal Provisions for the Prevention of Double Taxation and Fiscal Evasion' (League of Nations 1928) 40.
138. League of Nations, 'Double Taxation and Tax Evasion: Report and Resolutions Submitted by the Technical Experts to the Financial Committee of the League of Nations (Document F.212)' (n. 18) 4076.
139. However, Lepard thought the Report did not choose a side between formulary apportionment and arm's length standard, *see* Lepard (n. 46) 61.

what it renders is ad hoc and can destabilize the system in the long run. The personal versus impersonal division is not robust and coherent in and by itself; the technical experts used it only as an expedient proxy. To a large extent, the Report's allocation of income taxing rights between residence and source mirrors the outcome of the Academic Report's classification and assignment approach.[140] On the surface of it, the Technical Report was more generous to the source than the Academic Report,[141] yet the balance of revenue sharing between residence and source or the modern perception of source taxation primacy were mere fallacies. This result is first because the impersonal taxes assigned to the source, though exclusively, account for only a small portion of the taxes on the objects that should be contrasted with personal taxes;[142] second, the impersonal taxes as a revenue source are less important than the personal taxes.[143] The ad hoc nature of the technical design of what became the foundation of the first tax treaty models almost has all the clues of modern international tax problems.

Formulary apportionment, following the Technical Report, disappeared from the LON's future discussions of the solutions to the double taxation issue, which means that the pre-existing formulary practices were discouraged as well. However, employing formulary apportionment for the purposes of taxing cross-border businesses had just begun.

### 2.5.3 Formulary Apportionment in the First Model Double Taxation Conventions

The Committee of Technical Experts was enlarged following the completion of the Technical Report to develop the draft conventions of double taxation. The work of the enlarged Committee led to the completion of a report in 1927 (1927 Report),[144] which contained four draft tax conventions – one on general double taxation (hereinafter, the '1927 Draft Model'), and the other three were respectively on succession duties, administrative assistance and judicial assistance. In 1928, the League Council convened a General Meeting of Government Experts to further develop draft conventions. The Meeting agreed and endorsed the model draft Double Taxation Convention of 1927, yet it thought the draft was narrowly applicable to the scenario of one state imposing personal tax while the other imposes impersonal taxes. Therefore, the General Meeting presented a Report[145] containing three models in total (collectively '1928 Draft Models'): the previous one plus two additional models. The second model

140. The classification and assignment approach had been largely continued by the first Model Conventions, *see* Wells and Lowell (n. 98) 554.
141. For instance, the Academic Report assigned only physical and local operations to the origin.
142. Seligman, *Double Taxation and International Fiscal Cooperation* (n. 51) 65.
143. Jogarajan, *Double Taxation and the League of Nations* (n. 55) 35.
144. League of Nations, 'Double Taxation and Tax Evasion: Report Presented by the Committee of Technical Experts on Double Taxation and Tax Evasion (C.216 M.85.1927.II)' in United States Congress Joint Committee on Internal Revenue Taxation (ed.), *Legislative History of United States Tax Conventions*, vol. 4 (League of Nations 1927). reprinted in United States Congress Joint Committee on Internal Revenue Taxation (n. 18) 4111-4150.
145. League of Nations, 'Double Taxation And Tax Evasion-Report Presented by the General Meeting of Government Experts on Double Taxation and Tax Evasion (Document

was developed for two contracting states, both levying only personal taxes, and the third model was suited for cases other than those covered by the first two models. There are two findings to summarize from these first model double taxation conventions: one is the consensus on the approach to international double taxation, and another is an apparent preference for formulary apportionment to allocate income from multinational businesses.

The 1927 Draft Model is a product following the discussions among the experts on whether to develop a multilateral solution or a bilateral solution to prevent double taxation.[146] The Draft largely followed the resolutions of the Technical Report, in particular, the general approach of assigning personal taxes to the residence and impersonal taxes to the source. However, the 1927 Draft Model still has two historic innovations with regard to the concept of PE, both of which have profound implications for formulary apportionment.

One is the first explicit use of the concept of permanent establishment in Article 5, which filled in the blank area in the scope of impersonal taxes and thus demarcated the limitation of source taxing rights.[147] An explanation of what constituted permanent establishment was also provided in this article, and 'affiliated companies' were included as one of eight types of PE.[148] In addition, this Article further provided that where an undertaking has PEs in both contracting states, each state will tax the portion of the income produced therein.[149] In this case, an arrangement of apportionment was suggested as a fallback rule if no separate accounts existed recording the income in each state.[150] In the Commentary, factors including capital, employees, salaries and receipts were given as examples for the application of the apportionment rule.[151] These provisions combined lead to an alternative formulary apportionment system for international business taxation as envisaged by the ICC.[152] Another is the exclusion of an independent agent from the definition of permanent establishment.[153] Such provision not only had materially limited the source taxing rights[154] but also introduced the

---

C.562.M.178.1928.II.)' in United States Congress Joint Committee on Internal Revenue Taxation (ed.), *Legislative History of United States Tax Conventions*, vol. 4 (League of Nations 1928). reprinted in United States Congress Joint Committee on Internal Revenue Taxation (n. 18) 4151-4194.

146. As evidenced in the minutes of the meeting of experts, *see* Jogarajan, *Double Taxation and the League of Nations* (n. 55) 98.
147. Avi-Yonah, 'All of a Piece Throughout' (n. 8) 323.
148. 'The real centers of management, *affiliated companies*, branches, factories, agencies, warehouses, offices, depots, shall be regarded as permanent establishments.', Avi-Yonah, 'All of a Piece Throughout' (n. 8).
149. 'Should the undertakings possess permanent establishments in both Contracting States, each of the two States shall tax the portion of the income produced in its territory.', *Ibid.*
150. 'In the absence of accounts showing this income separately and in proper form, the competent administrations of the two Contracting States shall come to an arrangement as to the rules for apportionment.', *Ibid.*
151. 'These rules will vary essentially according to the undertakings concerned; in certain States account is taken, according to the nature of the undertakings, of the amount of capital involved, of the number of workers, the wages paid, receipts, etc.', United States Congress Joint Committee on Internal Revenue Taxation (n. 18) 4129.
152. Richard and Andrus (n. 10) para. 1.49.
153. 'The fact that an undertaking has business dealings with a foreign country through a bona-fide agent of independent status (broker, commission agent, etc.) shall not be held to mean that the

arm's length test.[155] The PE concept was claimed as the most important agreement reached by the Experts;[156] it is endurable and has become a central component of modern tax treaties. It accords with the spirit of source-based taxation, and it served as a foothold in the balance struggle between residence and source.

On the one hand, the formulary proposal through the PE provision was short-lived. In the 1928 Draft Models, affiliated companies were excluded from the definition of permanent establishment in all three Drafts,[157] largely due to the opposition of the US representative Adams to giving the source country access to the parent company's accounts.[158] On the other hand, formulary apportionment was insisted on for business income allocation. In determining the profits produced by the PE for the purpose of allocation, the default reliance on separate accounts was omitted by these Drafts; instead, a formulary apportionment method was provided as agreed upon by the competent tax authorities. Except for this, no substantial differences exist in the 1928 Models from the 1927 Draft Model in the formulary apportionment aspect, including the respective Commentaries of Article 5.[159]

In summary, the first Model Conventions of Double Taxation had concluded the debate on the approaches to double taxation relief. From then on, the methods to prevent double taxation and the general framework of tax treaties were established. In particular, the method of formulary division representing an alternative design of bilateral treaties has been buried ever since. However, the General Meeting's hesitating moves regarding the allocation of business profits foreshadowed another period of formulary apportionment, as an idea moulding not the general international tax system, but the regime of international business income allocation.

### 2.5.4 Carroll Report and the Defeat of Formulary Apportionment

The LON's work on tax treaties had gradually shifted its focus to the allocation of profits issue following the rollout of the first double taxation models. In 1929, the newly appointed Fiscal Committee discussed the allocation issue and concluded that more

undertaking in question has a permanent establishment in that country.', League of Nations, '1927 Draft Models' in United States Congress Joint Committee on Internal Revenue Taxation (ed.), *Legislative History of United States Tax Conventions*, vol. 4 (US GPO 1962) 4125.

154. Wells and Lowell (n. 98) 553, 557.
155. Graetz and O'Hear (n. 56) 1089.
156. Thomas S Adams, 'Interstate and International Double Taxation' (1932) 101 Lectures on Taxation 102, 108.
157. League of Nations, 'Draft Convention No. I-a' in United States Congress Joint Committee on Internal Revenue Taxation (ed.), *Legislative History of United States Tax Conventions*, vol. 4 (US GPO 1962) 4162. League of Nations, 'Draft Convention No. I-b' in United States Congress Joint Committee on Internal Revenue Taxation (ed.), *Legislative History of United States Tax Conventions*, vol. 4 (US GPO 1962) 4173.
158. Wells and Lowell (n. 98) 553.
159. League of Nations, 'Draft Convention No. I-a' (n. 157) 4166; League of Nations, 'Draft Convention No. I-b' (n. 157) 4172; League of Nations, 'Draft Convention No. I-c' in United States Congress Joint Committee on Internal Revenue Taxation (ed.), *Legislative History of United States Tax Conventions*, vol. 4 (US GPO 1962) 4175.

extensive knowledge of the existing practice was needed to achieve real progress.[160] At the second session of the Committee in 1930, it was agreed that the task of apportioning profits from multinational undertakings was complex and difficult.[161] Treating the apportionment issue as a serious risk point of double taxation, the Committee entrusted Mitchell B. Carroll, the assistant to Adams, to conduct a detailed study on it.

#### *2.5.4.1 Definition, Classification and Theoretical Basis of Formulary Apportionment*

What Carrol delivered through his extensive research during the period between 1930 and 1933 is a five-volume Report at the length of over a thousand pages.[162] Carrol, later on, in 1934, claimed that his study had contributed to the decided victory of separate accounting over formulary apportionment in the international field.[163] In fact, it has been widely acknowledged that the Carroll Report marks a turning point in the historical track of allocation rules for international business income.[164] Even though this overall is not a good story for formulary apportionment, the Report is still of great significance to the intellectual base of formulary apportionment.

---

160. League of Nations, 'Fiscal Committee Report to the Council on the Work of the First Session of the Committee. Held in Geneva from October 17th to 26th, 1929.' in United States Congress Joint Committee on Internal Revenue Taxation (ed.), *Legislative History of United States Tax Conventions* (US GPO 1962) 4199.
161. League of Nations, 'Fiscal Committee Report to the Council on the Work of The Second Session of the Committee Held in Geneva From May 22nd to 31st, 1930.' in United States Congress Joint Committee on Internal Revenue Taxation (ed.), *Legislative History of United States Tax Conventions* (US GPO 1962) 4207.
162. The first three volumes are country and US states investigations, the fourth volume is the general conclusion, and the fifth volume is of the accounting methods. League of Nations, 'Taxation of Foreign and National Enterprises Vol. 1. A Study of the Tax Systems and the Methods of Allocation of the Profits of Enterprises Operating in More than One Country in France, Germany, Spain, the United Kingdom, and the United States of America' (n. 39); League of Nations, 'Taxation of Foreign and National Enterprises Vol. 2. A Study of the Tax Systems and the Methods of Allocation of the Profits of Enterprises Operating in More than One Country in Austria, Belgium, Czechoslovakia, Free City of Danzig, Greece, Hungary, Italy, Latvia, Luxemburg, Netherlands, Romania and Switzerland' (League of Nations 1933) C.425.M.217.1933.II.A; League of Nations, 'Taxation of Foreign and National Enterprises Vol. 3. A Study of the Tax Systems and the Methods of Allocation of the Profits of Enterprises Operating in More than One Country in British India, Canada, Japan, Mexico, Netherlands East Indies, Union of South Africa, States of Massachusetts, of New York and of Wisconsin' (League of Nations 1933) C.425(a).M.217(a).1933.II.A; Mitchell B Carroll, 'Taxation of Foreign and National Enterprises Vol. 4. Methods of Allocating Taxable Income' (League of Nations 1933) C.425(b).M.217(b).1933.II.A hereinafter 'Carroll Report'; Ralph C Jones, 'Taxation of Foreign and National Enterprises, Vol. 5' (League of Nations 1933) C.425(c).M.217(c).1933.II.A 5.
163. Mitchell B Carroll, 'Allocation of Business Income: The Draft Convention of the League of Nations' (1934) 34 Columbia Law Review 473 https://doi.org/10.2307/1115876 accessed 26 August 2025.
164. Yoram Keinan, 'The Case for Residency-Based Taxation of Financial Transactions in Developing Countries' (2022) 9 Florida Tax Review https://doi.org/10.5744/ftr.2008.1001 and https://journals.upress.ufl.edu/ftr/article/view/365 accessed 26 August 2025; Alexander Nahum Sack, 'Taxation of International Business Upon Income and Problems of International Regulation of Such Taxation' (1934) 20 Bulletin of The National Tax Association 66 https://doi.org/10.1086/bullnattax41786583 accessed 26 August 2025.

One is, as stressed above, the Carroll Report, which is the final pronouncement in the authoritative forum of international tax law, making that the formulary apportionment had lost its prospect as one grand design of the international tax system. Formulary apportionment had already been employed in limited forms and scopes by nation-states before WWI, and the very idea of using formulary allocation in the larger system can be traced back to Schanz. It is the unanimous interest in countering double taxation that brings all stakeholders together to form the so-called international tax system. The ICC is the first mover to propose a turnover-based formulary apportionment for international business taxation. The LON-backed Academic Report in 1923 contemplated the economic allegiance theory that clearly underlay formulary apportionment, which was discussed as a holistic solution to double taxation relief, yet was finally rejected out of practical concerns. Subsequent to that, the LON had laid down the general skeletons of double taxation; for example, through the classification and assignment approach and the personal/impersonal taxes division, the formulary apportionment had been eviscerated as an option for constructing the general system of international taxation. In what follows, driven by the First Double Taxation Models, formulary apportionment was narrowed down to be the alternative to taxing multinational undertakings, including enterprise groups or single enterprises with multiple establishments, as the counterpart of separate accounting. The Carroll Report reflected the tension, the outcome of which would be seen in the ensuing developments. In any event, formulary apportionment had been cast aside as a grand alternative design of the international tax system.

Another is that the Report had explained the definition and theoretical basis of formulary apportionment. It may be for the first time that the formulary apportionment had been given a lucid account, which is also adopted by this chapter, and it is worth a full quote here: 'By fractional apportionment is meant the determination of the income of one establishment of an enterprise by dividing-total net income in the ratio of certain factors – for example, assets, turnover, pay-roll, or a fixed percentage.'[165] Formulary apportionment was thus defined originally in the context of permanent establishment, instead of a group of multinational enterprises. It depicted two basic types: one is the quintessential factor-based apportionment, and the other is the simple fixed percentage apportionment. Either type of formulary apportionment follows an aggregation (of total income)-apportionment methodology, in contrast with the separate accounting-independent entity methodology of ALS.

A different classification of formulary apportionment depending on the scope of income subject to apportionment was also adopted by the Report.[166] The apportionment method that applies to the total net income of the enterprise from all sources or transactions is classified as unlimited formulary apportionment. If the method only applies to a specific portion of income, for instance, a certain group of activities, then the method is classified as limited formulary apportionment.

More specifically, the net income subject to apportionment may be the total net income of the enterprise regardless of the sources or transactions to which it pertains,

165. Carroll, 'Carroll Report' (n. 162) 46.
166. *Ibid.*, 58.

and, for convenience, this method will be called unlimited fractional apportionment. However, the net income subject to apportionment may be that derived from specific combinations of activities, such as manufacturing and selling, and, for convenience, this method will be called limited fractional apportionment. The existent practices of formulary apportionment, as studied by the Report, were presented following this classification.

In addition to the definition and classification of formulary apportionment provided, the Report also sheds light on formulary apportionment's underlying rationale, which, it is believed, has four interrelated layers.[167] The first layer revealed was the unitary business principle, according to which the enterprise's home office and the foreign establishment form an organic unity. As a result, the enterprise should be taxed as a whole rather than fictitiously as separate components; thus, the income of the foreign establishment will be taxed in line with its economic significance relative to the whole enterprise. This finds an echo in the foregoing discussions of the affinity between formulary apportionment and economic allegiance theory. Besides this point, the report also corresponded with the economic allegiance theory, which states that income is the outcome of a whole apparatus rather than isolated stages of production. On these bases, economic allegiance is the second layer of the rationale. The third layer is regarding the geographic sources of income. What supports the formulary apportionment is the view that income cannot be geographically traced to a function or an establishment located somewhere. Thus, the most suitable methodology for taxing the multinational business is apportionment rather than separate accounting. The fourth layer is the ability to pay principle, which dictates full and proportional taxation of multinational enterprises.

#### *2.5.4.2 Unqualified Authority of Arm's Length Standard*

The foregoing sections have demonstrated that formulary apportionment was not only a serious alternative robust in theoretical basis for international double taxation relief but also had been historically used frequently in tax treaties and national systems and was what the first Model Double Taxation Conventions were heading towards for allocation of profits. The Carroll Report actually provided even more evidence in this

167. 'The two underlying theories of taxing foreign enterprises with local establishments are: ... 2. That the enterprise is an organic unity and consequently the tax should be assessed on that part of the enterprise's total net income (computed in accordance with the law of the taxing country) which corresponds to the relative economic importance of the local establishment. This method is known as unlimited fractional apportionment. The advocates of this method contend that, in a unitary business which, for example, produces raw materials, manufactures them into finished products and then sells them, no profit is realised by the enterprise as a whole until the goods have been sold. They contend furthermore that it is impossible to determine accurately what part of the profit is attributable to each function or establishment of the business and consequently the profit can only be apportioned on some empirical basis – for example, an arbitrary apportionment formula. Moreover, they say it is the only way of applying the fundamental principle of taxing the enterprise in accordance with its capacity to pay.', *Ibid.*, 187.

respect,[168] which makes it compulsory to know how the transformation happened. However, due to the limited space, a comprehensive presentation of the Report is skipped,[169] and the following turns to question its historical role of defeating formulary apportionment.

First, the Report is in and by itself not problem-driven. Carroll was entrusted by the Fiscal Committee with the general mission of inquiring into the methods of apportioning profits acquired by multinational undertakings.[170] The Committee, in general, seemed neither to harbour what the apportioning mechanism should be like nor to provide any guiding principles. This is because the Committee itself had never formulated what the exact problems caused by indefinite methods of apportionment are, except for the general and vague expression of double taxation. Examined closer, the Committee clearly endorsed a taxpayer-centred approach since it stressed that the apportioning method should be 'equitable and reasonable' and prevent double taxation from the point of view of the business, while the role of tax administrations was passive and accepted the method. As to the content of the inquiry, the Committee also mandated two major parts: one is the collection and analysis of pre-existing legislation, and the other is the study of the three methods of apportionment, namely, separate accounting, empirical methods,[171] and formulary apportionment. The Report closely followed this mandate,[172] yet failed to identify real problems of either double taxation,[173] infeasibility or inequity in the existent practices, of which the last almost had no weight of consideration in the Report. The major problem in relation to the apportionment issue in the modern scenario, that is, tax avoidance, was instead disregarded. The peril of a non-problem-driven inquiry of the apportionment issue often leads to biased and ad hoc solutions to real problems.

Second, not enough weight was assigned to the prevalent formulary methods. The large picture unfolded by the survey is that not many formal legislations were enacted on the issue of profits apportionment.[174] The regimes in place with statutory status largely involved formulary apportionment, such as those of US states Wisconsin, New York, and Massachusetts, Spain, Austria, Hungary, Czechoslovakia, and Switzerland, either by statutes or international treaty.[175] However, more countries had pronounced their preference for the method of separate accounting, which became the major basis for considering the relative value among the three methods.[176] However, as Langbein pointed out, the report improperly equated the importance of statutory norms

168. *Ibid.*, 173-288.
169. For this purpose, *see* the introduction in Richard and Andrus (n. 10) paras 1.68-1.88.
170. League of Nations, 'Fiscal Committee Report to the Council on the Work of The Second Session of the Committee Held in Geneva From May 22nd to 31st, 1930.' (n. 161) 4209-4230.
171. The formulary apportionment method in fact was not differentiated in substance from the empirical method, thus the later will not be given separate considerations, *see* Carroll, 'Carroll Report' (n. 162) para. 122.
172. With the first three volumes addressing the systems in place, the fourth volume providing summary and recommendations, and the last volume on the accounting practice of allocation.
173. Langbein believed it was because the domestic legislation was not developed enough to bring about double taxation problem. Langbein (n. 45) 635.
174. Carroll, 'Carroll Report' (n. 162) 37.
175. *Ibid.*, 81-87, 60-65, 67, 73-79, 94-96.
176. *Ibid.*, 88, 189.

with administrative practice.[177] The very few legislative norms for the apportionment question employed formulary apportionment, while separate accounting was only an administrative practice with no statutory status at all. The preference for separate accounting was proclaimed as an administrative method of assessment rather than a legislative choice of allocation methods, which explained why several countries enacting formulary apportionment also announced that they prefer separate accounting.[178] In fact, looking into those announcements, the so-called the majority's predilections for separate accounting were in many instances highly conditional and cautious, while those concerns were right on the mirror side of the strengths of formulary apportionment.[179] In short, the norm status of formulary apportionment in the country practices was not given adequate weight for considering the relative value of the three apportionment methods, and the majority preference for the separate accounting method was a story oversimplified.

Third, the Report's arguments for the superiority of separate accounting over formulary apportionment were far-fetched, if not untenable. In concluding all the information collected from the jurisdictions, the discussion of the basic methods of allocation had been transformed into a stage comparing theories underlying separate accounting/arm's length with formulary apportionment.[180] Before heading towards the comparison, the report bluntly revealed the truth that a separate accounting/arm's length combination had no sound theoretical basis at all, whereas formulary apportionment was based on the principles of unitary business and the ability to pay. As a result, the comparison that followed became a one-sided repudiation of formulary apportionment. Even so, the arguments were purely addressing administrative concerns that cannot hold up the superiority of separate accounting/arm's length, especially since these concerns overlooked the existent legislative sanctions adopting formulary apportionment while overestimating the weight of administrative constraints in their time and for the future. For example, differences among accounting methods, currency, language, and commercial laws were emphasized as obstacles to formulary apportionment, and so were the discrepancies in the computation of branch profits. These are not intractable difficulties, as the developments of the current economic, political and cultural integrations have evinced. Similarly, the reasoning

177. Langbein believed it was because the domestic legislation was not developed enough to bring about double taxation problem. Langbein (n. 45) 634-635.
178. Carroll, 'Carroll Report' (n. 162) 90.
179. For example, in the statement of Irish Free State as follows, 'The method of separate accounting is considered the best *if* the accounts truly reflect the British Indian income, *but it is not usually sufficient*, as the transactions of the head office and branches are generally so *closely interlocked* that it is *difficult to isolate* the British Indian income. Furthermore, the transactions between the head office and branches require a very close scrutiny, which entails the examination of the head-office accounts.' it was a reluctant interpretation to claim that the State truly preferred the separate accounting method, *see*, League of Nations, 'Taxation of Foreign and National Enterprises Vol. 2. A Study of the Tax Systems and the Methods of Allocation of the Profits of Enterprises Operating in More than One Country in Austria, Belgium, Czechoslovakia, Free City of Danzig, Greece, Hungary, Italy, Latvia, Luxemburg, Netherlands, Romania and Switzerland' (n. 162) 37. Similar expressions can also be found in the statements of Czechoslovakia, Japan, Austria, and Wisconsin.
180. Carroll, 'Carroll Report' (n. 162) 187-189.

also applies to the author's formalistic understanding of source-based taxation as strictly territorial taxation. The Report dismissed the feasibility of branch jurisdiction to access the information of foreign parents, which is another failure to foresee the trend. Even if these concerns were valid in the early era of globalization, many of them are resolved nowadays, for instance, the Country-by-Country (CbC) Reporting mechanism apparently contradicts the formalistic understanding of source taxation.

The next point relates to one of Langbein's most valuable but long-neglected arguments, that is, separate accounting is not equal to a separate entity or, more generally, the ALS of transfer pricing regulation. Separate accounting refers to the practice of tax authorities using the accounts maintained by the establishments of an enterprise as the starting point of taxation,[181] while ALS has been constructed as a rationale for using the prices of comparable transactions made between independent enterprises as the basis of readjusting the transfer (mis-)prices of transactions between associated entities.[182] Literally, they are distinct concepts. The ALS asks more than the separate accounting does, as it dictates the independent enterprise assumption, artificial comparability, and fictitious transactions. On this basis, it was argued that the countries' asserted preferences for separate accounting were actually addressing their repugnance for arbitrary assessment rather than substantive rules of profit apportionment among competing claims of multiple tax jurisdictions or anti-avoidance.[183] Another direct proof is that among the four methods of transfer pricing adjustment, the countries expressing a predilection for separate accounting vis-à-vis formulary apportionment did not have a particular preference, including for the first method as the predecessor of the modern arm's length provisions.[184]

Lastly, the conceptual gap between separate accounting as an administrative practice of tax assessment and the ALS as substantive interjurisdictional norms echoes another weakness of Carroll's arguments in the Report and the developments thereafter. The apportionment inquiry originally arose from the allocation scenario between the head office and permanent establishment or among the multiple permanent establishments, which can be traced to the PE article of the first Draft Models of Double Taxation.[185] In the First Session of the Fiscal Committee convened following the completion of the 1928 Draft Models, besides the issue of apportionment regarding permanent establishment, the 'holding companies' scenario as brought out by the ICC was discussed in detail, yet the Committee concluded that it 'only affected a small number of cases'.[186] This decision may be attributed to the prevalence of cross-border business carried out through PE rather than setting up local subsidiaries. Throughout the Report, the discussions of apportionment methods of either separate accounting or

181. *Ibid.*, 46.
182. OECD, 'OECD Transfer Pricing Guidelines for Multinational Enterprises and Tax Administrations 2017' (OECD 2017) 23.
183. Langbein (n. 45) 635.
184. *See* the discussions in the next section.
185. 'Should the undertaking possess permanent establishments in both Contracting States, each of the two States shall tax the portion of the income produced in its territory. The competent administrations of the two Contracting States shall come-to an arrangement as to the basis for apportionment.' League of Nations, 'Draft Convention No. I-a' (n. 157) 4162.
186. League of Nations, 'Fiscal Committee Report to the Council on The Work of the First Session of the Committee. Held in Geneva from October 17th to 26th, 1929.' (n. 160) 4199.

formulary apportionment were conducted against the default setting of permanent establishment instead of subsidiaries.[187] It is thus well noted that the study and the recommendations of the Carroll Report were directed at the case of a single enterprise and permanent establishment, whereas associated companies were of only collateral significance. Immediately following the wrap-up of the Carroll Report, the LON in explaining the new Draft Convention[188] reaffirmed the 'fundamental principle' of separate accounting/independent enterprise and ALS as laid down by the Report, but only in the context of permanent establishment and with no references to subsidiaries.[189] The similar expressions are evinced in the LON Models from then on, which left the question of associated subsidiaries open, and the 1963 OECD Model.[190] In modern cases, the application of ALS to subsidiaries within a group is the starting point, which is in deviation from the original trajectory. The unqualified engraftment, for one thing, the asserted customary status of the ALS in the context of affiliated companies is actually unverified.[191] For another, and more significantly, it unwittingly leads to the problem of stateless income. In the context of a permanent establishment, it is a typical 'one taxpayer, two taxing states' scenario where there will always be a parent or home office in the residence state and an establishment in the source state. The First Draft Models conferred global taxing rights upon the residence state under the personal-impersonal division methodology. Thus, any residues will be taxed on the parent by the residence state after the source state taxes on the local establishment. The case is different for affiliated companies because there will not always be a parent or home office, and the tax relationship is 'two taxpayers, two taxing states' that overruns the simple residence-source net of taxation. Taking into account Langbein's well-recognized indication of the continuum price problem,[192] transferring the ALS originating from the context of permanent establishment to associated companies could create favourable conditions for the integrated enterprise where the taxing states can only tax partial rather than all of its total profits accrued.[193]

#### 2.5.4.3 *Methods of Transfer Pricing Adjustment*

Besides the discussion of allocation methods, the Carroll Report also included two chapters on the 'allocation criteria' in the contexts of both permanent establishment

187. *See*, for example, Carroll, 'Carroll Report' (n. 162) 45-54.
188. *See* the discussions in the next section.
189. League of Nations, 'Fiscal Committee Report to the Council on the Fourth Session of the Committee. Held at Geneva from June 15th to 26th, 1933.' in United States Congress Joint Committee on Internal Revenue Taxation (ed.), *Legislative History of United States Tax Conventions*, vol. 4 (US GPO 1962) 4242.
190. Wolfgang Schön, 'International Tax Coordination for a Second-Best World (Part III)' (2010) 2 World Tax Journal 227, 231 https://doi.org/10.59403/2c2zh72 accessed 26 August 2025.
191. Reuven S Avi-Yonah, 'Does Customary International Tax Law Exist?' [2019] Michigan Public Law: Law Faculty Papers (Topic) https://www.ssrn.com/abstract=3382203 accessed 26 August 2025; Cees Peters, 'Critical Analysis of the General Court's "EU Arm's Length Tool": Beware of the Reflexivity of Transfer Pricing Law!' (2022) 31 EC Tax Review 30 https://doi.org/10.54648/ecta2022004 accessed 26 August 2025.
192. Langbein (n. 45) 636-637.
193. *Ibid.*, 637.

and subsidiaries.[194] No explanations were given as to what the allocation criteria meant exactly. With contextual analysis, it represented attribution of income to permanent establishment, yet in a different way from the transfer pricing adjustment of affiliated companies. Here, only the latter will be discussed.

In the introduction, the taxation of associated companies in the 'great majority of countries' was depicted, according to which the general practice followed the ALS. To verify the conformity with the ALS of the interlocking transactions, tax authorities usually only inquire into the current affairs of the business, while in difficult cases, they may resort to empirical methods such as formulary apportionment, consulting the experiences of permanent establishment.

The Report listed several examples of non-arm's length relations among associated companies. Although they are rather primitive compared to modern transfer pricing planning of MNEs, the Report summarized three general methods of transfer pricing adjustment, a question viewed as reaching the profits diverted from subsidiaries to foreign parent, which are in sharp contrast with the modern practices:

(i) readjusting the price to arm's length on the basis of independent enterprises and taxing the subsidiary;[195]
(ii) taxing the parent company directly on the basis of treating the subsidiary as an agent, thus permanent establishment of the parent;[196]
(iii) assessing the whole enterprise on the basis of subsidiary and parent forming a single economic unit or the subsidiary being an organ of the parent company;[197]
(iv) assessing the consolidated accounts of parent and subsidiary on the basis of the unitary business principle as well.[198]

As revealed in the survey, method (i), as the predecessor of modern transfer pricing provisions, is only one of the alternatives employed by countries to allocate the income of associate companies. Technically, what was reported is that counties did not express preferences among the four methods of transfer pricing adjustment, contrary to the probable impression from countries' asserted predilection for separate accounting.[199] The other three methods, though different in detail, do not respect the independent enterprise principle obstinately. They provided adequate theoretical justifications and application circumstances for these non-arm's length unitary methods. When the integration of the multinational groups, global capital mobility, the importance of intangibles, and residual profits generated were not comparable to nowadays, the unitary methods could be successfully adopted; then, what factors on what basis have rendered unitary methods a forbidden zone in transfer pricing regulations under contemporary circumstances?

194. Carroll, 'Carroll Report' (n. 162) 97-116.
195. *Ibid.*, 110.
196. *Ibid.*, 111.
197. *Ibid.*, 112.
198. *Ibid.*, 113.
199. Lepard (n. 46) 65; Langbein (n. 45) 633.

The survey unveiled not only an unqualified reasoning that the asserted preference of the countries for separate accounting leads to the authority of ALS but also, for transfer pricing regulation, there was no dogmatic adherence to either separate accounting, independent enterprise principle, or transaction/price centred approach that have been observed as golden rules contemporarily. Inspecting closer into the survey, the image was not that the separate accounting countries unanimously sided with the method (i) or the formulary apportionment countries unanimously sided with the other three methods, piercing the independent personality of companies, but that having evinced great dynamics and flexibility in their practices of transfer pricing. The question is hence raised as to interpreting the asserted preference for separate accounting into the repudiation of formulary apportionment and the justification of the subsequent developments leading to the contemporary transfer pricing regime that adheres to the ALS dogmatically.

### 2.5.5 1933 Draft Convention of Business Income Allocation

Based on the study and recommendations of the Carroll Report, the Fiscal Committee, in its Fourth Session in 1933, provided a report to the Council of LON, which contained a Draft Convention[200] only dealing with the allocation of business income. The Draft was then minorly amended, respectively, in 1935[201] and 1936[202] in the Fifth and Sixth Sessions. Collectively, they are named in this chapter as '1933 Draft Convention'.

#### *2.5.5.1 FA in the Three-Tier Approach in the Context of PE*

As referred to in the last section, the 1933 Draft Convention had already incorporated the separate accounting/independent enterprise principle and arm's length method in the context of permanent establishment,[203] which is the first time the term 'arm's length' was used in the LON Draft Conventions. Specifically, for the general purpose of determining the taxable income of permanent establishment, the Convention had set up a three-tier approach deploying both ALS and formulary apportionment.[204]

---

200. League of Nations, 'Fiscal Committee Report to the Council on the Fourth Session of the Committee. Held at Geneva from June 15th to 26th, 1933.' (n. 189) 4243-4247.
201. League of Nations, 'Fiscal Committee Report to the Council on the Work of The Fifth Session of the Committee Held in Geneva From June 12 to 17, 1935.' in United States Congress Joint Committee on Internal Revenue Taxation (ed.), *Legislative History of United States Tax Conventions* (US GPO 1962) 4249.
202. League of Nations, 'Fiscal Committee Work of the Fiscal Committee During Its Sixth Session Held at Geneva from October 15th to 21st, 1936.' in United States Congress Joint Committee on Internal Revenue Taxation (ed.), *Legislative History of United States Tax Conventions* (US GPO 1962) 4257.
203. It is held that the arm's length standard is a higher concept incorporating both the separate accounting/independent enterprise principle and arm's length method. The arm's length method refers to the transfer pricing adjustment focusing on rectifying the price and transactions to arm's length while respecting the independent enterprise/separate accounting principle.
204. League of Nations, 'Draft Convention for the Allocation of Business Income between States for the Purposes of Taxation' in United States Congress Joint Committee on Internal Revenue Taxation (ed.), *Legislative History of United States Tax Conventions* (US GPO 1962) Art. 3:

The first tier is the default rule of separate accounting, the independent enterprise fiction, and the arm's length method.

The second tier is that under several specified circumstances, the tax authority may use a fixed percentage of the turnover method. The third tier utilizes the formulary apportionment method, adopting the unitary enterprise approach as a last resort.

Both of the last two tiers should try to replicate the results of the first tier. In this respect, the 1933 Draft Convention evinced a sharp turn from the 1928 Draft Convention in which formulary apportionment had substantial weight, even though subordinate to separate accounting but not constrained by the arm's length method. Such a change was laid down by the Carroll Report.

#### 2.5.5.2 *Squeezed Living Space of FA*

Another breakthrough is the new Article 5, which introduced the ALS into the context of associated enterprises and is the close forerunner of the contemporary Article 9(1) of the OECD and UN Models. The Commentary of Article 5 provided the transfer pricing adjustment directly by rectifying the balance sheets.[205] While not specifying in detail the transfer pricing adjustment methods, the wording of Article 5 and its Commentary of the 1933 Draft Convention approximates the method (i) in the Carroll Report,

---

> If an enterprise with its fiscal domicile in one contracting State has permanent establishments in other contracting States, there shall be attributed to each permanent establishment the net business income which it might be expected to derive if it were an independent enterprise engaged in the same or similar activities under the same or similar conditions. Such net income will, in principle, be determined on the basis of the separate accounts pertaining to such establishment. Subject to the provisions of this Convention, such income shall be taxed in accordance with the legislation and international agreements of the State in which such establishment is situated.
>
> The fiscal authorities of the contracting Slates shall, when necessary, in execution of the preceding paragraph, rectify the accounts produced, notably to correct errors or omissions, or to re-establish the prices or remunerations entered in the books at the value which would prevail between independent persons dealing at arm's length.
>
> If an establishment does not produce an accounting showing its own operations, or if the accounting produced does not correspond to the normal usages of the trade in the country where the establishment is situated, or if the rectifications provided for in the preceding paragraph cannot be affected, or if the taxpayer agrees, the fiscal authorities may determine empirically the business income by applying a percentage to the turnover of that establishment. This percentage is fixed in accordance with the nature of the transactions in which the establishment is engaged and by comparison with the results obtained by similar enterprises operating, in the country.
>
> If the methods of determination described in the preceding paragraphs are found to be inapplicable, the net business income of the permanent establishment may be determined by a computation based on the total income derived by the enterprise from the activities in which such establishment has participated. This determination is made by applying to the total income coefficients based on a comparison of gross receipts, assets, number of hours worked or other appropriate factors, provided such factors be so selected as to ensure results approaching as closely as possible to those which would be reflected by a separate accounting.

205. Article 5 deals with subsidiaries which will be taxed as independent enterprises provided no profits or losses are transferred as a result of the relations between the affiliated companies. If such transfers are effected, the administration will make the necessary adjustments in the balance-sheets.

distinct from the other three non-arm's length methods. Consequently, the cornerstones of taxing associated enterprises have remained largely stable ever since.[206] From the beginning to the present, there are also two interpretations of this provision of taxing associated enterprises that remain valid.

First, the texts of both the original Article 5, including its Commentary and current Article 9(1) have no explicit reference to 'price' or 'transaction'; what has been really stressed is the broader 'conditions' as the only variable to the independent enterprise scenario and 'profits' as the ultimate implications to be considered and adjusted.[207] This actually contrasts with the current transfer pricing practice and the arm's length method presented as method (i) in the Carroll Report.[208]

Second, the provision is silent as to whether formulary apportionment is permissible to allocate the income among associated enterprises, which is different from the provision of permanent establishment. It is a matter of fact that the provision leaves ample space by stressing only the beginning - the 'relations' or 'conditions', and the end - the 'profits', and the overall constraint on the methods of allocation or adjustment that any of those should replicate the arm's length results as reached by independent enterprises are rather vague especially where comparable circumstances do not exist. This almost produces a consensus that the literal reading of the provision can provide the space to synthesize the ALS and formulary apportionment method.[209]

However, the interpretation which is faithful to history may give the opposite answer.

It is well known that the ALS of the provision was grafted from the permanent establishment context without adequate deliberation. Thus, it must mean that dropping the three-tier approach to taxing permanent establishment was a strategic move. Similarly, while the arm's length method and unitary business methods were juxtaposed in the Carroll Report, the Convention eventually only endorsed the former, even though it is generally based on the Carroll Report. The intention of the Fiscal Committee may have been to express a stronger commitment to separate accounting in the context of associated companies and the legalistic ratification of the independent personality of corporations. In this light, the historical leeway to endorsing formulary apportionment in the provision of associated enterprises is limited.

Last but not least, the prospect of allocating business income becomes a separate multilateral convention. The LON, in addressing the Draft Convention, also expressed

---

206. Richard and Andrus (n. 10) para. 1.105.
207. *Ibid.*, para. 1.107.
208. Jinyan Li, 'Soft Law, Hard Realities and Pragmatic Suggestions: Critiquing the OECD Transfer Pricing Guidelines' in Wolfgang Schön and Kai A Konrad (eds), *Fundamentals of International Transfer Pricing in Law and Economics* (Springer Berlin Heidelberg 2012) 80.
209. RS Avi-Yonah, 'The Rise and Fall of Arm's Length: A Study in the Evolution of US International Taxation' (1995) 15 Virginia Tax Review 89, 93; Li, 'Soft Law, Hard Realities and Pragmatic Suggestions' (n. 208) 81; Arnold McDonnell, 'Report on the Invitational Conference on Transfer Pricing: The Allocation of Income and Expenses Among Countries' [1993] Canadian Tax Journal 899, 907; Georg Kofler, 'The BEPS Action Plan and Transfer Pricing: The Arm's Length Standard Under Pressure?' (2013) 5 British Tax Review 646, 652; Langbein and Fuss (n. 74) 259-409; Jinyan Li, *International Taxation in the Age of Electronic Commerce: A Comparative Study* (Canadian Tax Foundation 2003) 543-546, 612-613.

its vision of a multilateral convention on the basis of the Draft Convention.[210] A multilateral convention had always been envisaged or preferred by the ICC and LON since they began to engage in eliminating double taxation,[211] but it seemed not to have aroused adequate consensus or interest. The LON's new attempt was based on the limited scope of the Draft Convention on business income allocation and the consistency of its provisions with the fundamental international tax principles.[212] The 1935 Report summarized the responses to the questions circulated in 1933 to governments as to whether they agreed to negotiate a multilateral convention on the basis of the Draft Convention. It turned out that the number of countries in favour of the idea was small and did not justify a separate agenda.[213] Since then, bilateral conventions have become the definite mainstream, even though the LON did not give up its vision of a multilateral convention.[214] This point is raised here as a side note to (re-)considering the prospect of entering into a multilateral convention focused on the taxation of MNEs, with the hope of improving the existing system of transfer pricing and countering the BEPS problems more effectively.

### 2.5.6 Tracing the Genesis, the Influence of the United States

The specific *influence* of the United States on the international tax system in its formative period is not the purpose of this chapter, but it is well-documented, for example, in the drafting of the First Model Conventions of 1927 and 1928.[215] The so-called influences refer to the adoption of opinions, concepts, ideas, and norms equivalent to those of the United States in the international field. It has already been noted that the incorporation of ALS in the context of permanent establishment is where the allocation question of taxing international businesses started, but its crossover to the associated enterprise context that led to the original Article 5 is less documented.[216] This section tries to sketch the influences of the United States on ALS in the LON Draft Conventions.

To encapsulate, the formulation of the ALS for the purpose of taxing associated enterprises in Article 5 of the 1933 Draft Convention had been latently influenced by the contemporaneous regulations and tax treaty of the United States. As a general matter, it is natural for Carroll to focus on the practices of the United States as a tax expert based and trained there. The main and original concern of the US tax rules of

210. League of Nations, 'Fiscal Committee Report to the Council on the Fourth Session of the Committee. Held at Geneva from June 15th to 26th, 1933.' (n. 189) 4242.
211. *See* the discussions on the legacies of the ICC, also in Richard and Andrus (n. 10) paras 1.27, 1.29., and the 1923 LON Academic Report's reference to general convention in the Introduction, and the 1927 LON Report's preference to 'Collective' Convention.
212. League of Nations, 'Fiscal Committee Report to the Council on the Fourth Session of the Committee. Held at Geneva from June 15th to 26th, 1933.' (n. 189) 4242.
213. League of Nations, 'Fiscal Committee Report to the Council on the Work of The Fifth Session of the Committee Held in Geneva From June 12 to 17, 1935.' (n. 201) 4251.
214. *Ibid.*, 4252; *see also* the relevant discussion in Mitchell B Carroll, *Global Perspectives of an International Tax Lawyer* (1st edn, Exposition Press 1978) 70.
215. Graetz and O'Hear (n. 56) 1085-1089.
216. Lepard (n. 46) 68.

associated companies was the manipulations of special relations between parent company and subsidiaries to avoid taxes in the United States.[217] Recalling that the Carroll Report listed four methods of transfer pricing adjustments, of which the first method was directly extracted from section 45 of United States Revenue Act of 1932,[218] as the predecessor of the current section 482 I.R.C.[219] 't provided the essential components of modern ALSs, including the circumstances where it operated, the recognition of the independent personality of subsidiaries, separate accounting, and the adjustment of income. However, the provision was only a rough predecessor of the ALS in Article 9, for the benchmark and outcome of transfer pricing adjustment were all conferred upon the decision of the Commissioner to counter anti-avoidance or reach the true income.

Besides the internal rules, the tax treaty entered by the United States and France in 1932 is the genesis of the modern Article 5. The treaty has been believed as the first bilateral tax treaty providing a separate provision of the allocation of profits between associated companies, which is also the first of such entered into by the US[220] What Article IV of this treaty had provided is succeeded by the Article 5 of the 1933 Draft Convention, which means that it must have served as the model provision of the Convention.[221] Article IV was itself modelled on section 45 but supplemented it with the fundamental component of the independent enterprise yardstick, which eventually constitutes the modern ALS contained in Article 9.

### 2.5.7 The Finale: The Divergence of the Mexico and London Models

Following the periods of the international tax evolution, the discussions have approached the end of the Revenue Phase. It is considered that the two Model Conventions of the LON, respectively, the '1943 Mexico Model' and the '1946 London Model', mark the end of the era when the LON dominated the norm-making of international taxation. The two Models, as the precursors of the OECD and UN Models, laid down the

217. Graetz and O'Hear (n. 56) 1060-1061.
218. It reads 'In any case of two or more trades or businesses (whether or not incorporated, whether or not organised in the United States and whether or not affiliated) owned or controlled directly or indirectly by the same interests, the Commissioner is authorised to distribute, apportion, or allocate gross income or deductions between or among such trades or businesses, if he determines that such distribution, apportionment, or allocation is necessary in order to prevent evasion of taxes or clearly to reflect the income of any of such trades or businesses.', League of Nations, 'Taxation of Foreign and National Enterprises Vol. 1. A Study of the Tax Systems and the Methods of Allocation of the Profits of Enterprises Operating in More than One Country in France, Germany, Spain, the United Kingdom, and the United States of America' (n. 39) 252.
219. Mitchell B Carroll, 'Evolution of U.S. Treaties to Avoid Double Taxation of Income: Part II' (1968) 3 International Lawyer 150.
220. Lepard (n. 46) 68-69.
221. 'When an American enterprise, by reason of its participation in the management or capital of a French enterprise, makes or imposes on the latter, in their commercial or financial relations, conditions different from those which would be made with a third enterprise, any profits which should normally have appeared in the balance sheet of the French enterprise, but which have been in this manner, diverted to the American enterprise, are, subject to the measures of appeal applicable in the case of the tax on industrial and commercial profits, incorporated in the taxable profits of the French enterprise.'.

general outlines of modern bilateral tax treaties. Compared to the First Model Conventions, a remarkable change is the removal of the texts of personal/impersonal tax division, but it did not materially affect the content or structure of the provisions.[222]

*The Three-tier Approach Reproduced.* The 1933 Draft Convention, which dealt particularly with business enterprises and later revised versions, was never approved by the LON and thus did not constitute genuine international tax models. However, taking the opportunity to revise the 1928 Models, the LON incorporated its major provisions into the Mexico and London Models. As a result, the ALS was, for the first time, formally adopted in a Double Taxation Model for the purpose of taxing the business income of enterprises. Consequently, the two Models were identical in providing essentially the same provisions as in the 1933 Draft Convention. The same three-tier approach embodying both separate accounting and formulary apportionment was adopted in the case of permanent establishment, while both Models added corresponding adjustment provisions to follow the arm's length provision for associated enterprises.

Equally important but having drawn less attention with respect to the Mexico and London Models, is their sharp difference in the allocation of business income between the residence and source. The Mexico Model, developed by a sub-committee comprised mostly of representatives from developing countries in Latin America,[223] advocated extensive taxation at source on the basis of both revenue claims of the source state and countering tax evasion.[224] Accordingly, the primary taxing right over interest, dividends, royalties, and annuities was assigned to the source. More significantly, the Mexico Model had essentially abandoned or sidestepped[225] the permanent establishment threshold of source taxation of business income. Instead, Article IV(1) provided a principle echoing the mantra of the BEPS Project that income should be taxed only where economic activities were carried out.[226] Article IV(2) enabled the source country to tax the profits derived from activities beyond isolated or occasional, even though not attributable to a permanent establishment.[227]

---

222. Cavelti (n. 82) 75.
223. There were only representatives from developed countries of the US and Canada in the Committee. League of Nations, 'Fiscal Committee: Model Bilateral Conventions for the Prevention of International Double Taxation and Fiscal Evasion. Second Regional Tax Conference, Mexico, D.F., July 1943' (League of Nations) C.2.M.2.1945.II.A.
224. League of Nations, 'Fiscal Committee London and Mexico Model Tax Conventions Commentary and Text' in United States Congress Joint Committee on Internal Revenue Taxation (ed.), *Legislative History of United States Tax Conventions* (US GPO 1962) 4333-4334.
225. 'the expansive scope of taxation of business profits that were not attributed to a PE made the PE inquiry somewhat meaningless. 1', Wells and Lowell (n. 98) 564.
226. '1. Income from any industrial, commercial or agricultural business and from any other gainful activity shall be taxable only in the State where the business or activity is carried out.', Article IV of the Mexico Model, League of Nations, 'Fiscal Committee London and Mexico Model Tax Conventions Commentary and Text' (n. 224) 4380.
227. '2. If an enterprise or an individual in one of the contracting States extends its or his activities to the other State, through isolated or occasional transactions, without possessing in that State a permanent establishment, the income derived from such activities shall be taxable only in the first State.', League of Nations, 'Fiscal Committee London and Mexico Model Tax Conventions Commentary and Text' (n. 224).

The London Model was a tit-for-tat response to the Mexico Model that aimed to bring residence-based taxation on track. Consequently, the primary taxing right over the same group of incomes originally assigned to the source country was surrendered to the residence country,[228] and the PE threshold of source taxation was re-established for business taxation at source.[229] In the combined Commentary of the two Models, the Fiscal Committee defended the position of the London Model that, first of all, the PE nomenclature had already been widely adopted; second, the existence of a permanent establishment is the prerequisite to make the taxation of foreign enterprises operable and equitable; third, tax evasion is in and by itself not a matter of international tax treaties but of domestic tax administration, since the tax not collected at source will always be topped up by the residence.[230] These points are clearly not robust. Under modern circumstances, the permanent establishment concept has been increasingly challenged and has become an important factor destabilizing the international tax system.[231] The inter-nation equity between residence and source had not been seriously contemplated in the formation of this threshold, as the foregoing discussions unveiled, and it originated to shield the source country from taxing extraterritorial business activities. With respect to tax evasion, the fallacy is that the Fiscal Committee considered the residence countries would all choose to tax their residents on a worldwide basis, which was not true back then or now. The stateless income proliferated at this point. The Fiscal Committee failed to recognize that it was the inherent framework of the Model Conventions rather than the mere internal tax administration that was crucial to the fiscal evasion issue.

## 2.6 THE EPILOGUE OF THE REVENUE PHASE

The retrospection of the Revenue Phase takes the largest space of this chapter. Technically, this phase only spreads a bit more than two decades, yet the clues of this period are the most informative as regards the genesis of the international tax system and, in particular, the evolution of formulary apportionment. One of the principal selling points of this chapter is that formulary apportionment is examined not as an isolated event but against the evolution of the general international tax system, with a particular focus on the components in relation to the BEPS problems or those generally under pressure. The foregoing discussions of the substantial developments ranging from the ICC contributions and the Academic and Technical Reports to the final Mexico and London Models have captured the process of how formulary apportionment had been elevated transiently and eviscerated while the skeletons of modern international taxation were simultaneously built up. The historical events revisited often had different focuses, and the theses discussed in each of them are various. This epilogue

228. *Ibid.*, 4383-4387.
229. *Ibid.*, 4381.
230. *Ibid.*, 4334.
231. João Francisco Bianco and Ramon Tomazela Santos, 'A Change of Paradigm in International Tax Law: Article 7 of Tax Treaties and the Need To Resolve the Source versus Residence Dichotomy' (2016) 70 Bulletin for International Taxation https://doi.org/10.59403/1g95w25 accessed 26 August 2025.

intends to serve two ends: one is to generalize the findings succinctly, and the other is to discuss the implications of this Phase for the subsequent phases of international taxation.

### 2.6.1 Historical Evolution of Formulary Apportionment

The above discussions have unveiled the changing position and purposes in the international tax forum. To encapsulate, formulary apportionment had been on a continual 'relegation'. The pre-existing statutory practices of formulary apportionment either in internal regulations or tax treaties were repelled; formulary apportionment was de-escalated from an overarching design of international taxation to an alternative to taxing the income of business enterprises; and it used to be recommended as the primary method of taxing business enterprises in the First Double Taxation Models,[232] but was eventually relegated as a secondary option in the narrow scenario of taxing permanent establishments. In these processes, the landslide defeats of formulary apportionment were conspired by two pivotal pieces of work championed by the LON, namely, the 1923 Academic Report that had contemplated but repudiated formulary apportionment as a potential option to eliminate double taxation, and the 1933 Carroll Report that drew a hard line between formulary apportionment and separate accounting for the purposes of taxing multinational enterprises.

### 2.6.2 Theoretical Basis of Formulary Apportionment

The discussions above have shed light on the theoretical justifications of formulary apportionment, which rebuts the claims that formulary apportionment is just superficial and arbitrary. The first of them was revealed when the Academic Experts in 1923 deliberated about the overarching principles of international taxation. They upheld the economic allegiance theory, originally contributed by Georg von Schanz who also advocated proportional allocation between residence and source state, that the whole faculty of a taxpayer should be divided among the tax jurisdictions according to the taxpayer's relative interests in each, which evinces a natural affinity with formulary apportionment. Based on the theory, the Experts enumerated the formulary apportionment as one of the alternatives to allocating taxing rights and eliminating double taxation but rejected it out of practical concerns. When formulary apportionment was relegated as the option to tax business enterprises, the Carroll Report in 1933 summarized four interrelated layers of the rationale of formulary apportionment, which are the unitary business principle, the economic allegiance theory, the geographic sources of income, and the ability to pay principle.

Part III of this research has more on this topic.

232. Particularly referring to that the 1927 Model that included affiliated companies into the categories of permanent establishment and suggested formulary apportionment to tax the permanent establishment.

### 2.6.3 Residence–Source Dichotomy

The Revenue Phase coincides with the formative period of international taxation. International taxation and international rules back then were embryonic, yet it is remarkable that the core institutions of the modern international tax system in the next century were mostly laid down in these two decades. Although the foregoing discussions were, in fact, formulary apportionment-centric, due to their global nature, the core institutions of the international tax system have already been touched upon, and they converge under the umbrella of the paradigm of residence–source dichotomy.

The basic connotation of the paradigm is that the residence state is imposing a global/personal income tax on its residents, while the source state is imposing a schedular/impersonal income tax on the non-residents. The paradigm was originally constructed for the taxation of individuals; the taxation of business enterprises is its natural extension. In modern times, the importance and complexity of international business taxation grows; in some aspects, it increasingly deviates from the classical individual-centred system. In particular, international tax competition has mobilized most developed economies to tax resident MNEs on a territorial rather than worldwide basis.[233] However, the residence of enterprises decides their overall tax circumstances because it is the prescriptive cornerstone of tax treaties. In contrast, source is a composite concept of legal, economic principles and administrative expedience. Considering the general economic realities and with more countries turning to a territorial system, source is at the centre of the disputes over the challenges of base erosion and profits shifting.

The concept of source, never formulated systematically in tax treaties or elsewhere, is an alternative expression of the jurisdictions to tax non-residents on all bases other than residence. Besides laying down the fundamental architecture, the residence-source paradigm has established a system of pro-residence and disfavouring-source through a set of institutions such as the classification and assignment approach, the personal/impersonal tax division, the ALS, and the permanent establishment threshold.

### 2.6.4 Permanent Establishment Threshold

The permanent establishment has been at the frontline of the 'power struggle' between the residence country and source country.

In retrospect, the very original purpose of introducing the concept into international taxation was to lock the source taxation in only the local and physical operations, in the interests of capital exporting countries against the mercantile economic model. In the current years since the formative period, the scope of permanent establishment has been under continual revision to reflect either the claims of residence or source

233. Through the widespread use of exemption method to eliminate double taxation, the participation exemption regime and the CFC rules. *See* Brian J Arnold, *International Tax Primer* (4th edn, Kluwer Law International 2019) 17-69.

countries.[234] The digitalization of the economy and the BEPS problems have altered the seesaw; multinational enterprises can be involved in the economic life of a country and earn profits from it without having a physical presence. The permanent establishment threshold has thus questioned whether it is still workable to maintain the 'balance' between the residence and source in the new normal. Specified proposals, such as the 'digital PE'[235] or the new Indian proposal of profit attribution PE,[236] and comprehensive proposals of European CC(C)TB, all aim to repeal or transform the permanent establishment threshold. Entering the emerging Allocation Phase in the post-BEPS era, it seems that for international taxation, the permanent establishment threshold will inevitably undergo fundamental reform.

### 2.6.5 Arm's Length Standard

The importance of the Carroll Report cannot be emphasized more with respect to its contributions to the status of ALS that becomes the foundation of the modern transfer pricing regime. Nevertheless, this is a prospect which was way beyond the expectations of Carroll himself. In drafting the Report, he did not foresee that establishing subsidiaries rather than permanent establishments would become the dominant form of carrying on international business, and it would involve the most complex and controversial aspects of international taxation. The mandate given to Carroll was to explore a proposal that, first of all, can be implemented expediently to prevent double taxation, the potential of being abused, and the fairness of tax sharing was incidental, if not nil. Another dimension of the Report's historical implication is regarding the prejudiced role of the ALS between the residence and source. It is argued that the Revenue Phase had laid down the foundation of an international tax system that favoured residents, largely the capital-exporting countries, while restricting or disparaging the taxation of source countries that primarily provided raw materials. The upholding of an ALS and separate accounting by the Report is a prepense choice to adapt the taxation of multinational enterprises to the narrow source concept, where, they are necessary to limit the concept of source to 'sources obviously within the jurisdiction of the state', so as to eliminate the need to trace profits through corporations created under the laws of another country and prevent the transgression of a country's jurisdiction over income definitely sourced to its territory.[237] For the same purposes of restricting the source, the Carroll Report had approved the 'remuneration of services' approach in the context of permanent establishment to justify the allocation

234. OECD, 'Model Tax Convention on Income and on Capital 2017 (Full Version)' (OECD Publishing 2019) Arts 5 and the following history of it http://dx.doi.org/10.1787/g2g972ee-en accessed 26 August 2025.
235. Hongler Peter and Pistone Pasquale, 'Blueprints for a New PE Nexus to Tax Business Income in the Era of the Digital Economy' (20 January 2015) https://papers.ssrn.com/abstract=259 1829 accessed 2 December 2023.
236. Reuven S Avi-Yonah and Ajitesh Kir, 'A Break in the Dam? India's New Profit Attribution Proposal and the Arm's Length Standard' [2019] SSRN Electronic Journal https://doi.org/10.2139/ssrn.3414266 and https://www.ssrn.com/abstract=3414266 accessed 18 November 2023.
237. Carroll, 'Carroll Report' (n. 162) 169.

of residual profits to capital exporting/residence countries where the centre of management considered the 'most vital' part of enterprises was located.[238] In addition, as touched upon earlier, it is attributed to the Carroll Report that the dichotomy of arm's length versus formulary apportionment is formed, and it precedes the 1935 Convention's literal equivocality at this point. The Report created an intense atmosphere that arm's length/separate accounting sits at one extreme end, while formulary apportionment sits at the other.

However, although Carroll saw contracts as pivotal to determining the content of transactions entered into by affiliated companies, contracts seemed to him more of a convenient instrument to analyse the functions thereby contained but less the contract in and by itself being the primary reason to price the functions.[239] Carroll dismissed the case where no comparables could be found as it would hardly occur;[240] hypothetical transfer pricing methods relying on fictional contracts did not gain his approval, contrary to the modern practices endorsed by the OECD. In another difficult scenario where different parts of the enterprise were highly interdependent or their functions were heavily intertwined, taking the example of research and development functions, Carroll had presented his thoughts of economic allegiance/value creation at the whole of the firm level as decisive to assign the profits globally. In this case, formulary apportionment was obviously the preferred option, which partly fuels the three-tier approach adopted by the 1935 Convention and the Mexico/London Models.

In summary, the ALS was constructed originally to serve the priorly established system that keeps source taxation at an 'unavoidable' minimum level. The Carroll Report's conception of the arm's length standard nevertheless deviates essentially from the economic allegiance theory that dictates the analysis from the internal and whole-of-enterprise perspectives of the value creation of the firm. The Carroll Report had set up the dichotomy of arm's length versus formulary apportionment, which had been vigorously defended by the OECD. Only for limited cases had the Report conceived the merits of unitary business principles that uphold formulary apportionment for the allocation of profits of the firm, but Carroll himself was constrained by the dichotomy. These cases may have been rare a century ago, but they are normal in modern times. While advocating the ALS, the Carroll Report did not give contracts, either real or hypothetical, a superior status for the analysis of transfer pricing.

## 2.7 FORMULARY APPORTIONMENT IN THE TRADE PHASE

As indicated in the very beginning, the Trade Phase stretched roughly from post-WWII to the late 1990s. It was characterized as a period in which international commerce began to proliferate and reached its apex in the late 1990s when the capitalism versus anti-capitalism rivalry ended. Benshalom characterized the Trade Phase as a stage during which the liberalization of investment and trade triumphed over the traditional

238. *Ibid.*, 192.
239. Langbein and Fuss (n. 74) 300.
240. In the context of permanent establishment, Carroll, 'Carroll Report' (n. 162) 191.

revenue and equity considerations of international taxation.[241] The emblem of the Trade Phase raised by the author is the dramatic reduction of withholding tax, especially with respect to interest payments. The predicament of formulary apportionment in this period also corresponded with the tenet of this Phase: the impetus of promoting cross-border trade and business as an end in itself essentially marginalized the orthodox considerations of international taxation.

### 2.7.1 The Decentralization of International Tax Norm-Making and the Supremacy of the Arm's Length Standard

Tracing the developments related to formulary apportionment in this period is not as convenient as in the Revenue Phase, since the key feature of the norm-making of international taxation in the Trade Phase has been decentralized from the hand of the LON to the OEEC/OECD, influential countries, especially the United States, and less so to the United Nations.[242] However, the common thread of the developments provided by these contributors is the primacy of the ALS established and incarnated in this Phase. Continuing the momentum since the 1930s, formulary apportionment was no more than a subscript in the grand memoir of its counterpart as in the aforementioned dichotomy, the ALS.

To encapsulate, the course through which the supremacy of the ALS was set up during this Phase can be further divided into three stages. The first stage, since the LON's formal adoption of the ALS prior to 1968, confirmed, through the 1963 OECD Draft Model[243] and the judicial decisions and legislations in the United States,[244] the ALS as the primary or exclusive basis of income allocation and transfer pricing. Most notably, the 1963 OECD Draft Model already provided the same expression of the ALS as the modern Article 9(1), based on and slightly revised from the provision in the 1933 Draft Convention. The second stage spread from 1968 to the 1980s, when the ALS was standardized for the first time from a sweeping and result-based guiding rationale to a concrete approach relying on transactional pricing analysis and directing specific transfer pricing methods. The 1968 US regulations[245] were groundbreaking in this respect by laying down the three traditional transfer pricing methods, including the CUP method, the Residual Profit Method (RPM) and the Comparable Price Method (CPM), and other methods as the fallback. The OECD internationalized and developed the US approach starting from the 1979 Transfer Pricing Report. In the third stage, till the 1990s, when the transfer pricing regime significantly expanded in scale, both the

241. Benshalom, 'The Quest to Tax Interest Income in a Global Economy: Stages in the Development of International Income Taxation' (n. 12) 652.
242. The LON was dissolved in 1946, and in the same year, the United Nations established the Fiscal Commission, which was disbanded in 1954 as well.
243. OECD, 'Draft Double Taxation Convention on Income and Capital 1963' (1963) https://www.oecd-ilibrary.org/content/publication/9789264073241-en accessed 26 August 2025.
244. Richard and Andrus (n. 10) paras 2.07-2.12.
245. TD 6952, 33 Fed. Reg. 5848. For the process of drafting the regulations, *see* Jens Wittendorff, *Transfer Pricing and the Arm's Length Principle in International Tax Law* (Kluwer Law International BV 2010) 33-39.

United States and the OECD confronted head-on the emerging problems of the ALS, especially in relation to the no-comparables scenarios and intangibles. The 1995 TPG, on the one hand, concluded the OECD's efforts in the decade and marked the formation of the OECD's central role in transfer pricing; on the other, it still absorbed the US developments while creating a schism in the interplay of the two contributors.[246]

In the Trade Phase, the international tax developments did not revolve around the competition between arm's length and formulary apportionment, but, under the established supremacy of the former, the exact means to crystallize the ALS and how far it can be stretched to cope with difficult problems. The following sketches the dimming role of formulary apportionment accompanying the above trajectory of the ALS.

### 2.7.2 Formulary Apportionment in the United States Regulations

The post-WWII era had seen a profound change in the global political economy. Among others, the European colonial empires were dissolved, while the United States had evolved as the engine of world production, the haven for portfolio capital, and the great exporter of direct investment. What ensued in the global economy is that the previous type of multinational enterprises in the mercantilist economic model was gradually taken over by the US types of MNEs organized through forward horizontal integration and expanding widely dispersed subsidiaries. Against such background, the United States began to exert even more significant influence than it already did in the Revenue Phase in terms of shaping and leading the international tax norm-making. The formation of a modern transfer pricing regime, as briefed above, is a salient example. However, in the process, when the ALS gained its dominance, the formulary apportionment was not absent.

Formulary apportionment was contemplated in the US as a more effective way to prevent tax avoidance but was eventually rejected out of the pre-existing authority of the ALS[247] in the interests of private businesses. Under the general mandate of countering the shifting of profits of US MNEs and defending the US tax base, the House of Representatives put forward in 1962, in addition to the historic CFC regulations, a proposal replacing the ALS with formulary apportionment applying to the cross-border sales of goods.[248] The proposal was repudiated without serious consideration, not only because of the reluctance of lawmakers to break the path dependence but also because of the lobbying of the business community against formulary apportionment.[249]

#### *2.7.2.1 PSM Versus Formulary Apportionment*

Even though the ALS's authority had been established several decades ago in the United States and globally as well, it remained an abstract norm of tax law while

246. *See* the analysis in the Ch. 2.
247. Namely, the s. 45 that is later on renumbered as the s. 482 from 1954.
248. House of Representatives 10650, 87th Cong., 2nd Sess. s. 6 (1962).
249. Richard and Andrus (n. 10) para. 2.09.

lacking detailed instructions as to its crystallization. Focusing on the transfer of tangible property, the new section 482 regulations in 1968 ended this situation by providing a comparable transaction-based and price-centred (collectively, 'transac tional pricing') set of rules to determine the arm's length results. The fallback method in the four-tier hierarchy is an exception that does not rely on transactional pricing and comparables, and most frequently in practice, it directs the use of the profit split method.[250] The subsequent developments throughout the 1990s relieved the hierarchy of four methods and the dependence on exact comparables by adopting the 'best method rule';[251] the PSM was thus accorded in the 1994 final regulations a formal and equal status with the traditional methods, not only for tangible property but also intangibles.[252]

Due to its distinct attributes compared to other specified methods, for instance, being two or multiple-sided, the PSM is often correlated with formulary apportionment, and it is often alluded to as a 'backdoor'[253] of formulary apportionment to accommodate the opposition.[254] The BEPS Project has also raised the importance of the PSM.[255] However, it is held that the ostensible affinity between 'split' and 'apportionment' cannot genuinely link the two contrasting concepts. Apart from the technical discrepancies,[256] such as the reliance on a pre-determined allocation formula, the PSM has key defining differences from the formulary apportionment: it is an alternative still within the framework of the ALS based on the comparison between related and unrelated transactions; it is still an indirect transactional pricing method using 'reverse engineering' to determine the arm's length price; and it inherently follows the independent enterprise principle with no unitary group perspective. Divergent allocation outcomes could be attributed to the distinct nature of the two approaches.[257]

250. Summary Study of International Cases Involving s. 482 of the Internal Revenue Code (Washington D.C.: Treasury Department, 8 January 1973).
251. First introduced by the 1993 regulations, *see* 58 Fed. Reg. 5263 (1993).
252. Treas. Reg. 1-482-6 (1994).
253. Kathryn A. Bell, 'U.S. Committed to Traditional Position on Profit Splits' [2017] *Bloomberg BNA* https://www.bna.com/us-committed-traditional-n73014453014/ accessed 26 August 2025.
254. Greil Stefan, 'The Dealing at Arm's Length Fallacy: A Way Forward to a Formula-Based Transactional Profit Split?' (2017) 45 Intertax https://doi.org/10.54648/taxi2017053 accessed 26 August 2025. Li, 'Global Profit Split: An Evolutionary Approach to International Income Allocation' (n. 114) 823.
255. OECD, 'Revised Guidance on the Application of the Transactional Profit Split Method: Inclusive Framework on BEPS: Action 10' (OECD/G20 Base Erosion and Profit Shifting Project 2018) https://www.oecd.org/tax/beps/revised-guidance-on-the-application-of-the-transactional-profit-split-method-beps-action-10.pdf accessed 20 November 2023.
256. Such as referred to in the OECD Transfer Pricing Guidelines, 'Global formulary apportionment would use a formula that is predetermined for all taxpayers to allocate profits whereas transactional profit methods compare, on a case-by-case basis, the profits of one or more associated enterprises with the profit experience that comparable independent enterprises would have sought to achieve in comparable circumstances.', in OECD, *TPG 2017* (n. 182) para. 1.18.
257. As evinced in the numerical example by Heinz-Klaus Kroppen, Roman Dawid and Richard Schmidtke, 'Profit Split, the Future of Transfer Pricing? Arm's Length Principle and Formulary Apportionment Revisited from a Theoretical and a Practical Perspective' in Wolfgang Schön and Kai A Konrad (eds), *Fundamentals of International Transfer Pricing in Law and Economics* (Springer Berlin Heidelberg 2012) 274-6.

Regardless of these arguments, the PSM, as endorsed in the OECD TPG, was also questioned as not being a 'method' in the first place but merely a negotiation tool.[258]

#### 2.7.2.2 *The US–UK/US Federal–States Collision over Formulary Apportionment*

There were conflicts of views regarding the role or scope of formulary apportionment among the government of the United Kingdom, the US federal government, and the US States, principally the State of California. The three-party scrimmage corresponded with the keynote of the Trade Phase that trade concerns tended to dominate over tax considerations and had revealed the underlying cause of the OECD's persistent opposition to formulary apportionment, albeit not a latent secret by itself.

In the 1960s, before the enactment of section 482 regulations that first laid down the enforcement framework of the ALS, the IRS had already recognized that transfer pricing had the effect of allocating income both between companies and between countries, which posed questions on the international implications of domestic transfer pricing regulations. In 1978, the problem was exposed when the US Senate refused to ratify Article 9(4) of the double tax treaty between the UK and the US, renegotiated in 1975, that inhibited US states from taxing UK MNEs on the basis of global formulary apportionment.[259] The UK businesses opposed vigorously by launching the 'The Unitary Tax Campaign' to lobby against the US global formulary apportionment,[260] and the British Parliament also added political pressure with the 1985 Finance Act,[261] so did the US Treasury with a report proposing the water's edge election in 1984.[262] The system of California was thus in the spotlight. The state of California, as the representative of US states employing formulary apportionment for sub-national taxation, had been involved in the legal controversy since the 1960s over the legality of including income earned abroad in the unitary income to be apportioned for state taxation purposes.[263] Within the United States, the states' use of formulary apportionment had been addressed in the courts over the years, and the US Treasury had endeavoured to overturn the state practices of formulary apportionment but ultimately failed. The Supreme Court in 1983 ruled against a US company's claim that California's global formulary apportionment was unconstitutional.[264] However, since the late 1980s, California, under pressure from both the US and the rest of the world, began to

258. Robert Couzin, 'The End of Transfer Pricing' (2013) 61 Canadian Tax Journal 159, 167.
259. Richard and Andrus (n. 10) para. 2.44.
260. Sol Picciotto, *International Business Taxation: A Study in the Internationalization of Business Regulation* (Weidenfeld and Nicolson 1992) 242.
261. Wittendorff (n. 245) 102.
262. Department of the Treasury, United States, *The Final Report of the Worldwide Unitary Taxation Working Group: Chairman's Report and Supplemental Views* (Office of the Secretary, Department of the Treasury 1984).
263. Michael C Durst, 'Analysis of a Formulary System for Dividing Income, Part II: Examining Current Formulary and Arm's Length Approaches' (2013) 22 Bloomsberg BNA Tax Management Transfer Pricing Report 270, 278.
264. *Container Corp. of America v. Franchise Tax Board*, 103 S. Ct. 2933 (1983).

introduce the possibility of 'water's edge' limitation,[265] exempting the income earned outside of the US from the application of the state formulary apportionment system. The issue culminated in becoming an international legal matter when the British bank challenged the constitutionality of global formulary apportionment by suing the California Franchise Tax Board, yet one more time, the global reach of the California formulary system was upheld by the Supreme Court in 1994.[266] The collision was eventually resolved when California and other states all provided the water's edge election of their formulary apportionment system under great political pressure from the federal government.

The sketch above is intended to capture the tripartite complexion among two national and one sub-national tax jurisdictions centred on the acceptable scope of formulary apportionment, which reflected the process of how US formulary apportionment retreated to being sub-national, cutting off its international reach. There are three observations from the process and the outcome of the experience.

First, the historical track itself is neither informative nor even pertinent to the relative merits between the ALS and formulary apportionment. This is a counterproductive situation, but it apparently echoed the motif of the Trade Phase of international taxation. It is evident that the direct decision-makers, the UK and US federal governments, and the stakeholder business communities, had common interests of removing the tax 'obstacles' to facilitate the cross-border trade and investment between the two partners, ignoring whether the 'obstacles' arose from inconsistent perceptions of a 'better' approach to tax MNEs or the potential implications from smoothing out these 'obstacles'. The decisive factors were not truly about tax as a separate issue itself but were embroiled in the power struggle of politics and private businesses. The MNEs are the victors, and the governments may be the victors in the trade respect, while the only thing to lose is the traditional considerations of international taxation, such as inter-nation equity and robustness against tax avoidance. Therefore, the retreat of US states' formulary apportionment has validated the thesis of the Trade Phase, in addition to Benshalom's original observation with regard to the taxation of interest.

Second, behind the scenes of the political struggle and the dominant trade concerns, the predicament of the states had revealed a fact that their supporters may not wish to acknowledge: the historical opportunity of implementing formulary apportionment with a global reach to tax MNEs was missed when the ALS supremacy and the foundations of international taxation were well-established. The taxation of MNEs, even if narrowed down to the transfer pricing between affiliated companies, is not a standalone field of international taxation. The US states' attempts to include the income earned outside of the United States in their formula had unavoidably collided with the 'traditional' perceptions of the territorial scope of the jurisdictions to tax and the constructed tax institutions such as the separate enterprise principle, permanent establishment threshold of source taxation and single tax principle. It is also strongly reminiscent of the latent objective of the ALS to restrict source taxation to only the

265. Stefan Mayer, *Formulary Apportionment for the Internal Market* (IBFD Publications 2009) s. 3.2.4.3.
266. *Barclays Bank PLC v. Franchise Tax Board of California*, 512 U.S. 298 (1994).

income obviously within the jurisdiction of the state; the global formulary apportionment in contrast reaches out across the border to tax a portion as calculated by the formula of every dollar of the MNE group.[267]

Third, back to reality, the stumbling of US states' formulary apportionment under those specific conditions can still foreshadow the prerequisites or paths, many of which are ranged over in the above sections, to consider, should the formulary apportionment play a larger role for international taxation of MNEs in the post-BEPS era. What comes first should be to clarify and recalibrate the reiterated unqualified authority of the standard rather than a principle of arm's length that gained such misposition with political opportunism. In addition, restructuring the taxation of MNEs using formulary apportionment may entail cognizing the myth of the independent enterprise principle and single tax principle, as well as adjusting the permanent establishment threshold. Besides this substantive content, it also reveals the pivotal role of tax treaties, either bilateral or multilateral, as the ideal instrument to implement international formulary apportionment, providing effective dispute resolution and legal and accounting coordination. Otherwise, the unilateral application will unavoidably encounter the same plight as the state of California did.

### 2.7.3 The Article 7(4) and the 'Seeds' of Formulary Apportionment

As described in the beginning, the developments in the US regarding transfer pricing had significant influences on the path of the OECD, especially in relation to the ALS that gained its dominant and exclusive status in this period. In contrast with the unilateral perspective of the US, the OECD had taken the torch from the LON to forge the multilateral consensus on the standard of allocation.

Before the OECD turned to focus on the transfer pricing issue, formulary apportionment was addressed in the discussions of drafting the OECD's bilateral tax treaty model. Formulary apportionment was reluctantly endorsed in the context of permanent establishment for transitional uses before the ALS' dominance was solidified. In comparison, formulary apportionment was utterly rejected on the grounds that it was not that tenable when preparing for the OECD TPG designed for associated enterprises, and such a position has been fully maintained ever since.

The OECD did not build from scratch the 1963 Draft Model or the subsequent model tax conventions; it just took over the torch from the LON. The 1963 Draft Model retained the essential elements of the developments regarding the taxation of multinational enterprises under the auspices of the LON, especially those achieved by the 1933 Draft Convention and adopted in the Mexico/London Models.[268] However, it deviated significantly from the LON's track with respect to formulary apportionment.

267. McIntyre, 'Contrasting Methodologies: A Systematic Presentation of the Differences between an Arm's-Length/Source-Rule System and a Combined-Reporting/Formulary-Apportionment System' (n. 70) 231.
268. Richard and Andrus (n. 10) para. 2.18.

The 1933 Draft Convention, as discussed earlier, had designed a three-tiered approach, reproduced in the Mexico/London Models, providing formulary apportionment as a fallback but normatively authorized approach to taxing the permanent establishments. Article 7 on business profits of the 1963 Draft adopted the permanent establishment threshold and the ALS in this context but abandoned the three-tiered approach of the LON while only allowing the use of apportionment methods to the extent of being customary.[269] Formulary apportionment method was thus viewed as an ad hoc exception rather than an authorized method. It is a transitional compromise to accommodate the practices in existence to prepare the exclusivity of the ALS, which explains why the Draft acknowledged in the Commentary of Article 7(4) that the method could render different results as under separate accounting,[270] unbundled from the arm's length result equal standard as following the three-tier approach.[271]

Such provision of Article 7(4) was formally adopted in the 1977 OECD Model and had remained unchanged until it was deleted by the 2010 Update.[272] As reported by Avi-Yonah and Tinhaga in 2014,[273] the provision has actually been included in a vast amount of bilateral tax treaties, especially between developing countries,[274] and is currently contained in the UN Model.[275] On this basis, the authors dismissed the claim that the authority of formulary apportionment had been undermined by the 2010 Update. More importantly, the wide existence of this provision is a rebuttal of the alleged customary law status of the ALS or separate accounting. It is thus contended that Article 7(4), in combination with interpreting subsidiaries into dependent agents under Article 5(5), has preserved the seeds of applying unitary formulary apportionment to taxing modern multinational enterprises.

### 2.7.4 Formulary Apportionment in the 1979 Report and Transfer Pricing Guidelines

The 1979 Report represents the OECD's first specialized contribution to the issue of transfer pricing, which laid down the essential elements of the following OECD Transfer Pricing Guidelines. The Report was a close replication of the US 1968

269. '4. Insofar as it has been customary in a Contracting State to determine the profits to be attributed to a permanent establishment on the basis of an apportionment of the total profits of the enterprise to its various parts, nothing in paragraph 2 shall preclude that Contracting State from determining the profits to be taxed by such an apportionment as may be customary; the method of apportionment adopted shall, however, be such that the result shall be in accordance with the principles laid down in this Article.', OECD, 'Draft Double Taxation Convention on Income and Capital 1963' (n. 243) Art. 7(4).
270. *Ibid.*, 86.
271. League of Nations, 'Draft Convention for the Allocation of Business Income between States for the Purposes of Taxation' (n. 204) Art. 3.
272. OECD, 'Model Tax Convention on Income and on Capital 2010 (Full Version)' (OECD Publishing 2012) M–23 https://doi.org/10.1787/9789264175181-en accessed 26 August 2025.
273. Reuven S Avi-Yonah and Zachée Pouga Tinhaga, 'Unitary Taxation and International Tax Rules' [2014] ICTD Working Paper.
274. Appendix – Current tax treaties with Art. 7-4 language, *Ibid.*, 12-26.
275. United Nations, 'Model Double Taxation Convention Between Developed and Developing Countries 2017 Update' (United Nations 2017) Art. 7(4).

Regulations; it shared the latter's exclusive preference for the ALS, but it intended to promote such an approach to build multilateral consensus. In addition, the Report was drafted against the background of the aforementioned US–UK/US Federal – States collision over formulary apportionment, which prompted the OECD to double down on the ALS.

Consequently, formulary apportionment has been vigorously and constantly opposed by the OECD since the 1979 Report.[276] The OECD's 1995 as the first version of the Transfer Pricing Guidelines fixed its opposing discourses on formulary apportionment,[277] and all of them were alluded to in the previous developments. The objections in relation to administrative aspects such as transitional cost, exchange rate movement, valuation, compliance cost or access to information were far-fetched, for administering the current system can by no means ignore these challenges; while the substantive aspects, including the concerns of double taxation and the potential profit 'mis-allocation' were the corollaries viewed with the lens of the ALS, yet cannot represent the genuine fundamental flaws of the formulary apportionment.[278]

### 2.7.5 Trade Phase and the No-Where Residual Profits

Facilitating the cross-border movement of capital and investment has always been the key consideration in the design of the international tax system, but in no sense are they exclusive or dominant relative to the revenue or distributive considerations. The difficult task of policymakers is to struggle for a balance to meet the needs of social developments in different historical periods. Under some circumstances, the equilibrium reached to further objectives at one end of the scale was at the patent cost of the objectives at the other end. The Trade Phase of international taxation features the marginalization of the conventional revenue and equity considerations of international taxation by the liberalization of trade and investment at the national and international level. Taking into account the fact that the institutional framework of the international trade regime comprising the GATT and the World Trade Organization (WTO) was also established during the same period, the Trade Phase can be said to be a result of the world trade regime encroaching upon the international tax field.

The dramatic reduction of withholding tax on interest income from inbound capital investment had been identified by Benshalom as a salient emblem of the Trade Phase. The periodization of international taxation and a particular component investigated are mutually corroborating. The evolution of allocation norms with respect to the taxation of MNEs is the additional validation of the thesis of the Trade Phase. On the other way round, the thesis of the Trade Phase as the periodization of international

276. OECD, 'Transfer Pricing and Multinational Enterprises: Three Taxation Issues' (OECD Publishing 1984) para. 14.
277. OECD, 'Transfer Pricing Guidelines for Multinational Enterprises and Tax Administrations 1995' (OECD 1995) paras 3.58-3.74 https://doi.org/10.1787/g2g7fa2a-en accessed 26 August 2025.
278. Reuven S Avi-Yonah, 'Between Formulary Apportionment and the OECD Guidelines: A Proposal for Reconciliation' [2009] SSRN Electronic Journal https://doi.org/10.2139/ssrn.1411649 and https://www.ssrn.com/abstract=1411649 accessed 18 November 2023.

taxation has provided a guiding light on analysing the seemingly standalone developments revolving around the surge of the ALS and the annihilation of formulary apportionment in the larger and diachronic context. To be specific, the changing tax treatment of the residual profit of MNEs following the 'wax' of the ALS and the 'wane' of the FA is thus identified as the embodiment of the Trade Phase, the finding of which is not only of value by itself but also reveals the far-reaching implications of the 'wax and wane'.

The Revenue Phase, also the formative period of international taxation, began from the 1923 Academic Report, which put forward the economic allegiance theory as the theoretical basis of constructing the international tax system. The economic allegiance theory was a grand design not particularly for the taxation of the modern MNEs, but it bears a natural but logical affinity with formulary apportionment. The contributions and developments that closely ensued did not strictly follow the economic allegiance or any other overarching theories, but formulary apportionment had been given ample leeway and normative status to operate, such as in the 1928 Draft Convention. The Carroll Report that laid down the foundations of taxing multinational enterprises sanctioned the ALS under the hard dichotomy between the ALS and the FA, and not without problems, the approach had been implemented in the 1933 Draft Convention and the 1940s Mexico/London Models. As to the treatment of residual profits, Carroll mainly contended that residual profits should be allocated to the controlling parent entity as the centre of management being the 'most vital' part of enterprises,[279] while the 1933 Draft Convention and the 1940s Mexico/London Models adopting the common three-tier approach that retained the use of formulary methods had assured that the residual profits would be assigned throughout the integrated MNE group. If not considered at the level of inter-national equity, both treatments are in general congruence with the logic of economic allegiance theory in the sense of taxing according to economic contribution.[280]

Entering the Trade Phase, when the US regulations and their internationalization pioneered by the OECD-championed ALS as the end in itself rather than a subsidiary part of a larger approach, the allocation of residual profits was substantially altered, and it deviated from the economic allegiance theory. According to the four-tier hierarchy of the transfer pricing methods laid down by the US regulations, the one-sided methods of the RPM or CPM will apply where no comparable uncontrolled prices can be found, which is often the case. These methods, rested on the economic conceptions of substitution, will only assign a marginal profit that induces the entity examined to enter the transaction; the residual profit will thus be allocated to the other party to the transaction. If applied to all members of the MNE group, the entire profit of the group was not definitively assigned. Thus, significant agnosticism exists with regard to where and to whom the group residuals were allocated. In the case of intangible property, both the 'developer-assister' approach that assigns the profits to the 'developer' (as 'designated' in discretion by the group) and the 'cost-sharing' approach that permits the group to divide the cost and risks of developing intangibles

279. Carroll, 'Carroll Report' (n. 162) 192.
280. Langbein and Fuss (n. 74) 339-341.

by agreements have given ample authority to the taxpayer in determining how the residuals were to be allocated. The OECD further developed the case by sanctifying the contractual allocation agreed among affiliated companies as the foundation of the transfer pricing system. It follows that the allocation of residual profits is at the discretion of the taxpayer, which essentially enables the taxpayer to avoid taxation on the residuals if the 'central' party was located in a tax haven.

Langbein and Fuss summarized the changing tax treatment of residual profits following the developments in the Revenue Phase and Trade Phase as undergoing three stages: the crude but defensible allocation, the indeterminate allocation, and the allocation at the discretion of taxpayers (effective tax exempt).[281] The latter two stages were both affected in the Trade Phase, and reflected a power shift from tax authority to private businesses, which was driven by the trade concerns that dominated the revenue or equity considerations and achieved in the course of the ALS marginalizing the formulary apportionment. Just as the dramatic reduction of withholding taxation on interest income, such a power shift also had a significant impact on the integrity of the corporate tax base.

## 2.8 FORMULARY APPORTIONMENT DOWNPLAYED IN THE ANTI-AVOIDANCE PHASE

The Anti-avoidance Phase depicts a period of developments of international taxation revolving around and driven by the dominant concern of countering the tax avoidance practices of MNEs. It started in the late 1990s when globalization entered a new stage characterized by the unprecedented rise of MNEs and culminated in the launch of the BEPS Project in 2012. As introduced above, the tacit tension at the multilateral level over the allocation norm of taxing MNEs was settled by the OECD in the Transfer Pricing Guidelines. In the ensuing years, the OECD firmly sustained the repudiation of formulary apportionment, though not free from critics of the ALS.

However, it does not mean that the Anti-avoidance Phase is not relevant to formulary apportionment. On the contrary, the Phase represents a turning point in the validity of the foundations of the international tax system established in the Revenue Phase and Trade Phase, which undergirds the formulary apportionment as an alternative to reforming the system in the emerging Allocation Phase. The only real impact of the 'factual' absence of formulary apportionment for this chapter is that the discussions of the Anti-avoidance Phase will not elaborate on the key developments directly shaping the trajectory of the FA as in the former Phases but turn to shed some light on the fundamental flaws of the anti-avoidance pattern.

### 2.8.1 The Taxation of MNEs as It Is, the Centrality of Transfer Pricing

Since the formative period of the international tax system, corporations were not dealt with as a separate subject of taxation but only as a special source from which

281. Langbein and Fuss (n. 74).

individuals derive their incomes. This was reflected in the early discussions and has been carved into tax treaties. Consequently, when discussing the taxation of MNEs, what was discussed was the adaptation of a system originally modelled for the taxation of individuals. That is to say, the taxation of MNEs has been fitted into a framework for taxing the income earned by individuals from various sources, comprising the foundational concepts such as residence and source and the mechanism of international double taxation relief. However, either in terms of the total volume of income involved or the idiosyncrasies of the applicable rules, the taxation of MNEs has increasingly become a self-governed regime. In that regime, the rules of transfer pricing have stood out as the decisive elements of determining the tax liabilities of MNEs, outweighing the importance of other basic rules.[282]

To explain the centrality of transfer pricing in the totality of taxing the MNEs, what comes first is the separation and dominant importance of corporate taxation from/over the taxation of members of the firm, namely, the shareholders. The position of the originators has been right in the first place that corporations are just legal fictions being a means of earning income used by individuals, and ultimately, it is the tax burden on individuals that matters. Nevertheless, few countries only tax individual shareholders of corporations on a look-through basis as in the case of partnerships. The reasons are threefold. First, income is generally taxed only when it is realized, and corporations have a legal personality; thus, as a theoretical matter, a complete look-through taxation at the level of shareholders is not supported. And second, linked to the first point, taxation at the corporate level is necessary to prevent indefinite deferral, the de facto exemption of income tax by retaining the income in the corporation. Last, and practically, tracking and taxing the ultimate individual shareholders are extremely burdensome and difficult to administer, especially for widely held and publicly listed MNEs. Taxation at both the corporate level and shareholder level is thus the international convention, which further raises the question of whether taxation on corporations or the shareholders plays a more significant role in international business taxation. The answer depends on many factors such as the considerations of administration and tax avoidance, the integration of corporate and shareholder taxation, the methods of international economic double taxation relief, the relative tax rate on inbound FDIs to individuals at home, and at the theoretical level, the indications of the theory of the firm.[283] All of them lead to the conclusion that most of the total taxes are taxed at the corporate level, while the taxes collected from shareholders are much smaller. The above has illuminated that the analysis of the taxation of MNEs should be focused on the corporation as a separate subject of taxation from its individual shareholders, which is the basis of unveiling the centrality of transfer pricing rules.

282. 'The arm's length principle governs the tax treatment of about 70% of cross-border trade in the world.', Hamaekers Hubert, 'Arm's Length: How Long?' (2001) 8 International Transfer Pricing Journal 30, 39; *see also* United Nations, 'Practical Manual on Transfer Pricing for Developing Countries (2017)' (United Nations 2017) para. 2.4.2.2.

283. For a comprehensive analysis following these lines, *see* Richard J Vann, 'Taxing International Business Income: Hard-Boiled Wonderland and the End of the World' [2010] World Tax Journal 291, 294-313 https://doi.org/10.59403/20k9xd3 accessed 26 August 2025.

The typical scenario of taxing an MNE involves a parent company and a foreign subsidiary or a PE. As is noted, the international taxation of corporations fits into the established framework of individual taxation; then there comes the question of the role of residence and source and the double taxation relief in determining the tax liabilities of the MNE, and where it is yet to be validated the decisive role of transfer pricing in the interaction with these foundations. First of all, transfer pricing relies on the residence rules of corporations and the close relative PE rules as a starting point to function. Assigning resident status to a company is obviously a personification of the legal fiction and an assimilation of the rule for individuals. Extending the logic of assimilation, it seems that the countries hosting the MNE either the parent or subsidiary/PE should be enforcing their quintessential taxing rights on the residents, but this is not the case. For the consideration of international taxation of an MNE as its separation from shareholders, the residence rule of corporations contrasts with the rule of individuals, at least in terms of theoretical justifications and policy connotations. The residence rule of MNEs serves essentially as a basic sourcing instrument, the rules of which are to reflect the economic connection to the jurisdiction. It accounts for, to some extent, the rare existence of using the residence of majority shareholders to determine the residence of companies, and even more, the rare case of taxing the worldwide income of resident headquarters. The territorial ('source') taxation on resident MNE is carried out through mechanisms such as exemption (as the worldwide trend), credit or deferral,[284] and can be justified on different grounds, but it is clear that the residence country of an MNE is principally collecting a source tax on the income deriving from local operations, just as in the 'true' source countries that host the PE or subsidiary.[285] Consequently, the corporate residence rules of both the parent and subsidiary and the PE rules are the basic sourcing tools to allocate incomes between the countries enforcing their nominal residence taxing rights. The transfer pricing rules, on top of the residence and source rules, are dedicated to determining the amount of income to be allocated to each country for their 'residence' taxation. The overall effect of the operation of these rules, including the double taxation relief methods, is that the majority of corporate tax is collected by the countries to which the transfer pricing rules have allocated the 'international income'. The nominal residence countries can collect, at best, little tax on the income thereby assigned elsewhere.[286]

### 2.8.2 Two Problematic Premises: The Malfunctioning Anti-avoidance Pattern

This section is not a comprehensive analysis of the tax planning strategies of MNEs that had proliferated during the Anti-avoidance Phase, but it intends to throw light on the unsustainability and ineffectiveness of the anti-avoidance pattern that has long been adhered to. It is argued that the interaction between MNEs' tax planning and the countering measures of tax authorities has been caught in a stopgap model that has led

284. Arnold (n. 233) 19-28.
285. Vann (n. 283) 310.
286. *Ibid.*, 313.

to indefinite ends. The BEPS Project represents that the model has reached its apex, but as evidenced in the previous chapters, it does not fundamentally alter the model, nor can it be expected to put an end to it. The BEPS Actions have generally intensified the methodologies that had been followed in the Anti-avoidance Phase, among which this section analyses two premises underlying the developments of the international fight against the tax avoidance of MNEs. First, at the macro level, the policy developments towards countering the tax avoidance practices of MNEs were structured upon a presumed unity of opposites of the residence and source. Second, from a micro perspective, the proliferation of anti-avoidance schemes as represented by the BEPS Project's engineering on recalibrating the ALS has strictly followed the premise that the taxpayers' abusive practices can be readily singled out and separately addressed, following which the MNE's transfer pricing manipulation can be successfully tackled without addressing the underlying sourcing conventions. Both of the premises will be elaborated below, and as it turns out, they are either misconceptions or ungrounded.

### *2.8.2.1 The Misconception of the 'Unity of Opposites' of the Residence and Source*

The so-called unity of opposites between the residence and source is coined to capture some basic misconceptions stemming from the residence-source paradigm of international taxation that have been embedded in the premise of the anti-avoidance methodologies in this Phase.

In taxation scenarios involving any categories of income, there will always be a country in which the taxpayer is a resident and a country where the income is sourced. As the discussions of the Revenue Phase have indicated,[287] the contributors in the formative period carried out the belief in constructing the residence-source paradigm that the residence and source are of perfect unity of opposite, which means that the taxation of the two sides are mutually complementary. Since the system has always been pro-residence, a long-held misbelief is that the portion gained through lowering the source tax will definitely fall in the net of the residence country, which is also (mis-)presumed to be proactive in catching the portion. However, it turned out that the MNEs have been successful in achieving an overall low or nil taxation, either escaping the residence and source taxation, or, correlatively, the residence country being unwilling to enforce its taxing right. The causes are multilayered, but such outcome of homeless income has been targeted continuously through stacked countering tax avoidance measures, at the domestic or treaty level, including enhancing transparency and information sharing, yet few, as exemplified by the United States earning stripping regime,[288] had rectified the misconception about the unity of opposite between the residence and source. The BEPS Project reached the closest point to making the breakthrough with a multilateral mandate of the G20, but the chance was missed in the end.

287. *See* Ch. 2.
288. Benshalom, 'The Quest to Tax Interest Income in a Global Economy: Stages in the Development of International Income Taxation' (n. 12) 686-697.

#### 2.8.2.2 *The Stopgap Game That Never Stops*

Second, turning to the micro and the practical area, transfer pricing is undoubtedly in the spotlight. Besides the normative reasons clarified in the above section, the actual role of transfer pricing planning in MNEs' strategies to minimize or escape tax liabilities can further confirm the centrality of transfer pricing in the international taxation of MNEs. The BEPS Action Plan summarized the challenges in the arena of transfer pricing and align them with the three Action items 8-10:[289] the profit shifting and allocation of income associated with the transfer of intangibles, the inappropriate accrual of income to a lowly taxed member through the transfer of risk and capital, and the treatment of affiliated transactions with no third-party comparables. The detailed evaluation of the reforms laid down in the BEPS Project has been conducted in the earlier chapters. Here, the transfer pricing regime with the ALS in focus is discussed against another premise of the Anti-avoidance Phase, that is, the tax avoidance practices of MNES can be singled out and addressed from the normal business practices. The premise naturally undergirds the BEPS Project's pragmaticism and conservatism and has actuated the large stopgap game ongoing during the Anti-avoidance Phase, in which new patching measures continually popped out in reaction to the problems. If the stopgaps had functioned effectively for their designed purposes, there would not be the high momentum for the BEPS Project. Reflected in the realm of transfer pricing, the premise has been stuck to where the BEPS Project further stretched the ALS to cope with the transfer pricing manipulations, insisting that the best course is to deal with the specific flaws by strengthening the standard's capabilities to separate the normal from the abusive practices. The efforts will be doomed to fail due to the inherent ineligibility and incompetence of the ALS to actualize the premise, which is rooted in the unsolved question of the fair allocation of the international incomes of MNEs, or in the words of Benshalom, the undetermined sourcing convention and the fair return to source contributions to the income.[290]

It should not raise questions as to whether the ALS has been 'recalibrated' to counter tax avoidance following the BEPS Project because it is the objective of the designers when contemplating the taxation of domestic cross-jurisdictional enterprises from the very beginning.[291] Yet, as introduced in the previous sections, the ALS' triumph over formulary apportionment was effected in the great debate about the appropriate norm for the allocation question and to the larger ends of preventing double taxation by multiple jurisdictions. The ensuing global economic landscape has long contrasted with the circumstances where the LON Committees and experts contemplated the allocation and double taxation concerns of cross-border business taxation. This may not mean that the ground of the earlier preference for the ALS was not solid anymore (if it ever was), but to indicate a fact that the priority of the

289. OECD, *BEPS Report* (n. 74) 19-21.
290. Benshalom, 'The Quest to Tax Interest Income in a Global Economy: Stages in the Development of International Income Taxation' (n. 12) 697.
291. For example, the US tax rules of associated companies in the 1930s, as discussed in Graetz and O'Hear (n. 56) 1060-1061.

anti-avoidance element in the original considerations was not 'high' in the first place. In this sense, the BEPS Project's anti-avoidance centric reform of the ALS is indeed a 'recalibration'.

However, such recalibration fell into the trap of the underlying premise of the anti-avoidance Phase again that the ALS is an effective means to dissect the affiliated businesses for profit manipulation from the alleged normal businesses utilizing the third-party unrelated outcome as benchmarks. The reasons are multifaceted, based on the problems in the ALS per se and its interpretation and applications, many of which have been reiterated by the critics of the ALS.[292] As illustrated in the example of debt financing, Benshalom had identified that the concept of the related debt under the control of the MNE group is fictional for its own sake, and so is the inquiry instructed by the ALS using the often artificially constructed comparables. The author went further than this. In fact, Benshalom dissented fundamentally from most of the critics or supporters of the ALS with respect to its validity as the very foundational allocation norm, which was reflected in his stance on the CUP method. The CUP method is fully committed to the rationale of the ALS, and even the most opposing critics of the standard generally do not question the validity of the method. This suggests that they do approve the ALS in limited conditions, such as for commodity transactions, including its validity or legitimacy in defining the accepted terms of the affiliated transactions and hence in rendering the outcomes of income allocation, which Benshalom had disagreed with.[293] It was simply contended by him that the third-party unrelated data, even if readily available, is not an adequate benchmark to assess the affiliated transactions, because an integrated enterprise acts essentially differently from those independent ones, which is true for financing options and many other decisions beyond. It is a view that questions comprehensively the validity of the ALS rather than only its application or practical difficulties, as regards using the standard to identify and 'correct' the abusive related businesses. This further suggests that the BEPS efforts of recalibration can hardly succeed in effectively countering transfer mispricing, but more than that, the general pattern of anti-avoidance relying on singling out abusive behaviours without addressing the validity of the underlying sourcing conventions undergirding the transfer pricing regime is problematic. The analyses in the earlier chapters of the prospective outcomes of the BEPS engineering on the ALS support the above conclusion as well, which have jointly announced the lack of validity of the anti-avoidance premise in question.

### 2.8.3 Closing Remarks: A System Craving for a New Age

Anti-avoidance is a grand narration of international taxation in both tax treaties and national tax systems, to which the major part of the expansion, growing complexity, and encumbrance of the international tax system in recent decades is attributed. The

292. For example, as summarized in Richard and Andrus (n. 10) Ch. 4.
293. Benshalom, 'The Quest to Tax Interest Income in a Global Economy: Stages in the Development of International Income Taxation' (n. 12) 697.

above discussion cannot be counted as a comprehensive analysis of the issue, but it bypasses the concrete problems that have already been analysed in extensive literature and instead unscrambles two broken premises underlying the anti-avoidance pattern adopted by policymakers. The two premises in question are not a random combination of rationales behind the universal anti-avoidance schemes. What the discussions have revealed cooperate and supplement with each other, and lead to the same end.

The first premise concerns a large state-business-state picture, a triangular power struggle among the residence state, the source state, and the MNE, which turns out to be built on sand. In the Revenue Phase of international taxation, what the contributors harboured is a leakproof tax net woven by their construction of residence and source taxation as integrated by the paramount mandate of eliminating double taxation and the single tax principle. And the general inclination of taxing right allocation was to favour residence taxation over the taxation at source. The residence state, usually the capital-exporting countries, could have continued to be the primary beneficiary of the international tax system should it function as originally designed. The developments of both the economic base and the institutional superstructure profoundly altered the conceived image. The Trade Phase unveiled an era of trade concerns of liberating trade and facilitating investment dominating the conventional international tax concerns, featured by the colossal reduction of withholding tax and the shift of discretion of residuals assignment to MNEs. The pioneering contributors should not be blamed for their probable lack of vision of the dramatic change of economic infrastructure upon which the international tax system operates; it is due to the obtuseness to overhaul the fundamentals in line with the latest circumstances to impute. Among others, the MNEs have become the dominant actors is emblematic of the global economy ever since the latter part of the Trade Phase, and the trend continued and culminated through the Anti-Avoidance Phase.

In the new normal that sees a high integrated corporate group, unprecedented capital mobility, paramount importance of intangibles, and a large amount of group residual returns, the century-old framework has malfunctioned to the extent that the income is attributed to neither the source state, initially accorded the taxing right of the first bite, nor the residence state initially assigned to the residual taxing right, while the MNEs always win. International taxation entails a reform proposal that can really integrate the tax claims on the MNEs by the residence and the source in a judicious way, a comprehensive means beyond solving the double taxation problem by achieving the single tax result. This would certainly raise a higher standard at all margins, rendering the international business tax system upgraded to 2.0.

The second premise complements the first premise's grand narration of the residence and source and focuses on the transfer pricing regime as the superstratum above the foundational architecture. It is already argued that transfer pricing is central to the overall system of allocating the income of MNEs among taxing authorities; however, transfer pricing planning has played a pivotal role in the tax avoidance strategies of MNEs. As a regime dedicatedly maintained by the OECD as the quasi-international tax organization, transfer pricing is the emblem of whether the international tax system could function as originally contemplated, fair, efficient, and upholding the national states, and in particular, whether the existing loopholes could be closed, continuing the stopgap game upon the second premise in question.

The discussions of the second premise have revealed that the problem-reaction model relying on sorting out the abusive business activities from those with normal terms is problematic, and so is its application to the realm of transfer pricing constructed by the ALS. More importantly, the discussions leveraging Benshalom's case study of the US earning stripping regime enlighten that the transfer pricing problems stemming from the ALS cannot be successfully addressed without reconsidering the validity of the undergirding sourcing conventions. The ALS has long been endorsed as having provided an objective benchmark for sourcing the incomes to the states where the group members are located. The allocation and revenue effect and its robustness for tax abuse would not be significant concerns if the economic landscape were not as it currently is, where giant MNEs dominate and the intangibles become the paramount production factors, let alone the sweeping digitalization. In this course, trade concerns have outweighed the traditional tax considerations, and the ostensible objective benchmark of arm's length has become the convenient instrument which the MNEs utilize to minimize their tax liabilities at marginal costs. The ALS' validity as the most important sourcing norm has been substantially undermined. The motley collection of anti-avoidance measures following the broken premise in question but with no consistent and sound guiding principles can hardly succeed, nor can the stretches of the ALS towards various directions by the BEPS Project.

The analyses of the two premises thus shed light on the judicious response to the intractable problems of tax avoidance. The first of the inspirations is that a tax avoidance problem is not solely the problem of tax avoidance, or, against the periodization of international taxation, it is not the problem exclusive to the Anti-Avoidance Phase either. The problem needs to be addressed with a global perspective. For one thing, the extensive tax avoidance practices of MNEs only expose the loopholes and defects of the larger international tax system, which cannot be effectively addressed and insulated from the issues at the root. For another, in temporal dimensions, the tax avoidance problem has its clues largely in the developments of the Revenue Phase and is exacerbated through the Trade Phase. It follows that, as the second inspiration, transfer pricing as the central issue should be reflected in the holistic perception of taxing MNEs, rather than through weaponizing the ALS in the ceaseless fight against tax avoidance. In summary, the international tax system craves an alternative design of sourcing convention that, in the microcosmic view, differentiates the allocation of real MNE profits from abusive tax avoidance prevention,[294] but is robust against transfer pricing planning and other tax avoidance strategies employed by MNEs, and in the macroscopic view, can reform the manner which the residence taxation and source taxation have interacted with and been integrated with each other. This is the subject to be discussed in relation to the emerging Allocation Phase.

294. Couzin (n. 258) 164.

## 2.9 THE EMERGING ALLOCATION PHASE AND FORMULARY APPORTIONMENT

The Allocation Phase is coined to capture the latent but profound changes evolving since the BEPS Project with respect to the bedrock of the allocation conventions of taxing the MNEs. As has been argued elsewhere in this research, the BEPS Project, in the sense of both the asserted objectives and outcomes, did not aim to alter the foundations of the international tax system, yet objectively, it had indeed introduced new thoughts and variations to the century-old system which may have contributed to the incremental shift of the existing patterns and paradigms. The ensuing developments at the multilateral level under the auspices of the OECD/G20 and individual country level have also corroborated the rising tide in which the old institutions and the new are intersecting with one another.

One of the major objectives of this chapter is to retrieve the role of formulary apportionment in the evolution of international tax system. The Allocation Phase represents the last episode in the four-stage periodization of the evolution of the international tax system over a hundred years, and it may also mark a fresh beginning of the international tax system in the next century. Among others, this part serves to explicate the core precursors that are profound but may also be obscure, of the upcoming Phase, embedded in the BEPS and post-BEPS developments.

They are the direct evidence that the shift is real, and they are indicative of the future directions the system will be heading towards. More importantly, within the scope of this chapter, the role of formulary apportionment in the emerging allocation phase is to be revealed. Formulary apportionment has undergone a continuous de-escalation since the LON repudiated it as an alternative to relieve double taxation, and the ensuing Phases witnessed its further retreat from the realm of assigning the income of MNEs. The deliverables of the BEPS Project have signified that the previous anti-avoidance pattern has been caught in an impasse, which reflects a deeper crisis of the established sourcing conventions and other international tax architectures. The emerging Allocation Phase is identified by this chapter as a period when formulary apportionment may re-emerge as an alternative with advantages of both theoretical coherence and more robustness against tax avoidance.

### 2.9.1 The Arm's Length Wedge Between a 'Principle' and a 'Standard'

Using Arm's length result as the benchmark of taxing cross-border enterprises is almost as perennial as the international tax system as a whole. It was explored and ultimately established as a norm, more accurately, a principle of tax treaties. The United States introduced a hierarchical array of transfer pricing methods since the 1960s, which was reproduced by the OECD in the Transfer Pricing Guidelines. The problem is that the formulation of arm's length as a principle and its commentary has remained static in the OECD MTC, while the principle's crystallization has been under unremitting and, particularly, unchecked redressal. It thus has been contended that there are actually two benchmarks of arm's length: one is the principle laid down in the tax treaties, and another is the standard incarnated by voluminous illustrations and methods.[295] Formulary apportionment has struggled to survive in the wedge between the ALP and ALS.

In the earlier sections, it was pointed out that the interpretation of ALP faithful to the history did not allow the leeway for the application of formulary apportionment, largely because of their dichotomized relationship shaped in the historical trajectory of the principle's emergence. However, the developments occurring in the wedge between the principle and the standard of arm's length have vitiated the asserted theological status of the ALP. Many of them have been alluded to elsewhere in this thesis; thus, the following does not intend to go into much detail.

### 2.9.1.1 Transfer Pricing Guidelines

The wedge between the principle and standard of arm's length is mostly accentuated by the OECD TPG. As a general matter, it has been considered that the ALP as a norm originated in assigning the income of cross-border business enterprises to multiple tax jurisdictions, had been overtaken[296] by mechanical and artful tools provided by the TPG to narrowly find the 'right' price of a particular transfer similar to that of involving third parties.[297] The history is important for denoting what the competition was originally for, in which the ALP was the victor over other alternatives: an allocation benchmark to be based on the established bedrock institutions of international taxation, in particular, the economic allegiance theory directing that income should be taxed where the taxpayer has economic allegiance. The subsequent developments, especially the landmark Carroll Report and the OECD TPG, jointly altered the original conception of such a benchmark. The ALS that dominated through the OECD TPG instead vested in the separate legal personalities of group members and contracts a paramount status for transfer pricing analysis. Put succinctly, the relationship between the principle and standard of arm's length is a 'tail wagging the dog' story where the ALS becomes the true norm, which is the basis of the arguments that the standard's toolbox is antithetically the decisive consideration of the real materialized ALP hotly debated and regularly maintained.

### 2.9.1.2 Profit-Based Methods

The profit-based methods could be leveraged to provide the leeway that the formulary apportionment needs to survive and operate.[298] The earlier discussions have

295. The differentiation between the principle and standard of arm's length was also emphasized in Jefferson VanderWolk, 'The Arm's-Length Standard Enters Its Second Century' [2019] Tax Notes International 961.
296. Put more bluntly by Hubert (n. 282) 39.
297. J Scott Wilkie, 'Reflecting on the "Arm's Length Principle": What Is the "Principle"? Where Next?' in Wolfgang Schön and Kai A Konrad (eds), *Fundamentals of International Transfer Pricing in Law and Economics* (Springer, Berlin, Heidelberg 2012) 144-147.
298. Richard J Vann, 'Reflections on Business Profits and the Arm's-Length Principle' in Brian J Arnold et al. (eds), *The Taxation of Business Profits under Tax Treaties* (Canadian Tax Foundation 2010) 168.

illuminated the schizophrenia between the profit split method and formulary apportionment.[299] However, several features of the PSM render it with the potential to serve as a backdoor for formulary apportionment.[300] The PSM, although it functions under the constant transactional rhetoric, starts with the aggregation of transactions, which effectively relaxes the strict transactional and comparability requirement. In addition, both the PSM and the TNMM have a group perspective, even though limited, thus the mechanical independent enterprise approach is counteracted as well. Regardless of the important divergence, it was argued that there was a trend of convergence of these methods towards formulary apportionment.[301] As a matter of fact, the profit-based methods have gained growing importance since the 2010 TPG; the BEPS Project authorized the trend by elaborating on the application of PSM for more scenarios.[302]

#### *2.9.1.3 Economic Substance Approach*

Another division of the ALP and formulary apportionment is the emphasis of economic substance, which has been softened as well over the updates of the OECD TPG. One of the most vigorous criticisms of ALP is that it often renders results of taxation in deviation from economic substance, which in turn leads to double non-taxation. The TPG has put increasing weight on the functional analysis, intending to capture the value creation of MNEs. Following the BEPS revisions, the ALS has been recalibrated to be a hybrid of pricing and substance over form standard, as embodied in the revamped General Guidance and the steps of comparability analysis.[303] To encapsulate, the less persistence of the forms of contracts and transactions, the closer the ALS approaches the formulary apportionment.[304]

#### *2.9.1.4 Formulaic Exceptions to the Arm's Length Standard*

There are some mechanisms of transfer pricing in practice that bear the characteristics of formulary apportionment, constituting exceptions to the arm's length approach. Most notably, the predetermined approaches or allocation keys have been long and increasingly used in the OECD TPG and national transfer pricing administration. These

---

299. *See also* similar views Vikram Chand, Alessandro Turina and Louis Ballivet, 'Profit Allocation within MNEs in Light of the Ongoing Digital Debate on Pillar I: A "2020 Compromise"?' (2020) 12 World Tax Journal https://doi.org/10.59403/3erex4g accessed 26 August 2025, s. 2.2.
300. Bell (n. 253).
301. Jeffrey P Owens and Romero JS Tavares, 'Human Capital in Value Creation and Post-BEPS Tax Policy: An Outlook' (2015) 69 Bulletin for International Taxation 690 https://doi.org/10.59403/15tknh7 accessed 26 August 2025.
302. VanderWolk (n. 295) 968.
303. Jens Wittendorff, 'BEPS Actions 8-10: Birth of a New Arms Length Principle' (2016) 87 Tax Notes International 331.
304. Mirna Screpante, 'Formulaic (or Formulary?!) Apportionment Wearing Value Creation Clothes: Is the Wolf Dressed in Sheep's Clothing?' (10 September 2019) Http://Kluwertaxblog.Com/2019/09/10/Formulaic-Or-Formulary-Apportionment-Wearing-Value-Creation-Clothes-Is-The-Wolf-Dressed-In-Sheeps-Clothing accessed 27 November 2023.

mechanisms are introduced as safe harbours superseding the regular transfer pricing procedures. Their wide applications in intra-group transactions of intangibles, services and financing due to the merits of simplicity and reliability reflect the incompetence of the ALP.[305]

### *2.9.1.5 Value Creation Nomenclature*

The injection of the value creation nomenclature into the transfer pricing regime could be a game-changer.[306] As alluded to in the introduction of the 1923 Academic Report, the economic allegiance theory has a natural affinity with the value creation conception. It is also noted elsewhere in this thesis that the value creation nomenclature is significant with the potential to:

(a) pull the international tax architecture from the over-legalist orientation, possibly redefining both residence and source;[307]
(b) substitute the previous transactional pricing and comparables-centred approach for income-based and taxpayer-centred approach of transfer pricing;[308]
(c) linked to the first point, incrementally incept the unitary group methodology that sees the multi-member MNE as an economic unity;
(d) demystify the factor-based contribution analysis of income production of MNEs, for it is yet to be acknowledged that assets, employees and revenue as typical elements of formulary apportionment have long been incorporated in

305. Chand, Turina and Ballivet (n. 299) s. 3.1-3.5.
306. *See* the debate on value creation, Susan C. Morse, 'Value Creation: A Standard in Search of a Process' (2018) 72 Bulletin for International Taxation 196 https://doi.org/10.59403/3dxa2wh accessed 26 August 2025; Johana Hey and Chen Xin, '"Taxation Where Value is Created" and the OECD/G20 Base Erosion and Profit Shifting Initiative' [2018] International Taxation in China; Michael P Devereux and John Vella, 'Value Creation As the Fundamental Principle of the International Corporate Tax System' [2018] European Tax Policy Forum Policy Paper; Lennard Michael, 'Act of Creation: The OECD/G20 Test of "Value Creation" as a Basis for Taxing Rights and Its Relevance to Developing Countries' (2018) 25 Transnational Corporations 55 https://doi.org/10.18356/3db18835-en accessed 26 August 2025; Becker Johannes and Joachim Englisch, 'Taxing Where Value Is Created: What's User Involvement' Got to Do with It?' (2019) 47 Intertax https://doi.org/10.54648/taxi2019015 accessed 26 August 2025; Werner Haslehner and Marie Lamensch (eds), *Taxation and Value Creation: EATLP Annual Congress Vienna, 18-20 June 2020* (IBFD 2021).
307. Mirna Screpante, 'Rethinking the Arm's Length Principle and Its Impact on the IP License Model After Oecd/G20 BEPS Actions 8-10: Nothing Changed but the Change?' [2019] World Tax Journal 425 https://doi.org/10.59403/3x7kjs6 accessed 26 August 2025, s. 5.3.2;Frans Vanistendael, 'An Octogenarian on Value Creation' [2018] Tax Notes International 1385.
308. Maik Heggmair, 'The New Interpretation of the Arm's Length Principle: A Post-BEPS Evaluation' (2017) 24 International Transfer Pricing Journal https://doi.org/10.59403/cbagcm and https://www.ibfd.org/shop/journal/new-interpretation-arms-length-principle-post-beps-evaluation accessed 19 November 2023.

the permanent establishment and business profits articles as subtle manifestations of value creation factors.[309]

These potentials are closely correlated, and many of them have already been effected through the BEPS updates regarding transfer pricing, such as the overlaid delineation of transactions process, the relaxed hierarchy of transfer pricing methods,[310] value chain analysis, the DEMPE ('development, enhancement, maintenance, protection, and exploitation') functions, the new documentation requirements and so forth.[311]

The above developments are non-exhaustive examples validating the surfacing trend that formulary apportionment has infiltrated the existing international tax system with its underlying theories, variants or peripheral architectures. It is recognizable that the changes leading to a new system sometimes happen in the name of defending or ameliorating the old system, which is the case with the BEPS Project's engineering of transfer pricing and other regimes.

As the analyses of Chapters 2 and 4 indicated, involuntary incrementalism could also create more unintended problems. Among others, the wedge between the principle and the standard of arm's length is already at the edge of fracture, largely because of the persistent reliance on the previous premises as discussed in the last section.

### 2.9.2 Digital Economy and the Unified Approach

The taxation of the digital economy has proved to be the most intricate issue of the BEPS Project. Unlike the rest of the BEPS items, the work on digitalization continued following the finalization of the BEPS Reports, which focused on recalibrating the existing allocation rules of international taxation to assign part of the MNE's income to the market jurisdictions. To that end, in February 2019, the OECD/G20 Inclusive Framework issued a Public Consultation Document containing three proposals for revising the profit allocation and nexus rules: the user participation proposal, the marketing intangibles proposal, and the significant economic presence proposal.[312] As a result of the consultation, in May it was published a Program of Work contemplating three proposals for the new profit allocation rules (Pillar One), including the modified

309. Wilkie (n. 297) 154. *See also* Wilkie's comments to the Pillar One, available at http://www.oecd.org/tax/beps/public-comments-received-on-the-secretariat-proposal-for-a-unified-approach-under-pillar-one.htm assessed 18 November 2019.
310. For detailed discussions, *see* Jamil Ahmadov, '"Most Appropriate Method" as the New OECD Transfer Pricing Standard: Has the Hierarchy of Methods Been Completely Eliminated' (2011) 18 International Transfer Pricing Journal https://doi.org/10.59403/23v4xmb accessed 26 August 2025.
311. Mirjam Koomen, 'Transfer Pricing in a BEPS Era: Rethinking the Arm's Length Principle – Part I' (2015) 22 International Transfer Pricing Journal 141-152 https://doi.org/10.59403/1w2n4ye accessed 26 August 2025. In addition to transfer pricing, the value creation concept also played its role in many aspects of the BEPS Project, such as Action 7 and Action 6, *see* Vanistendael (n. 307) 1385-6.
312. OECD, 'Addressing the Tax Challenges of the Digitalisation of the Economy: Public Consultation Document' (OECD 2019).

residual profit split method, the fractional apportionment method, and the distribution-based approaches.[313] In October, the Pillar One proposals were refined as a Unified Approach providing a three-tier mechanism that assigns the Amount A, Amount B and Amount C to the market jurisdictions.[314] In January 2020, the Inclusive Framework approved the Unified Approach and set up a program of work to develop the Pillar One issues, which is the latest multilateral configuration on this matter.

These developments in the context of digitalization signify the fact that the foundations underpinning the income allocation conventions of the international tax system for a century are crumbling, albeit they may vary in mechanics and details. In particular, formulary apportionment as an alternative design of international taxation with versatile potential is now officially resurrected.

First of all, these developments are mobilized by a common objective to address the tax challenges of digitalization. As pointed out by the previous chapters, the work under BEPS Action 1 failed to deliver substantive actions, but it had classified the digital challenges into those exacerbating BEPS issues and the broader ones beyond BEPS in relation to the fundamental allocation question of international taxation. The latter group of challenges has indicated that international taxation is once again contemplated de novo against an economic reality different from the previous models, just as the LON experts were faced with back in the 1920s. However, several important differences have determined the contrasting destinies of formulary apportionment under the two circumstances. The LON experts in the Revenue Phase were occupied with the imminent threat of double taxation. Although they reacted by ruminating about the allocation of taxing rights, the concerns of equity, legitimacy, and resilience against tax avoidance were dwarfed by double taxation, that is, in hindsight, simpler to counteract.[315] Nevertheless, the OECD/G20 are haunted by these concerns head-on and pushed to search for solutions with all possibilities, with formulary apportionment as the hidden gem that immediately pops up. In addition, the digitalization of the economy has, for the first time, presented intuitively the production of value in a jurisdiction without exploiting typical tangible resources, which dictates the taxpayer-centred perspective of value creation, the reconsideration of the source concept, and the inter-nation equity and legitimacy concerns. Other differences are also critical, for example, the maturity of information sharing, transparency and dispute resolution. When all these variables are taken into account, they echo the downslope trajectory of formulary apportionment in the past century and explain the U-turn around the corner laid down in the latest developments.

313. OECD, 'Programme of Work to Develop a Consensus Solution to the Tax Challenges Arising from the Digitalisation of the Economy, OECD/G20 Inclusive Framework on BEPS' (OECD 2019).
314. OECD/G20, 'Secretariat Proposal for a "Unified Approach" under Pillar One' https://web-archive.oecd.org/2019-11-15/532559-oecd-invites-public-input-on-the-secretariat-proposal-for-a-unified-approach-under-pillar-one.htm accessed 18 December 2023.
315. It has been widely acknowledged that unilateral measures already suffice to eliminate double taxation, *see* Tsilly Dagan, *International Tax Policy: Between Competition and Cooperation* (1st edn, Cambridge University Press 2017) https://www.cambridge.org/core/product/identifier/9781316282496/type/book accessed 25 February 2025.

Second, formulary apportionment is no longer alluded to piecemeal or installed in the Trojan horse; instead, it is introduced in its totality. In the original proposals of the Programme of Work, a classical formulary apportionment employing allocation keys, a formula and computation of relevant profits is presented as one of the alternatives. The proposal of the Modified Residual Profit Split method shares these features as well. In the three-tier mechanism of the Unified Approach that absorbs the above proposals, Amount A is particularly underpinned by the application of formulary apportionment.

An in-depth evaluation of the Unified Approach is beyond the scope of this section,[316] but it is evident that the use of formulary apportionment in the Unified Approach has important differences from an archetype formulary system.[317] The formulary mechanism is under consideration since the Programme of Work is restricted only for the purpose of assigning a certain amount of profits to the market jurisdiction, rather than as a general method for restructuring the residence and source. Nevertheless, the formulary apportionment component in the Unified Approach is still revolutionary in many aspects: (a) the allocation key directing incomes to market countries is the new nexus legitimizing the jurisdictional tax claims, running counter to the declaration of the BEPS Project; (b) the separate entity principle is given up where the consolidated profit of a whole group or a business line is the apportionment basis, which is unprecedented that a group's profit is assessed for allocation purposes; (c) the ALP is denounced as the allocation norm of taxing the MNEs at the multilateral level for the first time, for what the uncontrolled third party would do was no more the benchmark of income attribution to a tax jurisdiction.

To encapsulate, the digitalization of global economy has mobilized the long overdue reform towards a more direct and extensive use of formulary apportionment as an alternative strand of taxing MNEs.[318] The entrenched sourcing conventions were rooted in an economic reality that substantially contrasted with the current one in both quantitative and qualitative senses. The world economic landscape not only sees more mobile capital, intangibles, more integrated MNEs, explosive cross-border business

316. Hartmut Förster, Greil Stefan and Hilse Arnim, 'Taxing the Digital Economy–The OECD Secretariat's New Transfer Pricing ABC and Alternative Courses of Action' (2020) 27 International Transfer Pricing Journal https://doi.org/10.59403/1srez66 accessed 26 August 2025; Craig Elliffe, 'International Tax Frameworks: Assessing the 2020s Compromise from the Perspective of Taxing the Digital Economy in the Great Lockdown' (2020) 74 Bulletin for International Taxation https://doi.org/10.59403/3qpc7ms accessed 26 August 2025; Pasquale Pistone et al. 'The OECD Public Consultation Document "Secretariat Proposal for a 'Unified Approach' under Pillar One": An Assessment' (2020) 74(1) Bulletin for International Taxation, 14-27, available at SSRN: https://ssrn.com/abstract=5002961; Chand, Turina and Ballivet (n. 299) 2; Alessandro Samari, 'The OECD Secretariat Proposal for a "Unified Approach" under Pillar One: Strengths and Weaknesses of the New and Revised Nexus and Profit Allocation Rules' (2020) 27 International Transfer Pricing Journal https://doi.org/10.59403/3yggys5 accessed 26 August 2025.
317. Ana Paula Dourado, 'The OECD Unified Approach and the New International Tax System: A Half-Way Solution' (2020) 48 Intertax 3 https://doi.org/10.54648/taxi2020001 accessed 26 August 2025.
318. Sara L McGaughey and Pascalis Raimondos, 'Shifting MNE Taxation from National to Global Profits: A Radical Reform Long Overdue' (2019) 50 Journal of International Business Studies 1668 https://doi.org/10.1057/s41267-019-00233-9 accessed 26 August 2025.

volume and intra-group transactions, but also the essential way of doing business and value creation thanks to the digitalization. The Unified Approach has destroyed the theological status of the arm's length/separate entity principle and the residence-source dichotomy and unveiled the new allocation phase of international taxation.

### 2.9.3 Unilateral Perspectives of the Destabilized Inter-Nation Allocation Model

The international tax system governs two clusters of relationships: one is that between the tax jurisdiction and a non-resident taxpayer, and another is that between two tax jurisdictions with competing tax claims on the same taxpayer or income. Both clusters have far-reaching implications for the distribution of revenues between the taxing authorities. As to the taxation of MNEs, it has been illuminated that transfer pricing is the central regime allocating the profits of MNEs to the taxing states. The allocation question of international taxation has been a major concern, especially in the relationship between the source/capital-importing countries and the residence/capital-exporting countries. Developed and developing countries have struggled for a balance through asymmetric tax treaties for decades. It is generally acknowledged that the existing international tax system is maintaining a pro-residence bias, favouring developed countries over developing countries.[319] Nevertheless, with international taxation entering into the new Allocation Phase, the allocation question has come to the centre stage, which further destabilizes the established allocation model. The following intends to sketch the unilateral perspectives of the destabilized inter-nation allocation model, including China's endorsement of the contribution analysis approach to transfer pricing, India's new profit attribution proposal and the EU-US collision over the taxation of the digital economy. China and India represent the typical source countries that strive to demand a larger piece of international tax sharing with developed countries, while the European Union and the United States as traditional dominant powers also collide against the new economic reality. These examples have reflected the deep crisis of the existing allocation model of international taxation.

#### *2.9.3.1 The Chinese Approaches to Contribution Analysis and the Location Specific Advantages*

Since the launch of the BEPS Project, China has taken an active role in the international tax reform, even though it is not a member of the OECD. To further its strategic goals of enlarging the pie sharing from the perspective of a source country, China has been ambitious to promote innovative propositions but meanwhile pragmatic to support the efforts of the BEPS Project. Among others, with regard to transfer pricing policies, China has upheld and adhered to a contribution analysis approach and a particular approach to the location-specific advantages. They differ in nature and content, but

319. Yariv Brauner, 'Treaties in the Aftermath of BEPS' (2016) 41 Brooklyn Journal of International Law 973, 983.

both are the hallmarks of China's dissatisfaction with the existing allocation model of international taxation, and taken together, they seem to signify that China has already carried out a hybrid method of ALS and formulary apportionment.[320]

#### *2.9.3.1.1 The Chinese Approach to Contribution Analysis*

One of the major reforms of transfer pricing since the 2010 update of the OECD TPG is the increasing weight of risks in transfer pricing analysis.[321] In the General Guidance section of the TPG, the analysis of risks in commercial or financial relations equipped with a detailed mechanism leads the steps of the functional analysis.[322] Such a risk-based approach is the corollary to the transactional approach to the application of the ALP, as it links the assumption of risks to the expected return of the transaction in line with the regular commercial and market practice. The risk-based approach could be abused for tax avoidance purposes since risk assumption is under the control of the MNE group simply through contractual arrangements. Compared to functions and assets, risks are much easier to shift and manipulate between associated parties. The BEPS reforms of the TPG, such as the recharacterization of contracts, the enhanced risk analysis and the improved profit split method, already constituted a pull-out of the risk-based approach to restrict risk-related base erosion and profit shifting opportunities. From the perspective of income allocation, the risk-based approach is also a significant concern for source countries like China that host massive direct investments as they deem the approach having stripped unduly the incomes away, because risks are often closely related to the central management company or the member responsible for research and development or intangibles rather than the manufacturing or assembly affiliates located in the source countries.

China has expressed its concerns about the risk-based approach and has endorsed a formulaic contribution analysis approach in the country practice section of the UN Transfer Pricing Manual.[323] Based on this, China was recognized as the first country that had officially pronounced that it would support and explore the application of the global formulary apportionment as a realistic and appropriate alternative allocation method.[324] The specific scenario in consideration is the transfer pricing problems related to the electronic manufacturing services industry where, manufacturing and assembly operations, workforce, tangible assets, and high level operational staff usually concentrate in China, while the existing transfer pricing policies especially the risk-based approach have enabled the MNE group to under-compensate the Chinese affiliates as if they were contract or toll manufacturers. In this case, the contribution analysis approach has a global perspective of the MNE group and

320. Martin Hearson and Wilson Prichard, 'China's Challenge to International Tax Rules and the Implications for Global Economic Governance' (2018) 94 International Affairs 1287 https://doi.org/10.1093/ia/iiy189 accessed 26 August 2025.
321. Richard and Andrus (n. 10) para. 2.123.
322. OECD, *TPG 2017* (n. 182) s. 1.2.1.
323. United Nations, 'Practical Manual on Transfer Pricing for Developing Countries (2017)' (n. 282) s. D2.4.7.
324. Langbein and Fuss (n. 74) 398.

determines the proper remuneration to the Chinese entity according to its contribution to the entire value chain of the group. It is descriptively conceived that the contribution of the Chinese manufacturer, in turn, should be weighed by the relative assets and employees of the whole group. The approach is thus a roughly two-factor global formulary apportionment.

#### *2.9.3.1.2 The Chinese Approach to the Location-Specific Advantages*

The approach to location-specific advantages (LSA) is another example of China positing itself, as expressed in the above contribution analysis approach. It is another piece of proof at the centre of China's challenge to the pie-sharing of international taxation.[325] The concept of LSA is generally used to refer to the benefits an MNE can exploit from locating its businesses in a specific locality, thanks to its favourable conditions. The LSAs can take many forms, two of the most acknowledged being location savings and market premiums, which relate to cost and demand.[326] The exact term of LSA was not found in the OECD TPG; its essentials had been addressed only marginally before the BEPS update of 2017, expressed either as 'economic circumstances' and 'market differences'.[327] The TPG 2017 incorporated the location savings, presumably also including marking premiums, and other local market features as comparability factors.[328] The United Nations acted earlier but eventually converged with the OECD approach.[329]

China has put the LSA into the practice of transfer pricing as early as 2008, even prior to any formal regulations of the concept.[330] The most recent and authoritative statement of China's position on this matter rests in the China Country Practice section of the 2017 UN TP Manual.[331] With other materials as supplements, the approach to the LSA represents China's visible opposition to the current allocation model underpinned by the ALS as well as the challenges to the orthodoxy of the OECD despite China itself being a general supporter of the BEPS agenda. First of all, the issue of LSA was framed in the first place against China's discontent with the allocation of profits between developed and developing countries, where it was thought that developing countries had not been adequately remunerated from the locational rent the MNEs derived

325. Hearson and Prichard (n. 320) 1297.
326. Peng Claire, 'A Rethink of Location-Specific Advantages with an Analysis of the Chinese Approach' (2017) 24 International Transfer Pricing Journal 484 https://doi.org/10.59403/2tjyeah accessed 26 August 2025.
327. OECD, *TPG 1995* (n. 277) para. 1.30; OECD, 'OECD Transfer Pricing Guidelines for Multinational Enterprises and Tax Administrations 2010' (OECD Publishing 2010) para. 1.57.
328. OECD, *TPG 2017* (n. 182) para. D.6.
329. United Nations, 'Practical Manual on Transfer Pricing for Developing Countries (2017)' (n. 282) paras 5.3.2.38-5.2.3.45; Claire (n. 326) 491.
330. Notice of the STA's Work on the Anti-Tax Avoidance in 2008, Guo Shui Han [2009] 106, 6 March 2009 (国税函[2009]106号 国家税务总局关于2008年反避税工作情况的通报).
331. United Nations, 'Practical Manual on Transfer Pricing for Developing Countries (2017)' (n. 282) s. D.2.

thanks to the unique advantages thereby provided.[332] Second, the Chinese approach to the LSA internalizes the endowment of the market as an intrinsic value creation factor of a firm's profits, countering the OECD approach to the ALS that identifies it as an external comparability factor.[333] A former official of the STA saw it as a positive move that the weight of the market factor increased as the local affiliate's reliance on foreign intellectual property declined.[334] Third, antithetical to the conceptual foundation of the ALS, the Chinese approach to the LSA upholds the unitary business principle rather than the independent legal entity fiction.[335] The remuneration for local affiliates in

332. 'For a long time, developed countries have relied on their dominance in rule-making, technology and intangible assets to compete with developing countries for tax sources, and have obtained most of the benefits of multinational companies, while developing countries have used huge markets, cheap labor, and at the expense of energy consumption and environmental damage, little profit is shared to them ... . First, the market contribution must match the group's global profit distribution. As an emerging economy, China has a huge market and strong demand. The *particularity of this market* is of great significance to the realization of profits of multinational companies. It is hoped that multinational groups with important market shares in China should consider and reflect the *profit distribution* of Chinese subsidiaries at this point. The second is that the corporate function commitment and profit return must match. There must be a corresponding profit ratio for whatever function is undertaken. It cannot be said that the function has increased R&D, marketing, management, etc., but the profit is still positioned on the basis of simple processing, which is unreasonable. The third is that the *Chinese government's investment, supporting facilities, cost savings and corporate profit returns must match.* The Chinese government has invested heavily in land, factories, and public facilities to attract foreign investment. China's labor force is still relatively cheap and the industrial facilities are relatively complete. The contribution of these factors to the profits of multinational companies should not be underestimated, and the profit returns of Chinese subsidiaries must be matched. Fourth, the social image of multinational companies must match their tax contributions. In recent years, some well-known multinational companies in the world have continuously exposed tax issues. People are questioning that these companies, while occupying a large market share and obtaining high profits, use tax planning to pay very little tax, which violates social morality.', 'Interview of the Director of the State Taxation Bureau of Jiangsu Province' https://www.shui5.cn/article/13/73408.html accessed 27 November 2023; United Nations, 'Practical Manual on Transfer Pricing for Developing Countries (2017)' (n. 282) s. D.2.4.41.
333. Mark Melnicoe and Tizhong Liao, 'International Tax Rules Must Adapt to China's Rise' [2015] Tax Management Transfer Pricing Report; 'The BEPS report proposes that the results of transfer pricing should be consistent with value creation, and it is proposed that the analysis of value creation should be combined with the consideration of the distribution of income within each jurisdiction. *We believe that the market has a unique and significant meaning and role in the creation of corporate value and the realization of profits.* To this end, we first adhere to the concepts of cost saving and market premium proposed in the "United Nations Transfer Pricing Manual for Developing Countries", and reflect them in the global profit distribution of multinational companies; second, in transfer pricing surveys, advance pricing negotiations and corporate data In preparation, for example, when using the profit method to divide profits, consider market factors as an important factor in the division to reflect the profits that should be reflected; third, for multinational companies that have important market shares in China, *we not only hope that companies will be in the group market factors are added to the profit distribution of the value chain, and it is hoped that companies will fully consider the particularity brought about by the huge market and strong demand of China as an emerging economy, and reflect this "speciality" in profit distribution.*', Jiangsu Provincial Office of STA, 'Administration Plan for International Taxation Compliance in 2014-2015' 2014-2015 https://www.shui5.cn/article/03/71246.html accessed 27 November 2023.
334. Melnicoe and Liao (n. 333).
335. United Nations, 'Practical Manual on Transfer Pricing for Developing Countries (2017)' (n. 282) s. D.2.4.2.3.

consideration of the LSAs is undergirded by investigating the role of local operations vis-à-vis the whole group and the entire value chain, which enables China to collect the locational rent that falls out of the reach of the comparable-based methods.[336]

China's revamp of its transfer pricing regulations since 2016 has evinced a converging trend towards the OECD approach to location savings,[337] but the Chinese approach to the LSA in general still contrasts with the OECD TPG following the BEPS revisions. It was thus said that China had lost the battle over location savings,[338] or the 2017 TPG only met China halfway.[339] Either viewpoint captures the essential fact that the collision is fundamental. While the OECD's ALS had already been refined to incorporate the LSA, the Chinese approach harbours the challenges, both technical and conceptual, to the validity of the standard as the bedrock of the international allocation model. In addition, the approach contains evident affinities with the global formulary apportionment, such as the independent consideration of the market contribution to value creation and the unitary business principle. Taken together with the contribution analysis approach, China may have already been implementing a hybrid method of the ALS and formulary apportionment.

### *2.9.3.2 India's Profit Attribution Proposal*

India revised the taxable threshold nexus rule in 2018 to address the challenges of the digital economy.[340] In 2019, a Report by the Central Board of Direct Taxes of India was released for public consultation, which proposed to revamp the Indian rule of profit attribution to permanent establishment.[341] The proposal has echoed the *a priori* deficit of economic soundness of the creation of value as the interplay of supply and demand, and expressed the unsuitability of the ALS as materialized in the authorized OECD Approach (AOA) to underpinning the existing allocation model.

#### *2.9.3.2.1 Treaty and Domestic Law Background*

As cast in the trajectory of formulary apportionment, the profit attribution to permanent establishment, in fact, had mobilized the evolution of the allocation model of international taxation. It is a long-established convention that the separate

336. Hearson and Prichard (n. 320) 1300-1301.
337. Claire (n. 326) 495-497.
338. Ryan Finley, 'Panel Expects Increased Transfer Pricing Compliance Burdens' (2015) 80 Tax Notes International 488, 489. quoted in Brauner, 'Treaties in the Aftermath of BEPS' (n. 319) 982.
339. Hearson and Prichard (n. 320) 1301.
340. OECD, 'Tax Challenges Arising from Digitalisation: Interim Report 2018 – Inclusive Framework on BEPS' (OECD 2018) 138 https://www.oecd.org/en/publications/tax-challenges-arising-from-digitalisation-interim-report_9789264293083-en.html accessed 18 September 2023.
341. Government of India, Ministry of Finance, Department of Revenue, Central Board of Direct Taxes, Public Consultation on the proposal for amendment of Rules for Profit attribution to Permanent Establishment, F. No. 500/33/2017-FTD.I (18 April 2019), hereinafter, 'Profit Attribution Report'.

accounting/independent entity principle is the pillar of the allocation of income in the context of PE.

Pertinent to its pivotal importance as the front line of the power struggle between the residence and source, the existing provisions of income attribution to the PE in the worldwide tax treaties can be encapsulated into three strands. The first is laid down in the pre-2010 OECD Model Convention, succeeding the 1933 Draft Convention that provided a multilayered approach employing both separate accounting and formulary apportionment. The second strand is generated following the revision of the OECD Model Convention in 2010, which discarded the formulary apportionment option and injected the transfer pricing philosophy of relying on the FAR (functions, assets and risks) analysis known as the AOA approach. The third is contained in the UN Model Convention, which is similar to the pre-2010 OECD Model but more generous to the source by means of the force of attraction rules and limitations on the deduction of expenses.[342]

The Indian approach in tax treaties and domestic law rests closer to the first strand and the UN model that sanctions the use of formulary apportionment, while dissenting from the OECD AOA approach. According to the provision in almost all Indian tax treaties, the profits attributed to a PE are determined first of all by assessing the accounts maintained by the PE as if it were an independent enterprise, yet where accounts are not available or accurate, the provision and the Rule 10 of the Indian Income Tax Rules 1962 provide the formulary apportionment as a fallback method.

The proposal aims to provide greater certainty, consistency, and predictability regarding the Indian rule of profit attribution to the PE. However, the more profound inducements implicit in the Profit Attribution Report are the digitalization of the economy[343] that undermines the basis of the validity of the PE concept and the corollary of the destabilized allocation model of international taxation, which erodes the tax base of India as a typical source country, yet with a huge market potential.[344]

#### *2.9.3.2.2 Basic Design*

The Profit Attribution Report recommends a three-factor formulary apportionment method to determine the profits of a non-resident attributable to the operations in India. The general formula is as follows:[345]

342. Anna Binder and Viktoria Wöhrer (eds), *Special Features of the UN Model Convention* (Linde Verlag 2019) 95-153.
343. India had already amended its taxable threshold nexus rule as of 2019 incorporating the significant economic presence test. s. 4, Finance Act, 2018.
344. Profit Attribution Report, para. 6 and the discussions in the s. 6.
345. For more detailed summary of the proposal, *see* EY Global, 'Tax Alert Indian Tax Administration Invites Public Comments on Proposal to Amend Rules on Profit Attribution to Permanent Establishment' (1 May 2019) https://globaltaxnews.ey.com/news/2019-5580-indian-tax-administration-invites-public-comments-on-proposal-to-amend-rules-on-profit-attribution-to-permanent-establishment accessed 2 December 2023.

*Profits attributable to operations in India = Profits derived from India*[346] × *[India Sales/3 × Global Sales + (Indian Employees*[347]*/6 × Global Employees) + (Indian Wages/6 × Global Wages) + (Indian Assets/3 × Global Assets)]*

There is an exception for the user-facing digital businesses that adds a fourth factor of users to the above formula. Depending on the intensity of users in these business models, there are corresponding adjustments of the weight of each factor in the formula.[348]

#### *2.9.3.2.3 Significance and Implications*

The Indian proposal was recognized by Avi-Yonah as the first time a national government had officially sanctioned formulary apportionment and abandoned the ALS.[349] The comment is fair and underscores the fact that although the ALS has been continuously vitiated from all directions and various proposals employing formulary apportionment are contemplated at the multilateral level, it is this Indian proposal that first retrieves formulary apportionment as the alternative design of international taxation. In addition, the proposal indicates that formulary apportionment can be introduced in a unilateral but treaty-compatible way into the current system. While awaiting the ensuing progress, it preliminarily vindicates this chapter's earlier proposition that the seeds of formulary apportionment in tax treaties are alive.[350]

The Profit Attribution Report has set out several justifications for the proposal of employing formulary apportionment.[351] It cites the example in the 1923 Academic Report that the experts used to illustrate the economic allegiance theory,[352] in order to back sales factor in the formula acknowledging the value creation at the demand side. Besides corroborating the inner connection between the economic allegiance theory and formulary apportionment, it is more profound that the proposal adopts formulary apportionment for the general system rather than narrowly for digital businesses, which differs from the OECD/G20 unified approach but exploits the potential of formulary apportionment. However, the proposal is indicative of the seriousness of the crisis of the allocation model of international taxation, especially from the perspective of source countries.[353]

346. As calculated as the higher of the revenue derived from India x Global operational profit margin, and the 2% of the revenue derived from India.
347. Employees and Wages are components of the sales factor.
348. The user factor is assigned a weight of 10% in cases of low and medium user intensity, while in case of digital models with high user intensity, the factor should be assigned a weight of 20%.
349. Avi-Yonah and Kir (n. 236).
350. *See* Ch. 2.
351. Avi-Yonah and Kir (n. 236) 17-19.
352. 'The oranges upon the trees in California are not acquired wealth until they are picked, and not even at that stage until they are packed, and not even at that stage until they are transported to the place where demand exists and until they are put where the consumer can use them. These stages, up to the point where wealth reaches fruition, may be shared in by different territorial authorities.', Bruins et al. (n. 44) 4027.
353. For more comprehensive evaluation of the proposal, *see* Vishweshwar Mudigonda and Majmudar Suchint, 'Does India's Proposals on Attribution of Profits to Pes Solve the Issue?'

### 2.9.3.3 EU-US Collision over Taxation on the Digitalization

The above instances of China and India have captured the destabilized allocation model of international taxation from the source country's perspective. The great power struggle between residence and source countries has mobilized many developments of international taxation,[354] which is the key contradiction of international tax relations parallel to that of tax avoidance of MNEs. In contrast, this section intends to sketch the collision between the European countries that are largely members of the OECD and the United States over the changing tax environment of the digital economy.[355] Just as the above sections do, the focus is to unscramble the width and depth of the crisis of the existing conventions of inter-nation income allocation, as not only the asymmetry between the developed and the developing is threatened but also the intra-system symmetry within the developed community.

The collision in question stems from one basic fact that the United States is the world's largest exporter of digital businesses, while the European Union has been the market with the largest customer base in both absolute quantity and consumption potential of the US digital products. The juxtaposition of the US and EU in this respect cannot provide a more typical, and in fact, an unprecedented scenario for the inherent flaws of the allocation model to be exposed. And at least two facets of this collision are especially noteworthy.

#### *2.9.3.3.1 Digital Service Tax*

One is over the digital service tax (DST). The exact concept of DST is not referred to in the BEPS Action 1, but in essence, it is a kind of equalization levy as considered in the Final Report. The DST came under the spotlight when the European Commission announced in 2018 a two-fold proposal including the DST as the interim instrument to counter the challenges of the digital economy in the European Union.[356] The EU DST proposal was intended to be implemented in all Member States as an additional levy of 3% on the gross turnover of digital firms, largely from the United States. However, the DST is a unilateral solution that does not require the coordination of the third countries. While the EU proposal is currently on hold, the DST has spread worldwide,[357] especially in Europe. In short, as of October 2020, nearly half of all the European OECD

---

(20 May 2019) https://www.internationaltaxreview.com/article/b1fq9g90kbsyzv/does-indias-proposals-on-attribution-of-profits-to-pes-solve-the-issue accessed 27 November 2023.

354. As elaborated in Bianco and Santos (n. 231).

355. *See* relevant discussions at Ruth Mason, 'The Transformation of International Tax' (2020) 114 American Journal of International Law 353, 394-397 https://doi.org/10.1017/ajil.2020.33 accessed 26 August 2025.

356. European Commission, 'Proposal for a Council Directive on the Common System of a Digital Services Tax on Revenues Resulting from the Provision of Certain Digital Services.' COM (2018) 148 final.

357. KPMG, Taxation of the Digitalized Economy, Developments Summary, Updated: 15 October 2020.

Member States have achieved substantive developments in introducing the DST, though the specific progress may vary.[358]

The United States reacted vehemently. In July 2019, France's Parliamentary Commission agreed on the DST that applied retroactively from 1 January 2019. Almost immediately, the Office of the United States Trade Representative (USTR) initiated the section 301 investigation into the French DST and found it discriminatory, burdensome and inconsistent with the prevailing international tax principles.[359] Following that, the Trump Administration threatened to impose additional tariffs of up to 25% on some French products.[360] France did not succumb to the pressure.[361] With more countries following suit, the U.S. section 301 investigation expanded in June 2020 into the DST motions of nine countries, five of which are European states and the EU itself.[362]

#### *2.9.3.3.2 The Pillar One Amount A Safe Harbour*

The collision over the DST concurred with the United States rocking the boat of Pillar One.[363] Around two months after the OECD published its Pillar One proposal, U.S. Treasury Secretary Steven Mnuchin wrote a letter to OECD Secretary-General José Ángel Gurría.[364] Besides his vigorous criticism of the DST, Mnuchin set out that the United States has serious concerns over the departures from the ALS and the nexus rule and suggested a safe-harbour regime for Pillar One to address these concerns. As noted in Gurría's response, after two public consultations held on Pillar One, Mnuchin's letter was the first time that a safe harbour had been proposed.[365]

358. Elke Asen and Daniel Bunn, 'What European OECD Countries Are Doing about Digital Services Taxes' (2020) https://taxfoundation.org/digital-tax-europe-2020/ accessed 23 November 2023.
359. USTR, 'Section 301 Investigation Report on France's Digital Services Tax' https://ustr.gov/sites/default/files/Report_On_France%27s_Digital_Services_Tax.pdf. accessed 27 November 2023.
360. USTR, 'Notice of Action in the Section 301 Investigation of France's Digital Services Tax' https://www.federalregister.gov/documents/2020/07/16/2020-15312/notice-of-action-in-the-section-301-investigation-of-frances-digital-services-tax. accessed 28 November 2020.
361. Leigh Thomas, *France to Impose Digital Tax This Year Regardless of Any New International Levy* (14 May 2020), https://www.reuters.com/article/us-france-digital-tax/france-to-impose-digital-tax-this-year-regardless-of-any-new-international-levy-idUSKBN22Q25B accessed 26 August 2025.
362. Daniel Bunn, 'The U.S. Trade Representative Expands Its Digital Services Tax Investigations' (2 June 2020) https://taxfoundation.org/us-trade-representative-ustr-digital-services-tax-investigations accessed 26 November 2023.
363. Ryan Finley and Stephanie Soong, 'The U.S. "Safe Harbor" Proposal: Rocking the OECD's Pillar 1 Boat' (10 November 2019) https://www.taxnotes.com/featured-news/us-safe-harbor-proposal-rocking-oecds-pillar-1-boat/2019/12/09/2bns7 accessed 26 November 2023.
364. For the full text of the letter, *see* Tax Notes, 'U.S. Outlines Digital Services Tax Concerns in Letter to OECD' (3 November 2019) https://www.taxnotes.com/research/federal/other-documents/treasury-tax-correspondence/u.s-outlines-digital-services-tax-concerns-in-letter-to-oecd/2b61x accessed 26 August 2025.
365. For the full text of the letter, *see* Tax Notes, 'OECD Responds to U.S. Treasury Letter Outlining Digital Tax Concerns' (4 November 2019) https://www.taxnotes.com/research/federal/other-documents/treasury-tax-correspondence/oecd-responds-to-u.s.-treasury-letter-outlining-digital-tax-concerns/2b633 accessed 26 August 2025.

Different from a regular definition of 'safe harbour' in the taxation arena, a Pillar One safe harbour allows certain MNEs to opt out of the mandatory application of Amount A if they can demonstrate that an equivalent amount of tax is already being paid in the market jurisdictions.

The US demand was immediately reflected in the following workflow of the OECD. In the January 2020 statement, a work plan was set up to consider the safe harbour approach.[366] In June 2020, Steven Mnuchin wrote another letter to the finance ministers of France, Italy, Spain, and the UK to seek a pause of the OECD agenda of the Pillar One.[367] The US withdrew from the international negotiations,[368] but the wheel kept rolling.[369]

As a result, the Pillar One Blueprint indicated the concerns raised by the US demand for the safe harbour approach, especially the serious scepticism expressed by many jurisdictions,[370] and committed to bridging the divergent views on this matter. Since the Blueprint, and eventually in the Multilateral Convention,[371] the marketing and distribution safe harbour was formally introduced as a component of the Pillar One Amount A.[372]

## 2.10 CHAPTER CONCLUSION

The above narration of the formulary apportionment against the staged evolution of the international tax system argues that a historical analysis of formulary apportionment vis-à-vis the evolution of international taxation goes beyond just filling in a 'blank area'. To encapsulate, the above analyses have addressed the propositions including but not limited to the following.

366. OECD, 'Statement by the OECD/G20 Inclusive Framework on BEPS on the Two-Pillar Approach to Address the Tax Challenges Arising from the Digitalisation of the Economy: January 2020' (2020) para. 90 https://www.oecd.org/tax/beps/statement-by-the-oecd-g20-inclusive-framework-on-beps.htm accessed 26 August 2025.
367. KPMG, Treasury Secretary Mnuchin seeks 'pause' in OECD Pillar 1 discussions of digital economy, at https://assets.kpmg.com/content/dam/kpmg/us/pdf/2020/06/20399.pdf.
368. Jenny Leonard and Davison Davison, 'U.S. Pulls Out of Global Digital Tax Talks, Lighthizer Says' (18 June 2020) https://news.bloombergtax.com/daily-tax-report/u-s-pulls-out-of-global-digital-tax-talks-lighthizer-says?context=search&index=2 accessed 20 June 2021.
369. For a more focused story on the safe harbour and its relevant technical analysis, *see* Carol P Tello, 'OECD Works on Pillar 1 Technical Issues Despite Pause on Political Issue of Scope' https://www.lexology.com/library/detail.aspx?g=fb055cc8-20dc-493c-bafe-ac3547fd4c01 accessed 26 November 2023; for a more detailed story in this respect, *see also* Alex McNichol, 'Canterbury Law Review Student Prize 2020: An Analysis of the United States' Stance on BEPS: Pillar One' (2021) 28 Canterbury Law Review 161.
370. OECD, 'Tax Challenges Arising from Digitalisation: Report on Pillar One Blueprint' (n. 2) paras 165-170.
371. 'Multilateral Convention to Implement Amount A of Pillar One' https://www.oecd.org/en/topics/sub-issues/reallocation-of-taxing-rights-to-market-jurisdictions/multilateral-convention-to-implement-amount-a-of-pillar-one.html accessed 26 August 2025.
372. Vikram Chand and Camille Vilaseca, 'Pillar I: The Marketing and Distribution Safe Harbour (MDSH) as Applicable to Licensed Manufacturers and Centralized Business Models: Does It Fulfil Its Policy Objective?' (2023) 51 Intertax https://doi.org/10.54648/taxi2023053 accessed 26 August 2025.

A caveat is that such a conclusion should not be understood to put a pall over many other findings throughout the historical inspection, such as that countering tax avoidance is found to be an intrinsic purpose of the ALS, and a multilateral tax treaty for dealing with the allocation issues of MNEs had ever been seriously pursued in the formative period:

(1) The current century-old system of international taxation can be roughly divided into four stages according to the dominant themes, respectively. One has to understand the driving concerns within a certain period of time to capture the law of the system's evolution.
(2) Formulary apportionment has experienced a 'U' curve in the full picture of the evolution of the international tax system. In contrast to the prejudice of many that formulary apportionment is naïve and a chimera, it, in fact, has always been an actor in different stages of the trajectory of international taxation. Formulary apportionment had been employed as a statutory instrument and was a serious alternative contemplated in the formative period as a global design for double taxation relief. After being rejected out of practical concerns, formulary apportionment also lost the competition of the allocation norm of taxing the MNEs, in which separate accounting/independent entities triumphed and dominated. The authority of formulary apportionment has been undermined in the following Phases of Trade and Anti-avoidance, yet still, the seeds of it are alive and vigorous in the existing tax treaty network. The digitalization of the economy does not utterly metamorphose the economic infrastructure where the international tax system operates, but renders the bias and flaws inherent in the architecture of the system detrimental for almost all parties.[373] Under such circumstances, the comeback of formulary apportionment is no more a conception, but a reality that gradually emerges.
(3) Formulary apportionment is not an isolated mechanism but is the crystallization of a cluster of principles and concepts. Formulary apportionment has a natural affinity with economic allegiance theory, which assigns the taxing rights to jurisdictions according to the location of factors in the internal process of value creation. It follows that the international tax system was constructed in the first place to assimilate how value is created. The problem is that the fundamental components, such as the residence-source dichotomy and the ALS, are already beyond fine-tuning, which inevitably leads the system to base erosion and profit shifting.
(4) The dominance and theological status of the ALS is built on historical contingency rather than theoretical superiority. It is embedded in a system created for an economic and political reality far different from the current one. It is revealed that the modern ALS was in embryo in the Revenue Phase and

373. Yariv Brauner, *Between Arm's Length and Formulary Apportionment, in the Allocation of Multinational Business Income: Reassessing the Formulary Apportionment Option* (Kluwer Law International 2020) s. 8.04.

matured in the Trade Phase, which served the interest of MNEs and developed countries as their home states. The source states have been systematically exploited. Nevertheless, the proliferation of aggressive tax avoidance by MNEs makes the game difficult to continue, where the anti-avoidance pattern has been following a flawed pattern.

(5) The BEPS Project marks the culmination of stretching the established sourcing and allocation conventions that marginalized formulary apportionment. The theme of fairness and inter-nation equity of international taxation has never been more palpable when both developing and developed countries are discontent with the current allocation model.

# PART II Some Experience from the Real World

CHAPTER 3

# A Comparative Analysis of the 'Existing' Formulary Apportionment 'Regimes': US, Canada, (the Withdrawn) EU CCCTB Proposal, and the Pillar One Amount A

*This chapter is a pivotal component within the general framework of the thesis. First of all, it complements the discussions of the above chapters, which are largely theoretical, by looking into how formulary apportionment actually works in real tax systems. In addition to that, considering the overall status and progress of formulary apportionment in the present international tax agenda, experiences and insights gained from sub-national formulary apportionment regimes have never been more opportune.*

*To be specific, this chapter will contribute to three inter-related overarching questions that are haunting the evolution of international tax system in which formulary apportionment had been and resumes to be a pillar:*[374] *first, in light of the development under the auspices of OECD and G20 on the theme of digital economy, what can be seen as to the role of formulary apportionment in the international tax regime in the long future?; second, what are the internal and external conditions to be satisfied for a formulary system of international corporate taxation?; third, what is the good design of such formulary apportionment system?*

*The three questions entail close examination and analysis of the formulary apportionment regimes in the selected jurisdictions of the United States, Canada, and the European Union. Therefore, this chapter is not organized as a per-country study but adopts the methodology of dismantling the formulary apportionment regime into several structural components, based on which*

374. *See* the discussions in Ch. 4 about the historical trajectory of formulary apportionment.

*the selected formulary apportionment regimes are compared and analysed horizontally and per structural components.*

## 3.1 INTRODUCTION

The last chapter peripherally surveyed the historical existence of formulary apportionment, while the formulary apportionment regimes in current operation were left for future discussions. This chapter fills the gap by selecting and examining formulary apportionment regimes in the United States, Canada, the withdrawn CCCTB proposal of the European Union and the Pillar One Amount A solution.

This chapter is a pivotal component within the general framework of the thesis. First of all, it complements the discussions of the above chapters, which are largely theoretical, by looking into how formulary apportionment actually works in real tax systems. In addition to that, considering the overall status and progress of formulary apportionment in the present international tax agenda, it is the right time to learn the experiences and insights gained from sub-national formulary apportionment regimes.

To be specific, this chapter contributes to three inter-related overarching questions that are haunting the evolution of international tax system in which formulary apportionment had been and resumes to be a pillar:[375] first, in light of the development under the auspices of OECD and G20 on the theme of digital economy, what can be seen as the role of formulary apportionment in the international tax regime in the long future?; second, what are the internal and external conditions to be satisfied for a formulary system of international corporate taxation?; third, what is the good design of such a formulary apportionment system?

The three questions entail close examination and analysis of the formulary apportionment regimes in the selected jurisdictions of the United States, Canada, and the European Union. Therefore, this chapter is not organized as a per-country study but adopts the methodology of dismantling the formulary apportionment regime into several structural components, based on which the selected formulary apportionment regimes are compared and analysed horizontally and according to the structural components.

## 3.2 A TAXONOMY OF THE COMPONENTS OF FORMULARY APPORTIONMENT REGIME

The elements of a formulary apportionment regime can be infinite if not applying a taxonomy. This chapter sorts out five structural components of the formulary apportionment regime under two broad categories for a more organized analysis. The taxonomy is not based on some profound methodology; rather, it provides a convenient reference for comparative analysis.

375. *See* the discussions in Ch. 2 about the historical trajectory of formulary apportionment.

The first category serves to capture the elements of the formulary apportionment regime that are relatively peripheral, not in the sense of essentiality, but based on that, they are less frequently discussed by the commentators. Therefore, this category can be coined as 'external' components, which include the jurisdiction to tax rule and the territorial scope. Moreover, there will also be an additional section in this category regarding the historical trajectory and general information of formulary apportionment regimes in the three jurisdictions.

The second category captures the intrinsic components of formulary apportionment regime that are also most frequently debated in the relevant literature, which are essential to the system of all other taxes as well. Therefore, this category is named as 'internal', including the delineation of taxable unit, the harmonization and determination of tax base, and the choice and weight of apportionment factors.

## 3.3 COMPARATIVE ANALYSIS OF EXTERNAL COMPONENTS OF FORMULARY APPORTIONMENT REGIME

### 3.3.1 Historical Trajectory and General Information

#### *3.3.1.1 The United States*

The United States is among the pioneers of employing formulary apportionment in state tax systems. When the European Union was proposing its reform blueprint for CCCTB in 2011, the experiences of US states on formulary apportionment began to come under the spotlight for policymakers and commentators. Under the current circumstances of the international tax agenda and considering the special federal-state political system of the United States, there are abundant resources worth excavating from the application and operation of the US formulary apportionment systems.

In the state corporation tax area, formulary apportionment originated from the context of property taxation in the 1870s and was subsequently extended to corporation income tax since Wisconsin unveiled the modern era of general income taxation in 1911.[376] The income sourced to Wisconsin was originally determined by the capital assets and business within the state in proportion to the total assets and business. In response to the critique about the intricacy of business factors in the Wisconsin formula, Massachusetts introduced the so-called standard three-factor formula in 1919 for the first time, which employs tangible property, labour costs, and sales revenue for apportionment.[377] Formulary apportionment regimes have thus proliferated in state corporation tax systems since the early twentieth century, and it is confirmed that such a trend of adopting formulary apportionment in the US states concurred with the

376. Lutz (n. 28).
377. Shu-Chien Chen, 'Tax Avoidance in the Sales Factor: Comparison between the CCCTB and USAAs Formulary Apportionment Taxation' (2017) 3 Indian Journal of Tax Law.

outburst of income taxation itself. To date, all the US states that levy taxes on corporate income apply formulary apportionment to determine the tax liabilities of companies.[378]

The formulary apportionment regimes of the states have been diverse since they were designed for unilateral applications, for which the coordination of these regimes has been a vital subject. The discrete state applications of formulary apportionment have roots in the US political system, with particular respect to the fact that the states have wide autonomy on tax matters while the federal government's role is relatively marginal. The US Constitution and court decisions generally did not contribute to the consistency of state formulary apportionment systems. However, various efforts have been made towards nationwide uniformity. First of all, the National Tax Association, a non-government tax organization, called upon all states in 1922 to use a common formula but hardly saw positive reactions.[379] In 1957, the Uniform Law Commission issued a model law called the Uniform Division of Income for Tax Purposes Act (UDITPA) for the allocation of income among the states.[380] The UDITPA has made significant contributions to the convergence of the state formulary apportionment regulations, even though substantial divergences still exist. In 1967, the Multistate Tax Compact was agreed upon by the states to facilitate the equitable apportionment of tax bases and promote uniformity or compatibility of state tax systems.[381] The Compact also established the inter-governmental Multistate Tax Commission, comprising members from each participating state as a forum of cooperation and management agency. While playing advisory roles, the Multistate Tax Compact and the Commission have become the most important instrument or forum for the coordination of the state formulary apportionment regimes. As of 2020, fifteen states and the District of Columbia act as members of the Compact, and in total, forty-nine states participate in the Commission in various capacities.

The last facet to be outlined is the active role of judicial decisions in the development of US states' formulary apportionment regimes. Here, a table is provided to present how the landmark cases have shaped the trajectory from various aspects. It is noted that the judicial contributions were catalysed by the disputes revolving around the constitutional limitations on state taxation provided by the Due Process Clause and the Commerce Clause of the Constitution. The Due Process Clause[382] interpreted in the tax context is similar to the nexus rule of international taxation that prevents extraterritorial taxation without a minimum connection between the taxing state and the taxable income, property, persons or transactions.[383] The Commerce Clause[384] has been interpreted as granting Congress the prerogative to legislate in the area of foreign

378. Currently there are only six states do not levy corporate income taxes, *see* John C Healy, Michael S Schadewald and Bruce M Nelson, *Multistate Corporate Tax Guide*, vol. 1 (Wolters Kluwer 2024) 3., also in Hellerstein and Hellerstein (n .30) para. 8.11.
379. Mayer (n. 265) 68-69.
380. Joe Huddleston and Shirley Sicilian, 'The Project to Revise UDITPA' 2 https://www.mtc.gov/uploadedFiles/Multistate_Tax_Commission/Uniformity/Minutes/The%20Project%20to%20Revise%20UDITPA.pdf accessed 28 November 2021.
381. Multistate Tax Compact Art. 1.
382. It reads in the 14th Amendment to United States Constitution 1787 that 'No State shall ... deprive any person of life, liberty, or property without due process of law ...'.
383. *Miller Bros. Co. v. Maryland*, 347 US 340, 345, 74 S.Ct. 535 (1954).

or interstate commerce, while the states are prohibited from intervening in these fields. Specific to the tax context, the prerogative of Congress under the Commerce Clause has been 'dormant', for which courts are authorized to prevent the states from imposing an inappropriate burden on interstate commerce.

*Table 3.1 Landmark US Cases of FA*

| *Landmark Cases* | *Major Contributions* |
|---|---|
| State Railroad Tax Cases (1875); *Adams Express Company v. Ohio*, 165 US 194 (1897). | Developed the 'unit rule' for apportioning the property values of transportation and communication industries as the earliest multistate business forms. |
| *Butler Bros. v. McColgan*, 315 US 501 (1942). | The application of separate accounting and the results thereby provided do not impeach the validity or appropriateness of formulary apportionment. The court decision is also known for establishing for the first time the test of unity for applying the unitary business principle.[385] |
| *Moorman Mfg. Co. v. Bair*, 437 US 267 (1978).[386] | Upheld the constitutionality of the single sales factor formula, and thus unveiled the decline of equally-weighted three-factor state formulas. |
| *Mobil Oil Corp. v. Commissioner of Taxes*, 445 US 425, 439, 100 S.Ct. 1223 (1980) | Confirmed the 'unitary business principle' as the linchpin of using formulary apportionment in the field of income taxation. |
| *Container Corp v. Franchise Tax Board*, 463 US 159 (1983); *Barclays Bank International Ltd v. Franchise Tax Board of California* (1994) 129 L. Ed. 2d 244; *Colgate-Palmolive Co v. Franchise Tax Board of California* (1994) 114 S. Ct. 2268 | Upheld the constitutional validity of worldwide combined reporting. |

384. Article 1, s. 8[3] of United States Constitution reads as 'Congress shall have Power … To regulate Commerce with foreign nations, and among the several States …'.
385. Daniel Sandler, 'Slicing the Shadow–The Continuing Debate Over Unitary Taxation and Worldwide Combined Reporting' [1994] British Tax Review 574.
386. Walter Hellerstein and Charles E McLure, 'Lost in Translation: Contextual Considerations in Evaluating the Relevance of US Experience for the European Commission's Company Taxation Proposals' (2004) 58 Bulletin for International Fiscal Documentation 86, 96.

### 3.3.1.2 Canada

Canada is another example with a long history of using formulary apportionment in the area of corporate taxation. Similar to the United States, Canada also maintains a federal political system where provinces have ample autonomy for local affairs. In comparison to the US state systems, the Canadian formulary apportionment regimes have provided a contrasting image of a higher level of uniformity of provincial regimes and coordination between provinces and the federal government.

In Canada, both the provinces and the federal government tax corporate income, both of which can be traced back to the early 1900s.[387] The uncoordinated dual corporate tax systems coexisted till WWII, when the War Time Agreements ceded the provincial corporate income taxes to the federal government.

The coordination of the two-level corporate income tax systems was embarked on immediately after the war by means of two sets of federal-provincial tax arrangements. In the period from 1947 to 1962, the provincial and federal governments agreed on a model income tax act and the Tax Rental Agreements (TRA). The basic approach was that the compulsory provincial corporate income taxes were administered by the federal government, and the provinces received a per capita transfer payment in return. The inter-provincial allocation of taxable profits was achieved by introducing the equal-weighted two-factor formulary apportionment, but separate accounting was still allowed as an alternative, even though rarely used by provinces. From 1962 onwards, the new Tax Collection Agreements between the provincial and federal governments superseded the TRA, according to which the agreeing provinces would adopt the federal tax base and the federal formula.[388] The policies of the non-acceding provinces of Alberta and Québec also converge with the federal approach.[389] However, the provinces also had substantial autonomy in that they could decide the rate structure and post-allocation tax credits.[390]

Consequently, the Canadian provincial formulary apportionment regimes have accomplished a fair degree of consistency and uniformity. This resulted from multiple factors, such as the clear leadership of the federal government and the small number of provinces deviating from the federal-provincial agreements. In addition to these factors, the Canadian system is further stabilized by a mechanism of equalization payment, which was first introduced in 1957.[391] The equalization mechanism interacts

387. The first corporate income taxation was introduced by Prince Edward Island in 1894, the British Columbia was the first province did so in 1901, while the federal government introduced it in 1916. *See* Moore Albert Milton, Perry J Harvey and Beach Donald I, 'The Financing of Canadian Federation: The First Hundred Years' [1966] Canadian Tax Foundation.

388. Weiner, *Formulary Apportionment and Group Taxation in the European Union* (n. 28) 15.

389. Smart Michael and Vaillancourt Francois, *Formulary Apportionment in Canada and Taxation of Corporate Income in 2019: Current Practice, Origins and Evaluation, in The Allocation of Multinational Business Income: Reassessing the Formulary Apportionment Option* (Kluwer Law International 2009).

390. Ernest H Smith, *Federal-Provincial Tax Sharing and Centralized Tax Collection in Canada* (Canadian Tax Foundation Publications 1998) 378.

391. Ernest H Smith, 'Allocating to Provinces the Taxable Income of Corporations: How the Federal-Provincial Allocation Rules Evolved' (1976) 24 Canadian Tax Journal 545, 559.

closely with the operation of formulary apportionment, where the federal government will make an equalization transfer to the province whose fiscal capacity is below a target level. The payment will flatten the curve of discrepancies with respect to the allocation of the tax base as a result of the operation of the formulary apportionment.[392]

### *3.3.1.3 The EU CCCTB Proposal*

As a political and economic organization consisting of twenty-seven sovereign Member States, the European Union has been the most persistent explorer and upholder of the transnational formulary apportionment system. The CCCTB proposal was the product of the EU's work through nearly two decades on the reform of European business taxation. Although eventually withdrawn due to political and technical issues (as detailed below), the CCCTB proposal, with a journey extending over a decade, can still offer valuable insights into the design and implementation of FA.

The CCCTB was first published in 2011 by the European Commission;[393] it is a proposal harmonizing, consolidating and apportioning the income of corporate groups within the EU. With no visible progress achieved after its publication, the EU 'relaunched' and recalibrated the CCCTB proposal in 2016. Since then, the focus of EU tax policy making has revolved around the implementation of the BEPS Actions, while the CCCTB proposal has stalled once more.

Ultimately, amid global consensus and implementation of the Two Pillar Solution, the EU officially withdrew the CCCTB in 2023 and turned to the 'Business in Europe: Framework for Income Taxation' (BEFIT) proposal.[394] The withdrawal of the CCCTB proposal was influenced by three key issues.[395] First, there was an ongoing debate over whether the scope of the proposal should be broadened. Second, questions arose regarding the handling of the Allowance for Growth and Investment, as well as the super-deduction for R&D. Lastly, the approach to addressing anti-avoidance provisions remained unresolved.

While a thorough (comparative) analysis of the BEFIT proposal is out of the scope of this thesis, the withdrawal of the CCCTB does not mean that it is completely abandoned, nor does it allude to that FA sees no future in Europe. Therefore, this chapter still uses CCCTB as the object of the study. This may be understood from three perspectives.

First, the BEFIT, just as the CCCTB, serves the generally common goals of tax base harmonization and reduction of compliance costs in the EU, which are the crucial drivers of both reform plans.

---

392. Michael and Francois (n. 389) 97.
393. European Commission, 'Proposal for a Council Directive on a Common Consolidated Corporate Tax Base (CCCTB)' (2011) COM(2011) 121 final https://eur-lex.europa.eu/legal-content/EN/TXT/?uri=CELEX%3A52011PC0121&qid=1701759982858 accessed 5 December 2023 hereinafter 'CCCTB 2011'.
394. *See* relevant information at https://taxation-customs.ec.europa.eu/taxation/business-taxation/business-europe-framework-income-taxation-befit_en accessed 26 August 2024.
395. *See* https://www.europarl.europa.eu/legislative-train/package-action-plan-on-corporate-taxation/file-common-consolidated-corporate-tax-base-(ccctb) accessed 26 August 2024.

Second, though replacing the CCCTB, the BEFIT draws heavily from the ideas behind and within the CCCTB, which in turn, are also echoed in the Two Pillar Solution. The BEFIT aims to build on the agreement reached at the OECD/Inclusive Framework level of international corporate tax reform. The key concepts of FA and a common tax base, which were central to CCCTB, are already present in the OECD agreement. In addition, the BEFIT improves the CCCTB by enhancing tax certainty and reducing compliance cost. As such, the connections between the BEFIT and CCCTB are solid, and the international tax environment catalysed the BEFIT.

Third, in terms of allocation approach, the BEFIT does not rule out the application of FA. The BEFIT proposal introduces a transitional allocation rule to be used for the first seven years.[396] During this period, the aggregated tax base of a BEFIT group is allocated to each member based on their average taxable results over the previous three fiscal years. After this period, the European Commission may propose a permanent formulary apportionment method, likely considering factors such as sales, assets, and labour to distribute the tax base.[397] This means that the design of FA factors and apportionment will soon become the central issue for the BEFIT as well.

Therefore, the merits of the CCCTB in terms of the design of the FA may still be worth researching.

The CCCTB proposal was originally put forward within the general framework of constructing the EU 'single market' or 'internal market'.[398] The proposal serves to further two general objectives of stimulating investment and growth, and improving the fairness of corporation income taxation.[399] Specifically, the CCCTB proposal was designed to remove tax obstacles and distortions in the internal market, ameliorate both over-taxation and double taxation and reduce the compliance burden and administrative cost of corporate taxation within the EU. The CCCTB proposal apparently has endogenous driving forces in the unique context of the EU, in which integration and harmonization of EU corporate tax policies are catalysing the reforms for the most part. In comparison to the more 'modern' debate about formulary apportionment, the proposal has put less weight on the comparative advantages of formulary apportionment over separate accounting/ALP.[400]

In the EU's path towards the CCCTB, *before its final withdrawal*, the trajectory of formulary apportionment is marked by three prominent events.[401] The first is the

---

396. Article 45, Proposal for a Council Directive on Business in Europe: Framework for Income Taxation (BEFIT), COM (2023) 532 final (12 September 2023).
397. *See* https://ec.europa.eu/commission/presscorner/detail/en/qanda_23_4407 accessed 26 August 2024.
398. Erika Siu et al., *Unitary Taxation in Federal and Regional Integrated Markets* (ICTD 2014) 21.
399. European Commission, 'Proposals for a Council Directive on a Common Corporate Tax Base and a Common Consolidated Corporate Tax Base (CCCTB) (SWD(2016) 341 Final)' (2016) 23 https://eur-lex.europa.eu/LexUriServ/LexUriServ.do?uri=SWD:2016:0341:FIN:EN:PDF accessed 5 December 2023.
400. Only the 2011 proposal had made few references to them, European Commission, 'CCCTB 2011' (n. 393) 4.
401. As identified Joann M Weiner, *The Dream Is Alive: EU Tax Policy with a Common Consolidated Corporate Tax Base and Formulary Apportionment, in The Allocation of Multinational Business Income: Reassessing the Formulary Apportionment Option* (Kluwer Law International 2020) 105.

Ruding Report published in 1992, which is a study under the mandate of the European Community to examine company taxation within the EU.[402] The Report examined the distortionary effect of uncoordinated corporation tax policies of EU countries on investment and competition. Besides recommending a series of specific reform measures, the Report agreed that a common corporate tax system across the EU was a long-term objective but dismissed a full harmonization of the EU tax system at that stage. The Ruding Report discussed the formulary apportionment regimes used in Canada, the US, and Switzerland and concluded that there was 'no case' for it to be introduced in the foreseeable future. In the context of international tax planning, formulary apportionment was rejected on the grounds (myths) familiar to the critics, such as that it requires the renegotiation of double tax treaties and a higher degree of integration in legal and accounting standards and involves practical problems of transitioning from the existing arm's length practice.[403] In the context of tax harmonization, however, the three formulary apportionment regimes were presented as successful examples of cross-jurisdictional tax harmonization and tax base allocation.[404]

The second landmark is the study of 'Company Taxation in the Internal Market' conducted in 1999 and published in 2001 by the European Commission.[405] In a nutshell, the study featured the fervent approval for the common consolidated EU corporate tax base and the unprecedented approbation in the history of the EU for the formulary apportionment over the arm's length approach as the allocation method. Considering the predominant scepticism of formulary apportionment at that time, the Commission was discreet when repudiating the hybrid use of separate accounting for the allocation of the consolidated tax base.[406] The Communication[407] advocating the idea of a consolidated tax base and an allocation mechanism drawing on the study was later adopted by the European Parliament in a resolution in 2002.[408]

402. European Commission, *Report of the Committee of Independent Experts on Company Taxation* (Publications Office 1992) hereinafter 'Ruding Report'.
403. *Ibid.*, 130.
404. *Ibid.*, 188.
405. Commission of the European Communities, 'Company Taxation in the Internal Market (SEC(2001)1681 Final)' (2001) 23 https://taxation-customs.ec.europa.eu/system/files/2016-09/company_tax_study_en.pdf accessed 5 December 2023.
406. *Ibid.*, 407-408.
407. European Commission, 'Communication from the Commission to the Council, the European Parliament and the Economic and Social Committee: Towards an Internal Market Without Tax Obstacles: A Strategy for Providing Companies with a Consolidated Corporate Tax Base for Their EU-Wide Activities (COM(2001) 582 Final)' https://eur-lex.europa.eu/legal-content/EN/ALL/?uri=CELEX:52001DC0582 accessed 5 December 2023.
408. European Parliament, 'Report on the Commission Communication to the Council, the European Parliament and the Economic and Social Committee on Tax Policy in the European Union: Priorities for the Years Ahead (com(2001) 260 - C5-0597/2001 - 2001/2248(cos))' (2002) https://www.europarl.europa.eu/doceo/document/A-5-2002-0048_EN.html?redirect accessed 5 December 2023.

The EU embarked on a formal process of developing the CCCTB proposal after the setting up of the CCCTB Working Group in 2004.[409] The Group had met intensively and worked closely with Member States and tax experts till 2008. It is palpable that the focus of the Group had been on the apportionment mechanism to share the consolidated tax base, including the choice and delineation of factors in the formula. The full proposal of the apportionment mechanism was first presented by the Commission in 2007, which established the keynote of the current CCCTB proposal. In short, the Commission preferred: (1) micro-based formulary apportionment over macro-based or the value-added approach; (2) a multiple-factor formula over a single-factor formula; (3) the factors able to capture the value creation at both the demand side and supply side, preliminarily including property, payroll and sales; (4) the uniform formula across the whole EU Member States that prohibits domestic variations; (5) an all-inclusive consolidation of taxable income without the distinction of business or non-business income; (6) the attribution of incomes to member entities of the corporate group over the direct apportionment to the taxing jurisdictions.[410]

The 'last' episode is the official release of the CCCTB proposal in 2011 after nearly a decade of deliberations. The proposal formally adopted the equal-weighted three-factor formulary apportionment mechanism based on tax base consolidation to tax the multinational corporation groups within the EU. The European Parliament approved the proposal by vote in 2012 and suggested some amendments.[411] However, the European Council has not taken legislative action due to scepticism and objections from both Member State governments and business groups.[412] In 2016, the Commission revised the proposal, switching to a phase-in approach that first adopts the common tax base and then the full consolidation with formulary apportionment, namely, from CCTB (Common Corporate Tax Base)[413] to CCCTB.[414] In 2018, the EU launched a reform project targeting the tax challenges of the digital economy, which

---

409. 'Common Consolidated Corporate Tax Base Working Group (CCCTB WG), Draft Terms of Reference & Rules of Procedure' CCTB/WP\002\doc\en https://taxation-customs.ec.europa.eu/system/files/2016-09/cctbtorfinal_en.pdf accessed 6 December 2023.
410. 'European Commission, Common Consolidated Corporate Tax Base Working Group (CCCTB WG) CCCTB: possible elements of the sharing mechanism' CCCTB/WP057\doc\en 5-7 https://taxation-customs.ec.europa.eu/system/files/2016-09/ccctbwp057_en.pdf accessed 6 December 2023.
411. European Parliament, 'Report on the Proposal for a Council Directive on a Common Consolidated Corporate Tax Base (CCCTB)' (2011) COM(2011) 121 Final C7-0092/2011 – 2011/0058(CNS) A7-0080/2012 https://www.europarl.europa.eu/doceo/document/A-7-2012-0080_EN.pdf accessed 5 December 2023.
412. Daniela Pîrvu, 'Impact Assessment of the Common Consolidated Corporate Tax Base' in Daniela Pîrvu (ed.), *Corporate Income Tax Harmonization in the European Union* (Palgrave Macmillan UK 2012) 150, https://doi.org/10.1057/9781137000910_8 accessed 24 September 2025; Arjo van Eijsden, 'The One-Stop-Shop Approach: A Discussion of the Administrative and Procedural Aspects of the CCCTB Draft Directive' (2011) 20 EC Tax Review 217 https://doi.org/10.54648/ecta2011026 accessed 26 August 2025; Huelya Celebi, 'The CCCTB as a Proposed Solution to the Corporate Income Taxation Dilemma within the EU' (2013) 22 EC Tax Review 289 https://doi.org/10.54648/ecta2013032 accessed 26 August 2025.
413. European Commission, 'Proposal for a Council Directive on a Common Corporate Tax Base' (2016) COM(2016) 685 final 2016/0337(CNS) https://eur-lex.europa.eu/legal-content/EN/TXT/?uri=CELEX%3A52016PC0685 accessed 5 December 2023 hereinafter 'CCCTB Proposal of Tax Base'.

included an interim digital service tax and a long-term significant digital presence. The Commission envisaged the project to be incorporated into the comprehensive CCCTB proposal. In the same vote of the EU Parliament, the CCCTB proposal and the digital tax project were backed collectively.[415]

### *3.3.1.4 The Pillar One Amount A*

The TPS is acknowledged as the hallmark of the era of BEPS 2.0 or as the product of the 'great compromise' of international taxation in modern times.[416] It is no exaggeration in any sense that the TPS is the most significant reform of the international tax system, while its real impact is yet to be assessed. The TPS is essentially an extension of the BEPS Project, for which the key developments showing that connection are extracted as follows:

- **October 2015**: The Action 1 final report is released, the final outcome of BEPS 1.0 on the digital economy. Notably, the report does not give any recommendations on taxation of the digital economy that could be pursued for implementation, and is the only exception to all other Actions.
- **June 2016**: OECD and G20 member countries set up the Inclusive Framework, which aims to enable more countries, especially developing countries, to participate equally in the next phase of the BEPS Project.
- **January 2019**: The Inclusive Framework publishes a Policy Note on the tax challenges of economic digitization, presenting **for the first time** the idea of a TPS. Pillar One focuses on the issue of tax allocation and nexus, which involves a fundamental restructuring of the international tax system; Pillar II focuses on the issue of low-tax entities and low-tax jurisdictions.
- **May 2019**: Based on the draft released in March 2019, the OECD released the Programme of Work to Develop a Consensus Solution to the Tax Challenges Arising from the Digitalization of the Economy, which further refines the TPS conception. Pillar II does not differ significantly from the final proposal, but Pillar One discusses a total of three approaches on how to allocate tax rights to marketplaces, while two alternatives are also proposed for the new nexus rules.
- **November-December 2019**: The drafts of Pillar One 'Unified Approach' and Pillar II GLOBE are released. Pillar One consists of Amount A, Amount B and

414. European Commission, 'Proposal for a Council Directive on a Common Corporate Tax Base (CCCTB)' (2016) (COM(2016) 683 final) (2016/0336(CNS)) https://eur-lex.europa.eu/legal-content/EN/TXT/?uri=CELEX%3A52016PC0683&qid=1701768577832 accessed 5 December 2023 hereinafter, 'CCCTB Proposal of Consolidation'.
415. European Parliament, 'MEPS Approve New EU Corporate Tax Plan Which Embraces Digital Presence' (2018) https://www.europarl.europa.eu/news/en/press-room/20180309IPR99422/meps-approve-new-eu-corporate-tax-plan-which-embraces-digital-presence accessed 5 December 2023.
416. Maarten Floris De Wilde, 'Towards a "2020s Compromise" in International Business Taxation; Reflections on an Emerging New Tax Paradigm' (10 February 2022) https://papers.ssrn.com/abstract=4031417 accessed 16 September 2023.

Amount C. Pillar II includes the Income Inclusion Rule (IIR), the Switch-over Rule (SOR), the Subject-to-tax Rule (STTR) and the UTPR.

- **October 2020**: The draft of the Two-Pillar 'blueprints' and the economic impact assessment are released. Subsequent comments and discussions did not merge to form a formal 'blueprint', but the blueprint report is by far the most fully discussed document on the two pillars, although there are many differences in technical details from the current proposal on the ground.
- **July/October 2021**: Over 130 Inclusive Framework members agreed on key design elements for the two pillars in October 2021 ('2021 Agreements'). Thereafter, the two pillars entered the technical implementation phase. Most of the constituent rules of the two pillars have been released on a rolling basis. During this stage, the development of the rule-making of the pillars can be tracked in the Progress Reports of the OECD/G20 Inclusive Framework on BEPS published each year (with the latest in 2023).[417]
- **October 2023-August 2024**: In October 2023, the Inclusive Framework's Task Force on the Digital Economy approved the release of the Multilateral Convention to Implement Amount A of Pillar One, together with related materials. While the text of the Convention reflected the general consensus achieved among Inclusive Framework members, the real fruition of Amount A seems lacklustre as the formal signing of such convention is missing the deadline by the end of August 2024. Besides the Convention, most of the components of Amount A have been prepared to become law.

The above trajectory covers both Pillar One and Pillar Two. Within the ambit of considering FA, the Pillar One Amount A is the most relevant than the other Pillar or the components thereof. To be detailed in the following sections, the Amount A is a new tax liability for reallocating a portion of the residual profits of the largest and most profitable MNEs to market jurisdictions where they have substantial economic activities and consumer interactions, regardless of their physical presence in those jurisdictions.

The Amount A is in essence formulaic, for it uses sales revenue in both the numerator and denominator of the apportionment formula to allocate the amount calculated from the residual profits to each relevant market jurisdiction.

#### *3.3.1.5 Summary and Lessons*

In general, formulary apportionment as a means to tax corporations has been conventional in the United States and Canada, while the CCCTB proposal in the EU is a novel experiment in the new normal of the contemporary era.

To be specific, the development of the United States is expected to provide the most comprehensive and valuable experiences with respect to the design of formulary

417. 'OECD/G20 Inclusive Framework on BEPS: Progress Report September 2022-September 2023' https://web-archive.oecd.org/temp/2023-10-15/666424-oecd-g20-inclusive-framework-on-beps-progress-report-september-2022-september-2023.htm accessed 26 August 2025.

apportionment in international taxation. For one thing, in terms of political structure, while the US Constitution has mandated extensive authority to the federal government, the coordination and harmonization efforts made by the central government in the field of corporate tax have been limited, for which the inaction of Congress can largely be attributed to the states' resistance. For another, the status quo and the trajectory of the US states' formulary apportionment regimes are cumulatively shaped by the game among the states, the US Supreme Court, the federal government, and private businesses in respect of almost all essential elements. Even though considerable discrepancies exist, the circumstances in the international context resemble many of those of the United States for the purpose of considering formulary apportionment. For example, there is no global government for harmonizing and coordinating the worldwide tax policies either, where countries are engaging in both competition and cooperation; the US states and nation-states are both engaging in some voluntary scheme of coordination, such as the Multistate Tax Commission and the G20/OECD BEPS Project; formulary apportionment has been recognized as a conventional approach in the evolution of international taxation as well;[418] autonomy and sovereignty are also major but subtle factors in international tax policy making; and so forth.

Among the comprehensive experiences from the US, there is one aspect worth noting in comparison to the other two jurisdictions, that is, the unitary business principle. Unlike the Canadian provincial formulary apportionment regime that functions on the basis of separate companies and the EU CCCTB proposal that adopts the consolidation approach, the US states and the Supreme Court have developed a sophisticated unitary business principle as the theoretical foundation and practical guideline for the state formulary apportionment regimes. With its details to be unveiled in the ensuing discussions, the unitary business principle stems from the economic essence of the corporate group as an integrated unitary business, which has long been advocated as the theoretical basis of international corporate tax reform.

The US trajectory also shows a dynamic process of an evolving image of formulary apportionment. For example, the states have been recalibrating their formulary apportionment regimes with respect to the choice and weight of factors and the territorial scope. In contrast, the Canadian experience of formulary apportionment has been much more stable; this can be ascribed to the greater harmonization and the cooperation achieved through the province-central government tax agreement. In the case of the US, one needs to note that the state corporate income tax does not represent a significant portion of revenue, while in Canada, the equalization transfer has played an indispensable role in the operation of the provincial formulary apportionment regimes.

The EU CCCTB, though still a pending proposal, is unprecedented as it explores formulary apportionment for income allocation between sovereign states. The content and outcome of the CCCTB are thus strong precursors for the prospect of formulary apportionment for international taxation in the rest of the world beyond the EU, for which the concrete design of the various components may be emblematic of what to

418. *See* the Ch. 2 of historical analysis.

envisage as regards an international formulary apportionment regime. In addition, compared to the cases of the US and Canada, the EU CCCTB is also more contemporary and designed against the new realities of dominating MNEs, the digitalizing economy, and the aftermath of BEPS.

The TPS is the continuation of the BEPS Project. With the consensus reached in 2021 by the state members of the Inclusive Framework, the formulary apportionment regime is being actualized for the first time in the history of the international tax regime. However, the real significance and its degree of fulfilment with respect to formulary apportionment do not necessarily match its historical status.

### 3.3.2 Jurisdiction to Tax Rule

Formulary apportionment, albeit being a contrasting way of taxing the multi-jurisdictional business from the arm's length/separate accounting approach, still relies on the jurisdiction to tax rules for practical operation and theoretical justification.

At the theoretical level, there is significant leeway to construct the rules of jurisdiction to tax within formulary apportionment. On the one hand, formulary apportionment could employ the same framework of core concepts such as residence, source, and nexus. On the other hand, it could deviate from the pre-existing institutions and turn to construct its foundation with internally developed resources. Both approaches reflect the boundaries of contemporary conceptions of state sovereignty to varying degrees, which have different implications for personal jurisdiction and subject matter jurisdictions in international taxation. While taking the previous route is relatively smoother, it may compromise the marginal benefits brought by the transition from the 'old regime'. And redesigning the jurisdiction to tax rules for the formulary apportionment regimes may prove to be pivotal to its success, especially since it concerns the justification of the international tax system at the ground level. Accordingly, the issue of jurisdiction to tax under formulary apportionment requires careful consideration of what to achieve through the reform to formulary apportionment and what can be agreed upon in the process of transition.

At the practical level, jurisdiction to tax rules have served as the threshold for demarcating the state power to tax, and on the mirror side, for ascertaining to which and how many tax authorities the taxpayer is liable to pay tax. Without such a threshold, countries will be caught in chaotic scrambles for the pie of the international tax base, and the compliance burden will be unbearable since taxpayers will have to file for taxation in all the jurisdictions to which the international business has connections. These practical concerns apply to both the existing system and formulary apportionment.

#### *3.3.2.1 The United States*

##### *3.3.2.1.1 Residence, Source and Nexus*

The jurisdiction to tax rules under US state formulary apportionment systems stipulate the circumstances where multistate corporations are liable to pay the state corporate income taxes in the first place and where the state is allowed to demand a share in the combined/consolidated tax base.

Similar to the international taxation sphere, the US state taxing power is constructed upon two basic concepts: residence and source. A state may exert its tax jurisdiction over the taxpayer's income from whatever sources to the extent the taxpayer is domiciled in the state. For a corporation, the domicile is where it is incorporated. Residence, before the courts, has been recognized as a basis for taxation for the 'protection afforded to the recipient of the income by the state, in his person, on his right to receive the income, and in his enjoyment of it when received'.[419] Alternatively, for non-residents of the state, the only jurisdictional basis of state taxation is the concept of source, for which the state taxing power extends only to income having sources within the state. It is the source concept that sits at the centre of jurisdiction to tax rules over non-resident taxpayers.

In international tax literature, the concept of 'nexus' plays a large part in discussions of source taxation, which is used to delineate the threshold for taxing the income of non-residents. The existence of a permanent establishment has been used in tax treaties and national tax laws as the customary form of nexus. The US states do not replicate the PE threshold in the taxation of nondomiciled corporations; the state rules have been concurrently framed by the Constitution and jurisprudential interpretations.

#### *3.3.2.1.2 A Caveat: The Unitary Business in Itself Does Not Create Nexus*

As explained further in the next section, the constitutional linchpin of US state formulary apportionment regimes is the unitary business principle. Where separately incorporated companies form a unitary business, they will have to file a consolidated or combined tax return for the division of taxable income among states where the unitary business is conducted. Different from the consolidation that only includes taxable entities in the state, the application of the combined reporting has been viewed as having the effect of taxing the non-domiciled out-of-state group entities.[420] And there were also voices equating the economic presence of the unitary business in a state with the existence of a nexus therein.[421] However, in the context of the United States, as well as for general reference, it is clarified that unitary business does not create nexus, which is a caveat for contemplating the jurisdiction to tax rule in the design of the formulary apportionment regime.

First, the unitary business principle is the theoretical underpinning of formulary apportionment as a global alternative to sharing the income of MNEs among multiple jurisdictions, while nexus is the jurisdictional principle justifying the taxation of non-resident taxpayers in the first place. There is some conceptual ordering, and

419. *Lawrence v. State Tax Comm'n*, 286 US 276, 281, 52 S. Ct. 556 (1932).
420. Larry R Garrison, 'Toward a Consensus on Apportionable v. Allocable Income' (1975) 28 Tax Executive 41, 45; State Taxation of Interstate Commerce: Hearings Before the Subcomm. on State Taxation of Interstate Commerce of the Senate Comm. On Finance, 93d Cong., 1st Sess. 237 (1973) (testimony of C.R. Cahoon).
421. Michael J McIntyre, 'Designing a Combined Reporting Regime for a State Corporate Income Tax: A Case Study of Louisiana' 61 Louisiana Law Review 699-742, 717.

notably, a distinction between the two subjects. A state cannot consider demanding a share of the taxable income before confirming that it can subject the taxpayer or the income to its jurisdiction to tax. Determining the apportionable income by combining the income of unitary business members is not equivalent to directly taxing the non-domiciled members without a nexus to the state.

Second, as a matter of judicial principle, the jurisdiction over a subsidiary company does not create the same jurisdiction over its parent company, and *vice versa*.[422] The same reasoning applies to the jurisdiction to tax. It has been confirmed by the courts that the presence of a subsidiary in the state does not ordinarily create tax nexus over the non-domiciled parent, nor does so when the parent is within the state while the subsidiary is outside, even if in both cases, the parent and subsidiary constitute a unitary business.[423]

Third, the distinct inquiries of determining the existence of a unitary business and the nexus to tax do not preclude that they may share some common factors. For example, the business activities arranged within a company group may establish substantial economic nexus with a state that justifies the state's jurisdiction to tax both the in-state parent and the out-of-state subsidiaries, and in the meantime, these activities fulfil the criteria of unitary business that may justify the combined reporting of the group's income and application of formulary apportionment.[424]

#### *3.3.2.1.3 Constitutional Parameters: The Due Process and Commerce Clauses*

Both the Due Process Clause and the Commerce Clause of the US Constitution have a say on the parameters of nexus for interstate taxation. The Due Process Clause focuses on the fundamental fairness of taxation, while the Commerce Clause concerns the effect of taxation on interstate commerce.[425] There had been some distinction made by the Supreme Court as regards interpreting the two clauses in addressing the nexus issue; this, however, has elapsed, and the Clauses ultimately concur on the instruction of nexus.

First, rather than providing some bright-line test, which is often left to the role of states, the court had delineated the criteria of nexus in a series of decisions by focusing on the relationship between the business and the state. To exert taxing power, the state should bear 'fiscal relation to protection, opportunities and benefits given by the

422. Restatement (Second) of Conflict of Laws § 52, cmt. b, at 180-181 (1971).
423. *Comptroller of Treasury v. Gore Enter. Holdings, Inc.* (together with *Comptroller of Treasury v. Future Value, Inc.*), 437 Md. 492, 87 A3d 1263 (2014); Hellerstein and Hellerstein (n. 29) s. 6.14.
424. As happened in the case *Comptroller of Treasury v. Gore Enter. Holdings, Inc.*, *see* relevant analysis in *ibid.*, 6.14[1].
425. Shirley Sicilian and Joe Huddleston, 'The US States' Experience with Formulary Apportionment' in Krever Richard and Vaillancourt François (eds), *The Allocation of Multinational Business Income: Reassessing the Formulary Apportionment Option* (Kluwer Law International 2020) 59.

state',[426] it should have 'certain minimum contacts',[427] 'some definite link, some minimum connection'[428] with the business.

Second, different from the PE threshold of international taxation that mostly emphasizes the physical presence of a non-resident taxpayer for the purpose of corporate income tax, the Supreme Court had decided that physical presence is not necessary for taxing nondomiciled taxpayers. In the seminal case *Quill v. North Dakota*, the Court ruled revolving around the Due Process Clause that an out-of-state taxpayer's 'purposeful availment' of the benefits of the economic market of a state should suffice for being subjected to the state jurisdiction to tax without regard to its physical presence.[429] In the more recent case, *South Dakota v. Wayfair*, the physical presence requirement of nexus within the ambit of applying the Commerce Clause was removed unequivocally.[430] It was ruled that the nexus was fulfilled by 'carrying on business' regardless of the specific forms of the economic connections.[431]

#### *3.3.2.1.4 The State Statutes, the Multistate Tax Commission's Factor Presence Test, and the Public Law 86-272*

While the courts have delineated the constitutional requirements of nexus for state taxation, the states are accordingly in the position to provide enforceable standards to concretize the descriptive concepts such as 'minimum contacts', 'purposeful availment of benefits', and 'carrying on business'. The general case is that most states in their statutes do not require the existence of physical presence and instead adopt the facts and circumstances approach to defining the constituents of 'economic nexus', including but not limited to maintaining an office, using capital, owning or leasing property, hiring employees, and any other activities soliciting profits in the state.[432]

Such provisions of nexus in the state statutes are flexible, yet they may be subjective and create uncertainties. In view of this, the Multistate Tax Commission adopted in 2002 the proposal of 'factor presence nexus standard' as a bright-line test using the in-state values of the traditional apportionment factors, property, payroll, or sales as the *de minimis* threshold to establish the existence of nexus.[433] The factors used in the factor presence test follow the same definitions and sourcing rules as for the

426. *Wisconsin v. J.C. Penney*, 311 US 435, 444 (1940).
427. *Int'l Shoe Co. v. State of Wash.*, Office of Unemployment Comp. & Placement, 326 US 310, 316 (1945) (quoting *Milliken v. Meyer*, 311 US 457, 463 (1940)).
428. *Miller Brothers Co. v. Maryland*, 347 US 340, 344 -45 (1954).
429. *Quill Corp. v. North Dakota*, 504 US 298, 307 (1992).
430. *South Dakota v. Wayfair, Inc.*, 138 S. Ct. 2080, 2099 (2018).
431. Hellerstein and Hellerstein (n. 29) s. 19.02[2][c].
432. *Ibid.*, 6.16[2].
433. 'B. (1) Substantial nexus is established if any of the following thresholds is exceeded during the tax period: (a) a dollar amount of $50,000 of property; or (b) a dollar amount of $50,000 of payroll; or (c) a dollar amount of $500,000 of sales; or (d) twenty-five percent of total property, total payroll or total sales. ', Multistate Tax Commission, 'Factor Presence Nexus Standard for Business Activity Taxes' https://www.mtc.gov/wp-content/uploads/2022/12/Factor-Presence.pdf accessed 6 December 2023.

apportionment formula itself.[434] Property and payroll factors may still be weighed in consideration of the factor presence nexus even though the state used the sales-only formula. To date, roughly ten states have adopted the factor presence test to varying extents.[435] The constitutionality of the factor presence test has not been challenged before the US Supreme Court, which was nevertheless upheld in 2016 by the Ohio Supreme Court for the purpose of Ohio's commercial activity tax.[436]

At the federal government level, Public Law 86-272[437] enacted in 1959, was recognized as the most important congressional legislation in constraining the state taxing power over interstate business.[438] The Law provides immunity from state taxation to nondomiciled corporations for their solicitation of orders for sales of tangible personal property to be sent or delivered from outside the state.[439] Therefore, the main effect of the law is that it has protected mail-order businesses that frequently cross the lines. It is conceivable that the interpretation of 'solicitation of orders' often aroused disputes in the states and before the courts,[440] and so did whether the protection of remote sales still fits the new normal of the digital economy.[441] In light of the situation, the Multistate Tax Commission has targeted the vulnerability and stepped in since 1986, providing guidelines on the scope of solicitation of order as to what activities constitute 'protected activities' that do not create nexus and those 'unprotected activities' that do so.[442] In November 2020, the fourth revision of the guideline was finalized and ready to be formally approved.[443]

---

434. *Ibid.*, C(4).
435. Sicilian and Huddleston (n. 425) 60.
436. Bannasch Michael, 'Factor Presence Nexus: A Growing Trend in State Taxation' https://www.journalofaccountancy.com/issues/2017/jul/state-taxation-presence-nexus.html accessed 5 December 2023.
437. Codified as 15 USC §§381-384.
438. Hellerstein and Hellerstein (n. 29) s. 6.17.
439. '(a) No State, or political subdivision thereof, shall have power to impose, for any taxable year ending after the date of the enactment of this Act, a net income tax on the income derived within such State by any person from interstate commerce if the only business activities within such State by or on behalf of such person during such taxable year are either, or both, of the following:

    (1) the solicitation of orders by such person, or his representative, in such State for sales of tangible personal property, which orders are sent outside the State for approval or rejection, and, if approved, are filled by shipment or delivery from a point outside the State; and
    (2) the solicitation of orders by such person, or his representative, in such State in the name of or for the benefit of a prospective customer of such person, if orders by such customer to such person to enable such customer to fill orders resulting from such solicitation are orders described in paragraph (1). Pub. L. No. 86-272, 73 Stat. 555 (1959).'

440. Healy, Schadewald and Nelson (n. 378) 48-50; *ibid.*, 6.18-9.
441. Christopher T Lutz, 'What to Do with Public Law 86-272' [2019] Tax Notes State 781, 782.
442. Multistate Tax Commission, 'Statement of Information Concerning Practices of Multistate Tax Commission and Signatory States Under Public Law 86-272' https://www.mtc.gov/wp-content/uploads/2023/02/StatementofInfoPublicLaw86-272.pdf accessed 26 August 2025.
443. 'P.L. 86-272 Statement of Information Project' https://www.mtc.gov/uniformity/pl-86-272-statement-of-information-project/ accessed 6 December 2023.

#### 3.3.2.2 *Canada's PE Nexus*

Canada uses the traditional permanent establishment standard for the nexus rule. A company is taxable in a province only if it has a local permanent establishment. All the provinces use this common nexus standard, and the definition and scope of the permanent establishment generally follow those in international taxation.[444] As discussed in the following section of the taxable unit, the Canadian provincial formulary apportionment regimes apply to individual corporations without consolidation or combination. When a corporation is carrying on business in more than one province through branches or some other forms of permanent establishments, it will be subjected to the tax jurisdictions of multiple provinces. As a result, its income will be shared among these provinces according to a common formula.

#### 3.3.2.3 *The EU CCCTB Proposal*[445]

As one of the two 'international' applications of formulary apportionment for the comparative analysis, the EU CCCTB proposal seemed to avoid a drastic transition from the existing institutions of international taxation. With respect to nexus rules, the CCCTB proposed to use the same foundational concepts of residence and permanent establishment to construct the jurisdiction to tax rules.[446] Since formulary apportionment in the CCCTB is applied on a consolidation basis, the nexus issue should be addressed from a holistic perspective.

The CCCTB Proposal did not explicitly prescribe what jurisdiction to tax rules are adopted, which was achieved through demarcating the scope of the CCCTB rules. First of all, the CCCTB Proposal provided a dual-structure concept of residence as a pillar of the personal scope of CCCTB. For one thing, it is provided that the CCCTB proposal applies to companies 'established' in the EU, that is, companies that are residents in any of the EU Member States. This refers to the scope of the whole set of rules, mainly to delimit the boundaries of the CCCTB program. Using the term 'established' avoids the questionable intrusion into the Member State's tax authority of the liability to company tax.[447] For another, the definition of tax residence was further provided, adopting the incorporation and effective management standard from international

444. *See* Joann Martens Weiner, *Company Tax Reform in the European Union: Guidance from the United States and Canada on Implementing Formulary Apportionment in the EU* (Springer Science & Business Media 2006) 69.
445. The part was written around 2021, therefore was not able to take into account the latest development of business income taxation reforms with EU, such as the BEFIT proposal, which is going to be studied as a following research of this thesis. For more information of the latest status, *see* https://taxation-customs.ec.europa.eu/taxation-1/corporate-taxation/business-europe-framework-income-taxation-befit_en accessed 26 August 2025 for reference.
446. European Commission, 'CCCTB Proposal of Consolidation' (n. 413) Art. 14.
447. Krister Andersson, 'Comments on document CCCTB\WP\040 Common Consolidated Corporate Tax Base Working Group: Personal Scope of the CCCTB' 2 https://taxation-customs.ec.europa.eu/system/files/2016-09/unicecomments_personal_scope.pdf accessed 26 August 2025.

taxation, which, throughout the provisions, may principally serve to exclude companies that are not resident from the CCCTB as well as for administration purposes.[448]

The dual-structure connotation of residence delineated an identity of 'EU resident' for the water's edge operation of CCCTB. In addition, a permanent establishment located in the EU was recognized as quasi-resident status in the CCCTB Proposal. For a permanent establishment owned by a non-EU third-country corporation, the inclusion in the CCCTB was premised on the fact that there exists a consolidated group. Otherwise, the non-resident will not be subjected to the CCCTB.[449] This relates to the territorial scope of formulary apportionment, which is an issue intersecting with the jurisdiction to tax as well as the taxable unit subjects.

Taking into account the discussions of the delineation of taxable unit in the following section, the choice of nexus rules in the CCCTB seemed to echo the US constitutional restraints on the state jurisdiction to tax in the regime of consolidated reporting. The US states are constitutionally directed *not* to include corporations without nexus to the state, should they elect to use consolidated reporting instead of unitary combined reporting to tax the groups of companies.[450] Both the consolidation regimes in the EU and the US principally rely on legal control parameters to define the personal scope of the consolidation. However, the nexus rules in the CCCTB as a tentative program in the international sphere contrasted with the US state's approach to nexus that is essentially sub-national, especially in terms of the latter's wide employment of the factor present test for defining nexus. In this respect, one leg of the EU CCCTB stretched the horizon of international taxation by introducing consolidation and a common tax base, while the other leg still stayed in the old world represented by the nexus concepts of residence and permanent establishment.[451]

#### *3.3.2.4 The Pillar One Amount A*

For unveiling the normative meaning of the TPS for comparative analysis purposes, it has to be noted in the first place that the solution is, in nature, not a sweeping overhaul of the foundations of how MNEs are taxed, but rather an overlay upon the century-old system. All the analyses in this chapter should be understood under this caveat.

In consideration of the jurisdiction to tax rules, the 2021 Agreements decided that Pillar One will formally introduce and implement a new nexus rule narrowly applicable to Amount A, without implications for Amount B or Pillar Two. The new nexus functions to demarcate the in-scope of subjects of Amount A, including the taxpayer – the MNEs, and the taxing states – the market jurisdictions. Once the nexus threshold is

448. European Commission, 'CCCTB Proposal of Consolidation' (n. 413) Art. 6, Ch. IX.
449. *See* the discussions in the section of the territorial scope. The CCCTB applies to non-resident with PEs in the EU provided that they constitute a consolidated group.
450. Hellerstein and Hellerstein (n. 29) s. 8.11[1] and the accompanying note 1309.
451. Maarten De Wilde, 'Tax Competition Within the European Union-Is the CCCTB Directive a Solution' (2014) 7 Erasmus Law Review 24, 33 https://doi.org/10.5553/elr.000013 accessed 26 August 2025. Maarten Floris de Wilde, 'On the Future of Business Income Taxation in Europe' (2020) 12 World Tax Journal https://doi.org/10.59403/2t8y81e accessed 26 August 2025.

satisfied, the MNE will have to pay the local portion of Amount A to the market jurisdiction.

The nexus rule sits at the core of the modern international tax system in all ways. It can refer to the residency rules, source rules and the PE rules, etc. By early 2023, the new nexus should be understood on the basis of the draft model rules on nexus and revenue sourcing.[452]

The new nexus differs from current nexus rules in at least four aspects:

(1) The concept of 'market' being the place where the MNE derives sales revenue is explicitly introduced for the first time into the international tax norms. The existing nexus norm manifests to some extent the taxing right of 'market' jurisdiction as well, such as the withholding taxing right of interest payment states. The new nexus, however, was constructed with the direct purpose of engaging marketplaces in the justification of taxing right.
(2) The new nexus uses both qualitative and bright-line quantitative yardsticks, while the existing nexus rules principally rely on qualitative standards. The bright-line test of the new nexus extensively employs numeric values: the global turnover above EUR 20 billion, the profitability above 10%, the EUR 1 million revenue in market jurisdiction, and the GDP line of EUR 40 billion. Nevertheless, the new nexus also relies on qualitative standards as it still entails sourcing rules to determine the location where the sales revenue should be attributed to. The significance of the new nexus is not diminished as it openly announces that the nexus does not entail physical presence.
(3) Related to the last point, another breakthrough in the new nexus is the consideration of the wealth status of the taxing states, which is not seen in the existing international tax system. The new nexus draws a line of EUR 40 billion in GDP, and the nexus threshold will be lowered to EUR 250,000, vis-à-vis EUR 1 million for poorer countries being the place where the sales activities take place.
(4) The new nexus builds on the philosophy that value is created by supply-demand interplay. This immediately leads to the development of a series of so-called revenue-sourcing rules which basically purport to identify the location of the end-consumers/users.

### *3.3.2.5 Summary and Lessons*

The US approach to jurisdiction to tax rule for formulary apportionment can be encapsulated as follows: the constitutional Due Process Clause and Commerce Clause serve as the bottom line, the Supreme Court decisions interpreted and applied these Clauses to provide sketchy guidelines, and the states adopted the bright-line operable standards. Among all these contributions, three facets of insights can be drawn as

452. OECD, 'Pillar One: Amount A – Draft Model Rules for Nexus and Revenue Sourcing, 4 February 2022-18 February 2022' https://web-archive.oecd.org/2022-02-04/623615-public-consultation-document-pillar-one-amount-a-nexus-revenue-sourcing.pdf accessed 5 December 2023.

lessons for designing the jurisdiction to tax rules for international formulary apportionment. First, the nexus should be constructed by the economic connections between the state and the taxpayer. In all circumstances, it is the existence and substance of such connections that matter for establishing the jurisdiction to tax, rather than a specific form of physical presence. Second, the factor presence test is a desirable approach to materializing the nexus to tax. It is not only congruent with the overarching rationales but also convenient to administer as the factors are also recorded for apportionment purposes. Third, the jurisdiction to tax rule, it seems, should not impede the cross-border flow of trade, for which the various activities of remote sales should be examined and treated differentially.

The Canadian FA regime and the EU CCCTB proposal, though contrasting substantially, both adopt the nexus rules largely following the relevant conventions of international taxation. Permanent establishment and residence are the two pillars undergirding the jurisdiction to tax. Different from the case of the US and Canada,[453] the EU CCCTB's choice in this respect may reflect that the sovereign Member States agreed to stretch the conception of their taxing power, that is, they accept to share tax interests with other Member States but only subject to that all the states are where the group member resides, in the form of a corporation or permanent establishment; and permanent establishment, just as in international taxation, is given quasi-resident status even for a PE owned by foreign company. As stated above, while the nexus rules of the CCCTB may have accommodated the states' conception of sovereignty or the smoothness of transition, they also carry the long-argued criticism revolving around the reliance on residence for its artificiality and the permanent establishment for its incongruence with the modern economic reality to the new system, for which the major concerns are the misalignment of taxation and value creation and the risks of base erosion and profit shifting.[454]

The new nexus introduced by Amount A originates from the political agenda of addressing the remaining issues of taxing the digital economy under BEPS Action 1, which breaks the mantra that only physical presence can establish taxing right. The process of developing the new nexus seemingly compromises theoretical soundness for simplicity as the division between customer-facing activities and automated digital services.

While having to rely on multi-layered sourcing rules similar in many aspects to the current source rules, the new nexus is unprecedented as it forsakes the physical presence ideology and the tax residency rule. In addition, the nexus functions as part of Amount A, being, in essence, a sales-only factor formulary apportionment. The Amount A is, therefore, more revolutionary than the Canadian and EU-proposed versions of formulary apportionment regimes and closer to the United States parallels.

453. *See* the differentiation between apportioning income to states versus apportioning income to taxpayers made by Walter Hellerstein, 'Tax Planning under the CCCTB's Formulary Apportionment Provisions: The Good, the Bad and the Ugly' in Weber Dennis (ed.), CCCTB: Selected Issues (Kluwer Law International BV 2012) 223-236.
454. de Wilde, 'On the Future of Business Income Taxation in Europe' (n. 451) 101-103.

With that being said, the new nexus of Pillar One Amount A is a variant of the factor presence test employed by the American states, and the latter employs source rules as well. Nevertheless, in establishing taxing rights, the US factor presence test is not a special-purpose test as it does not aim at taxing a certain business sector but is a comprehensive system for taxing multi-state business.

### 3.3.3 The Territorial Scope of Formulary Apportionment

The territorial scope of formulary apportionment is one of the most pivotal aspects for designing a formulary apportionment system in the international arena as it sits between the theoretical foundation of formulary apportionment and the various realistic constraints. As discussed elsewhere in this thesis, formulary apportionment finds its justifications in the unitary business principle as developed in the US context and other interrelated principles such as substance over form and value creation. None of these rationales is directed at limiting the territorial scope of formulary apportionment, which, on the contrary, is opposed to setting up jurisdictional boundaries for applying formulary apportionment.[455] However, international business and politics and the conventional use of arm's length/separate accounting have all been significant hurdles for a worldwide formulary apportionment.

Before comparing the formulary apportionment regimes as to their various water's edge limitations, it is a prerequisite to enunciate what the territorial scope of formulary apportionment refers to. The territorial scope of formulary apportionment can be overly extensive if taking all aspects of the elements into account, such as the covering of reporting obligations. The essential factor within a tax system is always 'who is going to pay what'. As such, the territorial scope of formulary apportionment applies to determining first, the taxpayers subjected to formulary apportionment, and second, the taxable income included in the apportionable tax base.

The following comparison contributes to understanding three basic questions revolving around the jurisdictional boundaries of formulary apportionment, namely, why, in the first place, were geographic limitations introduced to the system of formulary apportionment ('why'); what are those limitations and how are they structured ('what'); and, at last, what are the general lessons for the operation of formulary apportionment ('how').

#### *3.3.3.1 The United States*

As the forerunner of employing formulary apportionment for multijurisdictional corporate taxation, the United States has also contributed extensive experience with respect to formulating the territorial scope of formulary apportionment, which sheds light on all three basic questions.

455. Michael J McIntyre, 'The Use of Combined Reporting by Nation States' (2004) 35 Tax Notes International 917, 945.

### *3.3.3.1.1 The* Container *Case*

The US state's approach to a water's edge formulary apportionment regime was rolled out by two cases decided by the Supreme Court. The first is the *Container* case that dealt with the application of California's combined reporting regime to Container, a US-based multinational company, including its foreign subsidiaries incorporated overseas. The controversy was aroused where Container contended that California's worldwide formulary apportionment regime was unconstitutional, for it created the risk of international multiple taxation and impaired the federal uniformity or congressional policy in the tax arena. The court repudiated both contentions.

It is noteworthy that the court laid the ground for the analysis of these contentions by confirming the existence of the unitary business of Container and its subsidiaries and the fairness of California applying its apportionment formula together with unitary combined reporting. For the contention of multiple taxation risks under worldwide combined reporting with formulary apportionment, the court claimed that the risks of double taxation were still existent even though the world nations all adopted the arm's length approach because the specific allocations rules of nation-states always differ, which meant that California's use of worldwide formulary apportionment did not necessarily create additional risks of double taxation.[456] In addition, the court seemed to draw a distinction between 'occasional' double taxation that was permissible as in the case of employing a disparate allocation method where both over-taxation and under-taxation could happen, and 'inevitable' double taxation, the risk of which was substantial and thus impermissible as presented in the *Japan Line* case.[457]

For the second contention, the court ruled that the unitary taxation of Container did not contravene the federal policy and should not cause foreign retaliation. First of all, California was not taxing a pure foreign company, but a domestic company that was incorporated in the US, which California was justified in taxing. Furthermore, while the tax treaties entered by the Federal Government imposed the restrictions of ALS for taxing multinational enterprises, the Court held that such restrictions did not generally apply to the extent the contracting nation taxes its own domestic corporations. Therefore, California's use of combined reporting was to calculate the tax liabilities of its domiciled corporation by 'counting' the income arguably attributable to foreign subsidiaries while not affecting the incidence of tax. At this point, the Court seemed to back the proposition that the unitary taxation without geographic limitations does not contravene the ALS to the extent that it is not a treaty provision constraining the domestic taxation of resident MNEs. Therefore, the conformity of unitary combined reporting formulary apportionment to the arm's length treaty provision was not addressed as others did based on the interpretation of Article 9 or Article 7,[458] but more

456. 'Or California could try to avoid double taxation by adopting some version of the "arm's-length" approach. That course, however, would not by any means guarantee an end to double taxation.', Container *Corp. of Am. v. Franchise Tax Bd.*, 463 US 159, 197, 103 S. Ct. 2933 (1983).
457. *Container Corp. of Am. v. Franchise Tax Bd.*, 463 US 159, 188, 103 S. Ct. 2933 (1983); *see* detailed analysis in Hellerstein and Hellerstein (n. 29) s. 8.17.
458. Avi-Yonah and Pouga Tinhaga (n. 273) 13-20.

on the local rather than international nature of state taxation. Nevertheless, the court's reasoning unveiled the restrictions imposed by the convention upon the taxation of resident corporations where it engages in business with its associated enterprise in the other contracting state. The collision between formulary apportionment and the arm's length convention is thus fundamental as they follow contrasting methodologies. It is thus conceivable that the priority of dealing with such collision is for the design of formulary apportionment in international taxation.

#### *3.3.3.1.2 The* Barclays *Case*

The *Barclays* case[459] did not give the Court the leeway to rule on the taxation of US-based multinational corporations without a foreign parent. Instead, the case involves a UK-headquartered multinational enterprise, Barclays Bank, which has hundreds of member corporations around the globe, and two of them were doing business in the state of California. The disputes arose where, similar to the Container case, California intended to tax the two Barclays subsidiaries again on the basis of worldwide combined reporting. In ruling the *Barclays* case, the Court put an end to the constitutionality controversies revolving around the worldwide unitary taxation regime adopted by the US states.

On similar grounds, the court disapproved of Barclays' contention about the risk of double taxation from California's allocation method, which is different from that widely adopted by other nation-states. Specifically, the change of context from the US-based MNE to a foreign-based MNE did not substantially alter the reasoning provided for the *Container*. The taxpayer also challenged California's approach, asserting that it constituted discrimination as it increased the tax return burdens and fell short of precision, allowing 'reasonable approximation' in determining the tax liabilities. The court acceded to these assertions to some extent but maintained that they were infirm to overthrow California's approach.

#### *3.3.3.1.3 Summary of the Two Cases*

The two cases sweep away the constitutional and judicial obstacles to the unitary formulary apportionment with the combined reporting regime of the US states. From the merits of the decisions, the collision in the context of the US between the unitary formulary apportionment with combined reporting regime adopted by a unit of tax authority and the arm's length/separate accounting regime adopted by the rest of the tax authorities in the world was manifested in:

(a) the risk of double taxation;
(b) the asserted discrimination between foreign MNEs and domestic companies;

459. *Barclays Bank PLC v. Franchise Tax Bd.*, 512 US 298, 114 S. Ct. 2268 (1994).

(c) the restrictions imposed by the arm's length provision upon the taxation of residents with foreign interest, which especially concerns the allocation method used; and
(d) the possible impairment of national uniformity in tax policy is due to the fact that the subnational policy differs from the federal one.

Except for the last point, all of them are also relevant to the international context, which ought to be meticulously considered.

### *3.3.3.1.4 What and Why: The States' Restrictions on Worldwide Combined Reporting*

Both the above seminal cases evinced positive messages regarding the worldwide unitary formulary apportionment method employed by the US states. However, the ensuing developments actually reversed the course sanctified by the courts. The various stakeholders exerted great pressure on the state's approaches. As a result, most of the states that once employed worldwide combined reporting turned to introducing water's edge limitations, which generally restricted the application of state formulary apportionment regimes within the territory of the United States. In this great redirection, of course, it is worthwhile to examine the driving factors behind the stakeholders to explore the relevant circumstances in the international context ('why'). Corresponding to the three basic questions posed in the beginning and for substantive considerations, the concrete design of the water's edge limitations ('what') is a key aspect of the following discussions, while the question of the general lessons for the operation of formulary apportionment ('how') will be touched on later.

#### 3.3.3.1.4.1 Why

To encapsulate, it is foreign governments, taxpayers, and the US federal government that jointly shaped the state's water's edge systems. The scrimmage can be unveiled by the confrontation between the United Kingdom and the US when the two parties were negotiating their first bilateral income tax treaty in 1975. One of the focuses of the negotiation was that the UK requested to incorporate a provision limiting the US state formulary apportionment method only to the income earned within the US.[460] Similarly, such 'anti-unitary' provision was also requested by Canada in the treaty negotiation process. Both the UK and Canada failed to achieve their aims, not because the US Treasury was a defender of the state's worldwide unitary approach, but because the states threatened not to ratify the tax treaties through the Senate vote.[461] In 1979, the UK multinational corporations even formed a Unitary Tax Campaign to lobby

460. Robert D Wallingford, 'British Retaliation Against the California Unitary Tax: The Needed Impetus for a Federal Solution' (1986) 8 Journal of Comparative Business and Capital Market Law 345.
461. Brown Robert D et al., 'Unitary Tax: At the Crossroads? – Part II' (1985) 55 The CPA Journal (pre-1986) 36, 40.

against the US worldwide unitary apportionment method. It is notable that the governmental confrontations in this respect were to echo the discontent of their MNEs. In the five years from 1983 to 1987, over a hundred MNEs in aggregation from Japan, the European Economic Community, and the US were challenged with different actions or threats to the US state's approach in question.[462]

The vigorous opposition stemmed from a series of concerns of MNEs regarding the worldwide unitary apportionment regimes. Their allegations can be refined as follows, many of which correspond to those that have been expressed in *Container* and *Barclays*:

*Table 3.2 Oppositions to the Use of FA*

| *Oppositions* | *Consequences* |
|---|---|
| (1) Deviating from the practices of the rest of the world | ... over taxation or under taxation may arise |
| (2) Administratively burdensome | ... especially for foreign-based MNEs where US subsidiaries may have limited access to the information of foreign parent and affiliates |
| (3) The distortions of measurement of taxable income and production factors | ... may impede the international trade and investment flows |
| (4) Unclear and inconsistent definition of unitary business | ... the uncertainty of being subjected to unitary taxation is unacceptable |

#### 3.3.3.1.4.2 What

Due to the pressure on the states and indirectly on the federal government, various actions were taken at both levels to reverse the use of worldwide unitary combined reporting. In 1983, the Reagan Administration convened a Worldwide Unitary Taxation Working Group comprising tripartite representatives from states, MNEs and the federal government. However, no agreement was reached on the legal actions for the states to take, apart from a Unitary Taxation Report[463] containing the consensus on the three general principles to follow:

(1) Water's-edge unitary combination for both US and foreign-based companies.
(2) Increased federal administrative assistance and cooperation with the states to promote full taxpayer disclosure and accountability.

462. Nancy Foran and Dahli Gray, 'The Evolution of the Unitary Tax Apportionment Method' (1988) 15 The Accounting Historians Journal 65, 80 https://doi.org/10.2308/0148-4184.15.1.65 accessed 26 August 2025.
463. Department of the Treasury, United States (n. 262) hereinafter 'Unitary Taxation Report'.

(3) Competitive balance for US multinationals, foreign multinationals, and purely domestic businesses.[464]

Instead, the Report only listed six Options respectively favoured by the different groups of members.[465] In general, these Options all focused on the definition or scope of the water's edge combined group, besides the administrative issues, and it is these elements that were in the spotlight:

(1) Corporations that are typically US-domestic, being part of a unitary business, including those owned or controlled by a third US corporation, are includable in the water's edge group, to which the worldwide combined reporting is applicable.[466]
(2) US corporations with substantial business operations overseas, usually weighed by the 80/20% of the payroll and property (known as 'foreign operating corporation', are preferred by business members to be excluded from the water's edge group.
(3) Foreign corporations with business activities in the US beyond the threshold of nexus and a threshold of payroll and/or property and/or sales and/or purchases assignable to a location in the United States are includable in the water's edge group.
(4) Tax haven corporations meeting some thresholds are treated as within the water's edge.
(5) The states and business groups were conflicting over the treatment of dividends, where the states sought to subject all the dividends to the apportionable tax base, while the business proposed to set up a threshold for the state taxation of dividends.

At the time of the convention of the Worldwide Unitary Taxation Working Group, there were thirteen states employing the worldwide unitary combined reporting, but they were still reluctant to take action following the work of the Working Group. In view of the situation, the US Treasury proposed the Unitary Tax Repealer Act specifically to curb the territorial scope of the state unitary taxation, which drew materially on the contributions of the Report.[467]
Ultimately, under all the political/diplomatic, economic, judicial, and legislative pressures, the states began to abandon or restrict their worldwide unitary regime. Till 1991, all the states introduced some water's edge limitations. Table 3.3 summarizes the legislative reactions.

464. *Ibid.*, 9-10.
465. *Ibid.*, 27.
466. For example, the corporations incorporate in the US and the domestic international sales corporations, and foreign sales corporations.
467. S. 1974, 99th Cong., 1st Sess. (1985); State Taxation, s. 8.18.

*Table 3.3 US States' Legislation Actions for Retreating from Worldwide Unitary FA*

| *States* | *Reacting Time* | *Main Approach to Water's Edge* | *Legislation Actions* |
|---|---|---|---|
| Florida | 1984 | Revoked the worldwide combination legislation and reestablished separate reporting requirements. | Fla. S.B. 1A, 1984 Leg., 1st Spec. Sess., 1984 Fla. Laws 84-549. |
| Oregon | 1984 | Substituted consolidated reporting for the worldwide unitary combined reporting, thus excluded foreign corporations and their incomes from the state consolidation regime. | Or. Rev. Stat. § 317.715 (Westlaw 2020) |
| Massachusetts | 1984 | Massachusetts Supreme Judicial Court invalidated the state unitary business approach | *Polaroid Corporation & others v. Commissioner of Revenue* |
| Arizona | 1985 | Excluded the income of 'foreign'[468] corporations from allocation and apportionment. | 1985 Ariz. Sess. Laws, Chapter 109 |
| Colorado | 1985 | Excluded the income of foreign operating corporations. | 1985 Colo. Sess. Laws, Chapter 309 |
| Montana | 1985 | Provided a constricted definition of business income and business activity to limit the taxation of foreign corporations. | Mont. S.B. 330, 49th Leg., 1985 Reg. Sess. |
| New Hampshire | 1985 | Adopted the Option Two listed in Unitary Taxation Report, namely, the Comprehensive Water's Edge Combination. | N.H. H.B. 431-FN, 1985 Gen. Ct. |
| Indiana | 1985 | Prohibited the mandatory application of combined reporting to foreign corporation or foreign operating corporation. | Ind. S.B. 75, 104th Gen. Assy., 1st Reg. Sess., 1985 Ind. S. Enr. Act 75. |

468. Foreign corporations were defined as including non-US incorporated companies, US domestic companies with less than 20% of income derived outside the US.

| *States* | *Reacting Time* | *Main Approach to Water's Edge* | *Legislation Actions* |
|---|---|---|---|
| Utah | 1985 | Adopted the Option Two listed in Unitary Taxation Report, namely, the Comprehensive Water's Edge Combination, and permitted a one-time election for excluding all foreign members from combined reporting. | Utah H. Con. Res. 25, 1985 Leg., Gen. Sess. |
| Idaho | 1986 | Repeal the provisions for combined reporting.[469] | Idaho S.B. 1145, 48th Leg., 1985 1st Reg. Sess. |
| California | 1986 | Introduced the taxpayer right of election to be subject to the water's edge limitation. | 1986 Cal. Stat., Chapter 660 |
| Minnesota | 1988 | The unitary approach was limited only to US domestic corporations, while income and factors of foreign members were excluded. | 1988 Minn. Laws, Chapter 719 |
| Alaska | 1991 | Adopted water's edge legislation providing detailed scope of the unitary group that largely followed the common elements of water's edge Option Two of the Unitary Taxation Report. | Alaska Sess. Laws 1991 Chapter 11 |

#### *3.3.3.2 Canada*

As discussed in the previous section on taxable unit, the Canadian provincial formulary apportionment is established on the basis of a separate corporation rather than a combination or consolidation. It is thus free from the conundrum of demarcating the boundaries of unitary business and unitary group. In this regard, such a system can also avoid many problems of setting up the territorial scope of the formulary apportionment regime as encountered in the US context. According to the above section, it is pointed out that the Canadian multi-provincial corporate income taxation relies on the existence of permanent establishment as the basis of jurisdiction to tax, which applies to both Canadian and non-resident corporations.

Due to the major objective of income distribution among the provinces, Canada also imposes water's edge limitations on its formulary apportionment regime. Compared to the diverse water's edge approaches of US states, Canadian federal law has provided uniform rules in this respect, and due to the considerations in the above paragraph, they are also straightforward.[470] The general principle is that only the

469. Foran and Gray (n. 462) 83.
470. Income Tax Reg. 402, 413.

income earned within Canada can be included in the apportionable tax base and shared among provinces where the corporation has permanent establishments. For income excluded from the apportionable tax base, the apportionment factors associated with the income are also disregarded from the formula. For example, for a non-resident corporation that has permanent establishments located in multiple provinces, the apportionable income includes only the income earned in Canada, and accordingly, the value of the two factors, including salaries and wages, and gross revenues, paid or attributed to a permanent establishment outside Canada, is not counted in the formula.

In addition, since the Canadian formulary apportionment is applied to single corporations and relies on the permanent establishment to establish jurisdiction to tax, the case where a resident corporation has income earned outside Canada does not cause tanglesome problems for setting up the water's edge bubble. Put in a simpler way, the communication between the Canadian formulary apportionment system and the system of the rest of the world is much better smoothed through the cornerstones of a single entity and permanent establishment in international taxation. For instance, where a resident corporation derives income from sales of goods shipped from Canada to customers in a foreign country, the gross revenue is generally attributed on a destination basis, namely, to the foreign country if the corporation has a PE there, or, if not, to the PE negotiating the sale or to the province of manufacturing and/or production.

#### *3.3.3.3 The EU CCCTB Proposal*

The EU's proposal of CCCTB was a novel experiment of regional formulary apportionment, hence naturally dictated water's edge limitations on the territorial scope. Besides the official text of the proposal, the deliberation and drafting process of CCCTB also provided valuable insights into the construction of water's edge international formulary apportionment within a political region.

The methodology of designing the territorial scope of CCCTB had been consistent from the very beginning under the general objective of establishing a formulary apportionment zone with the jurisdiction of the EU, which can be indicated in a four-quadrant diagram representing the exhaustive permutation of taxpayer and income:[471]

471. The diagram is revised from Ana Agundez-Garcia, 'The Delineation and Apportionment of an EU Consolidated Tax Base for Multi-Jurisdictional Corporate Income Taxation: A Review of Issues and Options' [2006] Working Paper 21.

*Figure 3.1 Four-Quadrant Diagram Representing the Exhaustive Permutation of Taxpayer and Income*

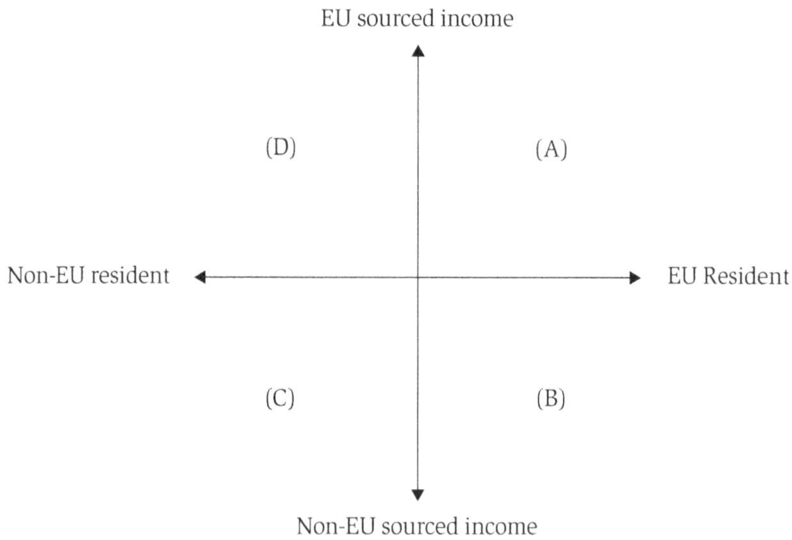


Quadrant A demonstrates the case where the EU resident earns income from the EU tax jurisdiction, which is the most basic scenario the CCCTB was designed to govern. The CCCTB Proposal provided that *all* income less exempt revenues and deductions from the *whole* EU were included in the tax base, which set out a hard and uniform border of the EU water's edge rather than a fluid border specific to each corporate group.[472] Therefore, it raises no specific issues within the ambit of the territorial scope question. The quadrant C deals with the scenario opposite to the quadrant A, and there is also not much ambiguity as the EU generally does not have the jurisdiction to tax the foreign income of non-residents.

The key circumstances are that the EU resident earns income outside the EU (quadrant B) and the non-EU resident earns income within the EU (quadrant D). For quadrant B, the CCCTB Proposal ultimately opted to exclude all income of non-EU sources from the consolidated tax base.[473] As in the case of the US state formulary apportionment regime, when faced with the question of whether to subject the income earned abroad to CCCTB, in general, there were no overarching principles or definite instructions but various conflicting considerations.

First of all, the CCCTB applied to a corporate group on the basis of consolidation rather than combination based on the identification of a unitary business; the treatment of foreign income under CCCTB does not involve the complexities of maintaining the consistency of unitary taxation. Instead, it is the practical concerns of residence

472. The differences between two kinds of water's edge are illustrated in *Ibid.*, 22-23.
473. European Commission, 'CCCTB 2011' (n. 393) 12; European Commission, 'CCCTB Proposal of Tax Base' (n. 413) 14.

taxation, the relief of double taxation, and the administrative burden that are at stake. Excluding the non-EU income of resident companies from CCCTB, on one hand, complies with the conventional residence principle that authorizes only the residence state to tax the worldwide income of its residents and thus avoids spreading the foreign income across the whole EU. On the other hand, dictates two separate systems of corporate taxation at the levels of the EU and Member States, which sacrifices consistency and simplicity. Nevertheless, in the text of CCCTB proposals, the only justification provided for this option is 'simplicity for business', which hardly makes sense as the taxpayer will have to prepare two separate records and tax returns.[474]

In comparison, while including the non-EU income in the consolidated tax base may prove to be simpler for taxpayer compliance, it hits the rocks of subverting the residence-based taxation, which is a line the CCCTB program did not intend to cross since the beginning.[475] In addition, the complexities arise from the double taxation relief before and after apportionment and the introduction of necessary anti-avoidance measures,[476] whereas in contrast, the alternative option of excluding non-EU income has advantages as recognized in the CCCTB Proposal.[477]

For quadrant D, the image is no simpler. Whether the CCCTB covers the case where a non-EU resident earns income from the EU echoes how the designers envisage the EU corporate taxation as in rem tax on the object matter 'income' or *in persona* tax on the taxpayer. As discussed in the ensuing section of the taxable unit, the CCCTB Proposal defined its scope by articulating the companies subject to the CCCTB. Therefore, the CCCTB's water edge can be roughly gauged as being framed along the boundary of persons. However, the exclusion of a resident's foreign income has set up an EU territorial source-based corporate tax system, which also casts some rationality on taxing the EU-sourced income of non-residents by the CCCTB.

To illustrate the EU Commission's decision in this respect, the following two diagrams represent the two most typical scenarios of non-EU resident earning EU-sourced income. The first is an EU parent holding indirectly through a subsidiary outside the EU, a permanent establishment in an EU Member State, and the second is simply a parent company outside the EU holding several permanent establishments in the EU. Both examples involve a non-EU resident earning income from sources within the EU through EU permanent establishments. It is provided that the CCCTB Proposal of Tax Base applies to a non-resident company 'in respect of' its EU PEs if the company is part of a consolidated group either as a qualifying parent or subsidiary.[478] The CCCTB Proposal of Consolidation provides that a resident taxpayer must form a group with all EU permanent establishments belonging to its third-country 'qualifying subsidiaries'

474. European Commission, 'CCCTB Proposal of Tax Base' (n. 413) 14.
475. 'Common Consolidated Corporate Tax Base Working Group, the Territorial Scope of the CCCTB' CCCTB\WP\026\doc\en para 22, 27 https://taxation-customs.ec.europa.eu/system/files/2016-09/ccctbwp026_territorial_scope_en.pdf. accessed 26 August 2025, paras 27, 22; Agundez-Garcia (n. 471) 23.
476. 'Common Consolidated Corporate Tax Base Working Group, the Territorial Scope of the CCCTB' (n. 475) para. 22; Agundez-Garcia (n. 471) 24.
477. European Commission, 'CCCTB Proposal of Tax Base' (n. 413) 13-14.
478. *Ibid.*, 2(2).

(Example 1),[479] and a non-resident must also form a group 'in respect of' its EU PEs (Example 2).[480] Cumulatively, the CCCTB clearly deems the EU-sourced income of non-residents to be taxable, subject to the requirement that the income is earned through EU permanent establishment within a qualified consolidated group. It is also noteworthy that these provisions repeatedly use 'in respect of', which can be understood as an emphasis on the Directive's intention to incorporate the income of the EU PEs rather than extend the personal scope of CCCTB. In this light, the CCCTB's nature of EU source taxation is strengthened.

The Directives' approach to the inclusion of EU-sourced income of non-EU residents has the advantage of being consistent with the theoretical basis of CCCTB as regards the economic integration of a corporate group, where the non-resident's business operations in the EU also contribute to the general profits of the group to be distributed within the EU. It also prevents the tax avoidance opportunities from escaping the CCCTB by indirectly holding an EU PE through a foreign subsidiary, should the PE be excluded from the scheme. However, this option is faced with the difficulty of reconciling the conflict between the ALP used in the tax treaty and the formulary apportionment used in the CCCTB with respect to the determination of income assigned to the EU PE. The CCCTB Proposal of Tax Base has only specified that dealings between the PE and its foreign parent follow the ALP, while the attribution of profits to the PE within the EU is out of the scope of the tax treaty between the PE host state and the foreign parent residence state.[481]

*Figure 3.2 Example of EU CCCTB Proposal*

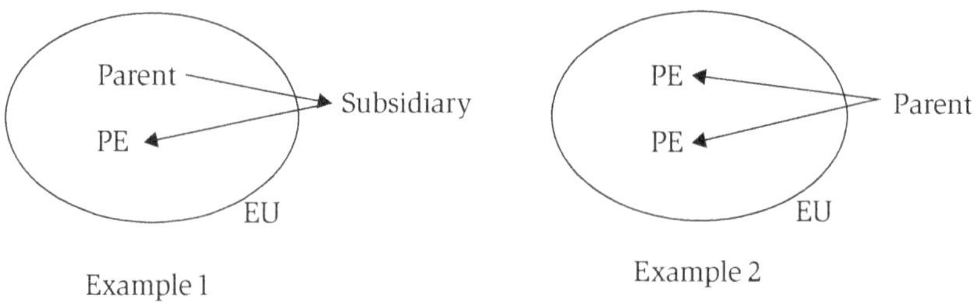


### 3.3.3.4 *Pillar One Amount A*

The TPS is the first international tax campaign that revamps the substantive aspects of the international tax system. Championed by the Inclusive Framework, it was created in the very first place as a global solution to address the global tax problems. As a result, such a design dispenses with the need to calibrate a water's edge system that demarcates the territorial scope of the formulary apportionment regime. Nevertheless, one may argue that the Inclusive Framework does not encompass all countries (142

479. European Commission, 'CCCTB Proposal of Consolidation' (n. 413) Art. 6(1)(b).
480. *Ibid.*, 6(2).
481. European Commission, 'CCCTB Proposal of Tax Base' (n. 413) Art. 56.

countries by early 2023) in the world,[482] so that territorial demarcation is still needed when MNEs are doing business or deriving sales revenue in these places.

This actually is not a problem as Pillar One Amount A is self-limiting for the TPS is implemented only in the participating countries which voluntarily legislate on the two pillars. Hence, the activities carried out in the non-participating countries will simply be disregarded. Another explanation is that the TPS is a supplement to the existing regime with no intention to replace the existing one. An add-on certainly entails no hard border.

### *3.3.3.5 Summary and Lessons*

The historical inclination to arm's length and separate accounting was based on its alleged comparative advantages over formulary apportionment with respect to the compatibility with double taxation relief, the popularity as the administrative practice of domestic taxation, and the orientation towards the interests of capital exporting countries in the mercantile economic model. None of them reflects the theoretical superiority of the ALS. The drastic change in political and economic realities has undermined the basis of that inclination. As validated in its applications at the very outset, formulary apportionment has the nature of fitting the multi-jurisdictional environment of business and taxation. At this point, any water's edge limitations on formulary apportionment will impair its theoretical consistency and practical merits.

However, the experiences of the US, Canada and the EU commonly validate that imposing water's edge limitations is inherently attributed to the coexistence of two heterogeneous systems of formulary apportionment and arm's length/separate accounting.[483] In the US, the states' use of worldwide unitary combined reporting had aroused vigorous opposition from political, diplomatic, and economic parties; in Canada, taxing only the income earned within Canada is the principle of Federal legislation; in the EU, the CCCTB has been an experiment of EU territorial corporate taxation in the first place. In this case, there are generally two solutions to this dilemma. Either it is that countries could cooperate through a multilateral organization or instrument to adopt formulary apportionment on a larger territorial scale, for which the more economies participate in a coordinated formulary apportionment regime, the fewer unintended effects such as tax planning will arise.[484] The TPS led by OECD/G20 Inclusive Framework is a two-way demonstration in this respect. First, it is that when the group of participating members is large enough, the consideration of introducing water's edge limitation would be redundant. Second, the world's commitment to formulary apportionment is conditional on it being in the form of Pillar One Amount A

482. OECD, 'What is BEPS?' https://www.oecd.org/tax/beps/about/ accessed 5 December 2023.
483. *See* the discussions in Chs 2 and 4 about the contrasting methodologies of formulary apportionment and arm's length.
484. Nadine Riedel and Marco Runkel, 'Company Tax Reform with a Water's Edge' (2007) 91 Journal of Public Economics 1533 https://doi.org/10.1016/j.jpubeco.2006.11.001 accessed 26 August 2025.

rather than anything else – being an add-on mechanism, dealing with residual profits, and having a relatively high threshold.

Therefore, it is hardly the case that countries outside the formulary apportionment bubble could unconditionally cooperate, no matter whether the regime is unilateral, bilateral, or regional. If the 'net' of formulary apportionment was not large enough to capture a substantial portion of economic flow, the water's edge system should be designed meticulously.

For the above purposes, the EU CCCTB Proposal has exemplified the design of the water's edge system of regional formulary apportionment, which should also be weighed considering the design of other components. The experiences of the US can provide many details in the design of water's edge system. The US experiences have embodied why water's edge limitations were introduced to demarcate the territorial scope of formulary apportionment in the first place, and what general approaches were taken to a water's edge system. The following summarizes or refines the lessons drawn from the US experiences for the design of formulary apportionment in the international context with respect to the territorial scope of formulary apportionment.

First, while the issue of territorial scope is not at the heart of formulary apportionment as the factors or formula used to be, it is no less critical for the success of a formulary apportionment regime. Sitting at the periphery, the territorial issue reflects the intersection of economic and political dimensions of formulary apportionment. Formulary apportionment can be deployed for subnational, national (unilateral), regional, and global applications in ascending order of geographic coverage. Correspondingly, in international taxation, there are unilateral, regional, and worldwide formulary apportionment, and at the very outset, the choice among them depends on political willingness. It is held that the larger scale which the formulary apportionment is deployed on, the greater the uniformity that can be achieved, and the fewer problems that may arise from the transition and administrations.

Second, under the current circumstances where an abrupt adoption of worldwide formulary apportionment is hardly attainable, there will undoubtedly be both unilateral and regional formulary apportionment requirements for the introduction of water's edge limitations for itself to be 'compatible' with the world outside the 'bubble'. Numerous issues can arise from establishing and maintaining the water's edge regime, among which are international considerations:

(1) resolving the collision at least at the theoretical level between arm's length convention and formulary apportionment as two contrasting methodologies is decisive as to whether setting up water's edge limitations on formulary apportionment is required;
(2) the risk of double taxation does not constitute a deterrent at the core for the use of worldwide unitary combination;
(3) where the collision in the point (a) was not resolved, establishing a water's edge bubble for unilateral and regional system of formulary apportionment seems to be necessary as the economic, political and judicial pressures could evolve again as in the case of US states;

(4) the water's edge regime should be constructed mainly by the standards for demarcating the personal scope of corporations together with their incomes subject to unitary combined reporting, for which a bright line test of 80/20% measured by apportionment factors is usually applied;
(5) for the purposes of preventing tax avoidance, tax haven corporations are usually included in the water's edge group;
(6) non-discrimination principle that provides a level playing field for both foreign MNEs and domestic corporations serves as a yardstick, even though sometimes it is not definitely clear what it directs;
(7) the treatment of foreign dividends is shaped by the complex conflicts among different policy aims and theoretical rationales.[485]

## 3.4 THE COMPARATIVE ANALYSIS OF INTERNAL COMPONENTS OF FORMULARY APPORTIONMENT REGIME

### 3.4.1 The Delineation of Taxable Unit

The taxable unit refers to the basic unit of entities subject to the application and administration of formulary apportionment, which is decisive to the process of how income is distributed among multiple jurisdictions. More than that, the delineation of a taxable unit reflects the diverging views on the theoretical basis of formulary apportionment as the method of taxing multi-jurisdictional corporations. Conceptually, the delineation of taxable units and formulary apportionment are separate issues, considering that the latter, in the narrower sense, only depicts how the pre-determined portion of income is distributed across tax jurisdictions. It thus creates a leeway for different approaches to delineating the taxable unit for the application of formulary apportionment. In practice, there are generally three categories of taxable units adopted by the existing or proposed formulary apportionment regimes: separate reporting, unitary combined reporting, and consolidated reporting.

The separate reporting approach does not rely on the consolidation of incomes of the members of a company group. Just as the separate accounting method, the separate reporting approach respects the separate identities of the member companies within a group.[486] It provides that the apportionable income of an enterprise within a jurisdiction is determined on an individualized basis by first inspecting the separate accounts of each member and then applying formulary apportionment respectively to each entity in line with the values of the factors as reflected in the accounts.[487]

485. *See* the discussions in Department of the Treasury, United States (n. 262) 39-41,45-47., and Mayer (n. 265) 91-94.
486. The separate reporting approach seems to be coined and constantly upheld by Walter Hellerstein, 'International Income Allocation in the Twenty-First Century: The Case for Formulary Apportionment' (2005) 728 Scholarly Works https://digitalcommons.law.uga.edu/fac_artchop/728 accessed 5 December 2023; *see also* Hellerstein and Hellerstein (n. 29) para. 8.03. In contrast, Weiner did not differentiate separate reporting from separate accounting, *see* Weiner, *Company Tax Reform in the European Union* (n. 444) 69-70.
487. McIntyre, 'The Use of Combined Reporting by Nation States' (n. 455) 938.

The 'unitary combined reporting' or 'combination' approach is the mirror side of the separate reporting approach, and its synthesis within the formulary apportionment is deemed to be the cardinal type of the latter. The unitary combined reporting approach disregards the legal form of doing business but is anchored to the economic substance of multicorporate activities. It defines, according to a set of standards, the affiliated companies or divisions within a corporate group as a combined unitary taxable entity engaging in integrated business operations, calculates the aggregated income of the entity, and distributes the income using a common formula to jurisdictions where the apportionment factors are located.

The 'consolidated reporting' or 'consolidation' approach is a variation, but shares the core features, of the unitary combined reporting approach. It requires the group led by a parent company to file a common tax report that aggregates the income of members, net of the outcome of intra-group transactions. The computation and deployment of factors and apportionment under the two approaches are generally the same.[488] What sets the two approaches apart is that the consolidated reporting, first, usually applies only to the group members that are subject to tax in the tax jurisdiction in the first place, and second, does not require the taxable members to engage in a *unitary business* so that as a result, different standards apply to the scope of 'consolidation' versus 'combination' where consolidation only needs to meet a legal ownership threshold while combination emphasizes economic relationship.[489]

#### *3.4.1.1 The United States*

##### *3.4.1.1.1 Apportionability and Unitary Business*

The US state corporation tax systems have provided fertile grounds for the use and development of formulary apportionment regimes that employ all three approaches to taxable units. As of 2020, twenty out of the forty-four states that levy corporate income taxes by formulary apportionment adopt the separate reporting approach to determining the income to be distributed to the states, and roughly the other half instead adopts the unitary combined reporting approach or the consolidated reporting approach.[490]

488. 'Taxing each member of a group on its share of the total income if the group attributable to a state is functionally the same as taxing the consolidated group on its total share of the income attributed to a state. E.g., a/3 + b/3 = 1/3(a + b)', in Michael J McIntyre, 'Combined Reporting with Formulary Apportionment: The Transfer Pricing System of the US States' (2012) https://www.taxjustice.net/cms/upload/pdf/Michael_McIntyre_1206_Helsinki.pdf accessed 5 December 2023 Slide 5.

489. E George Rudolph, 'State Taxation of Interstate Business: The Unitary Business Concept and Affiliated Corporate Groups' (1969) 25 Tax Law Review 171, 198., as cited by Walter Hellerstein, *The Application of Formulary Apportionment to Related Entities: Lessons from the US Experience, in the Allocation of Multinational Business Income: Reassessing the Formulary Apportionment Option* (Kluwer Law International 2020) 142. *see also* Weiner, *Formulary Apportionment and Group Taxation in the European Union* (n. 28) 26-27.

490. CCH, 'Combined Reporting Requirements' https://answerconnect.cch.com/app/acr/home/federal accessed 5 December 2023 Multistate Quick Answer Charts.

Apart from the differences pointed out earlier, the state consolidated reporting mechanisms, as usually based on the federal consolidated return filings, are generally optional for taxpayers to apply, whereas unitary combined reporting in the states adopting this approach is usually mandatory when the member company forms part of the unitary business.

The US states' diverse and complicated delineations of taxable unit for formulary apportionment regimes were not deemed exemplary. It can be attributed to both *historical contingency* and the special legal and political system. In the seminal case *Mobil Oil Corp. v. Commissioner of Taxes* as referred to above, the US Supreme Court had addressed the issue of 'apportionability' for state taxation, namely, the constitutional restraints on the state's power to tax the apportioned income of a unitary business group, originally in the context of separate reporting rather than unitary combined reporting.[491] Since then, the state has gradually elected to take on separate reporting for its formulary apportionment regimes. In the large part of this process, the multistate giant corporations did not proliferate yet, and this also fuelled the spread of a separate reporting approach.

The unitary combined reporting approach is the most developed as well as most widely discussed approach, in particular relation to the unitary business principle and the delineation of the unitary group. Compared to the separate reporting approach, the combined/consolidated reporting is obviously more consistent with the theoretical foundations of formulary apportionment, where it is oriented towards the economic substance rather than the legal forms used for economic activities, according to which the affiliated, associated and the commonly controlled companies will be deemed as an integrated unitary taxable entity for the application of formulary apportionment. In this respect, formulary apportionment with unitary combined reporting approach will encounter the problem of the legality of extending the tax jurisdiction to incomes or taxpayers that are not subject to taxation under separate reporting or separate accounting/arm's length approach, which is a constitutional question giving rise to the articulation of the unitary business principle and the scope of the unitary business group.

#### *3.4.1.1.2 The Delineations of Unitary Business*

The landmark *Mobil Oil Corp* case was filed in the US Supreme Court to adjudicate on two related issues: first, whether a state can tax the dividend income derived from the investment of a nondomiciled parent company in its subsidiaries by including them in the state apportionable tax base, and if so, second, whether unitary combined reporting is the precondition for such taxation? For the first issue, the Supreme Court declared that 'underlying activity', not legal forms, is the decisive factor, and that 'the linchpin of 'apportionability' in the field of state income taxation is the unitary business principle', following which the question was pinned down to whether the payor of

491. The Court ultimately rejected to require the state to apply unitary combined reporting, *Mobil Oil Corp. v. Commissioner of Taxes of Vermont*, 445 US, at 441.

dividends was engaged in a unitary business with the payee. The unitary business principle governs both the cases of an individual company and a group of affiliated companies. For the second issue, as already indicated, the Court repudiated the claim that the combined reporting is a prerequisite for the application of state formulary apportionment.

For one thing, the unitary business principle is not new. Long before the *Mobil Oil Corp* case articulated the unitary business principle and its centrality, it was the 'unit rule' that had served as the principle of formulary apportionment for the taxation of extraterritorial values, especially in the industries of transportation and communication.[492] While formulary apportionment had long been permitted for the distribution of taxable income across states, the constitutional doctrine of 'definite link' or 'minimum connection' had been casting a shadow over the legality of a state to tax the property, income or receipts of a multistate company.[493] The 'nexus' requirement was not forsaken by the introduction of the unitary business principle but was thereby insisted on and absorbed.[494] Following the principle, a state will be allowed to consider the economic activities both within and without the state as a unitary business and the members carrying out the business as forming a unitary group, and accordingly, apportion a share of the combined income, whether derived inside or outside of the state, to the state as calculated by comparing the in-state factors exploited in the unitary business to the total factors. The principle was not designed to mandate the taxation of the income of non-taxable affiliates, but this is indeed one of the effects.

For another, the views on the unitary business concept are not unitary.[495] Due to the federal system and the judicial system of the US, there are at least two strands of law for the delineation of the scope of a unitary business; one is federal, and another is state law. Both of them were mainly formulated by court decisions, and the state courts are free to delineate their own scope of unitary business to the extent consistent with the standards established by the Supreme Court.[496] In light of the centrality of this issue and its complexity, it is provided in Table 3.4 presenting comprehensively the contemporary views on it, including the standpoints of the prestigious tax scholars and the provisions of the UDITPA.

---

492. Elcanon Isaacs, 'The Unit Rule', 35 Yale Law Journal 838 (1926) https://doi.org/10.2307/789461 accessed 26 August 2025; *Western Union Tel. Co. v. Taggart*, 163 US 1, 18, 16 S. Ct. 1054 (1896); *Pullman's Palace Car Co. v. Pennsylvania*, 141 US 18, 26, 11 S. Ct. 876 (1891); *Adams Express Co. v. Ohio*, 165 US 194, 17 S. Ct. 305 (1897); State Railroad Tax Cases, 92 US 575, 608 (1875).
493. *Miller Bros. v. Maryland*, 347 US 340, 344-345, 74 S. Ct. 535 (1954); *Wisconsin v. JC Penney Co.*, 311 US 435, 444, 61 S. Ct. 246 (1940).
494. Hellerstein and Hellerstein (n. 29) s. 8.07[1]. 'being part of a unitary business conducted both within and without this state is what provides the constitutional due process "definite link and minimum connection" necessary for this state to apportion apportionable income of the unitary business, even if that income arises in part from activities conducted outside the state.', Model General Allocation & Apportionment Regulations as Amended 25 July 2018 Reg. IV. I.(b)(1)(A).
495. 'A final point that needs to be made about the unitary business concept is that it is not, so to speak unitary ...', *Container Corp. v. Franchise Tax Board*, 463, US 159 (1983).
496. Hellerstein and Hellerstein (n. 29) para. 8.09.

*Table 3.4 Views of Defining Unitary Business*

| | *Major Points* | *Principal Contributing Sources* |
| --- | --- | --- |
| Federal Law | - Three Unitary Indicators.Unitary business is characterized by: (a) functional integration; (b) centralized management; and (c) economies of scale, in contrast with a 'discrete business enterprise'. The three-indicator standard had been frequently cited as authority in the subsequent cases.[497] | *Mobil Oil Corp. v. Commissioner of Taxes (1980); Exxon Corp. v. Wisconsin Dep't of Revenue (1980)*[498](explored functional integration indicator); *ASARCO, Inc. v. Idaho State Tax Commissioner (1982)*[499](explored centralized management indicator); *Container Corp v. Franchise Tax Board* (1983) (explored economies of scale indicator) |
| | - Rejection of expansive definition.The scope of unitary business should not be defined over-expansively by reference to the corporate purpose or the activities generally furthering the corporate business. | *ASARCO, Inc. v. Idaho State Tax Commissioner (1982); F.W. Woolworth Co. v. Taxation & Revenue Department (1982)*[500] |
| | - 'Flow of Value' test.It was ruled that the *flow of value* instead of flow of goods is the prerequisite for identifying a unitary business.<br>- Rejection of bright-line test. The court also rejected to establish a simple bright-line test for that purpose. | *Container Corp v. Franchise Tax Board* (1983) |
| | - The Independent Considerations of both Enterprise Unity and Asset Unity; Operational Function Criterion.The cases had found that the 'apportionability' can be established that a unitary enterprise existed, as well as that the assets in the investment formed part of a unitary property organically connected to the corporate business. For Asset Unity, it was declared that an asset especially intangible investment was apportionable only when it served the operational function rather than the mere investment function. | *Container Corp v. Franchise Tax Board* (1983);[501] *Allied-Signal, Inc. v. Director, Div. of Tax'n* (1992);[502] *MeadWestvaco Corp. v. Illinois Dep't of Revenue* (2008).[503] |

| | *Major Points* | *Principal Contributing Sources* |
|---|---|---|
| State Law | - Three Unities test.The unitary nature of a business is manifested by three characteristics of the business: (a) unity of ownership; (b) unity of operation; and (c) unity of use. | *Butler Bros. v. McColgan* (1941) (1942);[504] Part 8019.0100, Subpart 2 Minnesota Administrative Rules. |
| | - Dependency and Contribution test.Where the in-state economic activities are dependent on or contribute/benefit to the out-of-state activities, they form a unitary business. | *Edison Cal. Stores, Inc. v. McColgan* (1947);[505] *Crawford Mfg. Co. v. State Comm'n of Revenue & Tax'n* (1956):[506] Section 1501(a)(27) Illinois Income Tax Act (35 ILCS 5/1501). |
| | - Necessity and Close Connection test.Where the components of business activities are closely connected and mutually necessary, they form a unitary business. | *John I. Haas, Inc. v. Comm'n* (1961).[507] |
| Multistate Tax Compact[508] | It largely adopts the guidelines established by the case laws of the Supreme Court as referred to above. In particular, it emphasizes the 'Flow of Value' as the pillar of the unitary business principle and provides description and illustration of the Three Unitary Indicators. It also sets out some 'hard' indicators to identifying those business activities as unitary business, including that are: (a) in the same type of | Model General Allocation & Apportionment Regulations that complements the Multistate Tax Compact.[509] |

497. It was also quoted by *F.W. Woolworth Co. v. Taxation & Revenue Dep't* (1982) and *Container Corp v. Franchise Tax Board*, 463 US 159 (1983).
498. *Exxon Corp. v. Wisconsin Dep't of Revenue*, 447 US 207, 224, 100 S. Ct. 2109 (1980).
499. *ASARCO, Inc. v. Idaho State Tax Comm'n*, 458 US 307, 102 S. Ct. 3103 (1982).
500. *F.W. Woolworth Co. v. Taxation & Revenue Dep't*, 458 US 354, 102 S. Ct. 3128 (1982).
501. *Container Corp. of Am. v. Franchise Tax Bd.*, 463 US 159, 180 n.19, 103 S. Ct. 2933 (1983).
502. *Allied-Signal, Inc. v. Director, Div. of Tax'n*, 504 US 768, 787, 112 S. Ct. 2251 (1992); Hellerstein and Hellerstein (n. 29) para. 8.07[2][a], 8.08[2].
503. *MeadWestvaco Corp. v. Illinois Dep't of Revenue*, 553 US 16, 128 S. Ct. 1498 (2008).
504. *Butler Bros. v. McColgan*, 17 Cal. 2d 664, 111 P2d 334, 341 (1941), aff'd, 315 US 501, 62 S. Ct. 701 (1942).
505. *Edison Cal. Stores, Inc. v. McColgan*, 30 Cal. 2d 472, 183 P2d 16, 21 (1947).
506. *Crawford Mfg. Co. v. State Comm'n of Revenue & Tax'n*, 180 Kan. 352, 304 P2d 504, 510 (1956).
507. *John I. Haas, Inc. v. Comm'n*, 227 Or. 170, 361 P2d 820, 822 (1961).
508. It can be considered state law since the sovereign members of the Commission adopted the Compact as statutory rules.
509. Model General Allocation and Apportionment Regulations – as of 2017 19-29.

| | Major Points | Principal Contributing Sources |
|---|---|---|
| | business; (b) part of different steps in a vertical business structure; (c) under strong centralized management. In addition, detailed definition of 'commonly controlled group' has been provided since the existence of which is deemed as the prerequisite for separate corporations to form a unitary business. | |
| Scholarly Views | (a) Basic Operational Interdependence Test.<br>(b) Operational Unity and Economic Unity.<br>(c) Three-stage Test examining in order the common control, the existence of economic interdependencies, and the substantiality economic interdependency. | (a) Jerome Hellerstein.[510]<br>(b) Keesling, Frank M. and John S. Warren.[511]<br>(c) Charles McLure.[512] |

### *3.4.1.2 Canada*

Canada is the representative of operating formulary apportionment regimes on the basis of separate reporting rather than consolidation or combination. Neither the federal government nor the provinces permit the consolidation of incomes of separate corporations. There were voices for transitioning to consolidation, but they were not acted upon due to the concerns of the negative revenue effect at the federal level and undermining the uniformity of the common tax base.[513] The tax rate differences between the provinces have created opportunities for multi-provincial enterprises to reduce overall tax burdens. In addition, since the separate reporting system retains the 'soil' of transfer pricing, it could be utilized by corporate groups to manipulate transfer prices.[514] However, the Canadian separate reporting-based formulary apportionment system diverges from the arm's length/separate accounting international taxation, where Canada does not recognize the separate identity of the divisions of a separate corporation.[515]

510. Jerome R Hellerstein, 'Allocation and Apportionment of Dividends and the Delineation of the Unitary Business' (1982) 14 Tax Notes; J Hellerstein, 'The Basic Operations Interdependence Requirement of a Unitary Business' (1983) 18 Tax Notes; Hellerstein and Hellerstein (n. 29) para. 8.09[4][c].
511. Frank M Keesling and John S Warren, 'The Unitary Concept in the Allocation of Income' (1960) 12 Hastings Law Journal 42.
512. Charles McLure, 'Defining a Unitary Business: An Economist's View' (May 1983). NBER Working Paper No. w1125, available at SSRN: https://ssrn.com/abstract=304841.
513. Daly, 'Tax Coordination and Competition in Canada', in Commission (n. 402) 390.
514. Jack Mintz and Michael Smart, 'Income Shifting, Investment, and Tax Competition: Theory and Evidence from Provincial Taxation in Canada' (2004) 88 Journal of Public Economics 1149, 2004 https://doi.org/10.1016/s0047-2727(03)00060-4 accessed 26 August 2025.
515. Weiner, *Company Tax Reform in the European Union* (n. 444) 69.

### 3.4.1.3 *The EU CCCTB Proposal*

According to the CCCTB Proposal, the EU formulary apportionment regime was designed to operate on a consolidation basis. The incomes of the group members are consolidated to reach a total tax base, which is to be shared between these members using a three-factor formula.

In contrast to the unitary combination approach, the EU consolidation approach adopted the 'bright-line' test, which has been constantly rejected in the United States. At the macro level, the CCCTB established mandatory consolidation if the group's consolidated turnover exceeds EUR 750 million so that the qualifying parent and subsidiaries will automatically be governed by the CCCTB rules.[516] Corporate groups below the turnover threshold can also opt for the CCCTB consolidation.[517] At the micro level, the CCCTB defined the inclusion of qualifying entities for consolidation using a two-part threshold test: one is the voting rights beyond 50%, another is the ownership right beyond 75% of the company's capital or of the rights giving entitlement to profit.[518] The permanent establishment of a resident taxpayer within the EU is automatically included in the group.[519]

In the preliminary stage of discussions, the unitary combination approach was discussed as an economic way of defining the group in parallel to the threshold test, and finally endorsed as a legal way.[520] The legal versus economic definition of a group epitomizes the comparative advantages and disadvantages between the consolidation approach and combination approach. The consolidation approach, as employed in the US states and proposed in the CC(C)TB, relies on clear-cut and quantifiable standards to demarcate the group that incorporates the member entities to be a unified taxable unit for the purpose of calculating and apportioning the consolidated tax base. It is thus convenient to implement, economical to administer and able to provide certainties to taxpayers.[521] On the other side, transparent and clear-cut standards are also susceptible to abuse and manipulation. The unitary combination approach is nevertheless more faithful to the unitary business principle, being the linchpin of formulary apportionment in terms of focusing on the economic rather than legal form facet that corporate groups use to form a unitary business because of integration and synthesis. The trickiest part of the unitary combination approach is, as has been exhibited in the US context, that it lacks objectivity and simplicity to implement, even though abundant in theoretical justification.

516. European Commission, 'CCCTB Proposal of Consolidation' (n. 413) Art. 2(1)(c).
517. *Ibid.*, 2(3).
518. *Ibid.*, 5.
519. *Ibid.*, 6.
520. Agundez-Garcia (n. 471) 11-15.
521. Hellerstein, *The Application of Formulary Apportionment to Related Entities: Lessons from the US Experience, in the Allocation of Multinational Business Income: Reassessing the Formulary Apportionment Option* (n. 489) 163.

#### 3.4.1.4 *Pillar One Amount A*

Since the release of the Pillar One Blueprint, it has been well-known that the reform purports to introduce a new taxing right for 'large' MNEs. The proposed model rules on the scope of Pillar One Amount A eventually adopts the approach similar to the EU CCCTB Proposal, that is, the bright-line test. The Pillar One Amount A applies to large and highly profitable companies, benchmarked by a global revenue of EUR 20 billion and 10% profitability measured against total revenue.

Such is certainly the road that has been chosen on the Amount A version of formulary apportionment. However, the OECD, in fact, had made a sharp turn on how to demarcate the scope of Amount A. It is not that the prospective approaches had ever been close to the rest of the other comparators, but that in the earlier stages of Pillar One, the discussions had focused on how to crystallize the G20 political mandate of taxing the digital economy. The Blueprint adopted both the 'activity test' and 'threshold test' for Amount A. The latter refers to the MNE's consolidated revenue, which is quite similar to the final model rules. The activity test, which was intended to restrict Amount A to automated digital services and consumer-facing businesses, was utterly abandoned in the later stages. Therefore, Amount A apportions part of all residual profits of the in-scope MNEs, rather than only the profits from digital businesses.

#### 3.4.1.5 *Summary and Lessons*

In a nutshell, both the US and EU/Pillar One formulary apportionment regimes apply to corporate groups, whether it is the unitary business group under the US combination approach, or the consolidated group under the CCCTB/Amount A consolidation approach, while the Canadian formulary apportionment regime applies to separate corporations.

The choice of taxable unit can be regarded as the core of formulary apportionment. In the modern context, it is the suspicions around arm's length/separate accounting that bring formulary apportionment back to the centre of the stage. Capturing the economic substance of separately incorporated companies as one single unity and crystallizing the economic allegiance principle, having been the foundation of international taxation, formulary apportionment spontaneously dictates the group reporting approach.

Using a separate reporting approach that renders formulary apportionment operating only on separate companies thus impairs the theoretical consistency and practical advantages in adopting formulary apportionment at the outset. For example, since the Canadian system of formulary apportionment does not apply to multi-province corporate groups, the transactions between associated enterprises are still governed by the arm's length/separate accounting practice. If transplanting to the international context, that will at best merely contribute to the conundrum of profit attribution to permanent establishment, while the larger part of the problem arising from the transfer pricing manipulation of associated enterprises is disregarded. Recognizing the corporate group as the taxable unit is thus the defining characteristic of formulary apportionment for international taxation.

The antithesis between the US combination approach and the EU/Pillar One consolidation approach can be simplified as the 'economic unity' test versus the 'legal unity' test of demarcating the corporate group under formulary apportionment. The diverse delineations of a unitary business group provide valuable lessons for contemplating the concrete standards of identifying the unitary group in an international context. As is evidently seen, the US economic way falls short of being accurate, objective, and simple to administer, which is just where the EU legal approach has advantages. In general, commentators have widely favoured the consolidation approach of adopting the legal unity test.[522]

However, the consolidation approach of either the US or EU CCCTB/Pillar One Amount A is not free from suspicion. At the theoretical level, the consolidation approach is too far-fetched to be consistent with the foundation of formulary apportionment, namely, the unitary business principle. While the US combination approach sticks to economic unity by providing sophisticated standards of unitary business principle, the consolidation approach at best captures the 'legal unity' in the same principle. For example, in the CCCTB Proposal of Consolidation, the consolidated group is explicitly recognized as a unitary single taxpayer only under several specified circumstances, such as interest deduction limitation and intra-group transfers of self-generated intangible assets.[523] In addition, the voting right and ownership right standards, as merely a strand of, thus overly simplify the requirements of a unitary business. As a result, a consolidated group does not necessarily overlap with a unitary combined group, especially at the margin. At this point, the combination approach outweighs the consolidation approach in terms of being a faithful application of the unitary business principle. Therefore, the marginal benefits gained in migrating from arm's length/separate accounting, such as the fairer attribution of income and fewer opportunities for transfer pricing manipulation, are more significant.[524]

An additional consideration adding to the complexities is the linkage between the choice of taxable unit and the jurisdiction to tax rule. As discussed in the earlier section, the change of nation-states' taxing power over subject or object matter is often the hardest rock on the way to the reform of international taxation. Countries have long-standing conceptions of what is theirs to impose taxes upon, such as the residents living within them, either individuals or companies. These conceptions are persistent to the extent that the jurisdiction to tax matters has been deemed as a solid domain of

522. Michael Aikins, 'Common Control and the Delineation of the Taxable Entity' (2011) 121 Yale L. J. 640-650. Walter Hellerstein and Charles E McLure, Jr., 'The European Commission's Report on Company Income Taxation: What the EU Can Learn from the Experience of the US States' (2004) 11 International Tax and Public Finance 199 https://doi.org/10.1023/b:itax.0000011400.45314.57 accessed 26 August 2025.
523. European Commission, 'CCCTB Proposal of Consolidation' (n. 413) Arts 9(4), 20, 69(1).
524. Hellerstein, *The Application of Formulary Apportionment to Related Entities: Lessons from the US Experience, in the Allocation of Multinational Business Income: Reassessing the Formulary Apportionment Option* (n. 489) 163.

the state sovereignty, which, in turn, is a concept commonly known as absolute, exclusive, and non-tradable. The consolidation approach to the taxable unit of formulary apportionment, either in the US or EU CCCTB, is constructed on the basis of 'fixed' conventional institutions of jurisdiction to tax.[525] To be specific, the consolidation-based formulary apportionment accommodates the residence/PE model of international taxation, whereas the combination-based formulary apportionment conflicts in many aspects with it.

### 3.4.2 The Harmonization and Determination of Tax Base

This section aims to discuss and compare mainly two strands of issues of tax base among the selected jurisdictions. One is the harmonization of the tax base, where it is to be considered how the harmonization of the tax base matters to the functioning of formulary apportionment regimes and how that harmonization has been worked on in the selected regions. Another is the determination of tax base, which deals with the standards for delineating the tax base for apportionment.

#### *3.4.2.1 The United States*

##### *3.4.2.1.1 The Harmonization of State Corporate Tax Base*

As a typical federal country, the United States allows the imposition of corporate income tax at both the federal level and the state level. Within the ambit of the Constitution, the states enjoy substantial freedom to define tax bases according to their preferences.[526] However, while the US states have exercised such a prerogative to provide individualized tax credit, net operating loss deduction, loss carry-over or depreciation rules, they have also achieved significant conformity in the essential elements of corporate tax base.

The conformity is created by at least three facets of the US tax system, and there are two observations that can be made from it. The first is that the existence of the federal corporate income tax has provided a template for the states to draft their corporate tax rules. In practice, the federal corporate income tax return is used by almost all the states as the starting point for calculating the state tax base.[527] The second is that the federal constitutional restraints on the state taxing power, especially in relation to the Commerce and Due Process Clauses of the Constitution and the Supreme Court's interpretations of 'apportionability' in the state application of formulary apportionment, have demarcated the contours within which the state practices are converging.[528] The third facet was recognized as the ultimate catalyst for the state harmonization of the corporate tax base. That is, the harmonization of the state tax base is in the interests of both taxpayers with multistate business by easing the

525. Weiner, *Company Tax Reform in the European Union* (n. 444) 65.
526. Hellerstein and McLure (n. 386) 91.
527. Weiner, *Company Tax Reform in the European Union* (n. 444) 65.
528. Hellerstein and McLure (n. 386) 92.

compliance burden and the state taxing authorities by easing the administration cost. Taxpayers and state governments thus share the communal benefits of contributing to a consistent corporate tax base across the state border lines. The states have also cooperated strategically through the National Tax Association and the Multistate Tax Commission to enhance the uniformity of the corporate tax base.[529]

#### *3.4.2.1.2 The Delineation of Tax Base*

For designing a formulary apportionment corporate tax regime, the first essential issue to be decided for taxing the base is how much of and on what basis the taxable income is to be included in the portion for apportionment. In the case of the United States, since a generally 'common' measurement of state corporate income tax base has been established, the states will have to decide what to apportion for the application of formulary apportionment. The basic question is whether the total base is apportionable, and if not, what is the threshold to decide on.

The US approach to the determination of tax base for the purpose of applying formulary apportionment can be conceptually grouped into two phases, divided by the Multistate Tax Commission's proposed revision of the Uniform Division of Income for Tax Purposes Act (UDITPA) in 2015. A caveat is that the two-phase understanding does not serve as a clear-cut line for the transition of the US approach.

First of all, as a general matter, the state practices of the determination of tax base are constrained by the constitutional requirement of the 'apportionability', which is the unitary business principle. Subject to such restraint, the states are allowed to adopt their own approach to dividing the tax base. Traditionally, only a few states, such as Maryland and Vermont subjected the entire tax base to formulary apportionment, while the majority practice is that part of the base is apportioned by the formula (the 'apportionment method') while the other part is allocated to specific location(s) such as where the property is located and where the taxpayer is resident (the 'allocation method').[530]

Prior to 2015, as in the state laws and the UDITPA, the business income and non-business income division is the fundamental methodology, according to which the business income is taxed by the apportionment method, while the non-business income is taxed by the allocation method. Business income is defined generally as any income 'arising from transactions and activity in the regular course of the taxpayer's trade or business', known as the 'transaction test', where the income is derived from a property, it constitutes business income if 'the acquisition, management, and disposition of the property constitute integral parts of the taxpayer's regular trade or business

529. Joann E. Weiner, 'Tax Coordination and Competition in the United States of America' in Commission European (ed.), *Report of the Committee of Independent Experts on Company Taxation* (Publications Office 1992) 425.
530. Hellerstein and Hellerstein (n. 29) para. 9.04. Weiner, *Company Tax Reform in the European Union* (n. 444) 66.

operations', known as the 'functional test'.[531] The definition was provided as consistent with the constitutional unitary business principle. There had been a heated debate as to whether the definition of business income dictated either the 'functional test' or the 'transactional test'.[532] In addition, the methodology of determining the tax base constructed upon the business/non-business income division has been criticized as well.[533]

The debates were gradually put to rest when the states increasingly replaced the 'business/non-business income' methodology with the 'apportionable/non-apportionable' methodology.[534] Income recognized as apportionable is subjected to formulary apportionment, while the non-apportionable (allocatable) income is subject to the allocation method. The wave of the new methodology can be seen as a direct application of the constitutional linchpin of 'apportionability'.

The Multistate Tax Commission responded to the trend and proposed revising the UDITPA in 2015, which provided a definition of apportionable income by effectively incorporating the definition of traditional business income.[535] However, beyond that, the new definition of apportionable income in the entirety adopts a 'specified – residual' structure by formulating apportionable income as all the residual income that is not specified as allocatable income.[536]

The major driver behind the transition to 'apportionable/non-apportionable' methodology is the disarray and confusion at the level of state laws and court decisions

531. UDITPA 1966 §1(a).
532. Hellerstein and Hellerstein (n. 29) para. 9.05. Richard W Crawford and Richard T Uzes, 'Income Taxes: The Distinction Between Business and Nonbusiness Income' Bloomberg BNA Tax Management Multistate Tax Portfolio Series, 2025.
533. William D Dexter, 'The Business Versus Nonbusiness Distinction Under the Uniform Division of Income for Tax Purposes Act' [1978] Urban Lawyer. James H Peters, 'The Distinction between Business Income and Nonbusiness Income' (1973) 25 Major Tax Plan 251. John R McGowan and Murray Dennis, 'The Business vs. Nonbusiness Income Controversy: Recent Developments' (1989) 8 Journal of State Taxation 303.
534. Sicilian and Huddleston (n. 425) 48-49.
535. (a) 'Apportionable income' means:
    (i) all income that is apportionable under the Constitution of the United States and is not allocated under the laws of this state, including:
        (1) income arising from transactions and activity in the regular course of the taxpayer's trade or business; and
        (2) income arising from tangible and intangible property if the acquisition, management, employment, development or disposition of the property is or was related to the operation of the taxpayer's trade or business; and
    (ii) any income that would be allocable to this state under the Constitution of the United States, but that is apportioned rather than allocated pursuant to the laws of this state. *See* Model Compact Art. IV. Division of Income. [UDITPA] As revised by the Multistate Tax Commission §1(a) (29 July 2015).
536. This is the approach upheld by the state of Louisiana. La. Rev. Stat. Ann. §47:287.92 (Westlaw 2019).

caused by the 'business/non-business income' division, which in turn causes substantial risks of over-taxation and under-taxation.[537] The problem of the 'business/non-business income' division is attributable to the poorly drafted business income definition but is inherent in that there is a lack of solid ground for introducing a standard independent of the constitutional division between apportionable and non-apportionable income.[538]

### *3.4.2.2 Canada*

In general, it is the provinces' constitutional discretion to design the corporate tax base and other tax matters as they wish. However, substantial harmonization has been achieved among the provinces, mainly attributed to the Tax Collection Agreements between the provinces and the federal government. In accordance with the Tax Collection Agreements, the eight contracting provinces explicitly proclaim the objective of maintaining a broad harmonized tax base.[539] In so doing, they all adhere to the federal definition of tax base. The provinces, Alberta and Québec, albeit not acceding to the Agreement, in practice rarely deviate from the federal tax base definition.[540] Under circumstances where deviations do exist, such as tax credits different from the federal base,[541] a mechanism called 'incremental cost pricing' is in place to smooth the discrepancies.[542]

The unique system underpinned by the Tax Collection Agreements and the use of separate reporting jointly differentiate the Canadian practice of the determination of tax base in the implementation of formulary apportionment substantially from that of the United States. It has already been discussed above that the Canadian provincial formulary apportionment corporate tax regimes have been operating on a separate reporting basis. This sidesteps the problem of defining unitary business as well as the closely related apportionable income conundrum. In addition, the contracting provinces to the Tax Collection Agreements have ceded the power to administer the corporate income tax, which means that the federal government is auditing regular tax returns and apportioning the taxable income of a multiprovincial taxpayer to provinces where the factors are located. The intra-group transactions are administered by the federal government in line with the ALS.

537. Walter Hellerstein, 'The Business-Nonbusiness Income Distinction and the Case for Its Abolition' (2001) 92 Tax Notes 1701-1714.
538. *Ibid.*, 1716.
539. Such as in the Comprehensive Integrated Tax Coordination Agreement between the Government of Canada and the Government of Ontario, *see* 'Ministry of Finance', Such as in the Comprehensive Integrated Tax Coordination Agreement between the Government of Canada and the Government of Quebec, available at https://www.finances.gouv.qc.ca/documents/Autres/en/AUTEN_Tax-agreement.pdf, accessed 24 September 2025; 'Reciprocal Taxation Agreement Between Canada and Manitoba' https://www.gov.mb.ca/finance/tao/pubs/signed_february24,2017.pdf accessed 5 December 2023.
540. Weiner, *Company Tax Reform in the European Union* (n. 444) 67-68.
541. M. Daly, 'Tax Coordination and Competition in Canada', in Commission (n. 402) app. 9A.
542. Michael and Francois (n. 389) 76-77.

#### *3.4.2.3 The EU CCCTB Proposal*

There is not much to say about the harmonization of the tax base under the CCCTB proposal since establishing a single set of tax rules for the internal market of the EU has been a major driver of the project.[543] The 2016 relaunch of the proposal made a compromise on the work of consolidation, but maintained the priority of securing the rules for the common base.

As the proposal provides, taxable income was defined as revenue less deductible expenses and other items.[544] As introduced in the section on taxable unit, the EU CCCTB proposal adopted a consolidation approach to designing the formulary apportionment regime. Therefore, in theory, the proposal should encounter the US state formulary apportionment regimes at the crossroads of harmonizing and, most notably, defining the tax base for apportionment. The CCCTB proposal thus provided an extra perspective on the tax base issues.

The common tax base does not make the differentiation between business income and non-business income. When entities are identified as members of the group applying the two thresholds, their entire tax base will be consolidated into the common tax base.[545] The scope of tax base thus largely relies on the thresholds of the consolidated groups. The consolidation of the tax base has the effect of disregarding the internal pricing of transactions within the group, therefore relieving the burden of transfer pricing administration and compliance.[546] In Articles 56 and 57, the CCCTB Proposal of Tax Base introduces the ALS as an anti-avoidance tool governing the transactions between associated enterprises that fall outside the contour of the consolidation.[547] The common tax base was designed to be broadly inclusive, where all revenues are assumed to be taxable unless explicitly exempted.[548] Article 8 of the CCCTB Proposal of Tax Base sets out the exempted revenues, such as the proceeds from a disposal of shares and the received profit distributions applying a participation exemption and permanent establishment income, with the purpose of preventing double taxation.[549]

#### *3.4.2.4 Pillar One Amount A*

Pillar One Amount A resembles the EU CCCTB regarding the tax base in many respects, as they both allocate the income of a consolidated MNE group. The Amount A relies on the general accounting standard and its equivalents to determine the adjusted profit

543. European Commission, 'CCCTB Proposal of Tax Base' (n. 413) 2.
544. *Ibid.*, 10.
545. European Commission, 'CCCTB Proposal of Consolidation' (n. 413) Arts 5, 7(1).
546. *Ibid.*, 9.
547. Daniel S Smith, 'The Arm's Length Standard: A Blind Spot in the CC(C)TB Proposals' in Weber Dennis and Jan Van De Streek (eds), *The EU Common Consolidated Corporate Tax Base: Critical Analysis* (Kluwer Law International 2016) 106.
548. European Commission, 'CCCTB Proposal of Tax Base' (n. 413) para. 7.
549. Hilkka Marjaana Helminen, 'The Participation Exemption' in Dennis Weber and Jan van de Streek (eds), *The EU Common Consolidated Corporate Tax Base* (Kluwer Law International 2018).

before tax and the group revenue. Using a similar set of accounting standards contributes significantly to the harmonization of the tax base, and the tax certainty efforts of Pillar One can help, too.

### *3.4.2.5 Summary and Lessons*

All four selected regimes/proposals have a significant degree of harmonization of taxable income under formulary apportionment. Canada and the EU proposal, and similarly, the Pillar One Amount A, purport to achieve the harmonization directly with centralized legislation. For the United States, two observations can be made from the US state corporate tax base harmonization. First, while generally not dictated by federal laws, the state definitions of corporate tax base have exhibited substantial conformity, which can be ascribed to the fact that the harmonization of state corporate tax base benefits taxpayers and the multistate business, and the state tax authorities themselves. Second, it is noted however that the state corporate tax base has not been fully harmonized, albeit the general conformity, which means that the state formulary apportionment regimes with an under-harmonized tax base, even though mixed with different approaches to taxable units, can successfully accommodate a state's fine-tuning of tax base to its peculiar needs.[550]

The US' experience in determining the tax base has provided three lessons. First, the existence of a constitutional mandate of unitary business principles for formulary apportionment has played a decisive role in the delineation of a taxable unit as well as the tax base. It demonstrates the overarching role of a guiding principle and how such a principle matters.[551] One has to take this factor into consideration for the design of formulary apportionment in the international context, where a constitution does not exist.[552]

Second, providing an abstract definition of income for apportionment is a difficult task and often problematic, especially the division between business income and non-business income. As the path of the US evinces, an apportionable/non-apportionable division seems more suitable, especially adopting the 'residual - specified' structure, following which all income having a nexus with the unitary business will be categorized as apportionable income unless specified as allocable income.[553]

Third, in demarcating the apportionable income, both the functional test and transactional test should be taken into account.

In the trajectory of the US and the EU CCCTB, it is evident that the scope of taxable income for apportionment is expanding, where the division made to filter out non-apportionable income is becoming less important. As a matter of fact, the fewer

550. McIntyre, 'Combined Reporting with Formulary Apportionment: The Transfer Pricing System of the US States' (n. 488) Slide 24.
551. As considered also for using 'taxing according to where income is earned' as a guiding principle in Agundez-Garcia (n. 471) 18.
552. Hellerstein and McLure (n. 386) 92.
553. This consistent with the recommendations in McIntyre, 'Designing a Combined Reporting Regime for a State Corporate Income Tax: A Case Study of Louisiana' (n. 421) 699-742, 726.

the distinctions that are made, the fewer the distortions and opportunities for manipulation are created.

### 3.4.3 The Choice and Weight of Apportionment Factors

Compared to taxable unit and tax base, the factors used in the apportionment formula and their relative weight seem to be even more central to the general functioning of the formulary apportionment system. When taxable unit and the apportionable tax base are determined, the factors in the formula will decide how the tax base is attributed and shared among tax jurisdictions or taxable units according to their cumulative proportions in relation to the total values of the factors. The relative weight of the factors matters not merely in the mathematical sense, but it represents the unsettled tension between competing policy objectives of formulary apportionment.

The following introduces the uses of different factors and weights thereto accorded in the selected formulary apportionment regimes. Based on this, the comparative analysis sheds light on the conceptual principles and practical considerations of determining the factors and their weight in the formula.

#### *3.4.3.1 The United States*

##### *3.4.3.1.1 The Decline of* Equal-Weighted Three-Factor *Formula*

As in other aspects, the case of the United States has provided the most extensive experiences of apportionment factors. Nevertheless, in contrast with the tax base and taxable unit, the states generally do not have the federal and judicial hurdles as to the choice of the apportionment formula.[554] Therefore, the United States presents the result of competition among different formulas within an ecology of minor harmonization.

To encapsulate, the states had almost uniformly adopted the equal-weighted three-factor formula of property, payroll, and sales but have increasingly assigned a greater or exclusive weight to the sales factor in the formula.[555] In the earlier time when formulary apportionment came to the stage, the states mostly employed the property as the single factor, but through the twentieth century, the states developed a consensus of favouring the equal-weighted three-factor formula commonly known as the Massachusetts formula. The modern development can be conceptually divided by the Moorman case in 1978 into two phases, in which the Supreme Court sanctioned the constitutionality of the single sales factor formula used by the state of Iowa.[556] Since then, the states have gradually abandoned the Massachusetts formula.

554. Hellerstein and McLure (n. 386) 94.
555. *See* the table showing in a dynamic way of the change of state formulas, in Kimberly A Clausing, 'The U.S. State Experience Under Formulary Apportionment: Are There Lessons for International Reform?' (2016) 69 National Tax Journal 353, 357 https://doi.org/10.17310/ntj.2016.2.04 accessed 26 August 2025.
556. *Moorman Mfg. Co. v. Bair*, 437 US 267, 98 S. Ct. 2340 (1978).

In reaction to the tendency, the Multistate Tax Commission in 2015 approved the changes that removed the requirement for the equal-weighted three-factor formula and recommended the double-weighted sales factor in the formula.[557] As of 2020, only five states still used the equally weighted three factors as the exclusive formula, while the majority of the states are using the single or weighted sales factor formula.[558] The traditional *'Massachusetts' equally-weighted three-factor* formula and the contemporary formulas with weighted sales factor are presented as follows.

*Equation 3.1 'Massachusetts' Equally-Weighted Three-Factor Formula*

$$\text{Income apportioned to the state} = \frac{1}{3}\left(\frac{Property^{state}}{Property^{all}} + \frac{Payroll^{state}}{Payroll^{all}} + \frac{Sales^{state}}{Sales^{all}}\right) * Total\ apportionable\ income$$

*Equation 3.2 Double Weighted Sales Factor*

Double weighted sales factor:

$$\text{Income apportioned to the state} = \frac{1}{4}\left(\frac{Property^{state}}{Property^{all}} + \frac{Payroll^{state}}{Payroll^{all}} + \frac{2 * Sales^{state}}{Sales^{all}}\right) * Total\ apportionable\ income$$

*Equation 3.3 Sales Only Formula*

Sales only formula:

$$\text{Income apportioned to the state} = \frac{Sales^{state}}{Sales^{all}} * Total\ apportionable\ income$$

#### *3.4.3.1.2 Judicial Opinions on Apportionment Formula*

Although the US judicial system has largely played a passive role in the development of state apportionment formulas, it has indeed provided thoughtful insights into the conceptual basis of determining the factors in the formula. For sanctioning the Massachusetts formula, the US Supreme Court observed that such a formula was justified in that it reflected a 'very large' share of value-generating activities, and it approximated the distribution of the sources of income or the social cost the income incurred.[559] In a more definitive tone, the Court noted that the 'factor or factors used in the apportionment formula must actually reflect a reasonable sense of how income is

557. Model Compact Art. IV. Division of Income. [UDITPA] As revised by the Multistate Tax Commission 29 July 2015, §9.
558. Federation Of Tax Administrators, 'State Apportionment of Corporate Income' https://www.taxadmin.org/assets/docs/Research/Rates/apport.pdf accessed 5 December 2023.
559. *Container Corp. of Am. v. Franchise Tax Bd.*, 463 US 159, 183, 103 S. Ct. 2933 (1983); *General Motors Corp. v. District of Columbia*, 380 US 553, 561, 85 S. Ct. 1156 (1965).

generated'.[560] Therefore, the conceptual basis in the Court's opinion as regards the choice of factors in the apportionment formula can be refined to three facets: first, it should reflect the activities that generate the value; second, the factors employed should correspond to the general understanding about the factors that produce income; third, the factors should correspond to the social cost incurred for the generation of the income.[561] It is thus observed that in constructing the conceptual basis of apportionment factors, the Court had put emphasis on the correspondence between the apportionable income and apportionment factors. As such, these characters of factors have been collectively dubbed 'factor representation'.

Prior to the *Container* case referred to above, in the *Moorman* case addressing the constitutionality of the single sales factor, however, the Court decision was criticized for being facile and simplistic.[562] The taxpayer, Moorman Manufacturing Co.'s contentions were that the single sales factor formula of Iowa led to extraterritorial taxation and multiple taxations, which is unconstitutional in violation of the Due Process Clause and the Commerce Clause. The Court's rejections of the two contentions evinced the presumptive validity of state tax apportionment[563] and the court's reluctance to engage in extensive judicial law-making in the area of state taxation.[564] The Court's decision on this case thus ran counter to its later statement of the conceptual basis of apportionment factors. The single sales factor formula indeed can hardly be justified on the basis of establishing adequate *factor representation* for the value creation activities, the sources of income, and the social cost incurred by the business. Besides the risk of multiple taxation, the single sales factor formula obviously creates undue advantages for the domiciliary multistate business vis-à-vis the out-of-state competitors since the in-state production activities are not taken into account. Therefore, the Moorman decision in 1978, as a matter of fact, unveiled the era of the single sales factor formula for the state formulary apportionment, but this is not accredited as an achievement but is imputed for introducing this distorting, discriminatory, and 'out of line' formula.[565]

#### *3.4.3.1.3 Change of Policy Objectives*

Behind the scenes of the intersection in 1978, there was a diversion of policy objective of formulary apportionment. For the equilibrium before the *Moorman* decision threw the stone into the water, the equal-weighted three-factor formula had been defended for fairly dividing the tax pie among the states. In contrast, the use of the single sales factor formula and its expansion are attributed to the logic that the formula can promote a state's economic development by providing a more favourable tax playing field and attracting investment and economic operations. In a nutshell, the transition in terms of apportionment factor echoed the changing focal point of state tax policy

560. *Container Corp. of Am. v. Franchise Tax Bd.*, 463 US 159, 169, 103 S. Ct. 2933 (1983).
561. Hellerstein and Hellerstein (n. 29) s. 9.15.
562. *Ibid.*, 8.14[2][b][ii].
563. *Ibid.*, 8.13.
564. *Moorman Mfg. Co. v. Bair*, 437 US 267, 278-279, 98 S. Ct. 2340 (1978).
565. *Ibid.* (Powell, J., dissenting).

objectives from maintaining the collective equilibrium of interests to furthering the unilateral interest of economic development.[566]

### *3.4.3.2 Canada*

As another jurisdiction with a relatively long history of employing formulary apportionment, the formula used by the Canadian provincial corporation income tax contrasts with its US counterpart in several aspects.

First, and most basically, the Canadian formula uses two equal-weighted factors of gross revenue factor and payroll (salaries and wages) formula. According to federal regulations, the levy of corporation income tax in a province relies on the existence of permanent establishment within the province. Where a corporation has permanent establishments in more than one province, the taxable income of the corporation will be apportioned to a province according to 50% of the share of gross revenue and 50% of the share of payroll associated with the province.[567] The formula is expressed as follows:

*Equation 3.4 Canada Formula*

$$TP = \tfrac{1}{2}\,[R/RC + P/PC] * TC$$

**TP**: taxable income of a corporation in a province for the year
**R**: apportionable *gross revenue* that is attributed to the province
**RC**: apportionable *gross revenue* of the corporation in total for the year
**P**: apportionable *payroll,* including salaries and wages paid in the province
**PC**: apportionable *payroll* paid by the corporation in total in the year
**TC**: the total taxable income of the corporation for the year

Second, different from the US experiences, the Canadian apportionment formula has been stable and uniform across the provinces. From a temporal perspective, the Canadian experiences do not present a dynamic tendency as the US states, which is mainly attributed to the federal government and the provinces having a long-standing agreement on a common formula.[568] When the federal rules were initially drafted, for example, balancing the apportionment result between the head office and permanent establishment as well as the complexities of the property factor had already been taken into account.[569] In addition, the non-agreeing provinces also adopted the same formula through autonomous legislation.

566. Hellerstein and McLure (n. 386) 95.
567. Siu et al. (n. 398) 19.
568. Section 402(3)(a), Income Tax Regulations.
569. Smith, 'Allocating to Provinces the Taxable Income of Corporations: How the Federal-Provincial Allocation Rules Evolved' (n. 391) 548, 550.

Apart from the general two-factor formula, the Federal Regulations also provide a special formula for nine sectors, including insurance, banks, trust and loan corporations, railways, airlines, grain elevator operators, bus and truck operators, ship operators, and pipeline operators.[570]

### *3.4.3.3 The EU CCCTB Proposal*

The EU CCCTB proposal employed a typical equal-weighted three-factor formula. The only variance is that the EU used the labour factor comprising the equal-weighted payroll and the number of employees at equal weights instead of the traditional payroll factor.[571] As such, the share in the consolidated tax base of a corporate group apportionable to, for example, a group member A is calculated by the member's share of sales, labour and assets in that of the entire group. The CCCTB formula is provided by the CCCTB Proposal as follows.[572]

*Equation 3.5 CCCTB Formula*

$$\text{Share A} = \left(\frac{1}{3}\frac{Sales^{A}}{Sales^{Group}} + \frac{1}{3}\left(\frac{1}{2}\frac{Payroll^{A}}{Payroll^{Group}} + \frac{1}{2}\frac{No\ of\ Employess^{A}}{No\ of\ Employess^{Group}}\right) + \frac{1}{3}\frac{Assets^{A}}{Assets^{Group}}\right)$$

$$* \ Con'd\ Tax\ Base$$

Both the original CCCTB proposal in 2011 and the relaunched proposal in 2016 were subjected to amendments by the EU Parliament, which is the due legal procedure of EU law-making. The Commission was thus called on to revise its proposals in line with the Parliament's request for amendments.

In April 2012, the Parliament passed a vote on a series of amendments to the original CCCTB proposal.[573] Many suggested changes in the amendments are significant, and the revision of the apportionment formula is one of them. The Parliament did not object to the choice of the sales, labour and assets factors, but proposed to assign a lower weight to the sales factor by adopting the 10% sales, 45% labour, and 45% assets weight structure. The EESC and the Committee on the Internal Market and Consumer Protection advocated taking out the sales factor completely.[574] The drivers for the change are to accord with the international tax convention that attributes major taxing right to the source state rather than the market state as well as to protect the taxing right of the states with a limited domestic market,[575] both of which have been

570. Section 402(4)(g) to (h), Income Tax Regulations.
571. European Commission, 'CCCTB Proposal of Consolidation' (n. 413) Art. 28.
572. *Ibid.* European Commission, 'CCCTB 2011' (n. 393) Art. 86.
573. European Parliament, 'Report on the Proposal for a Council Directive on a Common Consolidated Corporate Tax Base (CCCTB)' (n. 411).
574. EESC, 'Opinion of the European Economic and Social Committee' (2011) OJ C24/63-69 para. 4.6.3.
575. *Ibid.*, 21.

referred to several times in the CCCTB Working Group consultations.[576] The possibility of the manipulation of the sales factor is also a consideration.[577] The Parliament version of the CCCTB formula is expressed as follows.

*Equation 3.6 Parliament Version of the CCCTB Formula*

$$\text{Share A} = \left(\frac{1}{10}\frac{Sales^{A}}{Sales^{Group}} + \frac{9}{20}\left(\frac{1}{2}\frac{Payroll^{A}}{Payroll^{Group}} + \frac{1}{2}\frac{No\ of\ Employess^{A}}{No\ of\ Employess^{Group}}\right) + \frac{9}{20}\frac{Assets^{A}}{Assets^{Group}}\right) * Con'd\ Tax\ Base$$

In March 2018, following the same procedure, the Parliament proposed amendments to the re-launched CCCTB proposal again.[578] This time, the revision of the apportionment formula is also significant, mainly as a response to the challenges of the digital economy. The equal-weighted three-factor formula is revised to an equal-weighted four-factor one, adding the new 'data' factor that refers to the 'collection and use of personal data of online platforms and service users'.[579] The proposed formula is expressed as follows.[580]

*Equation 3.7 Parliament Amended Formula*

$$\text{Share A} = \left(\frac{1}{4}\frac{Sales^{A}}{Sales^{Group}} + \frac{1}{4}\left(\frac{1}{2}\frac{Payroll^{A}}{Payroll^{Group}} + \frac{1}{2}\frac{No\ of\ Employess^{A}}{No\ of\ Employess^{Group}}\right) + \frac{1}{4}\frac{Assets^{A}}{Assets^{Group}}\right.$$
$$\left. + \frac{1}{4}\left(\frac{1}{2}\frac{Data\ Collected^{A}}{Data\ Collected^{Group}} + \frac{1}{2}\frac{Data\ Exploited^{A}}{Data\ Exploited^{Group}}\right)\right) * Con'd\ Tax\ Base$$

### 3.4.3.4 *Pillar One Amount A*

The Pillar One Amount A is a sales-only factor form of formulary apportionment. The final formula employs the sales data of both the MNE group and those arising from market jurisdictions. The revenue sourcing rules function to pin down the location and amount of sales revenue.

576. 'Summary Record by the Chair of the Meeting of the Common Consolidated Corporate Tax Base Working Group (10-11 December 2007)' CCCTB/WP/64/en para. 47; 'Summary Record of the Meeting of the Common Consolidated Corporate Tax Base Working Group (Brussels, 12 December 2007)' CCCTB/WP/63/en para. 27. *See also* Jan Van de Streek, 'Some Thoughts on the European Parliament Amendments of the CCCTB' in Dennis Weber (ed.), *EU Income Tax Law: Issues for the Years Ahead* (IBFD Publications 2013) para. 4.4.3.
577. de Wilde, 'On the Future of Business Income Taxation in Europe' (n. 451).
578. European Parliament, 'Report on the Proposal for a Council Directive on a Common Consolidated Corporate Tax Base (CCCTB)' (2018) COM(2016)0683 – C8-0471/2016-2016/0336(CNS) A8-0051/2018 https://www.europarl.europa.eu/doceo/document/A-8-2018-0051_EN.pdf accessed 5 December 2023.
579. *Ibid.*, 14.
580. *Ibid.*, 28.

Such a choice of Amount A is based on the narrow political goals of expanding or creating the taxing right of market jurisdictions in the context of the digital economy. Besides, it is noteworthy that Amount A serves as an overlay rather than a sweeping reform.

### *3.4.3.5 Summary and Lessons*

Designing the apportionment formula is usually the last step in formulating the formulary apportionment regime when all other components, such as tax base and taxable unit, are decided so that the choice and weight of apportionment factors are the last of the issues.

In general, the formulas employed by the US, Canada and EU CCCTB have things in common as well as other aspects of variation. For example, the multi-factor formula has been unanimously preferred over the single-factor formula, at least at the outset, in the context of the US. Their formulas generally employ the factors of labour, sales, and assets in different forms and combinations, with the exception of the EU Parliament version proposing the 'data' factor. The variance is nevertheless substantial, especially where the US is trending toward the single sales factor formula or the variedly weighted sales factor in the EU CCCTB formulas.

Therefore, based on the existing systems, there should not be many controversies over the factors which are to be employed for formulary apportionment in the international context, which are just chosen from labour, sales and asset factors in their entirety or selectively. The rationales and specific considerations are illuminated in the following using the US experience as a blueprint. In addition, it is observed from the discrepancies that the sales factor has aroused the majority of the disagreement. The bottom line is that the sales factor should be included in the formula to attribute income to market states as a balance of interest with the production state. In economics, the sales factor is justified by the creation of income as an interplay of supply side and demand side. In practice, the sales factor and its weight in the formula are also implicated in the competing objectives of tax policy among the equitable allocation of income, attracting investment and countering tax avoidance, for which there is no golden rule providing commanding instructions.

Besides the US judicial input as to the conceptual basis of apportionment factors and the competing policy objectives pursued by the states, discussions revolving around the experiences of the US state formulary apportionment on the reference criteria of determining the choice and weight of apportionment factors in the formula have been abundant.[581] Based on these resources, a 'flow chart' is provided to simplify the thought process following the recommended criteria for designing the factors in the

581. Weiner, *Company Tax Reform in the European Union* (n. 444). Agundez-Garcia (n. 471). Weiner, *Formulary Apportionment and Group Taxation in the European Union* (n. 28). Charles E McLure, 'Replacing Separate Entity Accounting and the Arm's Length Principle with Formulary Apportionment' (2002) 56 Bulletin for International Fiscal Documentation 586-599. Hellerstein, 'International Income Allocation in the Twenty-First Century: The Case for Formulary Apportionment' (n. 486). Bharat N Anand and Richard Sansing, 'The Weighting

formulary apportionment. While stemming from the US context, the chart is made for reference in a generic sense. It is thus seen that deciding the factors and the weight in the apportionment formula is not an exact science but is at the cross-field of economics, tax theory, and political and administrative enforceability. From the perspective of real tax policy making, the considerations presented in the chart are to be weighed comprehensively, and where necessary, compromises are unavoidable:

> Step A-1: At the conceptual basis level, factor representation should be considered for the choice of factors in the apportionment formula. The factors should represent some essential correspondence with the apportionable tax base.
> Step A-2: The factor representation requirement thus precludes the use of arbitrary, irrational or frivolous
> factors, such as 'paper clips'[582] held by a company or 'macro' factors of country/industry specific averages.
> Step B-1: The choice and weight of factors also depend substantially on the context in which formulary apportionment is considered. In the unilateral setting where external constraints are discounted, tax policy makers can prioritize economic development goals and the minimization of tax distortions to the locations of business activities. In this case, additional factors other than sales may be repudiated.
> Step B-2: In contrast, in the setting where multiple jurisdictional actors compete and cooperate, the apportionment formula needs to be *practical* under *political* constraints. The equitable division of apportionable tax base becomes the collective objective as the concretization of agreeing on a feasible and acceptable formula, which in turn relates to the equity principle including inter-taxpayer equity and inter-nation equity. In light of the discussions in the chapter, both equity criteria are in concert with the conceptual basis of apportionment factor in that they both dictate the factor representation.[583] Arguably, a multiple-factor formula employing property, payroll and sales is in line with the equity criteria. In particular, the practical and political feasibility concerns under inter-nation equity command the balance of interest between production and market sides, which prompts the sales factor to be double weighted in the three-factor formula.
> Step C: As the US experiences exhibit, the general formula was developed for and out of the manufacturing and mercantile industries. There are many business forms, especially under modern circumstances, that do not fit in the conceptual framework of a general formula, which means that the factors in

Game: Formula Apportionment as an Instrument of Public Policy' 53 National Tax Journal 183 https://doi.org/10.17310/ntj.2000.2.01 accessed 26 August 2025. Hellerstein and McLure, Jr. (n. 522).

582. McIntyre, 'Contrasting Methodologies: A Systematic Presentation of the Differences between an Arm's-Length/Source-Rule System and a Combined-Reporting/Formulary-Apportionment System' (n. 70) 234.

583. Agundez-Garcia (n. 471) 46-59.

the general formula are unable to capture the value creation of these businesses and may render unacceptable division of income. In this case, the use of different factors reflecting the features of a specific business sector is suggested.

## 3.5 CLOSING REMARKS

This chapter is a comparative analysis of the existing formulary apportionment regimes in the US, Canada, the European Union CCCTB Proposal, and the new Pillar One Amount A. Rather than organized as a one-by-one country-specific comparison, this chapter first disassembles the formulary apportionment regime into several components, on the basis of which component-by-component comparative analyses and the lessons from them for the design of international formulary apportionment follow.

The comparative analysis of existing regimes of formulary apportionment does not aim to unearth some hidden truths but to provide a general framework and groundwork for exploring formulary apportionment in the contemporary international context. In some of the sections of the summary and lessons, some instructions which are quite unequivocal are provided; for example, the group approach is suggested over the Canadian separate reporting approach for the issue of the taxable unit, and the harmonization of the tax base is also preferable.

However, other than these, on top of the lessons drawn for each of the components, it is observable throughout the discussions that there are hardly any undisputable decisions with respect to the design of formulary apportionment. Controversies are widespread not only regarding what is 'good' or 'bad' but also what is 'achievable' or 'non-achievable'. The choices of the various alternatives in each component could render significantly different results of formulary apportionment.

## Part III

# Constructing the Analytical Framework for Formulary Apportionment

International tax law has a dual structure - comprising the tax distribution/ coordination relationship between states and the tax collection-payment relationship between state and foreign taxpayers. It was debated whether international tax law constitutes part of international law or is a separate field.[584]

Rather than confining international tax law strictly within international law, it is suggested to view international taxation as a global socio-legal phenomenon.[585] This allows drawing principles not just from legal orders but from broader sources like traditional tax policy criteria, observations of the current system, historical experiences, and strategic directions.

The principles of domestic tax law do not automatically become international tax principles. There needs to be reformulation and interpretation when applying domestic principles internationally. However, international tax principles have close contact with and need to consult domestic tax principles.

The principles provide value judgments and directional guidance rather than dictating specific rules. They may conflict, requiring prioritization based on weights. The principles aim to establish an analytical framework for analysing international tax considerations for formulary apportionment.

As such, a proposed outline of international tax principles covers legitimacy and equity (representing justice/fairness)[586] and neutrality (representing efficiency). These

584. Reuven S Avi-Yonah, *International Tax as International Law: An Analysis of the International Tax Regime* (Cambridge University Press 2007).
585. Allison Christians, 'Taxation as a Global Socio-Legal Phenomenon' (2008) 14 ILSA Journal of International and Comparative Law.
586. Before the finalization of this work, there was a separate chapter (and was taken out to cut the thickness of the research) on the selection of the principles or maxims of international taxation, for which fairness is one of the two pillars in parallel to efficiency. However, for focused discussion of fairness in international taxation, *see* Nancy H Kaufman, 'Fairness and the Taxation of International Income' (1997) 29 Law & Policy in International Business 145; Luuk

principles are derived from both endogenous (internal legal order) and exogenous (external evaluations) sources.

Equity and legitimacy not only support FA at a normative level but also provide guidelines for its prospective design and development. For neutrality, however, the usefulness of neutrality is contested and questioned, and the value falls more on *ex-post* evaluations.

*Figure 3.3 Analytical Framework*

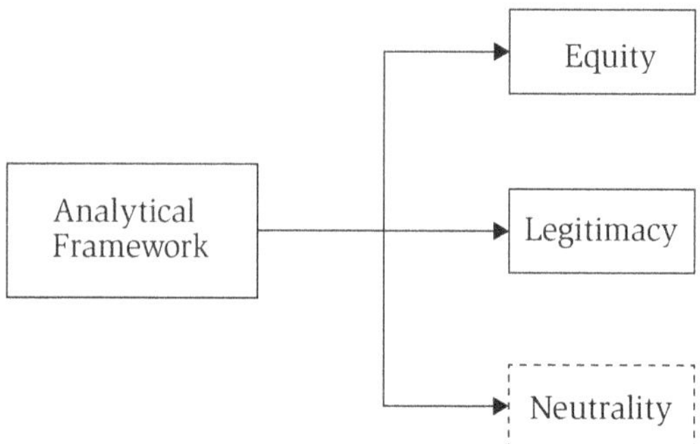


Bosch, 'Fairness in Allocating Taxation Right Between Source and Residence States' (2014) http://arno.uvt.nl/show.cgi?fid=134224 accessed 27 November 2023; Han Benshalom, 'Re-thinking International Distributive Justice: Fairness as Insurance' (2013) 31 Boston University International Law Journal 267; Jonathan Rhys Kesselman and Allan M Maslove, 'Fairness in Taxation: Exploring the Principles' (1994) 20 Canadian Public Policy-analyse De Politiques 99 https://doi.org/10.2307/3551841 accessed 26 August 2025.

CHAPTER 4

# The Principle of Equity

*This chapter explores the principle of equity in international taxation through a structured three-step approach, transitioning from a unitary fiscal setting to an international context, with a focus on both individual and corporate taxation. The first step examines inter-individual equity in a unitary fiscal setting, emphasizing the ability-to-pay and benefit principle as core mechanisms for equitable tax burden allocation among individuals. The second step analyses equity in the international setting, highlighting the limitations of directly applying domestic equity norms to international taxation due to the introduction of non-residents and foreign governments, which complicates horizontal and vertical relationships. It introduces inter-nation equity, as conceptualized by Peggy Musgrave, which focuses on equitable tax base allocation among nations rather than individuals, grounded in principles of sovereign equality and potential redistributive justice. The economic allegiance theory is proposed as a foundation for inter-nation equity, advocating for tax base distribution based on a taxpayer's economic interests across jurisdictions. The chapter distinguishes two approaches to inter-nation equity: the Equal Earned Income approach, which assumes geographically attributable income, and the Equal Allegiance approach, which uses economic allegiance as a proxy for tax base allocation. The third step extends these findings to corporate taxation, arguing that inter-nation equity remains applicable despite the shift in subjects, as corporate taxation ultimately serves individual tax fairness. The chapter concludes by applying inter-nation equity to formulary apportionment, suggesting it provides a critical framework for adopting and designing equitable tax systems for multinational enterprises, balancing tax rights among jurisdictions.*

## 4.1 INTRODUCTION: THE CONCEPT OF EQUITY AND METHODOLOGY

Like other terms of value, equity is also a concept that is difficult to define but can only be interpreted.[587] All principles of international tax law have roots in those developed in a domestic setting, and the discussions of equity in the unitary fiscal setting are also the 'standard' examinations.

Therefore, the study of the equity principle applied to individuals in the unitary fiscal setting serves as a starting point, which is the *first step* of the 'three-step' approach to examining the equity principle in international taxation.

Equity, as a fairness norm, concerns the even-handed allocation of the total tax burden of a country, which is different from the essence of tax legitimacy. Equity is inherently derived from the principle of equality, arguing that equal circumstances should be treated equally before the law, and this implies that, on the mirror side, unequal circumstances should be treated unequally.[588] The same applies to tax equity: *horizontal equity* requires taxpayers under the same circumstances to be taxed the same, while *vertical equity* requires taxpayers under different circumstances to be taxed differently. Both horizontal equity and vertical equity have no substantive content in themselves, but they are good 'prompters' to clarify equity.[589] Besides being a value perceived in the unitary setting, equity is also originally about individuals.

For the taxation of individuals, two groups of relationships are to be examined for the consideration of equity. First, it is the *vertical* relationship between the government and individuals; the tax authority needs to figure out how to spread the tax burden equitably among the general population. Second, equity is also felt when a taxpayer compares his tax liabilities with others. Such a relationship is *horizontal*. Although subjects in these two relationships are somewhat different, they are two sides of the same coin for equity considerations. They lead substantively to the same equity norm, inter-individual equity. The division of horizontal equity and vertical equity applies to inter-individual equity, but they lack independent significance.[590] The key, however, is how tax law evaluates the 'affinity' or 'difference' of the taxable circumstances as the

587. Klaus Vogel, 'Worldwide vs. Source Taxation of Income-a Review and Re-Evaluation of Arguments (Part III)' (1988) 16 Intertax 393, 393 https://doi.org/10.54648/taxi1988068 accessed 26 August 2025.

588. Maarten Floris de Wilde, '"Sharing the Pie": Taxing Multinationals in a Global Market' (2015) 43 Intertax 438 https://doi.org/10.54648/taxi2015040 accessed 26 August 2025.

589. David Elkinst, 'Horizontal Equity as a Principle of Tax Theory' (2006) 24 Policy Review https://doi.org/10.17310/ntj.2006.3.15 accessed 26 August 2025. Michael L Goetz, 'Tax Avoidance, Horizontal Equity, and Tax Reform: A Proposed Synthesis' (1978) 44 Southern Economic Journal 798 https://doi.org/10.2307/1057730 accessed 26 August 2025; Paul R McDaniel and James R Repetti, 'Horizontal and Vertical Equity: The Musgrave/Kaplow Exchange' (2022) 1 Florida Tax Review https://doi.org/10.5744/ftr.1993.1102 and https://journals.upress.ufl.edu/ftr/article/view/502 accessed 18 November 2023.

590. *See* different opinions, Kaplow Louis, 'Horizontal Equity: Measures in Search of a Principle' (1989) 42 National Tax Journal 139, 143-144 https://doi.org/10.1086/ntj41788784 accessed 26 August 2025. McDaniel and Repetti (n. 589) 607, 621. Richard A Musgrave, 'Horizontal Equity, Once More' (1990) 43 National Tax Journal 113-114 https://doi.org/10.1086/ntj41788830 accessed 26 August 2025.

basis of measuring the tax liability. There are two main principles concerning such measurement, which are the ability to pay (AtP) principle and the benefit principle (BP). In accordance with AtP and BP respectively, the tax systems are of different features in design. The study of equity in the unitary setting in relation to inter-individual equity is the first step for examining equity in the international setting.

The *second step* is to discuss equity for individuals in the international setting. When the setting is turned to an open economy and international setting, the underlying relationships and circumstances are different from those in the unitary setting. Then the question arises as to whether the above inter-individual equity is inclusive or suitable to guide the equitable design of the international tax system. If the answer is positive, it can be said that the direct international of inter-individual equity. If the answer is negative, then the equity standards should be refined in the international setting.

The *last step* is to build a smooth transition from the equity standards for individuals in the international setting to the equity standards in terms of corporate taxation in the same setting. The analysis in this phase mainly focuses on the potential influences brought by the change of subjects on the equity considerations developed through the second step.

*Figure 4.1 The Three-Step Approach Exploring Equity*

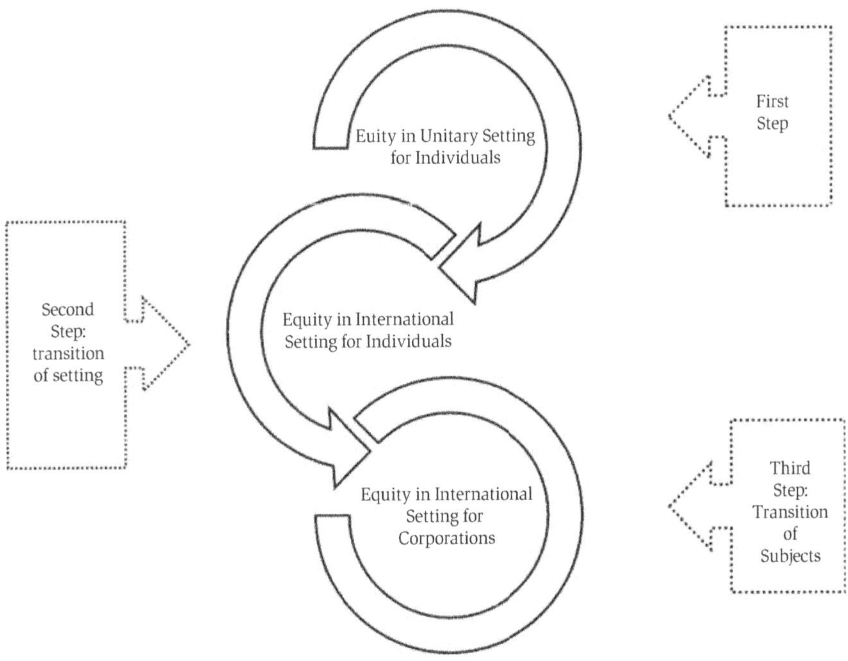

## 4.2 THE FIRST STEP: EQUITY IN UNITARY FISCAL SETTING

As shown and said above, the major content of equity in its original setting, the unitary fiscal setting, is inter-individual equity. As the two sides of a coin, if the governments allocate the tax burden equitably among the general population, an individual will see his tax obligation in accordance with equity in relation to the tax liabilities of other individuals.[591] The unitary fiscal setting means that equity is derived from and rooted in the setting of one taxing government, one fiscal system, and a closed economy. Such a setting is the birthplace of all ethical values, not limited to taxation, before the world is connected and an open economy emerges.

AtP and BP are the core theories that materialize the claims of inter-individual equity, by providing an 'index' to the government as the basis to distribute the tax burden. The AtP principle advocates that the distribution should be in line with the individual's ability to pay, whereas BP holds that the distribution is according to the individual's benefits gained from the public goods and services provided by the government. This study is not going to go deep into the intellectual history of AtP and BP, respectively, as has been well done by other researchers.[592] Instead, for the theme of this study, AtP and BP will be compared and jointly analysed in their applications to the real tax system.

The reasons for doing so are, first, the thoughts about AtP and BP were actually inseparable or 'unitary' themselves. In earlier times, the ideas about the justification of taxation and the tax fairness currently referred to were blended.[593] This can be illustrated by the famous statement concerning the general canons of taxation by Adam Smith: '*The subjects of every state ought to contribute towards the support of the government, as nearly as possible, in proportion to their respective abilities; that is, in proportion to the revenue which they respectively enjoy under the protection of the state.*'[594] More than 200 years later, when economists considered the future design of the modern international tax system, they said similar words: 'This ability-to-pay theory is more comprehensive than the preceding benefit theory *because it includes what there is of value in the benefit theory.*'[595] In short, before income was widely accepted as the index of ability to pay, one's benefit can be one's ability.

Second, after the separation of AtP from BP, their relationship is more competitive than cooperative. The *ability* to pay of the taxpayer has been viewed as different from the benefits he received from the government. Fundamentally, such separation

591. Kaufman (n. 586) 157.
592. For example, *see* Richard A Musgrave, *A Brief History of Fiscal Doctrine*, vol. 1 (Elsevier 1985). Joseph M Dodge, 'Theories of Tax Justice: Ruminations on the Benefit, Partnership, and Ability-to-Pay Principles' (2004) 58 Tax Law Review 399. Joachim Englisch, 'Ability to Pay in European Tax Law' in Cécile Brokelind (ed.), *Principles of Law: Function, Status and Impact in EU Tax Law* (IBFD Publications 2014) 439-464.
593. Englisch (n. 592) 1-2.
594. Adam Smith, *Wealth of Nations* (W. Strahan and T. Cadell, London 1776) 1103. 'Adam Smith defined the tax obligation, as did Hobbes and Petty, on the basis of an objective measure of benefit, and hence, ability to pay.', Miranda Stewart, 'The Tax State, Benefit and Legitimacy' (2015) TTPI – Working Paper 15.
595. Bruins et al. (n. 44) 18.

can be attributed to their different theoretical bases. The ideal of BP is ultimately a quid pro quo relationship between taxpayer and government; thus, in light of BP, a just or equitable tax system allocates the tax burden in accordance with the distribution of public goods or services.[596] AtP, however, disregards the potential link between the individual's interests in public goods or services and his liability to pay tax. The tax system advocated by AtP for a 'tax and welfare' state has the effect of distributive justice.[597] Over time and for various reasons, AtP has dominated BP as tax fairness standards.[598]

Third, the dominance of AtP as a tax fairness standard does not exclude BP's role in the legitimacy of taxation and the design of the fiscal system. To be discussed in Chapter 4, the benefit principle is one of the most enduring and 'waxed and waned' theories for tax justification, and now is still playing an important role in many areas of both domestic and international taxation. In fiscal systems other than tax, special-purpose levies and charges (*sonderabgaben*) are mostly justified by BP.[599]

### 4.2.1 An AtP Tax System and a BP Tax

The top issue for AtP is to determine an objective and measurable indicator of the ability of individuals to pay tax; it is a task searching for objectivity, which raises the foundational concept of income. The foundational concept of income contributed by Schanz-Haig-Simons (S-H-S) is one of the most enduring concepts in the development of tax knowledge. According to the SHS model, income is the algebraic sum of consumption and the net change in the value of all assets.[600] In the development of the concept of income, a few other methods were also put forward in service as indicators of an individual's ability to pay to make it possible to weigh everyone's tax liability in alignment with the objective of equity. They are wealth, consumption, or personal endowment of humans and so forth. However, apparently, the income as a tax base prevails.

Leaving aside temporarily the detailed considerations of the income concept, AtP suggests the following features of a national tax system:[601]

596. Kaufman (n. 586) 157.
597. 'The fact that redistributive justice had become a goal of the welfare State implied that taxes stopped being merely ad rem taxes and progressed towards being personal taxes (i.e., taxes which take into account the actual personal situation of taxpayers such as source of income, marital status, etc.).', Ribeiro João Sérgio, 'Distributive Justice Through Taxation: European Perspective' [2006] Jurisprudencija: mokslo darbai. Vilnius: Mykolo Romerio universiteto Leidybos centras, 2006, Nr. 2 (80). 81.
598. Kaufman (n. 586) 183-184. Dodge (n. 592) 400.
599. Qingxiu Chen, *General Theories of Tax Law* (Angle publishing Co., Ltd, 7th edn, 2012) 83.
600. For comprehensive study of income concept, *see* Kevin Holmes, *The Concept of Income: A Multi-Disciplinary Analysis* (IBFD Publications 2001).
601. Englisch (n. 592) 439-464. Kaufman (n. 586) 158-163.

(1) a comprehensive tax base. As an indicator of an individual's ability and thus liability to pay tax, the tax base needs to be as comprehensive as possible to capture the 'genuine' ability of the taxpayer;[602]
(2) a global tax system, meaning that all the incomes, regardless of their sources (not in geographic meaning), are aggregated and subject to a universal set of tax rules to calculate the taxable amount;[603]
(3) off-the-bottom exceptions, the ability to pay is the residual ability above the minimum subsistence of an individual. AtP income tax has usually been classified as in personam tax;
(4) a progressive tax rate to levy more tax on individuals with a higher ability to pay tax.[604]

In contrast, a BP-based tax system carries the following features:[605]

(1) no specific mandate for the choice of tax base, which can be either a poll tax or an income tax;
(2) a schedular income tax system, under which separate tax rules applied to income derived from different sources, such as interest and rent;[606]
(3) an in rem tax, which does not make adjustments for personal circumstances of individuals;
(4) special-purpose levies and charges are justified and constructed by BP.

Till now, AtP and BP as two pillars of equity, more specifically, inter-individual equity, in the unitary fiscal setting have been discussed in terms of their implications for the design of a concrete tax system. Three points can be further summarized or repeated from the above discussions:

(1) Equity in unitary fiscal setting concerns two sets of relationships, respectively the inter-individual and individual-government relationships. Equity in these

602. 'Theoretically, comprehensive income embodies net monetary increases in asset values by measuring changes in values of assets and liabilities between the beginning and the end of an income measurement period. Comprehensive income also captures the first five components (money received as a return on factors of production, monetary gifts and windfall gains, benefits in kind, and the net monetary increase in asset values) of Haig's income formulation.', Holmes (n. 600) Ch. 4.
603. A global tax system and a comprehensive tax base emphasize similar aspects but are of different nature, of which the former stresses that the income is taxed with a single rule, but the latter stresses that source of income is not important.
604. Even though progressivity of tax system has been attributed to equal sacrifice theory rather than ATP, but ATP still can generally justify a progressive tax system. Englisch (n. 592).
605. Here and the above about ATP only consider their implications in a pure theoretical background by deductions. In reality, the general tax system bears with both characteristics of ATP and BP systems. For more information about benefit taxes in reality, *see* David G Duff, 'Benefit Taxes and User Fees in Theory and Practice' (2004) 54 University of Toronto Law Journal 393 https://doi.org/10.1353/tlj.2004.0013 accessed 26 August 2025.
606. Ignatius Universitaire Faculteiten St- and Plasschaert Sylvain Rf, 'First Principles About Schedular and Global Frames of Income Taxation' (1976) 99 Bulletin International Fiscal Documentation.

two relationships is manifested by a single sub-concept of equity, the inter-individual equity.

(2) AtP and BP are two material fairness norms that support inter-individual equity by providing a yardstick for distribution of the tax burden.

(3) AtP and BP have direct implications on the design of a national tax system, mainly in relation to the tax base and the rate structure.

*Figure 4.2 Equity in the Unitary Setting*

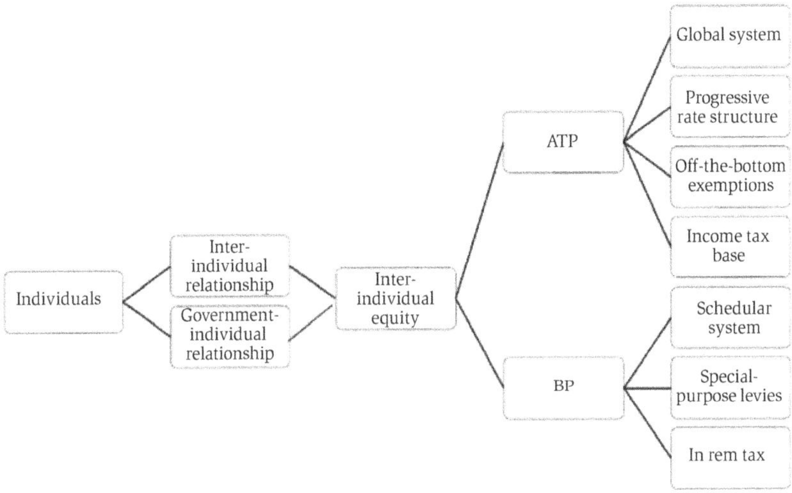


## 4.3 THE SECOND STEP: EQUITY IN THE INTERNATIONAL SETTING

After discussing equity in the unitary fiscal setting, as a template or starting point of equity, it is time to examine equity in the international setting. As the second step, the following study will continue to focus on the taxation of individuals.

In contrast to the unitary setting, where the relationships are somewhat simpler, in an international setting, at least the subjects are more than those in the unitary setting. The international setting has added two additional subjects to the unitary setting, which are the non-resident and the foreign government. However, for equity considerations, the changes are far more than that.

Even if the setting is now international, the factual changes still need to be observed from a single country's perspective as a foothold. To summarize briefly, for a country, some of its residents can earn income from abroad, while others cannot, and non-residents can earn income within its borders.

The equity question brought by the above factual changes is *ultimately* the same as the unitary setting, which is, what are the standards to achieve equity in the international setting?

### 4.3.1 Direct Internationalization Is Not the Way Out

The equity question raised by the transition from a unitary setting to an international setting is just like what has been discussed in the first part of this chapter about the validity of domestic principles in the international arena. It has been stated that the international tax principles derive from domestic principles but entail reinterpretation. The subjects and relationships are both divergent; thus, the adoption without reservation is problematic. Such a conclusion is still applicable to the equity question in this part. However, to make it more specific, further analysis of the new scenario is advisable. Based on the earlier discussions of equity in the unitary setting, it is natural to ask whether AtP and BP can still apply to the international tax system. Or if they can, are they enough?

Traditionally, in an international scenario, equity in the unitary setting, more specifically inter-individual equity, is directly called upon to provide a basis for the international tax system of individuals. As substantive equity norms, AtP is used to justify a country's taxation on its residents' worldwide income, namely, the system of worldwide taxation.[607] The underlying reasoning is that to satisfy equity, the taxpayer's entire ability needs to be taxed, while the geographic source of that ability (income) is of no relevance. Similarly, BP is used to justify a country's taxation of a non-resident's local source income, namely, a system of source taxation.[608] That is, if both residents and non-residents have benefited equally from the government, then non-residents should also be allocated the general tax burden according to the benefits they receive.

For the above, if paying attention to the details, it can be said simply as the application of AtP and BP to the international scenario. However, in the broader picture, it is the concept of equity or inter-individual equity being internationalized from a standard, traditional and unitary setting to a more complicated, open and international setting. Direct internationalization is one way to question the requirements of equity in an international setting, yet I will prove that such an approach is problematic.

607. Bradford David F and Policy US Treasury Tax, *Blueprints for Basic Tax Reform* (Revised edn, Tax Analysts 1984) 90; Musgrave and Musgrave (n. 7) 68. Vogel, 'Worldwide vs. Source Taxation of Income-a Review and Re-Evaluation of Arguments (Part III)' (n. 587) 395-397.

608. Please note that the 'source taxation' used here is not equivalent to the territorial tax system under which the resident country has no taxing right on the foreign income derived by its resident. The BP-based source taxation has no specific implication on the actual scope of taxation on residents. Arthur R Albrecht, 'The Taxation of Aliens under International Law' (1952) 29 British Yearbook of International Law 145, 145; Lokken Lawrence, 'The Sources of Income from International Uses and Dispositions of Intellectual Property' (1980) 36 Tax Law Reviwe 233, 239-240; Martha J Martha Rutsel Silvestre J, *The Jurisdiction to Tax in International Law: Theory and Practice of Legislative Fiscal Jurisdiction* (1st edn, Kluwer Law & Taxation Publishers 1989).

### 4.3.2 The Changes from Transitioning to International Setting

The three-step approach, as explained in the beginning, has limited the variables to the extent that in the transition of settings, the subject of the taxable person (individual) remains the same. However, even in doing so, the changes from the transition of settings, as briefly introduced above, are substantive in both quantity and quality.

For 'quantity', first of all, there are more taxable persons in the analysis framework than in a unitary setting because non-residents' circumstances must be considered. Other persons who are not directly involved in the taxable activity in question but are indirectly relevant should be accounted for as well, for equity considerations. In addition, not only do 'persons' increase, but the taxing authorities also increase. Both the home country and the foreign (host) country's positions in this scenario need to be considered. These subjects can be visualized in the following diagram. [A] is the home country to its resident [a], and [a] is doing business and earning income from the host country [B]. Furthermore, in the home country [A], [a'] is a pure[609] domestic taxable person without foreign income; in the host country [B], the same is for [b], as a resident of [B].

*Figure 4.3 Illustration of International Taxation*

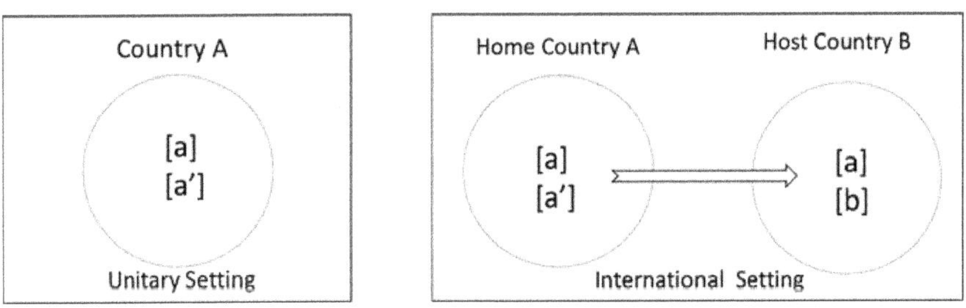


For 'quality', multiple groups of relationships are coming into sight. In the unitary setting, it is the horizontal inter-individual relationship, and the vertical individual-government relationship that are *substantializing* equity, giving equity its form as well as substance. The same methodology applies to equity in an international setting. In the above diagram, it can be seen that the original relationships in the unitary setting only exist partially for pure domestic persons (a) and (b) with their respective governments. In general, the vertical relationships: [A]-[a], [A]-[a']; and [B]-[b], [B]-[a], and the horizontal relationships: [a]-[a']; [a]-[b]. What is unique in an international setting is first the relationship [A]-[B] between the taxing home and host countries [A] and [B], which can also be grouped as a horizontal relationship. Moreover, the above paragraph has defined the introduction of A and B as a quantitative change, but actually, such change is qualitative as well. It is not simply the addition of two separate tax settings, but these settings are open and interrelated. The

609. Meaning that such tax person is without foreign source income.

interaction of two open tax environments in the end leads to an entirely new tax setting for the consideration of tax equity.

### 4.3.3 There Should Not Be Direct Internationalization

In search of equity standards in an international tax setting, the reliance on the direct internationalization of equity thoughts and norms in the unitary setting is not feasible. Another way out must be explored. The fundamental reason is that the underlying relationships that affect equity are different. As shown in the diagram, the conditions are standard and comprehensive in a unitary setting, whether in a horizontal or vertical relationship. The taxable persons have both political and economic ties with the taxing authority; equity under such circumstances has its origins either in the entitlement theory or economic justice,[610] or in the theories of the state. It is, however, difficult to consider welfarist distribution in relation to a state with non-residents.

In an international setting, it cannot be said that these theories are completely inapplicable, but it is for sure that they need substantial reinterpretation. Specifically, starting from the home country's perspective, the vertical relationship [A]-[a] and [A]-[a'], and the horizontal relationship [a]-[a'] are different from those in the unitary setting in both form and substance. If inter-individual equity drawn from a unitary setting holds as well in the home country tax setting, that must mean an equitable tax burden on [a] and [a'] will lead to an equitable relationship between [a] and [a']. However, one must note that the relative relationship between [a] and [a'] in the unitary setting, and the relative relationship between [a] and [a'] in the international setting are different. Based on the above, the direct internationalization of equity in the unitary setting is unreliable, if not unfeasible, for the underlying relationships in the country [A] are different.

The same is true for host country B. Compared to *Home Country* [A] versus *Country* [A], it is relatively easier to identify the divergence of *Country* [A] and *Host Country* [B]. The vertical relationship in the *Country* [A], [A]-[a] is obviously different from that of [B]-[a], for [a] in the international setting is not the resident of [B]. For horizontal relationship, the relative relationship between [a] and [a'] in the former setting is also different from that of [a] and [b] in the international setting. It is worth noting that this analysis is premised on the legitimacy of the host country [B]'s taxing right on [a].

Different from legitimacy, equity concerns the fair allocation of the tax burden; BP states that the more benefits the taxpayers derive from the source country, the higher the tax they should pay. As pointed out by Vogel, the equity question contains an underlying legitimacy question: 'a tax claim is equitable only if taxing the particular transaction or event by the state in question is legitimate or in other words can be justified'.[611] Nancy Kaufman briefly referred to Vogel's view, but she held that legitimacy lacks 'independent normative significance', and it is the good distribution of

610. Kaufman (n. 586) 157.
611. Vogel, 'Worldwide vs. Source Taxation of Income-a Review and Re-Evaluation of Arguments (Part III)' (n. 587) 394.

the tax burden that justifies the legitimacy of taxation.[612] Certainly, this is different from the view of this paper, yet since this study has a separate chapter about legitimacy, it is needless to repeat the discussion of legitimacy here.

The equity analysis in an international setting should also not neglect the role of taxing authorities, as they are undoubtedly protagonists in foreign-related taxable activities. The essence of the relationship between country [A] and country [B] can be temporarily put aside, but for sure, such a relationship is of a different nature and content from the inter-individual relationship as well.

### 4.3.4 Summary

The direct internationalization of equity norms AtP and BP is not the correct direction to construct an equitable international tax system.

On the one hand, the underlying relationships in the international setting are different from those in the unitary setting. The differences are not merely the addition of subjects, but the basis for constructing equity is different as well. This can also be seen even from the inter-relationship between AtP and BP themselves. Unlike competing and mutually exclusive relationships in the unitary setting, AtP and BP cooperate with each other in the international setting, following the direct internationalization of equity. For illustration, in the earlier diagram, AtP is utilized by country [A] to back its taxation on residents and its foreign source income; BP is upheld by country [B] to tax the local-source income of non-residents.

Separately, the proponents may hold that worldwide taxation achieves the AtP form of equity, while source taxation leads to the BP form of equity. It is generally safe to say that in a pure unitary setting, the AtP-based income tax embodies the good vision of equity, notwithstanding some realistic exceptions. However, in the international setting, neither AtP necessarily entails worldwide taxation, nor does the worldwide taxation actually evolve from AtP.[613] As for BP-based source taxation, if BP as inter-individual equity norms is internationalized directly, then 'it is only natural to extend to source taxation the same conceptual and technical objections made to benefit-based income taxes generally'.[614]

More fundamentally, international tax equity means an equitable international tax system, not a kind of equity in the home country, and another kind of equity in the host country. A commonly applicable equity norm is yet to be developed for guiding the design of the international tax system. Overall, the basic changes at the fact level are drastic, and the theoretical foundation for the original equity paradigm to sustain is, as far as the author sees, not yet found.

On the other hand, even accepting the split of equity into two pieces at two ends, the existing reality does not provide sound proof that the internationalization of equity norms can make a good case for its own justification.

612. Kaufman (n. 586) 166.
613. In Nancy Kaufman's words, the tax base need not encompass worldwide income and the tax base does not encompass worldwide income, *see ibid.*, 173, 175.
614. *Ibid.*, 184.

The above analysis has led to the conclusion that the direct internationalization of equity norms is not feasible.

To apply equity in the international setting, instead, the first thing to note is that the *status quo* should be no more than a backdrop, neither the destination. The current system is not the golden rule but more a fulcrum and a starting point to think about how to construct equity in the international setting. To be specific, one must unbundle the combinations of AtP-worldwide taxation and BP-source taxation.

There are possibilities and room to shuffle the combination of the equity norms and tax systems. For instance, there is no area that is forbidden to consider the possibility of a global AtP or a global BP-based tax system in order to reflect equity values in the international tax setting.

## 4.4 RESTART FROM EQUITY

As the fundamental shift of underlying relationships in the international setting has determined the failure of the internationalization of equity norms, the restarted attempt to construct international equity also requires a review of the relationships as well.

### 4.4.1 Missed Step: The Interaction of Taxing States

The above discussions centre on AtP and BP are dealing with only part of the relationships that lay the foundations to construct equity in an international setting, which are the relationships among taxpayers and taxing authorities, either horizontal or vertical. The missed step is to pay attention to the horizontal relationships between the taxing States. It is for 'intentionally left blank' that the above analysis does not touch upon this issue, in order to make the discussions more targeted. When taking into consideration such a relationship, the relevant views may become vulnerable.

In international taxation, there are two groups of relationships: the foreign-related tax collection-payment relationship and the tax distribution and coordination relationship. Putting them against the background of equity discussions, it is the former relationship that relates to the inter-individual equity. For the latter relationship that is inherently among taxing nations, the equity considerations established are apparently out of reach of inter-individual equity. The missed step in the earlier analysis is, for illustration in the above diagram, to consider the interaction (distribution and coordination) between country [A] and country [B]. In the unitary setting, the taxing State [A] or [B] is accounted in a vertical relationship, as in contrast to the international setting, where the two taxing States [A] and [B] are in a horizontal inter-nation relationship of distribution and coordination.

The inter-nation relationship analysis is indispensable for two reasons. First, and fundamentally, is that tax and redistribution are inherently a domestic issue, not an international issue. On the revenue side, the tax burden to be allocated is that of an independent state, for there is no normative international total tax burden. The tax burden of [A] and the tax burden of [B] cannot be aggregated to reach a normative total tax burden. On the spending side, budget decisions concerning individual welfare remain at the discretion of the independent state. It is the country [A] or [B] to be responsible solely for its own residents, not any other country's residents. Besides, for an individual, he or she can be a resident only for one country within the same period, which means that he or she belongs to a single and independent fiscal system. The above factors combined lead to the result that a tax payment to a country is inherently different from a payment to another country. For example, in the diagram, the individual [a] pays a sum of income tax to his resident country [A]. As an AtP-based income tax, such tax payment will become the resource of the country [A] to pursue a just distribution of public goods within [A]. In comparison, as a non-resident of country [B], his tax payment to [B] becomes the resource of [B] to maintain its own redistribution system, in which [a] typically has no role. This analysis has direct implications for the proposition of AtP. It is based on AtP that commentators advocate worldwide taxation by country [A] so as to equalize the tax burden between border-crossing taxpayer [a] and the domestic taxpayer [a']. This advocate wrongly presumes that a sum of money flows to [A] equals to the same sum of money flows to [B], for the purposes of AtP income tax to construct economic justice in country [A]. The ability to pay outside of the border is not the ability to pay within the border.[615]

Second, the integration of the global economy has outstripped the coordination of international taxation.[616] There are no supranational tax authorities and no global redistribution mechanism. The major existing international coordination on tax matters is in the form of bilateral tax treaties, which targets primarily the elimination of double taxation. A series of efforts, especially the BEPS Actions and the MLI led by OECD, might be the first step towards a global coordinated tax system. However, it is still far too early to say that material progress has been made toward establishing a global unified redistribution system. However, international taxation does affect wealth reallocation among nations directly; it is a significant factor. The widening wealth gap between rich countries and poor countries[617] necessitates the coordination and constructive arrangement of international taxation.

In conclusion, the status quo is on the one side, that the redistribution is inherently national, while on the other, international taxation has an important role in affecting the wealth distribution among rich and poor countries and, then, ultimately, the welfare of their residents.[618] As a result, reflections on equity without regard to the analysis of inter-nation relationships is problematic and biased.

615. The opposite opinion is 'The "ability to pay" principle is not limited by geographical or political borders', *see* Luuk Bosch, Fairness in allocating taxation right between source and residence, The Dutch perspective, comparative research and a rethinking of models, *see* Bosch (n. 586) 25.
616. Kaufman (n. 586) 177.
617. For example, typically, the North-Source division, RS Avi-Yonah, 'Bridging the North/South Divide: International Redistribution and Tax Competition' (2004) 26 Michigan Journal of International Law 371.
618. Jinyan Li, 'Improving Inter-Nation Equity Through Territorial Taxation and Tax Sparing' 9 http://digitalcommons.osgoode.yorku.ca/all_papers/252 accessed 27 November 2023.

### 4.4.2 The Emergence of Inter-Nation Equity

The equity reflections based on the inter-nation tax distribution and coordination lead to the concept of inter-nation equity. Such a concept was coined and refined by Peggy Musgrave along with a series of her outputs.[619] This study is not going to retrieve the full intellectual history of inter-nation equity, as it has been well done by others.[620] Instead, just like the above work for inter-individual equity, the following focuses on developing the standards for inter-nation equity and then identifying its relationship with inter-individual equity.

Before the inter-nation equity was extensively formulated by the Musgraves in 1972,[621] Peggy Musgrave had only made brief references to this concept.[622] Thus, the Musgraves' 1972 piece of work should be viewed as the real ground-breaking contribution to the concept of inter-nation equity and is also the basis to start the discussion here as well. Peggy Musgrave's later refinements relate more to the application of inter-nation equity.

Peggy Musgrave never tried to give a specific definition of inter-nation equity. Instead, she formulated inter-nation equity by setting the line between inter-nation equity and inter-individual equity,[623] which rightly coincides with the approach to equity as adopted in this section. Conforming to the common view of inter-individual equity, Peggy Musgrave considered it as 'a taxpayer's liability payable to his country of residence should be the same whether income is derived from foreign or domestic sources'. In short, inter-individual equity is the same tax treatment for the same incomes. She further divided the inter-individual equity into *international* inter-individual equity and *national* inter-individual equity, by a wide or narrow perspective

619. Musgrave and Musgrave (n. 7). Musgrave Peggy B, 'International Tax Differentials for Multinational Corporations: Equity and Efficiency Considerations' in United Nations (ed.), *The Impact of Multinational Corporations on Development and on International Relations, Technical Papers: Taxation* (United Nations 1974); Peggy B Musgrave, 'The OECD Model Tax Treaty: Problems and Prospects' (1975) 10 Columbia Journal of World Business 29. Peggy B Musgrave, 'Principles for Dividing the State Corporate Tax Base' in Charles E McLure (ed.), *State Corporation Income Tax: Issues in Worldwide Unitary Combination* (Hoover Institution Press 1984); Peggy B Musgrave, 'Fiscal Coordination and Competition in an International Setting' in Lorraine Eden (ed.), *Retrospectives on Public Finance* (Duke University Press 1991); Peggy B Musgrave, 'Substituting Consumption-Based Direct Taxation for Income Taxes as the International Norm: A Comment' (1992) 45 National Tax Journal 179. https://doi.org/10.1086/ntj41788958 accessed 26 August 2025; Peggy B Musgrave, 'Consumption Tax Proposals in an International Setting' (2001) 54 Tax Law Review 77; Peggy B Musgrave, 'Chapter 3 Interjurisdictional Equity in Company Taxation: Principles and Applications to the European Union' in Sijbren Cnossen (ed.), *Taxing Capital Income in the European Union: Issues and Options for Reform* (Oxford University Press 2000) https://academic.oup.com/book/51992. accessed 26 August 2025; Peggy B Musgrave, 'Sovereignty, Entitlement, and Cooperation in International Taxation' (2000) 26 Brooklyn Journal of International Law 1335.
620. Especially, *see* Kimberley Brooks, 'Inter-Nation Equity: The Development of an Important but Underappreciated International Tax Value' in Richard Krever and John G Head (eds), *Tax Reform In The 21st Century* (Wolters Kluwer 2009).
621. Musgrave and Musgrave (n. 7).
622. Peggy Brewer Richman, *Taxation of Foreign Investment Income, an Economic Analysis* (Johns Hopkins Press 1963) 49. Musgrave Peggy B, *United States Taxation of Foreign Investment Income: Issues and Arguments* (Law School of Harvard University 1969).
623. Musgrave and Musgrave (n. 7) 68-69.

of tax liability. If tax liability is defined in international terms, then it raises the international inter-individual equity, under which the foreign tax is equivalent to the home country tax. Thus, the home country should give a foreign tax credit to the taxpayer. Similarly, if tax liability is defined in national terms, the national inter-individual equity sees the foreign tax liability as expenses, then the home country gives a deduction. These two cases of home country, neither credit nor deduction for foreign tax payment,[624] involve a matter of inter-nation equity, which implies that inter-individual equity and inter-nation equity are of different values.

The inter-nation equity is then different from inter-individual equity in subjects, as the subjects are taxing states, not individuals. More fundamentally, the measurement of inter-nation equity is not the taxable income or tax revenue but the national gain or loss. It is presumed that if no tax is imposed by the source country, then the foreign income will be the national gain of the taxpayer's residence country.[625] The residence country's specific treatment of foreign tax through either credit or deduction is irrelevant to inter-nation equity, as indicated above, it is an intra-nation matter with effects on inter-individual equity and efficiency instead. What is at stake for inter-nation equity is the source country's decision to tax. The source country's tax always reduces the national gain of the residence country, but not the other way round.

As for the concept of national gain or loss, some commentators tend to reject it on theoretical or practical ground.[626] The concept of national gain is much broader than the taxable income in international taxation. For practical reasons, the discussions of inter-national tax base share, and ultimately tax revenue share rather than national gain or loss are more straightforward.[627] Yet the national gain formulation has mainly enlightened us to differentiate between intra-nation treasury transfer and that at the stake of inter-nation equity. The shift from national gain to tax base shares does not render the essential thoughts about inter-nation equity changed.[628] As a matter of fact, not only Peggy Musgrave herself, but a number of other commentators also rely on tax base shares rather than the original national gain concept in their studies.[629] Still, following Peggy Musgrave, the 'equity burden' is on the source country in relation to

624. Both only constitute a transfer from treasury to taxpayer within the home country, *see ibid.*, 68.
625. *Ibid.*, 71.
626. Vogel, 'Worldwide vs. Source Taxation of Income-a Review and Re-Evaluation of Arguments (Part III)' (n. 587) 398. Christoph Sommer, *Separate Accounting or Unitary Apportionment?: The Fairy Tale of Arm's Length Pricing and General Equilibrium Analysis of Multinational Enterprise Behavior under the Formulary Taxation Alternative* (Josef Eul Verlag Gmbh 2011) 33.
627. 'In fact, the significance of these tax arrangements for IJE (inter-jurisdiction equity) goes beyond the mere revenue share. As capital moves from one jurisdiction to another, this not only affects tax bases but also has its impact on factor earnings in both host and home jurisdictions. For developing countries in particular, the gain to labour from a capital inflow may outweigh in importance any revenue to its Treasury. At the same time, allowance for these secondary effects in determining an equitable distribution of tax bases would be administratively unmanageable, thus, for practical purposes, IJE has to be confined to revenue shares.', Musgrave, 'Chapter 3 Interjurisdictional Equity in Company Taxation: Principles and Applications to the European Union' (n. 619) 54.
628. Kaufman (n. 586) 190.
629. Kaufman (n. 586). Vogel, 'Worldwide vs. Source Taxation of Income-a Review and Re-Evaluation of Arguments (Part III)' (n. 587) 394. Li, 'Improving Inter-Nation Equity Through

whether and how much the source country decides to tax the income of non-residents, which concerns the legitimacy of the source jurisdiction to tax and its share of the international income.

### 4.4.3 In Search of Criteria

It is undeniable that the introduction of inter-nation equity is a milestone in the theories of international taxation. For the first time, the commentators have something more than inter-individual equity or efficiency to rely on to guide the design of an equitable international tax system. As said above, for inter-nation equity, the major concerns are the source country's right to tax the international income derived within the border, and the precise scope of the source taxation.

The source country's right to tax is, in other words, the legitimacy of source jurisdiction to tax. The source country's jurisdiction to tax can be legitimized by the foreign taxpayer's participation in the source country's 'State-Society-Economy' triangular system. Yet meanwhile, the legitimacy issue indeed does not relate to the specific allocation of the total tax burden. Thus, legitimacy is irrelevant to the extent of the source country's share of the international income. Peggy Musgrave's construction of the concept of inter-nation equity started from the standard model of worldwide taxation and source taxation, in particular, that it is at least the residual interest of residence country to tax the worldwide income of residents.[630]

Concrete criteria of inter-nation equity was then developed by Peggy Musgrave. To this end, she proposed four mechanisms to fulfil the objective of inter-nation equity. First, they are benefit-based taxation in the host country,[631] under which the inter-nation equity will be self-implementing.[632] However, it is not a realistic option because, as said above, the benefit taxation has shrunk to very limited application in the fiscal system. Second, it is a national rental (economic rent) system. Under the worldwide and source paradigm, Peggy Musgrave considered a case when the source country is capital-poor. To allocate the gain equitably, the source country can impose a national rental or benefit charge out of the regular tax system. The third one is that with the source taxation applied, which in turn is justified by territoriality and sovereignty, the general principle of equal treatment before the law can determine the source country's share of the international income. Specifically, the non-discrimination rule will determine that the source taxation on the non-resident's income will be equal to its own resident. At last, Peggy Musgrave turned to the distributional considerations. She proposed a reverse rate structure according to the per capita income. For poor source countries with low per capita income, it will impose a higher tax rate on non-residents

Territorial Taxation and Tax Sparing' (n. 618). Brian J Arnold and Michael J McIntyre, *International Tax Primer* (2nd edn, Kluwer Law International B V 2002) 4.

630. In the original words of Musgrave, the 'residence principle' and 'source principle', Musgrave and Musgrave (n. 7) 71. Kaufman (n. 586) 198.
631. Kaufman (n. 586) 190-191.
632. Musgrave and Musgrave (n. 7) 70.

from rich residence countries. Similarly, rich source countries with high per capita income will impose a lower tax rate on non-residents from poor residence countries.

## 4.5 RE-ASKING THE QUESTION

After dealing with the foundational contribution to inter-nation equity, and even exploring the criteria proposed by Peggy Musgrave, it seems that the definition of inter-nation equity is still ambiguous or absent. With the term 'definition' being used, it does not imply that inter-nation equity will have a clear-cut representation similar to defining an apple or a cat. Especially her theory of inter-nation equity was largely built on her reflections on worldwide and source taxation. As emphasized earlier, for constructing evaluation standards or guidelines of the international tax system, the status quo can serve as a fulcrum or backdrop, but it is better to keep a distance from it.[633] Otherwise, the standards may not be as universal as they should be.

The ambiguity of concept or definition is at the risk that inter-nation equity may become merely a 'slogan' or a symbol rather than some concept that has rich and clear substance. Taking inter-individual equity for a contrasting example, it has been clearly indicated that it is based on equality or equal treatment before the law. The horizontal or vertical aspect of equity is used to identify the contour of inter-individual equity. Then fundamentally, the norms to weigh the taxpayer 'inequality', namely, the substantive equity norms, including AtP and BP, were discretely analysed throughout the following text. For the case of inter-nation equity, there is no reason why the thinking process would, or need to, be different. It is natural to ask such a question after going through the current research references to inter-nation equity:

> The real challenge for tax scholars and tax policy-makers, however, seems not in comprehending the contours of the argument in favour of source taxation provided by the Musgraves, but rather in accepting that asking questions about inter-nation equity, is like asking questions about national redistribution with the tax system, requires discussing openly what a sensible distribution of revenue inter-nation is.[634]

Even before turning to the question, it can be imagined that asking the same questions about inter-nation equity will be more difficult than asking those for inter-individual equity. Because for the latter, a rich, complicated, yet clear set of theoretical arguments is there, the commentators only need to pick up what they think fits, for example, the entitlement theory, economic justice, or the theory of the state. However, for inter-nation equity, such arguments are not that readily available. Even so, re-asking the basic questions about inter-nation equity is the first step.

633. 'The real challenge for tax scholars and tax policy-makers, however, seems not in comprehending the contours of the argument in favor of source taxation provided by the Musgraves ...', Brooks (n. 620) 23.
634. *Ibid.*

### 4.5.1 First: The Subjects of Inter-Nation Equity

In search of a clear definition of inter-nation equity, one must take note of all the essential elements. The first element is the subjects. In a nutshell, the subjects are nations, or strictly speaking, different taxing jurisdictions. The key, is the scope of relevant taxing jurisdictions. Under Peggy Musgrave's original theoretical framework, the residence country and host country are subjects of inter-nation equity considerations. Because such a judgment is based on the fact that these two countries are the only ones with a reasonable claim to the international income.[635] However, the legitimacy framework constructed in the earlier section enables countries other than home and host places to have a reasonable tax claim. This extension of subjects is significant, for under Peggy Musgrave's original residence-source equity paradigm, the focus of inter-nation equity was on the source country; the residence country has a residual interest and has no effect on inter-nation equity.[636] However, when a third country was included in the analysis, how to manage the logical consistency of the original formulation of inter-nation equity was a challenge.

As stressed earlier, even though the status quo is the system of both worldwide and source taxation, it should be no more than a backdrop or a destination. To question how to construct equity in the international setting, the current system is not the golden rule but more a fulcrum and starting point.

Two possible directions exist to counter the subject issue indicated above. The first is to maintain the worldwide taxation of the residence country, and the third country is a second source country. In this case, the original inter-nation equity formulation is not affected in the part of the residence country; the key is still the circumstances of the source country and, in turn, the inclusion of the third country. The second is to drop the worldwide taxation of residence country, and then all the *subjects* for the purpose of inter-nation equity are on an equal footing. The focus of inter-nation equity will shift from reflecting the taxation of the source country to a holistic perspective of all the related countries.

It is still early to decide to follow either direction. For equity considerations, as discussed, the worldwide taxation of residence country was thought to be based on the claims of inter-individual equity. It has been demonstrated that the direct internationalization of inter-individual equity norms is not suitable to guide the design of the international tax system, nor is the status quo actually built on that. As a result, worldwide taxation lacks its ground on inter-individual equity. However, there is no clear basis in inter-nation equity to exclude worldwide taxation as well. It is believed that the motive for worldwide taxation lies elsewhere.[637]

---

635. Agundez-Garcia (n. 471).
636. Kaufman (n. 586) 198.
637. 'Where exercise of source entitlement is of primary importance for interjurisdictional equity, that of residence entitlement is of major concern with regard to efficiency, since it controls the degree of tax neutrality with respect to interjurisdictional capital resource allocation.', *see* Musgrave, 'Chapter 3 Interjurisdictional Equity in Company Taxation: Principles and Applications to the European Union' (n. 619) 48.

Considering that Peggy Musgrave's systematic formulation of inter-nation equity was built on the worldwide taxation of the home country, as a realistic solution, attention should turn to the construction of inter-nation equity without worldwide taxation of any country. The following will introduce the economic allegiance theory as both the materialized approach to legitimacy to tax and as the starting point of the criteria for international equity.

#### 4.5.1.1 *Economic Allegiance Theory*

The first theory to resort to as the beginning of the efforts is the economic allegiance theory, which was contributed by the four economists in their foundational work on the modern international tax system.[638] In the 1923 Report, when the authors were discussing the general principles governing international competence in taxation, they referred to the principle of domicile (residence) and that of location or origin. However, then they pointed out that the reason for the waver between these two principles is that they can be considered 'a part of the still broader principle of economic interest or economic allegiance, as against the original doctrine of political allegiance'.[639]

First of all, the authors expressed that the underlying theory of economic allegiance is the ability to pay theory. Based on that, the individual's whole ability should be taxed and taxed only once. Their conception of ability to pay was not as it has been articulated nowadays.[640] Their usage of AtP relates more to the legitimacy to tax rather than the sharing of international tax interests. As discussed above, the modern concept of AtP is mainly concerned with inter-individual equity. There is still some theoretical gap between the taxable ability to pay of an individual and his liability to pay to the relevant taxing jurisdictions, whereas the authors did not notice such a gap.[641] It was already concluded earlier that AtP and inter-individual equity are intra-nation matters. The economic allegiance theory constructed upon the four economists' reference to AtP has little to do with inter-individual equity, but should be interpreted against the current inter-nation equity concept, even though the authors did not explicitly formulate economic allegiance theory as a matter related to the equitable share of the international tax base.

Since the 1923 Report, the authors' formulation of AtP as the basis of economic allegiance theory was thought to contain 'what there is of value in the benefit theory',[642] thus it can be generally said that such theory is a benefit-like theory for its role in both legitimacy to tax and tax equity.[643] 'Inter-nation equity, the identification of the sovereign to whom the taxpayer should pay his or her tax (*note: the legitimacy*

638. Bruins et al. (n. 44). hereinafter, the [1923 Report].
639. *Ibid.*, 20.
640. Kaufman (n. 586) 197.
641. 'The ideal solution is that the individual's whole faculty should be taxed, but that should be taxed only once, and that the liability should be divided among the tax districts ...', *see* Bruins et al. (n. 44) 20. 'The League's experts failed to distinguish between inter-individual and inter-nation equity.', *see* Kaufman (n. 586) 197.
642. Bruins et al. (n. 44) 18.
643. Kaufman (n. 586) 198.

*to tax*) and the limits of that sovereign's tax base (*note: the inter-nation equity*), should be based on the taxpayer's economic interest in each country.'[644] It is Nancy Kaufman who had called our attention to the prospect of economic allegiance theory as a starting point of the criteria for inter-nation equity.[645] The issue of legitimacy to tax and that of inter-nation equity are inter-connected, for an equitable international tax system is only attainable when all the taxing authorities are justified to tax the international tax base.[646]

The original representation of economic allegiance theory is that 'tax liability should be divided among the tax districts according to his relative interests in each'.[647] From that, three aspects are the key: first, it is the 'tax liability' in question, which is, in essence, equivalent to the shareable international tax base; second, it is the taxpayer's 'interests', or the economic allegiance, in the tax districts are justifying their tax claims on the international tax base; third, and the most important aspect for inter-nation equity, economic allegiance theory advocates the distribution of tax liability or tax base according to the taxpayer's relative economic allegiance in each taxing State.

According to the 1923 Report, there are four elements of economic allegiance: (1) the acquisition of wealth; (2) the location of wealth; (3) the enforceability of the rights to wealth; and (4) the consumption of wealth. Each of these four elements corresponds to a place where the tax authorities have the reasonable right to tax. They are the places of: (1) the origin of the wealth; (2) the site of the wealth; (3) the enforcement of the rights to wealth; and (4) the residence or domicile. Among the four elements, the Report considered the acquisition of wealth and the consumption of wealth as more important than the rest.[648] Thus, the tax claims of origin and residence countries are more convincing than the other places. Then what follows is their analysis of in rem/*capital wealth/property* taxes. They have categorized the wealth into movables and immovables for the purpose of taxation, and discussed the relative proportion of economic allegiance of the above four places under each classification of wealth.[649] Their conclusion is that for some categories of wealth, the country of origin is 'preponderant' and 'more important', while for other categories, the country of domicile is so. In contrast, for income tax, the authors said that it is highly impractical to determine the classes of economic allegiance in the interested countries. The main reason is that income is a net and composite concept, and in practice the 'sequence of

644. 'economic allegiance is the basis upon which the total tax paid by the individual should reach the competing authorities, we have to ask ... what are the ways in which it can be subdivided.', *see* Bruins et al. (n. 44) 22. *See also* Kaufman (n. 586) 197.
645. Kaufman (n. 586) 194.
646. 'A tax claim is equitable only if taxing the particular transaction or event by the state in question is legitimate or in other words can be justified.', Vogel, 'Worldwide vs. Source Taxation of Income-a Review and Re-Evaluation of Arguments (Part III)' (n. 587) 394.
647. Bruins et al. (n. 44) 20.
648. 'It is clear, however, that the other two factors may sometimes become of importance, although in most cases, they are significant only in reinforcing the claims of either origin or domicile.', *Ibid.*, 25.
649. For further classification of movable and immovable wealth, *see ibid.*, 27-38. for the conclusion of this analysis, *see ibid.*, 39.

operations' to determine income across countries makes the regular analysis unworkable.[650]

Back to the subject issue, the insights for inter-nation equity from the economic allegiance theory are as follows. First, the economic allegiance analysis implies that all interested countries are on equal footing, with no country having the prime taxing right, which is an alternative to the worldwide source paradigm. The place of residence, specifically, is not interpreted as a country whose superior taxing power or political power to which the taxpayer is subordinate, but a place of 'the owner of the wealth who ultimately consumes it'.[651] Even though through the analysis, in many cases, it is still the residence or origin country that stands out, the underlying reasoning is that the proportion of economic allegiance in some places is more significant than any others. Second, it has been indicated in the report and also by Nancy Kaufman that the analysis of one element of economic allegiance of a particular matter may not only fall into one country, because it is totally possible that one element involves more than one country. Especially for the element of the acquisition of wealth, the corresponding place of origin is an open concept for income tax purposes, when the connotation of origin means 'the community the economic life of which makes possible the yield or acquisition of the wealth'.[652] When the origin or source of income is interpreted according to different approaches, it may not only cover more than one country but also cover the place of residence as referred to above.[653] Based on that, an individual's income earned abroad can be thought as originating from both where he lives and where he is doing the business, and where he lives is not superior to where he is doing the business in claiming the share of the international tax base. Third, as a theory containing the value of benefit analysis, however, the economic allegiance does not aim to quantify the taxpayer's consumption of public goods and services, nor the market value of the goods, services and protections provided by government. Consequently, the economic allegiance is a relative concept, its two-fold role of either justifying the countries' claims on the international income or determining the relative weight of each country does not require to directly calculate the specific amount of income a country should be apportioned.[654]

In conclusion, the economic allegiance theory can be relied upon to materialize the legitimacy propositions discussed in the earlier section, which mainly advocates that countries can be legitimized to tax international income by the alternative

650. 'It will be obvious that, in the case of the income tax, if our ideal of taxation is the tax on pure income, there is no such thing as the taxation of the separate stages until we have ascertained whether the whole sequence of operations has ended in a profit, and, if so, how much; and then we must go back and allocate that profit over all the different operations in the countries in which they may have taken place. In practice, such an allocation may be said almost to baffle analysis.', Bruins et al. (n. 44) 26.
651. *Ibid.*, 23.
652. *Ibid.*
653. Such deductions can be made under the supply-demand approach to the definitions of source, *see* Musgrave, 'Principles for Dividing the State Corporate Tax Base' (n. 619) 233.
654. 'It is important therefore to keep continually in mind the exact meaning of each of the four factors in economic allegiance, and in every particular case to attempt to estimate the *relative* weight to be attached to each of them.', Bruins et al. (n. 44) 25.

approach of the traditional worldwide source paradigm. The economic allegiance analysis has laid a level playing field for countries that have economic allegiance with taxable income. All the places that have economic allegiance with the international income are the 'sources' of the income. In addition, the economic allegiance theory has provided the solution to determine the relative shares of the taxing countries, that is, according to the relative weight of the elements of economic allegiance in the relevant places.

### 4.5.2 Second, the Connotation: The Revenue at Stake

Ever since the Musgraves came up with the concept inter-nation equity, commentators have gone quite far from the original starting point of the concept. They have resorted to inter-nation equity for various purposes. However, looking into the creation of inter-nation equity, it is seen that such a concept was popping up rather than being derived from the underlying theories. As is done for inter-individual equity, the following question applies: what is equity among nations?

Answering the question should be the logical starting point for constructing the concept of inter-nation equity, following the same process as inter-individual equity. Among individuals, the concept of equity is based on equality and *iustitia distributive* (distributive justice); there must be some theories which are the foundation of the concept of inter-nation equity. The foundational theories will give substantive content to the concept of inter-nation equity, a requisite to answer the reverse side of the above question: what is the inter-nation inequity?[655] When commenting on Peggy Musgrave's theory of inter-nation equity, Nancy Kaufman also pointed out that the 'foundation' is lacking for the relevant countries' entitlement to tax, and she resorted to the economic allegiance theory.[656] Yet, as far as the author can see, the reaction of Nancy Kaufman is still limited to providing a solution to inter-nation equity. Thus, the economic allegiance theory is said to be an 'alternative' to the home country and host country's entitlement to tax.[657] She did not touch on the underlying theory of equity or inequity among nations.

Through the earlier discussions, it is established that inter-nation equity concerns the share of tax base and, ultimately, tax revenue among nations. Answering the question of what equity is among nations will also contribute to figuring out the requirements to fulfil inter-nation equity, which may lead to different thinking processes or results compared to Peggy Musgrave's criteria.

#### *4.5.2.1 Inter-Nation Equity Based on Equality*

For individuals in the unitary fiscal setting, equity is constructed in terms of the fair allocation of the total tax burden. As the foundational value of equity, equality means

655. '... the whole concept of inter-nation equity is largely irrelevant in the absence of inter-nation inequity.' Brooks (n. 620).
656. Kaufman (n. 586) 194.
657. *Ibid.*, 195.

that taxpayers under equal circumstances should be treated equally, which automatically implies that taxpayers under unequal circumstances should be treated unequally. The substantive equity norm's ability to pay principle falls within the scope of national distributive justice. The income tax that conforms to equity is not merely a tool to sustain the government but an important tool to achieve distributive justice in society.

For 'equity' in the concept of inter-nation equity, because what is at stake is the share of tax base, if referring to the connotation inter-individual equity, then it can be interpreted that countries are equal in taxing the international income. More specifically, countries under the same circumstances should be allocated the same portion of taxable income, while countries under unequal circumstances should be allocated an unequal portion of taxable income. That is, inter-nation equity can also be divided into horizontal equity and vertical equity. Following a similar route, the key to inter-nation equity is to determine the circumstances that define the countries having the right to tax but to various extents as equal and unequal, and that key point can be said as the substantive norm for inter-nation equity, which deserves further study.

Leaving the above key point aside, the equality-based horizontal inter-nation equity advocates that countries under the same circumstances will tax the same portion of the international income, and the vertical inter-nation equity advocates that countries under different circumstances will tax a different portion of the international income. The inter-nation inequity will mean that countries under the same circumstances are apportioned different portions of the international income or different circumstances but the same portions. Digging deeper, for individuals within a country, the value of equality is one of the most fundamental principles of social justice. The inter-individual equity is the extension or application of the equality principle in the tax arena. For inter-nation equity, if it is also based on equality, some explanations must be given for such equality concerning the relationship among countries, not individuals.

The theoretical basis for the equality of countries at the closest reach is the international law theory and, more specifically, the sovereign equality of states. The principle of sovereign equality is a principle that finds its expression in the *Charter of the United Nations*, which says that the UN 'is based on the principle of sovereign equality of all its Members'.[658] The equality of sovereignty can be said to be the fundamental right of States, which is derived from either natural law, the nature of States, the international community, or the principle of independence of States.[659] The sovereign equality of states is not a guarantee for actual political or economic equality of states. Instead, such a principle is rather formal; it does not aim at states having the same rights but at states being recognized as having the same legal capacity for having rights as well as the equal capacity for realizing them. Whatever is lawful, just, or equitable for one State in a particular situation, should be equally lawful, just, and equitable for all other States in that situation.[660] It further implies that no State should

658. 'United Nations Charter' Art. 2 https://www.un.org/en/about-us/un-charter/full-text.
659. Lauri Mälksoo and Juliane Kokott, 'States, Sovereign Equality' 2 https://opil.ouplaw.com/display/10.1093/law:epil/9780199231690/law-9780199231690-e1113?print=pdf accessed 27 November 2023.
660. *Ibid.*, 5.

be privileged or discriminated against compared to other states under the same circumstances.

The implications of the sovereign equality principle are broader than merely for the construction of inter-nation equity. For example, it implies that a State is independent and free to choose its tax policy to the extent that it does not affect another State's tax sovereignty and that a State shall not discriminate against a third State in the tax policy-making for another State, and so forth. While applied to the construction of inter-nation equity, the principle of equality of states then means that it is the basic or fundamental right of taxing States to claim an equal share of the international tax base to the extent that the relevant circumstances are equal for the States. From that, it can be seen that the key to such equality lies not in the principle itself, nor in the theories of international law, but elsewhere in the specifics of tax theories. The demon is in the details. Even so, the theoretical foundations for inter-nation equity are necessary, and one of those is the equality of States.

#### *4.5.2.2 Inter-Nation Equity Based on Distributive Justice*

The inter-nation equity based on the equality of States cannot guarantee that the taxing States will approach the substantive equality of economic status. Even if an objective and independent proxy of equality (namely, to weigh the relevant circumstances of States) was used in inter-nation equity, it still does not necessarily mean that the States will become more economically equal in reality. Thus, it can be roughly said that inter-nation equity based on equality is the equality of opportunities, not the equality of outcome, because it does not relate to the actual wealth difference between states. The justice backed by inter-nation equity based on the equality of States is formal justice.

The inter-individual equity is grounded on the equality among individuals, while the inter-nation equity discussed above is based on the equality among States. In contrast, the equity norms of inter-individual equity, especially the ability to pay, advocate the domestic tax system to uphold substantive justice as opposed to formal justice. On the one hand, the AtP income tax is a personal tax that takes into account the actual economic circumstances of taxpayers. With such tax, the tax base is a net concept, which excludes the wealth for generating income and sustaining the basic needs. And the system is progressive in that the higher the income, the higher the marginal tax rate. At the end of the day, such a tax system is aimed at reaching the actual wealth equality of individuals. On the other hand, beyond the tax side, spending policy is of a redistributive nature as well.

Hence intuitively, one might imagine that whether inter-nation equity based on equality of States could or should include redistributive considerations. The inter-nation equity on redistributive justice grounds will preach the international tax system to incorporate elements from the redistributive national tax system.

For one thing and in a broader sense, exploring redistribution in an international tax system implies the global purview of economic justice. If economic justice is viewed as only within the borders of individual States, then inter-nation equity based on distributive justice is merely a groundless illusion. In comparison, if it is possible to conceive economic justice in the global sphere, then there will be room for constructing inter-nation equity based on international distributive justice. For the views on the scope of economic justice, at the two ends, it is the views of cosmopolitanism and nationalism.[661] It is claimed that a growing number of scholars are maintaining that principles of distributive justice should have a global purview; thus, room does exist for exploring inter-nation equity concepts based on global redistributive justice.

For another, as now the inter-nation equity advocates substantive equality rather than a formal one, the actual economic status of relevant taxing States needs to be considered. As for the implications of the conception of inter-nation equity, it means that the poorer States might instead be privileged over the richer States in their claims for the share of international income. In a system of a stricter redistributive nature, it is the duty of the rich States to assist the poor States.[662] For global redistributive justice for consideration of inter-nation equity, the subjects are States rather than individuals, even though, at the end of the day, only the well-being of individuals matters. And the yardstick for measuring the well-being of individuals may not be applicable to States. However, a yardstick for evaluating the 'well-being' of States is indispensable for materializing the propositions of inter-nation equity based on distributive justice.

The controversy around the scope of distributive justice has manifestations in the degree of inter-nation equity based on distributive justice as well. To the fullest extent of distributive justice in the international arena, inter-nation equity will entail a central taxing authority to be in charge of the distribution of wealth among States. This is exemplified by how the redistributive system within a country works. Without a central authority, a truly retributive international fiscal system is difficult, if not impossible. In reality, there is neither a worldwide taxing authority nor a multilateral organization to coordinate tax policies of over 200 taxing jurisdictions that are also competing with each other. As a compromise, the question can be turned into how to design the international tax system to reflect concerns of global distributive justice, which is premised on the belief that global distributive justice is beneficial for the world.[663] For inter-nation equity, the same reasoning applies; the question is, for the share of international income, what allocation mechanism will embody the redistributive objectives.

## 4.6 REDEVELOPING THE CRITERIA

Through the above discussion, there seems to be more uncertainty around inter-nation equity. The first issue is clearer, in that there is no basis in studies of equity thesis to back the worldwide taxation of residents, namely, the worldwide tax system. The crux

661. Simon Caney, 'International Distributive Justice' (2001) 49 Political Studies 974.
662. Tsilly Dagan, 'Just Harmonization' (2009) 42 University of British Columbia Law Review 331, 361.
663. The author holds that the international distributive justice has an insurance function for the world, *see* Benshalom, 'Rethinking International Distributive Justice: Fairness as Insurance' (n. 586).

is the conflict of equity with other norms, especially neutrality. As for neutrality itself, the neutrality chapter has adopted an inclusive method that does not exclude worldwide taxation. Turning to the theme of this study, the formulary apportionment system has been viewed as a source system where no country has a preferential entitlement to tax global income. Because of that, in the formulation of inter-nation equity, it will not presume that inter-nation equity is automatically or should be based on a pure system of source taxation. As a result, the following discussions of the criteria of inter-nation equity should be seen as in parallel to Musgrave's views summarized above, which means that the residence country and source countries are on equal footing.

The second issue is the question of whether equality of States or global distributive justice should be the foundation of inter-nation equity. My point of view is that the principle of equality of States is the baseline of the underlying theories of inter-nation equity. There will be no foothold for constructing inter-nation equity if the relevant States are not even equal in taxing the international income with all other circumstances equal. However, this study holds that formal equality is not where inter-nation equity should end; there are no reasons out of morality to preclude goals of global distributive justice in the international tax system. As such, distributive justice can work as the additional foundation of inter-nation equity as well. In the Musgraves' discourse of inter-nation equity, they did not explicitly relate to the concept of distributive justice among nations, but the non-reciprocal and the wealth-reverse rate structure are obviously the reflections of distributive justice in inter-nation equity. In addition to the growing global wealth gap,[664] the inclusion of distributive justice is not only a moral choice but also a realistic one.[665] However, it must be acknowledged that it is difficult to predict the distributional effect of a specific international tax arrangement.[666] Thus, the considerations derived from distributive justice are secondary and supplemental, where equality has laid the foundation for inter-nation equity.

In the above discussions, the concept of international income is used to depict a situation where an individual has derived income from foreign factors, and there are more countries than the residence country that have taxing rights on income. Then, according to the views of whether the sources of international income can be geographically determined, the criteria of inter-nation equity can be grouped into the Equal Earned Income approach and the *Equal Allegiance* approach.

664. Joe Hasell et al., 'Global Economic Inequality' (2018) https://ourworldindata.org/global-economic-inequality accessed 26 August 2025. Donghyun Park, 'Trends in the Income Gap between Developed Countries and Developing Countries, 1960-1995' https://ourworldindata.org/economic-inequality accessed 26 August 2025.

665. 'in the face of the growing global inequality, this question remains the most important one facing international tax scholars and policy-makers.', at Brooks (n. 620) 23; 'there appears to be no sound theoretical reason to restrict redistribution to members of any single tax jurisdiction. If there were a world taxing authority, it would be justified in redistributing wealth on a worldwide basis.', Reuven S Avi-Yonah, 'Globalization, Tax Competition, and the Fiscal Crisis of the Welfare State' (2000) 113 Harvard Law Review 1573, 1649 https://doi.org/10.2307/1342445 accessed 26 August 2025.

666. de Wilde, '"Sharing the Pie": Taxing Multinationals in a Global Market' (n. 588) 444.

### 4.6.1 Equal Earned Income Approach

First of all, supposing that an individual has earned a sum of income abroad, and some attributes of that income have enabled three countries to have the justified tax claims, including the residence country and two 'source' countries. Under these circumstances, the equality-based inter-nation equity is automatically fulfilled if the total income can be geographically attributed to its various sources. For the common international tax base, if objective and accurate portions of the relevant taxing states can be determined, then either horizontal or vertical inter-nation equity will be attained automatically. In fact, the inter-nation equity achieved in this way is not only relative equality but also absolute equality. As a result, if the same portions of the common tax base are determined for two or more taxing States, from the other side, the taxpayer has earned equal income from different locations, then those States will have an equal share of the tax base. Following that, this criterion for inter-nation equity can be named as *Equal Earned Income* approach.[667]

For the *Equal Earned Income* approach, for one thing, there is no clear distributional consideration in it. For another, as said, it is based on an important presumption that international income is generated from specific geographic sources, and the sources can be determined as well. Considering the disparity of individual income and corporate income generating, of which the latter has been frequently claimed as having no true geographic source, and the weaker mobility of individuals than corporations, it is needed to consider the case where it is not possible to pin down the income geographically.

Without being able to accurately ascertain the countries' 'genuine' and 'absolute' share of the international income tax base, there is strictly only one option left for inter-nation equity. That is, to construct inter-nation equity in a relative sense rather than an absolute sense. Because under the assumption that it is futile to track where income comes from, the calculation in absolute sense of the income sharing is unattainable as well. Consequently, the efforts for constructing inter-nation equity in the second-best sense will be to find some 'proxy' of the geographic source of the taxable income base, with the aim of approaching the optimal result achieved when the true source of income is known.

### 4.6.2 Equal Allegiance Approach

Efforts can then resort back to the economic allegiance theory. As discussed above, as a two-fold concept, the economic allegiance theory does have a role to play in constructing the criteria of inter-nation equity. It is not the goal of economic allegiance analysis to pin down accurately the income generated in a specific location but to provide an allocation mechanism for the relative 'bite' of all the countries that have

667. This term is coined by Agundez-Garcia (n. 471) 33.Although the author used this term in a different context and for different purpose, the underlying reasoning is similar to my discourse here. The same term can also be used here.

economic allegiance with the taxpayer.[668] Consequently, the inter-nation equity achieved by the economic allegiance theory is a kind of 'rough justice'.[669] Elements like those of the economic allegiance theory may be designed to act as proxies for the sources of income. Similar to the Equal Earned Income approach to inter-nation equity, the economic allegiance analysis can contribute to it by suggesting determining the countries that have economic allegiance with the income and the taxpayer and then weighing the relative portion of the economic interests in every country. The key insight is that if such a portion can be roughly reached, it can also be used to apportion the international income, presuming that the amount of income is certain and available. As a result, from the perspective of the taxpayer, for the international income, if he has equal economic allegiance with the countries, he will be considered to have earned equal income among the countries.

Naturally, countries with equal economic allegiance with the taxpayer or income will have an equal share of the total international income. Because such a method is in no sense to calculate the amount in each jurisdiction of the total international income the taxpayer has earned but to simulate a similar result, thus it cannot be captured by the aforesaid Equal Earned Income approach. In addition, the 'elements' in the original discourse of economic allegiance still lack some operable features, which makes the calculation of even the relative weight of economic allegiance in each place unattainable.

Consequently, there emerges the need to introduce some new elements to the economic allegiance theory, and the 'proxies' of the elements as well (proxy of the proxy of the true source of income). These proxies will make the new elements clearer, observable, and quantifiable. With these new elements, the core concept and thesis of 'economic allegiance' is still there. One must note that the original economic allegiance theory is aimed at the general tax system, which covers taxes far broader than income. The construction of such new elements should be based on the theory of the 'source of income', which addresses how and where income is generated itself. It can also be imagined that changes and adjustments will be invoked to the original discourse of economic allegiance theory. However, for the purpose here, the reformulated economic allegiance theory with new elements and the elements' proxies jointly contribute to a different approach to inter-nation equity, which can be named as 'Equal Allegiance' approach.

### 4.6.3 Possible Redistributive Considerations

Whether for equal earned income or equal allegiance approach, they do not bear with redistributive considerations in the first place. Thus, it can be said that the two approaches are both based on the equality of States. Although it is difficult to construct a coherent redistributive international tax system, taking a step back, it is advisable to make a memorandum for that in designing the system following inter-nation equity.

668. In the original discourse of economic allegiance, the analysis is around the wealth instead of the taxpayer.
669. Kaufman (n. 586) 199.

First, the very basic requirement of international distributive justice is to determine the wealth difference among countries. International redistribution only concerns the transfer of wealth from rich countries to poor countries. Thus, the yardstick of the inter-nation wealth gap is the key. The task of searching for such a yardstick is challenging in itself. If a global yardstick is unattainable, in a narrower scope, there needs to be the measurement of the relative wealth between one country and another country, or one group of countries and another group of countries.

Second, in choosing the specific international tax arrangements, the measures of a progressive nature should be preferred over those of a regressive nature to make the poorer countries gain more benefits. For inter-nation equity, progressive tax measures enable poorer countries to have a larger share of the international tax base. In the discourse of Musgrave's inter-nation equity, she proposed to link the share of international income inversely with the per capita income of countries. For the equal allegiance approach, a specially designed arrangement can be included as well, for example, to introduce elements that are 'heavier' in poorer countries than in richer countries.

## 4.7 SUMMARY OF THE SECOND STEP

The Figure 4.4 below shows the main thinking process and conclusions through the second step, which addresses which form of equity in the international setting should govern and guide international taxation. The summary is that the equity values developed in the unitary setting cannot be directly internationalized. Specifically, it is inter-nation equity constructed in the international setting rather than inter-individual equity started from a unitary/domestic setting that should be relied upon to guide the equitable design of the international tax system. The inter-individual equity and its sub-norms are inherently national matters. Inter-nation equity has been constructed from the underlying relationships in the international setting, and the equality of states and international distributive justice are brought out as two different foundations. These two foundations then lead to different approaches or criteria, which have been analysed respectively. The task of the last step is to study whether and to what extent the above conclusions are applicable to the international taxation of corporations.

*Figure 4.4 Illustration of Second Step of Equity Thinking*

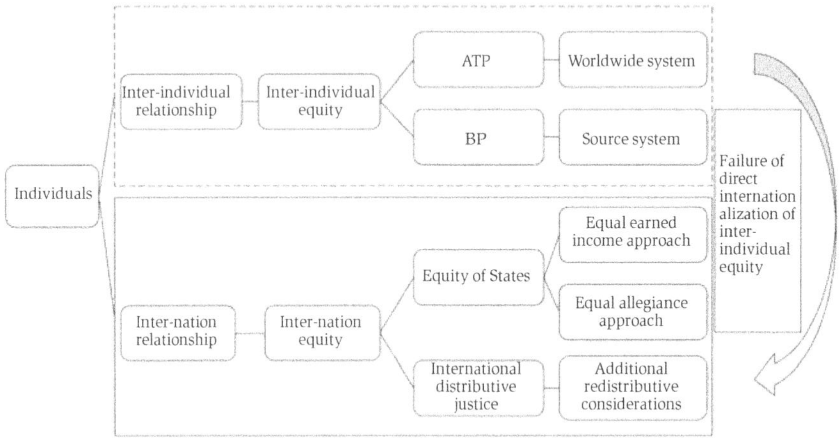


## 4.8 THE LAST STEP: INTER-NATION EQUITY FOR CORPORATE TAXATION IN INTERNATIONAL SETTING

The above discussions are all around the taxation of individuals, from the unitary setting to the international setting. The theme of this study, however, is the tax issue of companies. Therefore, there still lacks some conceptual linking as to whether this shift of subjects could render the above equity discourse different, to be specific, whether the theoretical framework of equity for individuals in an international setting still applies to that of corporations. Yet before the following, one can anticipate that the change of subjects from individuals to corporations will be less substantial for constructing inter-nation equity than that of tax settings from unitary to international.

### 4.8.1 Translating the Equity Discourse to Corporations

Similar to inter-individual equity, inter-taxpayer equity also has two aspects, horizontal equity and vertical equity, which also lead to substantive equity norms, the benefit principle and the ability to pay principle. Traditionally, in international tax literature of corporate taxation, the equity norms, the ability to pay, and the benefit principle have been relied upon to back respectively the worldwide tax system and source tax system, which is the same as the theoretical developments of inter-individual equity.[670]

The previous major claim that inter-individual equity cannot be directly internationalized is still valid when the subjects have shifted from individuals to corporations. Neither the worldwide nor the source tax system has a robust theoretical foundation in the propositions of inter-taxpayer equity because inter-taxpayer equity is inherently a

670. Kesselman and Maslove (n. 586).

domestic issue. It is the inter-nation equity that should dominate the equity considerations of international corporate income taxation, and there is no hindrance to applying the criteria of inter-nation equity to corporation taxation as well.

This is founded on two inter-connected reasons.

First, although various theories support the independent taxation of corporations (e.g., the separate entity principle and the fiscal unity principle),[671] as well as the independent significance of corporate tax as an important source of revenue, in essence, corporate tax primarily functions as a tool to counteract the deferral of personal income tax. When discussing tax justice or other aspects of tax fairness or justice, the fundamental starting point and ultimate focus are on individuals. The legitimacy of corporate taxation must ultimately be justified in terms of its impact on individuals, whether they are shareholders, employees or customers, for tax incidence considerations.[672] This, of course, aligns with the philosophical nature of tax equity discourse.

On this basis, the equity discourse outlined in this chapter, which begins with individuals in a unitary setting and extends to an international setting, can be applied to the context of corporate taxation without being altered by the existence of corporate taxation itself. In addition, the equity discourse addresses inter-nation equity rather than equity among individual taxpayers. Therefore, translating the equity discourse to the context of corporate taxation should not encounter significant obstacles.

Second, for either corporate taxation or individual taxation, the tax base is common: the income. Even though the income calculation varies in many details, they are both net concepts and bear the values of the ability to pay. According to the theory of the conception of income, the real 'ability' to pay is the subjective 'well-being' of individuals, but for practical reasons, it has come down to be objective, the modern S-H-S income.[673] The commonly referred to the ability to pay principle is, therefore, actually its own 'objective' version.[674] Using AtP to advocate a worldwide tax system for corporations, as many commentators do, is a further step. Because even though the objective AtP is a practical compromise, it was originally made for individuals, thus it further supports the progressivity and humane exemptions. In contrast, these features are normally non-existent in corporate income taxation.[675] Therefore, the AtP principle utilized for international corporate income taxation is even more objective. Identifying that can contribute to the inner consistency of the translation process.

671. Jinyan Li, 'The Future of the Corporate Form in Income Tax: A Case Study of Canada' [2023] Osgoode Legal Studies Research Paper No. 4459300 5-6 https://ssrn.com/abstract=4459300 accessed 26 August 2025.

672. Arnold C Harberger, 'The Incidence of the Corporation Income Tax' (1962) 70 Journal of Political Economy 215 https://doi.org/10.1086/258636 accessed 26 August 2025.

673. 'The Schanz-Haig-Simons model postulates that a practical concept of income is represented by a monetary increase in wealth plus imputed income and consumption expenditure over a period. That measure is a surrogate for immeasurable psychic income.', *see* Holmes (n. 600) Ch. 2; and Dodge (n. 592) 499.

674. Dodge (n. 592); Edoardo Traversa, 'Objective Ability to Pay: The Gerritse Case' [2015] Landmark Decisions of the ECJ in Direct Taxation https://www.academia.edu/41917849/Objective_Ability_to_Pay_The_Gerritse_Case accessed 2 May 2024.

675. Englisch (n. 592) 19-20.

Turning to the inter-nation equity that is finally addressed in the second step, the transition of subjects has not weakened the conclusion but, to the contrary, strengthened it in terms of some aspects.

First of all, even though the incomes earned by individuals are not all labour income (capital income is possible as well), yet compared to corporations, individuals as natural persons have far less mobility than corporations. For instance, partly attributed to the artificial nature of corporations, residence of corporations seems to be more prone to being manipulated than that of individuals. A corporation may be able to transfer its tax 'identity' to another jurisdiction through mere paperwork.[676] This has weakened the residence country's primary right to tax the worldwide income of corporations, which adds more force to the above result from denying the direct internationalization of inter-individual/taxpayer equity.

Moreover, related to inter-nation equity, multinational business practices have complicated the sources of business income even more, which renders the equal earned income or equal allegiance approach to inter-nation equity even more solid.

## 4.9 APPLYING INTER-NATION EQUITY TO FORMULARY APPORTIONMENT

As a key component of the analytical framework of this research, the principle of equity can shed critical insights into at least two aspects of formulary apportionment. First, the equity principle can provide the critical driving force to adopt formulary apportionment in the very first place. Second, it can also provide some instructions on the concrete design of formulary apportionment, where the latter embodies ambiguities.

To encapsulate the above analysis, this chapter looks into the intricate concept of equity within the context of international taxation, particularly focusing on the transition from a unitary fiscal setting to an international one. It begins by establishing the principle of equity, highlighting its inherent difficulty in definition but its importance in guiding tax allocation in a fair and just manner. It then introduces the 'three-step' approach to examining equity in international taxation. The discussion boils down to the construction of 'inter-nation equity', which considers the distribution of tax burdens among different taxing jurisdictions. This concept is distinct from inter-individual equity, with its subjects being nations rather than individuals. The chapter introduces the economic allegiance theory as a potential foundation for inter-nation equity, emphasizing the importance of a taxpayer's economic interests in various countries.

676. *See* further discussion at Piergiorgio Valente, 'Italian Tax Authorities Action Against Fictitious Corporate Tax Residence' (2017) 45 Intertax 353 https://doi.org/10.54648/taxi2017028 accessed 26 August 2025; Marian Omri Y, 'Jurisdiction to Tax Corporations' [2013] Tax Law: International & Comparative Tax eJournal; Shkumbin Asllani, 'The Definition of a "Place of Effective Management" at Article 4 Paragraph 3 of the 2014 OECD Model Tax Convention' [2017] 2017 UBT International Conference https://doi.org/10.33107/ubt-ic.2017.219 accessed 26 August 2025; David R Elkins, 'A Scalar Conception of Tax Residence for Individuals' [2021] SSRN Electronic Journal https://doi.org/10.2139/ssrn.3889245 accessed 26 August 2025.

It is important to note that at the foundational level, inter-nation equity can be further directed towards either the value of equality or redistributive justice. At the next level, the criteria for inter-nation equity can be distinguished by the Equal Earned Income approach and the Equal Allegiance approach. The former assumes that income can be geographically attributed to its sources, while the latter uses economic allegiance as a proxy for determining the distribution of tax revenue among nations.

Back to formulary apportionment, inter-nation equity is a key underpinning of formulary apportionment. As an alternative to taxing MNEs, the key barrier to its adoption may not be statistically what it renders, but the belief in the community that it can break the impasse of the current system underpinned by the ALP. In this respect, the (inter-nation) equity, including the legitimacy, if widely acknowledged, can significantly smooth the transition or exploration towards formulary apportionment. Inter-nation equity, regardless of its approaches, places the balance between the taxing states when taxing MNEs at the centre stage. The proponents posit that international business has to be taxed in a way that all states with a taxing right are placed on an equal footing, gauged by the optional approaches of either equal earned income or equal allegiance.

In addition, inter-nation equity, together with all the treatises, analyses and connotations delivered in this chapter, can also provide decisive instruction on the concrete design issues of formulary apportionment. For example, when contemplating the factors and the weight in the formula, the equity principle directly instructs that they should contribute to the balance of the residence-source scale (even though equity/legitimacy, in fact, opposes the dichotomy).

CHAPTER 5

# The Principle of Legitimacy

*The legitimacy principle rests on the bedrock of the international tax order and concerns the fundamental justice of international taxation. In the earlier discussions of the nature of international taxation and the mythology of international tax principles, a basic foothold is the extension of the horizon from the national tax order to the international tax order. This section of legitimacy adopts the same approach.*

*Corresponding to the dual relationship of international taxation, legitimacy affects not only the relationship between the taxpayer and tax authority but also the relationship between the taxing states. In addition, the connotation and instructions of the legitimacy principle will also be explored dynamically, taking into account the changing international tax order.*

*The ensuing discussions are structured into three parts. As the groundwork of what follows, the first part delineates the concept and taxonomy of the modern legitimacy principle in the modern international tax literature. The second part revisits the legitimacy principle in the domestic tax setting, which is the starting point where the theories of tax legitimacy evolve. The third part addresses the materialization of the legitimacy principle in the modern international tax setting. The last part concludes this section by summarizing the implications of the legitimacy principle for international tax law.*

## 5.1 INTRODUCTION

The legitimacy principle rests on the bedrock of the international tax order and concerns the fundamental justification of international taxation. In the earlier discussions of the nature of international taxation and the mythology of international tax principles, a basic foothold is the extension of the horizon from the national tax order to the international tax order. This chapter of legitimacy adopts the same approach.

Corresponding to the dual relationship of international taxation, legitimacy affects not only the relationship between the taxpayer and tax authority but also the relationship between the taxing states. In addition, the connotation and instructions of the legitimacy principle will also be explored dynamically, taking into account the changing international tax order.

The ensuing discussions are structured into three parts. As the groundwork of what follows, section 7.2 delineates the concept and taxonomy of the modern legitimacy principle in the modern international tax literature. Section 7.3 revisits the legitimacy principle in the domestic tax setting, which is the starting point where the theories of tax legitimacy evolve. Section 7.4 addresses the materialization of the legitimacy principle in the modern international tax setting. The last section concludes this section by summarizing the implications of the legitimacy principle for international tax law.

## 5.2 DIVISION BETWEEN NORMATIVE LEGITIMACY AND DESCRIPTIVE LEGITIMACY

In linguistics, legitimacy means conformity to sound reasoning and the quality of being based on a fair or acceptable reason. In law, legitimacy concerns the underlying logicality and justifiability of the right to govern and the making and interpretation of rules.

In line with such generic meaning, the law facet of legitimacy manifests the justification of the government's power to enact law to govern the constituents. Building on the insights of political science, a taxonomy of legitimacy for law can be established. First, it is the formal perspective that a law is legitimate if it reflects the will 'of the people', the arguments which underline the importance of participation and consensus in making the rules.[677] Since legitimacy in this respect focuses on whether the law is democratically made and gains the consent of the stakeholders beyond coercion, this dimension is commonly known as the 'input legitimacy'. In a similar vein, the input legitimacy does not concern whether the law is effective 'for the people' and promotes the common welfare of the stakeholders; it is thus also called the 'descriptive legitimacy'. In contrast, the second dimension of legitimacy, the 'output' or 'normative' legitimacy, fills the gap of 'input' or 'descriptive' legitimacy by giving normative substance to the subject matter, so as to ensure that the law and the outcome are justified by serving the common interest of the constituents.[678]

With this taxonomy, the descriptive and normative legitimacy are complementary, with one emphasizing the formal and procedural aspects of law and another

677. Fritz W Scharpf, *Governing in Europe: Effective and Democratic?* (Oxford University Press 1999) 6-8.

678. Patrizia Nanz, 'Democratic Legitimacy and Constitutionalism of Transnational Trade Governance: A View from Political Theory' in Christian Joerges and Ernst-Ulrich Petersmann (eds), *Constitutionalism, Multilevel Trade Governance and Social Regulation* (Hart Publishing 2006) 61.

focusing on the substantive aspect of law. They also form the integral of legitimacy of law, and the deficit of either one will undermine the legitimacy in its entirety.

For tax law, descriptive legitimacy is participation-oriented, which dictates that the process of law-making itself should be legitimate, while normative legitimacy is performance-oriented, which requires that the content and substance of tax law can effectively achieve the established goals. Within the ambit of domestic tax laws, both dimensions of legitimacy have been well explored. Normative legitimacy is manifested in the long-standing inquiry into the role of taxation in the relationship between the state and taxpayers and how tax is justified in such a relationship. Descriptive legitimacy has also been unfolded in the general legal-political discourse about the importance of participation, representation, and transparency applicable to tax law-making.

The case of both dimensions of legitimacy is different for international taxation. For one thing, while normative legitimacy is still partly anchored to the logicality of the relationship between the tax state and the taxpayer, the discrepancies are significant enough to alter the discourse. Taxing non-residents dictates separate legitimacy inquiries on whether to tax in the first place and the subject and object of taxation from those taxing residents or citizens in purely domestic scenarios. If to tax and the taxable subject are mirror questions on the circumstances where states are justified to tax non-residents, and the object of taxation examines the scope of the taxable income of residents and non-residents.

For another, the descriptive legitimacy is even more complicated for international taxation and is neither a comprehensive legal regime nor a subsystem of international law. The international tax law is arguably derived from two major sources including bilateral tax treaties and soft laws. Consequently, the participation-oriented descriptive legitimacy in international taxation is almost a new inquiry, which is drawing increasing attention in the (post-) BEPS era.

The following discussions proceed to elucidate international tax legitimacy following the above taxonomy. The two dimensions of legitimacy are not nascent topics in domestic tax law but they indeed raise idiosyncratic inquiries to the case of international tax law. Notwithstanding that both facets are indispensable for ruminating on the overall legitimacy of international taxation, the existing literature seemed to emphasize more on the descriptive legitimacy.[679] The ensuing parts instead attempt to give equal weight to descriptive legitimacy and normative legitimacy.

679. IJ Mosquera Valderrama, 'Legitimacy and the Making of International Tax Law: The Challenges of Multilateralism' (2015) 7 World Tax Journal https://doi.org/10.59403/3mqgt50 accessed 26 August 2025; Ivan Ozai, 'Institutional and Structural Legitimacy Deficits in the International Tax Regime' [2019] Law & Society: Public Law - Tax eJournal https://doi.org/10.59403/2ft4wzd accessed 26 August 2025; Linda Brosens and Jasper Bossuyt, 'Legitimacy in International Tax Law-Making: Can the OECD Remain the Guardian of Open Tax Norms?' [2020] World Tax Journal 313; IJ Mosquera Valderrama, 'Output Legitimacy Deficits and the Inclusive Framework of the OECD/G20 Base Erosion and Profit Shifting Initiative' (2018) 72 Bulletin for International Taxation https://doi.org/10.59403/se9pt3 accessed 26 August 2025; Sissie Fung, 'The Questionable Legitimacy of the OECD/G20 BEPS Project' (2017) 10 Erasmus Law Review https://doi.org/10.5553/elr.000085 accessed 26 August 2025.

## 5.3 NORMATIVE LEGITIMACY OF INTERNATIONAL TAXATION, THE 'FORGOTTEN' QUESTION

Normative legitimacy of international taxation is asserted as a forgotten question, not because that the substantive norms including the jurisdiction to tax rules, the nexus rules and allocation of taxing rights, and the worldwide versus territorial taxation under the legitimacy umbrella have not been adequately explored; but that first, it should be recognized and to be acted upon that the object of normative legitimacy has historical dimensions. Moreover, these issues have seldom been scrutinized under the lens of legitimacy as a principle of international taxation. The following content sheds light on these two reasons in order to figure out how normative legitimacy should be contemporarily approached and its instructions on the relevant substantive norms.

### 5.3.1 Normative Legitimacy Revisited in the Changing National Tax Order

The most important prerequisite of enunciating the legitimacy of (international) taxation is the awareness of its historical nature rooted in the constantly changing (international) tax order. International taxation has been unravelled as comprising two strands of relationships: one is between the taxing state and the taxpayer, and the other is between more than one taxing state, both of which in modern times contrast with themselves in the times when legitimacy was first conceived for international taxation. Based on the prior discussions of the relationship between the domestic tax principles and international tax principles, what follows first is the inquiry of how the normative legitimacy should be re-examined in the dynamics of the national tax order.

#### *5.3.1.1 Lorenz Von Stein's 'State-Individual' Model*

Table 5.1 below summarizes the popular principles or theories regarding the legitimacy of taxation over time. It can be clearly observed that all the theories introduced bear obvious characteristics of time. Yet, through this observation, Vogel pointed out that none of these theorists had realized that the concept of state as their basis of argument was historically contingent. Therefore, they may unconsciously think their theories of tax legitimacy are static, 'immutable' and 'universally valid', rather than what evolved in the perpetual motion of history.[680]

In contrast, according to Vogel, Lorenz von Stein was the first to take cognizance of the historical nature of tax legitimacy. The term 'tax' itself originated in monarchial times, and then, with the development of the form and organization of the state, the character of tax continued to change as well. From a patriarchal state to a constitutional

680. Klaus Vogel, 'The Justification for Taxation: A Forgotten Question' (1988) 33 The American Journal of Jurisprudence 19, 37 https://doi.org/10.1093/ajj/33.1.19 accessed 26 August 2025.

state, taxation has grown to be the centre of public finance, which corresponds to the rise of the 'tax state'.[681]

It is thus seen that the legitimacy of taxation is inherently based on the concept of the state and the state's relationship with the taxpayers. That being said, the legitimacy of tax is neither a static concept nor can the theories of it be universally valid. Both tax and the state have historical dimensions.[682] It is also a fact that the theories introduced above carried with them apparent characteristics of the dominant forms of the state at the times the authors lived in. It is understandable that in feudal times, when the state was more patriarchal, the emergency theory and sacrifice theory were more attractive. The form of state changes, the tax legitimacy changes with it, and this is a continuous process.

In addition, what Stein believed for the justification of taxation is a model based on the state-individual interaction. Stein held that because the measurement of the state is its constituents, taxation requires justification. He rejected both the sacrifice theory and benefit theory, for he believed they were based on the analogy of public economy to private economy, thus 'theoretically and practically worthless'.[683] Turning to his theory for the justification of tax, Stein observed two major conditions for 'all development'. The first is the individual's effort; the second is 'the community of human beings in the reciprocal activity of all individuals successively'.[684] For the latter, to make it possible for the community to provide the necessary conditions for individuals' development, individuals must return to the community part of their progress derived within it. It is a mutual relationship, for the state also contributes to the individuals' development through the law. As for such 'return' from the individuals to the community, it originates in the 'general human essence' of the community, 'taxes, however, in turn, originate from the development of the concept of the state'.[685] For Stein, taxation is justified on one side by the limitations on state activity in taxation, and on the other by the ultimate purpose of the state, the development and preservation of individual independence and personality. Vogel summarized Stein's theory for tax justification as follows: taxation is justified vis-à-vis 'individual independence' by arguing that it is only through taxation that the community is placed in the position to provide individuals with 'the economic conditions required for their development'.[686]

681. Schumpeter, Die Krise des Steuerstaates, (1918), reprinted in: Schumpeter, Aufsdtze zur Soziologie (1953).
682. Vogel, 'The Justification for Taxation: A Forgotten Question' (n. 680) 37.
683. *Ibid.*, 39.
684. *Ibid.*
685. Vogel, 'The Justification for Taxation: A Forgotten Question' (n. 680) 40.
686. *Ibid.*, 43.

*Table 5.1 Evolution of Benefit Theory*

| *Theories* | *Content* | *Comments* |
|---|---|---|
| **Emergency Theory** (Thomas Aquinas, Francisco Suarez, since the Middle Ages); **Public Necessity Theory** (Christoph Besold and Caspar Klock, since the seventeenth century) | Taxation is justified and permissible with an emergency as a prerequisite to levy such tax.[687] | Similar to the modern special-purpose tax or Pigouvian Tax. However, under these propositions, when the purpose is achieved or emergency settled, the tax needs to be refunded or credited, then the taxation will be an extraordinary rather than regular levy. The Public Necessity Theory maintained the purpose-justification of tax, yet emphasized that the continuous public necessity should be such purpose. |
| **Sacrifice Theory** (Karl Heinrich Rau, Otto Mayer, Adolph Wagner, F.J. Neumann, Schmoller, since the nineteenth-twentieth century)[688] | By reinterpreting the state as a higher and superior unity over the individuals, the tax is thought of as a mandatory sacrifice to the state needless of the consensual approval or mutual consideration. | This is based on a different view of the relationship between the state and the government. In this view, the state is 'organic', 'god-like' and 'transcendental'. The tax is thus viewed as an absolute necessity of the state, which makes it compulsory and actually clear of political and moral valuations. |

687. Francisco Suarez, Tractatus de legibus ac deo legislatore, Lib. V Cap. 13, 15 (1612), and *Ibid.*, 24-25.
688. *See* the relevant propositions in *Ibid.*, 27-31.

| *Theories* | *Content* | *Comments* |
| --- | --- | --- |
| **Social Contract Theory** (John Locke, Tomas Hobbes, since sixteenth-seventeenth century) | The integration of individuals into the political society is through a process of mutual consent in which individuals agree to abide by common rules and accept corresponding obligations to protect themselves and others from violence and other types of harm. And 'it is true that governments need a great deal of money for their support, and it is appropriate that each person who enjoys his share of the protection should pay his proportion of the cost'.[689] | They formulate the justification of tax from a higher level of abstraction, in the context of justification for the state or government. It can also be interpreted as containing some preliminary form of proportional taxation and benefit principle.[690] Furthermore, such benefit principle is premised on that a quid pro quo fiscal relationship exists between the individual and the state. |
| **(Newer) Benefit Principle** (James M. Buchanan, since twentieth century) | Tax is justified 'if and only if an equivalence between government services and the payments of individuals, collectively considered, exists'.[691] | Same with the older contractarian benefit principle, there should exist a quid pro quo relationship in the fiscal process of the state and the people. However, the difference is that such quid pro quo relationship is not between the state and an individual, but all individuals taken together. |

### *5.3.1.2 The Rise of Corporations and Klaus Vogel's 'State-Society-Economy' Model*

Based on Stein's 'state-individual' model, Vogel extended the dual relationship to a triangular relationship of 'state-society-economy' for his theory of tax legitimacy. First

689. John Locke, *Second Treatise of Government* (Columbia University Press 2016) https://www.earlymoderntexts.com/assets/pdfs/locke1689a.pdf accessed 28 November 2023.
690. Jane Frecknall-Hughes, *The Theory, Principles and Management of Taxation: An Introduction* (Routledge 2014) 23.
691. *Ibid.*, 32.

of all, Vogel defined society as the totality of individuals, which includes both the economic life (economy) and non-economic life (civil society, daily life) of all individuals.[692] Vogel restated Stein's 'state-individual' model as a 'state-society' model, which should be viewed as a refinement instead of a revision. However, the reality has changed, and as a result, the 'state-society' framework cannot provide a sound basis for tax legitimacy anymore. The predominant qualitative change, according to Vogel, is the rise of corporations.

Since the nineteenth century, economic relations have been increasingly among corporations instead of merely among individuals. Corporations are becoming the main actors in economic production and distribution. In particular, corporations have become separate from their owners and more and more in the hands of managers.[693] The original understanding of 'society' in the 'state-society' model is not able to capture such qualitative change. Conceptually and practically, the 'economy' contributed by corporations as organizations constitutes an independent system adding to the 'state-society' system. As in the 'state-individual' model, the justification of tax dictates the justification of the state in the first place; under the new reality, it then leads to the justification of the new relationship among state, society, and economy.

The key to the justification of tax is extended from solely the two-pronged relationship between state and individual, to the triangle of state-society-economy relationship. The question then is, first, what is the relationship between the new 'economy', 'state', and the redefined 'society', and how can tax be justified in the new reality? In the new reality, the individuals in the society belong to both the system of state as its citizens and the system of economy as producers and consumers. 'Everybody belongs to both empires.'[694] The relationship between state and society is no different from what has been discussed in the 'state-individual' model. The relationship between society and the economy they are not separate and distinct areas. They are connected and mutually dependent through the tie of individuals. As for the relationship between the state and the economy, Vogel used a lot of words to clarify this point.[695]

In summary, his conclusions are, first, that the state and economy should be separated and restricted to their own areas. It is not advisable for the state to participate directly in the economic production and distribution, and it is also 'not morally acceptable to build a social system on self-interest' because 'private business creates and encourages inequality and, therefore, injustice'.[696] As a result, the relationship between the state and society was established by Vogel and actually also by Schumpeter as an equilibrium.[697] By now, the triangular system of 'State-Society-Economy' has emerged and been justified.

692. Vogel, 'The Justification for Taxation: A Forgotten Question' (n. 680) 45.
693. Burnham James, *The Managerial Revolution: What is Happening in the World* (Lume Books 2021).
694. Schattschneider Elmer E and Adamany David, *The Semisovereign People: A Realist's View of Democracy in America* (1st edn, Cengage Learning 1975) 116.
695. Vogel, 'The Justification for Taxation: A Forgotten Question' (n. 680) 49-56.
696. *Ibid.*, 54.
697. *Ibid.*, 49.

In this triangular system of 'State-Society-Economy', tax touches upon the relationship of state and economy in terms of their functions and weights. To justify the tax, it is required to determine the place of tax in such a system. In this triangular system, tax is justified by being an indispensable element, a tache in the triangle. The state leaves production to the economy and depends on taxes. Moreover, applying the conclusion of Stein in his 'state-individual' model, the state is justified in its tax claim because taxation 'returns to the state a portion of the economic value that the state for its own part has assisted in producing'.[698]

### 5.3.1.3 *Implications for International Tax Legitimacy*

The legitimacy of taxation in the sphere of domestic taxation has long been viewed as a static image, for which different theories are competing at the same level with each other. The above discussions revealed that, to the contrary, the justification of taxation changes with the evolution of the concept of state and the state's relationship with taxpayers. As a result, the legitimacy of taxation should be revisited on the basis of changing tax order. In the same vein, the international tax legitimacy should be re-examined through the same lens, taking into consideration the new international tax order.

In addition, Stein and Vogel's discourses on tax legitimacy have cleared the shadows over the concerns brought by the rise of corporations regarding tax justification. Vogel's triangular system for justification of tax is built on his observation of the new reality in society: the rise of corporations leads to the subsystem of the economy. Tax is thus justified in the triangular system of 'State-Society-Economy', which covers both the taxation of individuals and corporations.

For a long time before Vogel, taxation on companies was justified according to the theories copied from those contractarian theories regarding individuals, which in turn depended on the political and moral theses of the state and individual. Such 'transplantation' is problematic, for the differences between a company and an individual are intrinsic. In addition, for the taxation of non-resident individuals, Vogel's 'State-Society-Economy' is also superior to the traditional theories in providing justification for taxing non-resident individuals. It gets rid of an obstinate character and actually an insolvable myth of the traditional theories, that is, the prerequisite of the political philosophy, which looks to the relationship between citizens and the state.

When the triangular system was put forward by Vogel, at least in this thesis, the international tax aspects were not implied at all. However, his theory is inclusive and able to unbundle our thoughts in the international arena and is 'compatible' with the new circumstances of international taxation. His theory is not differentiated according to the political ties that multinational corporations can easily acquire and manipulate. Rather, it looks at the role they play in the triangular system. To be specific, if the MNE participates in the economic system of a country in one way or another, then the country has the justification for taxing the relevant income derived within its triangular

698. *Ibid.*, 57.

system. Be that as it may, the triangular system is not responsible for determining the 'weight' of legitimacy if a country is justified thereby to tax a non-resident. That is, even if it is justified to tax in this case, it does not mean there will be actual tax liability incurred, nor can a specific amount of such liability be determined by the legitimacy theory.[699]

### 5.3.2 Modernizing Normative Legitimacy in the Changing International Tax Order

In the same spirit of the re-examinations of the tax legitimacy in the national tax order, the legitimacy of international taxation should also be contemplated based on the changing international tax order. The revisited normative legitimacy of international taxation is expected to shed light on many of the substantive norms of international taxation, as the current regime was legitimatized against the international tax order almost a century ago.

#### *5.3.2.1 The Scope of Normative Legitimacy of International Taxation*

Normative legitimacy concerns the justification of the substantive aspects of international taxation, and it evaluates the acceptability and logicality of the 'performance' of international taxation. One must be aware that while legitimacy can involve a wide variety of norms, its scope and boundaries should be properly demarcated.

As the basis of discussion, let's stylize a typical case of international taxation. Suppose the investor [a] of its home country [A] is doing a business and thus produces a certain amount of income from country [B].[700] The real world may be far more complicated, but the example captures all the basic elements of international taxation: the cross-border flow of business, a home state, a host state and the cross-border flow of income. The normative legitimacy, therefore, consists of two categories.

First, the home state [A]'s imposition of tax on its resident [a], and the host state [B]'s imposition of tax on the non-resident [a]. The tax relationship between investor [a] and the home country [A] is purely domestic if [a] does not cross the border and earn that foreign income; for state [B], it will not have any connections with [a] if [a] is not doing business in it. For the consideration of international tax legitimacy, the focus falls on analysing the justification of the existence and extent of taxation in the home and host states.

699. 'Yet even if one acknowledges the appeal of these principles (ABT and BP), they merely suggest *that* revenue should be allocated among residence and source countries, but not *how* the allocation should be made.', which is another reference that defines the scope of legitimacy. Wei Cui, 'Destination-Based Cash-Flow Taxation: A Critical Appraisal' (2017) 67 University of Toronto Law Journal 301 https://doi.org/10.3138/utlj.3796 accessed 26 August 2025.

700. For simplification of analysis, this case does not differentiate the direct investment and portfolio investment, which may render the analyses of two scenarios slightly different. In addition, the tax potentially levied by either country is limited to income tax, regardless of consideration of property tax or indirect tax.

Second, the operationalization of the legitimacy to tax. When the legitimacy to tax at both states is established at the conceptual level, it requires some substantive norms to operationalize the power to tax, which are commonly known as the jurisdiction to tax norms. At the residence side, the jurisdiction to tax norms is a set of rules defining the 'residence' status of corporations; at the source side, they are a set of rules defining the 'source' of some categories of income and the 'nexus' rules for the business income.

The above two categories thereby demarcate the scope of substantive international tax norms that fall within the ambit of normative legitimacy, which is also where the reconstructed international tax legitimacy sheds its light. The first facet corresponds to the residence-based taxation for which the taxpayer's residence is a pillar in the jurisdiction to tax paradigm. Moreover, this facet also involves the extent of residence taxation, that is, how legitimacy sees the debate between worldwide and territorial taxation. The second facet touches upon the normative basis of non-resident taxation, which is 'source' in relation to the 'residence' in the existing jurisdiction to tax paradigm. Similarly, the inquiry also extends to the 'nexus' employed to concretize the host state's legitimacy to tax non-residents.

An additional consideration beyond the above categories is separately discussed because what it depicts is hard to pin down as substantive norms but exerts substantial influence on the two categories. In a purely national scenario and as far as normative legitimacy is concerned, tax justice is inherently regarding the relationship between the taxpayer and the taxing state. In contrast, international taxation introduces the interaction of more than one taxing state as an additional factor in the legitimacy inquiry. The levy by either country would have a wealth (re-)distribution effect between the treasuries which leads indirectly to issues beyond what legitimacy should cover. While such 'after-effect' are spillovers beyond legitimacy that is concentrated on how tax can be justified, instead of how much tax to pay and the effect of tax, its reverse constraints on the state-taxpayer relationship should also be considered.

*Figure 5.1 Stylized Case of Cross-Border Business and Taxation*

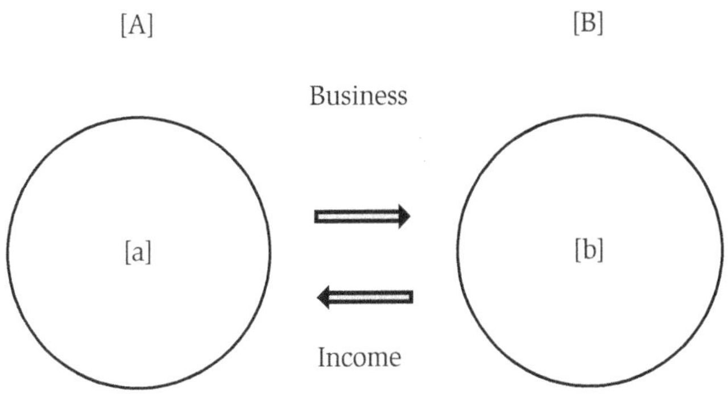

### 5.3.2.2 *Normative Legitimacy Revisited in the Changing International Tax Order*

Modernizing the international normative legitimacy and fathoming the instructions on the associated substantive norms thereunder jointly dictate, first of all, inspecting how legitimacy had been conceived in the germination of the international tax regime; second, exploring how the modern international tax order contrasts the old times and how it undermines the substantive norms within the framework of normative legitimacy; and third, applying and extending the theory of tax legitimacy developed from the national tax order.

#### *5.3.2.2.1 The Trivial Role of Legitimacy in the Formation Period*

The foundational components of the international tax regime, including the substantive norms within the legitimacy framework, were built up from the 1920s to World War II. In this period, the deliberations over the legitimacy of taxation in an international context have played a trivial role in the formation period of the international tax regime. Turning again to the work under the auspices of LON, the principal, if not the sole aim, is to seek solutions to double taxation arising from the exercise of competing jurisdiction to tax.[701] An implicit premise is that the pre-existing taxing power of either home or host state is acknowledged and legitimatized on whatever basis. The home state's taxing power over the resident and its global income and the host state's taxing power over the non-resident were taken as a fact, whereas political and ethical reflections were set aside. As a result, the discussions were hardly principle-based.

In the second part of the 1923 Academic Report that touched upon the principles governing international jurisdiction to tax, the authors made simple reference to the benefit principle derived from social contract theory. They also noticed the two dimensions of benefit theory as both the 'reason and measurement' of taxation,[702] yet later the theory was rejected not for theoretical deficiency but for practical complications. The authors, in the end, turned to the ability to pay principle as the theoretical basis of their 'economic allegiance' solution, which is a tax fairness norm concerning the distribution of a general tax burden typically in a closed society instead of a theoretical basis of a country's competence to tax in international tax setting.[703]

Regardless of the controversies surrounding the importance of the 1923 Academic Report, neither the earlier work of the Chamber of Commerce nor the asserted

701. There are three major tasks of the report, they are, to find out the economic consequences of double taxation, to formulate the general principles as the basis for an international convention to avoid the negatives of double taxation, and finally, the application issues of such principles. *See* Bruins et al. (n. 44) 4006.
702. *Ibid.*, 4022.
703. '... the principle of economic allegiance principle is not related to the ability of a taxpayer to pay but the territory from which benefits are derived.', *see* Rav Pratap Singh, 'International Taxation: The International Law Perspective' 8 http://www.publicinternationallaw.in/node/137 accessed 11 May 2019., and Peter Harris and David Oliver, *International Commercial Tax* (Cambridge University Press 2010) 43-86.

potent US international tax rules had ever thought about the legitimacy of international taxation.[704] The foundations of international taxation that have implications for normative legitimacy had been laid following the methodology of no more than accepting the competing taxing power as a fact and seeking a way to accommodate their coexistence. Why can the methodology make it through and persist till recently? The explanations lie in the contrasting international tax order in the early stages rather than the status quo.

##### *5.3.2.2.2 The Changing International Tax Order and the Undermined Normative Legitimacy*

At the surface of it, the ascendancy of the sovereignty institutions in international tax discourse since the early stage can account for the perception of the competing tax jurisdiction as a fact. Nevertheless, the root cause is still the transformation of international tax order, which in turn alters the sovereignty discourse.

International law can often account for things that tax thinking finds hard to do. The residence taxing right over the residents and source taxing right over the non-residents were deemed pre-wired in the formation period because both reflect a piece of state sovereignty, with one on the subject and another on the object. Albrecht had done research about the taxation of 'aliens' under international law.[705] He claimed that the right to taxation extended to aliens is generally accepted as an aspect of sovereignty. He then explored three main theories underlying such right to tax. He considered the contractual theory, the ethical theory, and the *sovereignty* theory. His final conclusion is that the 'right to tax aliens is sometimes influenced by contracts and occasionally affected by ethical principles; it is justified in international law *essentially* as an attribute of statehood or sovereignty'.[706]

The international tax literature on what the economic world and political world was like in the formation period of international taxation has been voluminous. Many of these that were captured have direct implications for the normative legitimacy inquiry, for example, the 'mercantilist economic model' depicting the international division of labour,[707] the clear-cut division between the capital exporting and capital importing countries, the 'bricks and mortar' form of economy, and so forth. These characteristics obviously differ sharply from the modern world, which undermines the factual basis of normative legitimacy that has not been constantly reviewed since the very beginning. The race to the bottom tax competition the mismatch between value creation and tax payment, and base erosion and profit shifting are the consequences of the undermined normative legitimacy of international taxation.

In addition to these phenomenal changes, the observations of the transformation of the international tax order are rather qualitative. This transformation can be approached abreast of the change of national tax order as discussed above. In the

704. Graetz and O'Hear (n. 56).
705. Albrecht (n. 608) 148.
706. *Ibid.*
707. Wells and Lowell (n. 56).

dynamics of national taxation, Stein and Vogel characterized the expansion of the market sector as epitomized by the rise of corporations. It follows that the traditional 'state-individual' dual relationship is restructured into a 'state-society-economy' triangular relationship.

In the same vein, Peters characterized the *traditional* international tax order with two elements: first, there was a clear borderline between the national field and international field of tax order, meaning that the national taxation was independent of the state-state interaction; second, international tax society was dominated by states that set the international norms by consent.[708] However, the traditional order of international taxation is transforming, and the two elements are also somewhat altered.[709]

For the first element, the world sees the diminishing boundary between what is purely domestic and what is international. It has been said that taxation is positioned in the triangular relationship in the national realm; the international tax order, however, is not the simple aggregation of the triangular unity of the national order. Recalling that in the earlier discussions, one of two components of international taxation is the state-state relationship. States cooperate and compete with each other and are mutually constrained as well. The days are long gone when, in a national domain, there remains a strict unity of state, territory, and market.[710] Taxation is now more and more international due to the increasing movement of persons, goods, and capital crossing the national border.

For the second element, Peters identified that in the changing international tax order, a state not only faces the constraints of other states but it also operates in a system of multi-layered governance that sees growing forces of the market.[711] It is arguable whether the states lose their dominance in the international tax governance, yet as a matter of fact, the states' power is dispersed and shared by the emerging multi-layered governance actors, such as the sub-national communities, the supranational political organizations, and the non-governmental organizations.

In addition, just as the national tax order has been through, the increasing power of the 'market' is also a key game changer for the international tax order. The 'market' in the international tax setting refers to not only the normal market that depicts the power of the private economy but also the 'public' market of tax law that captures the regulatory competition among states and the commercialization of tax sovereignty. In the new international tax order, the competition is not just limited to private market actors, and countries also participate in the game by marketing their public goods and regulatory tools.[712] The commercialization of tax sovereignty is the concretization of

708. CAT Peters, 'The Faltering Legitimacy of International Tax Law' (Doctoral Thesis, Tilburg University 2013) s. 2.2.3.
709. *Ibid.*, 3.
710. Wolfgang Schön, 'International Tax Coordination for a Second-Best World (Part I)' (2009) 1 World Tax Journal 67, 81 https://doi.org/10.59403/hzk01m accessed 26 August 2025.
711. Peters, 'The Faltering Legitimacy of International Tax Law' (n. 708) s. 2.3.1.
712. Matteo Ortino, 'The Notion of Economic Law and Regulatory Competition' in Karl M Meessen (ed.), *Economic Law as an Economic Good: Its Rule Function and Its Tool Function in the Competition of Systems* (European Law Publishers 2009).

the regulatory competition among states in the field of taxation. Dagan is the constant advocate of the proposition that the absolute, monopolistic and exclusive nature of sovereignty has been altered with respect to how the state's power to tax had been previously viewed.[713] In the market of international taxation, the states are becoming market actors competing with each other for economic resources (labour, capital, businesses, and tax revenue), by offering the entire package of public goods and services. The factual basis of the case is the high mobility of capital, business and resources, and according to Dagan, the decentralized structure of international tax governance is also a cause. At the other corner of this market, the taxpayers, in particular the MNEs, unbundle the sovereign 'goods' and shop around so as to minimize their tax liabilities. As such, the commercialization of sovereignty reshapes how the power to tax was perceived as a sovereign privilege. As far as the normative legitimacy of international taxation is concerned, the interaction between states and taxpayers in the traditional (inter-)national tax order has been profoundly altered. The sovereignty discourse underpinning the traditional international tax legitimacy is thus substantially weakened.[714]

#### *5.3.2.3 Modernizing and Operationalizing the Normative Legitimacy*

The normative legitimacy of international taxation is essentially the expression of value judgment on the relationship between the state and taxpayer, which in turn is shaped by the interaction between taxing states. The above discussions have revealed that the existing legitimacy paradigm is constructed upon the international tax order contrasted with the current one. It is also noted that in the formation period of the international tax regime, the reflections on legitimacy had been trivial, which may be explained by the dominant views that the power to tax the residents and non-residents are sovereign matters. However, the changing international tax order cannot accommodate the traditional sovereignty-based legitimacy discourse; thus, it dictates the modernization of the legitimacy theories. Based on this, the evaluations and instructions of normative legitimacy for the relevant substantive norms, as put into the two categories, should also be updated.

In fact, the key to the modernization of normative legitimacy of international taxation has been well explored. It lies in simply applying and extending the theory of tax legitimacy developed from the national tax order. In the legitimacy model contributed by Stein and Vogel based on the modern tax order in the national realm, taxation

713. Dagan Tsilly, 'The Marketization of Tax Sovereignty' (15 April 2017) https://papers.ssrn.com/abstract=2953220 accessed 2 December 2023. *See* similar view earlier at Philipp Genschel, 'Globalisation and the Transformation of the Tax State' (2005) https://www.econstor.eu/bitstream/10419/28260/1/497811359.PDF. However, views in respect of tax sovereignty under modern developments are mixed. *See* somewhat opposing view against Dagan at Mason (n. 355) 361-2.

714. Besides the arguments here, the role of sovereignty has been increasingly questioned, *see* Yariv Brauner, 'An Essay on BEPS, Sovereignty, and Taxation' in Sergio André Rocha and Christians Allison (eds), *Tax Sovereignty in the BEPS Era* (Kluwer Law International BV 2016). Kaufman (n. 586) 167-172.

is positioned as a mechanism undergirding the triangular interaction among the state, society, and economy. Turning to the international tax scenario as illustrated in the above example, the taxpayer [a]'s participation in its home state [A]'s triangular system is in nature not heterogenous from its participation in the host state [B]'s triangular system with respect to delineating the state-taxpayer relationship, principally on account of the interconnected system of 'economy' in states [A] and [B]. As stated earlier, the international tax order is not the simple aggregation of multiple national tax orders. The interconnection that makes the state-taxpayer relationships homogeneous between the states would not be possible if the international tax order was not as depicted above, referring particularly to the rise of the market and its integration, either of the private market or the 'public' market of tax law and sovereignty.

After establishing the homogeneity, the connotations of the modern normative legitimacy of international taxation are thus determined. The modernized normative legitimacy is centred on the taxpayer's role in the internal ecology of state, society, and economy and state-state interaction in the international tax order, and it serves as the common evaluative framework for the justification of taxation for ostensibly contrasting two groups of tax relationship, one is between the home state and the resident earning income worldwide, another is between the host state and the non-resident doing business in it. Following the theory, a level playing field of tax legitimacy is created for the border-crossing taxpayer.

The reconstructed normative legitimacy of international taxation, therefore, builds on the modernized legitimacy of taxation in the national domain. It stems from and adapts to the new realities at both national and international levels and thus redresses the justice of the international tax regime at the ground layer, which promotes both its sustainability and stability. These benefits are crystallized by the theory's instructions on the substantive norms as demarcated in the above.

First of all, modern normative legitimacy has established accordant fields for inspecting taxation in the states that have been partitioned and tagged as 'residence' states and 'source' states. The historical arguments focused on which state's taxing power takes precedence over the other under various circumstances and the coordination for double tax relief. This is inevitable because the sovereignty-based legitimacy for the taxing power of states is deemed as sovereign privilege; thus, they are exclusive and conflicting in nature. Under modern normative legitimacy, however, 'residence' and 'source' are not meaningful as they are in the existing framework. Residence is no longer a tacit mandate for worldwide taxation of residents, and source does not mean taxation of income only 'within' the border. Instead, the states are on a par with each other in their ordering to tax, and their power to tax is legitimatized by the participation of the taxpayer, either resident or not, in the triangular relationship of state, society, and economy. This corresponds to the first category of the substantive norms.

Second, as for the jurisdiction to tax norms, since the modern normative legitimacy proposes a different methodology for legitimatizing the power to tax in international taxation, the traditional jurisdiction to tax norms is no longer undergirded. The rules giving an artificial residence to MNEs are inherently arbitrary, and basing the power to tax solely on the status of residence falls short of substance in fulfilling the legitimacy requirements.[715] In comparison, the jurisdiction to tax norms at the side of the source state has more affinities with the modern normative legitimacy. Both the source of income rules and nexus rules have an economic basis that is anchored to the economic interaction between the taxpayer and the state. Yet still, the source and nexus rules are designed more for accommodating the practical and political compromises and economic realities in the formation period of the international tax regime, while lacking normative content,[716] as manifested in the classification and assignment approach, the withholding of tax regime, and the permanent establishment threshold. From the perspective of tax legitimacy, the liability to pay tax is determined by the taxpayer's degree of participation in the state's triangle of national tax order, which is true for both the home and host states. As such, first of all, an operable method for measuring such participation should capture the taxpayer's role in the tax order of the state, as being in the systems of economy and society and interacting with the state through the payment of tax; second, the method should eliminate the current disparity when establishing jurisdiction to tax. Thus it should be uniformly applicable to the home state and host state.

## 5.4 RE-ASKING THE QUESTION, THE DESCRIPTIVE LEGITIMACY PROBLEM

It was mentioned earlier that the legitimacy ruminations in international tax literature focus more on the procedural or formal aspects, in particular, the norm-making process. This section does not aim to repeat the existing discussions but rather asks a question that is relatively latent: is there a way to tax MNEs by *incentivizing* the descriptive legitimacy of international taxation? Or put in another way, this section analyses to what extent the current (ALP-based) system is compatible with or able to enhance the descriptive legitimacy of international taxation.

### 5.4.1 Deficit of Descriptive Legitimacy

The international tax system, as it has been since its formation in the 1920s, is a kind of negotiated international order where states tacitly follow some best practice or soft law and ultimately may implement the norm through their domestic laws or tax treaties. On the surface of it, states participate in international tax forums equally, rarely compelled to adopt a certain rule. However, the formal international tax system is mostly empowered by unilateral moves and bilateral tax treaties, while almost no multilateral or global agreement or formal forum exists (at least before the MLI, which

715. Irene Burgers, Raymond Adema and Maarten de Wilde, 'Residence, Multinational Enterprises and BEPS: Is Determining the Residence of Companies Belonging to Multinational Groups Mission Impossible?: 2017 European Association of Tax Law Professors Congress' in Edoardo Traversa (ed.), *Corporate Tax Residence and Mobility* (IBFD 2018).

716. Stephen E Shay, J Clifton Fleming and Robert J Peroni, 'The David R. Tillinghast Lecture What's Source Got to Do with It: Source Rules and U.S. International Taxation' (2002) 56 Tax Law Review 81, 139.

is also largely optional).[717] Countries, especially those low-income ones, had effectively been 'imposed' on an order of international taxation. They lack the resources and ability to influence rich countries. Thus, most times, they are left with few options but to follow the given instructions, and they play hand-raising machines where they are needed for their presence. The legitimacy deficit of the international tax regime has been heatedly discussed in the recent literature, which will not be repeated herein.[718]

### 5.4.2 The Possible Causes

The question is, therefore, triggered as to why the international tax system has fallen short of descriptive legitimacy as such. It is often recalled that the international tax system is a special realm of law, which makes coordinated and legitimate governance far too difficult to realize. Few analyses are conducted as to what exact differences distinguish tax law from other fields of law. Is it the sovereign nature of taxation, or simply the path dependency as the underlying framework of international taxation? It is rather submitted that the status quo in respect of descriptive legitimacy is the corollary of some core aspects of the existing international tax system, which is simply disincentivized from evolving to be more legitimate.

First, the international tax system was originally designed in the historical context where the morale for cooperation was limited. The very foundational essentials were laid down after or during the two world wars. It was, therefore, simply not realistic for an adequate number of countries to come together and conceive a mechanism for them to carry out norm-making effectively on a legitimate basis. Second, the main theme of eliminating double taxation in the formation period simply does not entail countries forming a multilateral regime in the first place. However, it is contended that the current system is a conscious and deliberate product for countries to interact in the tax arena on a unilateral, bilateral, or dispersed basis. Third, the existing system is built up by and for competition. To cooperate and form international rules in a way all states have equal and effective say that may impede the competition is difficult to imagine, and it at least requires potent internal or external drivers.[719]

The above are the indicators and explanations for why the system is disinclined to advance in the direction of descriptive legitimacy. The following unveils the crucial role of the ALP it.

### 5.4.3 The Crux, the Role of ALP

Focusing on the taxation of MNEs, the ALP is the cornerstone of the descriptive legitimacy problem as well. ALP is the winner over its competitors, which is an

717. *See* discussions at Ch. 2.
718. Bruno Peeters, Hans Gribnau and Jo Badisco, *Building Trust in Taxation* (Intersentia 2017) https://www.cambridge.org/core/books/building-trust-in-taxation/EB30499021E91393529827840D42900A; Ozai (n. 679); Valderrama (n. 679).
719. For the alternative analysis of the explanations of anti-multilateral international tax order, *see* Genschel and Rixen (n. 46); Thomas Rixen, 'The Institutional Design of International Double Taxation Avoidance' (2008) No. SP IV 2008-302 WZB Discussion Paper.

established fact as a historical matter. Based on the discussions earlier, the victory is also the mixed product of historical contingency, misunderstanding, and administrative considerations. The stable development of Article 9 seems to confirm that the choice was correctly made partly. However, digging deeper, ALP, in fact, has been the crux of the causes of the descriptive legitimacy problem.

First, as per the decisive work in the 1930s led by Mitchell B. Carroll, the modern ALP, and its dominant status are the unintended by-product of the preference for separate accounting over other alternatives, including formulary apportionment. Knowing this is critical to unravelling the underlying role of ALP in the international tax order. In the first instance, the decision makers at that time were faced with the problem of taxing MNEs with multiple PEs (instead of subsidiaries) across jurisdictions. There are several reasons why separate accounting was eventually chosen d for sharing a commonality, which is that it had already been widely in place as a national practice. In other words, the triumph of separate accounting was largely the outcome of path dependency. The path in question is right in the international tax order, where states' coordination was substantially limited to the extent of being organized on unilateral and bilateral bases. Separate accounting and the ensuing ALP are both the causes and effects of the descriptive legitimacy problem.

Besides the general explanations at the origin, there is one functionality of ALP further accounting for at the micro level, the status quo of descriptive legitimacy. The rationale of ALP and the regime of transfer pricing rely on the platform function thereunder for states to achieve minimal but requisite room for cooperation and coordination. Third-party unrelated data is a platform through which states with competing tax claims can agree on how much they may take from the pie. Otherwise, the case of taxing MNEs would be totally arbitrary and chaotic. With MNEs expanding exponentially, the 'platform' gains more and more weight and ultimately makes ALP the most important norm in international business taxation. For the consideration of descriptive legitimacy, the current state of play of international taxation is no longer simply path dependence but a deadlock in which states are deeply entangled by the platform functionality of ALP. As such, the degree of descriptive legitimacy relating to how and how 'much' the states are cooperating in forming international tax rules is largely decided by the elasticity of ALP. For the time being, states cooperate only to the extent where it perfects their competition, for which the explanation and application of ALP have played a central role. The norm of ALP has been the crux of the competition-based regime of international taxation. It is a product of the nascent system, but due to its platform functionality, it is unintentionally given great significance in subsequent development.

To encapsulate, the norm of ALP has been the crux of the competition-based regime of international taxation. It, on the one hand, is a product of the nascent system; on the other hand, it unintentionally attaches great significance in the subsequent development due to its platform functionality. The ALP is one of the most typical manifestations that the current system of international taxation has been disincentivizing descriptive legitimacy.

## 5.5 THE TWO-PRONGED LEGITIMACY AND FORMULARY APPORTIONMENT

Legitimacy, while less frequently discussed, is constructed in this chapter as a profound and comprehensive principle for international taxation. Similar to equity, legitimacy also undergirds formulary apportionment and provides instructions on the design specifics, even to a greater extent.

Legitimacy concerns not only the relationship between the taxpayer and the tax authority but also the relationship between taxing states. Legitimacy is distinguished between normative and descriptive forms. Normative legitimacy focuses on the justification of the government's power to enact laws and govern, while descriptive legitimacy emphasizes the democratic process and stakeholder consent in rulemaking. Both forms of legitimacy are complementary and essential for the overall legitimacy of law, with a deficit in either undermining the whole.

With respect to normative legitimacy, legitimacy's historical nature and its evolution with the changing concept of the state and its relationship with taxpayers are discussed. This chapter revisits normative legitimacy in the context of the national tax order and the rise of corporations, leading to the 'State-Society-Economy' model proposed by Klaus Vogel. It also explores the implications of these theories for international tax legitimacy, emphasizing the need to re-examine legitimacy in light of the new international tax order. It proposes that the traditional sovereignty-based legitimacy discourse is ill-suited for the current order and suggests a new evaluative framework for the justification of taxation that aligns legitimacy with the modern realities of both national and international tax systems.

With that being said, the modernized normative legitimacy entrenches formulary apportionment in two aspects.

First, modern normative legitimacy has established a framework where states are on a par with their ordering to tax, and their power to tax is legitimatized based on the taxpayer's participation in the triangular relationship of state, society, and economy. The traditional concepts of 'residence' and 'source' states are no longer meaningful within this framework.[720] This is effectively what formulary apportionment renders, as the taxing states are not determined by reference to residence and traditional sources.

Taking a further step, the traditional jurisdiction to tax norms are not supported anymore, as they lack normative content and are designed more for accommodating practical and political compromises. From the perspective of tax legitimacy, the liability to pay tax is determined by the taxpayer's degree of participation in the state's triangle of national tax order, which should be captured by an operable method uniformly applicable to both the 'home' and 'host' states.

It is therefore submitted that normative legitimacy contributes to the core of how formulary apportionment functions to distribute income among the states where MNEs do business. To be more specific, the current paradigm centred around nexus rule is superseded by some factor-test of formulary apportionment.

720. Burgers, Adema and de Wilde (n. 715).

In terms of descriptive legitimacy, formulary apportionment draws lots of force as it incentivizes cooperation and dictates the consensus shaping among the stake holders of international taxation. This has already been validated by the relevant developments of the two pillars.

The deficit of descriptive legitimacy has been widely identified partly due to the pro-competitive nature of the international tax system and the dominance of the ALP, which has become a platform for states to achieve minimal cooperation and coordination in tax matters that undermines legitimacy.

In contrast, formulary apportionment is naturally a system that demands a higher level of coordination. As discussed earlier, a relatively low level of coordination requirement of ALP is partly right, which makes it the winner over other alternatives. However, the implementation of formulary apportionment will have to deal with the same challenge the second time, should it be widely accepted. On the other side of the coin, descriptive legitimacy is also where formulary apportionment can significantly transform the international tax system.

CHAPTER 6

# Efficiency Considerations: The Questionable Usefulness of Neutrality

*This chapter critically examines the concept of tax neutrality in international taxation, questioning its prominence and utility as a guiding principle. It begins by exploring the foundational concerns of neutrality, highlighting its absence from Adam Smith's canons of taxation and its role in minimizing economic distortions caused by taxation. The chapter contrasts neutrality's limited role in domestic tax policy, where tax expenditures often overshadow it, with its elevated status in international tax discussions as a normative principle. It introduces scepticism about neutrality's significance, particularly in the context of pre-BEPS and uni-national frameworks, and proposes a re-evaluation of economic efficiency and neutrality. The chapter analyses Capital Export Neutrality and Capital Import Neutrality, detailing their economic rationales and the tax systems that support them – residence-based taxation for CEN and source-based taxation for CIN. It argues that these neutralities are mutually exclusive without global tax harmonization and critiques their practical applicability, noting CEN's preference in academic literature but highlighting its limitations, such as the opt-out problem and disconnect from real-world tax policies. The chapter also explores newer neutrality concepts like Capital Ownership Neutrality and Market Neutrality, finding them similarly constrained. Ultimately, it advocates for a new philosophy of neutrality, emphasizing global welfare over national welfare, an evaluative rather than instructional role for neutrality, and a shift from competition to cooperation among states. This framework informs a discussion on formulary apportionment, suggesting it prioritizes legitimacy and equity over efficiency, challenging traditional neutrality-driven tax system designs.*

## 6.1 THE BASIC CONCERNS OF NEUTRALITY

Neutrality, a sophisticated idea of taxation, is not one of Adam Smith's four canons of a good tax design.[721] Economists pick up the concept as they focus on the distortive effects of taxation on the economy. While the principal purpose of taxation is to raise revenue, it can simultaneously distort the decisions of individuals or firms that they could make where the tax does not exist. These distortions may vary substantially in form, such as the choices of consumption, the way to organize transactions and locations to do business, yet they all mean a less desirable outcome for the taxpayer, the economy or the general society.

In this case, the concept of neutrality is put forward by economists as part of their thinking on eliminating or minimizing the distortive effect of taxation. Therefore, the neutrality in taxation can be understood in three logical steps: first, tax is unavoidable, as it is the major, if not the only means to raise revenue for the treasury; second, tax is evil, for it distorts the perfect order of the world where tax does not exist; third, a neutral tax is good or at least acceptable since it minimizes or removes the distortions of taxation.

## 6.2 NEUTRALITY IN DOMESTIC AND INTERNATIONAL TAX SETTINGS

As for domestic taxation in the context of the United States, the tax neutrality concept was formulated by Stanley Surrey to address the differential tax treatment given to certain types of income or a group of taxpayers.[722] Whenever a preferential tax treatment is given, it, in effect, means that the government is making an expenditure to the taxpayer, which is called 'tax expenditure'. However, it can be readily perceived that the role of tax neutrality plays in domestic tax policymaking is limited as the tax expenditure schemes are prevalent if not always at the centre stage of tax policy deliberations.[723] Douglas A. Kahn concurs on this by questioning the validity of neutrality being a 'principle' for neutrality is in itself inconsistent with the modern Haig-Simons definition of income.[724]

While the basic meaning of the neutrality concept applies to the general context, it seems to be enjoying a different prestige in international tax than in domestic tax settings. Neutrality in international tax literature has been regularly referred to as a 'principle' and therefore given a normative status as the traditional ones like equity or equality. In simpler words, neutrality is becoming part of the standard discussions of

721. They are equity, certainty, convenience and economy.
722. Stanley S Surrey, 'Tax Incentives as a Device for Implementing Government Policy: A Comparison with Direct Government Expenditures' (1970) 83 Harvard Law Review 705 https://www.jstor.org/stable/1339837 and https://doi.org/10.2307/1339837 accessed 24 September 2025.
723. David A Weisbach, 'The Use of Neutralities in International Tax Policy' (2015) 68 National Tax Journal 2 https://doi.org/10.17310/ntj.2015.3.06 accessed 26 August 202.
724. Douglas A Kahn, 'The Two Faces of Tax Neutrality: Do They Interact or Are They Mutually Exclusive' (1990) 18 Northern Kentucky Law Review 1.

most international tax topics. This is already the case as academics are debating fiercely on what is the most meaningful proposition of neutrality and the corresponding system design of international taxation,[725] in which neutrality gives either *ex-ante* guidance or *ex-post* evaluations.

A basic starting point of this chapter is the scepticism of the current status of neutrality in international tax discussions. It is assumed that the true or the principal reason for the significance attached to neutrality is that, unlike competing or interlinked principles of justice, there seem to be few, if not nil, alternative and handy benchmarks of economic efficiency. For example, while 'administrability' or 'simplicity' mostly concern economic efficiency as well, yet both of them can hardly render measurable and objective suggestions. Therefore, the existing literature does not necessarily chart a conceptual route that this chapter has to follow, especially considering that the majority portion of the debate is conducted in the pre-BEPS era or in the uni-national context (mostly the United States). This chapter, instead, is a tentative contribution to re-launching the thinking on economic efficiency and neutrality on a roughly clean-slate basis.

## 6.3 THE BASIC PROPOSITIONS OF CEN AND CIN

### 6.3.1 The Economic Rationale of CEN

As with inter-nation equity, the neutrality concepts were originally introduced in international taxation by Peggy B. Musgrave in the 1960s.[726] In international tax literature, the efficiency analysis of the international tax system is mainly thought to be concerned with capital movement in the international market. Different economic analyses about the optimal taxation of capital rely on different assumptions of competition and capital flow in the global market. To provide a baseline of analysis, contemporary economic theory often hypothesizes that the competition is perfect and the capital flow is not restricted. It is assumed that the productivity of capital is the highest, and with that, also the fairest when production factors and consumption are distributed though free market mechanisms without public interference.[727] However, the imposition of tax incurs excess burden or deadweight loss. Thus, neutrality serves as one of the goals of international taxation.

What does worldwide economic efficiency imply or entail? 'Production is allocated efficiently throughout the world if it is not possible to reallocate resources

725. For example, Micheal S Knoll, 'Reconsidering International Tax Neutrality' (2010) 64 Tax Law Review 99; Fadi Shaheen, 'International Tax Neutrality: Reconsiderations' (2007) 27 Virginia Tax Review 203; Mitchell A Kane, 'Ownership Neutrality, Ownership Distortions, and International Tax Welfare Benchmarks' (2006) 53 Virginia Tax Review; Amos S Hershey, 'Neutrality and International Law' (1916) 26 International Journal of Ethics 168 https://doi.org/10.1086/intejethi.26.2.2376617 accessed 26 August 2025; Fadi Shaheen, 'International Tax Neutrality: Revisited' (2011) 64 Tax Law Review 131; Weisbach (n. 723).
726. Richard A Musgrave, *Criteria for Foreign Tax Credit, Taxation of Operation Abroad* (The Tax Institute, Princeton 1959). Richman (n. 622).
727. de Wilde, '"Sharing the Pie": Taxing Multinationals in a Global Market' (n. 588) 49.

between activities in a way that would increase total output.'[728] This implies that if the marginal rate of return in some country or asset is lower than in another country or asset, the investor will move the capital to where the marginal rate of return is higher.[729] Hence it further means that the movement of capital in a global market will render the marginal rate of return equal between assets or locations and enhance the total production of international capital. In this aspect, the imposition of tax should be neutral and not distort the flow of capital from lower productivity to higher productivity, and at last improve efficiency and equalize the marginal rate of return around the globe. The neutrality captures the perspective of outflow/export of capital, and naturally, this kind of neutrality is called 'Capital Export Neutrality' (CEN). In other words, the basic proposition of CEN is that tax considerations will not influence the investors of one country as to their decisions to invest at home or abroad.[730]

Yet it is still not clear as to the meaning of the marginal rate of return itself, and further analysis is needed to solve the puzzle. As is well known, the motivation for capital movement is to hunt for a higher post-tax rate of return instead of a pre-tax rate of return or marginal rate of return. With regard to the tax rate, 'the only economically meaningful concept of an income tax rate is the effective rate. This may be defined as the percentage by which the tax rules pertaining to that particular tax reduce the income of the taxpayer, income being defined as gross receipts less costs'.[731] Thus, if the tax system needs to be neutral to investment location choices of capital, the system should ensure that the effective tax rates are equal wherever the investments go. Under the assumptions of perfect competition and unrestricted capital flow, when the capital market is in equilibrium, the post-tax rates of return are equal everywhere;[732] this immediately implies that the pre-tax rates of return are also equal all across the world.[733]

### 6.3.2 The Tax System Satisfying CEN

With the same assumptions, the key condition left for the goal of CEN is that the effective tax rates faced by the investor in a country while investing at home or abroad should be the same. There are several possible ways to achieve this. The first is to let

728. *See* Michael P Devereux, 'Taxation of Outbound Direct Investment: Economic Principles and Tax Policy Considerations' (2008) 24 Oxford Review of Economic Policy 698, 700 https://doi.org/10.1093/oxrep/grn036 accessed 26 August 2025.
729. The most common measure used in economic theory is an effective marginal tax rate, which measures the percentage difference between the pre-tax and post-tax rates of return on a marginal investment. *See ibid.*, 716.
730. Richman (n. 622) 8.
731. *Ibid.*, 6.
732. 'In principle, each investor would want to invest in each asset up to the point at which the post-tax rate of return from each investment was the same: if the post-tax rate of return was not the same, then the investor could increase her overall return by switching from the investment with the lower rate of return to the investment with the higher rate of return.' *See* Devereux (n. 728) 702.
733. Because marginal rates of return (pre-tax rates of return – post-tax rates of return) are equal, post-tax rates of return are equal, and the effective tax rates are equal, then pre-tax rates of return must also be equal as well.

the source country (where the income is derived) exclusively tax the income, and the effective tax rates of the residence country should be equal to the source countries,[734] which means the same effective tax rates all across the world. In short, this tax regime is called source taxation with harmonized tax rates, which is obviously unrealistic by now. Another way is to let the residence country exclusively tax the income wherever the income is derived. The residence tax is indifferent to the investment destination and thus does not distort the capital location choice. Thus, CEN is immediately achieved.[735] Yet it is also not realistic that the foreign country where the investor is doing business (source country) has no share of the value created within its territory. The only option left is that, after the source country taxes the investor, the residence country taxes any portion left in case its effective tax rate is higher than that of the source country. If the effective tax rate of the source country is higher, to keep the tax burden undistorted by the investment locations, the residence country needs to rebate the tax difference to the investor. This regime is called unlimited credit system. As a result, the tax system that guarantees CEN is called 'Residence-based Taxation', 'Worldwide Taxation', or 'Unlimited Credit System'.[736]

### 6.3.3 The Tax System Satisfying CIN

Unlike the case of CEN, even though there are quite a few different interpretations of CIN, the options for achieving capital import neutrality are not that many. No matter which interpretation of CIN is used to consider the corresponding tax system design, the result is the same: a source-based tax system. For example, when choosing CIN in the sense of Origin Neutrality, which requires that the general tax system of the world should provide the same tax treatment regardless of where the investors come from, this leads to a tax system that confers taxing rights solely to the source country, which is a source-based or territorial tax system. This certainly cannot be achieved if the resident country does not give up its taxing rights on its residents. Thus, the system fulfilling CIN is also called the Exemption System if defining it from the residence countryside.[737] In addition, this further implies a difference between CEN and CIN which is worth mentioning. As said, CEN is a neutrality proposition based on worldwide efficiency, but capital export neutrality goals can be embodied and exercised by individual countries' policies. 'If all countries adopt the residence principle, then capital income taxation does not disturb the equality of the marginal product of

734. In this way, for pure domestic investment and foreign investment, the tax rates will be equal.
735. Some economic literature authors have urged that zero is the optimum tax rate on inward investment. *See, e.g.*, Roger H Gordon, 'Taxation of Investment and Savings in a World Economy' (National Bureau of Economic Research 1985) 1086 https://www.nber.org/papers/w1723 accessed 28 November 2023. Joel Slemrod, 'Effect of Taxation with Capital Mobility' in Henry J Aaron, Harvey Galper and Joseph A Pechman (eds), *Uneasy Compromise: Problems of a Hybrid Income-Consumption Tax* (Brookings Institution Press 1988).
736. Knoll (n. 725) 101. And these different names will be selectively used throughout this study.
737. These different names will be selectively used throughout this study.

capital across countries which is generated by a free movement of capital'.[738] Even if not all countries adopt the corresponding system satisfying CEN, one can still claim that capital export neutrality is promoted (not achieved) in that country if it adopts a credit tax system. However, for capital import neutrality, 'it is a feature of all tax systems analysed jointly'.[739] To achieve a complete CIN, all countries in the world have to embrace a territorial tax system.[740] Hence a capital import country cannot unilaterally claim that CIN is achieved without the residence countries of foreign investors exempting the foreign source income derived by its residents.

## 6.4 QUESTIONABLE GROUNDS FOR CHOOSING EITHER CEN OR CIN

### 6.4.1 Only One C'X'N Can Win in the Real World

Following the reasoning above, it is not difficult to draw the conclusion that without tax harmonization, it is impossible for a tax system to satisfy CEN and CIN at the same time. Because CEN requires a residence-based tax system, which provides credit for the tax paid to the foreign country with respect to the income earned abroad. In contrast, however, CIN requires a source-based tax system, which means the income earned abroad should be exempt. However, there are still some facts that need to be brought up; thus, let us suppose a case to illustrate this inconsistency further.

Assume that the corporate tax rates of China are 40%, and 30% in the Netherlands, and both countries adopt a residence-based tax system. A Chinese company, C, earns a taxable income of EUR 1 in the Netherlands, and it also earns a taxable income of EUR 1 in China. To be neutral for capital export, the tax system should not distort the business consideration of C as to whether to invest in China or the Netherlands. In other words, the capital export country China should not differentiate between the tax treatment of the EUR 1 earned in China and the Netherlands by company C. Therefore, the first thing is that the source country, the Netherlands, will tax according to its taxing right and rate at 30%, which leaves an after-tax income of EUR 0.7. Then, China will also tax, according to its residence tax jurisdiction, the foreign income EUR 1, that is EUR 0.4. However, CEN requires China to provide a tax credit for the tax paid to the foreign country with respect to the income earned abroad, in this case, it is EUR 0.3 paid to the Netherlands. After the credit, company C only needs to pay EUR 0.1 to China. In the end, the tax burden on the income earned abroad is EUR 0.4 (EUR 0.3 + EUR 0.1), which is equal to the parallel income EUR 1 earned within the home country China (EUR 1 × 40%).

This is the simplest version of the story, by simplifying the issues of tax base and type of income. Another important issue is that the source country tax may surpass the

738. Assaf Razin, 'International Tax Competition and Gains from Tax Harmonization' (1991) 37 Economics Letters 69, 70 https://doi.org/10.1016/0165-1765(91)90245-g accessed 26 August 2025.
739. Mihir A Desai and James R Hines Jr, 'Evaluating International Tax Reform' [2003] National Tax Journal 493 https://doi.org/10.17310/ntj.2003.3.03 accessed 26 August 2025.
740. Shaheen (n. 725) 135.

home country's, which poses the common limitation of the credit in reality. Based on the above case, assuming that a Dutch company N has earned EUR 1 in China, the tax burden in China (foreign tax paid) will be EUR 0.4, but the tax burden in the Netherlands (home country tax liability) will be EUR 0.3, which obviously means that the expected foreign tax credit (EUR 0.4) surpasses the home country tax, but there is only EUR 0.3 available for credit. It follows that the tax burden of each Euro which company N earns when investing in China will be EUR 0.1 more than the income earned in the Netherlands. A mere tax credit is not enough to guarantee the tax neutrality of outbound investment if the tax rate of the source country is higher than the resident country. In this case, to fulfil CEN, the resident country needs to further provide a tax rebate of EUR 0.1 for the investment across the border. This system is the unlimited foreign tax credit, which equals a tax credit plus a tax rebate system. If no tax rebate exists, 'because of the limitation on credits, investors are subject to the higher of the foreign and the domestic tax rate, whereas CEN requires that they should always face the same tax rate whether they invest at home or abroad'.[741]

Under the same assumptions, for CIN, if company C invests in the Netherlands, and also company N invests in the Netherlands. CIN should ensure that the tax burden of company C and company N in the Netherlands are the same. As discussed earlier, CIN will be achieved if the Netherlands solely taxes company C, which requires China neither to tax nor provide a rebate to the Netherlands source income earned by its resident company. In conclusion, a tax system that meets CIN is a territorial tax system adopted worldwide, while from the perspective of the resident country, it is an exemption tax system.

It is now explicit that CEN and CIN cannot be satisfied at the same time if the tax rates of the resident country and source country differ. However, what if the tax rates are the same? Based on the same case and assumption above, suppose that the tax rates of both China and the Netherlands are 40%. For CEN, the tax burdens calculated in the two countries are the same. Hence under the credit system necessary for CEN, the tax credit calculated by the resident country is zero. In effect, this is the case where the resident country exempts the foreign income, which is the right of the system requirement of CIN. Therefore, if the tax system is fully harmonized on tax base and tax rate, CEN and CIN can be satisfied simultaneously.

### 6.4.2 Difficult Choice to Uphold Either Neutralities

In general, the consideration of economic efficiency lies at the centre of neutrality, which has been shown in the normative and policy discussions of international income taxation, including not only the academic publications of both economists and lawyers

741. Rachel RU Griffith, James Hines and Peter Birch Sørensen, 'International Capital Taxation' in James A Mirrlees, Stuard Adam and Timothy Besley (eds), *Dimensions of Tax Design: the Mirrlees Review* (Oxford University Press 2010) 957 https://pure.manchester.ac.uk/ws/portalfiles/portal/33806113/FULL_TEXT.PDF accessed 26 August 2025.

but also most of the key serious government analyses.[742] As to CEN and CIN, however, their efficiency grounds are different and inconsistent. In order to attain maximization of worldwide efficiency, the marginal pre-tax rate of return needs to be equalized across the world, which will be the same as the case where at the margin and in the absence of taxation, competition drives the marginal pre-tax rate of return on all investments in a jurisdiction to be equalized.[743] That is, each individual investor faces the same effective tax rate on the returns from investments at home and abroad, which can only be achieved by worldwide taxation. Therefore, CEN is inherently pro-worldwide efficiency. Thus, 'typically, economists regard CEN as essential for world-wide economic efficiency, because the location of investments would be unaffected by capital income taxes'.[744] The worldwide efficiency in this sense can be specified as 'worldwide production efficiency'.[745]

In comparison, CIN does not pay attention to the location choices of investors, even though these choices may indeed be affected by differences in effective tax rates. The hypothetical case by Devereux can be directly used to further explore the traits of CIN.[746] In this case, and based on the worldwide efficiency standpoint, an important pre-condition is that 'each investor would want to invest in each asset up to the point at which the post-tax rate of return from each investment was the same: otherwise they could increase their overall return by switching from the investment with the lower rate of return to the investment with the higher rate of return'.[747] Following the reasoning of Devereux, if CIN holds, the marginal pre-tax rates of return will differ across jurisdictions, and there will be no capital production efficiency as can be achieved under CEN. However, investors in different jurisdictions will face the same post-tax rate of return on each of their investments.[748] Using a similar exemplifying case, Assaf Razin and Efraim Sadka found that the intertemporal marginal rate of substitution is equated across countries;[749] in economics, this implies that the international allocation of world savings is efficient. In short, the worldwide efficiency contained in CIN has been known as 'worldwide saving efficiency'.

In conclusion, though CEN and CIN can both be said to be based on efficiency grounds, their efficiency grounds are different and, thus, mutually inconsistent.

742. Graetz (n. 92) 270. and *see, e.g.*, Treasury US, 'The Deferral of Income Earned Through US Controlled Foreign Corporations A Policy Study' [2000] Office of Tax Policy, Annex. (hereafter Treasury Subpart F Study).
743. Devereux (n. 728) 701.
744. Graetz (n. 92) 270. and *see* Kimberly S Blanchard and Peter H Blessing, 'The Treasury's "Subpart F" Study' (February 2002) 23-24 https://papers.ssrn.com/sol3/papers.cfm?abstract_id=299123 accessed 28 November 2023., which contains a review of the economic literature.
745. Concluded from the reasoning in Razin (n. 738) 70.
746. Michael P Devereux, 'Taxing Foreign Profit: Economic Principles and Feasibility' (2008) https://www.ifs.org.uk/publications/4191 accessed 27 November 2023.
747. The reader may need read further into the case in the above reference literature.
748. Devereux (n. 746).
749. Razin (n. 738) 70.

### 6.4.3 The Problems of the Medal-Winner CEN

While CEN and CIN cannot be achieved simultaneously without global tax harmonization, at least in the academic literature of international taxation, CEN apparently draws more preferences from the commentators. A straightforward account is that capital, being geographically mobile, responds more swiftly to tax than savings, which means that the efficiency loss may be greater if CEN is violated. In addition, the CEN-sponsored tax system, namely, the worldwide residence-based tax is thought to be more accessible than that of CIN, as countries can, though not effectively so do, extend unlimited tax credits for the purposes of CEN, but face insurmountable difficulties to offset the existing residence-based tax to truly level the playing field for inbound investors for the purposes of CIN. A more notorious repercussion of CIN is essentially a pro-competition welfare benchmark that adds oil to the fire of global tax competition that already burns fiercely.

However, the story of CEN may not sound that good as its negative aspects are reflected upon by a small circle of commentators who jumped out of the competition between CEN and CIN.[750] Among others, there are primarily two aspects of criticism that substantially vitiate the credibility of CEN being the preferable benchmark of global welfare for international tax policy.

First, the opt-out problem. The reasoning is simple. The proposition of CEN regarding the realization of global production efficiency can easily fall where only a limited number rather than all or the majority of countries join the initiative of liberalizing capital flow by opting for the CEN-endorsed tax policy. This is because the widespread existence of territorial tax systems may impair or offset the gains of global production efficiency that could have been realized under a worldwide tax system, plus unlimited tax credits at the global scale.[751]

Second, there is a lack of connections to the real-world international tax policy. It has been contended from time to time that the significance of CEN has largely remained in the papers of academic debates since the construction of the idea does not give adequate consideration to how the states act and how the system, especially of the corporate taxation, works. Shaviro pointed out that the existence of corporate income tax at entity level substantially weakens the cogency of whichever neutrality proposes to be the proper efficiency benchmark, as in all circumstances corporations are separate taxpayers whose owners may not share the same residence and they can easily channel their investment through establishments in different jurisdictions (or, changing directly the residence of corporations) which effectively frustrate the sole purpose of CEN: laying a neutral ground for investment location choices.[752] Similar reasonings apply to CIN as well. Other realistic considerations include: the residence state's willingness to actually exercise its power to tax is naively presumed, how the

750. Generally *see* Luís Eduardo Schoueri and Ricardo Andre Jr Galendi, 'Justification and Implementation of the International Allocation of Taxing Rights: Can We Take One Thing at a Time?' in Sergio Andre Rocha (ed.), *Tax Sovereignty in the BEPS* (Wolters Kluwer 2017). Shaviro (n. 69).
751. *See* detailed analysis in this respect by Shaviro (n. 69) 127-129.
752. *Ibid.*, 129-30.

states may interact with the residence state is overlooked in the conceptual map of neutralities, so are the existence of other economic distortions, the differences in infrastructures among states, and tax competition that casts huge shadows all along.[753]

### 6.4.4 Inconsistent Interpretations of CIN

Compared to CEN, the interpretation of CIN has not gained that much consensus. As said in the earlier paragraphs, there are three different interpretations regarding CIN, namely, the *Origin Neutrality, Expansion Opportunity Neutrality* and *Saving Neutrality*. This, indeed, has posed a few inner inconsistencies to CIN itself. First of all, what are the efficiency contexts of these interpretations? It is well known that the Saving Neutrality advocates efficient allocation of world savings, because if CIN holds, all savers in a given jurisdiction get the same prices for present and future consumption.[754] As for the expansion opportunity neutrality, it is viewed as a competition-based argument made by businessmen craving a level playing field, rather than an efficiency-based neutrality theory.[755] In this respect, the neutrality concept is more like the meaning of tax-equality between different business competitors in a given jurisdiction, even it is not at the same value of equality itself.[756] For the Origin Neutrality, although it is mirror side of CEN focusing on not distorting the location choices of investments, the efficiency objective of this interpretation of CIN is not clear enough.[757]

In addition, the baselines of various interpretations of CIN are different. In the analysis of CEN, a non-tax world is frequently used as the baseline evaluating the neutrality effects of taxation. When CEN is fully satisfied, the outflow of capital will not be distorted by the imposition of tax, just as there is no tax imposed. This is the comprehension of neutrality in a complete way. Yet it can be found that some inconsistencies exist if looking into the interpretations of CIN. For the first understanding of CIN, the Origin Neutrality, as the 'flip side of CEN',[758] it is by nature a 'nontax world-based neutrality', it represents 'neutrality with respect to the location of investors (where capital comes from) assuming the location of the investment is fixed'.[759] For the second understanding of CIN, the Expansion Opportunity Neutrality, the situation is different. The expansion of business depends on the net profitability and available funds, and a non-tax world-based neutrality will guarantee that a tax imposed will not reduce or enhance them. However, as a matter of fact, even CIN, in this sense, holds that the mere imposition of tax will reduce in substance the funds available for business expansion. As a result, the Expansion Opportunity Neutrality is

---

753. Schoueri and Galendi (n. 750) 53-54.
754. *See* Razin (n. 738). *see also* Avi-Yonah, 'Globalization, Tax Competition, and the Fiscal Crisis of the Welfare State' (n. 665) 1573, 1605-1607. Desai and Hines Jr (n. 739) 492-493. Graetz (n. 92) 271.
755. Richman (n. 622) 8. Musgrave, *United States Taxation of Foreign Investment Income* (n. 622) 119; Shaheen (n. 725) 135.
756. Fadi Shaheen, 'International Tax Neutrality: Reconsiderations', 27 Virginia Tax Review 203 (2007), p. 210.
757. Shaheen (n. 725) 136.
758. *Ibid.*, 211.
759. *Ibid.*, 136.

not a non-tax world-based neutrality. CIN, in this sense, is aimed at achieving relative neutrality, which is similar to horizontal equity of taxation. Because rather than a pure sense of neutrality, CIN promotes that all businesses in a given jurisdiction suffer from the same reduction of expansion opportunity. In other words, the imposition of tax is indifferent to the expansion discrepancy between different investors.[760] The same reasoning goes to the last understanding of CIN, Saving Neutrality, because any income tax distorts the allocation of saving and consumption.[761] Hence the Saving Neutrality is not a non-tax world-based neutrality either.

### 6.4.5 A Bite of the Reality Sandwich

The following explores how the real-world corporate tax systems may respond to the debate over neutrality propositions. It reveals the tenuous link between the instructions of those 'buzz words' of neutrality and how the states are actually taxing the MNEs, with their inclination towards worldwide or territorial systems as the test.

Within a pure worldwide system, all foreign income of residents is taxed, while under a pure territorial system, all foreign income of residents is exempt. However, in practice, countries often have exceptions and trade-offs between these two extremes.

Exceptions to worldwide taxation include exempting certain types of foreign income and allowing deferral, whereby foreign earnings through foreign subsidiaries are not taxed until repatriated.[762,763]

Exceptions to territorial taxation, under 'participation exemption regimes', include: limiting the exemption based on the source country, limiting based on the type of income (e.g., active versus passive), imposing ownership percentage or holding period requirements for the exemption, and providing less than 100% exemption.[764,765,766]

760. *Ibid.*, 210-211.
761. Zhiyong Yang, *The Economics of Taxation* (Dongbei University of Finance and Economics Press 2011) 21-29.
762. Robert J Peroni, J Clifton Fleming and Stephen E Shay, 'Getting Serious about Curtailing Deferral of U.S. Tax on Foreign Source Income' 52 SMU Law Review 455, 457.
763. Graetz (n. 92) 323-324. Avi-Yonah, *International Tax as International Law: An Analysis of the International Tax Regime* (n. 584) 19. 'So long as earnings are not technically repatriated, they face only host country taxation, so a worldwide system with deferral can fairly mimic a territorial regime.', Ms Thornton Matheson and Victoria J Perry, *Territorial vs. Worldwide Corporate Taxation: Implications for Developing Countries* (International Monetary Fund 2013) 8.
764. Avi-Yonah, *International Tax as International Law: An Analysis of the International Tax Regime* (n. 584) 11.
765. Avi-Yonah, *International Tax as International Law: An Analysis of the International Tax Regime* (n. 584). Larking Barry and International Bureau of Fiscal Documentation, *IBFD International Tax Glossary* (5th edn, IBFD Publications 2005) 514.
766. PricewaterhouseCoopers LLP, 'Evolution of Territorial Tax Systems in the OECD' (2013) 5-6 prepared for The Technology CEO Council. Kyle Pomerleau and Kari Jahnsen, 'Designing a Territorial Tax System: A Review of OECD Systems' (1 August 2017) 15-18 https://taxfoundation.org/territorial-tax-system-oecd-review/ accessed 27 November 2023.

Therefore, while the worldwide versus territorial distinction provides a conceptual framework, in practice, countries blend elements of both systems with various exceptions and qualifications.

*Table 6.1 Basic Content of Worldwide and Territorial Tax Systems*

| *Classification* | *Taxation of Resident* | *Taxation of Non-resident*[767] |
|---|---|---|
| **Worldwide Tax System** | Domestic Source + Foreign Source | Domestic Source |
| **Territorial Tax System** | Domestic Source | Domestic Source |

## 6.5 THE NEW GENERATIONS OF NEUTRALITIES: ARE THEY BETTER ALTERNATIVES

CON focuses on neutrality regarding ownership of assets,[768] rather than just the location of investment (CEN) or the source of savings (CIN). However, CON relies on questionable assumptions like productivity depending solely on ownership, and runs into issues reconciling with CEN principles.

MN is an even broader concept that aims for neutrality across all potential competitors exploiting assets in any market, including aspects like international trade flows that CEN/CIN neglected.[769] But achieving full MN would require harmonizing all residence and source-based corporate tax systems globally, which would be very difficult.

While CON and MN introduce new perspectives beyond CEN/CIN, they also face conceptual limitations as practical guides for international tax policy. The author suggests the need to move beyond just debating different neutrality benchmarks and take a fresh approach to rethinking international tax rules.

However, a bigger picture was drawn by Michael J. Graetz in 2000,[770] who might be the first to conclude the limited role of neutralities. In this widely cited article, it is reasoned that the use of neutralities as the guiding norm is inadequate and unsatisfactory. However, he just provided us with a starting point, not a definite answer. As he said, the compromise is not the final answer either, because 'a "compromise" between CEN and CIN can justify virtually any policy outcome'. A qualified guiding norm of the international tax system should first have a clear connotation itself, and should have unambiguous policy direction. As discussed, the relationship between CEN and CIN

767. In fact, there are also wide variations in different tax jurisdictions among the taxation of the domestic source income earned by non-residents, but for the theme of this part, these variations will not be discussed.
768. Edward D Kleinbard, 'Stateless Income' (2011) 11 Florida Tax Review 114 https://doi.org/10.5744/ftr.2011.1009 and https://journals.upress.ufl.edu/ftr/article/view/349 accessed 18 November 2023.
769. *Ibid.*, 114-115.
770. Graetz (n. 92).

should be defined as 'competing' or 'either-or', and the neutralities satisfy neither of the above.

> Debating CEN versus CIN as a guide to international tax policymaking is a dead end. We need to change the conversation about international tax policy, and take a fresh look at our international tax rules. And in doing so, we should avoid fruitless policy debates where one side insists that any departure from worldwide taxation of U.S. residents, including corporate residents, is an unfortunate violation of CEN, while the other side demands that only territorial taxation of income will implement CIN.[771]

## 6.6 LAYING THE GROUND FOR A NEW PHILOSOPHY OF INTERNATIONAL TAX NEUTRALITY

The previous discussions are not meant to completely negate the value of neutrality, which rather serve to solicit and justify the stance of this thesis. That is, the various inconsistencies and weaknesses of either one proposition or the basic approach to neutrality have necessitated a new philosophy of neutrality to reflect on international tax system, specifically, the formulary apportionment proposal.

As revealed below, there are three relatively novel perspectives that jointly lay the ground for the new philosophy of neutrality: first, the 'championship' of neutrality really has to be ceased; second, global welfare rather than national welfare should be the guiding light of international taxation; third, neutrality should be redirected more as an 'evaluative' than an 'instructional' standard; fourth, global cooperation rather than competition may be the main theme of international taxation in the foreseeable decades.[772]

As a result, under the task of constructing an analytical framework for formulary apportionment regarding neutrality, based on the analysis and discussion of existing research on neutrality, this research tentatively and arguably claims that neutrality considerations may not be regarded as a core component in the FA analytical framework. Formulary apportionment may concern more the legitimacy and equity than the efficiency of the international tax system.

### 6.6.1 Ending the Race of Neutralities

> International tax is an extremely complex area of tax law. There are no straightforward answers based on intuition in this realm.[773]

771. *Ibid.*, 324.
772. J (Jingxian) Chen and Wilson Chow, 'Global Minimum Tax Reform and the Future of Tax Competition' (2023) 77 Bulletin for International Taxation https://doi.org/10.59403/24gqzfd and https://www.ibfd.org/doi/24gqzfd accessed 4 May 2024; Juliana Cubillos, Frederik Heitmüller and Irma Mosquera Valderrama, 'Multilateral Cooperation in International Tax Law' https://globtaxgov.weblog.leidenuniv.nl/files/2021/08/Multilateral-Cooperation-in-International-Tax-Law.pdf accessed 4 May 2024.
773. C Neil Stephens, 'A Progressive Analysis of the Efficiencies of Capital Import Neutrality' (1998) 30 Law and Policy in International Business 159.

Neutrality is a term frequently used in international law studies. 'Neutrality has been defined as the condition of those states which in time of war take no part in the contest, but continue pacific intercourse with the belligerents.'[774] Therefore, the core element of 'neutrality' in international law is 'to take no part in the contest'. In loose language, one can compare the cross-border business to the 'contest' in international law, and the normative goal of neutrality of the tax system can also be correlated to the 'pacific intercourse' by a neutral state. However, one of the different considerations in these two scenarios is that the cross-border business in tax neutrality consideration needs to be divided into two separate parts, namely, inbound versus outbound business, whereas the 'contest' in international law probably has no such 'movement direction' problem. This has dramatically increased the complexity of the issue.

When the 'contest' in international tax law is divided, the neutrality in the tax setting is also divided. The dichotomy itself is justified, but what is problematic is the either-or choice one is faced with. Based on the outcome of the inconsistency analysis of neutralities, it clearly follows that either CEN or CIN as the foundation of international tax design is acceptable. In the analytical framework of CEN and CIN, they are mutually exclusive. That means if following CEN, the merits indicated by CIN will be compromised, and vice versa. The general neutrality discussion in the international tax setting is redefined to the discussion about CEN or CIN, and the core question should be which one tends to be the governing building block of international taxation. However, in this extremely complex area of tax law, where there are no straightforward answers based on intuition, the 'one of two' answer clearly is against the reality of international tax law, even based on intuition.

Stephens has successfully identified the drawback of the 'either-or' model of neutralities. The 'existing tax system distorts along many margins. Neutralities pick a single margin and require that the distortions along that margin be eliminated instead of allowing trade-offs along all of the margins affected by existing law'.[775] It is a pity that Stephens did not provide more detailed explanations of this claim. However, according to my understanding, CEN addresses the tax distortion of capital locations, while CIN addresses the tax distortion of saving locations or investor residences. Similarly, CON addresses the tax distortion of investor identities.[776] Each of the neutralities only addresses one of the potential distortions of tax, which falls short of a panoramic view or considering the trade-offs among each other. For example, as de Wilde pointed out, the concerns of CEN and CIN over efficiency are, in fact, just mirror images.[777] Similarly, as Schoueri et al. put it, we are drowning in the 'alphabet soup' of

774. Hershey (n. 725) 172.
775. Weisbach (n. 723) 10.
776. Shaheen (n. 725) 136.
777. 'The concepts of export neutrality and import neutrality prove distortive when scrutinized from a perspective that is opposite to the production factor movements addressed by either the export or import neutrality concepts. That is, respectively when the concept of export neutrality is addressed from the perspective of the host state on an inward bound movement; and when the concept of import neutrality is addressed from the perspective of the home state on an outward bound production movement. It is just a matter of looking at the mirror image ... All export neutrality promoting credit systems distort inbound investment ... All import neutrality

neutralities, and one must get away with it in a way that is described in the remaining sections of this part.[778]

### 6.6.2 Global Efficiency over National Efficiency

The logic starting point of the goal to achieve neutrality in domestic taxation is the maximization of national welfare. When the tax system is not neutral, economic efficiency and welfare are reduced. Whereas for international taxation, there is controversy as to the starting point for efficiency and neutrality. The majority opinion is that the international tax system should seek to maximize global welfare, while some dissenting views hold that national welfare should be the guideline.[779] In a ground-breaking book about international tax neutrality, the author deems that 'the maximization of world welfare is considered as a logical extension of the criterion of maximization of national welfare'.[780] Besides that, a fair number of analyses are based on the proposition that a sovereign state should pursue global welfare and worldwide economic efficiency.[781]

However, the relationship between the national efficiency and global efficiency is not as straightforward as it looks. The economic discussions in this respect are abundant;[782] here it is instead some legal analyses are provided by restricting this issue to the scope of international tax law rather than a purely economic argument.

First, supposing that there is only one country in the world, the national efficiency is equivalent to global efficiency, and thus it is needless to consider the issue. Yet the reality is that the world is still with sovereign borders, and national efficiency has deviated from global efficiency. From this point, that the former should prevail over the latter seems to be reasonable. In addition, many tax scholars base their propositions advocating for national-favoured tax policies on this 'reality'.[783] However, in the sense of taxation, this is merely a partial reality. Notwithstanding that the fiscal

promoting territorial systems distort outbound investment.', de Wilde, '"Sharing the Pie": Taxing Multinationals in a Global Market' (n. 588) 79.

778. For example, Schoueri and Galendi (n. 750) 55-6.
779. Daniel Shaviro, 'Why Worldwide Welfare as a Normative Standard for U.S. Tax Policy?' (2007) 60 Tax Law Review 155; Graetz (n. 92) 277-82.
780. Richman (n. 622) 6.
781. *See* Klaus Vogel, 'Worldwide vs. Source Taxation of Income: A Review and Re-evaluation of Arguments (Part II)' (1988) 10 Intertax 310 https://doi.org/10.54648/taxi1988056 accessed 26 August 2025. Vogel Klaus, 'Which Method Should the European Community Adopt for the Avoidance of Double Taxation?' (2002) 56 Bulletin for International Fiscal Documentation 4, 5. *See* for a comparison Musgrave, 'Principles for Dividing the State Corporate Tax Base' (n. 619) 232-233.
782. Joseph Stiglitz and Robert M Pike, 'Globalization and Its Discontents' (2004) UEH University available at https://digital.lib.ueh.edu.vn/handle/UEH/69581 accessed 26 August 2025; Dani Rodrik, 'How Far Will International Economic Integration Go?' (2000) 14 Journal of Economic Perspectives 177.
783. Graetz (n. 92) 269-94; H David Rosenbloom, 'The David R. Tillinghast Lecture International Tax Arbitrage and the "International Tax System"' 53 Tax Law Review; Tsilly Dagan, 'The Tax Treaties Myth' (2000) 32 Journal of International Law and Politics; Keen Michael and Wildasin David, 'Pareto-Efficient International Taxation' (2004) 94 American Economic Review 259 https://doi.org/10.1257/000282804322970797 accessed 26 August 2025.

world is somehow divided by fiscal frontiers, there is still a tight net that is wide enough to cover most tax sovereign states. The author holds a secular belief that the international tax system is real, and that it is comprised of treaty networks, foreign-related domestic tax laws, and international tax customs.[784] Hence, the claim that tax is a solely domestic issue and cannot be international is untenable.[785] 'While some degree of freedom is plausible, norms tend to be strengthened by compliance and weakened by violation. Thus, nationalistically driven departures from promoting worldwide welfare may tend to feed on themselves and push overall policy in a direction where at some point it really would be noticed and become likely to provoke retaliation.'[786]

In addition, another objection to global efficiency is that it is indifferent about which country's well-being is increased. Thus, global efficiency 'urges the policy-makers to embrace the larger benefit without regard to where it occurs or who benefits. Worldwide economic efficiency does not heed love of country'.[787] This is because of the inadequate understanding of global efficiency.

Still supposing that there is only one country in the world, which means the national efficiency is global efficiency, and the global efficiency is national efficiency. Then the issue is simplified, if the economic efficiency is maximized, all the welfare thus created belongs to this country. In comparison, if there are two countries in the world with an open market, the situation is still simplified but also close to the reality. The national economic efficiency holds if one country issues a tax policy that maximizes its own interests without regard to its peer in an open economy, its peer clearly suffers a loss. Therefore, the national economic efficiency cannot hold at the same time for both countries. However, global economic efficiency focuses on maximizing the world production itself, in other words, making the cake in the global market bigger. It indeed gives less care to the sharing of the cake. To make it more explicit, national economic efficiency in this scenario addresses the efficiency of a resident multinational enterprise; thus, the state can directly benefit from it, and there is not much room left for dispute of allocation because each state focuses on the maximization of its own welfare. Whereas each one feeds on the welfare loss of the other, the end of the world will be a race to the bottom. While under global economic efficiency, to make the multinational enterprise prosper is the sole efficiency consideration. As to which of these two countries can claim from this enterprise or in what redistribution method are questions out of the scope of efficiency considerations. The

784. Avi-Yonah, *International Tax as International Law: An Analysis of the International Tax Regime* (n. 584) 1-8.
785. For example, in his rejection of worldwide perspective of taxation, Graetz claimed that 'economic and political unification of Europe has stumbled over issues of taxation', which is obviously inconsistent with the tax harmonization achievement that EU has made. Graetz (n. 92) 269-294.
786. Daniel Shaviro introduced a prisoner's dilemma analysis into the case where a state can either move for its own benefits thus incurs losses to others but finally incurs losses to all the parties, or, the states can cooperate with each other and bring benefits for the common community. Shaviro (n. 779) 17.
787. Graetz (n. 92) 280.

allocation method to be applied is the issue of equity or fairness in international.[788] Thus, the key point is that the national economic efficiency standard mixes the cake-making and cake-sharing but ends up all getting less, while global economic efficiency focuses on making the cake and subordinates the cake-sharing to other specific standards. Thus, the border is clearer, and the role is limited. One cannot deny the optimality of the latter simply because it cannot solve all the problems. When considering an efficiency or welfare goal of international taxation, global economic efficiency is obviously preferable.

### 6.6.3 Being More Evaluative Than Instructional

First of all, it would be problematic if solely examining the neutralities without any regard for other potential values in international tax design. Although disputes do exist as to the priorities and the exact meanings of those benchmarks, those used to assess the domestic tax policy generally include equality, certainty, convenience, and economy, especially since Adam Smith concluded them in the eighteenth century.[789] In the international tax setting, intuitive thinking is whether the benchmarks used in domestic tax policy consideration can be successfully transposed. In addition, one has good grounds to hold that those principles in domestic tax design should not be discarded merely because goods, services, labour, or capital have crossed national borders.[790] Yet it cannot be denied that the cross-border movements indeed have added a lot more complexities to the connotation and extension of the benchmarks.

Back to efficiency, it is an economic consensus that the only tax that is neutral to price is lump-sum tax (or poll tax, head tax).[791] Because a lump-sum tax does not react simultaneously to economic activities, the distortion effect of the tax is minimized. Therefore, 'if the government had no distributional objectives and was concerned solely with efficiency, it may employ only direct taxation and this would take the form of a poll tax'.[792] However, the lump-sum tax has not gained widespread application, and some experiments proved to be a 'political disaster'.[793] While it is beyond the scope of this study to question why the lump-sum tax fails, it is safe to say that the design of tax has more considerations than merely maximizing economic efficiency.

788. Richman (n. 622) 11.
789. Adam Smith, *An Inquiry Into the Nature and Causes of the Wealth of Nations* (Regnery Publishing, 1776) 1103-1106.
790. Graetz (n. 92) 296.
791. Simon R James and Christopher Nobes, *The Economics of Taxation* (7th edn, Xiaolin Luo tr, Chinese financial & Economic Publishing House 2002) 25.
792. Anthony Barnes Atkinson and Joseph Eugene Stiglitz, 'The Design of Tax Structure: Direct versus Indirect Taxation' (1976) 6 Journal of Public Economics 74 https://doi.org/10.1016/0047-2727(76)90041-4 accessed 26 August 2025.
793. *See, e.g.*, Peter Smith, 'Lessons from the British Poll Tax Disaster' (1991) 44 National Tax Journal 421 https://doi.org/10.1086/ntj41788932 accessed 26 August 2025. Eric M Zolt, 'Prospects for Fundamental Tax Reform: United States vs. Japan' (1999) 83 Tax Notes 903, 905.

However, one of the core issues about corporate taxation is whether income or consumption is optimal as tax base, both in domestic and international tax settings.[794] There have been arguments for substituting a cash flow tax based on consumption for the current corporate income tax, both from academia and politicians.[795] However, many dimensions remain unclear. One of the key oppositions to the radical change of tax base is that 'income is a better measure of ability to pay than the alternatives, notably consumption or wages'.[796] 'Deciding to tax income reflects a decision to place issues of fairness at the heart of tax policy debates. That commitment cannot be ignored simply because income traverses national borders.'[797] Therefore, in this respect, it is directed at another backbone of tax design, fairness.

Fairness of taxation, together with economic efficiency, are two indispensable pillars of tax design. As discussed in the efficiency grounds of international taxation, worldwide economic efficiency seems indifferent to the redistribution of income among relevant states, even though this is a necessary step of taxation. From this perspective, the efficiency standard does leave a hole that needs to be filled, for which the only alternative is fairness. It is not our task here to explore what fairness exactly requires, or the relations between fairness and efficiency. Nevertheless, following the discussion of fairness in domestic tax discussion, the fairness issue in international tax setting may primarily include the fair allocation of income between nations, in short, the inter-nation equity, and the fair tax burden on foreign taxpayers, namely, the inter-taxpayer equity.[798] One can clearly see that neither of these aspects can be fully covered by any efficiency benchmarks:

> Neutrality itself, of the types discussed, though desirable on general grounds, is not a totally sacrosanct objective, and there may be situations when government intervention in a freely operating capital market may be necessary to counteract other interferences with welfare criteria, or a deliberate departure from neutrality in the interest of other more important policy objectives (such as the diversion of capital investment toward the low-income countries) may be called for.[799]

The neutralities are misplaced by their traditional role. When discussing neutrality in international tax policy, it is a dead end if still following the route of: (1) choosing which neutrality proposition is the best of all, then; (2) which tax system should dominate according to (1). There is an underlying link between (1) and (2), which is the role neutrality plays when designing a tax system, and how one views such a role will directly render his reasoning and conclusion different. The specific role of

794. Auerbach Alan J, Devereux Michael P and Simpson Helen, 'Taxing Corporate Income' (National Bureau of Economic Research 2008); Atkinson and Stiglitz (n. 791) 55-75.
795. Republican Party (United States), 'A Better Way: Our Vision for a Confident America' https://www.novoco.com/public-media/documents/ryan_a_better_way_policy_paper_062416.pdf accessed 17 July 2018;Schutte Christian and Shome Parthasarathi, 'Cash-Flow Tax' (1993) 1993 IMF Working Papers 638-62; Auerbach Alan et al., 'Destination-Based Cash Flow Taxation' Oxford Legal Studies Research Paper No. 14/2017.
796. Graetz (n. 92) 295.
797. *Ibid.*, 307.
798. Jianwen Liu, *International Tax Law* (3rd edn, Peking University Press 2013) 39-42.
799. Richman (n. 622) 11.

neutrality embodied in the reasoning through (1) and (2) is that neutrality is *ex ante* and instructional principle for the design of the international tax system.

As to the role of neutralities in international tax policy discussion, Weisbach has postulated three possible roles of neutralities in international taxation.[800] The first is that one or more neutralities are correct and might maximize welfare, and the second is that neutralities might be a rule of thumb to provide simple guidance on the complex policy-making environment. However, he denied these possibilities on different grounds, which coincided with many weak forces pointed out in the previous parts. According to Weisbach, the third possibility is that the use of neutralities is simply a ritual before the real work. In other words, the neutralities should be abandoned thoroughly.

If looking backwards and aligning the reasoning of Weisbach, his reasoning contains a logic of 'all or nothing': combining the reasoning of the first and third possible roles, it conveys that all the existing neutrality propositions are imperfect, thus all of them are worthless. Following the same logic and combining the second and third roles, the neutralities cannot be used simply because, in many studies, they are not materially used. The thinking of 'all or nothing' clearly does not suit the complicated discussion of international tax policy. The reasonable approach is either to perfect the propositions of neutrality or to find a better way to utilize the neutralities in the international tax design, or both. However, to some extent, they are based on the role of neutralities, and one of the most important things that should be kept in mind is to abandon the thinking of 'all or nothing'.

Based on the above discussions, it is, therefore, necessary to draw a line between the two potential roles of neutrality in international taxation, that is, neutrality as an 'instructional' benchmark guiding the design of the international tax system in the first place and neutrality as an 'evaluative' benchmark providing insights into economic efficiencies. The differences between these two roles are a matter of degree, but the key spirit is that the instructional role means that neutrality will be relatively significant and decisive, while the evaluative role signifies that neutrality presents the economic advantages and disadvantages for the policymakers to weigh the decisions as instructed by other benchmarks, especially from the side of fairness. With that being said, it is upheld that different from the positions of existing discussions, neutrality, according to the new philosophy, effectively withdraws from a leading role and instead supports the application of other standards, values, or benchmarks. It provides additional insights to decision-makers and lets them know the economic cost of their preferences and accordingly determines how much to deviate from the model previously elected.

The revised role of neutrality means to take neutrality not as *ex ante* and an instructional factor in the international tax design, but as an *ex post* and evaluative benchmark. When rejecting the neutralities by proving their imperfections, Weisbach actually already identified that the neutralities should not be the only/primary approach for international policy choices – 'there is nothing wrong with a model that is

800. Weisbach (n. 723).

conditional on assumptions about policy choices – it should not be the only or primary approach to the problem given how restrictive the assumptions are'.[801] There is no reason that the 'all or nothing' method should dominate or that different weights of various values, standards, or benchmark objectives of international taxation cannot be conferred. For example, the long-argued conflict between efficiency and fairness does not render either useless, even if someone clearly leans towards one of them. The transition of the roles of neutralities from *ex ante* to *ex post* and from instructional to evaluative first implies that the weight of neutralities decreases.

It also liberates us from the puzzle of which neutrality proposition is the best because, as evaluative and *ex-post* benchmarks, they do not need to be perfect, thus contrasting the above reasoning of Weisbach. As cited at the beginning of this section, different types of neutrality, even desirable on good grounds, are not sacrosanct objectives. Departure from neutralities sometimes is both necessary and inevitable. This directly means that the traditional route of selecting the best neutrality proposition and then deciding the tax system should end; a correction of neutrality's misplaced role is thus necessary.

The revised role of neutrality further implies that the obstinate bond between neutralities and worldwide/territorial systems breaks. On the traditional route, the relevant reasoning is trapped by the mode of finding the best neutrality which leads to a definite system choice. For example, CEN adheres to that a universal worldwide tax system is ideal, while CIN advocates a universal territorial tax system. However, no matter what neutrality to side with, one is bound and trapped by these two systems. This way of thinking is thus unreliable as it cannot provide a wide vision. Through the above investigation of the real-world tax systems, it is clearly seen that neutrality is incompetent in explaining the popular exemption regimes and why they could differentiate the tax system materially. However, when the role of neutrality is revised as such, different neutrality propositions do not have to compete with each other and make a choice between worldwide/territorial systems either. Instead, their principal aim is to evaluate any system proposals on the table, no matter what grounds the proposals are justified thereby. The revised role opens our eyes to look for any other system options besides the worldwide or territorial ones.

After the role of neutralities is revised, the neutralities are weighed more as an *ex-post* evaluative benchmark instead of *ex-ante* guiding rule, a special question arises as to what to count on in the first place to contemplate the international tax policy. Besides neutrality, equity, simplicity and tax sovereignty are also known as basic principles of international taxation. Compared to neutrality, they have more weight because they are much closer to the reasons of taxation, but still, for directly guiding the designing issues, they are abstract and elastic. For design and reform in particular of international tax policy, 'the best way to make international tax policy is by setting forth the social goal and determining the best set of trade-offs for achieving it given the tools and information available'.[802] The problem-solving model for reform of international taxation has dominated discussions of the issue for a long time. However, this

801. *Ibid.*, 9.
802. *Ibid.*, 3.

model may be justified as well as evaluated by the above benchmarks including neutralities. In this sense, the roles of neutralities and even other principles are delineated completely. It follows that Weisbach's conclusion that neutralities are not helpful is based on the traditional role of neutralities. This is also why, after criticizing CEN and CIN comprehensively, Gratez did not explicitly contend that they should be thoroughly abandoned, whereas they just reminded us not to be confined by a commitment to CEN or CIN or to a compromise between them.[803] Another proof weakening the traditional role of neutralities from the real world is the credit method as the inherent feature of the worldwide tax system advocated by CEN, for the credit method was introduced in the first place as a correction mechanism for the inadequacies in the international tax regime resulting from the 1920s Compromise,[804] not to satisfy CEN.

### 6.6.4 States Are Heading Towards Cooperation Away from Competition

The fundamental premises that lay the foundation of all the discourses of international tax neutrality is that economic production can be maximized should capital compete freely with each other in the global market and that states best act as invisible hand instead of active participant.

First of all, it has long been recognized in the economic literature that competition of capital can increase welfare only to the extent that its positive externality outweighs the negative externality. Therefore, states never allow capital to compete utterly freely across and within their borders. Relevantly, states are increasingly becoming some market actors in themselves, which significantly complicates the original efficiency presumption.

As such, it is not wise to stick to efficiency considerations or make the hard choices among the alphabet of neutralities, while turning a blind eye to the fact that states are actually nitpicking the capital as well. States not only often impose controls on where the international capital is coming from but also instruct on the location, industry or generally the amount of the capital having been attracted.

However, and more importantly, the presumption that states interact with each other based on competition, similar to that of mobile capitals, is flawed, particularly as states increasingly cooperate and coordinate on tax matters. The trend emerged when states realized their competition sometimes was 'harmful' while they only wanted beneficial competition. This happened in the pre-BEPS era, when the market of taxing states remained in the shadow of the market of international capital, and the former actually served the latter. However, the BEPS problem has raised the issue to the level where most of the states agreed to cooperate in both procedural and substantive aspects; they, therefore, set fairly solid bottom lines and boundaries for the behaviour of capital. Certainly, the states are not commanding the capital directly, but they are now indeed restricting the competition of capital as the previous mode of competition

803. Graetz (n. 92) 336.
804. de Wilde, '"Sharing the Pie": Taxing Multinationals in a Global Market' (n. 588) 81.

renders no winner except the MNEs themselves. As such, either neutrality proposition concerning a margin of economic production or having to choose one to side with does not seem tenable when the states do not want that degree of competition in the first place.

## 6.7 UNDER THE LENS OF NEUTRALITY: FORMULARY APPORTIONMENT VERSUS ALP

Is arm's length neutral? The answer still depends on what neutrality is in question or what distortions of taxation are considered. In the literature of ALP, the neutrality considerations are rare. Yet, back to the origin, it is found that one of the key starting points of ALP is to achieve neutral treatment of associated business vis-à-vis uncontrolled business. The real achievement in this respect depends on the evaluation of how ALP has replicated the free market behaviour through the standards, methods and processes.

However, comprehensively, the rampant BEPS phenomenon is the most straightforward proof that the ALP contributes little to the neutrality of the international tax system. A core explanation that the ALP enables MNEs' manipulation of tax factors (not necessarily production factors) so as to artificially avoid taxes. Such a result not only manifests the distortive effect of the tax system but also impairs the system in the first place. In this regard, the ALP system is self-demolishing.

The neutrality story for formulary apportionment is relatively more complex. First, if considering neutrality as a principle with the same weight as legitimacy and equity within the analytical framework of this research, then neutrality simply and clearly points to two designs regarding FA.

One is the single sales factor formulary apportionment. The reason is that neutrality requires the least possible tax distortion, regardless of which proposition maximizes efficiency. This further requires that formulary apportionment adopt factors that are as difficult to manipulate as possible, which translates on the factor side to using immobile factors. Among the traditional apportionment factors, only sales is basically outside the total control of the company. Therefore, the single sales factor formulary apportionment is more in line with neutrality.

The second is a design of FA that conforms to neutrality but currently only exists in academic discussions,[805] which is to use some country-level macroeconomic indicators, such as the Human Development Index, to apportion taxable income. This is more progressive and aggressive than the sales-only factor above. Aggressive here means that this method completely abandons company-level indicators, decoupling from the company's actual performance in states, which may deviate from the principle of normative legitimacy. Progressive means that this kind of FA can distribute tax in a way that helps relatively poor countries, aligning with the redistributive thinking of the equity principle.

805. 'Progressive Formulary Apportionment: The Case for "Amount D" | Tax Notes' https://www.taxnotes.com/featured-analysis/progressive-formulary-apportionment-case-amount-d/2021/06/11/76k47 accessed 2 May 2024.

However, the new philosophy of international tax neutrality, as developed in section 6.6, has determined that neutrality is relatively inferior in the analytical framework established in this chapter that provides evaluative rather than instructional insights. As such, a pure neutrality-based design of formulary apportionment tends to maximize efficiency and stir competition. This would run counter to the prescriptions of legitimacy and equity because, at its core, an FA based purely on neutrality would still promote tax competition, and the evolution of US state FAs toward single sales factor formulary apportionment may be the example.

# Part IV
# Testing and Experimenting with Formulary Apportionment in China

First, as the culminating part of this research, its core function is to integrate the preceding discussions and propose an FA regime that this study considers to be better or more balanced, covering both substantive and procedural elements. It is worth noting that here China mainly provides a discussion background and a starting point from the perspective of national interests and strategic positions to demonstrate how to determine the specific design of FA. However, this does not mean that this study supports the so-called unilateral FA. On the contrary, the author believes that the FA design proposal for China is actually a universally applicable multilateral solution.

Second, in terms of the structure of the study, the preceding parts of this research discussed the complex story of ALP, the BEPS Project as a somewhat disappointing aspect of the most sweeping reform in the history of international taxation, the arising FA as part of its historical trajectory, the examination and comparison of existing FA regimes or proposals in today's world, and the analytical framework of FA. After all these, it is natural and necessary to discuss an exemplary FA design.

Lastly, China's international status determines that more research should focus on China, which is an essential part of international tax governance. However, relatively speaking, discussions on China's international tax system are much fewer compared to those in Europe and the United States. From this perspective, this part of the study also fills a certain gap. For example, Chapter 7 introduces the basic aspects of China's international tax system from the perspective of the Belt and Road Initiative and comprehensively utilizes various materials to reveal the strategic trends of China's tax system. In addition, based on China's international status, studying FA from China's perspective also has significant reference value for the vast majority of developing and transitional countries.

CHAPTER 7

# From Source-Oriented to Residence-Oriented: China's International Tax Regime Reshaped by BRI[806]

*This chapter examines the transformation of China's international tax regime (ITRC) under the influence of the Belt and Road Initiative (BRI), proposing that the ITRC is shifting from a source-oriented to a residence-oriented tax system. By analysing BRI-driven reforms in both domestic tax laws and bilateral double tax agreements, the study employs a conceptual approach to classify tax rules into source-based taxation (SBT) and residence-based taxation (RBT) modules, assessing their relative weight and maturity. Key domestic reforms include the enhancement of the foreign tax credit system, which now features a global credit mechanism and extended credit layers, and the activation of the controlled foreign corporation regime to counter tax avoidance. In terms of DTAs, the analysis highlights the expansion of China's tax treaty network (breadth) and substantive changes in treaty provisions (depth), such as the redirected role of sparing credits, reduced withholding tax rates, and the strategic use of most-favoured-nation clauses. These developments, accelerated by the BRI's focus on facilitating outbound investment, collectively support the proposition that China's ITRC is increasingly prioritizing residence-based taxation. This transformation reflects China's evolving role as a capital-exporting nation and has significant implications for international tax governance, particularly for developing and transitional economies.*

806. This chapter is revised from the author's working paper published elsewhere, which can be accessed at https://dspace.ceu.es/server/api/core/bitstreams/17280d81-251d-4ec5-82a7-bd0c1f4580ff/content accessed 26 August 2025.

## 7.1 INTRODUCTION

The Belt and Road Initiative[807] is a regional and transnational cooperative economic framework launched by China, which aims to revive its ancient economic ties with Eurasian countries.[808] Announced by the Chinese President Xi Jinping in 2013, the geographic coverage and economic data that the BRI has achieved are eye-catching. Up to July 2023, China signed the BRI 'Cooperation Agreements' with 152 jurisdictions, which showed the acceding parties' political commitment to further cooperating under the initiative. In the first five years (2013-2018) of BRI, the flow of FDI from China to BRI countries had surpassed USD 90 billion, and the newly signed engineering project contracts are valued at more than USD 600 billion, with an annual growth rate of 11.9%.[809]

For China, BRI has been the strategic focus of the government since its launch. The Party and the central government ministries have been enacting guiding documents frequently to reform and regulate, and ultimately to facilitate the construction of BRI. Their efforts have covered multiple fields, including but not limited to infrastructure, technology, energy, environment, economy and so forth. Among those areas of rules, taxation has also been a key in advancing BRI.

This chapter seeks to analyse the profound shifts in China's international tax regime catalysed by BRI. Specifically, it argues that China's tax system is transitioning from a predominantly source-oriented model, which prioritizes taxing income at its source, to a residence-oriented model, focusing on the global income of Chinese residents. This transformation has significant implications for both domestic tax laws and international tax treaties, which form the pillars of China's tax framework.

To start the verification of the proposition, section 7.2 lays down some background information about BRI and the ITRC. Section 7.3 elucidates the research proposition and the verifying approach. Sections 7.4 and 7.5 identify and analyse the BRI-driven changes of the two components of the international tax regime, respectively, the domestic tax laws and the double tax agreements. For the domestic part, the discussions will cover the foreign tax credit system and the CFC regime. For the tax treaty part, the changes are inspected in terms of the breadth and depth. For breadth, the analysis looks into the general picture of China's bilateral tax treaty network, while the depth part will discuss the content changes in terms of sparing credit, the withholding tax liability, and the most-favoured-nation clause. Based on all these discussions, section 7.6 concludes by revisiting the proposition and presenting the result of the verification.

---

807. The 'Belt' is for 'Silk Road Economic Belt', and 'Road' is for '21st-Century Maritime Silk Road'. In 2015, several ministries of China published the official English translation for BRI. Before that, the 'Belt and Road' was also mostly known as 'OBOR' for 'One Belt and One Road' or 'One Belt, One Road'. *See* Yawen Zheng, 'The Establishment of a Multilateral Investment Treaty for the "One Belt, One Road" Initiative' (2018) Special Issue Cambridge Law Review.

808. However, as shown in Figure 7.3, BRI reaches out further than Eurasia, which has embraced Africa, Oceania, North and South America into its scope.

809. *See* 'The Regular Press Conference of the Ministry of Commerce' (Ministry of Commerce of the People's Republic of China, 18 April 2019) https://www.mofcom.gov.cn/lsxwfbh/art/2023/art_1cd88617ff764fe496646138ced59b0c.html accessed 2 December 2023.

## 7.2 THE INTERNATIONAL TAX REGIME OF CHINA

### 7.2.1 BRI and International Taxation

Being a transnational framework, the key starting point of BRI is to connect the markets of China and its partners in the BRI. Yet, comparing the level of development of China and most BRI countries, the outbound investment from China outweighs China's inbound investment from BRI countries. As a result, such 'inter-connection' implicitly advocates more for the removal of barriers to the Chinese outbound investment from both the China side and BRI countries. The other way round, facilitating the inbound investment into China, however, only gains normative weight in the framework of BRI.

Based on the above, inspecting how China adjusts itself to the demand and reality of BRI may provide valuable insights into understanding China's strategy and foreseeing its future actions as well. The scope is limited to the area of taxation and, more specifically, to the international aspects of business taxation.

### 7.2.2 China's International Tax Regime

The international tax regime of China, or technically, China's foreign-related tax law has two components:[810] the domestic tax law and the double tax agreements (DTA) signed with other tax jurisdictions. The composition generally reflects the basic norm of international taxation. The following only lays down some background information for the purpose of later and deeper discussions.

The current international tax model has been commonly accredited to the contributions made in the 1920s by the LON.[811] To this day, if comparing the international tax law of China to the common international tax model, the former is still an 'infant' to the latter, which is going to celebrate its 100th anniversary. The ITRC was created in the 1980s because either its first DTA was signed in 1983 or the first foreign-related enterprise income tax law was enacted in 1980.[812] However, in modern times, China's international tax regime is closer to maturity after its 'adolescent' restlessness. That maturity can be partly explained by the so-called latecomer advantage, in that the Chinese international tax regime grows out of the modern international tax institutions.[813]

---

810. This relates to the nature of international tax law, *see* Brian J Arnold, 'Canada's International Tax System: Historical Review, Problems and Outlook for the Future' (2018) No. 8 Canada in International Law at 150 and Beyond Paper 1-2 https://www.cigionline.org/publications/canadas-international-tax-system-historical-review-problems-and-outlook-future/ accessed 2 December 2023.
811. de Wilde, '"Sharing the Pie": Taxing Multinationals in a Global Market' (n. 588) 12.
812. Sino-foreign Joint Venture Enterprise Income Tax Law of the People's Republic of China (中华人民共和国中外合资经营企业所得税法) 1980.
813. Jinyan Li, *International Taxation in China: A Contextualized Analysis* (IBFD Publications 2016) para. 1.3.2.2.

For one thing, the ITRC is consistent with the *residence-source* model of the international tax model. China taxes the worldwide income of residents while providing foreign tax credits to eliminate double taxation. For non-residents, the Chinese tax liability is limited to the income derived within China. As a result, to be well-functioning, the residence-source international tax model is, in turn, dependent on the delineation of residence and source concepts. For the concept of residence, China uses the test of place of incorporation and place of effective management,[814] which is further supplemented by provisions of its (usually Article 4). The identification of source is generally aligned with the categorization of incomes, of which the foundational division is between positive (business) incomes and passive (investment) incomes.

For another, China now has one of the largest tax treaty networks in the world. By the end of April 2019, China had concluded DTAs with 107 jurisdictions, even though the network has been 'weaved' only since 1983. The technical design of its DTAs draws on either the UN model or OECD model so that all these tax treaties are basically the same in structure, and the divergence of content is limited. It is expected that China's bilateral tax treaty network will further expand.

## 7.3 RESEARCH PROPOSITION AND VERIFYING APPROACH

This chapter, with a focus on the implications of BRI for the international tax law of China, proposes that under the influence of BRI, there is an emerging trend that the ITRC is shifting from *source-oriented* to *residence-oriented*. This pair of terms, the source-oriented tax (SOT) system and residence-oriented tax (ROT) system, will be refined in the following.

To validate the proposition, this chapter uses a conceptual approach as the core to identifying an international tax regime as SOT or ROT.

The division of SOT and ROT conceptualizes and aligns with a country's relative stance on the so-called inbound taxation and outbound taxation.

In the case of China, the inbound taxation is the taxation of non-residents on their incomes sourced from China, manifested as an outflow of taxable income from China, while the outbound taxation is the taxation of Chinese residents on their worldwide, especially foreign-source incomes, manifested as *inflow* of taxable income to China. As inbound taxation arises from the country being the source of taxable income outflow, it can be entitled 'source-based' taxation (SBT). In the same vein, the outbound taxation can be named as 'residence-based' taxation (RBT). In this chapter, SBT and RBT refer to the two integral modules of the international tax regime of a country.

SBT and RBT are inherently not overlapping or conflicting, for they are targeting different groups of taxpayers and incomes. They embody and reflect distinctive policy objectives and value orientations. The design of SBT rules aims to effectively tax the income of non-residents on one hand, on the other, they can play the role of attracting foreign investment. These two dimensions either echo the benefit principle that

814. Enterprise Income Tax Law of the People's Republic of China (中华人民共和国企业所得税法) 2007 Art. 2.

justifies the territorial taxation or relate to the CIN or the legal principle of non-discrimination. Correspondingly, besides effectively taxing the foreign income, the residence-based tax rules can be designed to facilitate outbound investment, by removing tax barriers or lowering tax burdens. Not free from controversies, the RBT is constructed upon ability-to-pay and capital export neutrality.

*Table 7.1 SBT Versus RBT Systems*

| | *SBT* | *RBT* |
|---|---|---|
| Policy objectives | Effective taxation on non-resident | Effective taxation on resident's foreign income |
| | Attracting foreign investments | Facilitating outbound investment |
| Foundations | Benefit principle | Ability-to-pay |
| | CIN | CEN |

Even though SBT and RBT are equally key to the integrality of an international tax regime, different countries or countries at different stages may waver between the two. In other words, the relative weight of SBT and RBT is discrepant. For example, a developing economy that has barely any outbound investment conceivably has less sophisticated outbound or RBT rules compared to that of a developed economy that relies much on foreign markets and overseas investment. Or reversely, a traditional capital exporting country is expected to have less sophisticated inbound or SBT rules.

For the purpose of ongoing discussions, and based on the above comparison of SBT and RBT, this chapter further categorizes two modules of taxation, in delineation of a country's general orientation towards international taxation. That is what has been mentioned in the beginning, the *SOT* or *ROT*, which is determined by a country's inclination to or particular emphasis on SBT or RBT.

Being equally important in the purported proposition, another focus falls on the 'trend'. That first means that the purported proposition is not final or once and for all, but is of the attribute of time, which is to catch the tendency of development within a certain period of time. In this chapter, it is for the period of the BRI's construction. In other words, the proposition and its validation are not to grab the 'destination', but the 'scenery' during the journey. The efforts throughout this chapter do not touch upon the model of ITRC before the BRI or demonstrate that the ITRC has *already* finished its transformation.

To catch the trend of SOT or ROT, the key challenge then is to measure the weight of SBT or RBT of an international tax regime. It is not feasible to accurately calculate their respective weight, either absolute or relative at an exact point of time. However, grasping the trend only entails inspecting the changes that are happening, and then distributes the changes to the weight of SBT or RBT to grasp the tendency.

In determining the trend of ITRC as source-oriented or residence-oriented, the *key* step is '*classification*', *meaning* the process of grouping a certain tax rule into either SBT or RBT. For that purpose, the policy objectives pursued by a relevant set of tax rules are accessible indicators for their classification. In cases where the rule is already in place, the focus is then to delineate the changes in the rule. As a result, the '*maturity*' is introduced as an index factor of the 'weight' of SBT or RBT. The maturity is, in turn, signified and materialized by the density or maturity of the rules in each camp, so factors like number, existence, robustness, or enforcement of rules are to be considered.

For illustration, it is supposed that a country introduces the CFC regime, being an anti-avoidance rule, of which the tenet is to safeguard the home taxing right of resident multinationals. The step classification groups the CFC regime into RBT, and it adds force to ROT. In comparison, if the country enhances the CFC regime to be more sophisticated, the classification step will be supplemented by the consideration of the maturity of RBT. The CFC regime will be inspected in terms of its competency, practical implementation or other elements. All these improved elements increase the weight of RBT. If within a certain period of time, many other reforms of similar kind are adopted, a trend towards ROT can be established.

## 7.4 BRI-DRIVEN REFORMS OF DOMESTIC TAX LAW

Compared to the investigation of China's DTAs, which often requires seeing things behind the articles, the adjustments of Chinese domestic tax laws are more transparent. Even though there are many more changes in law enforcement, however, the following will only focus on the rule-based reforms. To testify the proposition, one of the characteristics of ROT is that a state is taking tax actions encouraging its residents to invest overseas. On the opposite side, the growing outbound investment may also challenge the effectiveness of the home country's RBT. The countering tax measures, therefore, constitute another thread demonstrating the proposition. Accordingly, two aspects of rule changes will be introduced and discussed. The first is the perfected and activated CFC regime, the second is the improved foreign tax credit system.

### 7.4.1 Improved Foreign Tax Credit System

China's foreign tax credit (FTC) system has undergone substantial reform against the background of BRI. The tenet of the reform is to facilitate the going out of Chinese companies by providing more thorough credit for foreign tax. The original FTC system was effectively built up in 2009,[815] and it had imposed considerable restrictions on the sufficiency of tax credit. In 2017, STA reshaped the FTC system so as to adapt to the new situation brought about by BRI,[816] and that has released the restrictions tit for tat. Here the restrictions and the countering reforms are grouped as horizontal and vertical.

815. Notice on Issues Concerning the Foreign Income Tax Credit of Enterprises (财税〔2009〕125号 财政部 国家税务总局 关于企业境外所得税收抵免有关问题的通知) 2010 (Caishui No. 125 [2009]).
816. Notice on Issues Concerning Improving the Tax Credit Policy for Overseas Income of Enterprises (财税〔2017〕84号 财政部 税务总局关于完善企业境外所得税收抵免政策问题的通知) 2017 (Caishui No. 84 [2017]).

The horizontal feature of the old system, marking those restrictions, is the per-country credit mechanism. Within this mechanism, resident companies deriving incomes from more than one country cannot combine and re-use the credit balance across countries. As a result, taxpayers' credit balances in low-tax countries cannot be reused for the credit of high-tax countries. However, foreign tax paid to high-tax countries that exceed the credit limit as calculated by the Chinese tax rate cannot be credited currently. Therefore, insufficient credit exists under the per-country credit mechanism, which will adversely affect the cash flow of the taxpayer. The situation will be worse if one of the foreign branches has suffered losses, for under the mechanism such losses cannot be manipulated into calculating the taxable income in China or third countries.

The vertical restriction in the old FTC system is the three-layer credit mechanism, regarding the indirect credit for tax paid by the multi-layered foreign subsidiaries. Ideally, a perfect FTC system should provide unlimited credit to the end of the holding chain. Whereas, apparently, this cannot be the case in reality. In China's old FTC system, the taxpayer can file credit for foreign tax at most until the third layer subsidiary. There are detailed standards to identify the qualified layer and subsidiary.[817] With the popularity of outbound investment, the business model that extends further than three-layer holding becomes common as well.[818] Restricting the credit chain to three layers makes the FTC halfway to its purpose, for double taxation is only partially exempt.

The new system aiming at facilitating outbound investment has targeted loosening both the horizontal and vertical restrictions. First of all, the per-country credit is supplemented by a global credit mechanism, which provides combined FTC regardless of the country of the source. In this case, the FTC obtained by the taxpayer will be more sufficient. The same spirit is found in the reform of the five-layer credit. It literally means that the resident company can credit the foreign tax it has indirectly borne all the way to the fifth-layer subsidiary. Although it raises higher standards of tax administration and compliance, the elimination of double taxation will be achieved to a greater extent.

The two measures, in horizontal and vertical aspects, have the direct effect of easing the tax burden of outbound Chinese investors. Besides these, there are also peripheral actions serving the same purpose. For instance, STA abolished the *ex-ante* approval procedure for FTC in 2015;[819] now, the taxpayer only needs to file for a record of FTC. Another example is a BRI-tailored policy relevant to FTC. In general, for sub-contracting or consortium engineering projects, the entity that actually earns the

817. *Ibid.*, 5, 6.

818. *See* official reading of the new FTC policy at Interview with Senior Officials of STA, 'Senior Officials of STA and MOF Answering Questions on Improving the Tax Credit Policy for Enterprises' Overseas Income' (2 January 2018) http://m.mof.gov.cn/czxw/201712/t20171229_2790745.htm accessed 2 December 2023.

819. Announcement on Issues Concerning the Follow-up Administration after the Cancellation of the Approval Item of Confirmation of the Application of Simple Collection and Tax Sparing Credit to the Overseas Income of Enterprises (国家税务总局公告2015年第70号 国家税务总局关于企业境外所得适用简易征收和饶让抵免的核准事项取消后有关后续管理问题的公告) 2015 (STA Announcement No. 70 [2015]).

foreign income is not the entity that actually pays the foreign tax. The first entity then may not be eligible for Chinese FTC. STA issued a circular in 2017 to solve this inconsistency problem by adopting the principle of 'substance over form'.[820] These actions have provided firm support for improving the FTC system and facilitating the outbound investment of resident companies.

According to the conceptual approach, the foreign tax credit system should first be classified into the group of RBT rules. For that, the FTC is a basic method to eliminate double taxation, which is the key consideration for cross-border factor movement. Second, in the level of maturity, the above reform of China's FTC system has made it more competent to achieve its normative goal. The improvement of the FTC system has added weight to the RBT. Taken individually, it conforms to the trend in the research proposition regarding the ITRC's transformation to ROT.

### 7.4.2 Activated and Patched CFC Regime

The CFC regime is designed to combat the artificial tax avoidance of resident companies by using foreign-controlled entities, especially in low-tax jurisdictions. CFC denies the potential tax deferral or avoidance by taxing currently the resident's proportionate income share in its controlled foreign subsidiaries. CFC regime is not sensitive to the worldwide or territorial tax system, in that in either system resident companies have the incentive to abuse the tax laws. However, the CFC regime is rooted in the rightfulness of residence taxing rights and unreasonable tax deferral or tax avoidance by using the CFC challenges such rightfulness. In this sense, the CFC regime maintains the RBT, and its development may manifest the changing weight of RBT.

The evolution of China's CFC regime in recent years corresponds to the trend of strengthening RBT. The regime was introduced by China's first EITL (Enterprise Income Tax Law) in 2008,[821] and materialized by STA subsequently in 2009.[822] However, it was still far from perfection, for it lacked operational guidelines on various elements. For instance, there are no comprehensive standards of 'control'[823] in identifying controlled foreign entities. The same situation is there for 'reasonable business operation'. In addition, although the EITL refers to the individual holding CFC, STA cannot deal with the individual tax avoidance on behalf of the Individual Income Tax Law (IITL). The IITL then did not intend to cooperate with EITL on this point. Furthermore, at the practical level, STA lacked the experience of tackling the tax avoidance of residents using overseas resources.

---

820. Announcement on Issues Concerning the Tax Credit Vouchers for Overseas Contracted Engineering Projects of Enterprises (国家税务总局公告2017年第41号 国家税务总局公告关于企业境外承包工程税收抵免凭证有关问题的公告) 2017 (STA Announcement No. 41 [2017]).
821. *See* Enterprise Income Tax Law of the People's Republic of China (中华人民共和国企业所得税法) Art. 45.
822. Notice on Issuing the Measures for the Implementation of Special Tax Adjustments (for Trial Implementation) (国税发〔2009〕2号 国家税务总局关于印发《特别纳税调整实施办法（试行）》的通知) 2009 (Guoshuifa No. 2 [2009]).
823. In the above regulation, it is provided only the case of control by shareholding.

Due to the immaturity of legislation and the lack of realistic urgency, China's CFC regime had been frozen for a significant time. STA had never administered a CFC case until 2014 and 2015, when STA improved the tax information collection of residents investing overseas.[824] The reform was enacted expressly to serve the construction of BRI, signalling that the increasing outbound investment is the factual impetus. Later, in 2018, the new IITL also filled up the hole in CFC regime with respect to individual controlling cases.[825] While more patches can be put on the regime, the existing one can already basically function. It was found then a boost of CFC cases filed by STA since 2014, and by now, STA has managed to administer the CFC regime on a regular basis.

The above reforms around the CFC regime, either STA's legislative and administrative measures that have activated CFC or the patch made by IITL, have increased the effectiveness and competency of the regime. Being the rule of RBT in itself, the CFC regime, through the improvements, has contributed to the weighted RBT. In conclusion, the reforms of the CFC regime have added the persuasiveness of the research proposition, affirming again the ITRC's transformation to ROT.

## 7.5 CHANGES IN BILATERAL TAX AGREEMENTS

The bilateral tax treaty is entered traditionally for the purpose of eliminating double taxation and tax evasion. However, that purpose has extended to objectives like developing economic relationships and improving cooperation on tax matters.[826] The contracting parties' proactive intent must be triggered by the realistic economic intercourse of the two countries. This is the fundamental reason for their delegates to sit down and argue. The same applies to BRI, which aims to (re)build the economic ties along the Belt and Road. Consequently, with the revival of the Belt and Road, there must be a need to establish 'tax ties' as well.

When questioning the implications of BRI for the general ITRC, and for now in terms of tax treaties, both the breadth and depth of China's DTAs should be considered. In this chapter, the inspection of breadth, which refers to the extensiveness of China's tax treaty network, intends to explore the expansion of the treaty network. While for depth, the specific changes of treaties' articles are viewed as substantial evidence to knowing the tendency of ITRC under the influences of BRI. Only through the combination of both the breadth and depth aspects can the global transformation of China's stance on international taxation from the treaty perspective be mastered.

824. Announcement on Issues Concerning Resident Enterprises' Reporting of Information Relating to Overseas Investment and Income (国家税务总局公告2014年第38号 国家税务总局关于居民企业报告境外投资和所得信息有关问题的公告) 2014 (STA Announcement No. 38 [2014]); Notice on Effectively Conducting the Work of Resident Enterprises' Reporting of Information about Overseas Investment and Income (税总函〔2015〕327号 国家税务总局关于做好居民企业报告境外投资和所得信息工作的通知) 2015 (Shuizonghan No. 327 [2015]).

825. Individual Income Tax Law of the People's Republic of China (2018 version) (中华人民共和国个人所得税法 2018版) 2018 Art. 8.

826. *See* OECD, 'Multilateral Convention to Implement Tax Treaty Related Measures to Prevent BEPS' Art. 6 https://www.oecd.org/tax/treaties/multilateral-convention-to-implement-tax-treaty-related-measures-to-prevent-BEPS.pdf accessed 4 December 2023.

However, what needs to be explained is that the breadth part and depth part are not always and do not need to be aligned by the same tax treaties. In other words, the treaties that signify the specific tendency of expansion do not necessarily show noticeable content changes, which may lie elsewhere. This chapter views the two aspects as on equal footing and organically connected.

### 7.5.1 The Breadth of China's Tax Treaty Network

This section will be unfolded by three charts, which are, in turn, processed with the data regarding China's DTAs and the development of BRI.[827]

Figure 7.1 shows (in light grey area) the countries signing tax treaties with China. As can be seen, China's tax treaty network is already very comprehensive so far. With a few still not in force, China has signed bilateral tax agreements with 107 countries in the world, which makes China's tax treaty network one of the largest in the world. From the map in Figure 7.1, there are only two noteworthy grey areas, meaning that those are countries without tax agreements with China. One is in Africa, and another is in South America.

Figure 7.2 shows the number of tax treaties that China signed or updated with other countries each year from 1983 to 2019. This chart supplements Figure 7.1 in that it introduces the time dimension into the analysis of China's DTA network evolution.

Combining Figure 7.1 and Figure 7.2, the first thing to note is that over thirty years and with such extensive coverage, China's international tax treaty network is still growing, either by extending to new jurisdictions or refreshing the old treaties. Narrowing the lens down to only the period since the launch of BRI, it is found that even within only six years, BRI has clear influences on the expansion of China's treaty network. Since 2015, China's treaty network has extended to eight new countries, who are, at the same time, the new members of BRI as well.[828] Even in the first five months of 2019, the tax treaties with New Zealand and Italy, being the new BRI countries respectively in 2017 and 2019, were totally renegotiated, both in 2019.

Then, on the historical dimension, three more points of time are shown in Figure 7.2 that are worth considering. The first is 2001, when China joined the WTO, marking its integration into the world and its twenty-year rapid growth of the economy. The new century is literally the new age of economic China. The second point of time is that after seven years of attracting foreign capital, China's dual corporate income tax system ended in 2008.[829] The third one is in 2016, two years after the announcement of BRI, China has transformed from a capital-importing country to a net capital-exporting

827. *See* 'List of Countries That Have Signed "Belt and Road" Cooperation Document with China' (Jiangsu Belt and Road Portal, 12 June 2023) http://ydyl.jiangsu.gov.cn/art/2022/2/8/art_76283_10343080.html accessed 2 December 2023.and STA, 'List of Double Taxation Agreements Signed by China' http://www.chinatax.gov.cn/n810341/n810770/index.html accessed 23 November 2023.
828. They are Chile, Zimbabwe, Cambodia, Kenya, Gabon, The Republic of Congo, Angola and Argentina. Argentina does not officially sign the BRI cooperation documents with China, yet it already has substantial projects going on in the name of constructing BRI.
829. *See* Li, *International Taxation in China* (n. 813) para. 2.2.1.

country. As can be seen in Figure 7.2, nearly 70 out of 107 tax treaties were signed before 2001, when China had fewer capital outputs. The little triangle symbolizing the launch of BRI rests after the first two dash lines and ahead of the third one.

This has two aspects of instructions. For one thing, the status quo of China's tax treaties falls behind the fast-changing reality, both economic and legal, in that the basis of those treaties has shifted dramatically. The second instruction relates to how should one view BRI's role in China's evolving tax treaties. When evaluating the implications of BRI for both the scope and content of China's tax treaty network, the efforts of isolating BRI from its general economic and legal background are futile. The changes brought by BRI must be seen in conjunction with the background it grows in. Thus, it can be said that BRI has been accelerating the change of reality along the existing route and, in turn, making the tax rule changes faster and more observable.

*Figure 7.1 China's Tax Treaty Partners*

*Figure 7.2 Yearly Signed or Updated DTAs of China*

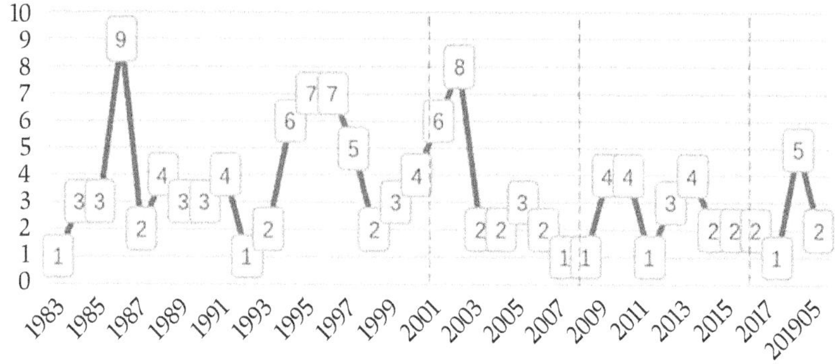


*Figure 7.3 Distribution of DTAs in BRI Countries*

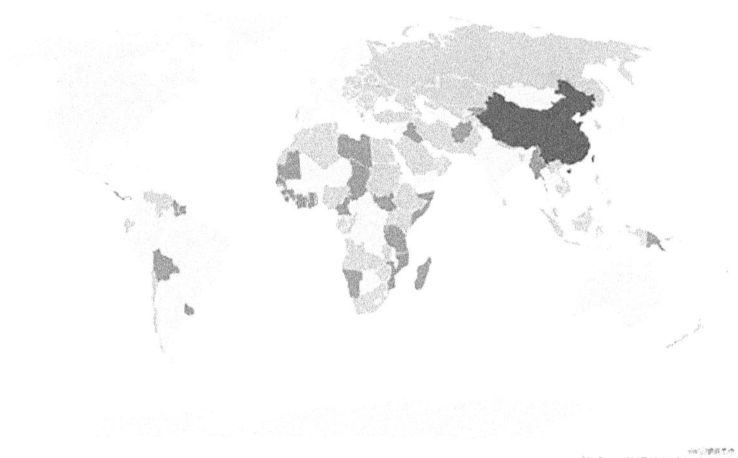

Figure 7.3 painted all the countries signing the BRI cooperation documents ('BRI Countries') with China in dark grey or light grey. The light grey areas in the map are the BRI countries with which China has a DTA, while the dark grey areas are the BRI countries without a DTA with China. By July 2023, the painted areas altogether consisted of 152 countries, which covered the majority of Africa and the Euro-Asia continent. The BRI countries are mostly developing countries, for the noteworthy grey areas are all rich North America, Australia, and West and North Europe.

In terms of the distribution of DTAs in the BRI countries, the majority of BRI countries, both in absolute number and geographic coverage, have already had bilateral tax treaties with China. That is attributed to the work done by STA largely before BRI.

#### *7.5.1.1 Summary*

The above analysis of the three diagrams has shown the network of China's current international tax treaties and the evident role of BRI in its expanding scope. The analysis also touches upon why a transition of ITRC in terms of tax treaties is destined to happen. This part only deals with the breadth of the ITRC, and the next session will turn to focus on the depth and content of tax treaties so as to reveal the material changes. That, nevertheless, does not mean the scope change of DTAs is of trivial significance. The key lies in that: first, the bilateral tax treaty is critical to distributing income between countries by allocating taxing rights; second, the bilateral tax treaty is itself an instrument to removing barriers to cross-border investment, which has been pointed out in the top design of BRI; third, BRI has made a difference in the expanding tax treaty network, for the increased treaty partners may be attracted in by BRI.

The first decade in the chronicle of China's international treaties witnessed the agreements with most of OECD countries.[830] Through the latter two decades and under the influences of BRI, the network has included more capital-poor countries than capital-rich countries, with China as a benchmark. Even though sometimes the tax treaties are called 'international', it is, in fact, only 'bilateral'. Yet, China's international tax treaties are seen as a whole, and the general position of China in the DTAs must have been different from what it ever was.

### 7.5.2 The Depth of China's Tax Treaties

As said, the depth part will deal with the content changes of China's DTAs, under the implications of BRI, with the aim of shedding some light on the research proposition of this chapter. This part is not going to do a blanket search of all the article changes of DTAs, but only to identify the key articles that are relevant to the proposition. The direct objective of a bilateral tax treaty, as usually stated in its preamble, is to eliminate double-taxation and combat tax avoidance. To those ends, tax treaty determines the two contracting parties as either source or residence, and then divides the taxing rights between them. The identification of ITRC as SOT or ROT, while manifested in tax treaty, is first dependent upon China's position as source or residence, and further on the interests vested in the source or residence by the treaty. In general, the taxing right of the source is prioritized, and the residence state has the residual right to tax. According to this judgment, this chapter does find proof of the ITRC's move from SOT to ROT.

830. Li, *International Taxation in China* (n. 813) para. 4.2.2.

#### 7.5.2.1 *The Flexible Sparing Credit*

Normally, in the double tax agreement, Article 23 specifies the methods adopted by the two contracting states for eliminating double taxation. In cases where they choose the credit method, there are options for the residence state to decide whether to view the de facto unpaid tax as the payable tax in the other state for the purpose of calculating the foreign tax credit. The unpaid tax is the tax that would have been paid but otherwise is spared (exempted or reduced) as a tax incentive to attract foreign investment.

Neither OECD nor UN Model Tax Conventions provide sparing credit in its articles as an option for double-tax elimination. However, sparing credit has been common for the DTAs between developed and developing countries. However, being counterproductive for the popular propositions of neutrality and equity, sparing credit has lost its appeal for developed countries.[831] However, sparing credit may still attract those countries, mainly because it increases their outbound investors' competitiveness.

For developing countries, however, the inclusion of sparing credit in their DTAs prevents the other contracting state from nullifying their tax incentives under the top-up effect of the credit method. The incentive benefits then accrue to investors rather than the treasury of their home states. Thus, the sparing credit method has been embraced as a tool for attracting and competing for capital from developed countries.

The sparing credit thus implicitly links SOT and ROT, for different countries or a country in different phases may adopt sparing credit from different starting points. When a country adopts sparing credit in its DTAs, it is not difficult to identify its purpose as attracting foreign investment or facilitating outbound investment. Based on that, sparing credit adds weight to either SOT or ROT, and is able to show dynamically the transformation process between SOT and ROT.

#### 7.5.2.2 *The Redirected Role of Sparing Credit*

The historical trajectory of sparing credit in tax treaties echoes the evolution of China's DTAs and is in concert with the tendency of ITRC from SOT to ROT.

Sparing credit was introduced by China as early as its first DTA in 1983, which was with Japan. Since then, sparing credit has sprung up in its tax treaty network. Put against the system background, China operated a dual tax system that gave institutional incentives to foreign investors until 2008. Consequently, by the end of 2007, forty-nine in all ninety-two China's DTAs contain sparing credit provisions, and most of them are treaties with developed countries.

In 2008, the first Enterprise Income Tax Law cancelled the systematic preferential treatment of foreign investors, and only sectorial and regional incentives existed thereafter. The institutional basis thus falls away. After 2008, only two among the

831. Xiong Yan, 'Thinking Over Questions Relevant to Sparing Credit (对饶让抵免有关问题的思考)' (2016) 12 International Taxation (国际税收).

thirty-three newly signed or updated tax treaties contain the sparing credit provisions. The first one with Ethiopia included a restricted sparing credit, which was claimed to be a reluctant compromise made by China in 2009.[832] The second one, however, came late in 2016 with Cambodia, which used a standard clause of sparing credit.

This chapter holds that the tax treaty with Cambodia manifests a shifted role of sparing credit, and to a certain extent, it marks a new stance of China's tax treaty negotiation, in contrast to that of a decade ago.

Needless to say, the mutual sparing credit, will be more attractive for Cambodia as an investment destination among other Southeast Asian countries. For China, the taxable income that would have accrued to the Chinese treasury due to the credit mechanism turns out to be the income of the Chinese investors in Cambodia. What makes this even more meaningful for those investors is that China operated a per-country credit mechanism until 2017. The credit balance for a specific country cannot be reused for another country's tax credit. Sparing credit thus reduces the 'waste' of credit balance and, in a certain way, alleviates the double taxation caused by the inadequate foreign tax credit. Therefore, the sparing credit included in the Cambodia-China DTA plays a redirected role from its predecessors that started from China being the location of investment, rather than an exporter of capital.

Following the conceptual approach, the classification of sparing credit is flexible. The way to classify is not to look at the content of provisions, but to look through the motives of adopting it. As analysed above, the redirected role of sparing credit renders itself into the category of RBT from the former SBT, which echoes China's shifted motives to facilitating outbound investment from attracting foreign investment. Compared to the arguments in section 7.5 that prove more the destination of the trend, the analysis here has shown where the transformation comes from and where it leads to.

### 7.5.3 Lowered Withholding Tax

In international taxation, the way to tax the income of foreign investors is generally aligned with the categorization of incomes as active income or passive income.[833] The country of source can tax the active or business income on a net basis with a normal corporate tax rate, while passive incomes are taxed at a reduced rate on a gross basis. More particularly, the source tax on passive incomes is paid by the payer rather than the recipient. The scope and the special way of taxing the international passive incomes result in a unique category within the corporate income tax, that is, the withholding tax.

#### *7.5.3.1 Withholding Tax and RBT/SBT*

Withholding tax is a key design for international income sharing. For business income derived by the permanent establishment, the source country has abundant resources to

832. *Ibid.*, 35.
833. Reuven S Avi-Yonah, *International Tax as International Law* (Cambridge University Press 2007) 1.

tax such income. In contrast, the passive income earner does not need a significant presence in the source country. Letting the payers pay the source tax out of the dividend, interest, or royalties to be received by foreign earners seems to be the best option. Withholding tax is thus key to realizing source taxing rights, leaving the residence country to tax the residual incomes. Withholding tax, together with other tax allocation regimes, affects the balance of income sharing between source and residence. The heavier liability of withholding tax results in a larger share in the source, and less income will accrue to the residence. Being a gross-based mechanism, withholding tax is more succinct than typical corporate income tax. Among others, the decisive factors of withholding tax liability are the scope and the tax rate, which is also simpler than the case of net-basis income tax.

On the other side of the mirror, the income sharing of residence and source directly concerns the interests of taxpayers. In the case where the residence state adopts the credit method, the withholding of tax affects the cash flow of the taxpayer. When the residence state uses the exemption method to eliminate double taxation, the withholding of tax will directly affect the overall tax burden. In either case, withholding taxation influences the interest of cross-border taxpayers.

Based on the above, it is reasonable to assess the changing position of a country by looking into the trend of withholding tax in its tax treaties. The trend can be a rising, declining or stable withholding taxation. If a tax treaty has provided lower withholding tax liability in the source state over a certain period of time, then that means the residence state has been sharing a larger share of the cross-border income. The residence country has gained a stronger position than the source state in the international tax pie-sharing. Translate that to contact the conceptual approach, the residence country that achieved lower withholding tax liability in a DTA obtains greater benefits for its residents. Consequently, the residence country has the motive to reduce the withholding tax liability for both the treasury and to facilitate overseas investment. In short, lower withholding tax liability adds weight to RBT.

For the theme of this chapter, a preliminary conclusion can be drawn that the residence country may be transforming to ROT if multiple such treaties can be found. Because any tax liability in a DTA is bilateral, the changing position as reflected by inspecting withholding tax should be considered with the underlying fact – the general stance of the contracting parties as exercising more source or residence taxing rights. For the tax treaties between China and BRI countries, as analysed above, China plays more as the residence states. Consequently, the trend of lower or higher withholding tax liability prescribed by the treaty means the larger or smaller income pie share of China, which in turn renders China closer to ROT or SOT.

#### *7.5.3.2 Cases of Lowered Withholding Tax*

Inspecting some of China's recent DTAs reveals a clear trend of lower withholding tax liability, which further supports the proposition that the ITRC is heading towards ROT. Such a trend also has an indelible connection with the construction of BRI. The following will introduce the details.

Non-exhaustively, this chapter has found some recent tax treaties that exhibit dynamically or statically the decreasing withholding tax liability. The DTAs with Russia and Romania are good examples of the dynamic demonstration. China's first tax treaty with Russia was signed in 1994, in which the rates set for the passive income dividend, interest and royalties were all 10%. In 2014, the DTA with Russia was renegotiated, and the same rates were reduced. For dividends, a 5% rate applies with a modest threshold. Otherwise, the rate is 10%. For interest and royalties, the rates were also reduced to 5% and 6%. This is not the end. In 2015, when China and Russia signed the BRI cooperation document,[834] the delegates of the two sides also signed a tax protocol amending the new DTA. According to the protocol, the withholding taxing right on interest payment was exclusively conferred upon the residence state, while the source state gave up its taxing right. All in all, from 1994 to 2015, China has gained more and more residence taxing rights relative to the source taxing rights of Russia. The same conclusion can be drawn based on the observation of the DTA with Romania, which has reduced the withholding rate to around 3%. For static demonstration, the first DTAs with BRI countries Gabon, Argentina, and the Republic of Congo all set the withholding tax rate to a relatively low level.

Besides the above, there are proofs demonstrating that the aforesaid trend is real and that such a trend is affected by BRI to a large extent. The proofs are the provisions in a number of DTAS exempting or lowering the withholding tax liability of the Silk Road Fund of China (SRF). Established in 2014, SRF is a state-owned fund with a focus on financing BRI projects. In DTAs with BRI countries, Italy (2019),[835] Argentina (2018), Congo (2018), Spain (2018), and Malaysia (2016), the withholding tax liabilities of SRF in those countries are set low or lowered, wholly or partially exempt. Although the preferential treatment can be attributed to sovereign immunity, that does not hinder it from adding strength to the trend and reflecting the straightforward role of BRI in ITRC.

### 7.5.4 Most-Favoured-Nation Clause

This part aims to link the changing position of the most-favoured-nation (MFN) clause in China's tax treaties over the years with the research proposition. The analysis in the following is expected to contribute to the proposition that China is indeed gaining more dominance in negotiating tax treaties, and the ITRC is, in turn, heading towards ROT.

In plain words, the MFN clause ensures in a bilateral agreement between A and B that party A will not be subjected to a less favourable treatment than what B accords to C in their agreement of the same kind. In international trade or investment law, MFN

834. Xinhua News Agency, 'Joint Statement between the People's Republic of China and the Russian Federation on the Construction of Silk Road Economic Belt and the Construction of Eurasian Economic Union' (GOV, 3 September 2015) https://www.gov.cn/xinwen/2015-05/09/content_2859384.htm accessed 4 December 2023.

835. The renegotiated DTA with Italy was also signed simultaneously with the BRI document.

is a 'standard' clause[836] for the major multilateral trade agreements, including GATT, GATS, TRIPS, and NAFTA. All contain it, and so do most bilateral investment treaties.[837] However, it is well known that these agreements virtually do not touch upon tax, especially direct tax issues.

Narrowing down the lens to tax treaties, the MFN clause has independent significance than that in international trade or investment law. For one thing, in international taxation, it is less possible for MFN to be a rule of customary international law. Unlike the popularity among international trade or investment agreements, MFN only exhibits limited existence in the global tax treaty network. Countries are not obliged to provide MFN treatment to their counterparty when negotiating bilateral tax agreements. As a matter of fact, either in academia or practice, the stances on MFN are far from united.[838] For another, taxation has a direct and immediate impact on national welfare, which explains partly why tax issues are usually reserved in trade or investment agreements and why a multilateral tax agreement is still staggering on its way. Therefore, it should be understood that the MFN clause enjoys a different status and serves different purposes in a tax treaty than those in a trade or investment agreement.

### *7.5.4.1 MFN and Non-discrimination: Deviated but Connected*

As reported by the International Law Commission, the MFN clause does not stem from a country's general right to non-discrimination.[839] The OECD MTC has never accepted the MFN clause in its articles, while only considering it in the commentary for a while and later on removing it without substitution.[840] The OECD in Article 24 has provided four forms of non-discrimination in five paragraphs.[841] They are the non-discrimination of nationality, permanent establishment, payment and capital. Being

836. OECD, 'Most-Favoured-Nation Treatment in International Investment Law' [2004] OECD Working Papers on International Investment 16 http://dx.doi.org/10.1787/518757021651 accessed 26 August 2025.
837. *See* The General Agreement on Tariffs and Trade (GATT 1947) Art. 1;General Agreement on Trade in Services (GATS) Art. 2;The Agreement on Trade-Related Aspects of Intellectual Property Rights (TRIPS) Art. 4;North American Free Trade Agreement(NAFTA) Art. 1103 (investment), Art. 1203 (services) and Art. 1403 (financial services).
838. *See* generally the discussions in Daniel Dürrschmidt, 'Tax Treaties and Most-Favoured-Nation Treatment, Particularly within the European Union' (2006) 60 Bulletin for International Taxation 202. Axel Cordewener and Reimer Ekkehart, 'The Future of Most-Favoured: Nation Treatment in EC Tax Law: Did the ECJ Pull the Emergency Brake without Real Need? – Part I' (2006) 46 European Taxation 239., and Dennis Weber, 'Most-Favoured Nation Treatment under Tax Treaties Rejected in the European Community: Background and Analysis of the D Case' (2005) 33 Intertax 429.
839. United Nations, *Yearbook of the International Law Commission 1978, Vol. II, Part 2* (UN 1978) Ch. 2, paras 47-50.
840. Article 24 OECD Commentary 1977, No. 55, 2nd sentence, and it was deleted in the 1992 commentary, *see* OECD, 'Model Double Taxation Convention on Income and Capital 1977' (OECD 1977) https://doi.org/10.1787/9789264055919-en accessed 26 August 2025. Ines Hofbauer, 'Most-Favoured-Nation Clauses in Double Taxation Conventions: A Worldwide Overview' (2005) 33 Intertax 445 https://doi.org/10.54648/taxi2005070 accessed 26 August 2025.
841. OECD, *MTC 2017* (n. 234).

separate aspects, the four lack an overarching rationale behind them.[842] The prevalence of non-discrimination clauses in tax treaties has contributed little to the status of the MFN clause in tax treaties, simply because a third state cannot require the most-favoured-nation treatment on account of the non-discrimination provisions. The status quo is that, among the MFN clauses that are included in the worldwide tax treaties, almost none of them are aligned with the non-discrimination article. In most circumstances, instead of being applied overarchingly, MFN treatments are provided only for particular aspects of international taxation, such as the transportation income or permanent establishment.[843] Resting uncomfortably among the general non-discrimination provisions, the current status of the MFN clause is closer to being an exception to them. For example, the tax treaty between countries A and B contains the standard non-discrimination article, which enumerates several situations where neither party shall discriminate against the other's residents. A's tax treaty with country C also has a similar non-discrimination arrangement. Now B has negotiated a more favourable condition in its treaty with A, the question arises of whether C is reasonable to claim for its residents the same treatment that B's residents are newly having in A. The answer, under the existing development of treaty law, is obviously negative.[844]

Consequently, the *opinio juris* of countries to include an MFN clause in their tax treaties barely exists. And, the autonomous revision of treaty conditions that may be triggered by MFN treatment with a third state poses risks to the reciprocal basis of a tax treaty unless the MFN clause is expressly provided in the treaty. In the above example, the claim of C will be justifiable if the A-C tax treaty has the MFN provisions written regarding its claim. Otherwise, the MFN treatment inappropriately derived from non-discrimination will blur the border of the 'two-sidedness' or 'privity' of the tax treaty.

While the realities of the non-discrimination article and MFN clause deviate, their underlying connections are real. First of all, the loosely aligned provisions of non-discrimination in the MTC target the same negative consequences that the general DTA aims to counter. Economic distortions can be caused by both double taxation and discriminatory taxation.[845] The equal tax treatment of nationals and non-nationals advocated by non-discrimination reflects part of the capital import neutrality.[846]

842. Guglielmo Maisto, Pasquale Pistone and Dennis Weber (eds), *Non-Discrimination in Tax Treaties: Selected Issues from a Global Perspective* (IBFD Publications 2016) 4.

843. For illustration, *see* the distribution of MFN clauses through the treaty articles at Hofbauer (n. 840) 449-453.

844. 'As tax conventions are based on the principle of reciprocity, a tax treatment that is granted by one Contracting State under a bilateral agreement to a resident or national of another Contracting State party to that agreement by reason of the specific economic relationship between those Contracting States may not be extended to a resident or national of a third State under the non-discrimination provision of the tax convention between the first State and the third State.', OECD Commentary 2007 on Art. 24 Concerning Non-discrimination, *see* OECD, *MTC 2017* (n. 234) C(24)-1.

845. Richman (n. 622).

846. CIN aims to lay down a level playing field for residents and non-residents, in the sense of the general international tax regime, which is wider than equal treatment in the source. Non-discrimination in the source states is necessary but not sufficient.

Discriminatory tax treatment in the source state hinders the free movement of capital and investment, and so does the double taxation of residence and source states.

Second, both non-discrimination in the MTC and MFN clauses lead to equal treatment, while only the former is for residents and non-residents, and the latter is for non-residents. In the same vein as the first point above, what justifies MFN is that discriminatory treatment among non-residents of different nationalities also creates distortions and reduces efficiency. Through the application of the MFN clause, the differential tax treatment in a certain aspect will be eliminated, and that aspect will not be a factor for foreign investors in their business decisions. As a result, the efficiency will be safeguarded for both the investor and the source state. In this regard, the MFN clause and non-discrimination article are connected by their common rationale and objective.

#### *7.5.4.2 Driving Forces Behind MFN*

Questioning why a country is driven to adopt MFN clauses in their tax treaties leads us to the purposes of those countries doing so. And, more importantly, the inquiry into the driving forces of the MFN clause will also provide fulcrums to testify the proposition. Since the relative scarcity of MFN clauses in the global tax treaty network, MFN is not a reliable instrument for achieving international tax harmonization, as MFN can effectively do in the international trade and investment system. The deviated nature of MFN and non-discrimination also decides their different outcomes in the practice. However, as discussed above, MFN shares the value of non-discrimination, which means that even though MFN gains far less application, the situation does not prevent MFN from radiating its appeal to a single state. It is held that the MFN clause, especially the unilateral type, is relied upon by a state as a tool to attract foreign investment.

To illustrate this point, the base case will be concretized by adding more details and another version. First of all, suppose that in Base Case 1, A, B and C all have tax treaties among each other, and all those treaties include the MFN clause regarding the withholding tax rate on interest. The original rates in the three treaties are identically 10%. Now, C has negotiated such a rate as lowered to 5% with A in their DTA, which means A will impose a preferable rate on investors of C. The MFN clause between A and B will then be triggered; the same rate will apply to B's investors in A. If these MFN clauses in this triangle scenario all provide the two-way treatment, the same change will happen to B and C as the source states. The cross-border investments from and to either A, B and C will face only a 5% withholding tax on interest, so that the overall tax burden on investment within the group of ABC will be decreased. The consideration of taxation will be less weighted in capital movement.

However, a more realistic version of the base case is that the 'conduction chain' of MFN clauses is often broken. When the mutual or group MFN treatment is not available, the unilateral MFN clause in a state's tax treaty with another country will especially attract investment from that country, for the preferable treatment will be maintained in the state. For example, in Base Case 2, A provides unilateral MFN treatment to B in their DTA, while C has MFN arrangements with neither A nor B. In this new situation, if A provides a lower rate from 10% to 5% to C, A will also accord such a rate to B. In contrast, if the rate for B further drops to 3%, C is not entitled to such favourable treatment. Base Case 2 has identified that in the real world, where bilateral or multilateral MFN is rare,[847] a unilateral MFN can guarantee the target country is treated no worse than any other country in the source state. The source country can thus gain an advantage over its competitors, attracting the target country's investment.

*Figure 7.4 Base Cases Illustrating MFN Clauses*

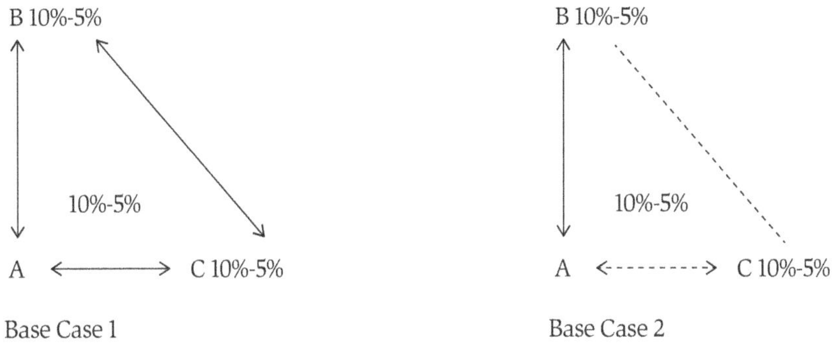


### *7.5.4.3 New Developments of MFN in China*

In general, China has few MFN clauses in its extensive tax treaty network, consistent with the overall situation in the world. However, the recent move in the DTA with Chile provides us with a new window to think through the implications of MFN. China and Chile signed their first tax treaty in 2015, and Chile officially endorsed BRI in 2018. The China-Chile tax treaty is annexed to a protocol, of which Article 10 has prescribed an MFN clause regarding the withholding rate on interest.[848] The MFN treatment is provided unilaterally by Chile to China, saying that in the case that Chile applies a lower rate in the treaty with a third country for interest payment from Chile, the same low rate will then be provided to China as well. In 2018, two years after the China-Chile DTA took effect, the MFN clause was triggered since Chile had negotiated a lower rate

847. For the comprehensive collection of the existing MFN clauses in the global bilateral tax treaty network, *see* IBFD website-Tax Research Platform-Treaties-MFN.
848. 'In the event that pursuant to an Agreement concluded with a country after the date of signature of this Agreement, Chile agrees to a lower rate of tax in paragraph 2 of Article 11, such new rate shall automatically apply under the same conditions as established in that other Agreement, for the purposes of this Agreement when the provision of the first-mentioned Agreement becomes applicable, in particular with reference to financial institutions wholly owned by the government. In such case, the competent authorities shall by mutual agreement settle the mode of application of this paragraph.', STA, 'Protocol to Agreement Between the Government of The People's Republic of China and the Government of the Republic of Chile for the Elimination of Double Taxation and the Prevention of Tax Evasion and Avoidance with Respect to Taxes on Income' https://www.chinatax.gov.cn/chinatax/n810341/n810770/c1644352/5027078/files/16443522.pdf accessed 4 December 2023.

with Japan and Italy.[849] As a result, the two countries through the Exchange of Notes modified the original interest article in 2018.

The implications of this new development should be considered by both signatory parties. On the one hand, it should be noted that before the treaty with China, Chile had already been a veteran in adopting the MFN clause in its DTAs. By now, there are twenty-two DTAs that contain the MFN clause, and the majority of them are with OECD countries. Combined with the earlier analysis, the intention of Chile to embrace the MFN is clear, especially considering most OECD countries use the exemption method to eliminate double taxation. Chile aims to level the playing field, at least in terms of certain tax aspects for those capital-exporting countries; the economic efficiency will be enhanced probably at the cost of reciprocity. The MFN clauses will increase the horizontal attraction over its fellow South American countries as well.

On the other hand, on the side of China, because of the successful application of the MFN clause with Chile, its competitive advantage of tax policy is sealed. The treaty with Chile is not the first that contains an MFN clause, even though the total number is indeed tiny. What makes the MFN clause with Chile of significance is not about the content, but it is the first of such being effectively activated and unilaterally given to China, which also denotes the willingness of China to innovate in DTA design.[850] The earlier MFN clauses are either bilateral like that with The Philippines,[851] or unilaterally given to other countries like The Netherlands.[852] In any event, the MFN clauses remain on the paper. The activated MFN clause will further add forces to the position of China as both the largest trade partner of and exporter to Chile, among other capital exporters including Japan and Italy. That particularly relates to BRI, which is expected to deepen the economic relationship between the two countries.

#### *7.5.4.4 The Shifted Position of China*

MFN clause has a special status in the general institutions of international tax law. In the current circumstances that a multilateral or regional tax treaty is not around the

849. 'I hereby inform you that the condition for this (MFN) clause to apply has been fulfilled, since Chile concluded after the date of signature of the Convention with China, a convention with Japan and another with Italy that contemplates lower source tax rates for interests than those contained in the Convention between Chile and China.', STA, 'Exchange of Notes of China and Chile Tax Authorities in 2018 (2018年中智税务机关照会文件)' https://www.chinatax.gov.cn/n810341/n810770/c1644352/5027078/files/16443521.pdf accessed 4 December 2023.
850. 'Coming of Age: China's Leveraging of BEPS' (10 December 2018) https://www.internationaltaxreview.com/article/2a68raha94goaj1osa4ff/coming-of-age-chinas-leveraging-of-beps accessed 25 November 2023.
851. Sta, 'Protocol to the Agreement Between the Government of The People's Republic of China and the Government of the Republic of the Philippines for the Avoidance of Double Taxation and the Prevention of Fiscal Evasion with Respect to Taxes on Income' Art. 2 https://www.chinatax.gov.cn/chinatax/n810341/n810770/c1153616/5027045/files/11536163.pdf accessed 4 December 2023.
852. Sta, 'Protocol to the Agreement between the Government of the People's Republic of China and the Kingdom of the Netherlands for the Avoidance of Double Taxation and the Prevention of Fiscal Evasion with Respect to Taxes on Income' Art. IX https://www.chinatax.gov.cn/chinatax/n810341/n810770/c1152939/5026985/files/11529391.pdf?eqid=af89a3b50000a9f8000000464377bcc accessed 4 December 2023.

corner, the reciprocity and privacy of DTA are material obstacles to the acceptance of the MFN clause. The adoption and practice of the MFN clause in the global tax treaty network are thus not common. In contrast, the non-discrimination article, which shares the equal treatment principle with MFN, is routine in DTAs. However, the deviated reality of non-discrimination and MFN does not cut the link that they both target the negative economic effect of unequal treatment. Based on that, countries should have been obsessed with the MFN clause. Due to the restrictions, though, countries may retreat to providing unilateral MFN treatment utilizing the MFN clause as an instrument to attract investment. On the mirror side, there may also be countries that demand the MFN treatment proactively in that it maintains their relative competitiveness.

The above case roughly echoes the track of the MFN clause in China, which sheds some light on the theme of this chapter, for the shifted position of China corresponds to the transition of ITRC from SOT to ROT. Before the China-Chile treaty, though remaining deactivated and with exceptions,[853] the MFN clauses of China were introduced for the sake of its value of attracting capital. For example, China unilaterally provided MFN treatment to the Netherlands in 1987. The case of the United States is not that straightforward, but according to 'substance over form', the MFN clause with the United States that specifies the sparing credit in their 1984 Exchange of Notes serves the same purpose for China.[854] In this phase, MFN is one of the characteristics that contribute to the so-called SOT system, when the focus of STA was to attract foreign capital or safeguard its source taxing rights. In more recent times, China either withdrew the unilateral MFN treatment to other countries; for example, the unilateral MFN treatment to the Netherlands was cancelled in their renegotiated treaty in 2014, or as discussed, China was taking MFN treatment from Chile. Especially for the latter, STA opened a new door out of the sight of OECD or UN MTC serving the redirected goals of ITRC towards ROT against the background of BRI.

## 7.6 CHAPTER CONCLUSION

The changes surveyed and analysed in accordance with the approach illuminated earlier have verified the proposition made in section 7.3. The international tax regime of China, propelled by the forces of BRI, shows a clear trend of transforming from a

853. For example, the exception is that with Vietnam, in which the MFN treatment is given unilaterally to China by Vietnam, *see* STA, 'Exchange of Notes Between Government of the People's Republic of China and Government of the Socialist Republic of Vietnam (中越照会文件)' https://www.chinatax.gov.cn/n810341/n810770/c1153436/5027029/files/11534367.pdf accessed 4 December 2023.

854. As analysed earlier regarding the function of sparing credit, here the MFN clause is a tool for China to attract investment from the United States. 'Both sides agree that a tax sparing credit shall not be provided in Article 22 of this Agreement at this time. However, the Agreement shall be promptly amended to incorporate a tax sparing credit provision if the United States hereafter amends its laws concerning the provision of tax sparing credits, or the United States reaches agreement on the provisions of a tax sparing credit with any other country.', STA, 'Exchange of Notes of between China and the United States (中美照会文件)' https://www.chinatax.gov.cn/n810341/n810770/c1153055/5026996/files/115305510.pdf accessed 4 December 2023.

source-oriented to a residence-oriented tax system. The STA, either in formulating domestic tax laws or negotiating double tax agreements, bears more and more residence than source thinking.

As explained in sections 7.4 and 7.5, from a domestic rule-making perspective, the improved tax credit system and CFC regime, respectively, ease the burden and defend against base erosion; from the perspective of bilateral tax treaties, the expanding breadth of China's tax treaty network, among other dimensions, is paving the way for Chinese companies to go global. In terms of depth, the changes in sparing credit, withholding tax liability and the MFN clause both signal the transformation of China's position in tax treaties.

The trend is real, and this chapter further anticipates that such transformation to residence-oriented taxation is an ongoing process. This does not mean China is loosening its taxing rights as the state of source. Actions have also been taken to attract foreign investment or combat source base erosion, but mostly they stay at the level of rule-administration rather than rule-making.[855] In contrast, the rule-based changes that lead to residence-oriented taxation have been revealed from top to bottom, and the construction of BRI has accelerated the transformation and made it more observable.

855. STA on Issues Concerning Expanding the Applicable Scope of the Policy of Temporary Exemption of Withholding Tax on the Direct Investment Made by Overseas Investors with Distributed Profits (国家税务总局公告2018年第53号 国家税务总局关于扩大境外投资者以分配利润直接投资暂不征收预提所得税政策适用范围有关问题的公告) 2018 (STA Announcement No. 53 [2018]).

CHAPTER 8

# Strategical Viability of China Exploring Formulary Apportionment

*This chapter examines the strategic viability of China adopting formulary apportionment in the context of international tax governance, positing that such an approach aligns with China's evolving international tax strategy and offers potential first-mover advantages in reshaping the global tax order. It begins by analysing China's multifaceted role in the international tax landscape as a follower, challenger, and reformist, highlighting its transition from a source-based to a residence-oriented tax policy, influenced by initiatives like the Belt and Road. The chapter explores China's dissatisfaction with the arm's length standard and its preference for contribution-based transfer pricing and location-specific advantages, which reflect a unique supply-demand philosophy of value creation. These policies, particularly the Value Contribution Apportionment Method, reveal China's inclination toward a three-factor formulary apportionment model, incorporating assets, labour, and sales. By harmonizing its dual roles as a 'world factory' and 'world market', China seeks to address inequities in the current origin-based tax regime. Despite tensions with OECD approaches, the chapter argues that China's strategic position and reformist ambitions make it well-suited to pioneer formulary apportionment, potentially advancing international tax governance toward greater fairness and robustness.*

## 8.1 INTRODUCTION

As global tax policies evolve, China's strategic role in shaping international tax governance is gaining prominence. This chapter investigates a pivotal question: Can China take the lead in pioneering formulary apportionment on the international stage With China's ongoing transformation from a source-based to a residence-based tax system and its rising influence in international tax matters, exploring formulary apportionment may offer the country substantial advantages, including the coveted position of a first-mover in this emerging tax policy area.

The previous chapter has captured the changes in China's international tax law under the direct implications of the BRI. Besides unravelling the concrete fact that China is on the verge of transforming from a typical source state to a residence-oriented state in terms of international tax policy, which is in itself an important backdrop for considering the prospect of Chinese formulary apportionment, it also implicitly denotes that the governance of international taxation of China is currently under strategical revamp to serve the interests and goals set at the top level.

In addition to this, the ensuing discussions of this chapter will first conduct closer examinations of China's international tax policy, especially in relation to transfer pricing which has been left untouched in the earlier chapters, to ascertain the presumptive congruence between formulary apportionment and China's overall strategies of international taxation.

The quest in the first component of this chapter, as described above, has its focal point on the 'particularity' of China attempting to be the first mover in exploring formulary apportionment. The second component, however, focuses on the 'universality' of China's tentative move. The prior chapters, especially those on the ALS, the historical trajectory of formulary apportionment and the evaluation of the BEPS Project, have depicted piecemeal how the general landscape of the international tax regime evolves.

This chapter contributes the final piece to the jigsaw by introducing the 'experimental' formulary apportionment by China against the international tax order under transformation. It serves to elucidate that by introducing formulary apportionment, in either form, China may advance international tax governance to the next level, both in terms of conceptual consistency and robustness against existing problems. In this course, China may also be reciprocated by the first-mover advantages as what the United States had historically undergone.

## 8.2 THE CONGRUENCE BETWEEN THE CHINESE INTERNATIONAL TAX STRATEGY AND FORMULARY APPORTIONMENT

In the very beginning, it should be noted that China's official stance on formulary apportionment was rather implicit. The unequivocal declaration that China should launch the campaign for international formulary apportionment can hardly be seen. However, the proof undergirding China's preference or at least support for formulary apportionment has been more than abundant, either in subjective or objective aspects. This section unveils them in order.

### 8.2.1 The Triple-Faced China in the International Tax Landscape

Unlike the major Western economies, China is not among the founders of the international tax regime. It has only been nearly four decades since China's international tax system was built from scratch. As pointed out in the prior chapter, therefore, China is a follower and norm taker of the West-centric international tax regime most of the time. However, the 'youth' in this respect does not prevent the integrity of the course of evolution of China's international tax system, which is instead condensed into this short period of time.

The 1980s is the 'Great Bang' emblematic of China breaking the isolation of the global economy and politics, when the first bilateral tax treaty and domestic tax law with foreign-related provisions were concluded.[856] Since then, China's international tax policy as a whole roughly assumes a phased trajectory. The first stage, extending till the 1990s, is characterized by China regarding its international tax policy as a tool for attracting foreign investment, as many of the tax treaties at this stage were entered with OECD countries, and the domestic tax law provided additional preferential treatment to foreign investors. The tax treaty network further expanded to developing countries in the 2000s, when China began to express its interest as a capital exporter by emphasizing its residence tax base and eliminating double taxation. In the meantime, China overhauled its enterprise tax law and abrogated the dual structure of income tax that differentiated between foreign corporate taxpayers and their Chinese counterparts. The third stage is marked by the advent of the global financial crisis. The global tax agenda turned to address the tax avoidance and evasion of large MNEs following the crisis. The repercussions on China's international tax strategies are that, on the one hand, the tendency continues that the treaty network further extends in which China's strategic intentions of facilitating outbound investment and preserving the residence tax base are increasingly seen; on the other hand, from 2012 onwards, China eventually sets out to seize the opportunity to participate in the campaign of international tax reform mandated by the G20.[857]

Ascertaining China's position in the current international tax order as in the currently ongoing third stage of its own trajectory is pivotal for contemplating China's international tax strategies that may harbour congruence with formulary apportionment that can corroborate the viability of this chapter's thought experiment. To encapsulate, China has multiple faces in the existing international tax landscape. China is simultaneously a *follower* of Western countries that set up and maintain the international tax regime, a *challenger* to the international tax order that has long been West-centric and partial to developed countries, and a *reformist* that carries out actions in line with the pre-established objectives and strategies. Ostensibly, these different faces conflict with each other, but they rest comfortably from the perspective of China's status quo and what it aims to achieve.

### 8.2.2 China as a Follower

China has a distinct culture, history and political and economic system from Western countries, especially Europe and the United States. Many areas of the Chinese legal

856. Japan is China's first tax treaty partner, *see* STA, 'Japan' (28 March 2011) https://www.chinatax.gov.cn/n810341/n810770/c1153042/content.html accessed 3 December 2023.
857. OECD, 'Los Cabos, Mexico 2012' (OECD) https://g20.org/summit-and-logos/2012-los-cabos/ accessed 25 November 2023.

system are idiosyncratic, such as the law of the land that strictly forbids the private sales of land. This is in accord with the official title of China's legal system as 'the socialist legal system with Chinese characteristics'. However, tax law, especially its international aspects, is among the closest mimicries of its Western counterparts. This is the case not just in terms of the content and structure of tax treaties, but even more in the design of domestic tax laws. The latter is evidenced in part by the discussions of the previous chapter, and the historical materials also reveal that the making of China's enterprise tax law was directly instructed by American specialists.[858] In the BEPS era, China sees the G20 mandate and the OECD BEPS Project as a valuable opportunity to make its voices heard and exert its influence on the future direction of the international tax regime. While not an official member of the OECD, China has been an active participator in 'hundreds of' meetings, consultations, and negotiations for the production of deliverables and outcomes of the BEPS Project.[859] According to the STA's own statistics, China had submitted fifty-two position papers and attended forty-two meetings simply for the output of the 2014 Deliverables,[860] and these numbers for the whole project are over a thousand and one hundred, respectively.[861] In addition, China took swift action by enacting new rules or amendments to immediately implement the outcomes of the seven actions in the Deliverables,[862] many of which only took months to be finalized, such as those on the general anti-avoidance rule, offshore indirect transfer and beneficial ownership.[863] To date, China has basically implemented the outcomes of all the BEPS minimum standards in its domestic laws.[864]

### 8.2.3 China as a Reformist with Ambitions

As President Xi Jinping once declared, China believes in the philosophy that 'the reform and opening up will always be an ongoing process but never be

858. Richard D Pomp and Stanley S Surrey, 'The Tax Structure of the People's Republic of China' (1979) 20 Virginia Journal of International Law 1.
859. Hearson and Prichard (n. 320) 1303.
860. General Office of STA, 'Reforming the Tax System: Seeking One Area and Living the Overall Situation: Part 3 of a Series of Reviews of National Taxation Work in 2014(改革税制:谋一域而活全局 – 2014年全国税务工作系列综述之三)' https://www.chinatax.gov.cn/n810219/n810724/n811741/c1440429/content.html accessed 4 November 2023.
861. Tizhong Liao, 'Actively Implement the Results of the G20 Tax Reform and Strive to Create a Fair and Modern International Tax System' [2017] International Taxation 10.
862. State Taxation Administration Order No. 32 General Anti-Tax Avoidance Management Measures (Trial) (国家税务总局第32号令 一般反避税管理办法（试行））2014.
863. Notice on Several Issues Related to Enterprise Income Tax Application to Indirect Transfers of Property between Non-resident Enterprises (国家税务总局公告2015年第7号 国家税务总局关于非居民企业间接转让财产企业所得税若干问题的公告) 2015 (STA Announcement No. 7 [2015]); Announcement on the Definition of 'Beneficial Ownership' under Entrusted Investments (国家税务总局公告2014年第24号 国家税务总局关于委托投资情况下认定受益所有人问题的公告) 2014 (STA Announcement No. 24 [2014]).
864. Diheng Xu, 'The Convergence and Divergence Between China's Implementation and OECD/G20 Beps Minimum Standards' [2018] World Tax Journal 471 https://doi.org/10.59403/8dmhs5 accessed 26 August 2025. NG Peter and Smith David, 'Chapter 19: China's Response to the BEPS Recommendations and the Impact on Taxpayers' in Sam Sim and Mei-June Soo (eds), *Asian Voices: BEPS and Beyond* (IBFD Publications 2017) 401-427.

completed'.[865] In the recent decade, China has launched a systemic tax reform to build up a 'modern fiscal and financial system',[866] which is a long-term goal still set in the *14th Five-Year Plan* (2021-2025).[867] Besides the reforms that aim to enhance the tax administration at all levels, the substantive reforms have at least overhauled the value-added tax, the business tax (abolished), the individual income tax and the consumption tax. With respect to international taxation, a national reform plan promulgated by the central government in 2015 clearly states China's ambitions in the arena of international taxation:[868]

(1) to become the leading force in the norm-making of international taxation. The party and the government are well aware that the influence and power of the discourse of China in international taxation are not potent. In this case, it was decided that China would proactively participate in the formulation of international tax rules, with particular reference to the G20 tax reform, the OECD Forum on Tax Administration, and the UN Committee of Experts on International Cooperation in Tax Matters. In addition, as the Western developed countries have done to China, China is now determined to take an active part in international tax assistance by providing knowledge training and technical support to help developing and low-income countries improve their tax collection and administration capabilities;
(2) to establish new international tax relationships to form a deeply integrated cooperation network for mutual benefits. China has elevated the emphasis on deepening international cooperation to an unprecedented level, based on economic globalization and the internal goal of building an open economic system. The concept of 'big country taxation' has been constantly advocated, and so has the idea of 'international vision'. It was also explicitly claimed that China would comprehensively and deeply participate in the BEPS Project. The international information exchange mechanisms concerning the Multilateral Convention on Mutual Administrative Assistance in Tax Matters and the Standard for Automatic Exchange of Financial Account Information were reinforced;
(3) China's international tax policy should proactively serve China's 'going global' strategy, which is a national scheme supporting China's business and

865. 王相坤, '改革开放只有进行时没有完成时(Reform and opening up can only be carried out but not completed)' http://theory.people.com.cn/n/2013/1128/c40537-23686027.html accessed 26 August 2025.
866. Peiyong Gao and Dehua Wang, 'The Reform and Development of Fiscal and Taxation System in "the 13th Five-Year" Period' (2016) 1 Finance Forum.
867. Xinhua News Agency, 'Outline of the 14th Five-Year Plan (2021-2025) for National Economic and Social Development and the Long-Range Objectives Through the Year 2035(中华人民共和国国民经济和社会发展第十四个五年规划和2035年远景目标纲要)' (13 March 2021) https://www.gov.cn/xinwen/2021-03/13/content_5592681.htm accessed 4 December 2023.
868. Xinhua News Agency, 'The General Office of the Communist Party of China Central Committee and the General Office of the State Council Have Issued the "Plan for Deepening the Reform of the National and Local Tax Collection and Management System" (中共中央办公厅 国务院办公厅印发深化国税、地税征管体制改革方案)' (24 December 2015) https://www.gov.cn/gongbao/content/2016/content_2979704.htm accessed 14 April 2023.

> capital-exporting overseas. The reform plan confirms the priorities of the 'going global' strategy, which are the 'Belt and Road' initiative and the international cooperation in production capacity and equipment manufacturing. For these purposes, the STA is required to accelerate the progress of negotiations on the conclusion or modification of double taxation agreements, enhance consulting services for overseas taxation policy, establish routine communication mechanisms with major foreign tax authorities, and help to settle tax-related disputes for companies going overseas timely.

The G20/OECD BEPS Project is opportune for China to put its own agenda into effect. The spirit of reformism and the ambitions were crystallized by China's swift actions to implement the outcomes of the BEPS Project through domestic laws or tax treaties. According to Liao, the former Director General of the International Department of the STA, China's deep involvement in the project has at least made a material difference to the guiding principles and the fields of digital economy, intangibles, common reporting standard and so forth.[869] China has also made substantial contributions to or exerted its influence on the UN or OECD double taxation models and transfer pricing guidelines.[870] In addition, China has been the initiator, founder and leader in the framework of tax cooperation under the Belt and Road Initiative. For the first time in history, China has played as a norm-maker rather than a norm-taker in the arena of international taxation.

### 8.2.4 China as a Challenger

Depicting China only as a follower in shaping the international tax institutions misses another half of the picture. The above discussions of China's ambitions in the field of international taxation have already elicited China's interest in shaking the international tax landscape. To be specific, China's face of a challenger is manifested in at least three interrelated aspects.

First, China's overall approach to its participation in the recent international tax projects is not playing hand-raising robot, which instead can be coined as *'confrontational cooperation'*:

> On the one hand, China has just been there for the meetings, negotiations and consultations for the agenda, its voices have been heard and indeed made some differences and most of its reform measures are in line with the OECD recommendations. Cooperation is China's keynote of its engagement with either G20, OECD or the United Nations, which contrasts with other large developing countries that have expressed discontent with the OECD approaches.[871]
>
> On the other hand, following the keynote of 'proactive' participation, China's involvement in international tax events has exerted real influences and strengthened China's power of discourse. More importantly, the changes in the

869. Liao (n. 861).
870. Liao Tizhong, 'A Fair and Modern International Tax System: Review and Exploration' [2019] International Taxation 5.
871. Hearson and Prichard (n. 320) 1303.

economic and geopolitical positions enable China to see itself differently from where it was before the last decade, when China was basically absent in the forum of international tax rule-making. In a nutshell, China has confronted the orthodox institutions of international taxation, especially in relation to some of the classic income allocation models that systematically favour the traditional powers in the West. This is manifested in China's steadfast propositions from the perspectives of China as a world factory and a world market, its rising position in the global value chain, and its national strategy to export business and capital, of which the details are unravelled in the ensuing sections.

Second, China's understanding of the value creation discourse diverges from the OECD's perception as reflected in the outcomes of the BEPS Project. The evaluations of the BEPS Project have revealed that the OECD was hesitant and equivocal on the normative interpretation of the guiding mantra 'income should be taxed where value is created' in the early stage. With the benefit of hindsight, it turns out that the OECD ultimately recalibrated the value creation principle as a *defensive* weapon targeting the tax avoidance strategies of MNEs and the complicit loopholes of tax treaties or domestic tax laws.[872] As coined by Mason, the OECD essentially utilizes the value creation nomenclature to endorse its 'full taxation' norm, which is notably supported by the four minimum standards.[873] At the core of the norm is that income should be taxed where and *wherever* real economic activities are located. The course has hardly been altered by the innovative post-BEPS work on digitization. For one thing, the output has scarcely referred to the mantra of value creation;[874] for another, the ring-fencing approach and the limited application of non-ALP allocation methods following the three-tier approach, to a large degree, vitiate the revolutionary significance of the work.

In contrast, China perceived the value creation mantra principally as a theoretical justification for enlarging China's pie in the international distribution of taxable income. Consistent with the confrontational cooperation approach, China has taken a discreet approach in championing this understanding.

To quote Liao, 'the proposition that profits should be taxed in places where economic activities originate and where values are created *led by* China has become the guiding principle of BEPS Project, which has made important contributions to safeguarding the interests of *developing countries* and promoting the smooth completion of various action items, and played a unique role for enhancing (China's) power of discourse'.[875] Therefore, China's perception of the value creation principle is an *offensive* instrument that seeks to ensure the interests of developing countries *vis-a-vis* the establishment, namely, the traditional Western powers in the existing international tax regime. This is in accord with China's Position Paper in the UN Transfer Pricing

872. Li, Bao and Li (n. 74). David Quentin, 'Corporate Tax Reform and "Value Creation": Towards Unfettered Diagonal Re-Allocation across the Global Inequality Chain' (2017) 7 Accounting, Economics, and Law: A Convivium. Langbein and Fuss (n. 74). Devereux and Vella (n. 306).
873. Mason (n. 355) 370.
874. Post-BEPS work on digitalization, *see* OECD, 'Action 1 Tax Challenges Arising from Digitalisation' https://www.oecd.org/en/topics/policy-issues/base-erosion-and-profit-shifting-beps.html accessed 4 December 2023.
875. Liao (n. 861).

Manual, which is an authoritative and comprehensive source unravelling its stance on value creation, which contrasts with that of the OECD.[876] China not only gives credit to the positive progress achieved under the light of the value creation rhetoric but also poses a series of fundamental questions from which China's systematic perception of value creation is readily observable: does our international tax system become 'fairer and less biased' after the BEPS reform? How should the incomes that are 'emancipated' from tax havens be distributed among non-tax haven countries? And, how should the pie of taxable income be shared between the place of real economic activities and the place of value creation? Value creation for China is a twofold principle that not only contains the 'full taxation' norm but also carries more inquiry into the modernization of the long-established income allocation model, especially as to its fairness between developed and developing countries. In relation to the second component, it is noteworthy that China points out that the locations of real business activity and value creation do not necessarily coincide, which implies that the OECD's full-taxation norm is only halfway fulfilment of the value creation mantra. It raises an open question as to how to further align taxation with value creation, to which China seems to already have the answers taking into consideration the rest of the content of the Position Paper. The ensuing discussions will shed more light on this.

Where does China put itself in light of its perception of the value creation mantra? The confrontational cooperation approach is vindicated again as China does not seek to weaponize value creation for 'vengeance' on the international tax 'establishment'.[877] While China often sees itself at the front line defending the interests of developing countries, which is pervasive in the UN Transfer Pricing Manual, the contemplation of China's circumstances has made China cautious to carry forward the classic dualism power struggle between residence and source. As stated above, China rather renews the inquiry on the basis of value creation starting from China's own unique position, as detached from the traditional discourse. This can be conveniently observed from the analysis of the Deputy Director of the STA Zhang when he was in office, which will be further examined in combination with China's dissatisfaction with the ALS:

> For many years, China has been one of the largest hosting states for foreign direct investment in the world, and it has assumed the role of '*world factory*'. In recent years, with the rapid economic development and the continuous improvement of people's purchasing power, China has become a 'world market'. As a place of production and consumption, China creates and contributes huge value to the world, and these contributions to value creation should get its due return in the profit distribution of transnational economic activities.

In the meantime, with the implementation of the 'going global' strategy, China will soon become a net capital exporter. In relation to the income from international

876. United Nations, 'Practical Manual on Transfer Pricing for Developing Countries (2017)' (n. 282) s. D.2.1.5.
877. Lee Sheppard, 'Revenge of the Source Countries?' [2005] *TNT* 54;Lee Sheppard, 'Revenge of the Source Countries? Part 2: Royalties' [2005] *TNT* 191; Lee Sheppard, 'Revenge of the Source Countries? Part 6: Subsidiary as PE' [2006] *TNT* 200; Lee Sheppard, 'Revenge of the Source Countries? Part 5: Throwing BRICs' [2006] *TNT* 123; Lee Sheppard, 'Revenge of the Source Countries? Part 4: Who Gets the Bill?' [2005] *TNT* 210.

investment and transactions, China acts as both the source country and the residence country. Therefore, when China participates in the international coordination of taxation, it is necessary to defend our taxing rights and interests as the source country, whereas one should also not go to another extreme so as to prevent future international taxation rules from being opposed to the outbound investment of China.[878]

The last facet of China being a challenger to the orthodox international tax order is its dissatisfaction with the ALS and the income allocation model underpinned by it. As discussed in Chapter 2, the ALS emerged originally for the taxation of a permanent establishment, and later on, as a national administrative practice, was transplanted to the taxation of separate enterprises, becoming a statutory norm in international taxation. Operating in combination with the other set of basic norms, the ALS is one of, if not the most, fundamental norm in the existing income allocation model of international taxation. At the core of the standard, there lies the fiction that the associated enterprises are commercially separate, and thus, the internal transactions can be priced by comparison to the true uncontrolled dealings. Since the OECD took the torch, the arm's standard has been deified, whereas the transfer pricing methods that materialize it are in constant turmoil which reflects the theoretical and practical constraints of the standard inherent in itself. The BEPS reforms are the latest efforts to 'modernize' the ALS by ingesting the value creation dictations. These reforms and the post-BEPS actions on the digital economy, to a certain extent, have undermined the theological status of the standard.

China has pioneered the tendency of incremental departures from the ALS before, during and after the BEPS Project, and deliberately calibrated the standard according to its own understanding of the standard's constraints and its strategical goals in the international tax landscape. Such is first manifested in China's preference for contribution-based transfer pricing analysis over the traditional risk-based analysis, which has been upheld by China since the pre-BEPS era. The contribution analysis is characterized by the accentuation of an entity's contribution to the value creation of the whole enterprise as the basis for determining the return to it from the internal transactions. This approach, therefore, has affinity with the post-BEPS ALS being economic substance and function-based as stretched by the BEPS reforms. It departs from the strict separate entity hypothesis and the risk-based approach of the pre-BEPS ALS. Second, what has already become a hallmark of the Chinese approach to transfer pricing is the adherence to location-specific advantages over the years, which is where China's perception of the value creation leitmotif plays its role. In a nutshell, China considers that value is created by the interplay of the supply side and demand side. Income is generated not simply by production, and price is determined by the interface of input and output. The BEPS items on transfer pricing eventually include the location advantages as a comparability factor, the methodology of which, however, contrasts

878. Interview with Zhang Zhiyong, 'Strengthen Global Tax Cooperation and Combat International Tax Evasion: Zhang Zhiyong, Deputy Director of the STA, Answered Reporters' Questions (加强全球税收合作 打击国际逃避税：国家税务总局副局长张志勇答记者问)' (1 December 2014) https://www.gov.cn/xinwen/2014-12/01/content_2785317.htm accessed 4 December 2023.

that of China's supply-demand view of value creation. These two aspects will be discussed in depth as separate sections.

### 8.2.5 China to Switch the Course: Between the World Factory and the World Market

The above section has revealed the multi-faced China with respect to its position in the international tax landscape and its strategies for international taxation. No more countries have simultaneously shown such a complex and ostensibly paradoxical picture. In order to unscramble the underlying congruence between China's international tax strategy and formulary apportionment, this section further examines some practical evidence with respect to China's international tax strategy harbouring that formulary apportionment could be a viable choice for China to further its goals of international taxation. The following discussions are organized into three parts. The first two address China's transfer pricing strategies that bear the methodology of formulary apportionment, and the third part delivers an integrated view.

#### *8.2.5.1 From the Perspective of a 'World Factory': The Contribution Analysis Approach and Formulary Apportionment*

One of the major reforms of transfer pricing since the 2010 update of the OECD TPG is the increasing weight of risks in transfer pricing analysis.[879] In the General Guidance of the TPG, the analysis of risks in commercial or financial relations equipped with a detailed mechanism leads the steps of the functional analysis.[880] Such a risk-based approach is the corollary to the transactional approach to the application of the ALP, as it links the assumption of risks to the expected return of the transaction in line with the regular commercial and market practice. The risk-based approach could be abused for tax avoidance purposes since risk assumption is under the control of the MNE group simply through contractual arrangements. Compared to functions and assets, risks are much easier to shift and manipulate between associated parties. The BEPS reforms of the TPG such as the recharacterization of contracts and the enhanced risk analysis and the improved profit split method already constituted a pull-out of the risk-based approach to restrict risk-related base erosion and profit shifting opportunities. From the perspective of income allocation, the risk-based approach is also a significant concern for source countries like China that host massive direct investments as they deem the approach having stripped unduly the incomes away because risks are often closely related to the central management company or the member responsible for research and development or intangibles rather than the manufacturing or assembly affiliates located in the source countries.

The contribution analysis is not a formal step in the process of comparability analysis as endorsed by the OECD in the newest Transfer Pricing Guidelines. Instead,

879. Richard and Andrus (n. 10) para. 2.123.
880. OECD, *TPG 2017* (n. 182) s. D.1.2.1.

it is one of the approaches to splitting the profits for the application of the transactional profit split method, according to which the profits from the related transactions are combined and then allocated between the associated parties on the basis of their relative contribution to the generation of the overall profit.[881] Considering the circumstances where the TPSM offers its solutions, the contribution analysis is accentuated and has advantages when: (1) all the related enterprises engaged in the controlled transactions are making unique and valuable contributions; or (2) there is a high degree of integration between the related enterprises, meaning that they are highly-related or inter-dependent on each other; or (3) there are substantial group synergies attributable to the deliberate concerted group actions, which should be distributed to all the involved group members.[882]

It can be derived from the above that the contribution analysis is specifically applicable to circumstances where it is difficult to determine the arm's length pricing by the traditional transactional approach under the separate accounting method. Against the background of the TPSM, the contribution analysis, therefore, contains the methodologies of formulary apportionment in seeing the examined group members as a whole and using some allocation key to split the overall or residual profit. Consequently, the contribution analysis, albeit being subsidiary to the TPSM, effectively sits at the tension area between the arm's length orthodoxy and the heterodox formulary apportionment. The OECD TPG confirms this point when introducing its repulsion for global formulary apportionment.[883]

As among the general efforts of the BEPS reform, the importance of the contribution analysis has been enhanced, at least on the face of it. First, the new TPG substitutes the most appropriate method for the strict hierarchy of transfer pricing methods, under which the TPSM was merely a last resort. Second, as another area where material progress was achieved, the transfer pricing documentation requires the taxpayer to analyse the individual entities' principal contributions to value creation within the group. However, the OECD, through these reforms, does not intend to seek qualitative changes in contribution analysis or the TPSM generally. The most appropriate method approach does not really establish an equal and free application of the non-traditional methods, including the TPSM; the previous hierarchy of transfer pricing methods is not erased by only loosened. In addition, even if the PSM was used, the application and outcome were designed to approximate the fictional arm's length result rather than being truly in line with the formulary apportionment methodology. For instance, the OECD TPG still recommends the use of any comparable data available while vigorously repudiating the use of a prescriptive list of criteria or profit-splitting factors.[884] Similarly, the documentation requirements merely see the contribution analysis as part of a brief written functional analysis in the master file.[885] The

881. *Ibid.*, 25.
882. *Ibid.*, 1.162.
883. *Ibid.*, 1.19.
884. *Ibid.*, 2.138.
885. OECD, *TPG 2017* (n. 182) Annex I to Chapter V Transfer Pricing Documentation – Master file.

contribution analysis, therefore, has limited significance in the transfer pricing regime, either practically or normatively.

China's approach to contribution analysis, however, contrasts that of the OECD and resembles much of the formulary apportionment methodologies, in that China not only sees the contribution analysis as a solution to the risk-based approach but also applies it to effectively accommodate a formulary apportionment method for transfer pricing analysis. China's choice in this respect validates the practical values of formulary apportionment vis-à-vis the theoretical/practical weakness of the ALS, which is, in turn, accentuated by the awareness of the economic realities of China being a world factory.

The contribution analysis is a pertinent lens through which to inquire into China's stance on formulary apportionment against its general international tax strategies as to the taxation of MNEs. First of all, China exhibits its face as a follower as it concurs with the OECD's reform spirit of altering the previous path of a risk-based approach to transfer pricing. China complained from the perspective of developing countries hosting MNEs' production operations or providing labour or natural resources that MNEs can under-compensate the local entities in the arrangements of toll or contract manufacturing, limited risk distribution and limited risk service provider. This is most notably the case for China as a world factory, which is a top destination for global MNEs to turn their R&D investment into real products. To tackle these challenges, China has upheld the contribution analysis or directly the global formulary apportionment. Based on this, China was recognized as the first country that had officially pronounced to support and explore the application of the global formulary apportionment as a realistic and appropriate alternative to the ALS.[886]

The first scenario in consideration is that the MNEs have established multiple affiliates in China and dispersed the functions and risks of the business among these entities, each of which is thus assigned a limited return. A mirror case is when all the functions, such as manufacturing, marketing, distribution, or R&D, are concentrated in a single entity, yet each of these functions is compensated with a limited routine return. In both situations, China tends to break the artificial boundaries set between the entities or the multiple functions of a single entity and take a holistic view of the group of entities or functions. Accordingly, the appropriate return to the single-function entities is determined by considering them as a whole, either in terms of functions or risks. It follows that the return to China as a manufacturing centre is deemed proper only in light of its contribution to the profitability of the MNE. The economic substance matters more than the arm's length presumptions.

China goes a step further in another scenario of transfer pricing relating to the electronic manufacturing services industry, which is an emblem of China's image as a world factory. This sector is characterized by foreign MNEs with headquarters outside of China meanwhile relying heavily on the manufacturing, assembly operations, labour and tangible assets in China. While the transactional net margin method is often used to determine the transfer price of the controlled manufacturing contracts, it is faced

886. Stanley I Langbein and Max R Fuss, 'The OECD/G20-BEPS-Project and the Value Creation Paradigm' (2018) 51 International Lawyer 259, 101.

with increasing challenges attributed to industrial centralization and, thus, the lack of comparable. China considers the uses of profit indicators whatsoever for the application of the TNMM underestimates the profit contribution of the Chinese manufacturers. It is the risk-based approach that gives China a sense of unfairness. On the one hand, these, mostly the western, MNEs have exploited huge value from the manufacturing resources, including workforce, factories, and management personnel. According to the Global Manufacturing Competitiveness Index published intermittently since 2010 by Deloitte, which weighs comprehensively the hard factors such as physical infrastructure, labour and materials and soft factors such as talent-driven innovation, legal and regulatory system, healthcare, and supplier network, China has ranked No. 1 for its competitiveness of manufacturing in the recent decade.[887] While China is often put in the group of BRICS, it leads the way ahead of another four countries, and this ascendancy sees no signs of vitiation as the position of China in manufacturing has been institutionalized from being scale-driven to competitiveness advantage-driven.[888] On the other hand, the Chinese affiliates are assigned a relatively low level of profit being contract or toll manufacturers that bear low risks, to which the application of either transactional or profit transfer pricing methods renders similar results. In comparison, MNEs are allowed to divert the majority of value to developed countries or tax havens where the headquarters or the intellectual properties are located.

In this case, China suggests the contribution analysis approach that has a global perspective of the MNE group and determines the proper remuneration to the Chinese entities according to their roles and contributions to the entire value chain of the group. It is descriptively conceived that the contribution of the Chinese manufacturers, in turn, should be weighed by the assets and labour relative to the whole group. The approach is thus a two-factor global formulary apportionment. This is further accentuated in a Report of the STA presenting that China understands the OECD BEPS value creation mantra as not only requiring 'taxation to align with economic activities' but also 'distribution of taxable income to align with economic activities', and that the economic activities are tested by the labour and assets employed in the business. This applies especially to the MNEs with no special intangible assets but mainly take orders for manufacturing. 'when the workers, wages, and fixed assets of its subsidiary in China account for a significant proportion of the global group, the profit distribution to the subsidiary must be adapted, synchronized, and matched with this proportion'.[889] In the domestic laws that internalize the outcomes of BEPS Action 13, China generalizes the application of contribution analysis beyond its subsidiarity to the TPSM by requiring taxpayers to disclose in the local file the principles and results of the group profit distribution in the global value chain, and the local entities' contributions to the

887. Deloitte, '2016 Global Manufacturing Competitiveness Index' (Deloitte) https://www2.deloitte.com/ch/en/pages/manufacturing/articles/global-manufacturing-competitiveness-index.html accessed 4 December 2023.
888. Gary Gereffi and Joonkoo Lee, 'Why the World Suddenly Cares About Global Supply Chains' (2012) 48 Journal of Supply Chain Management 24, 24-32 https://doi.org/10.1111/j.1745-493x.2012.03271.x accessed 26 August 2025.
889. 2014-2015 International Tax Compliance Management Plan (2014-2015年度国际税收遵从管理规划) 2014.

overall or residual profit of the group no matter which transfer pricing method is selected.[890]

This is also where China's perception of value creation is further elucidated and crystallized, in addition to the fairness view and supply-demand view. China disapproves of the view that the majority of value in the entire value chain is created by research and development activities while manufacturing is only assigned a routine return. As such, value creation activities should not be differentiated according to the subjective arrangements under the control of the taxpayer; rather, their contributions to value creation should be evaluated in a neutral and objective way, for which the input of labour, assets, or capital is a viable option. Alternatively, China also proposes to assign a routine level of profit to headquarters and allow the Chinese manufacturers to retain the residual profits. This additional perspective of value creation partly coincides and partly conflicts with the fairness view and supply-demand view, which is attributable to China's twofold role of world factory and world market.

#### *8.2.5.2 From the Perspective of a 'World Market': Location-Specific Advantages and the Additional 'P' Added to the 'DEMPE'*

As discussed above, China as a world factory has reflected on the fair return to the Chinese manufacturing industry in the global value chain and endorsed the contribution analysis approach to transfer pricing that is in congruence with the formulary apportionment methodology. China also steps further to suggest the production-factor-based formulary apportionment in lieu of the arm's length transfer pricing as an alternative, supplementing and materializing its perception of the value creation principle.

In addition to this perspective, China's emerging status as the world's largest consumer market vis-à-vis its established status as a world factory has propelled China to question further the validity of the current origin-based international tax regime as underpinned by the ALS. This is in line with the multi-faced China being a follower of the Western-centric international tax regime and simultaneously a cautious challenger with reform ambitions. To be specific, China has been harbouring opposing views against the existing allocation model of taxation on MNEs established that value is principally created by the input at the supply side, according to which the majority of income is attributed to the origin places where the value is added. While the challenges to the origin-based model against the backdrop of digitalization have been well cognized, this section aims to unveil China's deeply embedded repulsion of it from the position of an emerging world market, focusing on the policies on the location-specific advantages and transfer pricing of intangibles. This, in turn, adds to the substance of China's supply-demand view of value creation, which substantiates the necessary link between China's international tax strategy and the formulary apportionment.

890. Announcement on Matters Regarding Refining the Filing of Related Party Transactions and Administration of Contemporaneous Transfer Pricing Documentation (国家税务总局公告2016年第42号 国家税务总局关于完善关联申报和同期资料管理有关事项的公告) (STA Announcement No. 42 [2016]).

The origin versus destination discourse of international taxation is based on two relative economic views on the creation of value. One is the supply approach holding that value is created at the supply side by the input of production factors, another is the supply-demand approach seeing value as created by the interplay between supply and demand, according to which both the economic contributions of factors at the supply side and the ultimate sales at the demand side should be considered.[891] The existing international tax regime has been constructed following the supply approach to assign the income principally to the origin jurisdictions, while the return to the demand/destination jurisdictions has been constricted to a minimal level. This state of affairs is more a historical and political matter than a matter of economic reasoning, as the destination states are taken into account by the international tax law merely for consideration of passive incomes through a withholding tax mechanism,[892] which is in itself a political compromise reached in the formative period.[893] The origin-dominated model is embedded in the jurisdiction of tax rules, source rules, the E threshold, and the transfer pricing regime, accentuating functions, assets, and risks. This model has sustained the functioning of the international tax regime without major problems for roughly a century. However, when the international tax regime faces any crises, its theoretical soul bears the brunt of being questioned. The supply approach of value creation is being increasingly oppugned subsequent to the Global Financial Crisis and the digitalization of the economy. Its relative alternative, the supply-demand approach has 'resurfaced' to the centre stage.

In view of this, formulary apportionment is often the resort to introducing the demand side into the value creation matrix, due to its elasticity of accommodating either the supply or demand considerations or both. In contrast, the ALS by approximating the outcome of private market should in theory determine a fair return to the demand side, yet in reality, it has failed to do so because of the inherent incomparability between highly integrated MNEs and single companies, which is increasingly the case since the quantitative economic changes are still deepening. The BEPS reform has accentuated the economic substance to redress the problems of lack of comparable and transfer pricing manipulation, which, to the contrary, reinforces the pro-origin propensity of the transfer pricing regime.

As discussed above, China has realized its emerging status as the world's largest consumer market and its idiosyncrasies such as the unparalleled size of its population and its future potential. Cognizant of the inner tensions between the status as a world factory and a world market for their implications for contemplating international tax strategy, China still upholds that the contributions of the market for value creation should be recognized and compensated in international taxation. This is where China exhibits its multiple faces one more time. The alternative of endorsing formulary apportionment employing sales factor in the single or multiple-factor formula that

891. Musgrave, 'Principles for Dividing the State Corporate Tax Base' (n. 619) 234.
892. Maarten F de Wilde, 'Tax Jurisdiction in a Digitalizing Economy: Why "Online Profits" Are so Hard to Pin Down' (2015) 43 Intertax 6 https://doi.org/10.54648/taxi2015072 accessed 26 August 2025.
893. Graetz and O'Hear (n. 56).

replaces the arm's length transfer pricing, albeit being a straightforward solution, does not seem to fit well with China's confrontational cooperation approach and the image of a follower. However, consistent with the faces of a challenger and a reformist, China discreetly carries forward its supply-demand philosophy of value creation by insisting on the location-specific advantages and adding the 'P' representing promotion activities to the DEMPE analysis of intangibles, both of which are China's efforts to enhance the weight of market contributions within of the OECD framework of transfer pricing and thus are moderate rectification of the origin-based international tax regime.

The location-specific advantages (LSA) is an umbrella concept denoting the economic features of a specific market that enable MNEs to gain enhanced financial benefits (location rents) rather than locating their businesses in alternative places.[894] The LSA can take many forms, such as location savings, market premiums, skilled labour, access to a growing market, access to a massive consumer base, advanced infrastructure, and so forth, either of which reflects the power of the market itself.[895] The issue of LSA falls within the purview of transfer pricing because the price or profitability of the intra-group transactions needs to be determined in accordance with the ALS, from which the proper return to local affiliates is achieved and the contributions of the market jurisdiction are properly compensated in light of the LSA it provided. The exact term of LSA was not found in the OECD TPG; its essentials had been addressed only marginally before the BEPS update of 2017, expressed either as 'economic circumstances' or 'market differences'.[896] The TPG 2017 incorporated the location savings, presumably also including marking premiums, and other local market features as comparability factors.[897] The United Nations acted earlier but eventually converged with the OECD approach.[898] In the post-BEPS transfer pricing regime, LSA thus becomes one of the comparability factors, and the location rents from it are determined and allocated by the normal transfer pricing methods.

As a result, the LSA is a restrained means for the market to have its weight in the international allocation of income through the transfer pricing regime, which fits well with the triangular faces of China's international tax strategy. In fact, China's emphasis on and the actual exploitation of the LSA has been topical in international tax literature.[899] Following the implementation of the BEPS outcomes, China has established an 'expansionist' approach to determining the return to the market from the existence of LSA, from which it is seen that the LSA is not the purpose in itself but a tool

894. Arnaud Ferraton, 'Location-Specific Advantages and Transfer Pricing' 26 International Transfer Pricing Journal 2019 https://doi.org/10.59403/4ecvff accessed 26 August 2025.
895. United Nations, 'Practical Manual on Transfer Pricing for Developing Countries (2017)' (n. 282) para. 2.3.2.53.
896. OECD, *TPG 1995* (n. 277) para. 1.30. OECD, *TPG 2010* (n. 327) para. 1.57.
897. OECD, *TPG 2017* (n. 182) s. D.6.
898. United Nations, 'Practical Manual on Transfer Pricing for Developing Countries (2017)' (n. 282) paras 5.3.2.38-5.3.2.45; Claire (n. 326) 491.
899. MA de Lange and PWH Lankhorst, 'The Impact of Location Advantages on the Transfer Pricing of Multinationals: On the Chinese Love for European Designer Handbags and Lower Production Costs in India' (2014) 21 International Transfer Pricing Journal https://doi.org/10.59403/3y21myg accessed 26 August 2025.
Jinyan Li, 'Location Specific Advantages: A Rising Disruptive Factor in Transfer Pricing' (2018) 71 Bulletin for International Taxation 259 https://doi.org/10.59403/bx6n4e accessed 26

to incarnate the Chinese philosophy of value creation that accentuates the separate contribution of market.

China had put the LSA into the practice of transfer pricing as early as 2008, even prior to any formal legislation of the concept itself.[900] The full picture of China's approach to LSA is assembled by the Position Paper in the UN Transfer Pricing Manual, the domestic tax legislation, and the reports of the STA. The prescriptive details of how China manages the LSA in its transfer pricing administration are provided only in the UN Transfer Pricing Manual, including the definition and the identification of LSA, and the calculation of additional profits from LSA and the methods of allocation. It also provides examples of the automotive industry and contract research and development services to illustrate the full process of managing the LSA. In domestic tax law, the post-BEPS revamp of China's international tax rules, for the first time, was legislated on the issue of LSA. The Revision Draft of the 'mini-constitution' of China's transfer pricing regime released in 2015 proposed to embed LSA in the entire chains of transfer pricing administration, including the comparability analysis, the application of the TPSM, intangibles, and cost-sharing arrangements.[901] As such, the analysis of LSA was expected to become a mandatory and prioritized requirement in the general transfer pricing audit. The final text of the revision substantially condensed the reform of LSA to ultimately conform to the OECD approach that puts the issue of LSA within the comparability factor of economic circumstances.[902] It was thus said that China had lost the collision over location savings,[903] or the 2017 TPG only met China halfway.[904]

However, this should not be interpreted as China having retreated from its stance based on its philosophy of value creation. For one thing, China adopts more stringent standards than the BEPS Actions with respect to the documentation requirements by incorporating LSA in the Local File for general information and for value chain analysis.[905] Similarly, China also formalized the analysis of LSA for the negotiation and

August 2025; Anis Chakravarty, Shanto Ghosh and Eunice Kuo, 'Location-Specific Advantages' [2015] Global Transfer Pricing; Claire (n. 326).

900. 'Jiangsu, Shanghai, Beijing, Guangdong, Ningbo, Xiamen, Tianjin, Shenzhen, Fujian, Dalian National Taxation Bureau, Guangdong, Shenzhen Local Taxation Bureau and other units have done a lot in the negotiation and signing of advance pricing arrangements and bilateral transfer pricing negotiations in accordance with the deployment of the State Administration of Taxation by conducting careful review, evaluation and analysis work, actively researching and exploring the latest transfer pricing concepts and applications such as intangible asset pricing, *location saving, cost saving*, etc ...' Notice of the STA's Work on the Anti-Tax Avoidance in 2008 (国税函〔2009〕106号 国家税务总局关于2008年反避税工作情况的通报) 2009.

901. Implementation Measures for Special Tax Adjustment (Draft for Soliciting Opinions) (特别纳税调整实施办法(征求意见稿)) 2015 Arts 29, 34, 73, 105.

902. Announcement on the Administration Measures for Special Tax Investigation Adjustment and Mutual Negotiation Procedures (国家税务总局公告2017年第6号 国家税务总局关于发布〈特别纳税调查调整及相互协商程序管理办法〉的公告) 2017 (STA Announcement No. 6 [2017]).

903. Finley (n. 338)., quoted in Brauner, 'Treaties in the Aftermath of BEPS' (n. 319) 982.

904. Hearson and Prichard (n. 320) 1301.

905. Announcement of the State Administration of Taxation on Matters Concerning Improving the Administration of Affiliation Reporting and Contemporaneous Documentation (国家税务总局公告2016年第42号 国家税务总局关于完善关联申报和同期资料管理有关事项的公告) 2016 (STA Announcement No. 42 [2016]) Art. 12.).

conclusion of advance pricing arrangement (APAs).[906] Besides the legislative languages, the reports and the speeches of the STA high-level officials are also important sources for comprehending China's strategic inducement for embracing the concept of LSA. As the following excerpts prove, the LSA is not the purpose in itself, but one of China's tentative initiatives shaking the origin-based international tax allocation model from the position of the 'world market', to the same extent as the challenges posed to the ALS by the contribution analysis approach from the position of the 'world factory'. While the LSA or the DEMPE-P (the last 'p' for 'promotion', *see* the following) discourses are both moderate responses, the underlying reasoning regarding the Chinese philosophy of value creation is intrinsically correlated with the principles of formulary apportionment.

First of all, the issue of LSA is framed in the first place against China's discontent with the allocation of profits between developed and developing countries, where it is thought that developing countries had not been adequately remunerated from the locational rent the MNEs derived from the locational advantages. 'For a long time, developed countries have relied on their dominance in rule-making and advantageous positions in technology and intangible assets to compete with developing countries for source of taxation, and have obtained most of the interests of multinational enterprises, while developing countries only gain a minor portion of these interests at the expense of huge markets, cheap labour, energy consumption and damage to the environmental. This situation should no longer continue,' averred the head of the STA of Jiangsu Province in an interview.[907]

Second, the Chinese approach to the LSA internalizes the endowment of the market as an intrinsic factor of value creation, countering the OECD's perception of value creation that further stretches the origin-based system by externalizing the LSA as a comparability factor for the ALS. In addition to the sources referred to in the former section, the following excerpts from a Report by the STA of Jiangsu Province are the most straightforward declaration of the Chinese philosophy of value creation that underlies China's insistence on the LSA:

> The BEPS report proposes that the results of transfer pricing should be consistent with value creation, and it is proposed that the distribution of income among jurisdictions should be combined with the analysis of value creation. *We believe that the market has a unique and significant impact and role in the corporate value creation and the realization of profits.* To this end, we first adhere to the concepts of *cost saving* and *market premium* as proposed in the UN Transfer Pricing Manual, and apply them in the global profit distribution of MNEs; second, in transfer pricing audits, APA negotiations and documentation requirements, we consider the market as an *important factor* for the division of profits especially when TPSM is selected; third, for multinational companies that have significant market shares

906. Announcement of the State Administration of Taxation on the Issues Concerning Improving the Administration of Advance Pricing Arrangements (国家税务总局公告2016年第64号 国家税务总局关于完善预约定价安排管理有关事项的公告) 2016 (STA Announcement No. 64 [2016]) Arts 5-7.

907. China Taxation News, 'Jiangsu Provincial State Taxation Bureau Formulates an International Tax Compliance Management Plan (江苏省国税局制定国际税收遵从管理规划)' (Shui5, 2014) https://www.shui5.cn/article/13/73408.html accessed 2 December 2023.

in China, *we not only hope that market factors are added to the profit distribution of the value chain of the group, it is hoped that they fully consider the particularity of China's huge market and strong demand as an emerging economy, and reflect this particularity in their profit distribution.*[908]

Third, antithetical to the conceptual foundation of the ALS, the Chinese approach to the LSA upholds the unitary business principle rather than the independent legal entity fiction, which shares a similar leitmotif of the contribution analysis approach.[909] To be specific, the remuneration for Chinese affiliates in consideration of the LSA is undergirded by investigating the role of Chinese affiliates vis-à-vis the whole group and the entire value chain, which enables China to collect the locational rent that falls out of the reach of the comparable-based methods.[910] 'The Chinese government's investment, supporting facilities, cost savings and corporate profit returns to China must match. The Chinese government has invested heavily in land, factories, and public facilities to attract foreign investment. China's labour force is still relatively cheap and the industrial facilities are relatively complete. The contribution of these factors to the profits of multinational companies should not be underestimated, and the profit returns to Chinese affiliates must be matched.'[911] In China's Position Paper of the UN Transfer Pricing Manual, it is illustrated by the example of the luxury goods industry that the sales revenue realized from Chinese consumers buying in overseas stores should be reasonably attributed a portion to the marketing contributions made by Chinese affiliates, which is a claim based on the unitary business principle.[912] 'We pay close attention to the profit distribution share of Chinese companies in the whole MNE group, and the MNE should also pay attention to it.'[913]

Besides LSA, China's emphasis on the contribution of the market to the value creation that contrasts the traditional OECD orthodoxy of origin-based value creation methodology is additionally manifested in the transfer pricing policy of intangibles with respect to the concept of DEMPE-P.[914] The DEMPE, short for 'development, enhancement, maintenance, protection and exploitation', was newly introduced by the BEPS Actions 8-10 to deal with the abusive practices of MNEs in relation to intangibles. The reform invalidates the profit shifting allowed by the pre-BEPS transfer pricing system, which focuses on the legal ownership of intangibles. The DEMPE is the materialization of the BEPS value creation mantra requiring taxation to be aligned with economic activities. China generally followed the OECD DEMPE approach to intangibles, yet added an additional 'P', denoting 'promotion' that provided a Chinese

908. 2014-2015 International Tax Compliance Management Plan (2014-2015年度国际税收遵从管理规划).
909. United Nations, 'Practical Manual on Transfer Pricing for Developing Countries (2017)' (n. 282) s. D.2.4.2.3.
910. Hearson and Prichard (n. 320) 1300-1301.
911. China Taxation News (n. 907).
912. United Nations, 'Practical Manual on Transfer Pricing for Developing Countries (2017)' (n. 282) s. D.2.4.4.12.
913. 2014-2015 International Tax Compliance Management Plan (2014-2015年度国际税收遵从管理规划).
914. Claire (n. 326) 496-497.

'DEMPE-P' approach.[915] The same logic applies here to the LSA that the Chinese affiliate's activities promoting the foreign intangibles should be compensated corresponding to their contributions to the value of intangibles. It follows that both the China market promotion and the brand-awareness building are recognized as value-creation drivers.[916] The STA further strengthened the DEMPE-P approach by providing that the royalties from intangibles should be adjusted according to the subsequent contributions by the promotions in China, which indicates that China, principally on the demand side of intangibles, thinks it deserves a larger portion of intangible-related income based on value contributions of the Chinese consumers and market.[917]

## 8.3 THE HARMONIZATION GROWN OUT OF CONTRADICTION

The above discussions have dismantled China's multiple identities in the international tax landscape and two basic starting points for contemplating its international tax strategy, from which it can be seen that both the identities and the starting points harbour fundamental contradictions within themselves. China remains a follower of the classical international tax order, and it has also become an active participant in its recent update through the BEPS Project. However, either in public affirmation or deduced from policy actions, China does not sit comfortably with the existing international tax system and harbours the cognition that it needs to be recalibrated in line with its perception of value creation. Meanwhile, the status of world factories in recent decades has prompted China to rethink the contributions of labour and assets in the creation of value, whereas the emerging status of the world market pushes China to reflect on the role of the market. These contradictions, however, are the drivers of China's introduction of formulary apportionment.

To encapsulate, China's face as a follower of the Western establishment is not to defend the classical international tax order in itself but is subsidiary to the realities of world politics and China's overall strategy of calibrating the international tax landscape to the interest of China's long-term goals. China's active participation in the BEPS Project is in line with its internal agenda of modernizing the tax system. As a member of the G20 that provided worldwide political endorsement to the BEPS Project, China is well aware of its practical vision of countering the abusive behaviour of giant MNEs. Few principled yardsticks were established and the value creation discourse of 'profits should be taxed where economic activities deriving the profits are performed and where value is created' has been exploited as theoretical backing for various reform proposals that carefully circumvented the core columns of international tax system. China claims itself as a major victim of BEPS so closing the gaps of BEPS meets the

915. Announcement on the Administration Measures for Special Tax Investigation Adjustment and Mutual Negotiation Procedures (国家税务总局公告2017年第6号 国家税务总局关于发布〈特别纳税调查调整及相互协商程序管理办法〉的公告) Art. 30.
916. Cheng Chi et al., 'China's New Transfer Pricing Guidelines and BEPS' https://www.internationaltaxreview.com/article/2a68rfy5bw2ycq0s5btri/chinas-new-transfer-pricing-guidelines-and-beps accessed 5 December 2023.
917. STA, 'Announcement on the Administration Measures for Special Tax Investigation Adjustment and Mutual Negotiation Procedures' (n. 902) Art. 31.

immediate objectives of China's tax policy. Through the lens of historical analysis, it has been revealed that foundational institutions of the modern international tax system were established by and to the advantage of roughly the same group of Western developed countries that dominated the agenda-setting and norm-making of the BEPS initiative. While China participated proactively in the meetings and consultations, the real differences between China and other developing countries are dubious. In hindsight, the outcomes of the BEPS Actions still primarily dealt with the concerns of developed countries rather than developing countries.[918] As discussed in Chapter 5, the descriptive and normative legitimacy of the project are questionable. An additional backdrop is that China has been carrying out systemic reform to modernize its tax system, for which involvement in the international project is an indispensable component as well as an external catalyser.[919] As discussed above, China's international tax strategy is guided by a contrasting philosophy of value creation as manifested in the efforts to orient China at the cross-point of the world factory and the world market, which pose fundamental challenges to the columns of classical international tax institutions. As a result, it can be inferred that China's face as a follower cannot be equated with a defender of the classical international tax institutions. The more accurate truth is that following the OECD-set agenda is both expedient for political realities and a 'hitchhike' for modernizing the tax system of China. At the end of the day, China's ostensibly contradicting faces of a challenger and a follower converge to the third face of reformist, as the seeds of formulary apportionment, namely, the world factory and world market-related policies, and the nutrition for it to grow, the Chinese philosophy of value creation are already in place.

The contradiction between the world market and world factory for directing China's horizon of international tax system is not well-founded, and the different perceptions of value creation behind each, in fact, amalgamate into a harmonized philosophy of value creation, which in turn underpins China to experimenting formulary apportionment. The first thing to note is that China's unique stances on international taxation from the position of either world factory or world market have their roots in its dissatisfaction with the classical international tax system, especially in relation to the ALS, the risk-based approach, and the origin-based foundations. This discontent is not static; it grows as China's position in the global value chain climbs.[920] It is China forced to squeeze into the century-old system, the elasticity and stability of which are increasingly questionable. The international tax system has not been tested since its formation by a giant developing country morphing into a major economic and political force. It has been evaluated that the BEPS Project cannot be counted on in that

918. IBFD, 'Implementing OECD/G20 BEPS Package in Developing Countries: An Assessment of Priorities, Experiences, Challenges and Needs of Developing Countries' https://www.giz.de/en/downloads/wp_implementing_beps_package_developing_countries.pdf accessed 1 December 2023.
919. Tianlong Hu, 'An Acute Queening Move for China's Taxation Legal Reform: Issues and Proposals' (2017) 11 Frontiers of Law in China 616; Cameron Rotblat, 'Chinese State Capitalism and the International Tax Regime' (2019) 10 Columbia Journal of Tax Law 77.
920. Tizhong Liao and Hanli Li, 'China: International Taxation in the Post-BEPS Era' in Yong Sup Sim and Mei-June Soo (eds), *Asian Voices: BEPS and Beyond* (IBFD Publications 2017) Ch. 5.

the guiding light of value creation has been dwarfed without touching on the pillars undergirding the income allocation pattern.

Technically, the Chinese philosophy of value creation is not truly groundbreaking in itself; what is unprecedented is that China's unique status in the global economic landscape has brought it to real life, which has not been seen in the past. The positions of the world factory, featuring the large scale of the labour force and manufacturing assets, and the world market, featuring the vast amount of consumer base and huge spending capacity, seem not to have overlapped in a single place before. In the same vein, the separate spirits of value creation, respectively with the starting points of the world factory and world market, in fact, can be harmonized into what paves the way for China to pioneer introducing formulary apportionment in international taxation. It seems more reasonable to regard China's philosophy of value creation, as manifested in the public declarations and policy actions, as filling the gap left by the BEPS Project. The fairness view of value creation poses questions to the lack of attention paid to the balance between developed and developing countries in the pre-BEPS and post-BEPS world, and the supply-demand view serves to recalibrate the existing origin-based nature as strengthened by the BEPS Project. Starting from the perspective of world factory, China as the manufacturing hub is providing labour, lands, machines, and energies to produce for Western MNEs, for example, the iconic Apple and the more recently Tesla, whereas it asserted that China has been under-compensated as a result of the modern transfer pricing regime and a set of basic rules being the operating environment. This is reminiscent of the mercantilist paradigm dominating in the colonial era when the colonies that received capital and technology were assigned merely routine profits for their local operations.[921] The case has barely changed except that the western countries nowadays achieved this outcome through more sophisticated system design, such as what China publicly complained, the emphasis on 'people functions', the risk-based approach and the ALS, both of which have been intensified in the BEPS era. From the perspective of the world market, the supply-demand view of value creation instead reflects on China's contribution to value creation, not emphasizing that of the input as in the former fairness view but the output that closes the full cycle of value generation. China's suggestions and actions from these two perspectives are slightly divergent, as one advocates both the contribution analysis approach and the two-factor formulary apportionment, and another is more restrained to the unilateral spectrum. Should these two perspectives originate severally from different countries, they could have become opposing or competing propositions that are difficult to reconcile. However, the corresponding views of value creation behind them are subjected to harmonization due to China's unprecedented dual statuses of world factories and world markets. As such, a (Chinese) value creation philosophy synthesizes the origin approach as crystallized by the contribution analysis approach and, more accurately, the two-factor formulary apportionment and the destination approach that regards the market at the demand side for separate consideration of international taxation. Once this harmonized philosophy is established, the

921. Wells and Lowell (n. 56).

formulary apportionment that employs labour, assets and sales factors in the formula is one if not the only route China sees optimal that leads to the international taxation facing the future, since it is able to bridge the rift between China's slightly diverging conceptions of international taxation from the perspectives of the world market and world factory and it harmonizes the corresponding value creation perceptions as well.

The three-factor formulary apportionment is not pure logical deduction; it is harmonization growing out from realistic contradictions. First, it is China's fairly intricate roles in the international tax landscape, for it is simultaneously a follower, a challenger and a reformist. It has been determined that the face of the follower is subordinate to the face of the challenger, which in turn serves China's internally driven international tax strategies as a reformist. This reconciliation breaks the hurdle at the margin that any 'unorthodox' experiments may not fit China's overall position in international tax order. It turns out that the exploration of formulary apportionment sits comfortably with the ternary faces of China, being an actionist with ambitions to challenge the existing institutions. Second, there is the discordancy between China's perceptions of value creation, starting from the statuses of world factory and world market and the divergent specific approaches to each. Through some conceptual integration, this discordancy gives rise to a unified Chinese philosophy of value creation, which in turn undergirds the three-factor formulary apportionment as the optimal option of reform.

## 8.4 THE CHINA-OECD COLLISIONS AND THE CHINESE VALUE CONTRIBUTION APPORTIONMENT METHOD AS THE TROJAN HORSE

It can be imagined with respect to the resistance and oppositions that may arise should China carry through its philosophy of value creation in its involvement with the BEPS Project as a Western-led initiative with pragmatic visions. While China had been an overall follower, the discrepancy between the Chinese understanding of value creation and the OECD's perception of value creation is substantial. An inspection into the collisions of actions at the policy side can not only provide additional proof substantiating the conceptual discrepancies between the two groups of perceptions but more importantly, it is also expected to demonstrate the above deduction with regard to the three-factor formulary apportionment being the optimal option in congruence with China's international tax strategy.

For the first purpose, many of these collisions have already been ranged over in the above discussions, such as the contribution analysis approach and the issue of LSA, both of which are implemented and depth and globally in China's transfer pricing regime. The case of LSA, in particular, contrasts with that of OECD. China released the draft legislation to systemically upgrade the approach to LSA following the conclusion of the final reports of BEPS, which means China obviously sought to challenge the OECD's minor magnitude given to the LSA. As analysed above, the eventual simplification of the legislation may be highly attributable to the resistance of foreign tax authorities and MNEs due to its deviation from the OECD recommendations. While it has been said that this move is not necessarily a retraction, the collisions between China and the OECD on the nature, theoretical basis and implications of LSA are real, so is the discrepant perception of value creation.

In relation to the second purpose, unlike the issue of LSA having drawn heated discussions, there is a piece of gold hiding in the sand that few commentators notice, let alone its revolutionary connotation, that is, the Value Contribution Apportionment Method (VCAM). The VCAM epitomizes the Chinese philosophy of value creation as unscrambled above against the tension between the world factory and world market, to which the three-factor formulary apportionment being the spontaneous path is also validated. To be more intuitive, China's VCAM is metaphorically a Trojan Horse bringing the three-factor formulary apportionment incubating from the Chinese value creation philosophy into the real world of international taxation.[922]

The VCAM is among other proposals being part of the systemic revamp of China's transfer pricing regime. In the draft revision of China's mini-constitution of transfer pricing, the VCAM was structured as one of 'other transfer pricing methods' subsequent to the five OECD-authorized methods. From the perspective of comparing China's approach to that of the OECD recommendations, there are several observations that can be made about the VCAM. First, the draft did not provide a hierarchy of the transfer pricing methods, either within the five OECD methods or between them and the other methods. Second, in literal reading, 'the other methods' seemed not constrained by the ALS. In comparison to the wording of the original regulation,[923] this should be interpreted as a strategic move to ease the chain of the arm's length. Third, besides functions, assets, and risks, the 'value creation factors' were added for general analysis. These are sporadic embodiments of China's perception of value creation that deviates from the OECD's.

The provision of the VCAM is worth quoting intact:

> The VCAM is a method that analyses the contribution of value creation factors to the profits of multinational groups and apportions the consolidated profits among affiliated companies located in different countries. The apportionment should consider the factors individually or in a combination of the assets, costs, expenses, sales, number of employees, etc. related to the value contribution. The VCAM is usually applicable to transactions where it is difficult to obtain information of comparable transactions but the combined profit and the contribution of value creation factors can be reasonably determined.

From the wording of the provision, the VCAM is obviously a 'pseudonym' of formulary apportionment, though the term formula was not explicitly used. All elements of a formulary apportionment mechanism were provided, including the factors, the combination of profits and the apportionment itself. The application of VCAM was limited to the circumstances where comparables are not readily available. However, this does not effectively narrow down the scope of its application, since the

922. For perspectives of domestic law of China's responses to the value creation concept, *see* Na Li, 'Chapter 14: China (People's Rep.)' in Werner Haslehner and Marie Lamensch (eds), *Taxation and Value Creation: EATLP Annual Congress Vienna, 18-20 June 2020* (IBFD 2021).
923. STA, 'Implementation Measures for Special Tax Adjustment (Trial Implementation)' Art. 21.

lack of reliable comparables is almost the new normal of transfer pricing. Taking the inexistence of hierarchy between the transfer pricing methods into account, it can be gauged that the VCAM was introduced strategically as a 'bomb', and the law did not intend to contain the potential repercussions in the first place. Therefore, the resolution of China to carrying out its philosophy of value creation is firm.

Another breakthrough of the VCAM is the introduction of the sales factor into the formula. While turnover or revenue has been employed in the formula for the taxation of domestic corporate group, the sales factor was officially endorsed for the first time in the context of international taxation. In line with its understanding of value creation from the perspective of world factory, China suggested the assets and labour-factor formula in the UN Transfer Pricing Manual. From the perspective of the world market, China's reactions are rather less systemic; either the LSA or the DEMPE is a specific measure within the system. The inclusion of the sales factor in the formula is unified and systemic solution, and it has validated the inference based on China's perception of the role of market in value creation for the consideration of international taxation. One also has to note that while the provision of VCAM did not restrict itself to the fixed combination of assets, labour and sales for the formula, it does not hinder the understanding that the VCAM is roughly equivalent to the three-factor formulary apportionment considering the equal magnitude given to the factors. The link of the VCAM to the three-factor formulary apportionment and, in turn, to the Chinese philosophy of value creation is well-established.

At this point, China's faces of a challenger and a reformist are thoroughly exhibited, and so are the China-OECD collisions on how taxation should be aligned with value creation. The consultations were not made public, but the opposition can be imagined since the mini-constitution was ultimately disassembled into separate pieces of legislation. The epilogue of the VCAM is even gloomier than the LSA. Not only was the provision completely removed but the general clause of the transfer pricing methods was also finalized, requiring all methods to comply with the ALS. The only vestige of the VCAM may be that the 'other transfer pricing methods' include any methods able to reflect the principle that the jurisdictions where economic activities take place should be aligned with the jurisdictions of value creation.[924] The principle is also where the Chinese perception of the value creation principle contrasts that of the OECD's.

This legislative outcome of the VCAM should not be read as a setback in itself because, politically, the introduction of the VCAM was more like a pressure test. What is important is the information it sent to the world, that is, China's discontent with the foundations of the classical international tax system even after the BEPS reforms and how China perceives the value creation and its implications for international taxation. The ephemeral VCAM has vindicated the major theses of this chapter: it incarnates the Chinese philosophy of value creation; it unveils the three-factor formulary apportionment, which is a harmonized future path growing out of the contradictions in China's

924. STA, 'Announcement on the Administration Measures for Special Tax Investigation Adjustment and Mutual Negotiation Procedures' (n. 902) Art. 22.

multiple faces in international taxation and tensions between the starting points of the world factory and world market.

## 8.5 CLOSING REMARKS

This chapter is not a comprehensive effort to demonstrate that formulary apportionment is an immediate reform action for China to take, which is in itself a tough task even under a global mandate as echoed by the Pillar One Amount A. Instead, it narrowly focuses on the question of whether China is in a good position to explore formulary apportionment further and presents the analysis by unveiling China's international tax strategy and the possible principles underlying it.

The presentation captures both the explicit announcement from China's state tax authority, as well as its status of being the intersection point of an origin state and a market state. Such contradiction, however, should empower China's strategical momentum to explore multi-factor formulary apportionment. It is therefore briefly touched upon the viability of the classical three-factor formula for China.

In the end, the chapter unveils even more of China's implicit aim to challenge the route of the OECD with respect to how value is created and how to tax profits accordingly. It further substantiates the thesis in the earlier parts.

CHAPTER 9

# China Biting the 'Wolf Peach': The Possible Design and the Roadmap

*This chapter examines China's potential adoption of formulary apportionment as an alternative to the arm's length standard for taxing multinational enterprises, metaphorically likened to overcoming the historical misperception of the tomato as a 'wolf peach'. It explores the substantive design of a formulary apportionment system tailored to China's economic and political context, drawing on comparative analyses of existing regimes, international tax principles, and insights from the BEPS Project. The design addresses key elements: jurisdiction to tax rules, territorial scope, taxable unit delineation, tax base harmonization, and apportionment factor selection. Recommendations include adopting a factor presence test, a water's edge system to limit extraterritorial application, a unitary business approach for taxable units, a harmonized tax base, and a double-weighted sales factor formula. The chapter also proposes a roadmap for implementation, advocating for a multilateral tax convention and leveraging trade frameworks like the Belt and Road Initiative and the Regional Comprehensive Economic Partnership, supported by China's 'Community with a Shared Future for Mankind' ideology. These strategies aim to align formulary apportionment with global economic integration and fairness in international taxation.*

## 9.1 INTRODUCTION

A 'fruit' once feared as the 'wolf peach' is now common worldwide. Once thought poisonous, its reputation changed after American farmer Robert Gibbon Johnson publicly ate it, proving it safe. Today, it's known globally as tomato.[925]

925. 'Robert_Gibbon_Johnson', Wikipedia https://en.wikipedia.org/wiki/Robert_Gibbon_Johnson accessed 4 December 2023.

The anecdote of tomato metaphorizes to a certain extent of the status quo of formulary apportionment. While the OECD has latently softened its opposition, formulary apportionment has been demonized for decades as an alternative to taxing the MNEs. Most notably in the OECD-TPG, formulary apportionment has been labelled as unfeasible for being arbitrary and burdensome. The Article 9 of the model tax treaty has been interpreted as underpinning an exclusive relationship between formulary apportionment and the ALS. As such, formulary apportionment may also be wrongly perceived as a 'wolf peach'. Unravelling whether formulary apportionment is, in fact, a 'tomato' first of all, dictates the analysis of the 'nutrition' of the wolf peach, which has been dealt with in the previous chapters. In addition, an actual 'bite' on it to test its taste is also essential to the rediscovery.

Based on all the previous discussions, this chapter, as the piece concluding the revisiting of formulary apportionment, revolves around China's experimental 'bite' on formulary apportionment, focusing on the substantive design of the formulary apportionment proposal and the possible roadmap China can follow to implement it within the economic and political realities. Accordingly, this chapter is structured into two components. The first component recaptures the previous discussions of the elements of formulary apportionment and succinctly sheds light on how China may design its formula by adding some technical, practical and China-specific thoughts. The second component briefly explores the possible roadmap China may adopt to implement its formulary plan.

## 9.2 THE SUBSTANTIVE DESIGN OF CHINA'S FORMULARY APPORTIONMENT EXPERIMENT

When discussing China's way to the future of formulary apportionment, the two interrelated issues should better be addressed separately. One is the substantive design that captures the essential elements of a formulary apportionment system; another is the actual means to put the design into effect in the real legal and political systems. The consequences of the Chinese experiment of formulary apportionment depend on both the decisions on the basic elements and the roadmap to implement them.

The following discussions of the substantive design applicable to the case of China follow the same methodology of the comparative analysis of the existing formulary apportionment regimes in Chapter 3. The Chinese formulary apportionment regime is thus conceived along the division of the external components comprising the jurisdiction to tax rules and the issue of the territorial scope, and the internal components comprising the delineation of taxable unit, the harmonization and determination of tax base and the choice and weight of apportionment factors.

The suggestions for the case of China are the applications of or largely draw on the prior discussions of formulary apportionment from various perspectives, particularly the comparative analysis and the insights from the international tax principles, including the historical analysis and the evaluations of the BEPS Project. By focusing on the substantive design of formulary apportionment specifically for China, the previous motley reflections are, therefore, homogenized.

### 9.2.1 The Jurisdiction to Tax Rules

That the jurisdiction to tax rule was categorized as an external component of formulary apportionment is not to denote it being peripheral to the international tax system. On the contrary, the jurisdiction to tax rules are foundational to any alternatives to taxing the multinational enterprises. A significant portion of reflections on the modern international tax system has revolved around the relative pros and cons at the practical level between the ALS and the formulary apportionment while underestimating the significance of the jurisdiction to tax rules for either alternative as well as the difficulties of modulating them for international tax reform. In a nutshell, this is because the jurisdiction to tax rules sits in the intersection area between the concepts of the state and sovereignty and the ever-changing economic realities.

Besides the comparative analysis of the existing formulary apportionment regimes, the issue of jurisdiction to tax rules is also one of the focuses in the previous discussions of the international tax principles, particularly the principle of legitimacy. The principle of legitimacy, more technically, the normative legitimacy has comprehensively investigated the changing concepts of state and its interaction with taxpayers and the metamorphosis of the nature of sovereignty. It is concluded that in the modern international tax order, the jurisdiction to tax norm is dictated by the normative legitimacy to correspond with the taxpayer's participation in the state's triangle of national tax order, which challenges the current residence and source-based norm embedded in the classical international tax order. Therefore, the jurisdiction to tax norm is expected to be modernized to establish accordant fields for inspecting the MNE's liability to pay vis-à-vis the state's power to collect taxes.

The comparative analysis chapter provides straightforward suggestions to the jurisdiction to tax norm for the design of formulary apportionment. The Canadian provincial formulary apportionment regime and the EU CCCTB proposal both rely on the traditional institutions of jurisdiction to tax, including the status of residents, the permanent establishment, and designated sources of income. In comparison, the constitutional and judicial contributions at the US federal and states level have provided the insights that the factor presence test is more desirable, being the alternative congruent with formulary apportionment both theoretically and practically.

As a latecomer to the international tax system, there is no doubt that China adopts the jurisdiction to tax rules in line with international conventions. Most notably, while China is gradually turning to a source-oriented international tax policy, as investigated against the backdrop of the BRI, it remains one of the few major economies that tax the worldwide income of resident enterprises without providing participation exemption. The reform to formulary apportionment adopting the factor presence test will abrogate the 'nationality' of MNEs, which is currently fundamental to establishing the jurisdiction to tax at the 'residence' state. Similarly, the concept of permanent establishment will also be superseded as a key pillar of 'source' jurisdiction to tax.

The situation of the source of income rules is relatively more complex. In general, China only taxes the non-residents' incomes sourced within China. For this purpose, the incomes are classified into six categories with each assigned a proxy to determining the source, the principles of which are consistent with the international conventions.[926] In another regular way of categorization, these categories of income are largely non-active business income. To what extent are these sources of income rules affected by the proposed jurisdiction to tax norms? This depends on the related issue of tax base under formulary apportionment. If the apportionable base is the global income or if the apportionable income includes the non-active business incomes, the existing source of income rules as a trunk of jurisdiction to tax norm is nullified; if otherwise, the source of income rules may still be retained for the taxation of non-apportionable income.

The technical details of the factor presence test can only be pinned down based on the assessment of economic impact and administrative burden. Moreover, as one of the integral components of formulary apportionment, the design of the factor presence test being the jurisdiction to tax norm should additionally take the following considerations into account:

> The first caveat is that the jurisdiction-to-tax norm is at the surface of the eclectic interface between the taxpayer and the taxing state. This interface is composed of layers of economic, political/ethical, and practical reasoning superimposed or intersected with each other. Compromises and trade-offs are avoidable when deciding on the specifics of the factor presence test. There is simply no golden rule here.

Besides the above considerations, the other elements of formulary apportionment, as well as the roadmap to implement it, also bear upon the concrete design of the factor presence test. For example, since the unilateral formulary apportionment proposal is ruled out, the bilateral or multilateral implementation means that the participating states need to agree on a formula. This relates to the coordination between the apportionment factors and the factors in a test of jurisdiction to tax. As China is suggested to embrace the three-factor formula, the factor presence test may also employ them to maintain the consistency between the elements of formulary apportionment.

The factor presence test is essentially a bright-line test. It provides tangible benefits of simplicity and certainty. On the mirror side, however, it is also prone to be manipulated. As such, the design of the test may adopt an 'either-or' structure and an absolute-value plus proportion approach, drawing insights from the experiences of the United States. In plain words, the new nexus is established if any of the factors exceeds an absolute value, or, the proportion of the value of a factor in the jurisdiction exceeds a certain ratio of the total value of the factor.

Additional considerations should be paid to prevent the factor presence test from distorting or impeding the operations of business. First of all, it seems necessary to demarcate the *de minimis* activities that do not fall within the concerns to establishing the jurisdiction to tax, which requires examinations into the economic realities to set out qualitative as well as quantitative standards. In addition, by referring to the US experiences, activities for the solicitation of orders or auxiliary to the customer-facing

926. Regulation on the Implementation of the Enterprise Income Tax Law of the People's Republic of China (2019 revision) (中华人民共和国企业所得税法实施条例 (2019年修订)) 2019 Art. 7.

sales are 'protected' from taxation, which can be specified in a list together with the activities that are 'unprotected'. In the same spirit, the activities conducted using the internet or digital technologies should also be meticulously scrutinized for purposes of determining the establishment of nexus.

### 9.2.2 The Territorial Scope

The territorial scope is a practical and empirical area of formulary apportionment. It is essentially an issue of real politics in which any initiative to introduce formulary apportionment into the international tax landscape will have to deal with the rift it creates in the world undergirding by the arm's length institutions. The territorial scope issue is thus equivalent to the proper design of water's edge limitations to the proposed formulary apportionment regime.

There is hardly any abstract thinking around what is an ideal water's edge system, it is rather the pragmatic and technical concerns which dominate as is touched upon in the comparative analysis of the existing formulary apportionment regimes. The experiences of the United States, Canada and the EU CCCTB proposal have provided abundant lessons for the design of the water's edge system for the fundamentally different designs of formulary apportionment. The discussions of the case of the United States have elucidated why delimiting the border of formulary apportionment is necessary in the first place and the practical concerns in forming the water's edge limitation; the Canadian experiences corroborate that the water's edge limitations on the formulary apportionment based on single corporations are relatively simpler than that on unitary enterprise; and the EU CCCTB proposal provides the prototype of the water's edge design for truly international formulary apportionment on the basis of consolidation.

The lessons need to be refined, taking into account the suggestions for other elements of formulary apportionment in China's case. For example, the smooth boundary of Canadian formulary apportionment is largely attributed to it being established on a separate company basis, which contrasts what is suggested for China as discussed in the following. Similarly, the experiences of the water's edge limitations on US formulary apportionment, while being sophisticated, lack the real 'bloc' thinking since the regimes are separately operated by the states. At this point, the EU CCCTB proposal exhibits its comparative strength since it is constructed for a supranational political group.

Back to the starting point, the sole purpose of the water's edge system is to establish a bubble to keep the formulary apportionment regime operating in a predetermined sphere. As discussed previously, this is achieved by demarcating the interrelated personal (the water's edge group) and objective (the includable income) scope of the application of formulary apportionment. As such, the following suggestions are given for the design of water's edge limitations on China's tentative initiative to introduce formulary apportionment:

> Beyond all practical concerns, the overarching principle of designing a water's edge system is that the proposed formulary apportionment will be implemented

only within the group of countries to be participating in the initiative, so as to minimize the potential frictions with the outer world dominated by the arm's length institutions.

From the perspective of personal scope, should China uphold the unitary business rather than the consolidation approach, the focus of the water's edge limitations is on the standards to exclude the 'extraterritorial' parts of the unitary business from the application of formulary apportionment. In this case, the water's edge group should be delineated by inspecting the facts and circumstances of the members of the MNE. First, the 'third-country' corporations, as identified under the existing residence rules, are excluded from the water's edge group. In addition, resident corporations with substantial business operations located outside of the formulary apportionment bloc as determined by, for example, the location of at least 80% of payroll, property or sales will also be excluded. At last, while the permanent establishments are the extension of 'third-country' corporations, for the consideration of the water's edge issue, they are treated as 'residents' rather than being 'naturally' excluded.

Not all incomes of the water's edge group can be included for apportionment, which introduces the demarcation of the objective scope. The general principle is to apportion only the income produced or derived within the formulary apportionment bloc. Therefore, formulary apportionment does not apply to: (1) the income earned in third countries by residents, including the dividends paid by the foreign subsidiaries;[927] (2) the income earned within the bloc by the third-country corporation, which nonetheless should be differentiated from the case of 'domestic' permanent establishments.

For the consideration of tax avoidance, the corporations incorporated in tax havens or low-tax jurisdictions are included in the water's edge group if they are effectively connected with the unitary business.[928]

As an endnote, while being an indispensable component, the water's edge is subsidiary to the internal elements of formulary apportionment. The details of the water's edge limitations should be determined with systemic thinking.

### 9.2.3 The Delineation of the Taxable Unit

From a macro perspective, the reflections on the taxation of MNEs can be seen as a part of the 'autonomous' transformation of the international tax order. At the 'micro' level, the MNEs have metamorphosed into highly integrated, specialized, massive-in-scale economic organizations operating in the world economy that is globalized, digitalized, and dominated by intangibles. It is a well-established knowledge in economics and other disciplines with respect to what the MNEs are and why they exist and succeed, international taxation needs to follow suit. The way the MNE is treated, as either an

927. This thus concurs with the business representatives' opinion in the 1984 Report. *See* Dept. of The Treasury, United States (n. 262) 38.
928. *Ibid.*, 51.

economic unity or separate entities in coalition, is the very basic starting point of international taxation, not only for the competition between arm's length and formulary apportionment but also for the specific options to the taxable unit within the formulary apportionment.

The chapter on historical analysis has put formulary apportionment in the periodized evolution of the international tax system, and it reveals how formulary apportionment as an alternative to taxing MNEs waxed and waned. One of the most valuable findings is that at the formative period of the allocation model of international taxation, when the ALS and formulary apportionment were put on the same table, it was a motley collection of myths, administrative concerns, judgments contingent on historical circumstances, and the motif of international taxation in germination that ultimately edged out the formulary alternative. From where we stand at present, it is erroneous to reckon this historical resolution as abysmal, but safe to conclude that in almost every aspect, what undergirds the century-old system in which the arm's length stand is a key pillar has been long gone.

Chapter 2 presents point-by-point the fact that the methodologies of formulary apportionment and arm's length standard as competing options for sharing the international tax pie are contrasting. Chapter 2 has revealed the changing connotations and applications of the ALS. It is evidently seen that while the differences from formulary apportionment are qualitative, the boundaries of the ALS are being constantly stretched. The OECD's softening position on the separate status of member entities is one of the examples, which justifies that the 'whole-of-enterprise' approach has been increasingly gaining force. Based on the newest developments including the BEPS suggestions and the blueprint of the two Pillars for the Inclusive Framework, the path to concretizing the whole-of-enterprise approach is a challenge both for the reforms under the existing system and the more revolutionary third way of formulary apportionment.

The chapter on comparative analysis has unveiled that formulary apportionment is an inclusive solution in the sense it can apply to separate corporations as well as the corporate group. However, this Canadian way of formulary apportionment does not match the plight of international taxation. Hence, it is the American unitary business approach and the European consolidation approach being the competing delineation of the taxable unit under formulary apportionment. The two alternatives both have relative advantages over one another, but none of them is free from problems in application. Comparatively, the analysis approves the unitary business approach on the grounds that, first, the unitary business principle is one of the key foundations underpinning the strength of formulary apportionment, while the consolidation approach reflects only the legal unity of MNEs, second, although demarcating the unitary enterprise requires inspecting the facts and circumstances, the case of the United States has provided abundant experiences, and lastly, the bright-line test of the consolidation approach unavoidably creates the risk of being abused.

The following suggestions are provided to determine whether the member entities within a corporate group form a unitary enterprise. They can be taken into consideration in totality or selectively for the purposes of simplicity:

> As a prerequisite, the separate entities can form a unitary business enterprise only if they are members of a commonly controlled group. For this purpose, the law should provide the conditions of the commonly controlled group, which can generally rely on drawing the line of the stock ownership and voting power to be calculated cumulatively.[929]

The unitary enterprise is characterized by functional integration, centralization of management, and economies of scale. The functional integration depicts the interdependence and interconnection in the economic process of the enterprise. The member entities of the group may engage in different steps, but there is no reasonable way to separate the contributions of each step to the profit of the entire economic process. Centralized management refers to the business of the enterprise, albeit spreading among the group members, being centrally managed, coordinated, and controlled. It is noteworthy that such consideration is beyond the legal right to control, but more to the actual exercise of control over or between the members. Compared to the former factors, the economies of scale are the *ex-post* evidence of the existence of the unitary enterprise, which can be observed by the favourable conditions gained by group members compared to that of the discreet business.

The flow of value test determines the unitary business enterprise by examining whether the activities carried on between the related members represent the flow of value within the group. The law can enumerate the flow of value activities to increase certainty. In so doing, what the US state laws have set out can be drawn on: assisting the procurement of equipment, filling the personnel needs, interacting for the expansion of corporate business, providing technical, operational or strategic guidance, the joint use of goodwill, trade name, and patens. It is worth noting that the mere flow of funds by passive investment, the flow of goods and the occasional financial oversight are not enough to constitute the flow of value.[930]

A common practice is, for ease of administration, that the law should provide some presumptions for the existence and scope of the unitary business enterprise. The presumptions can largely be refined from the above tests of unitary business. For example, the unitary business is presumed to be established if the business activities are vertically structured or in the same general line, or there is strong centralized management.[931]

### 9.2.4 The Harmonization and Determination of Tax Base

After the unitary business is established and the scope of the unitary enterprise is determined, the closely following question is how to determine the income for combination and apportionment, and whether the tax base needs to be harmonized across the different tax jurisdictions is a question to be answered in advance. The

929. *See* the provisions of Model General Allocation and Apportionment Regulations – as of 2017 24-29.
930. Minnesota Administrative Rules pt. 8019.0100.
931. McIntyre, 'The Use of Combined Reporting by Nation States' (n. 455) 939.

harmonization and determination of tax base is an issue of both practical and theoretical concerns.

First of all, as to the harmonization of tax base, there is not much to debate except the realistic hurdles to consider to achieve it. The US states, the Canadian provinces, and the EU CCCTB formulary apportionment regimes all achieve a high degree of harmonization of the tax base. In other words, the calculation of taxable income of the unitary business group follows roughly a uniform rule even though the group members may be located in different tax jurisdictions. Achieving uniformity in the essential elements of tax base is in the interests of both taxpayer and tax administration. The formulary apportionment regime cannot run smoothly without creating duplicative or under-taxation if the tax jurisdictions within the bloc maintain divergent rules on the basic rules of taxable income. With respect to whether the harmonization of tax base allows some leeway of customized rules as incentive policies, which is the case of the US state formulary apportionment regimes, the decision is suggested to be made based on the difficulties of negotiating the full harmonization of tax base. The EU CCCTB Proposal generally does not allow it, which may be the reason why it is at a standstill.

The determination of tax base deals with the scope of income to be apportioned for taxation using the formula. As the comparative analysis in Chapter 3 has enunciated, the current trend of income inclusion in the tax base as observed in the US and the EU CCCTB proposal is 'expansionism', meaning that the income is generally apportionable unless explicitly exempt. However, the US approach is preferable for it being more consistent with the unitary business foundation of formulary apportionment.

For one thing, at the root of the question of which part of the unitary enterprise's income is apportionable lies the issue of why to combine and apportion in the first place, which directs to the theoretical basis of formulary apportionment, the unitary business principle. All incomes should be included in the combined tax base if they are generated by the unitary business. The most recent practice in the US is the apportionable/non-apportionable division, based on the 'nexus' of the underlying business activities with the unitary business.

For another, the unitary business principle-based determination of tax base corresponds with a key hypothesis throughout this thesis, especially in relation to the discussions of the two normative principles of legitimacy and equity. The legitimacy principle directs that tax is one of the edges in the triangular relationship between state, taxpayer, and taxation. The liability to pay tax is not necessarily based on the geographic source of income, which is presumed to be unattainable, but that the taxpayer is in the triangle. Therefore, the income is combined and apportioned on the basis that the underlying activity is a part of the unitary business. Similarly, the equity principle embraces the equal allegiance approach rather than the equal earned income approach because income cannot be geographically pinned down.

For the harmonization and determination of tax base, the following suggestions are given:

(1) A harmonization of tax base is preferable. The formulary apportionment bloc should endeavour to reach the consensus on the definition and calculation of tax base, for which the CCTB proposal can provide a sophisticated model.

Where the participating states intend to retain the autonomy to set up incentive measures, it should be allowed only in exceptional cases.

(2) Demarcating the scope of apportionable income is the application of the unitary business principle in its objective aspects. The general principle is thus the income arising from transactions and activities in the regular course of the unitary business and the income arising from the property effectively connected with the unitary business should be included in the combined tax base.

(3) The legal provisions of the scope of tax base should adopt a 'specified-residual' structure, meaning that the law provides guidelines to identify apportionable income, while the rest of all other income will not be included in the combined base.

(4) Based on the experiences from the United States, it is recommended to adopt the transactional test and functional test to determine the apportionable income, and both of them concretize the requirements of the unitary business principle. The transactional test dictates that the apportionable income is derived from transactions or functions in a 'normal, typical, customary or accustomed policy or procedure' of the unitary business, for which the frequency and regularity of the activities are important signposts. The functional test is used to address the income from tangible and intangible property. If the 'acquisition, management, employment, development and disposition' of the property is an integral part of or related to the unitary business, the income thereby derived should be included for apportionment.[932]

### 9.2.5 The Choice and Weight of Apportionment Factors

The choice and weight of apportionment may be the most important decisions to make in the design of a formulary apportionment regime. When the tax base for apportionment is determined and combined, the choice and weight of apportionment will decide both the numerator, denominator and the multiplier in the formula. Therefore, its implications for the actual outcomes of allocations of taxable income and revenue to the tax jurisdictions are immediate and direct. On account of the centrality of apportionment factors, the issue is widely relevant to previous discussions.

The issue concerns the contrasting methodologies of the ALS and the formulary apportionment for the allocation of income between the tax jurisdictions. As discussed in Chapter 2, the arm's length institutions comprising residence, source and transfer pricing rules follow a bottom-to-top and activity-by-activity approach, the objective of which is to attribute income to where it is thought derived. Chapter 2 has touched upon why the arm's length institutions or, generally, the international corporate tax system

932. Model General Allocation and Apportionment Regulations – as of 2017 15-9.

fails, and Chapter 2 has revealed the full circle of the trajectory of formulary apportionment. Based on these discussions, formulary apportionment is a factor-based top-to-bottom approach that presumes no geographic source of income, according to which the income allocation between taxing states is constructed in line with a set of normative principles of international taxation. The choice and weight of apportionment factors are the emanations of what underpins formulary apportionment being an alternative preferable to the traditional arm's length institutions. The normative principles of international taxation have forthright guidance for the choice and weight of factors in the formula.

Both dimensions of the principle of legitimacy shed some light on the significance and choice of factors. As discussed in Chapter 5, normative legitimacy addresses the justification of the state's power to tax and puts forward the model of the triangular relationship of state, taxation, and taxpayer. The modern legitimacy theory is then operationalized to dictate the jurisdiction to tax norms to be accordant in evaluating the power to tax of the states. The factor-based formulary apportionment achieves more than that. Regardless of the specific factors used, it annuls the residence, permanent establishment, and artificial source rules as the yardsticks of jurisdiction to tax. Instead, it uses a consistent factor-based approach that interlinks taxpayers' roles across the states. In addition, the factor-based formulary apportionment maintains the consistency between what is used for 'qualifying' the power to tax and what is used for 'quantifying' the tax liabilities to pay. This is also enabled by the 'factor representation' requirement for choosing the factors for the formula. The descriptive legitimacy expects the international tax system to be compatible with the 'internationality' of cross-border businesses; the reform, therefore, should be able to promote multilateralism over unilateralism or bilateralism that has dominated international taxation for over a century. In addition to the apportionment mechanism that directly gathers the tax authorities around the table, the formulary apportionment conforms to this requirement by employing the factors that spread over multiple locations in a real and discernable way but, in the meantime, correspond with the creation of value.

The principle of equity also has close contact with the apportionment factors, or more accurately, it guides and evaluates formulary apportionment by inspecting the role of factors. The equity principle is unfolded as inter-taxpayer equity and inter-nation equity, where the former requires that taxpayers with equal capacity pay equal taxes and the latter generally dictates that countries should get a fair share in the profits of MNEs. Formulary apportionment systematically transforms the debate about equity in international taxation. For inter-taxpayer equity, the employment of factors ensures that MNEs are treated equally regardless of their 'residence' and the locations of business operations, both in establishing nexus and determining the payable taxes. For inter-nation equity, the equality-based equal allegiance approach considers the factors that incarnate the taxpayer's interaction with the state and economy.

The most straightforward observation from the chapter of comparative analysis is the diversity of the choice and weight of factors in the formulas, not only in the static sense of horizontal comparisons between the selected regimes but also in a dynamic sense of the changing apportionment formulas over time. The US states formulary apportionment regimes at the very outset employed the equal-weighted factors of property, payroll, and sales; the Canadian regimes employ the equal-weighted factors of revenue and payroll, while the EU CCCTB proposal employs the equal-weighted three factors. However, the US states gradually turned to the single or double-weighted sales factor formula, and in the case of the CCCTB, it was suggested to change the weight of the three factors or add the additional 'data' factor to the formula.

Based on all relevant discussions as restated above, in particular, the thought process provided for deciding the choice and weight of factors, the following suggestions are given for the formulary apportionment experiment championed by China:

(1) The chapter on the viability of China introducing formulary apportionment has argued for the traditional property, payroll and sales formula considering the centrality of China in the experiment and its circumstances of international taxation. Beyond that, these factors are also approvable by the tests of the legitimacy and equity principles essentially because they reflect the supply-demand view of the creation of value thus fulfilling the 'factor presentation' requirement.

(2) Assigning weight to each of the three factors is at the complex intersection between the guiding principles and policy priorities that often compete or conflict with each other. The lessons from the BEPS Project lead to taking legitimacy and equity as the first principles, while the efficiency considerations will be compromised. As such, the double-weighted sales factor seems to be the most preferable choice. For one thing, the double-weighted sales factor formula establishes a balance between the origin and destination states by giving equal weight to their contributions to the value creation at the supply side and demand side, and there are tenable reasons to favour one side over another.[933] For another, from the perspective of efficiency, the heavier weight of sales factor than the traditional one-third weight theoretically can retain some of the merits of the sales only factor through the lens of neutrality propositions. The formula recommended is thus as follows.

*Equation 9.1 Recommended Formula by This Thesis*

$$\text{Income apportioned to the state} = \frac{1}{4}\left(\frac{Property^{state}}{Property^{all}} + \frac{Payroll^{state}}{Payroll^{all}} + \frac{2 * Sales^{state}}{Sales^{all}}\right) * Total\ combined\ income$$

(3) While the 'soul' and 'general skeletons' have been set up, a functional formulary apportionment regime requires to be filled with 'blood and flesh' as well, in which the operational rules of the apportionable factors take a large part. Discussing these rules in depth is beyond the space of this thesis, but at the core is the rule to determining the items includable or excludable for the calculation the value of the factors. The same principle of 'factor representation' for choosing the factors as developed in the US context should apply to

933. McIntyre, 'The Use of Combined Reporting by Nation States' (n. 455) 920.

calculating the value of factors. Providing comprehensive suggestions on the operational rules under such principle is beyond the scope of this thesis, but both the US states' formulary apportionment regimes and the EU CCCTB proposals have provided abundant resources for making the detailed provisions.

## 9.3 WAYS TO ROLL OUT CHINA'S FORMULARY APPORTIONMENT REGIME

### 9.3.1 When a Concept Falls Down to the Ground

As revealed in Chapter 4, formulary apportionment has never been implemented in an international context until the yet-to-be-adopted TPS. With that being said, formulary apportionment stays mostly as a conception that exists only in the papers of academia. When this conception falls down to the ground, the problems of all aspects instantly arise, and this can be grouped into two categories: first, those surrounding the concept per se; second, the puzzles of the ways to implementation that are generally irrelevant to the concept.

Specific to formulary apportionment, discussions on the first category of problems are already voluminous, while how on earth China, or any other country may initiate a formulary apportionment system has rarely been covered.[934] This section intends to make that up by exploring the possible ways that China can utilize to roll out formulary apportionment.

### 9.3.2 Multilateral Tax Convention of Formulary Apportionment

The ideal instrument for dealing with international tax matters has always been an MLC, as it is hard law imposing legal obligations on the contracting states and also a strong political announcement for deference to the common goal or standards. China can initiate a negotiation of such a convention for participating countries to agree on critical terms of a common formulary apportionment regime.

The EU CCCTB proposal intended to adopt this approach essentially under the unique EU legal system. The TPS also relies on MLC to implement some of its aspects such as the multilateral convention provisions on digital services taxes. This was not as common as it seemingly be before the introduction of the MLI, which is the first real MLC that the world has ever seen.

However, an MLC is also extremely difficult to negotiate. This is understandable as even a bilateral tax agreement usually takes years to finalize, let alone a multilateral one. For an MLC with the theme of promoting formulary apportionment, it will

934. Kerrie Sadiq, 'Unitary Taxation with a Global Formulary Approach as a Realistic and Appropriate Option for Developing Nations: A Chinese Case Study' (2016) 6 Journal of Chinese Tax and Policy 25-52.

necessarily encounter more resistance or at least difficulties, as the idea is relatively new and its global adoption is unprecedented.

The difficulty of bargaining also depends on what countries are in the circle to negotiate. Considering that the formula design recommended above suggests a relatively balanced perspective, China can choose the negotiating parties that are expected not to significantly lose revenue due to the transition to formulary apportionment. The list can be shortened by inspecting China's trading partners and the trade volume to provide a quantitative basis for negotiation.

### 9.3.3 Utilizing Investment and Trade Schemes

The above multilateral treaty approach is depicted as the 'orthodox' way to deal with international tax matters. The crux is that it still entails a way to further determine at what scale the FA experiment should extend, and on what basis to initiate the agenda.

It is submitted that China may utilize the existing investment and trade relations as leverage to promote formulary apportionment. To be concrete, employing investment and trade relations as the channel to advance formulary apportionment has the following advantages:

(1) First, countries with close trade and investment ties are more likely to cooperate in tax matters, as tax relations and trade relations are both important economic associations between countries. Countries with closer economic ties have more mutual trust, and tend to have similar economic system through integration or even similar level of development. These conditions all lay a preferable ground for cooperation in tax matters.
(2) Second, trade and investment flow have the effect of closing the international wealth gap. Production factors flow to where the rate of return is the highest until it is the same as everywhere else. In the long run, countries doing business tend to have balanced international payments. This is critical as the recommended formula adopts a balanced production-sales approach in itself. No party would like to be an instant loser in the new regime.
(3) Third, relying on trade and investment can also help determine the geographic scope of FA. The experiment of FA can be conveniently pinned down to a certain trading bloc or a group of countries with close trade relationships.

To be specific to China, as the leading developing country, China has a large trade network, if not the widest. China is asserted as the top trading partner to more than 120 countries in the world.[935] Among others, the following trade network can be further explored and utilized:

935. Ambassador Mark A Green, 'China Is the Top Trading Partner to More Than 120 Countries' (Wilson Center) https://www.wilsoncenter.org/blog-post/china-top-trading-partner-more-120-countries accessed 3 December 2023.

#### 9.3.3.1 *The Belt and Road Initiative*

Chapter 7 has covered in detail of this Belt and Road Initiative. The BRI's advantages of becoming the medium of promoting formulary apportionment lie in the strong political endorsement for establishing a China-centred trade regime and the high resemblance of economic development status. The over 150 countries that either signed a memorandum or a contract with China vowed to deepen their economic ties with China. In addition, the BRI originated from cooperation in infrastructure projects, so the participating countries are mostly developing countries. Traditionally, these countries also have difficulties in administering the increasingly complex ALP regime. Therefore, these factors cumulatively make the lobbying of formulary apportionment more promising.

#### 9.3.3.2 *The Regional Comprehensive Economic Partnership*

The Regional Comprehensive Economic Partnership (RCEP) is a free trade agreement among Asia-Pacific nations in which the ten Southeast Asian countries are the majority parties, but they may be weaker in negotiation power. Entering into force in January 2022, the RCEP immediately established the largest free trade bloc in the world. The RCEP group is also comprised of a few developed economies, such as Japan and Australia, yet China seems to be the dominant power, considering its size and close ties with Southeast Asia.

With respect to taxation, the RCEP principally serves to eliminate or relieve the tariff barriers of cross-border transactions. This is different from the income tax subject discussed herein. However, as stated in the preamble of the RCEP agreement, the parties desire to 'broaden and deepen economic integration in the region', which makes it consistent with the properties and values of formulary apportionment.[936] In other words, the reform towards formulary apportionment can serve as a component in the regional integration and harmonization framework in which the RCEP is a key milestone.

#### 9.3.3.3 *The Ideology of 'Community with a Shared Future for Mankind'*

The ideology of the 'Community with a Shared Future for Mankind'(CSFM), proposed by the Communist Party of China in its 18th National Congress in 2012, is a vision for global development and cooperation aimed at achieving common prosperity, common development, peace, and stability in the international community. The idea of CSFM can be the conceptual basis of China's campaign for formulary apportionment, even

936. Interests in the potential of RCEP becoming the instrument of harmonizing the national tax systems across the region have been growing, *see* Jiang Yuesheng, 'Reflections on the Relationship Between Multilateral Free Trade Agreements and Tax Measures: Taking RCEP and CPTPP as Reference (关于多边自由贸易协定与税收措施关系的思考：以RCEPCPTPP为参照)' [2022] Journal of International Taxation(国际税收) 9.

though it is constructed for far broader purposes. The CSFM can be relevant in the following aspects.

First, the concept emphasizes the interdependence and common interests of human society, calling for joint efforts by countries to address global challenges and build a world of lasting peace, universal security, common prosperity, openness, inclusiveness, and environmental sustainability. This corresponds to the underlying factual bases of invoking formulary apportionment. The need to (re)consider formulary apportionment arises where the ALP fails to deal with the unprecedented integration of the global economy and the common pursuit of a fair international tax system.

Second, the concept calls for mutual benefit and win-win cooperation. The Communist Party of China advocates promoting open and inclusive economic development to achieve shared prosperity for people in all countries. This entails enhancing economic cooperation, advancing trade and investment liberalization and facilitation, eradicating poverty and inequality, and promoting the fair distribution of global resources. This is relevant to tax arena considering the competition-based international tax regime is doomed. The international community is already acting on this and the high-profile BEPS Project is the hallmark.

Furthermore, a community with a shared future for mankind emphasizes mutual respect, fairness, justice, and multilateralism among nations. Through the CSFM, China advocates resolving disputes through equal dialogue and consultation, promoting fairness and justice in the international order, upholding multilateralism, and safeguarding the international system with the United Nations at its core. These connotations correspond with the core values or elements of formulary apportionment, such as the multilateralism and democratic rule-making concerning the principle of legitimacy and the equity principle in the international tax order. Multilateralism is in the blood and bones of formulary apportionment as it not only requires a substantial level of coordination for implementation but also is intrinsic multi-sided decided by the multilateralism of the factors and the formula.

In short, the concept of the CSFM, proposed by China, has gained broad recognition and support in the international community.[937] It calls on all countries to unite and cooperate beyond ideological, cultural, and historical differences to jointly address global challenges and build a more harmonious, stable, and sustainable world. It is asserted that the concept provides a new framework for international cooperation, promotes the reform and improvement of the global governance system, and offers valuable ideas and pathways for achieving common human development and lasting peace.

In addition to the concrete paths discussed above, it is believed that the concept or ideology of the CSFM, which China has championed for a decade in various venues,

937. For example, this concept was incorporated by the United Nations into the resolution on the UN Commission for Social Development, and used by the UN Disarmament Commission, the Human Rights Council, and the UN General Assembly First Commission, *see* Jun Ding and Hongjin Cheng, 'China's Proposition to Build a Community of Shared Future for Mankind and the Middle East Governance' (2017) 11 Asian Journal of Middle Eastern and Islamic Studies 1, 270 https://doi.org/10.1080/25765949.2017.12023314 accessed 26 August 2025.

can provide an additional conceptual basis for promoting formulary apportionment by China.

## 9.4 CLOSING REMARKS

This chapter explores theoretical aspects of the thesis. Following the detailed analysis of the practical elements of formulary apportionment, it becomes necessary to engage in conceptual thinking to envision potential future developments.

Assuming China is the subject country of the test with leading the advancement of formulary apportionment, this chapter concludes the thesis by drawing the picture along two lines. One is the substantive design of the prospective regime; another is the actual route that may be employed. The substantive aspects of the elements of formulary apportionment draw on the thoughts of the discussions in the previous chapters, especially the principal part in Chapters 4-6 and the comparative part in Chapter 3. The recommendations in this part do not claim to represent the optimal design but are instead based on a series of compromises and considerations, reflecting the author's analytical judgment.

As for the possible routes to roll out the tentative regime, the discussions touch on two contrasting approaches: one is the multilateral tax treaty, and another is employing the existing trade and investment relations. Both of them have yet to be seen in the real world and thus are of pure thought experiment nature. While their realistic relevance is unpredictable, hopefully, these visions may contribute to the situation when the day finally comes.

# PART V The Epilogue

# CHAPTER 10
# Conclusion

## 10.1 INTRODUCTION

As stated in the very beginning, this work serves to answer this main research question:

> **Main Question**: Should formulary apportionment be reconsidered a fundamental reform option in the evolving context of international taxation?

To answer this main question, the following subsidiary questions have been derived:

> Research Question 1: Is formulary apportionment, as opposed to the dominant ALP, something 'real', or in other words, a practical reality or merely a theoretical construct?
> Research Question 2: To what extent does FA exist in the current tax landscape, and if it does, what insights can the various forms of FA provide for designing an international FA system, envisioning a positive future for FA?
> Research Question 3: What is the analytical framework for the normative analysis of formulary apportionment, and what does it inform for formulary apportionment?
> Research Question 4: Is China in a position to adopt formulary apportionment, and if so, what could be the potential pathway for its implementation, and what formula would be recommended?

Consistent with the ordering of the research questions, the research was divided into five parts. This conclusion, as the last part, is to present the conclusions of this research corresponding to the Main Question and subsidiary questions.

## 10.2 FORMULARY APPORTIONMENT BEING REAL

The changes in the international tax system may seem to be driven by a series of random, unpredictable events, but when viewed through the roles played by the ALP and formulary apportionment within it, a coherent narrative emerges. The examination of the entire process makes it clear that the ALP's theological status is substantially ungrounded.

In the universe of FA, a misconception is that FA is a fancy and illusory idea confined to academic research. However, Chapter 2 reveals an opposite truth in the context of the staged evolution of the international tax regime.

### 10.2.1 FA Throughout the Phases of International Taxation

The evolution of international taxation can be understood through four distinct phases, each shaped by different economic and political pressures. While formulary apportionment has not been the predominant method within the existing international tax system, it has been a persistent and influential concept that has shaped discussions and proposals for reforms throughout the phases of international tax evolution. Its historical trajectory and the current reconsideration of its potential highlight the dynamic and evolving nature of international tax policies in response to global economic changes.

To be specific, formulary apportionment has played distinct roles throughout the evolution of international taxation, emerging and fading in relevance as the global tax landscape has shifted. Its influence can be observed across four major phases of development in international taxation: the Revenue Phase, the Trade Phase, the Anti-Avoidance Phase, and the Allocation Phase.

In the Revenue Phase (spanning from the end of World War I to the post-World War II period), formulary apportionment was primarily used to address the allocation of revenues between capital-exporting and capital-importing countries. At this time, global tax concerns were largely driven by the need to allocate profits in industries such as transportation, where businesses operated across multiple jurisdictions. Formulary systems were often applied at sub-national levels, such as in the United States and Germany, to determine tax liabilities based on a proportion of business activities, such as the length of railway tracks within a state. However, its international application remained limited, as double taxation was not yet a widespread concern.

As global commerce expanded in the Trade Phase (post-WWII to the 1990s), the focus of international taxation shifted towards facilitating cross-border investment and trade. In this period, the trend favoured the reduction of withholding taxes and the expansion of tax treaties, which marginalized the role of formulary apportionment. The ALP, which allocates profits based on the idea that related entities should be taxed as if they were independent, became the preferred method for transfer pricing, gradually replacing the use of formulary apportionment in the global tax framework.

By the Anti-Avoidance Phase (1990s to ~2015), the increasing complexity of global trade and the rise of MNEs led to growing concerns over tax avoidance. Although formulary apportionment was revisited as a potential solution to profit shifting and tax avoidance, it was not widely adopted. Practical concerns, such as the administrative complexity of implementing a formulary system across different jurisdictions and the difficulty of coordinating tax policies between countries, prevented it from becoming a standard method in international tax regimes. Instead, the ALP continued to dominate, despite its limitations in addressing modern tax avoidance strategies.

In the current Allocation Phase (post-2015), spurred by the OECD BEPS Project, formulary apportionment has experienced renewed interest. The BEPS Project exposed significant flaws in the international tax system, particularly the inability to adequately tax MNEs where value is truly created. This has led to discussions about the potential of formulary apportionment to provide a more equitable solution by allocating profits based on real economic activity rather than artificial transactions between subsidiaries. However, despite this renewed attention, formulary apportionment remains an alternative rather than a mainstream approach to international taxation, as countries grapple with the complexity of implementing such a system on a global scale.

For answering the Research Question 1 and the related secondary questions, while formulary apportionment has offered a theoretically sound and, in some cases, practical alternative for addressing cross-border tax challenges, its role has been largely overshadowed by the rise of the ALS. Nevertheless, its periodic resurgence in discussions – especially in the post-BEPS environment – demonstrates that it remains a viable option for the future of international taxation, particularly in an era where tax fairness and equity are increasingly emphasized.

### 10.2.2 The Rise of the ALP

The dominance of the ALP in the international tax system is a product of historical developments, institutional momentum, and political compromises rather than any inherent theoretical superiority. Its adoption was shaped by the interests of powerful economies, the influence of international organizations like the OECD, and the administrative simplicity it offered.

In the 1920s and 1930s, the LON initiated efforts to create a uniform approach to international taxation, seeking ways to address double taxation. During these discussions, formulary apportionment was considered, but the ALP was favoured due to its simplicity and its alignment with the prevailing economic thought, which emphasized treating corporations as separate entities. Mitchell Carroll's extensive report for the LON in the 1930s contributed to the shift in favour of separate accounting and the ALP, marginalizing formulary apportionment as too complex and difficult to administer.

The adoption of the ALP was solidified in the post-war era, particularly through the efforts of the OECD. In the 1960s, the OECD 'codified' the ALP in its transfer pricing guidelines, establishing it as the default method for taxing MNEs. The ALP's simplicity and alignment with the interests of developed economies made it an attractive option for many countries, reinforcing its dominance through bilateral tax treaties.

Thereafter, once the ALP became entrenched in the tax systems of major economies and embedded in international tax treaties, it gained inertia. Policymakers and tax authorities became accustomed to using it, and the global tax infrastructure was built around it. This created a path dependency that made it difficult to switch to alternatives like formulary apportionment.

The ALP's rise was not due to its theoretical strengths. Its appeal lay largely in practical and political considerations. Developed countries, especially capital-exporting ones, saw the ALP as a means of preserving their tax base by taxing profits where corporations were legally headquartered, rather than where economic activity occurred. It also required less international cooperation and fewer administrative changes compared to alternatives like formulary apportionment. For MNEs, the ALP provided flexibility in profit allocation and created opportunities for tax planning, often leading to profit shifting and base erosion.

The ALP's theoretical shortcomings – especially in the modern, digitalized global economy – continue to fuel debates about whether alternatives like formulary apportionment might offer a more equitable and effective solution in the future.

## 10.3 LESSONS OF FORMULARY APPORTIONMENT FROM THE REAL WORLD

Chapter 3 confirms a fundamental fact, that FA offers a viable alternative to the ALP, and its application is heavily influenced by the political, economic, and legal landscapes of each region. The US experience underscores the importance of judicial and legislative balancing in creating consistency across states, whereas Canada demonstrates the advantages of centralized coordination. The CCCTB proposal exemplifies the complexities of implementing FA across sovereign nations, and the OECD's TPS illustrates the potential for FA to reshape international tax rules in response to globalization and digitalization.

There are material differences in the existence of formulary apportionment across these four samples, including subnational *versus* regional application and implementation versus proposal status. This research extracts the most critical elements from these samples, categorized as internal and external factors. These include jurisdiction to tax rule and territorial scope, delineation of taxable unit, harmonization and determination of tax base, and choice and weight of apportionment factors. Within these elements, each of the four samples can offer valuable lessons at a fundamental level, which may provide insights into the design of a future international FA regime.

The United States' state-level FA system, rooted in its federalist structure, presents a unique blend of historical precedent and complexity of law realities. The jurisdiction to tax, governed by constitutional principles such as the Due Process and Commerce Clauses, emphasizes the importance of economic nexus and physical presence in determining tax liabilities. The unitary business principle serves as a conceptual foundation that allows the aggregation of income across multiple jurisdictions, though it remains constrained by state-specific variations in apportionment formulas and the boundaries of combined reporting.

In contrast, Canada's FA system, though similarly federal, achieves a greater degree of uniformity due to centralized coordination between provinces and the federal government. The use of permanent establishments as a nexus rule and a harmonized approach to the allocation of taxable income reflects a stable, collaborative structure that minimizes inter-provincial discrepancies. The apportionment factors in Canada focus primarily on payroll and property, highlighting the simplicity and coherence of the system.

The EU's CCCTB proposal marked a bold attempt to integrate FA into a transnational context. The territorial scope of the CCCTB, which excluded non-EU income, reflects a pragmatic approach to balancing Member State sovereignty with the need for EU-wide tax harmonization. By adopting a three-factor apportionment formula (sales, payroll, and assets) with equal weighting, the CCCTB proposal aligned with modern corporate tax principles but also faced challenges in implementation, particularly in relation to double taxation treaties and compliance burdens.

The OECD's TPS, particularly Pillar One, introduces an unprecedented global FA mechanism aimed at reallocating taxing rights in the digital economy. Pillar One's reliance on a new nexus concept based on significant economic presence (without the need for physical presence) represents a significant departure from traditional jurisdictional rules. By introducing a revenue-based apportionment model for residual profits, the TPS attempts to address the long-standing criticisms of the ALP. However, its effectiveness in resolving tax base erosion and profit shifting remains to be fully assessed.

Building on these detailed and specific lessons and the analytical framework tailored for FA, three fundamental principles must be adhered to in designing an international FA system:

> First, in the specific technical choices for each element, although different choices have their pros and cons, they should align with the core principles of FA. This entails recognizing MNEs as unitary businesses and allocating profits across jurisdictions based on the presence of value-creation factors. The relative weight of these factors should be determined according to a 50-50 split between supply and demand sides.
>
> Second, in any sense, more harmonization of FA elements is advisable than less harmonization. While jurisdictions may retain some freedom to choose specific elements within certain limits, FA remains a centralized system, reliant on a higher degree of coordination and cooperation.
>
> Third, the design of FA should prioritize the values of international tax equity and legitimacy rather than neutrality or efficiency. Under the current system, the issue of unfair profit allocation between developed and developing countries remains unresolved, which is also a persistent problem with the ALP-based system. To some extent, the application of FA in Pillar One, Amount A, addresses this issue but is still far from being sufficient. Additionally, addressing tax avoidance represents a different level of consideration that should not dominate the design of FA.

## 10.4 THE ANALYTICAL FRAMEWORK CONSISTING OF EQUITY AND LEGITIMACY, BUT LESS OF NEUTRALITY

This research envisages a framework of international tax principles based on two primary pillars. One pertains to efficiency, dealing with the role of taxation in fostering social welfare; the other concerns morality, examining to what extent taxation can promote social justice.

International tax law is an intersection field, where transitioning from domestic to international tax law and from international law to international tax law involves a transformation not just of the objects in scope but also of the underlying relationships. Therefore, the research identifies a possible gap in the current literature, which is the unanalysed and unrevised transplantation of tax principles born within the context of domestic law into the realm of international tax law. This is problematic. As such, in discussing each principle, the research generally contemplates the principle's transition from domestic to international law context, then elucidates these principles against the backdrop of international law.

Under the categories of economic and moralistic pillars, this research does not treat the commonly seen principles as *a priori* assumptions but instead engages in a 'clean-slate' discussion of neutrality, legitimacy, and equity. The research ultimately selects legitimacy and equity as the principles within the analytical framework of international taxation, while neutrality is placed in an inferior position that provides *ex-post* evaluative insights.

### 10.4.1 The Rise of Inter-Nation Equity

Rather than accepting direct internalization of taxation principles, it explores the concept of equity in a step-by-step manner, adapting it for the international tax system.

The first step addresses equity in a unitary fiscal setting, where inter-individual and individual-government relationships are central. The principles of ability to pay and benefit guide national tax system design, particularly concerning tax bases and rate structures.

In the international setting, additional subjects - non-residents and foreign governments - complicate equity considerations. The transition from unitary to international frameworks requires reinterpreting equity, as direct internationalization of norms like the ability to pay is inadequate. Instead, the concept of inter-nation equity emerges, focusing on sovereign equality and international distributive justice, which diverge from domestic inter-individual equity.

The final step examines these equity principles in the context of international corporate taxation. This approach is supported by the equal allegiance theory, which posits that taxpayers should face equal taxation based on their economic allegiance within a jurisdiction, irrespective of geographic income attribution.

Throughout the above three steps, the key insights reveal that the direct internationalization of domestic equity principles, such as the AtP and BP, is not feasible due to the fundamentally different nature of relationships in an international setting. This difference necessitates the principle of inter-nation equity – which shifts the focus from individuals to nations, emphasizing the equitable distribution of tax burdens among countries rather than among individual taxpayers.

Additionally, the economic allegiance theory is introduced as a foundational concept for inter-nation equity, emphasizing that a taxpayer's economic interests across different jurisdictions should influence the allocation of tax rights. This theory supports two proposed approaches for achieving inter-nation equity: the Equal Earned Income approach, which assumes that income can be geographically attributed to its sources, and the Equal Allegiance approach, which uses economic allegiance as a proxy for determining tax revenue distribution.

The principles of equity, originally developed for individual taxation, can be effectively extended to corporate taxation within an international context. Corporate taxation, despite its complexities, fundamentally connects to individual taxation, with its legitimacy grounded in the impact on shareholders, employees, and customers. The increased mobility and complex structures of MNEs demand a more nuanced application of equity principles, leading to the rejection of the direct internationalization of inter-individual equity norms.

Inter-nation equity not only provides justification for adopting formulary apportionment as an alternative to the ALP but also offers clear guidance on its design. By focusing on the equitable distribution of tax rights among nations – whether through the Equal Earned Income or Equal Allegiance approaches – formulary apportionment emerges as a more just method for taxing MNEs.

Furthermore, inter-nation equity informs the selection of factors and weights in the apportionment formula, ensuring a balanced allocation of taxing rights between residence and source countries. This approach addresses existing imbalances in the international tax system, aiming for a fairer distribution of tax revenues that accurately reflects the economic realities of global business operations.

### 10.4.2 Legitimacy: Normative and Descriptive Variables

The principle of legitimacy in international taxation is fundamental to the justice and efficacy of tax laws on a global scale. Legitimacy in this context is multifaceted, encompassing both normative and descriptive dimensions. Normative legitimacy pertains to the justification of the government's power to enact and enforce laws, while descriptive legitimacy focuses on the processes through which laws are created, emphasizing stakeholder participation and democratic principles. Both aspects are critical, any deficit in either can undermine the overall legitimacy of a tax system, and both aspects support formulary apportionment by providing a more equitable and cooperative framework for international taxation, in contrast to the current ALP-based system.

Historically, the legitimacy of taxation has evolved alongside the changing nature of states and their relationships with taxpayers. Early models, such as the 'state-individual' model introduced by Lorenz von Stein, were expanded into more complex frameworks like the 'state-society-economy' model proposed by Klaus Vogel. These developments reflect the rise of corporations and the transformation of economies, which necessitate a re-examination of tax legitimacy in both national and international contexts.

The current international tax order has revealed limitations in the traditional sovereignty-based discourse on tax legitimacy. In response, a new evaluative framework is suggested, one that aligns legitimacy with the interconnected systems of state, society, and economy at both national and international levels.

Modern normative legitimacy is presented as a more robust foundation for international tax systems, particularly in the context of formulary apportionment. This approach, which allocates tax liabilities based on a formula rather than relying solely on traditional concepts of residence and source, is seen as more aligned with the realities of a globalized economy.

Within this updated paradigm of normative legitimacy, the traditional concepts of 'residence' and 'source' lose their conventional significance. 'Residence' no longer implicitly confers the right to tax a resident's global income, and 'source' transcends the simplistic notion of taxing income solely within a nation's borders. Rather, states stand on equal footing regarding their entitlement to tax, and their taxing rights are justified through the taxpayer's engagement in the intricate relationship between the state, society, and the economy. This approach posits that a taxpayer's tax liability is contingent upon their level of involvement within the state's triumvirate structure of governance, applicable to both the country of source and the country of residence. As such, formulary apportionment aligns more naturally with normative legitimacy because it allocates taxing rights based on the economic reality of an MNE's activities across multiple states, rather than formalistic notions of residence or source. On the other side, by focusing on the MNE's participation in the economy of each state, formulary apportionment modernizes normative legitimacy. This framework ensures that taxation is justified by the degree of the MNE's involvement in the triangular system of state, society, and economy, rather than outdated notions of residence or territoriality.

In terms of descriptive legitimacy, this research adopts the notion of a legitimacy deficit, positing that the international tax regime has long been plagued by a crisis of insufficient legitimacy. Subsequently, the analysis identifies one of the critical contributors to this deficit, which is the dominant status of the ALP. The rationale of ALP and the regime of transfer pricing rely on the 'platform function' thereunder for states to retain minimal yet requisite room for cooperation and coordination. The norm of ALP has been the crux in the competition-based regime of international taxation. It, on the one hand, is a product of the nascent system; on the other hand, it unintentionally attaches great significance in the subsequent development due to its platform functionality. The ALP is one of the most typical manifestations that the current system of international taxation has been disincentivizing descriptive legitimacy.

Formulary apportionment, in contrast, is proposed as a system that inherently requires and incentivizes higher levels of coordination among states, thus enhancing descriptive legitimacy. The adoption of formulary apportionment has the potential to transform the international tax system, making it more cooperative and equitable.

By aligning both normative and descriptive legitimacy with the current global economic landscape, the international tax system can become more just, sustainable, and stable. The modernization of tax legitimacy principles, particularly through the adoption of approaches like formulary apportionment, is essential to address the challenges posed by the evolving international tax order.

### 10.4.3 Neutrality, Meaningful but Not That Useful

Neutrality in taxation, particularly in the context of international tax policy, has long been regarded as a tool for minimizing the distortive effects of tax systems on economic activities. The analysis of CEN and CIN demonstrates the inherent tension between these two principles, as both aim to achieve different forms of economic efficiency but cannot coexist without significant global tax harmonization. CEN, which promotes worldwide production efficiency, often receives more academic support due to its focus on minimizing distortions in capital movement. However, it faces practical challenges in its implementation, particularly when tax rates differ across jurisdictions.

The role of neutrality as a guiding principle is also questioned, suggesting a shift from its use as an instructional benchmark in tax policy design to a more evaluative role. Neutrality can provide insights into the economic consequences of tax policies, but its limitations in addressing the complexities of real-world tax systems are evident. Moreover, global trends toward tax cooperation, as seen in the post-BEPS landscape, may reflect a move away from tax competition and challenge the traditional reliance on neutrality as a central principle.

First, the race concerning neutrality must be terminated, and the focus of the discussion should not be on a 'winner takes all' paradigm; second, global efficiency is preferable to national efficiency; third, and arguably, it is seen more cooperation among states under the mechanism of the OECD/G20 Inclusive Framework, and lately, the efforts at the United Nations towards a global tax convention;[938] lastly, the more appropriate positioning of neutrality is as an *ex-post* evaluative rather than an instructional guideline.

In this context, neutrality is seen as one of several considerations in international tax policy, rather than the defining framework. Neutrality does not contribute much as a principle within the analytical framework of this research. Its value lies in providing a lens through which economic efficiency can be assessed, while other principles such as legitimacy, equity, and global cooperation take on greater importance. The pursuit of a more comprehensive approach to tax policy, one that moves beyond the binary choice between CEN and CIN, appears necessary for addressing the complexities of global taxation in an increasingly interconnected world.

938. *See* relevant developments at https://financing.desa.un.org/unfcitc accessed on 28 August 2024.

## 10.5 THE 'CASE STUDY' OF CHINA IMPLEMENTING FORMULARY APPORTIONMENT

### 10.5.1 Understanding China's International Tax Position Through BRI

The analysis has demonstrated the increasing complexity and sophistication of China's tax policies within the international legal framework, reflecting its growing participation in global economic networks. Tax policy has become a strategic tool for fostering cross-border investment and economic integration, rather than a solely domestic concern.

Furthermore, the findings point to a clear shift from a predominantly source-based taxation system towards a more residence-oriented framework. This transition underscores China's effort to balance its role as both a capital-exporting and capital-importing nation.

The BRI emerges as a crucial driver of these changes, with significant impacts on domestic tax laws and international tax agreements. The initiative has spurred greater harmonization and cooperation between the participating countries, aligning tax policies with broader economic goals. Specific reforms, including the following adjustments at both domestic law and treaty level, exemplify how China's tax regime is evolving to meet the demands of a globally integrated economy.

The reforms in China's foreign tax credit system are designed to support outbound investment by Chinese enterprises, offering a more comprehensive mechanism to eliminate double taxation and thus encourage global expansion. These changes indicate China's desire to position its tax policies to better facilitate the international flow of capital, particularly for Chinese companies expanding overseas.

Moreover, the CFC regime has been a key feature of the regulatory framework that addresses tax avoidance by Chinese companies operating abroad. By strengthening and expanding the scope of the CFC regime, China has enhanced its ability to combat tax deferral strategies, securing the taxation of income from foreign subsidiaries and reinforcing its residence-based taxation principles. This development points to a broader trend of safeguarding the taxing rights of Chinese authorities while supporting the international competitiveness of Chinese enterprises.

In addition to domestic reforms, the international dimension of China's tax regime has undergone substantial changes. The expansion of China's tax treaty network, particularly with countries involved in the BRI, signals the growing breadth of China's engagement with global tax norms. This network has facilitated cross-border investment and reduced barriers to trade by aligning tax obligations more effectively between China and its partner countries. By negotiating more comprehensive agreements, including provisions that reduce withholding tax rates and adopt flexible tax credit systems, China is positioning itself to attract investment while simultaneously fostering its outbound economic activities.

Key policy tools, such as sparing credits and reduced withholding tax rates, reflect China's broader strategic shift. These tools, initially designed to attract foreign investment into China, have evolved to serve the needs of Chinese investors abroad, illustrating the move towards a more residence-oriented system. The inclusion of such provisions in treaties with BRI countries highlights the initiative's influence on China's tax policy, encouraging not only the inflow of foreign capital but also facilitating the outward flow of Chinese investment.

The role of the MFN clauses in China's tax treaties further illustrates the country's increasingly global tax strategy. The adoption and implementation of MFN provisions, particularly in treaties with key BRI partners, reflect China's growing influence in shaping the terms of international tax cooperation to its benefit, ensuring competitive conditions for its domestic enterprises on the global stage.

Overall, China's international tax regime is undergoing a significant transformation, influenced by both domestic economic imperatives and its expanding global presence.

### 10.5.2 China's Position Towards Formulary Apportionment

Chapter 8 answers whether China is in a good position or the viability thereof to explore formulary apportionment. For this purpose, Chapter 8 utilizes a combination of historical analysis, policy examination, and strategic evaluation to assess China's role in the international tax landscape. It deeply analyses China's tax policies, international agreements, and the evolution of its tax law to understand its strategic fit for formulary apportionment.

The exploration of China's potential role in advancing FA in the international tax landscape reveals a strategic opportunity aligned with its evolving economic status. As China shifts from a traditional source country to a residence-based tax system, driven by its growing outbound investments, it positions itself at a critical junction in global tax reform. The BRI plays a pivotal role in this transformation, not only enhancing China's economic reach but also providing a framework for rethinking its international tax strategy. This shift underscores the need for innovative tax governance models that can reconcile China's dual roles as both a world manufacturer and an emerging world market.

The strategic viability of FA becomes evident in this context. China's dissatisfaction with the current ALP, which inadequately reflects its significant contributions to global value chains, suggests a need for reform. Traditional transfer pricing models often assign limited returns to production entities, under-compensating countries like China that play a central role in manufacturing. As a remedy, China's approach to transfer pricing, particularly its use of contribution analysis, reflects the principles of formulary apportionment. This approach allows for a more holistic view of value creation, considering both production and market demand in the allocation of profits.

China's evolving perception of value creation further strengthens the case for reform. By recognizing the contributions of both supply and demand sides in global economic activities, China challenges the origin-based international tax system. The incorporation of market demand into value creation offers a more equitable distribution of profits, particularly for countries that, like China, represent significant consumer markets. This perspective aligns with the use of multi-factor formulary apportionment, which includes sales, assets, and labour as key factors in determining tax liabilities. Such a model could rectify imbalances in the current system that disproportionately benefit developed economies.

China's active participation in global tax initiatives, such as the BEPS Project, highlights its role as both a follower and a reformist in the international tax order. While adhering to established norms, China has also positioned itself to challenge the current framework, advocating for changes that reflect its unique status as both a world factory and an emerging market. This dual role enables China to push for reforms that better serve its long-term economic goals, particularly in securing a fairer distribution of taxable profits.

The congruence between China's international tax strategy and formulary apportionment is further reinforced by its efforts to recalibrate income allocation models through concepts like location-specific advantages and an expanded DEMPE framework. These policies reflect China's broader philosophy of value creation, which seeks to align taxation more closely with the realities of global production and consumption. By advancing these ideas within the framework of existing global tax governance, China is laying the groundwork for more substantive reforms in the future.

Ultimately, China's unique position in the global economy, as both a manufacturing hub and a consumer market, creates a compelling case for its exploration of formulary apportionment. This approach offers a pathway to harmonize China's dual roles in the international tax landscape while addressing its dissatisfaction with the current system's failure to fairly distribute profits. Through its evolving tax strategy, China is poised to influence the future of global tax governance, potentially leading the way toward a more equitable international tax system that better reflects the realities of a globalized economy.

To encapsulate, the following factors make China well-positioned to explore formulary apportionment in international taxation:

(1) China's presumed exploration of formulary apportionment is not just a technical tax matter but also a strategic move reflecting its broader economic and political ambitions on the global stage.
(2) The dual role of both a major global manufacturer (world factory) and a significant consumer market (world market) allows China to challenge the existing international tax norms and potentially pioneer a new approach in international tax governance, and it also provides a strong incentive for China to seek a taxation system that more fairly allocates taxing rights between these two aspects, which formulary apportionment may offer.
(3) The reform towards formulary apportionment will be in alignment with the global tax reform trend.
(4) China's exploration of formulary apportionment also reflects its broader role in representing the interests of developing countries in global tax matters.

### 10.5.3 Substantive Design Recommended for China's Exploration of Formulary Apportionment

The research underscores the importance of a strategic approach in designing a formulary apportionment system tailored to China's unique economic landscape. The analysis reveals that both external components, such as jurisdiction to tax rules, and internal components, like the determination of taxable units and apportionment factors, require careful consideration.

First, jurisdiction to tax rule intersects with state sovereignty and economic realities, making its modulation for tax reform challenging. The principle of legitimacy, especially normative legitimacy, examines the evolving concept of the state and its interaction with taxpayers and sovereignty transformation. Jurisdiction to tax is dictated by the legitimacy principle, aligning with taxpayers' participation in the national tax order. This challenges the classical residence and source-based norms in the international tax order. In the era of formulary apportionment, jurisdiction to tax norm is expected to evolve to align MNEs' tax liabilities with states' tax collection powers. As the outcome of the comparative analysis, Traditional jurisdiction to tax concepts like residency, permanent establishment, and specific income sources are used in Canadian and EU regimes. In contrast, it is concluded that The US factor presence test is a more congruent alternative for formulary apportionment.

Adopting the factor presence test would replace the 'nationality' based jurisdiction to tax in the 'residence' state and redefine the concept of a permanent establishment in the 'source' state. China taxes non-residents' incomes sourced within its borders, categorized into six types with specific proxies for determining the source. The impact of the proposed jurisdiction to tax norm on these rules depends on the tax base design under formulary apportionment.

The concrete design of the factor presence test should consider other elements of formulary apportionment and implementation roadmaps. It is a bright-line test offering simplicity but can be manipulated; its design might include an 'either-or' structure and a value-proportion approach. To prevent business operation distortions, *de minimis* activities, and internet/digital technology uses need scrutiny.

Second, when exploring the practical and empirical areas of formulary apportionment in international taxation, the focus often falls on the concept of territorial scope. The key challenge lies in effectively designing water's edge limitations within the formulary apportionment regime. Abstract theories on the ideal water's edge system are subordinate to more pragmatic and technical concerns. This approach is evident in the comparative analysis of formulary apportionment regimes across different jurisdictions. Notably, the experiences of the United States, Canada, and the EU CCCTB proposal, or the TPS all provide valuable insights. These examples highlight the complexities and variations in designing water's edge limitations, tailored to the specifics of each formulary apportionment model.

In the United States, for instance, the need to define the boundaries of formulary apportionment and the practicalities of establishing water's edge limitations become apparent. Canada's experiences, however, reveal that applying water's edge limitations to single corporations within a formulary apportionment regime is relatively straightforward compared to dealing with unitary enterprises. The EU's CCCTB proposal, designed for a larger supranational entity, offers a model for a more internationally oriented formulary apportionment system.

Turning to China's potential implementation of formulary apportionment, it becomes clear that lessons from these jurisdictions need careful adaptation. The Canadian model, for instance, contrasts starkly with the suggested approach for China. The United States, while advanced in its implementation, shows a lack of cohesive 'unitary' thinking due to its state-centric approach, unlike the EU's CCCTB, which benefits from being designed for a unified political group.

The overarching goal of a water's edge system is to define the operational boundaries of a formulary apportionment regime. In the context of China, this involves ensuring that the system operates within a select group of participating countries to minimize conflicts with the established ALP. This necessitates a focus on personal and objective scopes, determining which parts of a business and which types of income should be included or excluded from formulary apportionment. Specific considerations include the exclusion of income from third countries and the inclusion of corporations in tax havens if they are closely linked to the main business.

In short, while the water's edge concept is a vital component of formulary apportionment, its design should not overshadow the overall framework. This necessitates a systemic approach to defining water's edge limitations, one that takes into account the broader objectives and workings of the formulary apportionment system and its interaction with existing international tax structures.

Third, in terms of the delineation of the taxable unit, formulary apportionment may apply to both individual corporations and corporate groups. However, the Canadian approach to formulary apportionment doesn't fully align with international tax challenges, leading to a preference for the American unitary business approach and the European consolidation approach. Each has its advantages and limitations. The unitary business approach is favoured due to its foundational role in formulary apportionment, its focus beyond legal unity, and its practical experience in the United States, though it carries risks of misuse.

To determine if corporate group members constitute a unitary enterprise, several criteria are suggested from the perspective of methodological coherence and administrative ease.

Fourth, harmonizing and determining the tax base for MNEs is both a practical and theoretical issue, focusing on how to define and calculate income for tax purposes. A harmonized tax base is crucial for reducing tax complexity and avoiding issues like double taxation or under-taxation. This harmonization has been effectively achieved in the US states, Canadian provinces, and the EU's CCCTB regimes. The trend is towards 'expansionism', where income is generally considered apportionable unless explicitly exempt, as seen in the US and EU CCCTB proposals.

The determination of the tax base involves deciding which incomes of the unitary enterprise are subject to apportionment. The US approach, which is more aligned with the unitary business foundation of formulary apportionment, is preferred. This approach is based on the unitary business principle, suggesting that all incomes generated by the unitary business should be included in the combined tax base. The determination of apportionable income in the US relies on the 'nexus' of underlying business activities with the unitary business.

Regarding the principles of legitimacy and equity, the research argues that tax liability is not solely based on the geographic source of income, but rather on the taxpayer's involvement in the unitary business. This view supports the idea that income should be combined and apportioned based on its connection to the unitary business, adhering to the equal allegiance over equal earned income approach.

Last, in terms of the choice and weight of apportionment factors, the apportionment factors directly influence the allocation of taxable income and revenue to different tax jurisdictions by determining the formula's numerator, denominator, and multiplier. Unlike the ALS, which attributes income based on specific activities and locations, formulary apportionment uses a broader, more holistic approach, assuming no specific geographic source of income. This approach aligns with normative principles of international taxation, offering an alternative to traditional methods.

The principles of legitimacy and equity are key in selecting apportionment factors. Legitimacy challenges the traditional yardsticks of tax jurisdiction like residence and source rules, advocating for a consistent factor-based approach that considers the taxpayer's roles across different states. This approach ensures alignment between the criteria for establishing the tax power and quantifying tax liabilities. Equity, however, emphasizes fair treatment among taxpayers and equitable profit sharing among nations. It argues for a system where MNEs are taxed equitably, irrespective of their location, promoting fairness in international taxation.

Observations on the existing regimes present diversity in the choice and weighting of factors in different tax regimes, with shifts over time from equal-weighted factors like property, payroll, and sales to more sales-centric formulas. This reflects an evolving understanding of value creation and the need to balance different principles and policy priorities.

Considering China's unique position in international taxation, traditional factors like property, payroll, and sales are suggested for China's experimentation with formulary apportionment. These factors meet legitimacy and equity principles by representing the supply-demand view of value creation. However, balancing these factors with efficiency considerations leads to favouring a double-weighted sales factor. This formula achieves a balance between origin(source) and destination states in value creation and additionally retains some neutrality benefits.

Operational rules for implementing these factors are critical, requiring clear guidelines on what items to include or exclude when calculating the value of each factor. Drawing from experiences in the US and the EU can provide valuable insights for developing these detailed provisions.

### 10.5.4 The Roadmap That China Can Take for the Formulary Adventure

Until the launch of the TPS, formulary apportionment was a concept not implemented internationally. The practical application of this concept raises numerous problems, categorized into two groups: issues inherent to the concept and challenges related to its implementation. While there is extensive discussion on the former, strategies for initiating a formulary apportionment system by a single country are less explored. When China or any other country is exemplified as taking the lead, what could be the feasible route to take?

One approach is through an MLC, a legal framework imposing obligations on states and signalling a commitment to common goals or standards. China could spearhead negotiations for an MLC, agreeing on key terms for a shared formulary apportionment regime. The EU's CCCTB proposal and the TPS on digital taxation illustrate this approach. However, negotiating an MLC is challenging due to the novel and globally unprecedented nature of formulary apportionment.

Another strategy involves utilizing investment and trade relations. Countries with strong economic ties are more likely to collaborate on tax issues. For China, leading in global trade, leveraging these relationships could be advantageous. Specifically, initiatives like the BRI and the RCEP offer platforms to promote formulary apportionment. BRI focuses on infrastructure cooperation with developing countries, while RCEP, the world's largest free trade bloc, includes Asia-Pacific nations with diverse economic statuses.

The ideology of the CSFM, proposed by the Communist Party of China, emphasizes global cooperation and common prosperity. This concept aligns with the goals of formulary apportionment, advocating for a fair and integrated international tax system, mutual benefit, and win-win cooperation. CSFM's focus on mutual respect, fairness, justice, and multilateralism resonates with the principles of formulary apportionment, making it a suitable conceptual basis for China's promotion of this tax approach.

In conclusion, while formulary apportionment faces conceptual and implementation challenges, China's strong trade networks and commitment to global cooperation through initiatives like BRI, RCEP, and CSFM offer potential pathways for its successful implementation.

# Bibliography


Adams TS, 'Interstate and International Double Taxation' (1932) 101 Lectures on Taxation 102.

Agundez-Garcia A, 'The Delineation and Apportionment of an EU Consolidated Tax Base for Multi-Jurisdictional Corporate Income Taxation: A Review of Issues and Options' [2006] Working Paper.

Ahmadov J, '"Most Appropriate Method" as the New OECD Transfer Pricing Standard: Has the Hierarchy of Methods Been Completely Eliminated' (2011) 18 International Transfer Pricing Journal.

Aikins M, 'Common Control and the Delineation of the Taxable Entity' (2011) 121 Yale Law Journal

Albrecht AR, 'The Taxation of Aliens under International Law' (1952) 29 British Yearbook of International Law 145.

Anand B and Sansing R, 'The Weighting Game: Formula Apportionment as an Instrument of Public Policy' 53 National Tax Journal 183.

Arnold BJ, 'Canada's International Tax System: Historical Review, Problems and Outlook for the Future' (2018) No. 8 Canada in International Law at 150 and Beyond Paper https://www.cigionline.org/publications/canadas-international-tax-system-historical-review-problems-and-outlook-future/ accessed 2 December 2023.

Arnold BJ, *International Tax Primer* (4th edn, Kluwer Law International 2019).

Arnold BJ and McIntyre MJ, *International Tax Primer* (2nd edn, Kluwer Law International B V 2002).

Asen E and Bunn D, 'What European OECD Countries Are Doing about Digital Services Taxes' (2020) https://taxfoundation.org/digital-tax-europe-2020/ accessed 23 November 2323.

Asllani S, 'The Definition of a "Place of Effective Management" at Article 4 Paragraph 3 of the 2014 OECD Model Tax Convention' [2017] 2017 UBT International Conference.

Atkinson AB and Stiglitz JE, 'The Design of Tax Structure: Direct versus Indirect Taxation' (1976) 6 Journal of Public Economics.

Auerbach A et al., 'Destination-Based Cash Flow Taxation' Oxford Legal Studies Research Paper No. 14/2017.

Auerbach AJ, Devereux MP and Simpson H, 'Taxing Corporate Income' (National Bureau of Economic Research 2008).

Ault HJ, 'Corporate Integration, Tax Treaties and the Division of the International Tax Base: Principles and Practices' (1991) 47 Tax Law Review 565.

Avery Jones JF, 'Sir Josiah Stamp and Double Income Tax' in John Tiley (ed.), *Studies in the History of Tax Law*, vol. 6 (Hart Publishing 2013).

Avi-Yonah R, 'The Rise and Fall of Arm's Length: A Study in the Evolution of US International Taxation' (1995) 15 Virginia Tax Review 89.

Avi-Yonah R, 'The Structure of International Taxation: A Proposal for Simplification' (1996) 6 Texas Law Review 1301.

Avi-Yonah R, 'Globalization, Tax Competition, and the Fiscal Crisis of the Welfare State' (2000) 113 Harvard Law Review 1573.

Avi-Yonah R, 'Bridging the North/South Divide: International Redistribution and Tax Competition' (2004) 26 Michigan Journal of International Law 371.

Avi-Yonah R, 'All of a Piece Throughout: The Four Ages of U.S. International Taxation' (2005) 25 Virginia Tax Review 313.

Avi-Yonah R, *International Tax as International Law: An Analysis of the International Tax Regime* (Cambridge University Press 2007).

Avi-Yonah R, 'Between Formulary Apportionment and the OECD Guidelines: A Proposal for Reconciliation' [2009] SSRN Electronic Journal https://www.ssrn.com/abstract=1411649 accessed 18 November 2023.

Avi-Yonah R, 'Does Customary International Tax Law Exist?' [2019] Michigan Public Law: Law Faculty Papers (Topic) https://www.ssrn.com/abstract=3382203 accessed 26 August 2025.

Avi-Yonah R and Kir A, 'A Break in the Dam? India's New Profit Attribution Proposal and the Arm's Length Standard' [2019] SSRN Electronic Journal https://www.ssrn.com/abstract=3414266 accessed 18 November 2023.

Avi-Yonah R and Pouga Tinhaga Z, 'Unitary Taxation and International Tax Rules' [2014] ICTD Working Paper.

Avi-Yonah RS, *International Tax as International Law* (Cambridge University Press 2007).

Bannasch M, 'Factor Presence Nexus: A Growing Trend in State Taxation' https://www.journalofaccountancy.com/issues/2017/jul/state-taxation-presence-nexus.html accessed 5 December 2023.

Barry L and International Bureau of Fiscal Documentation, *IBFD International Tax Glossary* (5th edn, IBFD Publications 2005).

Bell KA, 'U.S. Committed to Traditional Position on Profit Splits' [2017] *Bloomberg BNA* https://www.bna.com/us-committed-traditional-n73014453014/ accessed 26 August 2025.

Benshalom H, 'Rethinking International Distributive Justice: Fairness as Insurance' (2013) 31 Boston University International Law Journal 267.

Benshalom I, 'The Quest to Tax Interest Income in a Global Economy: Stages in the Development of International Income Taxation' (2007) 27 Virginia Tax Review 631.

Benshalom I, 'Taxing the Financial Income of Multinational Enterprises by Employing a Hybrid Formulary and Arm's Length Allocation Method' (2008) 28 Virginia Tax Review 619.

Benshalom I, 'The Quest to Tax Financial Income in a Global Economy: Emerging to an Allocation Phase' (2008) 28 Virginia Tax Review 165.

Bergsten CF, 'The Backlash Against Globalization' (2000) https://www.piie.com/commentary/speeches-papers/backlash-against-globalization accessed 24 November 2023.

Bianco JF and Santos RT, 'A Change of Paradigm in International Tax Law: Article 7 of Tax Treaties and the Need To Resolve the Source versus Residence Dichotomy' (2016) 70 Bulletin for International Taxation.

Binder A and Wöhrer V (eds), *Special Features of the UN Model Convention* (Linde Verlag 2019).

Blanchard KS and Blessing PH, 'The Treasury's "Subpart F" Study' (February 2002) https://papers.ssrn.com/sol3/papers.cfm?abstract_id=299123 accessed 28 November 2023.

Bosch L, 'Fairness in Allocating Taxation Right Between Source and Residence States' (2014) http://arno.uvt.nl/show.cgi?fid=134224 accessed 27 November 2023.

Bradford DF and Policy USTT, *Blueprints for Basic Tax Reform* (Revised edn, Tax Analysts 1984).

Brauner Y, 'An Essay on BEPS, Sovereignty, and Taxation' in Sergio André Rocha and Christians Allison (eds), *Tax Sovereignty in the BEPS Era* (Kluwer Law International BV 2016).

Brauner Y, 'Treaties in the Aftermath of BEPS' (2016) 41 Brooklyn Journal of International Law 973.

Brauner Y, *Between Arm's Length and Formulary Apportionment, in The Allocation of Multinational Business Income: Reassessing the Formulary Apportionment Option* (Kluwer Law International 2020).

Break G and Pechman J, 'Relationship Between the Corporation and Individual Income Taxes' (1975) 28 National Tax Journal 341.

Brooks K, 'Inter-Nation Equity: The Development of an Important but Underappreciated International Tax Value' in Richard Krever and John G Head (eds), *Tax Reform In The 21st Century* (Wolters Kluwer 2009).

Brosens L and Bossuyt J, 'Legitimacy in International Tax Law-Making: Can the OECD Remain the Guardian of Open Tax Norms?' [2020] World Tax Journal 313.

Brown RD et al., 'Unitary Tax: At the Crossroads? – Part II' (1985) 55 The CPA Journal (pre-1986) 36.

Bruins G et al., 'Report on Double Taxation Submitted to the Financial Committee by Professors Bruins, Einaudi, Seligman, and Sir Josiah Stamp' in Joint Committee on Internal Revenue Taxation (ed.), *Legislative History of United States Tax Conventions* (US GPO 1962).

Bunn D, 'The U.S. Trade Representative Expands Its Digital Services Tax Investigations' (2 June 2020) https://taxfoundation.org/us-trade-representative-ustr-digital-services-tax-investigations accessed 26 November 2023.

Burgers I, Adema R and de Wilde M, 'Residence, Multinational Enterprises and BEPS: Is Determining the Residence of Companies Belonging to Multinational Groups Mission Impossible?: 2017 European Association of Tax Law Professors Congress' in Edoardo Traversa (ed.), *Corporate Tax Residence and Mobility* (IBFD 2018).

Burnham J, *The Managerial Revolution: What is Happening in the World* (Lume Books 2021).

Canada Revenue Agency, 'T2 Corporation: Income Tax Guide – 2019' https://www.canada.ca/en/revenue-agency/services/forms-publications/publications/t4012/t2-corporation-income-tax-guide-2016.html accessed 12 September 2023.

Caney S, 'International Distributive Justice' (2001) 49 Political Studies 974.

Carroll MB, 'Observations on Report of The Committee of the National Tax Association on Uniformity and Reciprocity on State Tax Legislation, Especially with Regard to the Allocation of Income of International Enterprises' (1931) 24 Proceedings of The Annual Conference on Taxation Under the Auspices of The National Tax Association.

Carroll MB, *Taxation of Business in France* (US Government Printing Office 1931).

Carroll MB, 'Taxation of Foreign and National Enterprises Vol. 4. Methods of Allocating Taxable Income' (League of Nations 1933) C.425(b).M.217(b).1933.II.A.

Carroll MB, 'Allocation of Business Income: The Draft Convention of the League of Nations' (1934) 34 Columbia Law Review 473.

Carroll MB, *Prevention of International Double Taxation and Fiscal Evasion: Two Decades of Progress Under the League of Nations* (League of Nations 1939).

Carroll MB, 'Evolution of U.S. Treaties to Avoid Double Taxation of Income: Part II' (1968) 3 International Lawyer.

Carroll MB, *Global Perspectives of an International Tax Lawyer* (1st edn, Exposition Press 1978).

Cavelti LU, *International Tax Cooperation: The Sovereignty Conflict between the Residence and the Source Country* (Stämpfli Verlag 2016).

CCH, 'Combined Reporting Requirements' https://answerconnect.cch.com/app/acr/home/federal accessed 5 December 2023.

Celebi H, 'The CCCTB as a Proposed Solution to the Corporate Income Taxation Dilemma within the EU' (2013) 22 EC Tax Review 289.

Chakravarty A, Ghosh S and Kuo E, 'Location-Specific Advantages' [2015] Global Transfer Pricing.

Chand V, Turina A and Ballivet L, 'Profit Allocation within MNEs in Light of the Ongoing Digital Debate on Pillar I: A "2020 Compromise"?' (2020) 12 World tax journal.

Chand V and Vilaseca C, 'Pillar I: The Marketing and Distribution Safe Harbour (MDSH) as Applicable to Licensed Manufacturers and Centralized Business Models: Does It Fulfil Its Policy Objective?' (2023) 51 Intertax.

Chen J (Jingxian) and Chow W, 'Global Minimum Tax Reform and the Future of Tax Competition' (2023) 77 Bulletin for International Taxation https://www.ibfd.org/doi/24gqzfd accessed 4 May 2024.
Chen Q, *General Theories of Tax Law* (Angle publishing Co., Ltd, 7th edn, 2012).
Chen S-C, 'Tax Avoidance in the Sales Factor: Comparison between the CCCTB and USAAs Formulary Apportionment Taxation' (2017) 3 Indian Journal of Tax Law.
Cheng Chi et al., 'China's New Transfer Pricing Guidelines and Beps' https://www.internationaltaxreview.com/article/2a68rfy5bw2ycq0s5btri/chinas-new-transfer-pricing-guidelines-and-beps accessed 5 December 2023.
China Taxation News, 'Jiangsu Provincial State Taxation Bureau Formulates an International Tax Compliance Management Plan (江苏省国税局制定国际税收遵从管理规划)' (Shui5, 2014) https://www.shui5.cn/article/13/73408.html accessed 2 December 2023.
Christians A, 'Taxation as a Global Socio-Legal Phenomenon' (2008) 14 ILSA Journal of International and Comparative Law.
Claire P, 'A Rethink of Location-Specific Advantages with an Analysis of the Chinese Approach' (2017) 24 International Transfer Pricing Journal.
Clarke C and Kopczuk W, 'Business Income and Business Taxation in the United States since the 1950s' (2016) 31 Tax Policy and The Economy 121.
Clausing KA, 'The U.S. State Experience Under Formulary Apportionment: Are There Lessons for International Reform?' (2016) 69 National Tax Journal 353.
Coates WH, 'Double Taxation and Tax Evasion' (1925) 88 Journal of the Royal Statistical Society 403.
'Coming of Age: China's Leveraging of BEPS' (10 December 2018) https://www.internationaltaxreview.com/article/2a68raha94goaj1osa4ff/coming-of-age-chinas-leveraging-of-beps accessed 25 November 2023.
Commission European Communities, *Report of the Committee of Independent Experts on Company Taxation* (Publications Office 1992).
Commission of the European Communities, 'Company Taxation in the Internal Market (SEC(2001)1681 Final)' (2001) https://taxation-customs.ec.europa.eu/system/files/2016-09/company_tax_study_en.pdf accessed 5 December 2023.
'Common Consolidated Corporate Tax Base Working Group (CCCTB WG), Draft Terms of Reference & Rules of Procedure' CCTB/WP\002\doc\en https://taxation-customs.ec.europa.eu/system/files/2016-09/cctbtorfinal_en.pdf accessed 6 December 2023.
'Common Consolidated Corporate Tax Base Working Group, the Territorial Scope of the CCCTB' CCCTB\WP\026\doc\en https://taxation-customs.ec.europa.eu/system/files/2016-09/ccctbwp026_territorial_scope_en.pdf accessed 26 August 2025.
Cordewener A and Ekkehart R, 'The Future of Most-Favoured: Nation Treatment in EC Tax Law: Did the ECJ Pull the Emergency Brake without Real Need? – Part I' (2006) 46 European Taxation 239.
Couzin R, 'The End of Transfer Pricing' (2013) 61 Canadian Tax Journal 159.

Crawford R and Uzes R, 'Income Taxes: The Distinction Between Business and Nonbusiness Income' Bloomberg BNA Tax Management Multistate Tax Portfolio Series, 2025.

Cubillos J, Heitmüller F and Valderrama IM, 'Multilateral Cooperation in International Tax Law' https://globtaxgov.weblog.leidenuniv.nl/files/2021/08/Multilateral-Cooperation-in-International-Tax-Law.pdf accessed 4 May 2024.

Cui W, 'Destination-Based Cash-Flow Taxation: A Critical Appraisal' (2017) 67 University of Toronto Law Journal 301.

Dagan T, 'The Tax Treaties Myth' (2000) 32 Journal of International Law and Politics.

Dagan T, 'Just Harmonization' (2009) 42 University of British Columbia Law Review 331.

Dagan T, 'The Marketization of Tax Sovereignty' (15 April 2017) https://papers.ssrn.com/abstract=2953220 accessed 2 December 2023.

Dagan T, *International Tax Policy: Between Competition and Cooperation* (1st edn, Cambridge University Press 2017) https://www.cambridge.org/core/product/identifier/9781316282496/type/book accessed 25 February 2025.

de la Feria R, 'What Is Tax Fairness?' (1 July 2024) https://papers.ssrn.com/abstract=4881240 accessed 13 July 2024.

de Lange MA and Lankhorst PWH, 'The Impact of Location Advantages on the Transfer Pricing of Multinationals: On the Chinese Love for European Designer Handbags and Lower Production Costs in India' (2014) 21 International Transfer Pricing Journal.

de Streek JV, 'Some Thoughts on the European Parliament Amendments of the CCCTB' in Dennis Weber (ed.), *EU Income Tax Law: Issues for the Years Ahead* (IBFD Publications 2013).

De Wilde M, 'Tax Competition within the European Union-Is the CCCTB Directive a Solution' (2014) 7 Erasmus Law Review 24.

de Wilde MF, '"Sharing the Pie": Taxing Multinationals in a Global Market' (2015) 43 Intertax 438.

de Wilde MF, 'Tax Jurisdiction in a Digitalizing Economy: Why "Online Profits" Are so Hard to Pin Down' (2015) 43 Intertax.

de Wilde MF, 'On the Future of Business Income Taxation in Europe' (2020) 12 World Tax Journal.

De Wilde MF, 'Towards a "2020s Compromise" in International Business Taxation; Reflections on an Emerging New Tax Paradigm' (10 February 2022) https://papers.ssrn.com/abstract=4031417 accessed 16 September 2023.

Deloitte, '2016 Global Manufacturing Competitiveness Index' (Deloitte) https://www2.deloitte.com/ch/en/pages/manufacturing/articles/global-manufacturing-competitiveness-index.html accessed 4 December 2023.

Dept. of the Treasury, United States, *The Final Report of the Worldwide Unitary Taxation Working Group: Chairman's Report and Supplemental Views* (Office of the Secretary, Department of the Treasury 1984).

Desai MA and Hines JR Jr, 'Evaluating International Tax Reform' [2003] National Tax Journal.

Devereux MP, 'Taxing Foreign Profit: Economic Principles and Feasibility' (2008) https://www.ifs.org.uk/publications/4191 accessed 27 November 2023.

Devereux MP, 'Taxation of Outbound Direct Investment: Economic Principles and Tax Policy Considerations' (2008) 24 Oxford Review of Economic Policy 698.

Devereux MP and Vella J, 'Value Creation As the Fundamental Principle of the International Corporate Tax System' [2018] European Tax Policy Forum Policy Paper.

Dexter WD, 'The Business Versus Nonbusiness Distinction Under the Uniform Division of Income for Tax Purposes Act' [1978] Urban Lawyer.

Ding J and Cheng H, 'China's Proposition to Build a Community of Shared Future for Mankind and the Middle East Governance' (2017) 11 Asian Journal of Middle Eastern and Islamic Studies 1.

Dodge JM, 'Theories of Tax Justice: Ruminations on the Benefit, Partnership, and Ability-to-Pay Principles' (2004) 58 Tax Law Review 399.

Donghyun Park, 'Trends in the Income Gap between Developed Countries and Developing Countries, 1960-1995' https://ourworldindata.org/economic-inequality accessed 26 August 2025.

Dourado AP, 'The OECD Unified Approach and the New International Tax System: A Half-Way Solution' (2020) 48 Intertax 3.

Duff DG, 'Benefit Taxes and User Fees in Theory and Practice' (2004) 54 University of Toronto Law Journal 393.

Dürrschmidt D, 'Tax Treaties and Most-Favoured-Nation Treatment, Particularly Within the European Union' (2006) 60 Bulletin for International Taxation 202.

Durst MC, 'Analysis of a Formulary System for Dividing Income, Part II: Examining Current Formulary and Arm's Length Approaches' (2013) 22 Bloomsberg BNA Tax Management Transfer Pricing Report 270.

EESC, 'Opinion of the European Economic and Social Committee' (2011) OJ C24/63-69.

Eijsden AV, 'The One-Stop-Shop Approach: A Discussion of the Administrative and Procedural Aspects of the CCCTB Draft Directive' (2011) 20 EC Tax Review 217.

Elkins DR, 'A Scalar Conception of Tax Residence for Individuals' [2021] SSRN Electronic Journal.

Elkinst D, 'Horizontal Equity as a Principle of Tax Theory' (2006) 24 Policy Review.

Elliffe C, 'International Tax Frameworks: Assessing the 2020s Compromise from the Perspective of Taxing the Digital Economy in the Great Lockdown' (2020) 74 Bulletin for International Taxation.

Englisch J, 'Ability to Pay in European Tax Law' in Cécile Brokelind (ed.), *Principles of Law: Function, Status and Impact in EU Tax Law* (IBFD Publications 2014).

European Commission, 'Communication from the Commission to the Council, the European Parliament and the Economic and Social Committee: Towards an Internal Market without Tax Obstacles – A Strategy for Providing Companies with a Consolidated Corporate Tax Base for Their EU-Wide Activities (COM(2001) 582 Final)' https://eur-lex.europa.eu/legal-content/EN/ALL/?uri=CELEX:52001DC0582 accessed 5 December 2023.

European Commission, 'Proposal for a Council Directive on a Common Consolidated Corporate Tax Base (CCCTB)' (2011) COM(2011) 121 final https://eur-lex.europa.eu/legal-content/EN/TXT/?uri=CELEX%3A52011PC0121&qid=1701759982858 accessed 5 December 2023.

European Commission, 'Proposal for a Council Directive on a Common Corporate Tax Base' (2016) COM(2016) 685 final 2016/0337(CNS) https://eur-lex.europa.eu/legal-content/EN/TXT/?uri=CELEX%3A52016PC0685 accessed 5 December 2023.

European Commission, 'Proposal for a Council Directive on a Common Corporate Tax Base (CCCTB)' (2016) (COM(2016) 683 final) (2016/0336(CNS)) https://eur-lex.europa.eu/legal-content/EN/TXT/?uri=CELEX%3A52016PC0683&qid=1701768577832 accessed 5 December 2023.

European Commission, 'Proposals for a Council Directive on a Common Corporate Tax Base and a Common Consolidated Corporate Tax Base (CCCTB) (SWD(2016) 341 Final)' (2016) https://eur-lex.europa.eu/LexUriServ/LexUriServ.do?uri=SWD:2016:0341:FIN:EN:PDF accessed 5 December 2023.

European Commission, 'Common Consolidated Corporate Tax Base Working Group (CCCTB WG) CCCTB: Possible Elements of the Sharing Mechanism' CCCTB/WP057\doc\en https://taxation-customs.ec.europa.eu/system/files/2016-09/ccctbwp057_en.pdf accessed 6 December 2023.

European Parliament, 'Report on the Commission Communication to the Council, the European Parliament and the Economic and Social Committee on Tax Policy in the European Union: Priorities for the Years Ahead (com(2001) 260 - C5-0597/2001 - 2001/2248(cos))' (2002) https://www.europarl.europa.eu/doceo/document/A-5-2002-0048_EN.html?redirect accessed 5 December 2023.

European Parliament, 'Report on the Proposal for a Council Directive on a Common Consolidated Corporate Tax Base (CCCTB)' (2011) COM(2011) 121 Final C7-0092/2011 - 2011/0058(CNS) A7-0080/2012 https://www.europarl.europa.eu/doceo/document/A-7-2012-0080_EN.pdf accessed 5 December 2023.

European Parliament, 'Report on the Proposal for a Council Directive on a Common Consolidated Corporate Tax Base (CCCTB)' (2018) COM(2016)0683 - C8-0471/2016-2016/0336(CNS) A8-0051/2018 https://www.europarl.europa.eu/doceo/document/A-8-2018-0051_EN.pdf accessed 5 December 2023.

European Parliament, 'MEPS Approve New EU Corporate Tax Plan Which Embraces Digital Presence' (2018) https://www.europarl.europa.eu/news/en/press-room/20180309IPR99422/meps-approve-new-eu-corporate-tax-plan-which-embraces-digital-presence accessed 5 December 2023.

Evers M, 'Tracing the Origins of the Netherlands' Tax Treaty Network' (2013) 41 Intertax.

EY Global, 'Tax Alert Indian Tax Administration Invites Public Comments on Proposal to Amend Rules on Profit Attribution to Permanent Establishment' (1 May 2019) https://globaltaxnews.ey.com/news/2019-5580-indian-tax-administration-invites-public-comments-on-proposal-to-amend-rules-on-profit-attribution-to-permanent-establishment accessed 2 December 2023.

Federation of Tax Administrators, 'State Apportionment of Corporate Income' https://www.taxadmin.org/assets/docs/Research/Rates/apport.pdf accessed 5 December 2023.

Ferraton A, 'Location-Specific Advantages and Transfer Pricing' 26 International Transfer Pricing Journal 2019.

Finley R, 'Panel Expects Increased Transfer Pricing Compliance Burdens' (2015) 80 Tax Notes International 488.

Finley R and Soong S, 'The U.S. "Safe Harbor" Proposal: Rocking the OECD's Pillar 1 Boat' (10 November 2019) https://www.taxnotes.com/featured-news/us-safe-harbor-proposal-rocking-oecds-pillar-1-boat/2019/12/09/2bns7 accessed 26 November 2023.

Foran N and Gray D, 'The Evolution of the Unitary Tax Apportionment Method' (1988) 15 The Accounting Historians Journal 65.

Förster H, Stefan G and Arnim H, 'Taxing the Digital Economy–The OECD Secretariat's New Transfer Pricing ABC and Alternative Courses of Action' (2020) 27 International Transfer Pricing Journal.

Frecknall-Hughes J, *The Theory, Principles and Management of Taxation: An Introduction* (Routledge 2014).

Fung S, 'The Questionable Legitimacy of the OECD/G20 BEPS Project' (2017) 10 Erasmus Law Review.

'G20 Rome Leader's Declaration' https://www.governo.it/sites/governo.it/files/G20ROMELEADERSDECLARATION_0.pdf accessed 1 June 2024.

Gao P and Wang D, 'The Reform and Development of Fiscal and Taxation System in "the 13th Five-Year" Period' (2016) 1 Finance Forum.

Garrison R, 'Toward a Consensus on Apportionable v. Allocable Income' (1975) 28 Tax Executive 41.

General Office of STA, 'Reforming the Tax System: Seeking One Area and Living the Overall Situation - Part 3 of a Series of Reviews of National Taxation Work in 2014(改革税制:谋 - 域而活全局 - 2014年全国税务工作系列综述之三)' https://www.chinatax.gov.cn/n810219/n810724/n811741/c1440429/content.html accessed 4 November 2023.

Genschel P, 'Globalisation and the Transformation of the Tax State' (2005) https://www.econstor.eu/bitstream/10419/28260/1/497811359.PDF accessed 26 August 2025.

Genschel P and Rixen T, 'The International Tax Regime: Historical Evolution and Political Change' [2012] SSRN Electronic Journal http://www.ssrn.com/abstract=2139665 accessed 18 November 2023.

Gereffi G and Lee J, 'Why the World Suddenly Cares About Global Supply Chains' (2012) 48 Journal of Supply Chain Management 24.

Goetz ML, 'Tax Avoidance, Horizontal Equity, and Tax Reform: A Proposed Synthesis' (1978) 44 Southern Economic Journal 798.

Gordon RH, 'Taxation of Investment and Savings in a World Economy' (National Bureau of Economic Research 1985) https://www.nber.org/papers/w1723 accessed 28 November 2023.

Graetz MJ, 'The David R. Tillinghast Lecture Taxing International Income: Inadequate Principles, Outdated Concepts, and Unsatisfactory Policies' (2000) 54 Tax Law Review 261.

Graetz MJ and O'Hear MM, 'The Original Intent of US International Taxation' (1996) 46 Duke Law Journal 1021.

Green AMA, 'China Is the Top Trading Partner to More Than 120 Countries' (Wilson Center) https://www.wilsoncenter.org/blog-post/china-top-trading-partner-more-120-countries accessed 3 December 2023.

Griffith RRU, Hines J and Sørensen PB, 'International Capital Taxation' in James A Mirrlees, Stuard Adam and Timothy Besley (eds), *Dimensions of Tax Design: the Mirrlees Review* (Oxford University Press 2010) https://pure.manchester.ac.uk/ws/portalfiles/portal/33806113/FULL_TEXT.PDF accessed 26 August 2025.

Harberger AC, 'The Incidence of the Corporation Income Tax' (1962) 70 Journal of Political Economy 215.

Harris P and Oliver D, *International Commercial Tax* (Cambridge University Press 2010)

Hasell J et al., 'Global Economic Inequality' (2018) https://ourworldindata.org/global-economic-inequality accessed 26 August 2025.

Haslehner W and Lamensch M (eds), *Taxation and Value Creation: EATLP Annual Congress Vienna, 18-20 June 2020* (IBFD 2021).

Hattingh J, 'On the Origins of Model Tax Conventions: 19th Century German Tax Treaties and Laws Concerned with the Avoidance of Double Taxation' (2013) 6 Studies in the History of Tax Law 31.

Healy JC, Schadewald MS and Nelson BM, *Multistate Corporate Tax Guide*, vol. 1 (Wolters Kluwer 2024).

Hearson M and Prichard W, 'China's Challenge to International Tax Rules and the Implications for Global Economic Governance' (2018) 94 International Affairs 1287.

Heggmair M, 'The New Interpretation of the Arm's Length Principle: A Post-BEPS Evaluation' (2017) 24 International Transfer Pricing Journal https://www.ibfd.org/shop/journal/new-interpretation-arms-length-principle-post-beps-evaluation accessed 19 November 2023.

Hellerstein J, 'Allocation and Apportionment of Dividends and the Delineation of the Unitary Business' (1982) 14 Tax Notes.

Hellerstein J, 'The Basic Operations Interdependence Requirement of a Unitary Business' (1983) 18 Tax Notes.

Hellerstein JR and Hellerstein W (eds), *Hellerstein & Hellerstein: State Taxation (WGL)* (Thomson Reuters 2010) https://www.westlaw.com/Browse/Home/SecondarySources/TaxSecondarySources/TaxTextsTreatises/HellersteinHellersteinStateTaxationWGL?rs = tran3.0&vr = 3.0&originationContext = vendcc accessed 6 December 2023.

Hellerstein W, 'The Business-Nonbusiness Income Distinction and the Case for Its Abolition' (2001) 92 Tax Notes.

Hellerstein W, 'International Income Allocation in the Twenty-First Century: The Case for Formulary Apportionment' (2005) 728 Scholarly Works https://digitalcommons.law.uga.edu/fac_artchop/728 accessed 5 December 2023.

Hellerstein W, 'Tax Planning under the CCCTB' s Formulary Apportionment Provisions: The Good, the Bad and the Ugly' in Weber Dennis (ed.), *CCCTB: Selected Issues* (Kluwer Law International BV 2012).

Hellerstein W, *The Application of Formulary Apportionment to Related Entities: Lessons from the US Experience, in The Allocation of Multinational Business Income: Reassessing the Formulary Apportionment Option* (Kluwer Law International 2020).

Hellerstein W and McLure CE, 'Lost in Translation: Contextual Considerations in Evaluating the Relevance of US Experience for the European Commission's Company Taxation Proposals' (2004) 58 Bulletin for International Fiscal Documentation 86.

Hellerstein W and McLure CE, Jr, 'The European Commission's Report on Company Income Taxation: What the EU Can Learn from the Experience of the US States' (2004) 11 International Tax and Public Finance 199.

Helminen HM, 'The Participation Exemption' in Dennis Weber and Jan van de Streek (eds), *The EU Common Consolidated Corporate Tax Base* (Kluwer Law International 2018).

Herndon JG, *Relief from International Taxation, the Development of International Reciprocity for the Prevention of Double Taxation* (Callaghan & Co 1932).

Hershey AS, 'Neutrality and International Law' (1916) 26 International Journal of Ethics 168.

Hofbauer I, 'Most-Favoured-Nation Clauses in Double Taxation Conventions: A Worldwide Overview' (2005) 33 Intertax 445.

Holmes K, *The Concept of Income: A Multi-Disciplinary Analysis* (IBFD Publications 2001).

Hongler P and Pistone P, 'Blueprints for a New PE Nexus to Tax Business Income in the Era of the Digital Economy' (20 January 2015) https://papers.ssrn.com/abstract=2591829 accessed 2 December 2023.

Hu T, 'An Acute Queening Move for China's Taxation Legal Reform: Issues and Proposals' (2017) 11 Frontiers of Law in China 616.

Hubert H, 'Arm's Length: How Long?' (2001) 8 International Transfer Pricing Journal 30.

Huddleston J and Sicilian S, 'The Project to Revise UDITPA' https://www.mtc.gov/uploadedFiles/Multistate_Tax_Commission/Uniformity/Minutes/The%20Project%20to%20Revise%20UDITPA.pdf accessed 28 November 2021.

IBFD, 'Implementing OECD/G20 BEPS Package in Developing Countries: An Assessment of Priorities, Experiences, Challenges and Needs of Developing Countries' https://www.giz.de/en/downloads/wp_implementing_beps_package_developing_countries.pdf accessed 1 December 2023.

Ignatius UFS- and Plasschaert SR, 'First Principles About Schedular and Global Frames of Income Taxation' (1976) 99 Bulletin International Fiscal Documentation.

International Chamber of Commerce, *Proceedings Organization Meeting, Paris, France, June 23-30, 1920* (International Headquarters 1920).

International Chamber of Commerce, *First Congress, London (June 27-July 1, 1921) Double Taxation, Brochure No. 11. Double Taxation, Part I, Report of the Select Committee of the Chamber* (International Headquarters 1921)

International Chamber of Commerce, *First Congress, London (June 27-July 1, 1921) Double Taxation, Brochure No. 12. Double Taxation, Part II, Special Report by the British National Committee* (2nd edn, International Headquarters 1921).

International Chamber of Commerce, *Second Congress, Rome (March 18-25, 1923) Brochure No. 23 Programme of the Congress and Drafts of Resolutions* (International Headquarters 1923).

International Chamber of Commerce, *Second Congress, Rome (March 18-25, 1923) Brochure No. 25 Double Taxation* (International Headquarters 1923).

International Chamber of Commerce, 'About ICC' https://iccwbo.org/about-icc-2/ accessed 26 November 2023.

'Interview of the Director of the State Taxation Bureau of Jiangsu Province' https://www.shui5.cn/article/13/73408.html accessed 27 November 2023

Interview with Senior Officials of STA, 'Senior Officials of STA and MOF Answering Questions on Improving the Tax Credit Policy for Enterprises' Overseas Income' (2 January 2018) http://m.mof.gov.cn/czxw/201712/t20171229_2790745.htm accessed 2 December 2023.

Interview with Zhang Zhiyong, 'Strengthen Global Tax Cooperation and Combat International Tax Evasion: Zhang Zhiyong, Deputy Director of the STA, Answered Reporters' Questions(加强全球税收合作 打击国际逃避税：国家税务总局副局长张志勇答记者问)' (1 December 2014) https://www.gov.cn/xinwen/2014-12/01/content_2785317.htm accessed 4 December 2023.

James SR and Nobes C, *The Economics of Taxation* (7th edn, Xiaolin Luo tr, Chinese Financial & Economic Publishing House 2002).

Jiang Y, 'Reflections on the Relationship Between Multilateral Free Trade Agreements and Tax Measures: Taking RCEP and CPTPP as Reference (关于多边自由贸易协定与税收措施关系的思考：以RCEP CPTPP为参照)' [2022] Journal of International Taxation (国际税收) 9.

Jiangsu Provincial Office of STA, 'Administration Plan for International Taxation Compliance in 2014-2015' https://www.shui5.cn/article/03/71246.html accessed 27 November 2023.

Jogarajan S, 'Prelude to the International Tax Treaty Network: 1815-1914 Early Tax Treaties and the Conditions for Action' (2011) 31 Oxford Journal of Legal Studies 679.

Jogarajan S, 'Stamp, Seligman and the Drafting of the 1923 Experts' Report on Double Taxation' (2013) 5 World Tax Journal 368.

Jogarajan S, *Double Taxation and the League of Nations* (1st edn, Cambridge University Press 2018).

Johana H and Chen X, '"Taxation Where Value is Created" and the OECD/G20 Base Erosion and Profit Shifting Initiative' [2018] International Taxation in China.

Johannes B and Englisch J, 'Taxing Where Value Is Created: What's User Involvement' Got to Do with It?' (2019) 47 Intertax.

Jones RC, 'Taxation of Foreign and National Enterprises, Vol. 5' (League of Nations 1933) C.425(c).M.217(c).1933.II.A.

Kahn DA, 'The Two Faces of Tax Neutrality: Do They Interact or Are They Mutually Exclusive' (1990) 18 Northern Kentucky Law Review.

Kane MA, 'Ownership Neutrality, Ownership Distortions, and International Tax Welfare Benchmarks' (2006) 53 Virginia Tax Review.

Kaufman NH, 'Fairness and the Taxation of International Income' (1997) 29 Law & Policy in International Business 145.

Keen M and Wildasin D, 'Pareto-Efficient International Taxation' (2004) 94 American Economic Review 259.

Keesling FM and Warren JS, 'The Unitary Concept in the Allocation of Income' (1960) 12 Hastings Law Journal 42.

Keinan Y, 'The Case for Residency-Based Taxation of Financial Transactions in Developing Countries' (2022) 9 Florida Tax Review https://journals.upress.ufl.edu/ftr/article/view/365 accessed 26 August 2025.

Kemmeren EC, 'Principle of Origin in Tax Conventions: A Rethinking of Models' (Tilburg University, School of Economics and Management 2001).

Kesselman J and Maslove A, 'Fairness in Taxation: Exploring the Principles' (1994) 20 Canadian Public Policy-analyse De Politiques 99.

Kleinbard ED, 'Stateless Income' (2011) 11 Florida Tax Review https://journals.upress.ufl.edu/ftr/article/view/349 accessed 18 November 2023.

Knoll MS, 'Reconsidering International Tax Neutrality' (2010) 64 Tax Law Review 99.

Kobetsky M, *International Taxation of Permanent Establishments: Principles and Policy* (Cambridge University Press 2011).

Kofler G, 'The BEPS Action Plan and Transfer Pricing: The Arm's Length Standard Under Pressure?' (2013) 5 British Tax Review 646.

Koomen M, 'Transfer Pricing in a BEPS Era: Rethinking the Arm's Length Principle – Part I' (2015) 22 International Transfer Pricing Journal.

Krever R and Vaillancourt F (eds), *The Allocation of Multinational Business Income: Reassessing the Formulary Apportionment Option* (Wolters Kluwer 2020).

Krister Andersson, 'Comments on document CCCTB\WP\040 Common Consolidated Corporate Tax Base Working Group: Personal Scope of the CCCTB' https://taxation-customs.ec.europa.eu/system/files/2016-09/unicecomments_personal_scope.pdf accessed 26 August 2025.

Kroppen H-K, Dawid R and Schmidtke R, 'Profit Split, the Future of Transfer Pricing? Arm's Length Principle and Formulary Apportionment Revisited from a Theoretical and a Practical Perspective' in Wolfgang Schön and Kai A Konrad (eds), *Fundamentals of International Transfer Pricing in Law and Economics* (Springer Berlin Heidelberg 2012).

Langbein SI, 'The Unitary Method and the Myth of Arm's Length' (1986) 30 Tax Notes 630.

Langbein SI and Fuss MR, 'The OECD/G20-BEPS-Project and the Value Creation Paradigm' (2018) 51 International Lawyer 259.

Langbein SI and Fuss MR, 'The OECD/G20-BEPS-Project and the Value Creation Paradigm: Economic Reality Disemboguing into the Interpretation of the "Arm's Length" Standard' (2018) 51 International Lawyer 259.

Lauri M and Kokott, J, 'States, Sovereign Equality' https://opil.ouplaw.com/display/10.1093/law:epil/9780199231690/law-9780199231690-e1113?print=pdf accessed 27 November 2023.

League of Nations, 'Double Taxation and Tax Evasion: Report and Resolutions Submitted by the Technical Experts to the Financial Committee of the League of Nations (Document F.212)' in United States Congress Joint Committee on Internal Revenue Taxation (ed.), *Legislative History of United States Tax Conventions,* vol. 4 (US GPO 1925).

League of Nations, 'Double Taxation and Tax Evasion: Report Presented by the Committee of Technical Experts on Double Taxation and Tax Evasion (C.216 M.85.1927.II)' in United States Congress Joint Committee on Internal Revenue Taxation (ed.), *Legislative History of United States Tax Conventions,* vol. 4 (League of Nations 1927).

League of Nations, 'Double Taxation and Fiscal Evasion. General Meeting of Government Experts October 1928' (League of Nations 1928) C.495.M.147.1928.II.

League of Nations, 'Double Taxation And Tax Evasion-Report Presented By The General Meeting of Government Experts on Double Taxation and Tax Evasion (Document C.562.M.178.1928.II.)' in United States Congress Joint Committee on Internal Revenue Taxation (ed.), *Legislative History of United States Tax Conventions,* vol. 4 (League of Nations 1928).

League of Nations, 'Double Taxation and Fiscal Evasion Collection of International Agreements and Internal Legal Provisions for the Prevention of Double Taxation and Fiscal Evasion' (League of Nations 1928) C.345 M.102.

League of Nations, 'Double Taxation and Fiscal Evasion Collection of International Agreements and Internal Legal Provisions for the Prevention of Double Taxation and Fiscal Evasion' (League of Nations 1928).

League of Nations, 'Taxation of Foreign and National Enterprises Vol. 1. A Study of the Tax Systems and the Methods of Allocation of the Profits of Enterprises Operating in More than One Country in France, Germany, Spain, the United Kingdom, and the United States of America' (League of Nations 1932) C.73.M.38.1932.II.A.

League of Nations, 'Taxation of Foreign and National Enterprises Vol. 2. A Study of the Tax Systems and the Methods of Allocation of the Profits of Enterprises Operating in More than One Country in Austria, Belgium, Czechoslovakia, Free City of Danzig, Greece, Hungary, Italy, Latvia, Luxemburg, Netherlands, Romania and Switzerland' (League of Nations 1933) C.425.M.217.1933.II.A.

League of Nations, 'Taxation of Foreign and National Enterprises Vol. 3. A Study of the Tax Systems and the Methods of Allocation of the Profits of Enterprises Operating in More than One Country in British India, Canada, Japan, Mexico, Netherlands East Indies, Union of South Africa, States of Massachusetts, of New York and of Wisconsin' (League of Nations 1933) C.425(a).M.217(a).1933.II.A.

League of Nations, '1927 Draft Models' in United States Congress Joint Committee on Internal Revenue Taxation (ed.), *Legislative History of United States Tax Conventions* vol. 4 (US GPO 1962).

League of Nations, 'Draft Convention for the Allocation of Business Income between States for the Purposes of Taxation' in United States Congress Joint Committee on Internal Revenue Taxation (ed.), *Legislative History of United States Tax Conventions* (US GPO 1962).

League of Nations, 'Draft Convention No. I-a' in United States Congress Joint Committee on Internal Revenue Taxation (ed.), *Legislative History of United States Tax Conventions,* vol. 4 (US GPO 1962).

League of Nations, 'Draft Convention No. I-b' in United States Congress Joint Committee on Internal Revenue Taxation (ed.), *Legislative History of United States Tax Conventions,* vol. 4 (US GPO 1962).

League of Nations, 'Draft Convention No. I-c' in United States Congress Joint Committee on Internal Revenue Taxation (ed.), *Legislative History of United States Tax Conventions,* vol. 4 (US GPO 1962).

League of Nations, 'Fiscal Committee London and Mexico Model Tax Conventions Commentary and Text' in United States Congress Joint Committee on Internal Revenue Taxation (ed.), *Legislative History of United States Tax Conventions* (US GPO 1962).

League of Nations, 'Fiscal Committee Report to the Council on the Fourth Session of the Committee. Held at Geneva from June 15th to 26th, 1933' in United States Congress Joint Committee on Internal Revenue Taxation (ed.), *Legislative History of United States Tax Conventions*, vol. 4 (US GPO 1962).

League of Nations, 'Fiscal Committee Report to the Council on the Work of The Fifth Session of the Committee Held in Geneva From June 12 to 17, 1935' in United States Congress Joint Committee on Internal Revenue Taxation (ed.), *Legislative History of United States Tax Conventions* (US GPO 1962).

League of Nations, 'Fiscal Committee Report to the Council on The Work of the First Session of the Committee. Held in Geneva from October 17th to 26th, 1929' in United States Congress Joint Committee on Internal Revenue Taxation (ed.), *Legislative History of United States Tax Conventions* (US GPO 1962).

League of Nations, 'Fiscal Committee Report to the Council on the Work of The Second Session of the Committee Held in Geneva From May 22nd to 31st, 1930' in United States Congress Joint Committee on Internal Revenue Taxation (ed.), *Legislative History of United States Tax Conventions* (US GPO 1962).

League of Nations, 'Fiscal Committee Work of the Fiscal Committee During Its Sixth Session Held at Geneva from October 15th to 21st, 1936' in United States Congress Joint Committee on Internal Revenue Taxation (ed.), *Legislative History of United States Tax Conventions* (US GPO 1962).

League of Nations, 'Fiscal Committee: Model Bilateral Conventions for the Prevention of International Double Taxation and Fiscal Evasion. Second Regional Tax Conference, Mexico, D.F., July 1943' (League of Nations) C.2.M.2.1945.II.A.

Leonard J and Davison D, 'U.S. Pulls Out of Global Digital Tax Talks, Lighthizer Says' (18 June 2020) https://news.bloombergtax.com/daily-tax-report/u-s-pulls-out-of-global-digital-tax-talks-lighthizer-says?context = search&index = 2 accessed 20 June 2021.

Lepard BD, 'Is the United States Obligated to Drive on the Right: A Multidisciplinary Inquiry into the Normative Authority of Contemporary International Law Using the Arm's Length Standard as a Case Study' (1999) 10 Duke Journal of Comparative & International Law 43.

Li J, 'Global Profit Split: An Evolutionary Approach to International Income Allocation' (2002) 50 Canadian Tax Journal.

Li J, *International Taxation in the Age of Electronic Commerce: A Comparative Study* (Canadian Tax Foundation 2003).

Li J, 'Improving Inter-Nation Equity through Territorial Taxation and Tax Sparing' http://digitalcommons.osgoode.yorku.ca/all_papers/252 accessed 27 November 2023.

Li J, 'Soft Law, Hard Realities and Pragmatic Suggestions: Critiquing the OECD Transfer Pricing Guidelines' in Wolfgang Schön and Kai A Konrad (eds), *Fundamentals of International Transfer Pricing in Law and Economics* (Springer Berlin Heidelberg 2012).

Li J, *International Taxation in China: A Contextualized Analysis* (IBFD Publications 2016).

Li J, 'Location Specific Advantages: A Rising Disruptive Factor in Transfer Pricing' (2018) 71 Bulletin for International Taxation 259.

Li J, 'The Future of the Corporate Form in Income Tax: A Case Study of Canada' [2023] Osgoode Legal Studies Research Paper No. 4459300 https://ssrn.com/abstract = 4459300 accessed 26 August 2025.

Li J, Bao J and Li H, 'Value Creation: A Constant Principle in a Changing World of International Taxation' (2019) 67 Political Economy: Taxation 1107.

Li N, 'Chapter 14: China (People's Rep.)' in Werner Haslehner and Marie Lamensch (eds), *Taxation and Value Creation: EATLP Annual Congress Vienna, 18-20 June 2020* (IBFD 2021).

Liao T, 'Actively Implement the Results of the G20 Tax Reform and Strive to Create a Fair and Modern International Tax System' [2017] International Taxation 10.

Liao T, 'A Fair and Modern International Tax System: Review and Exploration' [2019] International Taxation 5.

Liao T and Li H, 'China: International Taxation in the Post-BEPS Era' in Yong Sup Sim and Mei-June Soo (eds), *Asian Voices: BEPS and Beyond* (IBFD Publications 2017).

'List of Countries That Have Signed "Belt and Road" Cooperation Document with China' (Jiangsu Belt and Road Portal, 12 June 2023) http://ydyl.jiangsu.gov.cn/art/2022/2/8/art_76283_10343080.html accessed 2 December 2023.

Liu J, *International Tax Law* (3rd edn, Peking University Press 2013).

Locke J, *Second Treatise of Government* (Columbia University Press 2016) https://www.earlymoderntexts.com/assets/pdfs/locke1689a.pdf accessed 28 November 2023.

Lokken L, 'The Sources of Income from International Uses and Dispositions of Intellectual Property' (1980) 36 Tax Law Review 233.

Louis K, 'Horizontal Equity: Measures in Search of a Principle' (1989) 42 National Tax Journal 139.

Lutz C, 'What to Do with Public Law 86-272' [2019] Tax Notes State 781.

Lutz HL, 'The Progress of State Income Taxation Since 1911' (1920) 10 American Economic Review 66.

Maisto G, Pistone P and Weber D (eds), *Non-Discrimination in Tax Treaties: Selected Issues from a Global Perspective* (IBFD Publications 2016).

Marian OY, 'Jurisdiction to Tax Corporations' [2013] Tax Law: International & Comparative Tax eJournal.

Martha JMRSJ, *The Jurisdiction to Tax in International Law:Theory and Practice of Legislative Fiscal Jurisdiction* (1st edn, Kluwer Law & Taxation Publishers 1989).

Mason R, 'The Transformation of International Tax' (2020) 114 American Journal of International Law 353.

Matheson MT and Perry VJ, *Territorial vs. Worldwide Corporate Taxation: Implications for Developing Countries* (International Monetary Fund 2013).

Mayer S, *Formulary Apportionment for the Internal Market* (IBFD Publications 2009).

McDaniel PR and Repetti JR, 'Horizontal and Vertical Equity: The Musgrave/Kaplow Exchange' (2022) 1 Florida Tax Review https://journals.upress.ufl.edu/ftr/article/view/502 accessed 18 November 2023.

McDonnell A, 'Report on the Invitational Conference on Transfer Pricing: The Allocation of Income and Expenses Among Countries' [1993] Canadian Tax Journal 899.

McGaughey SL and Raimondos P, 'Shifting MNE Taxation from National to Global Profits: A Radical Reform Long Overdue' (2019) 50 Journal of International Business Studies 1668.

McGowan JR and Dennis M, 'The Business vs. Nonbusiness Income Controversy: Recent Developments' (1989) 8 Journal of State Taxation 303.

McIntyre MJ, 'Contrasting Methodologies: A Systematic Presentation of the Differences between an Arm's-Length/Source-Rule System and a Combined-Reporting/Formulary-Apportionment System', *Proceedings of the Annual Conference on Taxation Held under the Auspices of the National Tax Association-Tax Institute of America* (National Tax Association 1994).

McIntyre MJ, 'The Use of Combined Reporting by Nation States' (2004) 35 Tax Notes International 917.

McIntyre MJ, 'Combined Reporting with Formulary Apportionment: The Transfer Pricing System of the US States' (2012) https://www.taxjustice.net/cms/upload/pdf/Michael_McIntyre_1206_Helsinki.pdf accessed 5 December 2023.

McIntyre MJ, 'Designing a Combined Reporting Regime for a State Corporate Income Tax: A Case Study of Louisiana' 61 Louisiana Law Review.

McLure C, 'Defining a Unitary Business: An Economist's View' (May 1983). NBER Working Paper No. w1125, available at SSRN: https://ssrn.com/abstract=304841.

McLure CE, 'Replacing Separate Entity Accounting and the Arm's Length Principle with Formulary Apportionment' (2002) 56 Bulletin for International Fiscal Documentation.

McNichol A, 'Canterbury Law Review Student Prize 2020: An Analysis of the United States' Stance on BEPS: Pillar One' (2021) 28 Canterbury Law Review 161.

Melnicoe M and Liao T, 'International Tax Rules Must Adapt to China's Rise' [2015] Tax Management Transfer Pricing Report.

Michael L, 'Act of Creation: The OECD/G20 Test of "Value Creation" as a Basis for Taxing Rights and Its Relevance to Developing Countries' (2018) 25 Transnational Corporations 55.

Michael S and Francois V, *Formulary Apportionment in Canada and Taxation of Corporate Income in 2019: Current Practice, Origins and Evaluation, in The Allocation of Multinational Business Income: Reassessing the Formulary Apportionment Option* (Kluwer Law International 2009).

'Ministry of Finance', Such as in the Comprehensive Integrated Tax Coordination Agreement between the Government of Canada and the Government of Quebec, available at https://www.finances.gouv.qc.ca/documents/Autres/en/AUTEN_Tax-agreement.pdf, accessed 24 September 2025.

Mintz J and Smart M, 'Income Shifting, Investment, and Tax Competition: Theory and Evidence from Provincial Taxation in Canada' (2004) 88 Journal of Public Economics 1149.

Moore AM, Perry JH and Beach DI, 'The Financing of Canadian Federation: The First Hundred Years' [1966] Canadian Tax Foundation.

Morse SC, 'Value Creation: A Standard in Search of a Process' (2018) 72 Bulletin for International Taxation 196.

Mosquera Valderrama IJ, 'Output Legitimacy Deficits and the Inclusive Framework of the OECD/G20 Base Erosion and Profit Shifting Initiative' (2018) 72 Bulletin for International Taxation.

Mosquera Valderrama IJ, 'Legitimacy and the Making of International Tax Law: The Challenges of Multilateralism' (2015) 7 World Tax Journal.

'Multilateral Convention to Implement Amount A of Pillar One' https://www.oecd.org/en/topics/sub-issues/reallocation-of-taxing-rights-to-market-jurisdictions/multilateral-convention-to-implement-amount-a-of-pillar-one.html accessed 26 August 2025.

Multistate Tax Commission, 'Factor Presence Nexus Standard for Business Activity Taxes' https://www.mtc.gov/wp-content/uploads/2022/12/Factor-Presence.pdf accessed 6 December 2023.

Multistate Tax Commission, 'Statement of Information Concerning Practices of Multistate Tax Commission and Signatory States Under Public Law 86-272' https://www.mtc.gov/wp-content/uploads/2023/02/StatementofInfoPublicLaw86-272.pdf accessed 26 August 2025.

Musgrave PB, *United States Taxation of Foreign Investment Income: Issues and Arguments* (Law School of Harvard University 1969).

Musgrave PB, 'International Tax Differentials for Multinational Corporations: Equity and Efficiency Considerations' in United Nations (ed.), *The Impact of Multina tional Corporations on Development and on International Relations, Technical Papers: Taxation* (United Nations 1974).

Musgrave PB, 'The OECD Model Tax Treaty: Problems and Prospects' (1975) 10 Columbia Journal of World Business 29.

Musgrave PB, 'Principles for Dividing the State Corporate Tax Base' in Charles E McLure (ed.), *State Corporation Income Tax: Issues in Worldwide Unitary Combination* (Hoover Institution Press 1984).

Musgrave PB, 'Fiscal Coordination and Competition in an International Setting' in Lorraine Eden (ed.), *Retrospectives on Public Finance* (Duke University Press 1991).

Musgrave PB, 'Substituting Consumption-Based Direct Taxation for Income Taxes as the International Norm: A Comment' (1992) 45 National Tax Journal 179.

Musgrave PB, 'Sovereignty, Entitlement, and Cooperation in International Taxation' (2000) 26 Brooklyn Journal of International Law 1335.

Musgrave PB, 'Chapter 3 Interjurisdictional Equity in Company Taxation: Principles and Applications to the European Union' in Sijbren Cnossen (ed.), *Taxing Capital Income in the European Union: Issues and Options for Reform* (Oxford University Press 2000) https://academic.oup.com/book/51992 accessed 26 August 2025.

Musgrave PB, 'Consumption Tax Proposals in an International Setting' (2001) 54 Tax Law Review 77.

Musgrave RA, *Criteria for Foreign Tax Credit, Taxation of Operation Abroad* (The Tax Institute, Princeton 1959).

Musgrave RA, *A Brief History of Fiscal Doctrine*, vol. 1 (Elsevier 1985).

Musgrave RA, 'Horizontal Equity, Once More' (1990) 43 National Tax Journal.

Musgrave RA and Musgrave PB, 'Inter-Nation Equity' in Richard M Bird and John G Head (eds), *Modern Fiscal Issues: Essays in Honour of Carl S. Shoup* (University of Toronto Press 1972).

Nanz P, 'Democratic Legitimacy and Constitutionalism of Transnational Trade Governance: A View from Political Theory' in Christian Joerges and Ernst-Ulrich Petersmann (eds), *Constitutionalism, Multilevel Trade Governance and Social Regulation* (Hart Publishing 2006).

OECD, 'Draft Double Taxation Convention on Income and Capital 1963' (1963) https://www.oecd-ilibrary.org/content/publication/9789264073241-en accessed 26 August 2025.

OECD, 'Model Double Taxation Convention on Income and Capital 1977' (OECD 1977) https://doi.org/10.1787/9789264055919-en accessed 26 August 2025.

OECD, 'Transfer Pricing and Multinational Enterprises: Three Taxation Issues' (OECD Publishing 1984).

OECD, 'Transfer Pricing Guidelines for Multinational Enterprises and Tax Administrations 1995' (OECD 1995) https://doi.org/10.1787/g2g7fa2a-en accessed 26 August 2025.

OECD, 'Most-Favoured-Nation Treatment in International Investment Law' [2004] OECD Working Papers on International Investment http://dx.doi.org/10.1787/518757021651 accessed 26 August 2025.

OECD, 'OECD Transfer Pricing Guidelines for Multinational Enterprises and Tax Administrations 2010' (OECD Publishing 2010).

OECD, 'Model Tax Convention on Income and on Capital 2010 (Full Version)' (OECD Publishing 2012) https://doi.org/10.1787/9789264175181-en accessed 26 August 2025.

OECD, 'Addressing Base Erosion and Profit Shifting' (OECD Publishing 2013) https://doi.org/10.1787/9789264192744-en accessed 26 August 2025.

OECD, 'The Dealing at Arm's Length Fallacy: A Way Forward to a Formula-Based Transactional Profit Split' https://www.oecd-ilibrary.org/taxation/addressing-the-tax-challenges-of-the-digital-economy-action-1-2015-final-report_9789264241046-en accessed 18 November 2023.

OECD, 'OECD Transfer Pricing Guidelines for Multinational Enterprises and Tax Administrations 2017' (OECD 2017).

OECD, 'Revised Guidance on the Application of the Transactional Profit Split Method: Inclusive Framework on BEPS: Action 10' (OECD/G20 Base Erosion and Profit Shifting Project 2018) https://www.oecd.org/tax/beps/revised-guidance-on-the-application-of-the-transactional-profit-split-method-beps-action-10.pdf accessed 20 November 2023.

OECD, 'Tax Challenges Arising from Digitalisation: Interim Report 2018: Inclusive Framework on BEPS' (OECD 2018) https://www.oecd.org/en/publications/tax-challenges-arising-from-digitalisation-interim-report_9789264293083-en.html accessed 18 September 2023.

OECD, 'Addressing the Tax Challenges of the Digitalisation of the Economy: Public Consultation Document' (OECD 2019).

OECD, 'Model Tax Convention on Income and on Capital 2017 (Full Version)' (OECD Publishing 2019) http://dx.doi.org/10.1787/g2g972ee-en accessed 26 August 2025.

OECD, 'Programme of Work to Develop a Consensus Solution to the Tax Challenges Arising from the Digitalisation of the Economy, OECD/G20 Inclusive Framework on BEPS' (OECD 2019).

OECD, 'Tax Challenges Arising from Digitalisation: Report on Pillar Two Blueprint' (2020) https://www.oecd.org/en/publications/2020/10/tax-challenges-arising-from-digitalisation-report-on-pillar-two-blueprint_4c7eaa3d.html accessed 26 August 2025.

OECD, 'Statement by the OECD/G20 Inclusive Framework on BEPS on the Two-Pillar Approach to Address the Tax Challenges Arising from the Digitalisation of the Economy: January 2020' (2020) https://www.oecd.org/tax/beps/statement-by-the-oecd-g20-inclusive-framework-on-beps.htm accessed 26 August 2025.

OECD, 'Tax Challenges Arising from Digitalisation – Report on Pillar One Blueprint: Inclusive Framework on BEPS' (OECD 2020) https://www.oecd.org/en/publications/tax-challenges-arising-from-digitalisation-report-on-pillar-one-blueprint_beba0634-en.html accessed 29 April 2025.

OECD, 'Statement on a Two-Pillar Solution to Address the Tax Challenges Arising from the Digitalisation of the Economy' (2021) https://www.oecd.org/tax/beps/statement-on-a-two-pillar-solution-to-address-the-tax-challenges-arising-from-the-digitalisation-of-the-economy-october-2021.pdf accessed 26 August 2025.

OECD, 'Pillar One: Amount A – Draft Model Rules for Nexus and Revenue Sourcing, 4 February 2022-18 February 2022' https://web-archive.oecd.org/2022-02-04/623615-public-consultation-document-pillar-one-amount-a-nexus-revenue-sourcing.pdf accessed 5 December 2023.

OECD, 'Action 1 Tax Challenges Arising from Digitalisation' https://www.oecd.org/en/topics/policy-issues/base-erosion-and-profit-shifting-beps.html accessed 4 December 2023.

OECD, 'Los Cabos, Mexico 2012' (OECD) https://g20.org/summit-and-logos/2012-los-cabos/ accessed 25 November 2023.

OECD, 'Multilateral Convention to Implement Tax Treaty Related Measures to Prevent BEPS' https://www.oecd.org/tax/treaties/multilateral-convention-to-implement-tax-treaty-related-measures-to-prevent-BEPS.pdf accessed 4 December 2023.

OECD, 'What is BEPS?' https://www.oecd.org/tax/beps/about/ accessed 5 December 2023.

OECD/G20, 'Secretariat Proposal for a "Unified Approach" under Pillar One' https://web-archive.oecd.org/2019-11-15/532559-oecd-invites-public-input-on-the-secretariat-proposal-for-a-unified-approach-under-pillar-one.htm accessed 18 December 2023.

OECD/G20 Base Erosion and Profit Shifting Project, 'Addressing the Tax Challenges of the Digitalisation of the Economy: Policy Note' (2019) https://www.oecd.org/tax/beps/policy-note-beps-inclusive-framework-addressing-tax-challenges-digitalisation.pdf accessed 26 August 2025.

'OECD/G20 Inclusive Framework on BEPS: Progress Report September 2022-September 2023' https://web-archive.oecd.org/temp/2023-10-15/666424-oecd-g20-inclusive-framework-on-beps-progress-report-september-2022-september-2023.htm accessed 26 August 2025.

Ortino M, 'The Notion of Economic Law and Regulatory Competition' in Karl M Meessen (ed.), *Economic Law as an Economic Good: Its Rule Function and Its Tool Function in the Competition of Systems* (European Law Publishers 2009).

Owens JP and Tavares RJS, 'Human Capital in Value Creation and Post-BEPS Tax Policy: An Outlook' (2015) 69 Bulletin for International Taxation.

Ozai I, 'Institutional and Structural Legitimacy Deficits in the International Tax Regime' [2019] Law & Society: Public Law – Tax eJournal.

Peeters B, Gribnau H and Badisco J, *Building Trust in Taxation* (Intersentia 2017) https://www.cambridge.org/core/books/building-trust-in-taxation/EB30499021E91393529827840D42900A accessed 26 August 2025.

Peroni RJ, Fleming JC and Shay SE, 'Getting Serious about Curtailing Deferral of U.S. Tax on Foreign Source Income' 52 SMU Law Review 455.

Peter NG and David S, 'Chapter 19: China's Response to the BEPS Recommendations and the Impact on Taxpayers' in Sam Sim and Mei-June Soo (eds), *Asian Voices: BEPS and Beyond* (IBFD Publications 2017).

Peters C, 'Critical Analysis of the General Court's "EU Arm's Length Tool": Beware of the Reflexivity of Transfer Pricing Law!' (2022) 31 EC Tax Review 30.

Peters CAT, 'The Faltering Legitimacy of International Tax Law' (Doctoral Thesis, Tilburg University 2013).

Peters JH, 'The Distinction between Business Income and Nonbusiness Income' (1973) 25 Major Tax Plan 251.

Picciotto S, *International Business Taxation: A Study in the Internationalization of Business Regulation* (Weidenfeld and Nicolson 1992).

Pistone P et al. 'The OECD Public Consultation Document "Secretariat Proposal for a 'Unified Approach' under Pillar One": An Assessment' (2020) 74(1) Bulletin for International Taxation, 14-27, available at SSRN: https://ssrn.com/abstract=5002961.

Pîrvu D, 'Impact Assessment of the Common Consolidated Corporate Tax Base', in Daniela Pîrvu (ed.), *Corporate Income Tax Harmonization in the European Union* (Palgrave Macmillan UK 2012) 150, https://doi.org/10.1057/9781137000910_8 accessed 24 September 2025.

'P.L. 86-272 Statement of Information Project' https://www.mtc.gov/uniformity/pl-86-272-statement-of-information-project/ accessed 6 December 2023.

Plucknett TFT, *A Concise History of the Common Law* (The Lawbook Exchange, Ltd 2001).

Pomerleau K and Jahnsen K, 'Designing a Territorial Tax System: A Review of OECD Systems' (1 August 2017) https://taxfoundation.org/territorial-tax-system-oecd-review/ accessed 27 November 2023.

Pomp RD and Surrey SS, 'The Tax Structure of the People's Republic of China' (1979) 20 Virginia Journal of International Law 1.

PricewaterhouseCoopers LLP, 'Evolution of Territorial Tax Systems in the OECD' (2013).

'Progressive Formulary Apportionment: The Case for "Amount D" | Tax Notes' https://www.taxnotes.com/featured-analysis/progressive-formulary-apportionment-case-amount-d/2021/06/11/76k47 accessed 2 May 2024.

Quentin D, 'Corporate Tax Reform and "Value Creation": Towards Unfettered Diagonal Re-Allocation across the Global Inequality Chain' (2017) 7 Accounting, Economics, and Law: A Convivium.

Razin A, 'International Tax Competition and Gains from Tax Harmonization' (1991) 37 Economics Letters 69.

'Reciprocal Taxation Agreement Between Canada and Manitoba' https://www.gov.mb.ca/finance/tao/pubs/signed_february24,2017.pdf accessed 5 December 2023.

Republican Party (United States), 'A Better Way: Our Vision for a Confident America' https://www.novoco.com/public-media/documents/ryan_a_better_way_policy_paper_062416.pdf accessed 17 July 2018.

Ribeiro JS, 'Distributive Justice Through Taxation: European Perspective' [2006] Jurisprudencija: mokslo darbai. Vilnius: Mykolo Romerio universiteto Leidybos centras, 2006, Nr. 2 (80).

Richard C and Andrus JL, *Transfer Pricing and the Arm's Length Principle After BEPS* (Oxford University Press 2017).

Richman P, *Taxation of Foreign Investment Income, an Economic Analysis* (Johns Hopkins Press 1963).

Riedel N and Runkel M, 'Company Tax Reform with A Water's Edge' (2007) 91 Journal of Public Economics 1533.

Ritzer G and Paul D, *Globalization: The Essentials* (John Wiley & Sons 2019).

Rixen T, 'The Institutional Design of International Double Taxation Avoidance' (2008) No. SP IV 2008-302 WZB Discussion Paper.

'Robert_Gibbon_Johnson', Wikipedia https://en.wikipedia.org/wiki/Robert_Gibbon_Johnson accessed 4 December 2023.

Rodrik D, 'How Far will International Economic Integration Go?' (2000) 14 Journal of Economic Perspectives 177.

Ronald S, *Income Tax Relief: Dominion (Including the Irish Free State) Income Tax Relief, Law and Practice, Over Seventy Examples; Appropriate Rate Tables* (Gee & Co 1925).

Rosenbloom HD, 'The David R. Tillinghast Lecture International Tax Arbitrage and the "International Tax System"' 53 Tax Law Review.

Rotblat C, 'Chinese State Capitalism and the International Tax Regime' (2019) 10 Columbia Journal of Tax Law 77.

Rudolph EG, 'State Taxation of Interstate Business: The Unitary Business Concept and Affiliated Corporate Groups' (1969) 25 Tax Law Review 171.

Sack AN, 'Taxation of International Business Upon Income and Problems of International Regulation of Such Taxation' (1934) 20 Bulletin of The National Tax Association 66.

Sadiq K, 'Unitary Taxation with a Global Formulary Approach as a Realistic and Appropriate Option for Developing Nations: A Chinese Case Study' (2016) 6 Journal of Chinese Tax and Policy 25.

Samari A, 'The OECD Secretariat Proposal for a "Unified Approach" under Pillar One: Strengths and Weaknesses of the New and Revised Nexus and Profit Allocation Rules' (2020) 27 International Transfer Pricing Journal.

Sandler D, 'Slicing the Shadow–The Continuing Debate Over Unitary Taxation and Worldwide Combined Reporting' [1994] British Tax Review.

Scharpf FW, *Governing in Europe: Effective and Democratic?* (Oxford University Press 1999).

Schattschneider EE and Adamany D, *The Semisovereign People: A Realist's View of Democracy in America* (1st edn, Cengage Learning 1975).

Schön W, 'International Tax Coordination for a Second-Best World (Part I)' (2009) 1 World Tax Journal 67.

Schön W, 'International Tax Coordination for a Second-Best World (Part III)' (2010) 2 World Tax Journal 227.

Schoueri LE and Galdino G, 'Single Taxation as a Policy Goal: Controversial Meaning, Lack of Justification and Unfeasibility' in Jonna Wheeler (ed.), *Single Taxation?* (IBFD Publications 2018).

Schoueri LE and Galendi RA Jr, 'Justification and Implementation of the International Allocation of Taxing Rights: Can We Take One Thing at a Time?' in Sergio Andre Rocha (ed.), *Tax Sovereignty in the BEPS* (Wolters Kluwer 2017).

Schutte C and Shome P, 'Cash-Flow Tax' (1993) 1993 IMF Working Papers.

Screpante M, 'Rethinking the Arm's Length Principle and Its Impact on the Ip License Model After Oecd/G20 BEPS Actions 8-10: Nothing Changed but the Change?' [2019] World Tax Journal 425.

Screpante M, 'Formulaic (or Formulary?!) Apportionment Wearing Value Creation Clothes: Is the Wolf Dressed in Sheep's Clothing?' (10 September 2019) http://Kluwertaxblog.Com/2019/09/10/Formulaic-Or-Formulary-Apportionment-Wearing-Value-Creation-Clothes-Is-The-Wolf-Dressed-In-Sheeps-Clothing accessed 27 November 2023.

Seligman ERA, 'The Taxation of Corporations. III' (1890) 5 Political Science Quarterly 636.

Seligman ERA, *Essays in Taxation* (The Macmillan Company 1905).

Seligman ERA, *Double Taxation and International Fiscal Cooperation* (Macmillan 1928).

Shaheen F, 'International Tax Neutrality: Reconsiderations' (2007) 27 Virginia Tax Review 203.

Shaheen F, 'International Tax Neutrality: Revisited' (2011) 64 Tax Law Review 131.

Shaviro D, 'Why Worldwide Welfare as a Normative Standard for U.S. Tax Policy?' (2007) 60 Tax Law Review 155.

Shaviro DN, *Fixing U.S. International Taxation* (Oxford University Press 2014).

Shay SE, Fleming JC and Peroni RJ, 'The David R. Tillinghast Lecture What's Source Got to Do with It: Source Rules and U.S. International Taxation' (2002) 56 Tax Law Review 81.

Sheppard L, 'Revenge of the Source Countries? Part 4: Who Gets the Bill?' [2005] *TNT* 210.

Sheppard L, 'Revenge of the Source Countries?' [2005] *TNT* 54.

Sheppard L, 'Revenge of the Source Countries? Part 2: Royalties' [2005] *TNT* 191.

Sheppard L, 'Revenge of the Source Countries? Part 5: Throwing BRICs' [2006] *TNT* 123.

Sheppard L, 'Revenge of the Source Countries? Part 6: Subsidiary as PE' [2006] *TNT* 200.

Sicilian S and Huddleston J, 'The US States' Experience with Formulary Apportionment' in Krever Richard and Vaillancourt François (eds), *The Allocation of Multinational Business Income: Reassessing the Formulary Apportionment Option* (Kluwer Law International 2020).

Singh RP, 'International Taxation: The International Law Perspective' http://www.publicinternationallaw.in/node/137 accessed 11 May 2019.

Siu E et al., *Unitary Taxation in Federal and Regional Integrated Markets* (ICTD 2014).

Slemrod J, 'Effect of Taxation with Capital Mobility' in Henry J Aaron, Harvey Galper and Joseph A Pechman (eds), *Uneasy Compromise: Problems of a Hybrid Income-Consumption Tax* (Brookings Institution Press 1988).

Smith A, *Wealth of Nations* (W. Strahan and T. Cadell, London 1776).

Smith A, *An Inquiry Into the Nature and Causes of the Wealth of Nations* (Regnery Publishing, 1776)

Smith DS, 'The Arm's Length Standard: A Blind Spot in the CC(C)TB Proposals' in Weber Dennis and Jan Van De Streek (eds), *The EU Common Consolidated Corporate Tax Base: Critical Analysis* (Kluwer Law International 2016).

Smith EH, 'Allocating to Provinces the Taxable Income of Corporations: How the Federal-Provincial Allocation Rules Evolved' (1976) 24 Canadian Tax Journal 545.

Smith EH, *Federal-Provincial Tax Sharing and Centralized Tax Collection in Canada* (Canadian Tax Foundation Publications 1998).

Smith P, 'Lessons from the British Poll Tax Disaster' (1991) 44 National Tax Journal 421.

Sommer C, *Separate Accounting or Unitary Apportionment?: The Fairy Tale of Arm's Length Pricing and General Equilibrium Analysis of Multinational Enterprise Behavior under the Formulary Taxation Alternative* (Josef Eul Verlag Gmbh 2011).

Speaker of the House, 'A Better Way: Our Vision for a Confident America' (2016).

STA, 'Exchange of Notes of between China and the United States (中美照会文件)' https://www.chinatax.gov.cn/n810341/n810770/c1153055/5026996/files/115305510.pdf accessed 4 December 2023.

STA, 'Protocol to the Agreement Between the Government of The People's Republic of China and the Government of the Republic of the Philippines for the Avoidance of Double Taxation and the Prevention of Fiscal Evasion with Respect to Taxes on Income' https://www.chinatax.gov.cn/chinatax/n810341/n810770/c1153616/5027045/files/11536163.pdf accessed 4 December 2023.

STA, 'Japan' (28 March 2011) https://www.chinatax.gov.cn/n810341/n810770/c1153042/content.html accessed 3 December 2023.

STA, 'Protocol to the Agreement between the Government of the People's Republic of China and the Kingdom of the Netherlands for the Avoidance of Double Taxation and the Prevention of Fiscal Evasion with Respect to Taxes on Income' https://www.chinatax.gov.cn/chinatax/n810341/n810770/c1152939/5026985/files/11529391.pdf?eqid=af89a3b50000a9f80000000464377bcc accessed 4 December 2023.

STA, 'Protocol to Agreement Between the Government of The People's Republic of China and the Government of the Republic of Chile for the Elimination of Double Taxation and the Prevention of Tax Evasion and Avoidance with Respect to Taxes on Income' https://www.chinatax.gov.cn/chinatax/n810341/n810770/c1644352/5027078/files/16443522.pdf accessed 4 December 2023.

STA, 'Exchange of Notes of China and Chile Tax Authorities in 2018 (2018年中智税务机关照会文件)' https://www.chinatax.gov.cn/n810341/n810770/c1644352/5027078/files/16443521.pdf accessed 4 December 2023.

STA, 'Exchange of Notes Between Government of the People's Republic of China and Government of the Socialist Republic of Vietnam (中越照会文件)' https://www.chinatax.gov.cn/n810341/n810770/c1153436/5027029/files/11534367.pdf accessed 4 December 2023.

STA, 'List of Double Taxation Agreements Signed by China' http://www.chinatax.gov.cn/n810341/n810770/index.html accessed 23 November 2023.

Stefan G, 'The Dealing at Arm's Length Fallacy: A Way Forward to a Formula-Based Transactional Profit Split?' (2017) 45 Intertax.

Stephens CN, 'A Progressive Analysis of the Efficiencies of Capital Import Neutrality' (1998) 30 Law and Policy in International Business 159.

Stevenson D, 'Europe Before 1914' https://www.bl.uk/world-war-one/articles/europe-before-1914 accessed 11 November 2020.

Stewart M, 'The Tax State, Benefit and Legitimacy' (2015) TTPI – Working Paper

Stiglitz J and Pike RM, 'Globalization and Its Discontents' (2004) UEH University available at https://digital.lib.ueh.edu.vn/handle/UEH/69581 accessed 26 August 2025.

'Summary Record by the Chair of the Meeting of the Common Consolidated Corporate Tax Base Working Group (10-11 December 2007)' CCCTB/WP/64/en.

'Summary Record of the Meeting of the Common Consolidated Corporate Tax Base Working Group (Brussels, 12 December 2007)' CCCTB/WP/63/en.

Surrey SS, 'Tax Incentives as a Device for Implementing Government Policy: A Comparison with Direct Government Expenditures' (1970) 83 Harvard Law Review 705 https://www.jstor.org/stable/1339837 accessed 24 September 2025.

Tax Notes, 'U.S. Outlines Digital Services Tax Concerns in Letter to OECD' (3 November 2019) https://www.taxnotes.com/research/federal/other-documents/treasury-tax-correspondence/u.s-outlines-digital-services-tax-concerns-in-letter-to-oecd/2b61x accessed 26 August 2025.

Tax Notes, 'OECD Responds to U.S. Treasury Letter Outlining Digital Tax Concerns' (4 November 2019) https://www.taxnotes.com/research/federal/other-documents/treasury-tax-correspondence/oecd-responds-to-u.s.-treasury-letter-outlining-digital-tax-concerns/2b633 accessed 26 August 2025.

Taylor A, 'Globalization, Trade, and Development: Some Lessons From History' (National Bureau of Economic Research 2002) w9326 http://www.nber.org/papers/w9326.pdf accessed 18 November 2023.

Taylor CJ, 'Twilight of the Neanderthals, or Are Bilateral Double Taxation Treaty Networks Sustainable' (2010) 34 Melbourne University Law Review.

Tello CP, 'OECD Works on Pillar 1 Technical Issues Despite Pause on Political Issue of Scope' https://www.lexology.com/library/detail.aspx?g=fb055cc8-20dc-493c-bafe-ac3547fd4c01 accessed 26 November 2023.

'The Regular Press Conference of the Ministry of Commerce' (Ministry of Commerce of the People's Republic of China, 18 April 2019) https://www.mofcom.gov.cn/lsxwfbh/art/2023/art_1cd88617ff764fe496646138ced59b0c.html accessed 2 December 2023.

Tomashot SR, 'Selling Peace: The History of the International Chamber of Commerce, 1919-1925' (PhD Dissertation, Georgia State University 2015).

Traversa E, 'Objective Ability to Pay: The Gerritse Case' [2015] Landmark Decisions of the ECJ in Direct Taxation https://www.academia.edu/41917849/Objective_Ability_to_Pay_The_Gerritse_Case accessed 2 May 2024.

Treasury US, 'The Deferral of Income Earned Through US Controlled Foreign Corporations A Policy Study' [2000] Office of Tax Policy, Annex.

United Nations, *Yearbook of the International Law Commission 1978, Vol. II, Part 2* (UN 1978) https://www.un-ilibrary.org/international-law-and-justice/yearbook-of-the-international-law-commission-1978-vol-ii-part-2_4b67af8d-en accessed 25 November 2023.

United Nations, 'Model Double Taxation Convention between Developed and Developing Countries 2017 Update' (United Nations 2017).

United Nations, 'Practical Manual on Transfer Pricing for Developing Countries (2017)' (United Nations 2017).

United Nations, 'List of Non-member States, Entities and Organizations Having Received a Standing Invitation to Participate as Observers in the Sessions and the Work of the General Assembly' (2019) A/INF/74/3 https://undocs.org/en/A/INF/74/3 accessed 26 August 2025.

'United Nations Charter' https://www.un.org/en/about-us/un-charter/full-text accessed 26 August 2025.

United States Congress Joint Committee on Internal Revenue Taxation, *Legislative History of United States Tax Conventions,* vol. 4 (US GPO 1962).

USTR, 'Notice of Action in the Section 301 Investigation of France's Digital Services Tax' https://www.federalregister.gov/documents/2020/07/16/2020-15312/notice-of-action-in-the-section-301-investigation-of-frances-digital-services-tax. accessed 28 November 2020.

USTR, 'Section 301 Investigation Report on France's Digital Services Tax' https://ustr.gov/sites/default/files/Report_On_France%27s_Digital_Services_Tax.pdf. accessed 27 November 2023.

Valente D, 'Italian Tax Authorities Action Against Fictitious Corporate Tax Residence' (2017) 45 Intertax 353.

VanderWolk J, 'The Arm's-Length Standard Enters Its Second Century' [2019] Tax Notes International.

Vanistendael F, 'An Octogenarian on Value Creation' [2018] Tax Notes International 1385.

Vann RJ, 'Reflections on Business Profits and the Arm's-Length Principle' in Brian J Arnold et al. (eds), *The Taxation of Business Profits under Tax Treaties* (Canadian Tax Foundation 2010).

Vann RJ, 'Taxing International Business Income: Hard-Boiled Wonderland and the End of the World' [2010] World Tax Journal 291.

Vishweshwar M and Majmudar S, 'Does India's Proposals on Attribution of Profits to Pes Solve the Issue?' (20 May 2019) https://www.internationaltaxreview.com/article/b1fq9g90kbsyzv/does-indias-proposals-on-attribution-of-profits-to-pes-solve-the-issue accessed 27 November 2023.

Vogel K, 'The Justification for Taxation: A Forgotten Question' (1988) 33 The American Journal of Jurisprudence 19.

Vogel K, 'Worldwide vs. Source Taxation of Income: A Review and Re-Evaluation of Arguments (Part I)' (1988) 16 Intertax.

Vogel K, 'Worldwide vs. Source Taxation of Income: A Review and Re-Evaluation of Arguments (Part II)' (1988) 10 Intertax 310.

Vogel K, 'Worldwide vs. Source Taxation of Income: A Review and Re-Evaluation of Arguments (Part III)' (1988) 16 Intertax 393.

Vogel K, 'Which Method Should the European Community Adopt for the Avoidance of Double Taxation?' (2002) 56 Bulletin for International Fiscal Documentation 4.

von Schanz G, 'Zur Frage Der Steuerpflicht' (1892) 9 FinanzArchiv/Public Finance Analysis.

Wallingford RD, 'British Retaliation Against the California Unitary Tax: The Needed Impetus for a Federal Solution' (1986) 8 Journal of Comparative Business and Capital Market Law 345.

Wang KC, 'International Double Taxation of Income: Relief Through International Agreement 1921-1945' (1945) 59 Harvard Law Review 73.

Wardell-Burrus H, 'Pillar Two and Developing Countries: The STTR and GloBE Implementation' (16 September 2022) https://papers.ssrn.com/abstract=4221115 accessed 21 September 2024.

Weber D, 'Most-Favoured Nation Treatment under Tax Treaties Rejected in the European Community: Background and Analysis of the D Case' (2005) 33 Intertax 429.

Weiner JE, 'Tax Coordination and Competition in the United States of America' in Commission European (ed.), *Report of the Committee of Independent Experts on Company Taxation* (Publications Office 1992).

Weiner JM, 'Company Taxation for the European Community: How Sub-National Tax Variation Affects Business Investment in the United States and Canada' (PhD dissertation, Harvard University 1994).

Weiner JM, *Formulary Apportionment and Group Taxation in the European Union: Insights from the United States and Canada* (Directorate General Taxation and Customs Union, European Commission 2005).

Weiner JM, *Company Tax Reform in the European Union: Guidance from the United States and Canada on Implementing Formulary Apportionment in the EU* (Springer Science & Business Media 2006).

Weiner JM, *The Dream Is Alive: EU Tax Policy with a Common Consolidated Corporate Tax Base and Formulary Apportionment, in The Allocation of Multinational Business Income: Reassessing the Formulary Apportionment Option* (Kluwer Law International 2020).

Weisbach DA, 'The Use of Neutralities in International Tax Policy' (2015) 68 National Tax Journal.

Wells B and Lowell C, 'Tax Base Erosion and Homeless Income: Collection at Source Is the Linchpin' (2011) 65 Tax Law Review.

Wells B and Lowell CH, 'Income Tax Treaty Policy in the 21st Century: Residence vs. Source' (2014) 5 Columbia Journal of Tax Law 1.

Wilkie JS, 'Reflecting on the "Arm's Length Principle": What Is the "Principle"? Where Next?' in Wolfgang Schön and Kai A Konrad (eds), *Fundamentals of International Transfer Pricing in Law and Economics* (Springer, Berlin, Heidelberg 2012).

Wilkins M, 'Chapter 1 The History of Multinational Enterprise' in Alan M Rugman and Thomas L Brewer (eds), *Oxford Handbook of International Business* (Oxford University Press 2001).

Wittendorff J, *Transfer Pricing and the Arm's Length Principle in International Tax Law* (Kluwer Law International BV 2010).

Wittendorff J, 'BEPS Actions 8-10: Birth of a New Arms Length Principle' (2016) 87 Tax Notes International 331.

Woodward R, 'Chapter 1: The Evolution of the International Corporate Tax Regime, 1920 – 2008' in Richard Eccleston and Ainsley Elbra (eds), *Business, Civil Society and the 'New' Politics of Corporate Tax Justice* (Edward Elgar Publishing 2018).

Xinhua News Agency, 'Joint Statement between the People's Republic of China and the Russian Federation on the Construction of Silk Road Economic Belt and the Construction of Eurasian Economic Union' (GOV, 3 September 2015) https://www.gov.cn/xinwen/2015-05/09/content_2859384.htm accessed 4 December 2023.

Xinhua News Agency, 'The General Office of the Communist Party of China Central Committee and the General Office of the State Council Have Issued the "Plan for Deepening the Reform of the National and Local Tax Collection and Management System" (中共中央办公厅 国务院办公厅印发深化国税、地税征管体制改革方案)' (24 December 2015) https://www.gov.cn/gongbao/content/2016/content_2979704.htm accessed 14 April 2023.

Xinhua News Agency, 'Outline of the 14th Five-Year Plan (2021-2025) for National Economic and Social Development and the Long-Range Objectives Through the Year 2035(中华人民共和国国民经济和社会发展第十四个五年规划和2035年远景目标纲要)' (13 March 2021) https://www.gov.cn/xinwen/2021-03/13/content_5592681.htm accessed 4 December 2023.

Xiong Y, 'Thinking Over Questions Relevant to Sparing Credit(对饶让抵免有关问题的思考)' (2016) 12 International Taxation (国际税收).

Xu D, 'The Convergence and Divergence Between China's Implementation and OECD/G20 Beps Minimum Standards' [2018] World Tax Journal 471.

Yang Z, *The Economics of Taxation* (Dongbei University of Finance and Economics Press 2011).

Zheng Y, 'The Establishment of a Multilateral Investment Treaty for the "One Belt, One Road" Initiative' (2018) Special Issue Cambridge Law Review.

Zolt EM, 'Prospects for Fundamental Tax Reform: United States vs. Japan' (1999) 83 Tax Notes 903.

王相坤, '改革开放只有进行时没有完成时 (Reform and opening up can only be carried out but not completed)' http://theory.people.com.cn/n/2013/1128/c40537-23686027.html accessed 26 August 2025.

Announcement of the State Administration of Taxation on Matters Concerning Improving the Administration of Affiliation Reporting and Contemporaneous Documentation (国家税务总局公告2016年第42号 国家税务总局关于完善关联申报和同期资料管理有关事项的公告) 2016 (STA Announcement No. 42 [2016]).

Announcement of the State Administration of Taxation on the Issues Concerning Improving the Administration of Advance Pricing Arrangements (国家税务总局公告2016年第64号 国家税务总局关于完善预约定价安排管理有关事项的公告) 2016 (STA Announcement No. 64 [2016]).

Announcement on Issues Concerning Resident Enterprises' Reporting of Information Relating to Overseas Investment and Income (国家税务总局公告2014年第38号 国家税务总局关于居民企业报告境外投资和所得信息有关问题的公告) 2014 (STA Announcement No. 38 [2014]).

Announcement on Issues Concerning the Follow-up Administration after the Cancellation of the Approval Item of Confirmation of the Application of Simple Collection and Tax Sparing Credit to the Overseas Income of Enterprises (国家税务总局公告2015年第70号 国家税务总局关于企业境外所得适用简易征收和饶让抵免的核准事项取消后有关后续管理问题的公告) 2015 (STA Announcement No. 70 [2015]).

Announcement on Issues Concerning the Tax Credit Vouchers for Overseas Contracted Engineering Projects of Enterprises (国家税务总局公告2017年第41号 国家税务总局公告关于企业境外承包工程税收抵免凭证有关问题的公告) 2017 (STA Announcement No. 41 [2017]).

Announcement on Matters Regarding Refining the Filing of Related Party Transactions and Administration of Contemporaneous Transfer Pricing Documentation (国家税务总局公告2016年第42号 国家税务总局关于完善关联申报和同期资料管理有关事项的公告) (STA Announcement No. 42 [2016]).

Announcement on the Administration Measures for Special Tax Investigation Adjustment and Mutual Negotiation Procedures (国家税务总局公告2017年第6号 国家税务总局关于发布〈特别纳税调查调整及相互协商程序管理办法〉的公告) 2017 (STA Announcement No. 6 [2017]).

Announcement on the Definition of 'Beneficial Ownership' under Entrusted Investments (国家税务总局公告2014年第24号 国家税务总局关于委托投资情况下认定受益所有人问题的公告) 2014 (STA Announcement No. 24 [2014]).

Enterprise Income Tax Law of the People's Republic of China (中华人民共和国企业所得税法) 2007.

General Agreement on Trade in Services (GATS).

Implementation Measures for Special Tax Adjustment (Draft for Soliciting Opinions) (特别纳税调整实施办法(征求意见稿)) 2015.

Implementation Measures for Special Tax Adjustment (Trial Implementation) (特别纳税调整实施办法(试行)) 2009.

Individual Income Tax Law of the People's Republic of China (2018 version) (中华人民共和国个人所得税法 2018版) 2018.

Minnesota Administrative Rules.

Model General Allocation & Apportionment Regulations as Amended 25 July 2018.
Model General Allocation and Apportionment Regulations – as of 2017.
Multistate Tax Compact.

North American Free Trade Agreement(NAFTA).

Notice of the STA's Work on the Anti-Tax Avoidance in 2008 (国税函〔2009〕106号 国家税务总局关于2008年反避税工作情况的通报) 2009.

Notice on Effectively Conducting the Work of Resident Enterprises' Reporting of Information about Overseas Investment and Income (税总函〔2015〕327号 国家税务总局关于做好居民企业报告境外投资和所得信息工作的通知) 2015 (Shuizonghan No. 327 [2015]).

Notice on Issues Concerning Improving the Tax Credit Policy for Overseas Income of Enterprises (财税〔2017〕84号 财政部 税务总局关于完善企业境外所得税收抵免政策问题的通知) 2017 (Caishui No. 84 [2017]).

Notice on Issues Concerning the Foreign Income Tax Credit of Enterprises (财税〔2009〕125号 财政部 国家税务总局 关于企业境外所得税收抵免有关问题的通知) 2010 (Caishui No. 125 [2009]).

Notice on Issuing the Measures for the Implementation of Special Tax Adjustments (for Trial Implementation) (国税发〔2009〕2号 国家税务总局关于印发《特别纳税调整实施办法（试行）》的通知) 2009 (Guoshuifa No. 2 [2009]).

Notice on Several Issues Related to Enterprise Income Tax Application to Indirect Transfers of Property between Non-resident Enterprises (国家税务总局公告2015年第7号 国家税务总局关于非居民企业间接转让财产企业所得税若干问题的公告) 2015 (STA Announcement No. 7 [2015]).

Regulation on the Implementation of the Enterprise Income Tax Law of the People's Republic of China (2019 revision) (中华人民共和国企业所得税法实施条例(2019年修订)) 2019.

Sino-foreign Joint Venture Enterprise Income Tax Law of the People's Republic of China (中华人民共和国中外合资经营企业所得税法) 1980.

STA on Issues Concerning Expanding the Applicable Scope of the Policy of Temporary Exemption of Withholding Tax on the Direct Investment Made by Overseas Investors with Distributed Profits (国家税务总局公告2018年第53号 国家税务总局关于扩大境外投资者以分配利润直接投资暂不征收预提所得税政策适用范围有关问题的公告) 2018 (STA Announcement No. 53 [2018]).

State Taxation Administration Order No. 32 General Anti-Tax Avoidance Management Measures (Trial) (国家税务总局第32号令 一般反避税管理办法（试行）) 2014.

The Agreement on Trade-Related Aspects of Intellectual Property Rights (TRIPS).

The General Agreement on Tariffs and Trade (GATT 1947).

United States Constitution 1787.

2014-2015 International Tax Compliance Management Plan (2014-2015年度国际税收遵从管理规划) 2014.

## SERIES ON INTERNATIONAL TAXATION

1. Alberto Xavier, *The Taxation of Foreign Investment in Brazil,* 1980 (ISBN 90-200-0582-0).
2. Hugh J. Ault & Albert J. Rädler, *The German Corporation Tax Law with 1980 Amendments,* 1981 (ISBN 90-200-0642-8).
3. Paul R. McDaniel & Hugh J. Ault, *Introduction to United States International Taxation,* 1981 (ISBN 90-6544-004-6).
4. Albert J. Rädler, *German Transfer Pricing/Prix de Transfer en Allemagne,* 1984 (ISBN 90-6544-143-3).
5. Paul R. McDaniel & Stanley S. Surrey, *International Aspects of Tax Expenditures: A Comparative Study,* 1985 (ISBN 90-654-4163-8).
6. Kees van Raad, *Nondiscrimination in International Tax Law,* 1986 (ISBN 90-6544-266-9).
7. Sijbren Cnossen (ed.), *Tax Coordination in the European Community,* 1987 (ISBN 90-6544-272-3).
8. Ben Terra, *Sales Taxation. The Case of Value Added Tax in the European Community,* 1989 (ISBN 90-6544-381-9).
9. Rutsel S.J. Martha, *The Jurisdiction to Tax in International Law: Theory and Practice of Legislative Fiscal Jurisdiction,* 1989 (ISBN 90-654-4416-5).
10. Paul R. McDaniel & Hugh J. Ault, *Introduction to United States International Taxation* (3rd revised edition), 1989 (ISBN 90-6544-423-8).
11. Manuel Pires, *International Juridicial Double Taxation of Income,* 1989 (ISBN 90-6544-426-2).
12. A.H.M. Daniels, *Issues in International Partnership Taxation,* 1991 (ISBN 90-654-4577-3).
13. Arvid A. Skaar, *Permanent Establishment: Erosion of a Tax Treaty Principle,* 1992 (ISBN 90-6544-594-3).
14. Cyrille David & Geerten M.M. Michielse (eds), *Tax Treatment of Financial Instruments,* 1996 (ISBN 90-654-4666-4).
15. Herbert H. Alpert & Kees van Raad (eds), *Essays on International Taxation,* 1993 (ISBN 90-654-4781-4).
16. Wolfgang Gassner, Michael Lang & Eduard Lechner (eds), *Tax Treaties and EC Law,* 1997 (ISBN 90-411-0680-4).
17. Glória Teixeira, *Taxing Corporate Profits in the EU,* 1997 (ISBN 90-411-0703-7).
18. Michael Lang et al. (eds), *Multilateral Tax Treaties,* 1998 (ISBN 90-411-0704-5).
19. Stef van Weeghel, *The Improper Use of Tax Treaties,* 1998 (ISBN 90-411-0737-1).

20. Klaus Vogel (ed.), *Interpretation of Tax Law and Treaties and Transfer Pricing in Japan and Germany,* 1998 (ISBN 90-411-9655-2).
21. Bertil Wiman (ed.), *International Studies in Taxation: Law and Economics; Liber Amicorum Leif Mutén,* 1999 (ISBN 90-411-9692-7).
22. Alfonso J. Martín Jiménez, *Towards Corporate Tax Harmonization in the European Community,* 1999 (ISBN 90-411-9690-0).
23. Ramon J. Jeffery, *The Impact of State Sovereignty on Global Trade and International Taxation,* 1999 (ISBN 90-411-9703-6).
24. A.J. Easson, *Taxation of Foreign Direct Investment,* 1999 (ISBN 90-411-9741-9).
25. Marjaana Helminen, *The Dividend Concept in International Tax Law: Dividend Payments Between Corporate Entities,* 1999 (ISBN 90-411-9765-6).
26. Paul Kirchhof, Moris Lehner, Kees van Raad, Arndt Raupach & Michael-Rodi (eds), *International and Comparative Taxation: Essays in Honour of Klaus Vogel,* 2002 (ISBN 90-411-9841-5).
27. Krister Andersson, Peter Melz & Christer Silfverberg (eds), *Liber Amicorum Sven-Olof Lodin,* 2001 (ISBN 90-411-9850-4).
28. Juan Martín Jovanovich, *Customs Valuation and Transfer Pricing: Is It Possible to Harmonize Customs and Tax Rules?,* Second Edition, 2018 (ISBN 978-90-411-6134-5).
29. Stefano Simontacchi, *Taxation of Capital Gains under the OECD Model Convention: With Special Regard to Immovable Property,* 2007 (ISBN 978-90-411-2549-1).
30. Michael Lang, Josef Schuch, & Claus Staringer (eds), *Tax Treaty Law and EC Law,* 2007 (ISBN 978-90-411-2629-0).
31. Duncan Bentley, *Taxpayers' Rights: Theory Origin and Implementation,* 2007 (ISBN 978-90-411-2650-4).
32. Sergio André Rocha, *Interpretation of Double Taxation Conventions: General Theory and Brazilian Perspective,* 2008 (ISBN 978-90-411-2822-5).
33. Robert F. van Brederode, *Systems of General Sales Taxation: Theory, Policy and Practice,* 2009 (ISBN 978-90-411-2832-4).
34. John G. Head & Richard Krever (eds), *Tax Reform in the 21st Century: A Volume in Memory of Richard Musgrave,* 2009 (ISBN 978-90-411-2829-4).
35. Jens Wittendorff, *Transfer Pricing and the Arm's Length Principle in International Tax Law,* 2010 (ISBN 978-90-411-3270-3).
36. Marjaana Helminen, *The International Tax Law Concept of Dividend,* Second Edition, 2017 (ISBN 978-90-411-8394-1).
37. Robert F. van Brederode (ed.), *Immovable Property under VAT: A Comparative Global Analysis,* 2011 (ISBN 978-90-411-3126-3).
38. Dennis Weber & Stef van Weeghel, *The 2010 OECD Updates: Model Tax Convention & Transfer Pricing Guidelines - A Critical Review,* 2011 (ISBN 978-90-411-3812-5).
39. Yariv Brauner & Martin James McMahon, Jr. (eds), *The Proper Tax Base: Structural Fairness from an International and Comparative Perspective— Essays in Honour of Paul McDaniel,* 2012 (ISBN 978-90-411-3286-4).
40. Robert F. van Brederode (ed.), *Science, Technology and Taxation,* 2012 (ISBN 978-90-411-3125-6).

41. Oskar Henkow, *The VAT/GST Treatment of Public Bodies*, 2013 (ISBN 978-90-411-4663-2).
42. Jean Schaffner, *How Fixed Is a Permanent Establishment?*, 2013 (ISBN 978-90-411-4662-5).
43. Miguel Correia, *Taxation of Corporate Groups*, 2013 (ISBN 978-90-411-4841-4).
44. Veronika Daurer, *Tax Treaties and Developing Countries*, 2014 (ISBN 978-90-411-4982-4).
45. Claire Micheau, *State Aid, Subsidy and Tax Incentives under EU and WTO Law*, 2014 (ISBN 978-90-411-4555-0).
46. Robert F. van Brederode & Richard Krever (eds), *Legal Interpretation of Tax Law*, 2014 (ISBN 978-90-411-4945-9).
47. Radhakishan Rawal, *Taxation of Cross-border Services*, 2014 (ISBN 978-90-411-4947-3).
48. João Dácio Rolim, *Proportionality and Fair Taxation*, 2014 (ISBN 978-90-411-5838-3).
49. Paulo Rosenblatt, *General Anti-avoidance Rules for Major Developing Countries*, 2015 (ISBN 978-90-411-5839-0).
50. Gaspar Lopes Dias V.S., *Tax Arbitrage through Cross-Border Financial Engineering*, 2015 (ISBN 978-90-411-5875-8).
51. Geerten M.M. Michielse & Victor Thuronyi (eds), *Tax Design Issues Worldwide*, 2015 (ISBN 978-90-411-5610-5).
52. Oktavia Weidmann, *Taxation of Derivatives and Cryptoassets*, Second Edition, 2024 (ISBN 978-94-035-2383-5).
53. Chris Evans, Richard Krever & Peter Mellor (eds), *Tax Simplification*, 2015 (ISBN 978-90-411-5976-2).
54. Reuven Avi-Yonah & Joel Slemrod (eds), *Taxation and Migration*, 2015 (ISBN 978-90-411-6136-9).
55. Alexander Bosman, *Other Income under Tax Treaties: An Analysis of Article 21 of the OECD Model Convention*, 2015 (ISBN 978-90-411-6610-4).
56. John Abrahamson, *International Taxation of Manufacturing and Distribution*, 2016 (ISBN 978-90-411-6664-7).
57. Frederik Boulogne, *Shortcomings in the EU Merger Directive*, 2016 (ISBN 978-90-411-6713-2).
58. Angelika Meindl-Ringler, *Beneficial Ownership in International Tax Law*, 2016 (ISBN 978-90-411-6833-7).
59. Andreas Waltrich, *Cross-Border Taxation of Permanent Establishments: An International Comparison*, 2016 (ISBN 978-90-411-6832-0).
60. Sergio André Rocha & Allison Christians (eds), *Tax Sovereignty in the BEPS Era*, 2017 (ISBN 978-90-411-6707-1).
61. Peter Antony Wilson, *BRICS and International Tax Law*, 2018 (ISBN 978-90-411-9435-0).
62. Louise Otis, Brigitte Alepin & Blanca Moreno-Dodson (eds), *Winning the Tax Wars: Tax Competition and Cooperation*, 2018 (ISBN 978-90-411-9460-2).

63. Marta Castelon, *International Taxation of Income from Services under Double Taxation Conventions: Development, Practice and Policy*, 2018 (ISBN 978-90-411-9594-4).
64. D.M. Broekhuijsen, *A Multilateral Tax Treaty: Designing an Instrument to Modernise International Tax Law*, 2018 (ISBN 978-90-411-9872-3).
65. John Abrahamson, *International Taxation of Energy Production and Distribution*, 2018 (ISBN 978-90-411-9101-4).
66. Leopoldo Parada, *Double Non-taxation and the Use of Hybrid Entities*, Second Edition, 2024 (ISBN 978-94-035-4666-7).
67. Richard Snoeij, *International Tax Aspects of Sovereign Wealth Investors: A Source State Perspective*, 2018 (ISBN 978-90-411-9431-2).
68. Aleksandra Bal, *Taxation, Virtual Currency and Blockchain*, 2019 (ISBN 978-94-035-0103-1).
69. Werner Haslehner, Georg Kofler, Katerina Pantazatou & Alexander Rust (eds), *Tax and the Digital Economy: Challenges and Proposals for Reform*, 2019 (ISBN 978-94-035-0361-5).
70. Eva Escribano, *Jurisdiction to Tax Corporate Income Pursuant to the Presumptive Benefit Principle: A Critical Analysis of Structural Paradigms Underlying Corporate Income Taxation and Proposals for Reform*, 2019 (ISBN 978-94-035-0640-1).
71. Jérôme Monsenego & Jan Bjuvberg (eds), *International Taxation in a Changing Landscape: Liber Amicorum in Honour of Bertil Wiman*, 2019 (ISBN 978-90-411-9234-9).
72. Kasper Dziurdź, *Non-discrimination in Tax Treaty Law and World Trade Law: The Impact of Formal, Substantive and Subjective Approaches*, 2019 (ISBN 978-94-035-0904-4).
73. Félix Daniel Martínez Laguna, *Hybrid Financial Instruments, Double Nontaxation and Linking Rules*, 2019 (ISBN 978-94-035-1074-3).
74. Jan Gooijer, *Tax Treaty Residence of Entities*, 2019 (ISBN 978-94-035-1301-0).
75. John Abrahamson, *International Taxation of Banking*, 2020 (ISBN 978-94-035-1094-1).
76. Richard Krever & François Vaillancourt (eds), *The Allocation of Multinational Business Income: Reassessing the Formulary Apportionment Option*, 2020 (ISBN 978-94-035-0614-2).
77. Ajit Kumar Singh, *Exploring the Nexus Doctrine in International Tax Law*, 2021 (ISBN 978-94-035-3363-6).
78. Galya Savir, *Regulation and Tax in Space*, 2021 (ISBN 978-94-035-3393-3).
79. Rita Julien, *Credit Method Compatibility and Constraints under EU Law: An Analysis of the Case Law of the CJEU*, 2022 (ISBN 978-94-035-2363-7).
80. Sergio André Rocha & Allison Christians (eds), *A Multilateral Convention for Tax: From Theory to Implementation*, 2022 (ISBN 978-90-411-9428-2).
81. Brigitte Alepin, Lyne Latulippe & Louise Otis (eds), *Coordination and Cooperation: Tax Policy in the 21st Century*, 2022 (ISBN 978-94-035-3740-5).
82. Chunyang Zhang, *The Role of Tax Law in Mergers and Acquisitions: A Chinese Perspective*, 2022 (ISBN 978-94-035-3741-2).

83. Florian Navisotschnigg, *Substance in International Tax Law: DEMPE Approach, Substantial Activity Requirement and Beneficial Ownership*, 2022 (ISBN 978-94-35-4895-1).
84. Mees Vergouwen, *The Effect of Directives Within the Area of Direct Taxation on the Interpretation and Application of Tax Treaties*, 2023 (ISBN 978-94-035-0907-5).
85. Rachna Matabudul, *Tax Treaty Dispute Resolution: Lessons from the Law of the Sea*, 2023 (ISBN 978-94-035-3407-7).
86. David Orzechowski-Zölzer, *The Taxation of Fees for Technical Services on the Basis of Article 12A UN Model Convention*, 2024 (ISBN 978-94-035-4297-3).
87. David Rüll, *The Resolution of International Tax Disputes: From the Established Mechanisms Towards an Institutionalised International Instrument*, 2024 (ISBN 978-94-035-2088-9).
88. Savvas Kostikidis, *Residence and Economic Substance of Subsidiary Corporations in International and European Tax Law*, 2024 (ISBN 978-94-035-3858-7).
89. Céline Braumann, *Customary International Law and Tax Jurisdiction*, 2025 (ISBN 9789-40-353-888-4).
90. Sophia Piotrowski, *Fiscal State Aid Schemes: Selectivity and Limits to Enforcement*, 2025 (ISBN 978-94-035-0389-9).
91. Benjamín Sevilla Bernabéu, *General Anti-Avoidance Rules: A Comparative, International and European Perspective*, 2025 (ISBN 978-94-035-2489-4).
92. Jie Wang, *Reconsidering Formulary Apportionment in the Post-BEPS Era*, 2026 (ISBN 978-94-035-2729-1).

www.ingramcontent.com/pod-product-compliance
Ingram Content Group UK Ltd.
Pitfield, Milton Keynes, MK11 3LW, UK
UKHW020231290926
15470UKWH00002B/473

9 789403 527291